SYMBOLS AND ACRONYMS

1. Uppercase letters are used for asset prices, including currency values.
2. Lowercase letters are used for rates of change except in Chapters 10–13.
3. Superscripts indicate the asset being traded or the currency units.
4. Subscripts indicate a point in time. Subscripts are dropped when unnecessary.
5. Continuously compounded returns are in italics.
6. Return statistics are either in Greek letters or abbreviated in English (for example, σ_j^2 or $Var(R_j)$).

P_t^d and P_t^f	Price of an asset at time t in the domestic (d) and foreign currencies (f), respectively
p^d and p^f	Domestic and foreign inflation, respectively (that is, the rate of change in P)
$S_t^{d/f}$	Spot exchange rate between currencies d and f at time t
$s_t^{d/f}$	Change in the spot exchange rate between currencies d and f during period t
$F_t^{d/f}$	Forward exchange rate between the domestic and foreign currencies priced at time 0 and for delivery at time t (sometimes denoted $F_{0,t}^{d/f}$)
$Fut_t^{d/f}$	Price in domestic currency of a futures contract on foreign currency priced at time 0 and for delivery at time t (sometimes denoted $Fut_{0,t}^{d/f}$)
i^d and i^f	Nominal interest rate in the domestic and foreign currencies, respectively
r^d and r^f	Real interest rate in the domestic and foreign currencies, respectively
$Call_t^{d/f}$	Value of a call option on foreign currency at time t
$Put_t^{d/f}$	Value of a put option on foreign currency at time t
$K^{d/f}$	Exercise (or striking) price of a currency call or put option
$X_t^{d/f}$	Real exchange rate at time t (nominal rate adjusted for inflation since a base period)
$x_t^{d/f}$	Rate of change in the real exchange rate during period t
V	Value of an asset or security
R_t^d and R_t^f	Return in the domestic and foreign currencies, respectively, during period t (used in Chapters 10–13)
μ_j	Mean return on asset j
σ_j or $SD(R_j)$	Standard deviation of return on asset j
σ_j^2 or $Var(R_j)$	Variance of return on asset j
$\rho_{j,k}$ or $Corr(R_j, R_k)$	Return correlation between assets j and k ($\rho_{j,k} = \sigma_{j,k}/(\sigma_j\sigma_k)$)
$\sigma_{j,k}$ or $Cov(R_j, R_k)$	Return covariance between assets j and k ($\sigma_{j,k} = \rho_{j,k}\sigma_j\sigma_k$)
β_j	Systematic risk (beta) of asset j ($\beta_j = \rho_{j,m}(\sigma_j/\sigma_m)$)

Continuously compounded rates:

$p = \ln(1+p)$ = continuously compounded inflation rate

$i = \ln(1+i)$ = continuously compounded interest rate

$r = \ln(1+r)$ = continuously compounded real interest rate

$s_t^{d/f} = \ln(1+s_t^{d/f}) = \ln(S_t^{d/f}/S_{t-1}^{d/f})$ = continuously compounded nominal spot rate change

$x_t^{d/f} = \ln(1+x_t^{d/f}) = \ln(X_t^{d/f}/X_{t-1}^{d/f})$ = continuously compounded real spot rate change

MULTINATIONAL
FINANCE

KIRT C. BUTLER
Michigan State University

SOUTH-WESTERN College Publishing

An International Thomson Publishing Company

Acquisitions Editor: Christopher Will
Developmental Editors: Kurt Gerdenich and Lois Boggs-Leavens
Production Editor: Sharon L. Smith
Production House: Jonathan Peck Typographers, Ltd.
Interior Designer: Craig LaGesse Ramsdell
Cover Design: Paul Neff
Cover Illustration: © Robert Bergin/SIS
Marketing Manager: Scott D. Person

Library of Congress Cataloging-in-Publication Data

Butler, Kirt Charles.
    Multinational finance / Kirt C. Butler.
        p.   cm.
    Includes bibliographical references and index.
    ISBN 0–538–85385–9
    1. International business enterprises—Finance.   2. Foreign exchange
    3. International finance.   I. Title.
HG4027.5.B88   1997
658.15'99—dc20   96–34787
                                                              CIP

2 3 4 5 6 7 8 D 1 3 2 1 0 9 8 7 6

Printed in the United States of America

I(T)P™

International Thomson Publishing
South-Western College Publishing is an ITP Company. The ITP trademark is
used under license.

To Erika, Rosemarie, and Vincent

Brief Contents

Detailed Contents

Preface

Writing a book is an adventure. To begin with, it is a toy and an amusement.
Then it becomes a mistress, then it becomes a master, then it becomes a tyrant.
The last phase is that just as you are about to be reconciled to your servitude,
you kill the monster, and fling him to the public.

Winston Churchill

It is the job of business schools to train tomorrow's managers. As the pace of evolution in the world's markets increases, so too must innovation in the world's business schools. Keeping pace with new developments in business and finance is the single biggest challenge facing both businesses and business schools. Finance in particular has been transformed by increases in cross-border ownership and trade and by the emergence of derivative securities for hedging risks and exploiting opportunities in our increasingly global marketplace. Ensuring that business education is up-to-date and state-of-the-art is crucial to success both in business schools and in the businesses that they serve.

The Challenge Facing This Book

There are two predominant approaches to teaching multinational financial management in the classroom. Most teachers would agree that the ideal method would be to integrate international finance material into the traditional finance curriculum. This is being done more effectively today than it was even a decade ago in the introductory finance textbooks. Yet it is difficult enough to cover just the algebra of discounted cash flow and the rudiments of the firm's investment and financing decisions in a first course in finance. The rather foreign terminology of international finance and the algebra of exchange rates and international parity conditions are usually left for later coursework. International money and capital markets, cross-border investment and financing decisions, and multinational financial strategy and execution are either covered in haphazard fashion in subsequent courses in finance or not at all. This integrated approach to covering the material in multinational finance is usually more successful in theory than in practice.

The next best alternative to a fully integrated approach is to have a specialized course in multinational financial management. A "specialized" course in international finance is a bit of an oxymoron, because courses in every area of international business must of necessity encompass a much broader range of issues and problems than their domestic counterparts. *Multinational Finance* is designed to satisfy the needs of this specialized course in multinational financial management. The challenge facing this text is to present a broad range of international finance topics in sufficient detail to be useful to the finance practitioner and in a manner that allows the reader from another discipline to see beyond the algebra and terminology to the general principles at the heart of multinational financial management.

To this end, *Multinational Finance* will appeal to two audiences, both of which may be represented in the same classroom in a course in multinational finance. Business students pursuing non-finance degrees will find the material in this book of enormous benefit as they apply the concepts and techniques to their own functional areas. *The text provides a concise treatment of foreign exchange, currency and derivative markets, currency risk, international portfolio management, and multinational corporate financial management.* Each of these topics helps students (and managers) to understand the financial fundamentals that drive the behaviors of firms operating in the international arena. The good news for this audience is that a single introductory course in finance is the only necessary prerequisite for this text.

The second audience is students pursuing a concentration in finance. Finance majors are exposed to the domestic equivalents of many of the international finance topics in the standard finance curriculum. Traditional courses in investments, for example, do a good job on stock and bond valuation. The traditional investments course usually does not provide adequate coverage of cross-border differences in national debt and equity markets, the presence and effect of restrictions on cross-border capital flows, exchange rate risk, or international asset pricing. Each of these topics impacts the international finance practitioner. Similarly, courses in speculative markets tend to emphasize interest rate markets and not currency markets. And the most popular advanced corporate finance textbooks relegate multinational corporate finance topics to a chapter near the end. While finance cases can be used to develop international issues in the classroom, the most popular corporate finance texts fail to cover differences in national taxes and corporate governance systems, the nature and management of foreign exchange risks, barriers to cross-border investment and financing, and strategies for the creation and transfer of value across national boundaries.

The Goal of This Book

The goal of this book is to provide coverage of each of the topics of multinational corporate finance so that an individual involved in or managing foreign operations can do so successfully. This individual could be the owner/manager of a small business just beginning relations with a foreign customer or supplier, a sales representative looking for new markets to conquer, a new business or finance graduate working in the procurement office of a firm engaged in foreign sourcing, or even the financial manager of a multinational corporation. Individuals in each of these positions will find the topics in this book to be timely, relevant, and of enormous benefit in the execution of their duties.

We'll generally assume the role of the financial manager of a large multinational corporation in *Multinational Finance*, but the financial management tools that you will learn apply equally well to any enterprise in most any country. The enterprise could just as well be a partnership, a proprietorship, a collective, a kibbutz, a governmental agency, a trustee, or an individual. The enterprise could just as well be operating in a capitalist as in a socialist country. If nothing else, you should find yourself relating the topics in this text to your own investment objectives and retirement goals, for the topics in this book are as germane to personal investing as they are to big business.

Key Features

- **An emphasis on the basics.** Intended for senior undergraduate and MBA classes, *Multinational Finance* requires only a single preparatory course in finance.

- **A visual approach.** *Multinational Finance* uses extensive graphs and figures that complement the verbal and algebraic coverage and assist the reader in understanding key concepts.

- **Coverage that corresponds to the functional areas of finance.** After a discussion of the foreign exchange and Eurocurrency markets, *Multinational Finance* is organized to cover the international dimensions of
  - money markets
  - capital markets and portfolio investment
  - corporate finance

- **Comprehensive coverage of multinational finance topics.** *Multinational Finance* provides comprehensive coverage of all of the conventional topics of multinational financial management including
  - the international monetary system and the international balance of payments
  - foreign exchange and Eurocurrency markets and their linkages
  - foreign exchange movements and the nature of foreign exchange risk
  - derivative securities including separate chapters on futures, options, and swaps
  - international debt and equity markets
  - international portfolio diversification
  - the theory of the multinational corporation
  - international capital budgeting
  - international taxation
  - the multinational corporation's capital structure and cost of capital
  - multinational treasury management
  - measuring and managing exposure to currency risk

- **Unique chapters on key topics.** In addition to the usual topics of multinational financial management, entire chapters are devoted to topics of special interest to practitioners of multinational finance
  - the rationale for hedging financial price risks
  - international asset pricing
  - managing an international investment portfolio

- strategy in the multinational corporation
- the real investment options of the multinational corporation
- the international market for corporate control
- **An emphasis on financial management.** *Multinational Finance* engages the reader by emphasizing the managerial aspects of multinational corporate finance.

Intended Audience

Multinational Finance is intended for senior-level and graduate courses in international finance or multinational financial management. The book is written to be accessible to anyone that has had a first course in finance. Advanced topics are placed in appendices to the chapters so that instructors can tailor the textbook assignments to their course objectives and to the students' level of preparation.

Organization of the Book

The book is organized into five major parts.

PART 1   Overview and Background
PART 2   Foreign Exchange and Exchange Rate Determination
PART 3   Hedging Currency Risk with Derivative Securities
PART 4   International Capital Markets and Portfolio Investment
PART 5   Multinational Corporate Finance

Part 1 introduces the topics that will be covered in the text and describes the international economic environment.

Part 2 describes the spot and forward foreign exchange and Eurocurrency markets, presents the international parity conditions, and introduces foreign exchange risk and foreign exchange risk exposure. Foreign exchange is the single common denominator of cross-border trade, so this important material is required reading for the remainder of the text.

Part 3 provides the rationale for hedging currency risk and describes derivative instruments that can be used to hedge currency risk exposures including futures, options, and swaps.

Part 4 describes the international capital markets and the portfolio diversification and asset pricing considerations that contribute to international portfolio management. An entire chapter is devoted to international asset pricing. Part 4 is important to the financial manager of a multinational corporation because debt and equity funds are increasingly being raised in foreign markets.

Part 5 covers financial management of the multinational corporation and is split into three sections. Section 5-A describes the environment of international business and introduces a theory of the multinational corporation. The two chapters in this section draw heavily on the academic literature on international business and business strategy. Section 5-B describes the multinational corporation's investment decisions including multinational capital budgeting and tax considerations. The chapters on real options and on the international market for corporate control are far more extensive than in competing texts in international finance. Section 5-C covers three topics from the liability side of the balance sheet. Entire chapters are devoted to multinational capital structure and cost of capital, multinational treasury management, and measuring and managing exposure to foreign exchange risk.

Study Aides

A number of learning aides highlight the main points in each chapter.

- *Sidebars* run in the margins alongside the text and highlight key concepts and definitions.
- *Boxed essays* provide interesting practical insights and real-world examples of the conceptual material in the text.
- *Key Terms* at the end of each chapter compile the essential terms found in the chapter. These key terms are found in boldface the first time they appear in the text. Key terms are defined in a comprehensive *Glossary* at the end of the book.
- *Conceptual Questions* at the end of each chapter summarize the key ideas in each chapter and allow students to test their understanding of the material.
- *Problems* at the end of each chapter provide exercises in implementing the material in each chapter. Solutions to these end-of-chapter problems are provided in a *Solutions Manual* that is available to instructors adopting *Multinational Finance* for classroom use.
- *Suggested Readings* are listed at the end of each chapter and are annotated to indicate the topic that is addressed by each article.

Supplements

A comprehensive *Instructor's Manual* is available to adopters of *Multinational Finance*. It contains

- *Lecture Notes and Overhead Transparencies* that review the key elements in each chapter. The lecture notes and overhead transparencies are flexible enough so that they can be geared to undergraduate or to graduate courses. (See the *Instructor's Manual* for details.)
  - Over 250 *Powerpoint Slides* can be copied from the *Instructor's Manual* or used as a slide show with the accompanying diskette.
  - Separate *Notes Pages* accompany the slides and provide additional insights and examples of the concepts on the slides.
- A *Solutions Manual* that provides answers to the end-of-chapter *Conceptual Questions* and to the end-of-chapter *Problems*.
- A *Test Bank* with over 600 test questions including objective questions (true-false, multiple choice, matching), problems, and essays. The test bank is also available in disk format via MicroExam, a complete computerized testing program.

- A list of *Suggested Cases* that examine the issues in each chapter. These cases are available through South-Western College Publishing's *CaseNet* program and other sources.

The objective in providing this comprehensive Instructor's Manual is to allow the instructor to spend his or her time where it is most useful—in teaching the students.

Acknowledgments

My gratitude goes to my students who, over the last three years, have suffered through preliminary drafts of the book. Ruperto (Tito) Carpio, Rich Coskey, Stephanie Gaide, Mehool Kakabalia, Katherine McIntyre, Eray Tukenmez, and Daphne Turner were especially helpful. Many colleagues and industry contacts also helped me refine the book into its current form. Here is a partial list of these contributors.

Richard Ajayi	Wayne State University
Anne Allerston	Bournemouth University, United Kingdom
Bruce Benet	Michigan State University
Jeffrey Bergstrand	University of Notre Dame
Rita Biswas	SUNY—Albany
Donald J.S. Brean	University of Toronto, Canada
Robert A. Clark	University of Vermont
David B. Cox	University of Denver
Miranda Detzler	University of Massachusetts—Boston
Dora Hancock	Leeds Metropolitan University, United Kingdom
Kwang Nam Jee	Korea Development Bank
Kurt Jesswein	Texas A&M International University
H.S. Kerr	Washington State University
Naveen Khanna	Michigan State University
Theodor Kohers	Mississippi State University
Chuck Kwok	The University of South Carolina
Michael Mazzeo	Michigan State University
Kathleen McIntyre	Ford Motor Company
Blaire Miller	Comerica Bank
Richard M. Osborne	Michigan State University
Hakan Saraoglu	Bryant College
Anil Shivdasani	Michigan State University
Richard R. Simonds	Michigan State University
Jacky C. So	Southern Illinois University at Edwardsville
Michael Solt	San Jose State University
Wei-Ling Song	Michigan State University
Richard Stehle	Humboldt University, Germany
Dean Taylor	University of Colorado at Denver

Tamer Cavusgil and the Center for International Business Education and Research (CIBER) at Michigan State University provided support and encouragement throughout the project. Leadership and direction were provided by my Sensei, Seikichi Iha.

The Finance team at South-Western College Publishing proved their worth in bringing this project to fruition. My heartfelt thanks go to developmental editor Kurt Gerdenich, production editor Sharon Smith, and graphic artist Craig Ramsdell. Production of the book was painstakingly performed by Jonathan Peck Typographers of Santa Cruz, California. I am deeply indebted to the copyediting team of Jeff Lachina at Lachina Publishing, Cleveland, Ohio, for their careful attention to detail. My editor, Chris Will, put the whole project together and provided encouragement at all the right times.

Finally, and most importantly, I wish to thank my wife, Erika, and my two children, Rosemarie and Vincent, for their tolerance of my many early mornings and late nights. My family is my inspiration and my refuge.

About the Author

Kirt C. Butler is an Associate Professor in the Department of Finance at Michigan State University where he teaches international and corporate finance and global strategy in MSU's Eli Broad Graduate School of Management. He joined the faculty in 1985 after completing his doctorate in finance at Michigan State University. He also holds a M.S. degree in Computer Science from the College of Engineering and a B.A. in Psychology from the Honors College at Michigan State University.

Professor Butler is the current Midwest (U.S.) Regional Chairperson of the Academy of International Business. He has served as a consultant on international financial issues for U.S. and foreign corporations and for the legislature of the State of Michigan. He was a Guest Professor at Augsburg University in Germany during 1992.

Professor Butler's research has appeared in a variety of academic and practitioner journals including the *Journal of Finance, Journal of Accounting Research, Journal of Portfolio Management, Journal of Banking and Finance, Journal of International Financial Management and Accounting*, and the *Journal of Teaching in International Business*, among others.

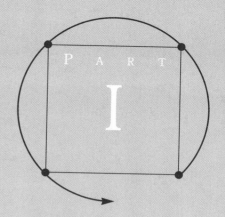

Overview and Background

*The more we learn of the possibilites
of our world, and the possibilites of ourselves,
the richer, we learn, is our inheritance*

H.G. Wells

The global economy is not just an Orwellian prediction of a possible future reality—it is already here. The world's financial markets are linked in a global network of securities exchanges, financial institutions, government agencies, news services, and corporate and private enterprises. Information that is relevant to asset values is transmitted nearly instantaneously and impacts asset prices in many markets around the world.

The world's goods markets face greater physical and institutional barriers to trade than financial markets do. Yet significant progress has been made toward free trade through international agreements such as the North American Free Trade Agreement (NAFTA), the European Union (EU), the Andean and Mercosur trade pacts in Latin America, the Association of Southeast Asian Nations (ASEAN) pact, the Asia-Pacific Economic Cooperation (APEC) pact, and the creation of the World Trade Organization (WTO) to oversee the General Agreement on Tariffs and Trade (GATT). In this rapidly changing global economy, business competition is as likely to come from China or Central Europe as from your own backyard. Part 1 gives a quick tour of the economic and monetary landscape of multinational business and finance.

Introduction to Multinational Corporate Finance

*Even if you're on the right track,
you'll get run over if you just sit there.*

Will Rogers

1.1 FINANCIAL MANAGEMENT OF THE MULTINATIONAL ENTERPRISE

Financial management refers to management of the corporation's real and financial assets and liabilities. In this book we'll typically assume the viewpoint of the financial manager of a **multinational corporation (MNC)** and address the financial manager's concerns, including short- and long-term investment and financing decisions and the costs and characteristics of various sources of capital. The corporation's financial decisions and the environment within which they are made are shown in Figure 1.1. Topics that impact the financial manager's decisions include the characteristics and efficiency of the world's financial markets, national tax and regulatory environments, and local, national, and international investment and financing opportunities.

Multinational finance is conducted across more than one cultural, social, political, legal, or economic environment.

Multinational financial management is nothing more than domestic financial management conducted in an environment that is influenced by more than one cultural, political, or economic environment. As such, multinational financial management takes place in an environment that is loaded both with more opportunities and with more obstacles and risks than purely domestic financial management. At the heart of both the opportunities and the risks of international business are the differences among peoples of the world.

The challenge facing the financial manager of a global enterprise is to be able to successfully implement and execute business strategies in more than one culture. Because of this cross-border orientation, multinational financial management lies at the crossroads of international business, international economics, and finance. For this reason,

3

Economic Environment
Goods and capital markets
and the international
monetary system

Business and Financial Risk
including the risk of
unexpected changes in
currency values

Cultural Environment
People—languages, social
customs, and culture

Cultural Risk
the risks of dealing with
an unfamiliar culture

Political Environment
Governments, their public
policies and constraints

Political Risk
the risk that a foreign
government will unexpectedly
change the rules of the game

The Multinational Corporation

Investment decisions
1. export-import trade
2. foreign investment
3. cross-border partnerships
4. foreign sourcing
5. global asset diversification

Financing decisions
1. hedging of currency risk
2. foreign sources of debt and
   equity capital
3. trade credit and trade financing
4. taxes and repatriation
   of foreign-source income

**Environmental Factors Affecting
Financial Management and Performance**

Market efficiency
Corporate governance

National tax environments
National trade policies and practices

FIGURE 1.1
Overview of Multinational
Financial Management

financial management in a global marketplace requires at least a passing familiarity with each of these fields. The field of international business examines business strategy and execution in the presence of cultural, political, and economic differences among nation-states and peoples. International economics focuses on macroeconomic interactions between nation-states and encompasses such topics as fiscal and monetary policy, balance-of-trade theory, trade patterns, the distribution of income, the causes and consequences of budget and trade deficits, inflation, and the effect of inflation differences between countries. Financial management takes a microeconomic perspective with an emphasis on asset and liability management within the broader macroeconomic environment.

Today's financial manager must also be well versed in each of the traditional fields of business, including marketing, management, business law and taxes, and accounting. Business problems are rarely the province of a single discipline, and the challenges facing multinational businesses are prone to be multidisciplinary. Practitioners of each of the functional fields of business—including finance—need to be cognizant of international differences in marketing, management of people and resources, law, taxes, and accounting.

To be effective in a multinational enterprise, today's financial manager must also be an expert in several fields within finance. Management of the multinational corporation requires a thorough knowledge of each of the areas of finance. Management of foreign exchange risk requires a thorough knowledge of financial markets, especially the international money markets conducted in interest rates and foreign exchange. To be able to recognize attractive investment opportunities in foreign lands, the multinational financial manager must understand the limitations of traditional investment analysis, must have a plan of attack for entry and exit into foreign markets, and must be able to value the growth and abandonment options presented by foreign markets. In many ways, the financial manager of today must be a jack of all trades as well as master of one—finance.

The goal of financial management is to make decisions that maximize the value of the enterprise to some group of stakeholders. The form of corporate governance in the United States and in many other industrialized countries is such that "stakeholder wealth maximization" is taken to mean "shareholder wealth maximization."

No enterprise today is untouched by foreign affairs. Even if an enterprise conducts its business solely within a single economy, it is nearly inevitable that one day its suppliers, customers, and competitors will come from other countries. Businesses that consider themselves to be purely domestic cannot ignore the trend toward globalization in the world's markets. If they do, they will soon enough find themselves with sorrow near at hand.

1.2 GLOBALIZATION OF THE WORLD'S MARKETS

In the last several decades, the world's goods, services, and financial markets have become increasingly integrated across national boundaries. In the goods markets, the world's businesses are turning to foreign sales, foreign sourcing, foreign direct investment, and cross-border partnerships as paths toward business consolidation and expansion. The market for services has also seen an explosion of cross-border trade, especially in services such as telecommunications and information services. As the markets for goods and services become more internationally integrated, foreign markets are playing an increasingly important role in the viability of domestic industries.

The world's markets are increasingly being integrated across national borders.

The pessimistic tone of daily news reports on efforts to integrate world trade highlights the substantial barriers to, and our halting progress toward, a truly global economy. Yet viewed in the long lens of history, trade barriers today are lower than ever. The fall of barriers to international trade in goods and services has been hastened by many trends and events, including

- The global trend toward free-market economies
- The rapid industrialization of the Far East and Pacific Rim
- The entry of China into international trade
- The fall of the Iron Curtain and the emergence of a diverse set of central and eastern European countries
- Reunification of East and West Germany
- The expiration of England's lease on Hong Kong and Hong Kong's return to Chinese control on July 1, 1997

- The rise of regional economic linkages and trade pacts (see Figure 1.2) including:
  - The **North American Free Trade Agreement (NAFTA)** among Canada, Mexico, and the United States
  - Western European economic convergence and integration through the **European Union** (formerly called the European Economic Community)
  - Growing economic cooperation and integration among the countries of Southeast Asia and the Far East (including China) through the **Asia-Pacific Economic Cooperation (APEC)** pact

WTO World Trade Organization	121 nations signed the Uruguay Round of the General Agreement on Tariffs and Trade (GATT) on April 15, 1994. GATT slashes tariffs globally by roughly 40 percent, protects intellectual property, and sets up a dispute resolution system. The World Trade Organization (WTO) oversees the trade agreement.
NAFTA North American Free Trade Agreement	United States, Canada, and Mexico. With more than $7 trillion in combined GNP, NAFTA covers a huge market.
EU European Union	Belgium, France, Germany, Italy, Netherlands, Portugal, Spain, United Kingdom (England, Wales, Northern Ireland, Scotland). Economic integration requires convergence of member nations' fiscal and monetary policies, with plans for a single European currency in the early twenty-first century. Central European states may join as their fiscal and monetary policies stabilize.
ASEAN Association of Southeast Asian Nations	Brunei, Indonesia, Malaysia, Philippines, Singapore, Thailand, Vietnam. A loose geopolitical affiliation rather than a trade accord. Burma, Laos, and Cambodia may soon join.
APEC Asia-Pacific Economic Cooperation	A loose economic affiliation of Southeast Asian and Far East nations including China, Japan, Korea, and many others
Mercosur the "common market of the South"	Argentina, Brazil, Paraguay, Uruguay. Begun in 1995, this pact allows 90 percent of trade among these four countries to be tariff-free.
Andean Pact	Venezuela, Colombia, Ecuador, Peru, Bolivia.
Group of Three	Colombia, Mexico, Venezuela.

FIGURE 1.2 The World's Major Economic Cooperation and Free Trade Accords

- Closer economic and political ties among the countries in the **Association of Southeast Asian Nations (ASEAN)** including Singapore, Brunei, Malaysia, Thailand, Philippines, Indonesia, and Vietnam. (ASEAN is a loose geopolitical affiliation rather than a trade accord per se. Burma, Laos, and Cambodia are scheduled to join soon.)

- The emergence of regional trade pacts in the Americas, such as **Mercosur** (Mercado Commun del Sur, "the common market of the south," including Argentina, Brazil, Paraguay, and Uruguay) and the **Andean Pact** (Venezuela, Colombia, Ecuador, Peru, and Bolivia)

- Completion of the Uruguay Round of the **General Agreement on Tariffs and Trade (GATT)** and creation of the **World Trade Organization (WTO)**

Largely because of the reduction in physical and governmental barriers to trade, foreign trade has assumed an increasing importance for nearly all nations. Exports as a percentage of GNP have grown over time for the vast majority of countries. Figure 1.3 shows this growth for the United States, Germany, and Japan. Foreign trade also has become increasingly important to **less developed countries (LDCs)** as these countries struggle to increase their national wealth and the living standards of their citizens. Cross-border investment has grown along with the importance of exports over the last several decades. Figure 1.4 displays trends in the international investment position of the United States. Other nations have experienced similar growth in cross-border investment.

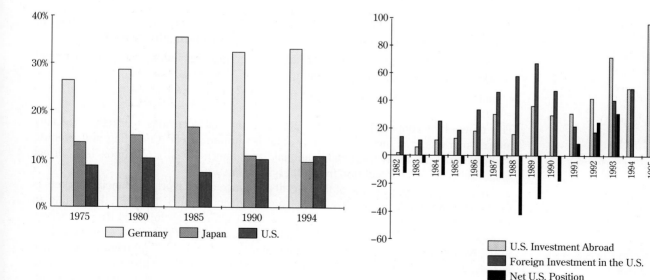

FIGURE 1.3 Exports as a Percentage of GNP

FIGURE 1.4 International Investment Position of the United States ($billions)

*Economic,
political,
& social
consequences*

The economic, political, and social consequences of these changes have an enormous influence on individuals and societies. Some of the economic consequences of globalization in the world's goods and service markets are:

- An increase in cross-border investment in real assets (land, natural resource projects, and manufacturing facilities)
- An increasing interdependence between national economies leading to global business cycles that are shared by all nations
- Changing political risk for multinational corporations as nations redefine their borders as well as their national identities

Financial market integration has been facilitated by advances in electronic communication and data processing.

Despite (and, in some cases, because of) the reduction of imperfections in the markets for goods and services, significant opportunities still exist for businesses to increase returns while lowering risks through cross-border operations, investment, and diversification.

Integration is proceeding at an even faster pace in the world's financial markets as advances in electronic communication and data processing reduce physical and institutional barriers to the flow of capital. Developments in computers and telecommunications have been especially important in hastening the integration of both domestic and international capital markets. Currency trading, in particular, has undergone explosive growth in the latter half of the twentieth century. Some of this growth is a consequence of the growth in import and export trade. But a considerable portion of this growth is due to the introduction of new financial instruments that facilitate both currency trading and import/export trade.

Along with the reduction of barriers in the world's goods markets, the demise of capital flow barriers in international financial markets has had several consequences:

- An increase in cross-border financing as multinational corporations raise capital in whichever market and in whatever currency offers the most attractive rates
- An increasing number of cross-border partnerships, including many international mergers, acquisitions, and joint ventures
- Increasingly interdependent national financial markets

The number of cooperative linkages between national securities markets, especially futures markets, has increased rapidly. The institution of early morning and evening trading hours at many regional, national, and international exchanges is a direct response to market competition from other time zones.

The most striking example of the interdependence of the world's financial markets is the worldwide stock market crash that occurred on October 19, 1987. Beginning in Asian markets late on the afternoon of October 19, the crash followed the sun across Europe, the United States, and finally back to Asia as each of these markets opened for trade. Nearly all of the world's major stock markets fell at least 20 percent in both local currency and in U.S. dollars during the month of October 1987.[1] This historic event provided a graphic reminder that today, more than ever, we all live on the same small planet.

---

1 Richard Roll chronicles the 1987 global stock market crash in "The International Crash of October 1987," *Financial Analysts Journal,* 1988.

According to the **discounted cash flow (DCF)** approach to valuation, the market value of an asset is equal to the present value of expected future cash flows discounted at a rate appropriate for the level of systematic risk. Let CF_t represent a firm's or a project's expected cash flows over T future periods and i_t the appropriate risk-adjusted discount rate over holding period t. Then value is determined by

$$V = \sum_{t=1}^{T} [E[CF_t]/(1+i_t)^t] \tag{1.1}$$

With respect to the MNC's investment decisions, the DCF approach states that the firm should continue to invest until its marginal cost of capital is equal to its marginal rate of return on investment.

This valuation equation has an important implication for the firm's financial decisions. If a corporate decision has no impact on the firm's expected future cash flows or discount rate, then the decision also has no impact on the value of the firm. Conversely, if a decision is to add value to the owners of the firm, then the decision must either increase expected cash flows or decrease the cost of capital or both.

Multinational Investment Policy

In investment theory, the set of investments available to a corporation is called the **investment opportunity set**. The investment objective of the corporation is to identify and invest in the set of investments that maximizes the value of the firm to its stakeholders. In terms of equation (1.1), the investment objective of the firm is to choose that set of investments that maximizes the present value of expected future cash flows.

The objective of investment policy is to select those investments that maximize the value of the firm

Suppose a firm obtains its financing in the domestic market but augments its domestic investment opportunities with foreign investment alternatives. Relative to the purely domestic firm, the MNC has more flexibility in the location and timing of its investments. With greater access to foreign markets, the MNC can shift sales toward those international markets willing to pay the highest price for its products. Higher demand in foreign markets can arise for a number of reasons, including consumer preferences, lack of competition in the foreign market, and changes in the purchasing power of foreign currencies. If the MNC has foreign manufacturing capacity, it can shift production to low-cost sites. The MNC is better able to weigh the pros and cons of investment in various foreign and domestic sites, including the impact of taxes and access to financial incentives provided by host governments. The MNC is better able to take products that are in the mature stage in its domestic markets and transform these into growth products in foreign markets. Also, the MNC has greater flexibility in the timing of these activities. These **real options** can be a large part of the additional value of the MNC relative to its domestic competitors.

Figure 1.5 depicts the internal rates of return on domestic and on multinational investments along with the domestic cost of capital on these investments. The value of the domestic corporation is represented by the darkened area between the domestic firm's investment opportunity set and cost of capital. This area represents the domestic firm's positive-NPV investment opportunities.

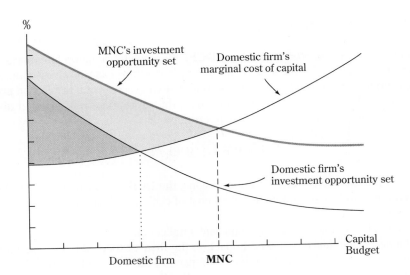

FIGURE 1.5
The Multinational
Corporation's Investment
Opportunity Set

Simple point →

The investment opportunity set of the MNC is shifted up and to the right in Figure 1.5 to represent the expanded opportunities available to the MNC. The increase in value is represented by the larger wedge-shaped area between the domestic cost of capital and the MNC's international investment opportunity set. The MNC has more investment opportunities than its domestic rivals because of its activities in markets other than its home market. While these opportunities come with some unique currency, political, and cultural risks, the international experience of the MNC places it in a better position than its domestic rivals to evaluate and manage these risks. If the risks are too great, of course, the MNC can choose not to invest in foreign projects. It is then no worse off than its domestic counterpart.

It would be inappropriate to use a single cost of capital or hurdle rate to compare investment alternatives of different risk, so this graph must be interpreted to represent the capital costs for investment opportunities of similar risk. Subject to this limitation, the graph makes a simple point: The MNC derives at least a portion of its additional value over the domestic firm from its expanded set of investment opportunities.

Multinational Financial Policy

The objective of financial policy is to maximize the value of the firm through the mix of financing instruments.

The objective of **financial policy** is to maximize the value of the firm by selecting the most appropriate mix of financing instruments. Financial policy includes decisions regarding the mix of debt and equity, the currency of denomination of debt and equity, the maturity structure of debt, the markets in which to raise capital, the method of financing both domestic and foreign projects, and hedging of currency risks. The corporation's choices in these areas determine investors' required returns and, hence, the corporation's cost of capital.

Through its access to international financial markets, the MNC is in a unique position to minimize its cost of capital—and thereby maximize its value—by raising funds from foreign investors who are willing to pay a premium over domestic investors. If the

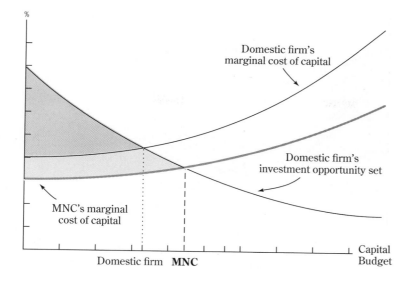

FIGURE 1.6
The Multinational
Corporation's Cost of Capital

multinational corporation can get a higher price for its debt or equity securities on international markets than in domestic markets, then for a given set of investments it can capture a lower cost of capital than a comparable domestic firm can. The option to raise funds in foreign markets is especially valuable when credit conditions are tight in the home market but not in one or more foreign markets. As with investment policy, the MNC also has more flexibility in the location and timing of its financing choices than the domestic firm has. The expanded financing set of the MNC is represented in Figure 1.6 as a marginal cost of capital that is shifted downward and stretched to the right relative to a comparable domestic firm. The multinational corporation can increase the value of the firm by reducing the cost of capital (or discount rate) in equation (1.1).

Figure 1.7 combines the expanded investment opportunity set of the MNC with the lower capital costs arising from the MNC's greater access to capital markets. The increment to value enjoyed by any single firm will vary with the MNC's lines of business, the competitors faced in domestic and international markets, the competitiveness of the home country economy relative to foreign economies, and the competencies and competitive advantages of the MNC itself. Figure 1.7 merely provides a graphical illustration of the potential gains from multinational operations.

1.4 THE MULTINATIONAL'S EXPOSURE TO FOREIGN EXCHANGE RISK

The world's goods and financial markets present unique opportunities to individuals and businesses involved in international trade. As individuals and businesses increasingly take advantage of the cross-border opportunities made possible by the reduction of barriers to trade in the world's goods and financial markets, they expose themselves to a wide variety of new risks. A good portion of this book is devoted to the measurement

Benefits to the MNC...

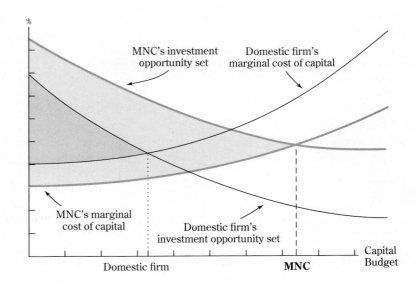

FIGURE 1.7
The Advantages of
Multinationality

and management of a form of financial price risk called foreign exchange risk.

The single common denominator of international business is foreign currency exchange. Whenever goods pass national boundaries in a transaction, foreign currency changes hands. Trading volume in the foreign exchange market is immense, usually surpassing one trillion dollars per day in the interbank market that comprises the majority of foreign exchange transactions. In this environment, the behavior of foreign exchange rates plays a key role in a firm's success or failure in both domestic and foreign markets. It is no longer enough to build a better mousetrap if your revenues or costs can be severely damaged by volatile foreign exchange rates. An understanding of foreign exchange risk exposure as well as the techniques used to manage foreign exchange risk is essential for both large and small firms competing in today's global marketplace. We will spend much of our time in this book developing a framework for evaluating these risks and opportunities.

Foreign Exchange Risk: A Form of Financial Price Risk

Risk exists whenever actual outcomes can differ from expected outcomes.

Risk exists whenever actual outcomes can differ from expected outcomes. In finance, we are often interested in how an asset's value changes in response to changes in other factors. Some of these factors are controllable, such as changes in the firm's investment mix and financial policy. Factors outside managers' control include unexpected changes in commodity prices, interest rates, and foreign exchange rates.

Assets and liabilities are exposed to **financial price risk** when their values can change with unexpected changes in a financial price. The most prominent financial price risks are interest rate risk, commodity price risk, and foreign exchange (or currency) risk. An example of an asset exposed to **interest rate risk** is a fixed-rate bank deposit. An example of a company exposed to **commodity price risk** is a trucking firm whose expenses depend heavily on gasoline prices. Every corporation with assets, liabilities, revenues, or expenses denominated in a foreign currency is exposed to **foreign**

exchange risk (or **currency risk**). While fluctuations in interest rates, foreign currency exchange rates, and commodity prices arise from different sources, the methods used to manage these risks are essentially the same. **Financial innovation**—designing new products with a goal toward reducing exposures to financial risk—has become a cornerstone of foreign currency trading.

There was a global increase in foreign exchange risk during the 1970s. This increase was largely due to the advent of floating exchange rates in 1971, although one could argue that floating exchange rates are a consequence rather than a cause of increasing foreign exchange risk. Figure 1.8 shows the volatility of monthly changes in the value of the U.S. dollar against the Japanese yen over the period 1970 to 1995.

Under a floating exchange rate system, currency values are determined by supply and demand in the currency markets rather than by government policy or decree. Financial price risk reveals itself under floating exchange rate systems through frequent and unpredictable (but usually small) fluctuations in currency values. In fixed exchange rate mechanisms, governments attempt to set their currency values either by edict, through fiscal and monetary policy, or by market intervention. A contemporary example of a fixed exchange rate system is the European Exchange Rate Mechanism (ERM) in which rates are managed within a relatively narrow band by European Union central banks through cooperative monetary and fiscal policies. Changes in currency values under fixed exchange rate systems are much less frequent but are much larger than under floating exchange rate systems.

Along with the increase in the globalization of the world's goods and financial markets has come an increase in exposure to all three forms of financial price risk. For this reason, financial risk management has become a necessary and integral part of the operation of large multinational corporations from every country. Risk management is also critical to the financial health and viability of smaller enterprises just beginning to enter the global marketplace. Profits on overseas transactions can quickly be wiped out by unexpected changes in currency values.

As firms increase their international operations, they become more exposed to currency risk.

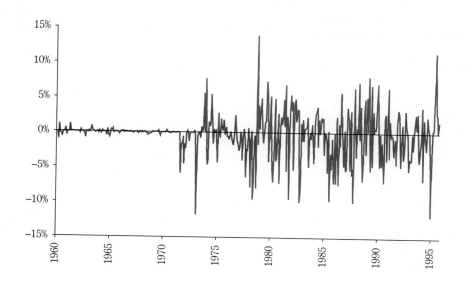

FIGURE 1.8
Monthly Percentage
Changes in the Nominal
Yen/Dollar Exchange Rate,
1970 to 1995

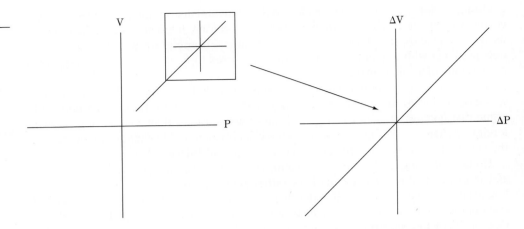

FIGURE 1.9
Risk Profile in (P,V) and
(ΔP, ΔV) Space

Risk Measurement

The left-hand graph in Figure 1.9 presents a **risk profile** that captures the relation between an asset's value, V, and some underlying factor or financial price, P. The right-hand graph in Figure 1.9 translates this risk profile into the relation between changes in asset value (ΔV) and changes in the underlying factor (ΔP).

Here's a more familiar application of this general framework. In your introductory finance course, you learned that the risk of an asset held in a diversified portfolio depends on its covariances with other assets (σ_{jM}) and not solely on its individual risk or standard deviation (σ_j). The risk of a share of stock is then the sensitivity of stock returns to market portfolio returns (see Figure 1.10). This sensitivity can be estimated by the slope of a regression equation:

$$R_j = \alpha_j + \beta_j R_M + e_j \qquad (1.2)$$

where R_j is security j's return, R_M is the market portfolio return, α_j and β_j are intercept and slope coefficients, and $e_j \sim N(0,\sigma_{ej}^2)$ captures any variation in R_j not explained by

FIGURE 1.10
Risk Profile of a Share of
Stock As Measured by Beta

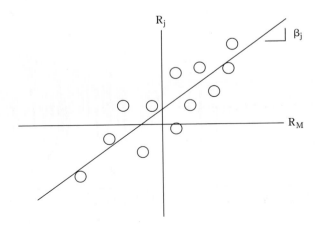

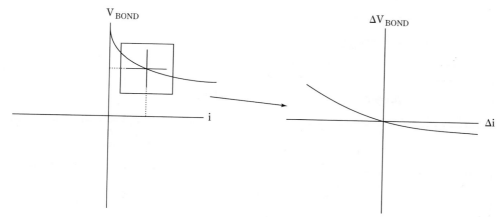

FIGURE 1.11 Risk Profile of a Fixed Income Bond

variation in R_M. The slope coefficient, or beta (β_j), measures the sensitivity of security j's returns to changes in the market and is equal to σ_{jM}/σ_M^2. The percent of the variation in R_j explained by variation in R_M is measured by the square of the correlation coefficient (called the coefficient of determination, or r^2).

For securities that are linked contractually to a financial price or rate of return, 100 percent of the variation in value can be explained by variation in the underlying price. In this case the risk profile is deterministic. Examples are the value of a foreign currency obligation in the domestic currency, a forward foreign exchange contract whose value depends on spot rates of exchange, a fixed income bond whose value depends on the level of interest rates, and an oil futures contract whose value is linked to the price of oil. Each of these contracts is exposed to financial price risk. As another example, Figure 1.11 depicts the value of a bond as a function of the level of interest rates. We apply the framework of Figure 1.9 to financial price risks including foreign exchange risk, interest rate risk, and commodity price risk. Careful monitoring and management of these risks are keys to the success of the multinational corporation.

1.5 CORPORATE GOVERNANCE AND THE POTENTIAL FOR GOAL CONFLICT

The Set-of-Contracts Perspective Toward Corporate Governance

Business enterprises in countries around the world share some common elements. Figure 1.12 presents the basic structure of management and ownership that is typical of companies in market economies. In every country, the firm can be viewed as the nexus of a set of contracts between the various stakeholders in the firm. In this **set-of-contracts perspective**, the corporation is defined by a legal framework of contracts. Important contracts include those with customers, suppliers, labor, debt, and equity.

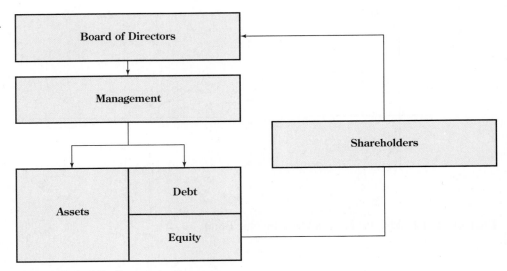

FIGURE 1.12 Corporate Governance

Since each of these contracts is executed within the laws of the society in which the firm operates, the society itself helps determine the form of these contracts and the rights and responsibilities of the various parties. Each country has a unique cultural, social, political, legal, and economic environment. International business is a partnership among the MNC, the suppliers of factor inputs such as labor, the suppliers of capital, and the host country.

The Potential for Goal Conflict in the Multinational Enterprise

The traditional goal of financial management is to maximize shareholder wealth. This works fine as a starting point, especially in economies such as that of the United States. Shareholder wealth maximization has the advantage of focusing the financial manager's attention on cash flows rather than accounting income or market share, because the timing and riskiness of expected future cash flows determine value.

But shareholder wealth maximization is far from the only objective followed by those with a stake in the firm. Suppliers, customers, debtholders, management, and employees have objectives that are often in conflict with shareholder wealth maximization, especially during periods of financial distress. **Agency costs** are the costs of contracting and monitoring between the various stakeholders to reduce potential conflicts of interest. The presence of agency costs does not mean that management will not act in the best interests of shareholders, only that it is costly to make them do so. Since it is shareholders' objective to maximize shareholder wealth, it is shareholders who ultimately bear these agency costs.

Viewing the firm as a pie is useful in a discussion of how one stakeholder's actions or inactions can affect the value of other stakeholders. Figure 1.13 represents the various

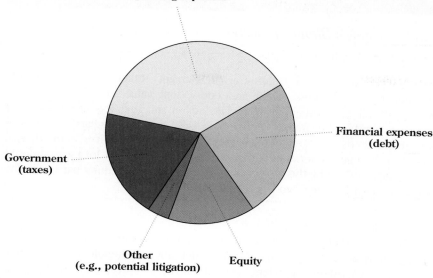

$$V_{Revenues} = V_{Expenses} + V_{Govt} + V_{Other} + V_{Debt} + V_{Equity}$$

FIGURE 1.13 Claimants on the Revenues of the Firm

claimants on the value of expected future revenues. In this view, the total market value of expected future revenues, $V_{Revenues}$, can be split up as follows:

An Income Statement View of the Stakeholders of the Firm

$$V_{Revenues} = V_{Expenses} + V_{Govt} + V_{Other} + V_{Debt} + V_{Equity}$$

Stakeholders
(narrowly defined)

Stakeholders (broadly defined)

Stakeholders are usually narrowly defined as the owners of the firm's debt and equity securities. These marketed claims are paid out of operating income and are represented by V_{Debt} and V_{Equity} in the above equation. Debt holders put their claims in writing through restrictive covenants in the bond indenture. As the residual owner, the value of equity's claim depends on the laws and legal conventions of the nations within which the multinational corporation operates.

Many other groups of individuals have a stake in the company, most but not all of whom have explicit claims on revenues. The objectives of these stakeholders are not identical with those of shareholders. For example, labor is more concerned with wages and job security than with shareholder wealth. The objective of "maximize shareholder

MNCs have many stakeholders, each with their own unique objectives.

Union Carbide Corporation is a diversified U.S. company with worldwide operations in a variety of industry segments. Union Carbide's 50.9 percent–owned subsidiary, Union Carbide India Limited, operated a chemical plant in Bhopal, India. In 1984, deadly gases were inadvertently released from the plant, causing the deaths of more than two thousand people and injuries to nearly a quarter of a million people. This disaster resulted in losses for nearly all of Union Carbide's major stakeholders (broadly defined). Debt and equity lost value in anticipation of a settlement of a class action suit that was eventually held in Indian (rather than U.S.) courts. The careers and self-esteem of managers and employees involved in the Bhopal operation suffered directly. The biggest loss was suffered by the government (Union Carbide's equity partner in the deal) and by the people of India.

wealth" can also be in conflict with host countries' cultural, economic, political, social, ecological, and religious goals. By adopting a broad definition, stakeholders are taken to include the firm's customers, suppliers, and employees, represented by $V_{Expenses}$. Another set of stakeholders is the governments that have an explicit interest in the taxes paid by the firm (represented by V_{Govt}) and an implicit interest in all activities of the firm that influence the societies in which the firm operates (represented by V_{Other}). While not all of these activities appear in the income statement, some of them can and do impact other stakeholders. For example, if the firm violates the laws of one or more of the countries in which it operates, it may be liable for civil or criminal penalties or both. Union Carbide's disaster at their plant in Bhopal, India, (see box) resulted in a potentially huge claim that adversely affected all stakeholders, but especially the debt and equity claimants.

Countries differ in the extent to which they protect each of these stakeholders. Countries tending toward socialism tend to place a greater emphasis on employee welfare. Some industrialized countries place a great emphasis on environmental concerns; others take a laissez-faire or hands-off attitude, allowing their industries to compete unfettered in the world marketplace. Most countries protect or subsidize key industries or selected sectors of their economies. These industries are deemed to be of vital importance to the nation's economy or to the national identity. Protected industries often include products related to agriculture. Protected industries include rice in Japan, beer in Germany, and wine in France. In the United States, various agricultural products that are vulnerable to foreign competition are protected through price supports and other subsidies.

It is up to sovereign nations to determine the nature of the playing field on which companies operate within their borders. Chief financial officers and their representatives must work within the rules and respect the sensibilities and sensitivities of the societies in which they operate.[2] Businesses ignoring the local rules of the game do so at their own peril.

---

2 On this topic, Mark Twain wrote: "Always do right. This will gratify some people, and astonish the rest."

An understanding of global financial management is crucial to success in today's, and inevitably in tomorrow's, marketplace. This is unquestionably true for firms competing directly with foreign firms, such as the U.S. auto industry in competition with Asian and Western European automakers. Yet it is also true for domestic firms whose suppliers, customers, and competitors are increasingly likely to be from foreign countries. In today's business environment, the success of firms in service and manufacturing industries depends on two things—their ability to recognize and exploit imperfections in national markets for products and factors of production and their ability to work effectively within the political and economic constraints imposed by foreign governments.

This book develops a framework for evaluating the risks and opportunities presented by the world's diverse goods and financial marketplaces. While we usually take the perspective of the financial manager of a large multinational corporation, keep in mind that this framework works just as well for individuals, small businesses, and government entities. Along the way, we provide a tour of businesses and business environments in many countries around the world. Bon voyage.

Key Terms

Agency costs
Andean Pact
Asia-Pacific Economic Cooperation (APEC)
Association of Southeast Asian Nations (ASEAN)
Commodity price risk
Discounted cash flow (DCF)
European Union (EU)
Financial innovation
Financial policy
Financial price risk
Foreign exchange (currency) risk
General Agreement on Tariffs and Trade (GATT)

Interest rate risk
Investment opportunity set
Less developed countries (LDCs)
Mercosur
Multinational corporation (MNC)
North American Free Trade Agreement (NAFTA)
Real options
Risk profile
Set-of-contracts perspective
Stakeholders
World Trade Organization (WTO)

Conceptual Questions

1.1 Describe how multinational financial management is different from domestic financial management.

1.2 What is the goal of financial management? How might this goal be different in different countries? How might the goal of financial management be different for the multinational corporation than for the domestic corporation?

1.3 List several world and/or regional trade pacts in which your country is involved. Do these trade pacts impact all residents of your country in the same way? On balance, are these trade pacts good or bad for residents of your country?

1.4 Do countries tend to export more or less of their gross national product today than in years past? What are the reasons for this trend?

1.5 How has globalization in the world's goods markets affected world trade? How has globalization in the world's financial markets affected world trade?

1.6 What is a financial price risk? Describe several forms of financial price risk.

1.7 List the MNC's key stakeholders. How does each have a stake in the MNC?

SUGGESTED READINGS

The following article chronicles the global stock market crash of 1987.

Richard Roll, "The International Crash of October 1987," *Financial Analysts Journal,* Sept./Oct. 1988, pages 19–35.

The World's Largest Industrial Corporations

1994 Rank	1993 Rank	1984 Rank	Name	Country	Sales ($M)	Profits ($M)	Assets ($M)
1	1	3	General Motors	U.S.	154,951	4,901	198,599
2	2	5	Ford Motor	U.S.	128,439	5,308	219,354
3	3	1	Exxon	U.S.	101,459	5,100	87,862
4	4	2	Royal Dutch/Shell Group	Brit./Neth.	94,881	6,236	108,300
5	5	16	Toyota Motor	Japan	88,159	1,185	98,037
6	6	24	Hitachi	Japan	76,431	1,147	105,258
7	8	21	Matsushita Electric Industrial	Japan	69,947	911	94,441
8	9	11	General Electric	U.S.	64,687	4,726	194,484
9	10	35	Daimler-Benz	Germany	64,169	650	60,365
10	7	8	Intl. Business Machines	U.S.	64,052	3,021	81,091
11	11	4	Mobil	U.S.	59,621	1,079	41,542
12	12	28	Nissan Motor	Japan	58,732	(1,672)	82,820
13	15	71	Philip Morris	U.S.	53,776	4,725	52,649
14	19	22	Chrysler	U.S.	52,224	3,713	49,539
15	17	30	Siemens	Germany	51,055	1,068	50,579
16	13	6	British Petroleum	Britain	50,737	2,416	48,699
17	18	32	Volkswagen	Germany	49,350	92	52,329
18	20	60	Toshiba	Japan	48,228	450	62,905
19	21	18	Unilever	Brit./Neth.	45,451	2,389	28,438
20	16	17	IRI	Italy	45,389	(1,086)	116,626
21	22	49	Nestlé	Switzerland	41,626	2,378	34,563
22	26	46	Fiat	Italy	40,851	627	59,128
23	27	149	Sony	Japan	40,101	(2,953)	48,635
24	24	73	Honda Motor	Japan	39,927	619	34,708
25	23	22	ELF Aquitaine	France	39,459	(981)	48,916
26	29	95	NEC	Japan	37,946	356	47,799
27	33	91	Daewoo	S. Korea	35,707	761	50,029
28	30	9	E.I. Du Pont de Nemours	U.S.	34,968	(2,727)	36,892
29	41	*	Mitsubishi Motors	Japan	34,370	127	32,544
30	28	7	Texaco	U.S.	33,768	910	25,505

(continued)

1994 Rank	1993 Rank	1984 Rank	Name	Country	Sales ($M)	Profits ($M)	Assets ($M)
31	32	27	Philips Electronics	Netherlands	33,517	1,168	27,720
32	36	153	Fujitsu	Japan	32,795	453	42,761
33	37	99	Mitsubishi Electric	Japan	32,726	424	39,594
34	25	14	ENI	Italy	32,566	1,994	54,569
35	35	52	Renault	France	32,188	656	42,357
36	31	13	Chevron	U.S.	31,064	1,693	34,407
37	39	40	Hoechst	Germany	30,604	546	26,187
38	34	50	Procter & Gamble	U.S.	30,296	2,211	25,535
39	40	*	Alcatel Alsthom	France	30,224	653	51,257
40	44	65	Peugeot	France	30,112	559	26,267
41	38	*	ABB Asea Brown Boveri	Switzerland	29,718	760	29,055
42	45	53	Nippon Steel	Japan	29,004	(40)	52,360
43	43	43	Mitsubishi Heavy Industries	Japan	28,676	784	46,222
44	48	86	Pepsico	U.S.	28,472	1,752	24,792
45	42	23	PEMEX (Petroleos Mexicanos)	Mexico	28,195	986	37,844
46	46	12	Amoco	U.S.	26,953	1,789	29,316
47	50	42	BASF	Germany	26,928	792	25,078
48	49	36	Bayer	Germany	26,771	1,215	27,340
49	64	177	BMW (Bayerische Motoren Werke)	Germany	25,973	427	24,971
50	56	130	Hewlett-Packard	U.S.	24,991	1,599	19,567

* Mitsubishi Motors first appeared in 1987. Amoco was called Standard Oil until April 1985. ABB Asea Brown Boveri was created in 1988 from ASEA (Sweden) and Brown Boveri (Switzerland). These firms were ranked 194 and 161 in 1987, respectively. Alcatel was a part of CGE (Cie General D'electricite) and was ranked 85 in 1984.

Source: *Fortune*, "Fortune's Global 500" from the August 7, 1995, issue as well as the April 29, 1985, and August 19, 1985 issues; © 1995 Time Inc. All rights reserved.

The World's Largest Service Corporations

1994 Rank	Name	Country	Sales ($M)	Profits ($M)	Assets ($M)
1	Mitsubishi	Japan	175,836	219	109,256
2	Mitsui	Japan	171,491	264	82,462
3	Itochu	Japan	167,825	82	74,063
4	Sumitomo	Japan	162,476	73	58,974
5	Marubeni	Japan	150,187	104	78,803
6	Nissho Iwai	Japan	100,876	53	56,413
7	Wal-Mart Stores	U.S.	83,412	2,681	32,819
8	Nippon Life Insurance	Japan	75,350	2,682	422,351
9	AT&T	U.S.	75,094	4,676	79,262
10	Nippon Telegraph & Telephone	Japan	70,844	768	146,777
11	Tomen	Japan	69,902	10	27,014
12	Nichimen	Japan	56,203	40	24,635
13	Kanematsu	Japan	55,856	(153)	19,431
14	Dai-Ichi Mutual Life Insurance	Japan	54,900	1,823	299,470
15	Sears Roebuck	U.S.	54,825	1,454	91.896
16	Tokyo Electric Power	Japan	50,359	870	154,097
17	U.S. Postal Service	U.S.	49,383	(914)	46,416
18	Sumitomo Life Insurance	Japan	49,063	2,061	259,372
19	Deutsche Telekom	Germany	41,071	794	107,486
20	Allianz Holding	Germany	40,415	(594)	152,723
21	Veba Group	Germany	40,072	824	38,629
22	State Farm Group	U.S.	38,850	(244)	76,670
23	Prudential Ins. Co. of America	U.S.	36,946	(1,175)	211,902
24	Oesterreichische Post	Austria	36,766	1,859	178,323
25	Meiji Mutual Life Insurance	Japan	36,344	1,455	180,334
26	Union Des Assur De Paris	France	34,597	283	160,212
27	Kmart	U.S.	34,313	296	17,029
28	Electricite De France	France	33,467	227	125,867
29	Deutsche Bank	Germany	33,069	824	369,811
30	Daiei	Japan	32,062	(504)	22,964

(continued)

1994 Rank	Name	Country	Sales ($M)	Profits ($M)	Assets ($M)
31	Citicorp	U.S.	31,650	3,366	250,489
32	Industrial Bank of Japan	Japan	31,072	299	470,446
33	Fuji Bank	Japan	30,103	47	615,189
34	Mitsubishi Bank	Japan	29,991	254	592,447
35	Sumitomo Bank	Japan	29,621	(2,857)	613,856
36	Sanwa Bank	Japan	28,799	225	624,394
37	Ito-Yokado	Japan	28,632	709	17,131
38	RWE Group	Germany	28,628	547	39,745
39	CIE Generale Des Eaux	France	28,153	603	41,805
40	Credit Agricole	France	27,753	1,045	328,244
41	ING Group	Netherlands	26,926	1,265	206,607
42	Asahi Mutual Life Insurance	Japan	26,506	717	135,306
43	Dai-Ichi Kangyo Bank	Japan	26,500	282	622,927
44	Credit Lyonnais	France	26,388	(2,182)	327,995
45	Sakura Bank	Japan	26,069	226	600,514
46	France Telecom	France	25,706	1,787	53,919
47	Kansai Electric Power	Japan	25,585	444	75,869
48	East Japan Railway	Japan	24,643	660	83,951
49	Long Term Credit Bank of Japan	Japan	24,605	71	392,681
50	Carrefour	France	24,573	383	11,058

Source: *Fortune,* "Fortune's Global 500," August 7, 1995; © 1995 Time Inc. All rights reserved.

CHAPTER

2

World Trade in Goods and Capital

*"Merchants have no country. The mere spot they stand on does
not constitute so strong an attachment as that from
which they draw their gains."*

Thomas Jefferson

OVERVIEW

In the previous chapter we discussed the trend toward globalization and the reduction of trade barriers in the world's goods, services, and capital markets. This chapter begins with a discussion of world trade and the balance-of-payments accounting system used to measure trade flows. The International Monetary Fund publishes a monthly summary of each nation's balance of payments and of cross-border trade flows.

The remainder of this chapter is devoted to the international monetary system. The **international monetary system** refers to the global network of governmental and commercial institutions within which currency exchange rates are determined. This financial system is influenced by market forces; by supranational organizations, including the World Bank and the International Monetary Fund; by national policies, laws, regulations, and practices; and by government intervention.

Appendix 2-A gives an example of how free trade can improve the economic welfare of the world's citizens. There is an old joke that goes "If you laid all the economists in the world end to end, they still would not reach a conclusion." The belief that trade can benefit all parties is as close to a fundamental tenet as there is in economics. The Ricardian free trade model in the appendix is a two-asset, two-country model of comparative advantage in which the inputs to production are country specific and cannot cross national borders. By relaxing the assumption of immobile factors of production, we are able to review some arguments (pro and con) revolving around the tenet that free trade can benefit everyone.

Foreign trade is becoming increasingly important for all countries. The most advanced industrialized countries, such as Japan and the United States, are struggling for market share in an increasingly competitive global marketplace. Many *less developed countries* (LDCs) are attempting to promote their industrial bases as a way of improving the welfare of their people.

The term *newly industrializing countries* (NICs) has been coined to describe the countries that have been most successful in nurturing their local manufacturing industries. These high-growth countries include Argentina, Brazil, Mexico, Singapore, South Korea, and Taiwan. These NICs undergo a "life cycle" of industrial growth that is initially based on low labor costs. As these countries industrialize and labor costs rise, the types of industries that led to early advances can lose their advantage relative to other low-cost producers. Labor-intensive manufacturing industries, such as clothing and footwear, continue to migrate toward countries with even lower labor costs, and the NICs often find themselves competing in the same products and markets as industrialized economies. The transition from an economy based on low labor costs into a globally competitive, capital-intensive, high-technology economy is very difficult. Many of these countries face vexing social and public policy issues as the workforce lays its claims to the country's new-found wealth.[1]

Government policymakers, business forecasters, and financial market participants in both developed and developing economies share a need for accurate and timely information regarding cross-border economic and financial transactions. The **International Monetary Fund** (IMF) compiles statistics on cross-border transactions and publishes *Balance of Payments Statistics*, a monthly summary of each country's **balance-of-payments**. This international accounting system tracks each country's cross-border flow of goods, services, and capital.[2]

Table 2.1 presents balance-of-payments accounts for the United States on an annual basis since 1989. Inflows are reported with a positive sign and are often listed as a "Credit." Outflows have a negative sign and often appear as a "Debit." The accounts of most interest are the trade balance, the current account, the financial account, and the overall balance.

The **trade balance** measures whether a particular country is a net importer or exporter of goods. Figure 2.1 plots the U.S. balance of trade since 1971. Exports are a positive number while imports are negative, so a *trade surplus* (a trade balance greater than zero) indicates that residents are exporting more than they are importing. A *trade deficit* (a trade balance less than zero) means that residents are importing more than they are exporting. The trade balance is followed closely by fiscal and monetary authorities because higher exports of goods translate into higher employment in the domestic economy and a more valuable domestic currency.

> The IMF's Balance of Payments
> Statistics track cross-border trade
> in goods, services, and capital.

---

1 As Winston Churchill observed: "The problems of success are preferable to, but no less difficult than, the problems of failure."

2 The IMF changed the way it constructs its balance-of-payments accounts beginning with the September 1995 issue of *International Financial Statistics*. For a complete description of the system in use today, see the *Balance of Payments Manual*, International Monetary Fund, 5th ed., September 1993.

TABLE 2.1 UNITED STATES BALANCE OF PAYMENTS
(BILLIONS OF U.S. DOLLARS), 1989–1995

	1989	1990	1991	1992	1993	1994	1995
Goods: Exports f.o.b.	362.16	389.31	416.91	440.35	458.72	504.54	576.76
Goods: Imports f.o.b.	−447.30	−498.34	−490.98	−536.45	−590.11	−668.86	−749.77
Trade Balance	−115.14	−109.03	−74.07	−96.10	−131.39	−164.32	−173.01
Services: Credit	127.27	147.70	164.15	178.44	185.72	196.52	206.79
Services: Debit	−102.50	−117.63	−118.46	−120.79	−128.01	−137.48	−143.93
Balance on Goods & Serv.	−90.37	−78.96	−28.37	−38.45	−73.68	−105.28	−110.16
Income: Credit	152.63	160.42	137.16	118.58	119.37	137.77	181.47
Income: Debit	−139.90	−140.71	−123.07	−109.55	−111.53	−148.26	−194.11
Bal. on Goods, Serv., & Income	−77.63	−59.25	−14.28	−29.42	−65.84	−115.78	−122.80
Current Transfers: Credit	4.09	8.79	46.84	6.50	5.28	5.15	5.74
Current Transfers: Debit	−30.43	−42.45	−40.28	−39.08	−39.18	−40.31	−35.93
Current Account	−103.97	−92.91	−7.72	−62.00	−99.73	−150.93	−152.98
Capital Account: Credit	.24	.26	.28	.43	.47	.48	.53
Capital Account: Debit	–	–	–	–	−.67	−1.08	−.43
Capital Account	.24	.26	.28	.43	−.20	−.60	.10
Direct Investment Abroad	−36.83	−29.95	−31.38	−42.66	−72.60	−49.37	−96.90
Dir. Invest. in Reporting Economy	67.73	47.92	22.02	17.58	41.13	49.44	74.70
Portfolio Investment Assets	−22.10	−28.80	−45.69	−46.43	−141.80	−49.80	−93.77
Portfolio Investment Liabilities	65.60	−4.20	53.29	61.74	103.30	92.35	191.39
Other Investment Assets	−83.40	−13.73	13.81	17.79	31.20	−32.03	−79.69
Other Investment Liabilities	74.00	43.19	2.24	31.24	35.61	110.22	54.61
Financial Account	65.00	14.42	14.30	39.26	−3.16	120.81	50.35
Net Errors and Omissions	53.98	44.52	−28.94	−26.39	35.98	−14.27	6.66
Overall Balance	15.25	−33.71	−22.07	−48.70	−67.11	−45.00	−95.88

Adapted from the International Monetary Fund publication *International Financial Statistics,* May 1996,
page 622. The term "f.o.b." stands for "free-on-board" and indicates that the values of import/export
goods are measured at the border of the exporting country.

The **current account** is a broader measure of import-export activity that includes
services, royalties, payments for the use of patents, travel and tourism, employee compensation, individual investment and interest income, gifts, and grants, along with the
trade balance on goods.

The **financial account** in Table 2.1 covers cross-border transactions associated with
changes in ownership of financial assets and liabilities. Within the financial accounts,
the "Direct Investment Abroad" account includes cross-border outflows of direct investment capital, where direct investment capital is defined as equity capital, reinvested
earnings, and intercompany transactions between affiliated enterprises. The "Direct
Investment in the Reporting Economy" category includes inflows of direct investment
capital. (Recent U.S. history in these direct investment categories appears in Figure 1.4
on page 7 of chapter 1.) The "Portfolio Investment" accounts include cross-border

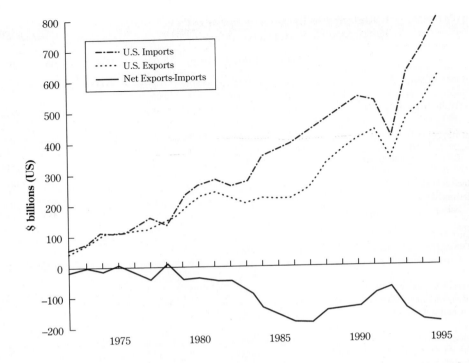

FIGURE 2.1
U.S. Merchandise Trade,
1972–1995

transactions associated with long-term debt and equity securities, money market instruments, and derivative instruments. The "Other Investment" accounts reflect a variety of other cross-border financial transactions, including foreign currency transactions, deposits, loans, and trade credits. The financial account is the net sum of these direct, portfolio, and other investment transactions. Transactions between affiliated financial intermediaries, such as commercial banks, appear in the portfolio investment or other investment accounts.

As the name suggests, the IMF's balance-of-payments is a double-entry system that is intended to record both sides of every cross-border transaction. Because only one side of a transaction is typically reported to the monetary authorities, the balance-of-payments includes a "Net Errors and Omissions" account to ensure that inflows equal outflows. This account is an attempt to infer short-term and long-term cross-border activity from imbalances elsewhere in the balance of payments. Illegal drug trafficking, for example, is typically left unreported by the traffickers. Purchases and sales of short-term financial claims are also often unreported and can account for a sizable proportion of the "Net Errors and Omissions" account.

The **overall balance** is the sum of all of the other accounts. This balance measures the sum of all private financial and economic transactions of the reporting economy with the rest of the world. Deficits and surpluses in the overall balance are associated with changes in foreign exchange rates. A surplus in the overall balance suggests that the quantity of the domestic currency demanded in international markets is greater than the supply, and such a surplus typically is associated with an increase in the value of the domestic currency. A deficit in the overall balance can be interpreted as excess supply of the domestic currency (or as a lack of demand), and such a surplus typically is associated with a drop in the value of the domestic currency.

The Uruguay Round of the General Agreement on Tariffs and Trade was completed in April 1994 after seven years of contentious negotiations. National governments around the world are still in the process of ratifying the treaty. A major point of debate is the extent to which farm tariffs and subsidies would be reduced. A healthy and stable agricultural community is a priority for many governments. For this reason, farmers are often subsidized by their governments and are particularly vulnerable to foreign competition. Here is one account of the GATT negotiations:

There was nothing to do in that cold, cold meeting
Except grouse about trade and some fondue we were
*   eating.*
Too proud to concede and too mad to play ball,
We sat at the meeting. We did nothing at all.

So all we could do was to sit, sit, sit, sit.
And we did not like it, not one little bit.
But then something went bump and that bump made us
*   jump.*
We looked, then we saw him with red, white, and blue hat.
We looked and we saw him, the cat at the GATT.

And he said to us, "Why do you sit there like that?
I know it is boring and the sun is not sunny,
But we can have lots of good trade and make money.
I know some good rules we could have," said the cat.
"I know some new tricks," said the cat at the GATT.

"A lot of good tricks. I will show them to you.
Maggie Thatcher will not mind at all if I do."
But the French said, "No, no, make that cat go away,

Tell that cat at the GATT farmers should not have to pay.
He should not be here. He should not be about.
He should not be here, oh, the farmers will shout."

"Now, now, have no fear, have no fear," said the cat.
"Free trade is not bad," said the cat at the GATT.
"Why you can have a much freer market I found,
With the structure I call the Uruguay Round."
"Sacre bleu," said the French, and the Germans said, "Nein,"
With the Swiss, Dutch, and Belgians all starting to whine.

"Have no fear," said the cat, "I will not let you fall.
Just give us our way and we'll let you play ball.
I can balance free trade with real politique.
I can ram through these rules and lots of new tricks.
You let us sell crops and compete with your farms
And welcome our products with wide-open arms.

Then, in exchange, we'll make it quite easy
For you to hock software to make U.S. firms queasy.
And that is not all. Oh no, that is not all.
If you open your trade and let us compete,
U.S. banks will start up on each European street.
Complete overhaul of copyright laws,
If you simply remove your EEC flaws."

It sounded real good. It had magical charm,
This radical deal from the fellows of Cairns.
Then our farmers came in and they said to us all,
"Will you sell us all out? Tell us what will you do?"
Should we tell them the truth? Now what should we do?
Now what would you do if this happened to you?

Written by Art Silverman and aired on National Public Radio's *All Things Considered* on November 20, 1990.

2.2 THE INTERNATIONAL MONETARY SYSTEM

An Economist's Classification of Exchange Rate Systems

The range of possible international monetary systems runs the gamut from freely floating systems, in which currency values are determined without government intervention in a competitive marketplace, to fixed rate systems, in which governments set exchange

FIXED RATE system ↓ .

In a fixed exchange rate system, governments stand ready to buy and sell currency at official exchange rates.

• Reduce Risk
  To companies
• Gov't assumes Risk

Drawbacks
1. Links inflation Rates

2. Hard to support if value is Questioned

rates and attempt to enforce their acceptance on buyers and sellers. The freely floating and fixed rate exchange rate systems are at the two endpoints of the range of exchange rate systems in use today. The way in which inflation in different countries is linked through the exchange rate system is most easily understood using these two textbook extremes.

Fixed Rate Systems In a **fixed exchange rate system**, governments stand ready to buy and sell currency at official exchange rates. Fixed-rate systems are attractive because, if they can be maintained, they reduce foreign exchange risk for those companies doing business internationally. For instance, if a U.S. exporter agrees to supply goods to a foreign importer in exchange for a certain amount of foreign currency payable in two years, the U.S. exporter knows exactly how much the foreign currency will be worth in dollars in two years under a fixed-rate system. The problem with fixed-rate systems is that by standing ready to buy or sell currencies at the stated exchange rate, the government is assuming the foreign exchange risk of its constituent businesses. If the market values of the currencies are not equal to the fixed exchange rate, the government must in essence pay the difference from market value. This results in a transfer of wealth from the society at large to those businesses that would otherwise have had to pay (or receive) a cash flow based on the market exchange rate.

We saw in Chapter 1 how an increase in financial risk has accompanied the rapid globalization of the world's capital markets in recent years. Because it is difficult to maintain fixed exchange rates in the presence of high volatility in exchange rates, the international monetary system of today is closer to a freely floating system than to a fixed-rate system, although many governments attempt to manage or peg their currencies to other currencies or to currency baskets such as in the **European Exchange Rate Mechanism**, (ERM).

There are two drawbacks to a fixed exchange rate system. First, fixed exchange rates forge a direct link between domestic and foreign inflation rates. Suppose German inflation rises because of the cost of East German reunification while French inflation remains low. With a fixed exchange rate between deutsche marks and francs, German products become more expensive than French products. German consumers will buy less of the high-priced German produce, resulting in rising unemployment in Germany, while French prices will rise and unemployment will fall due to the increased demand for French products. This system creates a direct link between inflation, wage levels, and unemployment conditions in countries with fixed exchange rates. The major impediment to European monetary union is the fact that the members of the European Union (EU) have such divergent economic, fiscal, monetary, and social conditions at home.[3] Member states are unwilling to surrender their national sovereignty on matters of social and economic policy to the European parliament in Brussels.

The second drawback to a fixed exchange rate system is the difficulty of maintaining the fixed exchange rates when market participants believe that the true values are otherwise. Because governments cannot impose their will on financial markets indefinitely, markets ultimately get their way when market rates and government rates disagree. And when changes in currency values arrive in fixed rate systems, they are whoppers.

---

3 Prior to 1994, the European Union was called the European Economic Community or EEC

From 1985 to 1991, Japanese companies invested more than $75 billion in U.S. real estate, largely funded by aggressive Japanese banks that were flush with cash from several years of uninterrupted prosperity. These investments appear in the "Direct Investment in the Reporting Economy" category in the U.S. Balance of Payments accounts in Table 2.1. Among the properties purchased were such U.S. landmarks as the Rockefeller Center (by Mitsubishi Estate Co.), Pebble Beach Golf Links (financed by Sumitomo Bank), and the 1,241-room Hyatt Regency Waikoloa in Hawaii (financed by Mitsubishi Bank). Timing is everything, and these investments were, unfortunately, very poorly timed. The U.S. real estate market collapsed in the late 1980s with many commercial properties falling more than 25 percent in value. As if a fall in U.S. property values were not enough, the Japanese stock market fell 40 percent during 1990. Unlike U.S. banks, Japanese banks are allowed to own stock, and a large part of the value of a Japanese bank comes from its stock holdings. The yen also fell against the dollar during this period. All three of the above purchases as well as many others ended up in default, leaving Japanese banks holding the empty bag.

Japanese officials have estimated the size of problem loans at Japanese banks to be about ¥40 trillion, or $469 billion at the June 1995 exchange rate.* This is equal to approximately 10% of Japan's gross domestic product. Because of the size of the bad debt problem, the Japanese government is being forced into a bail-out much like that in the U.S. banking system during the 1980s.

* "Japan admits bad debts problem totals $469bn," *London Financial Times*, June 7, 1995, page 14.

Governments are most adamant about maintaining fixed rates when their fixed rate systems are under the most pressure. Devaluations and revaluations typically come on the heels of a claim by the head of state that the government has full confidence in the value of their currency and will maintain the fixed rate system at all costs. When currency values do fall out of a fixed exchange rate system, government officials are quick to blame currency speculators for precipitating the collapse.[4] Because changes come infrequently but in large increments in a fixed exchange rate system, the apparent absence of foreign exchange risk in a fixed rate system is an illusion.

Exchange rate changes in a fixed rate system are called **devaluations** when a currency falls in value relative to another currency and **revaluations** when that currency rises in value relative to another currency. For example, if the official exchange rate between the French franc and the German deutsche mark is changed by government fiat from FF2/DM to FF3/DM, the deutsche mark has had a revaluation against the French franc. At the same time, the franc has had a devaluation from DM.5000/FF (the reciprocal of FF2/DM) to DM.3333/FF against the deutsche mark. An increase in a currency value under a floating exchange rate system is called an **appreciation** and a

---

4 A formal analysis of this phenomenon is presented by Dean Taylor in "Official Intervention in the Foreign Exchange Market, or Bet against the Central Bank," Journal of Political Economy, April 1982, pages 356–368. A popular treatment appears in "Days of the one-way currency bet are over," James Blitz, London Financial Times, August 18, 1993, page 13.

FLOATING

Exchange rates in a floating
rate system change with
market conditions.

Advantage

Disadvantage

Classifications

fall in a currency value is called a **depreciation**. As under fixed exchange rates, when currency rises in value another must fall.

Floating Rate Systems **Freely floating exchange rate systems** allow currency values to fluctuate according to supply and demand forces in the market without direct interference by government authorities. The major advantage of a freely floating system is that changes in inflation, wage levels, and unemployment in one country are not forced on another country through currency values as they are in the fixed exchange rate system. Consider our example of a rise in German inflation. With floating exchange rates, the value of the franc will tend to rise as both German and French consumers buy more of the lower-priced French goods. As the franc rises in value relative to the deutsche mark, French goods will lose some of their price advantage to German consumers and unemployment in Germany will not fall as rapidly as under a fixed rate system. French consumers will continue to buy German goods because their francs will buy more marks. In a freely floating system, the exchange rate adjusts for the inflation differentials between countries. In general, a freely floating system tends to insulate countries from changes in inflation, wage levels, and unemployment in other countries.

The major disadvantage of a freely floating system is the flip side of its major strength. Because exchange rates change continuously, it is difficult to know how much a future payment or receipt in a foreign currency will be worth. This means that multinational enterprises must monitor their foreign exchange positions and, if necessary, hedge their exposures to foreign exchange rate changes.

The IMF's Classification of Exchange Rate Systems

Recognizing that no currencies are truly either freely floating or fixed rate, the International Monetary Fund (IMF) classifies currencies into one of the following categories:

1. More flexible (usually a freely floating system)
2. Flexibility limited in terms of a single currency or group of currencies
3. Pegged system

The advantages and disadvantages of these systems are summarized in Figure 2.2. A recent classification of the world's currencies, reprinted from the IMF publication *International Financial Statistics,* appears in Table 2.2. The rest of this section describes some of the features of the exchange rate systems found in practice.

More Flexible Exchange Rate Systems Some countries, such as the United States and Japan, are in a **more flexible exchange rate system** in which currency values are allowed to float in relation to each other. These currencies are not in a truly freely floating system because government intervention can and does have a significant impact on currency values, especially in the short term.

Managed float exchange rate systems are similar to a free float in that there are no official bounds on currency values. In contrast to their "hands off" stance in a freely floating system, however, governments do intervene in managed float systems in order to accomplish their policy objectives. Managed float systems allow governments to

More flexible (floating rate) system

Foreign exchange rates are allowed to fluctuate according to market supply and demand without direct interference by monetary or fiscal authorities.

Advantages   Countries are at least partially insulated from unemployment and inflation in other countries.

Disadvantages   Exchange rates change continuously, making it difficult to know how much a future payment or receipt in a foreign currency will be worth in the domestic currency.

Limited flexibility system

Currencies exhibit limited flexibility with respect to a single currency (such as the dollar) or to a basket of currencies (such as the ECU).

Advantages   Allows governments to implement broad policy objectives within a relatively flexible exchange rate system; attempts to combine the benefits of a fixed rate system with enough flexibility to make the system manageable.

Disadvantages   There is still a chance that the currency will undergo a significant change in value or fall out of the exchange rate system.

Pegged (fixed rate) system

An exchange rate system in which governments are willing to both buy and sell currency only at an official exchange rate that is pegged to another currency or currency basket.

Advantages   If the system can be maintained, residents face less exchange rate risk and trade will flourish.

Disadvantages   The absence of exchange rate risk can be an illusion—when exchange rate changes (devaluations or revaluations) come they are huge.

Summary

FIGURE 2.2
The IMF's Classification of Exchange Rate Systems

implement their policy objectives within a relatively flexible exchange rate system and to coordinate monetary policies with other governments if they choose. The flip side of this flexibility is that if government intervention helps one country, it is likely to hurt another. The world's economy is, after all, a closed system. Financial risk management in a managed system is much like that in a freely floating system, although financial managers must always be conscious of the possibility of government intervention and its influence on foreign exchange rates.

Limited Flexibility Exchange Rate Systems The category of **limited flexibility** comprises two groups. The first group includes several Persian Gulf countries with currencies that have shown limited flexibility in terms of the U.S. dollar. The reason that these currencies have shown limited flexibility in terms of the dollar is because oil is priced around the world in U.S. dollars. The second group includes the countries in the European Exchange Rate Mechanism, or ERM. The ERM attempts to combine the best

TABLE 2.2 Exchange Rate Arrangements as of December 31, 1995[a]

Currency pegged to					Flexibility limited in terms of a single currency or group of currencies		More flexible		
U.S. dollar	French franc	Other currency	SDR	Other composite[b]	Single currency[c]	Cooperative arrangements[d]	Adjusted according to a set of indicators[e]	Other managed floating	Independently floating
Antigua and Barbuda	Benin	Bhutan (Indian rupee)	Libya	Bangladesh	Bahrain	Austria	Chile	Algeria	Afghanistan, Islamic State of
Argentina	Burkina Faso	Bosnia and Herzogovina (deutsche mark)	Myanmar	Botswana	Qatar	Belgium	Nicaragua	Angola	Albania
Bahamas, The	Cameroon	Estonia (deutsche mark)	Seychelles	Burundi	Saudi Arabia	Denmark		Belarus	Armenia
Barbados	C. African Rep.	Kiribati (Australian dollar)		Cape Verde	United Arab Emirates	France		Brazil	Australia
Belize	Chad	Lesotho (South African rand)		Cyprus		Germany		Cambodia	Azerbaijan
Djibouti	Comoros	Namibia (South African rand)		Czech Republic		Ireland		China, P.R.	Bolivia
Dominica	Congo	San Marino (Italian lira)		Fiji		Luxemborg		Columbia	Bulgaria
Grenada	Côte d'Ivoire	Swaziland (South African rand)		Iceland		Netherlands		Costa Rica	Canada
Iraq	Equatorial Guinea			Jordan		Portugal		Croatia	Ethiopia
Liberia	Gabon			Kuwait		Spain		Dominican Rep.	Finland
Lithuania	Mali			Malta				Ecuador	Gambia, The
Marshall Islands	Niger			Morocco				Egypt	Ghana
Micronesia, Fed. States of	Senegal			Nepal				El Salvador	Guatemala
Nigeria	Togo			Slovak Republic				Eritrea	Guinea
Oman				Solomon Islands				Georgia	Guyana
Panama				Thailand				Greece	Haiti
St. Kitts and Nevis				Tonga				Guinea-Bissau	India
St. Lucia				Vanuatu				Honduras	Italy
St. Vincent and the Grenadines				Western Samoa				Hungary	Jamaica
Syrian Arab Rep.								Indonesia	Japan
Venezuela								Iran, I.R. of	Kazakhstan
Yemen, Rep. of								Israel	Kenya
								Korea	Lao P.D. Rep.
								Kyrgyz Rep.	Lebanon
								Latvia	Madagascar
								Macedonia, FYR of	Malawi
								Malaysia	Mauritania
								Maldives	Mexico
								Mauritius	Moldova
								Norway	Mongolia
								Pakistan	Mozambique
								Poland	New Zealand
								Russia	Papua New Guinea
								Singapore	Paraguay
								Slovenia	Peru
								Sri Lanka	Philippines
								Suriname	Romania
								Tunisia	Rwanda
								Turkmenistan	São Tomé & Principe
								Turkey	Sierra Leone
								Ukraine	Somalia
								Uruguay	South Africa
								Uzbekistan	Sudan
								Vietnam	Sweden
									Switzerland
									Tajikistan, Rep. of
									Tanzania
									Trinidad and Tobago
									Uganda
									Ukraine
									United Kingdom
									United States
									Zaire
									Zambia
									Zimbabwe

a For members with dual or multiple exchange markets, the arrangement shown is that in the major market.
b Comprises currencies that are pegged to various "baskets" of currencies of the members' own choice, as distinct from the SDR basket.
c Exchange rates of all currencies have shown limited flexibility in terms of the U.S. dollar.
d Refers to the cooperative arrangement maintained under the European Monetary System.
e Includes exchange arrangements under which the exchange rate is adjusted at relatively frequent intervals on the basis of indicators determined by the respective member countries.

Source: Adapted from *International Financial Statistics* published by the International Monetary Fund, May 1996.

of the fixed and floating exchange rate systems. First and foremost, because foreign exchange rates tend to remain relatively stable within the ERM, short-term foreign exchange risk is reduced. And because pegged systems usually have an allowable band for movement around the central rate, these systems do not require the restrictive monetary policies necessary to ensure a single fixed rate. This limit varies in the ERM for different currencies and at different times. The German deutsche mark, historically the most stable of the European currencies, is usually kept within a band of ±2.5 percent around its ERM central rate. As a currency begins to fall below its ERM floor, EU central banks usually cooperate in buying the currency (selling other foreign exchange reserves in the process), thus, they hope, keeping the currency within the ERM bands.

Pegged Exchange Rate Systems In this exchange rate arrangement, currency values are **pegged** to another currency such as the U.S. dollar, French franc, or Russian ruble, or to a currency basket such as the special drawing right (SDR) or the European currency unit (ECU). **Special drawing rights** are an international reserve created by the International Monetary Fund and allocated to member countries to supplement foreign exchange reserves. SDRs are merely bookkeeping units of account and are traded only between central banks. Since 1981, the SDR has been constructed of 41 percent U.S. dollar and 19 percent German deutsche mark, with the remaining 40 percent divided equally among the British pound, French franc, and Japanese yen. Prior to 1981, an SDR included sixteen currencies. The value of an SDR is quoted in the financial pages of the newspaper, so it is convenient to peg currencies to the SDR.

TABLE 2.3 EMS EUROPEAN CURRENCY UNIT (ECU) RATES

May 23, 1996	Ecu cen. rates	Rate against Ecu	Change on day	%± from cen. rate	% spread v weakest	Div. Ind.
Spain	162.493	159.356	+0.138	−1.93	3.39	13
Netherlands	2.15214	2.13999	+0.00087	−0.56	1.97	4
Belgium	39.3960	39.3250	+0.0106	−0.18	1.58	1
Germany	1.91007	1.91329	+0.00062	0.17	1.22	−2
Austria	13.4383	13.4630	+0.0042	0.18	1.21	−1
Portugal	195.792	196.359	+0.116	0.29	1.10	−2
Ireland	0.792214	0.794750	−0.001443	0.32	1.07	−2
France	6.40608	6.47385	−0.00244	1.06	0.33	−9
Denmark	7.28580	7.38745	+0.0029	1.40	0.00	−10
Non ERM Members						
Greece	292.867	302.584	+0.092	3.32	−1.86	—
Italy	2106.15	1935.68	−0.43	−8.09	10.32	—
UK	0.786652	0.820491	−0.000842	4.30	−2.79	—

Ecu central rates set by the European Commission. Currencies are in descending relative strength. Percentage changes are for Ecu; a positive change denotes a weak currency. The Divergence Indicator (Div. Ind.) shows the ratio between two spreads: the percentage difference between the actual market and the Ecu central rates for a currency, and the maximum permitted percentage deviation of the currency's market rate from its Ecu central rate. (September 17, 1992) Sterling and Italian Lira suspended from ERM. Adjustment calculated by the *Financial Times.*

Source: Adapted from the *London Financial Times,* May 24, 1996, page 33.

Several countries in the "Other composite" category (see Table 2.2) peg their currencies to the **European currency unit (ECU)**. The ECU is a trade-weighted basket of currencies in the European Exchange Rate Mechanism (ERM) of the European Union. Like the SDR, the ECU represents a basket of currencies and, hence, it is a unit of account rather than an actual currency. The ECU weights each member's foreign exchange rate by a measure of that member's relative gross national product and volume of trade within the EU. Table 2.3 displays the May 23, 1996 values of the EMS currencies against the European currency unit.

The primary disadvantage of a pegged system is that central banks must still fight the market to maintain the system. Even if inflation in two countries is the same, the ebbs and flows of business fortune will result in fluctuations in currency values. Consequently, there is still a chance that currencies will undergo significant changes in value or even "fall out" of a pegged exchange rate system. Changes in currency values in a pegged system lie somewhere between the large and infrequent variations of a fixed rate system and the smaller but persistent variations in a freely floating system.

Government Intervention in the Foreign Exchange Market

Suppose Italy wishes to intervene in a freely floating currency market in order to increase the value of the Italian lira. To increase the price of its domestic currency, the Italian government can either increase the demand for the domestic currency or decrease the supply of the domestic currency. The effect of either action is an appreciation of the lira as shown below.

To increase value either:
1. Decrease supply
or
2. Increase Demand

1. Increase the demand for the domestic currency (for example, from D_0 to D_1)

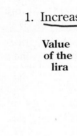

2. Decrease the supply of the domestic currency (for example, from S_0 to S_1)

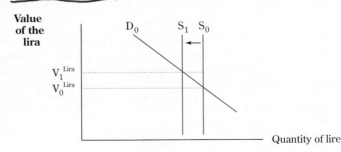

Several roads lead to Rome. First, the Italian government can buy lire in order to remove lire from the international currency markets. It now must decide what foreign exchange reserve currency it will sell for lire. If the Italian government sells German deutsche marks for lire, it is simultaneously decreasing the demand for deutsche marks and increasing the demand for lire. The lira will tend to rise in relation to the deutsche mark. If Italy sells dollars rather than deutsche marks, the lira will tend to rise relative to the dollar and perhaps also against the deutsche mark and other currencies. As Italy intervenes in the foreign exchange market, the balance of various assets in its foreign exchange reserves changes. Foreign exchange reserves include gold, domestic and foreign currencies, and currency baskets such as the European currency unit (ECU) and the IMF's special drawing rights (SDRs).

A Brief History of the International Monetary System

The history of the international monetary system leads us on a circuitous path through several exchange rate systems. A brief review of this history will help you to understand how alternative exchange rate systems affect asset values across national borders. This is essential knowledge for managing value and financial risk within the present and future international monetary systems.

The International Monetary System before 1944 Prior to 1914, the major countries of the world operated on what is known as the **classical gold standard**, in which gold was used to settle national trade balances. World War I upset this standard and threw the international monetary system into turmoil. In 1925, a **gold exchange standard** was instituted in which the United States and England were allowed to hold only gold reserves while other nations could hold either gold, U.S. dollars, or pound sterling as reserves. Reserves are assets available to central banks for use in managing balance of payments and foreign exchange positions. The gold exchange system lasted until 1931, at which time England was forced to withdraw from the system under pressure from massive demands on its reserves as a result of an unrealistically high exchange rate. To maintain the competitiveness of their products on world markets, most other nations followed England in devaluing their currencies. Many nations also instituted protectionist trade policies in this era.

The gold exchange standard lasted until 1931.

Protectionist trade policies and the breakdown of the international monetary system helped to fuel the global depression of the 1930s. During this period, currency exchange rates fluctuated wildly. Speculators sold weak currencies and purchased strong currencies, thus causing further fluctuations in currency values. Because there was not an established forward exchange market, there was no way to hedge foreign exchange risk, and businesses were at the mercy of a very fickle monetary system.

Protectionism fuels depression

Bretton Woods: 1946–1971 After World War II, representatives of the Allied nations convened at Bretton Woods, New Hampshire, to create a postwar monetary system that would promote world trade and impose some structure on the near-anarchy that had ruled the financial markets during the previous fifteen years. Under the Bretton Woods system, the price of an ounce of gold was set at $35 (U.S.). Each nation agreed to maintain a fixed (or pegged) exchange rate for its currency in terms of the dollar or gold. For example, the German deutsche mark was set equal to 1/140 of an

The Bretton Woods System lasted from the end of WWII until 1971.

ounce of gold, or $0.25/DM. Under this form of gold exchange standard, only U.S. dollars were convertible into gold at the official par value of $35/ounce. Other member nations were not required to exchange their currency for gold, but they pledged to intervene in the foreign exchange markets if their currency moved more than 1 percent from its official rate.

The Bretton Woods conference created two well-known institutions to implement this fixed-rate system. The International Monetary Fund (IMF) was created to provide temporary assistance to countries trying to defend their currencies against supply/demand imbalances or working to correct "structural" trade problems. The IMF is a very large international organization with 1995 funding of more than $150 billion (U.S.). The Bretton Woods conference also created the **International Bank for Reconstruction and Development**, popularly known as the **World Bank**, to help in the reconstruction and development of its member nations.

The Bretton Woods system worked passably well from 1946 until the late 1960s. The market periodically imposed its own agenda on the world's economies, and devaluations were common, but by and large the system served to facilitate cross-border trade and to stimulate economic development. During the 1960s, U.S. inflation rose as the government borrowed money to finance the war in Vietnam and the expensive social programs of Lyndon Johnson's Great Society. High U.S. inflation caused the market price of gold to rise above $35 per ounce and the market value of the U.S. dollar to fall below the official rate relative to foreign currencies. A run on the U.S. dollar ensued as speculators (including investors, financial institutions, and governments) rushed to buy gold with dollars at the $35 per ounce price. Finally, on August 15, 1971, President Nixon surrendered to market forces and took the United States off the gold standard. Many currencies were already floating by this time. Nixon also imposed a price freeze on domestic U.S. prices. Not surprisingly, this price freeze was ineffective in curbing U.S. inflation.

Exchange Rates since the Fall of Bretton Woods Table 2.4 lists the Bretton Woods agreement and important international monetary agreements signed since 1971. To interpret the context within which these agreements were formed, the value of the U.S. dollar relative to the Japanese yen and U.K. pound sterling appears in Figure 2.3.

After the collapse of Bretton Woods, several unsuccessful attempts were made to resurrect a gold exchange standard. The first of these, the Smithsonian Agreement, was signed in Washington, D.C., by the Group of Ten during December 1971.[5] This agreement devalued the U.S. dollar to $38 per ounce of gold and revalued other currencies relative to the dollar. A 4.5 percent band was established to promote monetary stability. In April 1972, members of the European economic community (EEC) established a pegged exchange rate system known as "the snake" or "the snake within the tunnel." The term "snake" referred to the fact that the pegged currencies floated as a group against non-EEC currencies. The "tunnel" refers to the band allowed around the central currency rates in the system. Both the Smithsonian Agreement and the snake proved unworkable in the presence of continued volatility in the currency market. Countries

---

5 Also called the Paris Club, the Group of Ten included Belgium, Canada, France, Italy, Japan, the Netherlands, Sweden, the United Kingdom, the United States, and West Germany.

TABLE 2.4 BRETTON WOODS AGREEMENT AND MAJOR EXCHANGE RATE AGREEMENTS SINCE 1971

Date	Event	Repercussions
1946	Bretton Woods Agreement	The U.S. dollar was convertible into gold at $35/ounce. Other currencies were pegged to this price. Agreement also created the IMF and the World Bank.
1971	President Nixon takes the U.S. off the gold standard	The dollar was no longer convertible into gold, forcing the dollar and other major currencies to float on world currency markets.
1971	Smithsonian Agreement	Dollar was devalued to $38/ounce of gold; Group of Ten (Belgium, Canada, France, Italy, Japan, the Netherlands, Sweden, the United Kingdom, the United States, and West Germany) revalued currencies against the dollar and agreed to maintain these values within a 4.5 percent band. Agreement lasted barely six months before the U.K. pound fell out of the system.
1972	European Joint Float Agreement	"The snake within the tunnel," a pegged exchange rate system, was adopted by the European Economic Community. Pound fell out of the system two months later.
1976	Jamaica Agreement	Floating rates declared acceptable, officially acknowledging the system already in place.
1979	European Monetary System (EMS) created	European Exchange Rate Mechanism (ERM) intended to maintain currencies within a 2.25 percent band around central rates. Created European Currency Unit (ECU).
1985	Plaza Accord	Group of Ten agreed to cooperate in controlling volatility in currency exchange rates and bring down the value of the dollar.
1987	Louvre Accord	The dollar had fallen from its 1985 high. The Group of Five (France, Germany, Japan, the United Kingdom, and the United States) agreed to promote stability in currency markets around current levels.
1991	Treaty of Maastricht	European community members agreed to pursue a broad agenda of economic, financial, and monetary reforms. A single European currency was proposed as the ultimate goal of monetary union.

frequently were forced to either devalue their currency or fall out of these pegged systems until an agreement could be reached on a new target price. Realignments were the rule of the day. The pound sterling lasted only until June 1972 before the Bank of England was forced to allow it to float against other currencies. The Swiss franc lasted until January 1973 before it too floated. The dollar was devalued to $42.22 per ounce of gold in February 1973. Currency values fluctuated even more severely following the

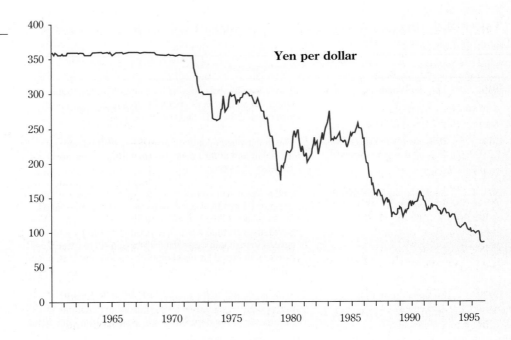

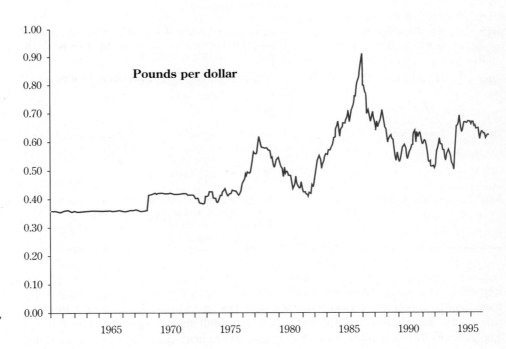

FIGURE 2.3
Nominal Value of the U.S.
Dollar under Floating Rates,
1961–1995

1973–1974 OPEC oil embargo, and pegged systems such as the snake experienced troubled times.

This was a period of unprecedented financial risk. Many economists expected floating exchange rates to lead to less volatility in the monetary system. Instead, floating rates seemed to lead to even more volatility. Whether floating rates were the cause or the effect of monetary instability is the subject of continuing debate. In any case, floating exchange rates and high volatility combined to create high levels of foreign exchange risk. Interest rate risk was also on the rise as inflation grew in many countries. And the OPEC oil embargo caused a great deal of oil price risk. Participants in the financial and goods markets faced a nemesis—financial price volatility—for which they were ill-prepared.

In January 1976, the IMF convened a monetary summit in Jamaica to reach some sort of consensus on the monetary system. Exchange rate volatility was still too high (and policy objectives too diverse) for governments to form an agreement on a fixed-rate or pegged system. However, participants did agree to disagree. Under the Jamaica Agreement, floating exchange rates were declared acceptable, officially acknowledging the system already in place and legitimizing the basis for a system still used today.

Under the 1976 Jamaica Agreement, floating exchange rates were officially accepted by most nations.

In March of 1979, the EEC's snake was superseded by the **European Monetary System (EMS)**. This system was based on central bank cooperation to maintain currency values within a ±2.25 percent band around the central rates. The United Kingdom (comprising England, Northern Ireland, Scotland, and Wales) was subsequently admitted with a 6 percent band. The European Exchange Rate Mechanism (ERM) of the EMS is centered around the European currency unit (ECU), which is a basket of currencies weighted by each member's proportion of intra-European trade and the relative size of GNP. The ERM is still in operation today, although member nations fight a constant battle to keep their currencies within the limits of the ERM. Occasionally, countries are forced out of the ERM by market forces. Reentry into the system is usually at a much lower exchange rate than when the country left, resulting in a currency devaluation.

During the mid-1980s, the dollar rose in value relative to other currencies. During this time, foreign governments complained that the high dollar was causing inflation in their economies because the price of U.S. imports was high. The U.S. government complained that the trade deficit was widening because of the poor competitive position of high-priced U.S. goods on the world market. The dollar reached its high against most currencies in early 1985, climbing as high as DM3.50/dollar (or $0.286/DM) against the German deutsche mark.

In September 1985, the Group of Ten met at the Plaza Hotel in New York and agreed to cooperate in controlling volatility in currency exchange rates. A principal objective of the Plaza Accord was to bring down the value of the dollar. The dollar had already begun falling during the spring and summer of 1985. By February 1987, the dollar had fallen to what many believed to be equilibrium. At that time, the Group of Five (France, Germany, Japan, the United Kingdom, and the United States) met in France and agreed to promote stability in currency markets around current levels in the Louvre Accord.

Another crisis occurred during the autumn of 1992. The Treaty of Maastricht, named after the Dutch city that hosted the European summit, had been signed by European Union governments in December 1991. Government leaders were optimistic that the road to economic and financial unification would proceed, despite the protests and warnings of numerous Euro-skeptics. However, in May 1992 Denmark failed to ratify the Maastricht Treaty in a close popular vote. By early September, the success of the French referendum on the treaty, scheduled for September 20, was also in doubt. Calamity hit Europe's currency markets on September 17, 1992. On that day, the British pound sterling fell below its ERM floor of £2.778/DM. Despite increasing a key interest rate from 10 percent to 12 percent and threatening a boost to 15 percent, Prime Minister John Major and Chancellor of the Exchequer Norman Lamont could not keep the pound within its ERM range. Italy also suspended the lira from the ERM after the lira fell below its ERM floor. Italy and Spain eventually devalued their currencies before being readmitted to the ERM.

Even non-EU countries were affected. Finland and Sweden wished to share in European integration and had been maintaining informal links between their currencies and the ECU. When the value of their currencies plummeted against the German mark, both countries initially intervened in an attempt to maintain their link with the ECU and establish credence that they belonged in the ERM. Finland eventually gave up resistance and allowed the Finnish markka to float. Sweden refused to give in and eventually raised its key lending rate to 500 percent per annum (inflation was less than 10 percent at the time) in an effort to defend the value of its currency.

A currency crisis in August 1993 caused the ERM bands to be widened to ±15 percent, making the ERM much more of a floating rate system on the fixed/floating continuum. Because of the fixed rate characteristics of the original ERM, the system helped equalize inflation across European community members. The wider bands in the August 1993 system allow more divergence in monetary policies within the ERM. Instituting wider bands within the ERM can be viewed as a breakdown of the system. It can also be viewed as a natural response to existing differences in inflation, interest rates, and monetary policies within the ERM members. Since monetary convergence is a central goal of the European Union, the continuing struggles of the ERM suggest that the original timetable for EU economic and monetary convergence will be delayed.

2.3 SUMMARY

We began this chapter with a description of the International Monetary Fund's balance of payments statistics. The balance-of-payments accounting system tracks the flow of goods, services, and capital into and out of each country. The accounts of most interest to financial managers are:

• Current account	Measures a country's international trade in goods and services, including merchandise imports and merchandise exports
• Capital account	Measures changes in cross-border ownership of most long-term financial assets
• Trade balance	The net balance on merchandise trade
• Current account balance	A broader measure of import-export activity that includes services, travel and tourism, transportation, investment income and interest, gifts, and grants, along with the trade balance on goods

Important Accounts [handwritten annotation]

- Overall balance   Measures the sum of all private financial and economic transactions with the rest of the world

Keeping abreast of the international balance of payments can allow multinational financial managers to identify opportunities as well as potential problem areas in the conduct of their foreign and domestic operations.

We then described two categorizations of exchange rate systems—the classical economist's classification scheme and the International Monetary Fund's classification scheme. Exchange rates under fixed-rate and pegged systems have occasional large devaluations and revaluations, while exchange rate changes under a floating rate or flexible system have smaller but more continuous depreciations and appreciations.

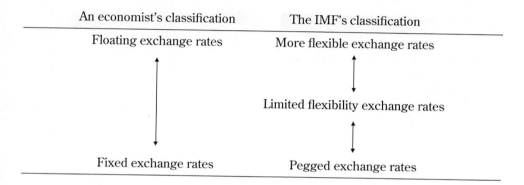

The chapter concluded with a brief history of the international monetary system. Most exchange rates have been floating since the currency crises of 1971. Attempts to limit exchange rate fluctuations through mechanisms such as the European Exchange Rate Mechanism have met with some success, although in the long run currency values are determined by market forces and not by government fiat.

KEY TERMS

Balance of payments

Capital account

Currency revaluations/devaluations and
  appreciations/depreciations

Current account

Current account balance

European currency unit (ECU)

European Exchange Rate Mechanism (ERM)

European Monetary System (EMS)

Fixed versus freely floating exchange rate
  systems

Gold standard and gold exchange standard

International Monetary Fund (IMF)

International monetary system

Overall balance

Pegged, limited flexibility, and more flexible
  exchange rate systems

Special drawing rights (SDRs)

Trade balance

World Bank (the International Bank for
  Reconstruction and Development)

Conceptual Questions

2.1 What distinguishes developed, less developed, and newly industrializing economies?

2.2 Describe the International Monetary Fund's balance-of-payments accounting system.

2.3 How would an economist categorize systems for trading foreign exchange? How would the IMF make this classification? In what ways are these the same? How are they different?

2.4 In what ways do national governments intervene in the foreign exchange markets?

2.5 Describe the Bretton Woods agreement. How long did the agreement last? What forced its collapse?

Suggested Readings

An accessible discussion of the arguments for and against free trade appears in

Paul R. Krugman, "Is Free Trade Passé," *Economic Perspectives* Vol. 1, No. 2, Fall 1988, pages 131–144.

A graphical analysis of equilibrium in international trade appears in

Wassily Leontief, "The Use of Indifference Curves in the Analysis of Foreign Trade," *Quarterly Journal of Economics* 47, May 1933, pages 493–503.

The Theory of Comparative Advantage: A Game in Which Everybody Wins?

In his essay *Principles of Political Economy,* David Ricardo (1772–1823) originated what is now known as the Classical Theory of Comparative Advantage.[6] According to this early international trade theory, everyone gains if each nation specializes in the production of those goods that it produces relatively most efficiently and imports those goods that other countries produce relatively most efficiently. This seems like plain commonsense—and it is. It is useful to develop this commonsense notion a little further in order to identify the nature (and perhaps fragility) of the potential gain from cross-border trade.

Suppose there are two countries, A and B. The only goods consumed in these countries are food (F) and clothing (C). The only factor required in the production of food and clothing is labor, but the production technologies for food and for clothing differ between the countries. Country A is able to produce ten units of food per day of labor input ($^A\alpha^F$ = 10 food units/day) and ten units of clothing per day's labor ($^A\alpha^C$ = 10 clothing/day). Country A has one thousand days of labor available (^AL = 1,000 days). The numbers of days that Country A spends on food and on clothing production are $^AL^F$ and $^AL^C$, respectively, such that $^AL^F + {}^AL^C = {}^AL$. Country B is able to produce only two units of food per day of labor ($^B\alpha^F$ = 2 food/day) and eight units of clothing per day's labor ($^B\alpha^C$ = 8 clothing/day). Country B also has one thousand labor-days available (^BL = 1,000 days). The production coefficient $^A\alpha^F$ is Country A's food productivity stated in terms of one day's labor. The reciprocal, $1/(^A\alpha^F)$, is the number of labor days needed to produce one unit of food.

We'll consider two interesting cases. The first case, called "autarky," involves no trade between Countries A and B. In the second case, all barriers to trade are removed and free trade is allowed. We will see that both countries benefit from free trade in this model.

---

6 *The Principles of Political Economy and Taxation* (Cambridge: Cambridge University Press, 1981), Chapter 7. This work was first published in 1817. Carlyle first referred to Ricardo and Thomas Robert Malthus (another early nineteenth-century economist) as the "respectable professors of the dismal science" because of their belief that the world must forever struggle over scarce resources.

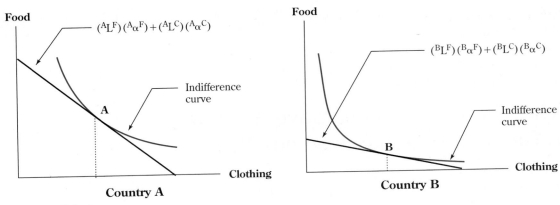

FIGURE 2A.1
Production Possibilities Schedules for Food and Clothing

Autarky (No Trade) Equilibrium

A closed economy must choose how much food and clothing to produce based on its own production capacities and consumer tastes. Given consumer tastes, how much of each good it will produce depends on the relative efficiency of its production technologies.

If Country A devotes all of its labor to food production, so that $^AL = {}^AL^F = 1{,}000$ days, it will produce $(^AL)(^A\alpha^F) = (1{,}000 \text{ days})(10 \text{ food/day}) = 10{,}000$ food units. Likewise, if Country A devotes all of its labor to clothing production, it will produce $(^AL)(^A\alpha^C) = 10{,}000$ clothing units. Suppose Country A devotes $^AL^F$ of its ^AL labor units to production of food and $^AL^C$ to the production of clothing, such that $^AL^F + {}^AL^C = {}^AL$. Country A's production possibilities schedule is given by $(^AL^F)(^A\alpha^F) + (^AL^C)(^A\alpha^C)$ in Figure 2A.1 and represents the maximum combination of food and clothing that Country A is able to produce, given its labor supply.

In Country B, both food and clothing production are less efficient than in Country A. In comparison to Country A, however, Country B's clothing production is relatively more efficient than its food production. A worker in Country B can produce either two units of food or eight units of clothing in a day. With one thousand days of labor supply, this economy can produce a maximum of two thousand units of food, eight thousand units of clothing, or any linear combination of the two. The production possibilities of Country B fall along the line $(^BL^F)(^B\alpha^F) + (^BL^C)(^B\alpha^C)$ in Figure 2A.1.

Suppose consumer preferences in these economies are governed by $U(F,C) = FC$ where $U(F,C)$ represents utility, given consumption in food and clothing. For this utility function, consumers' preferred trade-off between food and clothing turns out to be equal to $-F/C$.[7] An indifference curve conforming to this utility function appears in Figure 2A.1. Higher utilities are farther from the origin. The slope of this indifference curve is equal to $-F/C$ at each point, so consumers are willing to give up (hence the negative sign) one

---

7 For readers familiar with calculus, the marginal utilities $dU/dF = C$ and $dU/dC = F$ yield consumers' preferred trade-off between food and clothing: $dF/dC = (dU/dC)/(dU/dF) = -F/C$.

47

Appendix 2-A The Theory of
Comparative Advantage:
A Game in Which
Everybody Wins?

unit of clothing for F/C units of food. In Country A, both food and clothing require the same labor inputs. In Figure 2A.1, the indifference curve tangent to the production possibility schedule at point A is the highest level of welfare attainable in Country A. At this point, equal amounts of labor are expended on food and clothing production.

Although consumer preferences in these economies are identical, the production processes are quite different. Country A enjoys an absolute advantage over Country B in both food ($^A\alpha^F > {}^B\alpha^F$) and clothing ($^A\alpha^C > {}^B\alpha^C$) production. Country A enjoys a relative advantage in food production, because clothing production per unit of food production in Country A, $(^A\alpha^F)/(^A\alpha^C) = 1$, is greater than that in Country B, $(^B\alpha^F)/(^B\alpha^C) = 1/4$. Conversely, Country B is relatively more efficient at clothing production.

For Country B, a unit of food requires four times as much labor to produce as a unit of clothing. The indifference curve is tangent to the production possibilities schedule at point B, which reflects the higher cost of producing food in Country B. At this point, the slope of the production possibilities schedule is equal to the slope of the indifference curve, $dF/dC = -F/C = -1/4$. Given consumer preferences and the production processes in this economy, four days of labor will be expended on clothing production for every one day of labor expended on food production.

A closed economy must rely on its own production to satisfy its consumption needs. By comparing the amount of labor required to produce a unit of each good, we can determine the relative price of food and clothing in each country. In a closed economy,

TABLE 2A.1 OPTIMAL PRODUCTION IN TWO CLOSED ECONOMIES

			No trade			
Country (labor)	Output consumption	Available labor	Labor productivity	Total production		Total
A $^AL=1000$ days	Food	$^AL^F$ =500 days	$^A\alpha^F$ =10/day	$(^AL^F)(^A\alpha^F)$ =5,000		5,000
	Clothing	$^AL^C$ =500 days	$^A\alpha^C$ =10/day	$(^AL^C)(^A\alpha^C)$ =5,000		5,000
B $^BL=1000$ days	Food	$^BL^F$ =200 days	$^B\alpha^F$ =2/day	$(^BL^F)(^B\alpha^F)$ =400		400
	Clothing	$^BL^C$ =800 days	$^B\alpha^C$ =8/day	$(^BL^C)(^B\alpha^C)$ =6,400		6,400

			Free trade				
Country (labor)	Output consumption	Available labor	Labor productivity gain	Total production	Total trade	Total	Net
A $^AL=1000$ days	Food	$^AL^F$ =600 days	$^A\alpha^F$ =10/day	$(^AL^F)(^A\alpha^F)$ =6,000	Export 600	5,400	+400
	Clothing	$^AL^C$ =400 days	$^A\alpha^C$ =10/day	$(^AL^C)(^A\alpha^C)$ =4,000	Import 1,200	5,200	+200
B $^BL=1000$ days	Food	$^BL^F$ =0 days	$^B\alpha^F$ =2/day	$(^BL^F)(^B\alpha^F)$ =0	Import 600	600	+200
	Clothing	$^BL^C$ =1000 days	$^B\alpha^C$ =8/day	$(^BL^C)(^B\alpha^C)$ =8,000	Export 1,200	6,800	+400

48

Appendix 2-A The Theory of
Comparative Advantage:
A Game in Which
Everybody Wins?

relative prices are determined by the slope of the production possibilities schedule. One possible production-consumption pattern in the absence of trade is provided in the top panel of Table 2A.1 for Countries A and B. In Country A, if just as many days are required to produce a unit of food as to produce a unit of clothing, then a unit of food should be just as expensive as a unit of clothing. That is, the price of a unit of food in terms of a unit of clothing is $^AP^{F/C} = (^A\alpha^F)/(^A\alpha^C) = 1$ food unit per clothing unit. In Country B, four times as many labor units are required to produce a unit of food as to produce a unit of clothing. That is, $^BP^{F/C} = (^B\alpha^F)/(^B\alpha^C) = 1/4$, so that one food unit is as valuable as four clothing units, and food is four times more expensive than clothing. These prices represent the relative cost of producing food and clothing in each country.

Free Trade and Comparative Advantage

The rule of comparative advantage states that each country should specialize in producing those goods that it is able to produce relatively most efficiently. Suppose we allow free trade between the two economies. Country A has a comparative advantage in food production if and only if the ratio of food productivity to clothing productivity is greater than the same ratio in Country B. That is,

- Country A exports food if and only if $(\alpha_{F/A}/\alpha_{C/A}) > (\alpha_{F/B}/\alpha_{C/B})$.

Conversely,

- Country A exports clothing if and only if $(\alpha_{F/A}/\alpha_{C/A}) < (\alpha_{F/B}/\alpha_{C/B})$.

In our example, $(\alpha_{F/A}/\alpha_{C/A}) = 1 > 1/4 = (\alpha_{F/B}/\alpha_{C/B})$, so Country A has a comparative advantage in food production. To utilize each country's comparative advantage, Country A should export food and Country B should export clothing.

Country A should be willing to export food and import clothing so long as it can get at least as many units of clothing as it gives up in food. That is, its minimum price for exporting food and its maximum price for importing clothing are determined by its production trade-off: $\alpha_{F/A}/\alpha_{C/A} = 1$ unit of food per unit of clothing. Similarly, Country B should export clothing and import food so long as it receives at least one unit of food for four units of clothing. This minimum acceptable price is determined by Country B's relative costs of producing food and clothing in the absence of trade: $\alpha_{F/B}/\alpha_{C/B} = 1/4$ unit of food per unit of clothing. Because Country B is willing to sell clothing at any price more than $P_{F/C} = \alpha_{F/B}/\alpha_{C/B} = 1/4$ and Country A is willing to buy clothing at any price less than $P_{F/C} = \alpha_{F/A}/\alpha_{C/A} = 1$, there is a lot of room for negotiation between the countries and a great deal can be gained by cross-border trade.

For both countries to gain, Country A should produce more food and Country B more clothing than they do in the autarky case because they produce these goods relatively most efficiently. At least some of the excess production can then be traded to the other country. One of the many possible scenarios in which both countries gain is shown in the bottom panel of Table 2A.1. The equilibrium price $P_{F/C}$ = one-half unit of food per unit of clothing was chosen arbitrarily. This price is greater than 1/4 and less than 1, so it is beneficial to both parties. In this example, Country A consumes 8 percent more food and 4 percent more clothing, while Country B consumes 50 percent more food and 16% more clothing than in the no-trade case.

In Ricardo's model of international trade, final goods are transportable, but factor inputs are confined within national boundaries. Although one country may have an absolute advantage in one or more products, production and international patterns of trade are determined by comparative advantage. Poor climate, for example, may conspire against labor productivity in both food and clothing production in a foreign country. But if inefficiency is relatively less pronounced in clothing than in food production, then the foreign country will make and export clothing despite an absolute disadvantage in the clothing sector.

This discussion of comparative advantage is not intended to make you an expert in international trade theory. A thorough study of international trade should include at least one course in international economics, but this is well beyond the scope of this text. This simple Ricardian world is intended only to illustrate the manner in which international trade can add to the wealth of nations.

49

Appendix 2-A The Theory of
Comparative Advantage:
A Game in Which
Everybody Wins?

Relaxing the Assumptions of the Classical Theory

International trade theory has come a long way since Ricardo developed his simple argument for free trade. Real-world complications that scholars have added to Ricardo's world include

1. Multiple input factors and the mobility of at least some of these factors
2. The effects of selective government interference on trade through differential taxes, quotas, tariffs, and other restrictions
3. Goods market imperfections, such as information costs, transportation costs, and imperfect competition
4. Capital market imperfections, such as information costs, transactions costs, taxes, and restrictions on cross-border investment
5. The effects of uncertainty
6. Competitive response to trade policy

This list is not exhaustive nor are the listed categories mutually exclusive. As these types of real-world complications are included, the benefits of free trade are not quite so universally allocated as in the classical Ricardian model. World trade is still, on balance, beneficial to all nations, but the balance is not evenly distributed across nations or across populations within each nation.

Consider the issue of factor mobility. In the Ricardian world, it was assumed that labor could switch freely between food and clothing production. If labor either cannot or will not switch professions ("My parents were farmers, so I'm a farmer"), then some segments of the population may suffer despite overall gains from free trade. This is precisely the issue when special interest groups lobby against European monetary and economic union or the North American Free Trade Agreement (NAFTA). In today's highly technical and industrialized society, retooling for another profession is a difficult and time-consuming task.[8]

---

8 I've always followed the advice of Henry David Thoreau: "Never take a job for which you have to change clothes." Thoreau recognized the innate immobility of labor.

Labor Costs and Labor Immobility

Labor is far less mobile than capital for two reasons. First, it is hard to get people to move from their homeland. Second, the host country is often less than hospitable to immigrants or to foreign labor. Because of the immobility of labor, the cost of labor (as well as the quality of that labor) exhibits wide variation around the world. Here is a sample of national hourly labor costs:

Despite the wide differences in labor wage rates (even within the EU), people find it inconvenient, difficult, or even impossible to move to countries that pay higher wages.

Source: United States Department of Labor Statistics

Country	1994 hourly wage rates in U.S. dollars
United States	$17.10
Asian NICs	$5.77
European Union countries	$19.47
Belgium	$22.97
Denmark	$20.44
France	$17.04
Germany	$27.31
Ireland	$6.94
Italy	$12.16
Netherlands	$20.91
Portugal	$4.57
Spain	$11.45
United Kingdom	$13.62

The only input factor to the production technologies of the Ricardian model is labor. This input factor is immobile in that it cannot be relocated to another country with higher labor productivity. Consequently, differences in labor productivity are responsible for the pattern of trade in the Ricardian model. In reality, some factors of production are mobile while other factors are not. Land and climate, for example, are difficult or impossible to transport. Other factors, such as capital, are very mobile. Education is also transportable, but the mobility of technology depends on the particular technology, on the impediments to its duplication, and on its method of dissemination. Still other factors, such as human labor, are relatively less mobile and fall somewhere between the extremes of climate and capital.

KEY TERMS

Autarchy
Comparative advantage
Production possibilities schedule

51

Appendix 2-A The Theory of
Comparative Advantage:
A Game in Which
Everybody Wins?

2A.1 You were asked the following questions at the end of Chapter 1:

- Do trade pacts impact all residents in the same way?
- On balance, are trade pacts good or bad for residents of your country?

Answer these questions again now that you have read this appendix to Chapter 2.

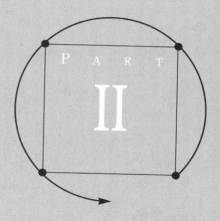

Foreign Exchange and Exchange Rate Determination

Uncertainty and expectations are the joys of life
Congreve

The behavior of foreign exchange rates plays a key role in the success or failure of the multinational corporation. Exposure to foreign exchange risk is an inevitable consequence of cross-border operations in today's global marketplace. For this reason, effective financial management of the multinational corporation requires an understanding of exchange rate movements and of the multinational's exposure to exchange rate risk.

Chapter 3 introduces the foreign exchange market and describes how trade is conducted in the interbank market for foreign exchange. Chapter 3 also introduces the Eurocurrency markets, which trade interest rate contracts denominated in various currencies. Chapter 4 describes a set of international parity conditions that link the foreign exchange and Eurocurrency markets. These international parity conditions capture the equilibrium relationship among currency values, interest rates, and inflation rates. Chapter 5 investigates the behavior of foreign exchange rates and introduces the concept of currency risk exposure.

Because of the importance of foreign exchange to the multinational corporation, the material in Part 2 is a prerequisite for the remainder of the book.

The Foreign Exchange
and Eurocurrency Markets

So much of barbarism, however, still remains in the transactions of most civilized nations, that almost all independent countries choose to assert their nationality by having, to their own inconvenience and that of their neighbors, a peculiar currency of their own.

John Stuart Mill

OVERVIEW

At the center of the international financial markets is a set of international banks that make markets in foreign exchange and Eurocurrency deposits and loans. The market for foreign exchange allows one currency to be exchanged for another. The spot foreign exchange market is a market for immediate exchange of currencies. Exchanges of foreign currency that are to take place in the future are traded in a forward market. The Eurocurrency market is a market in bank deposits and loans that allows value to be shifted over time within each currency. These foreign exchange and Eurocurrency markets are linked through a global network of international money-center banks.

3.1 INTERNATIONAL BANKING AND INTERBANK MARKETS

Commercial Banks as Financial Intermediaries

The traditional role of commercial banks is as **financial intermediaries**, borrowing from individuals and institutions with a desire to save and lending to those with a need for funds. For domestic banks, the bulk of this activity comes from local depositors and borrowers.

The need for international banking activities arose as commercial banks followed

······························

*Commercial banks have
"followed the customer" to
international markets.*

······························

their local customers into foreign markets. As cross-border investment became more common early in this century, large banks found themselves taking deposits and making loans in currencies other than their domestic currency. Individuals and businesses engaged in foreign activities have a need to exchange foreign currency, so international banks developed **trading (or dealing) desks** for spot and forward foreign exchange transactions. As more and more foreign and domestic customers exchanged currencies, banks gradually began to assume the role of **market maker** in foreign exchange trading. Market makers stand ready to buy and sell currencies at their quoted bid (buy) and offer (sell) prices. Large international banks thus found themselves operating in the foreign exchange market as well as in credit markets in various currencies.

The United Kingdom's Standard Chartered Bank is an example of an international bank. Standard Chartered conducts more of its business outside its country of incorporation than any of the other top one hundred global banks.[1] Standard Chartered began by financing colonial Britain's trade with Asia, using Hong Kong as the conduit. As its overseas business grew, so did Standard Chartered's overseas lending and foreign exchange operations. In 1992, Standard Chartered conducted 75 percent of its business outside the United Kingdom, mostly in Hong Kong and Southeast Asia.

Internal credit markets are markets for deposits and loans by local residents; hence, they are governed by the rules and institutional conventions of the local country. These deposits and loans can be denominated in the domestic currency or in foreign currency. A U.S. resident depositing dollars with a U.S. bank is an example of an internal market transaction. Another example of an internal market transaction is a Korean subsidiary of a Japanese firm borrowing Korean won from a Korean bank. Each of these transactions is regulated by local authorities. Because of their foreign exchange activities, international banks are well placed to serve as financial intermediaries in the credit markets of two or more countries.

External credit markets trade interest rate contracts that are denominated in a single currency but are traded outside the borders of the country issuing that currency. Because these markets grew up in Europe, they are usually referred to as **Eurocurrency markets**. Dollar-denominated deposits held in a country other than the United States are called **Eurodollars**. As an example of a Eurodollar transaction, a Swiss bank with a branch in London might accept a dollar deposit from a Belgian dentist. Eurocurrency markets remain relatively unencumbered by government regulation because the government issuing the currency has no direct jurisdiction over the deposit, the lending bank, or the depositor.

······························

*External credit markets trade
interest rate contracts outside the
country issuing a currency*

······························

Figure 3.1 illustrates the linkages between the domestic credit markets of the United Kingdom, Japan, and the United States. The Eurocurrency markets provide competitively priced interest-bearing deposits and loans in each currency. The interbank spot and forward foreign exchange markets allow currencies to be exchanged at competitive rates. Because of the close association between the foreign exchange and Eurocurrency markets, international banks usually conduct trading in these markets out of the same trading room.

---

1 A list of the world's top global banks appears in Chapter 10.

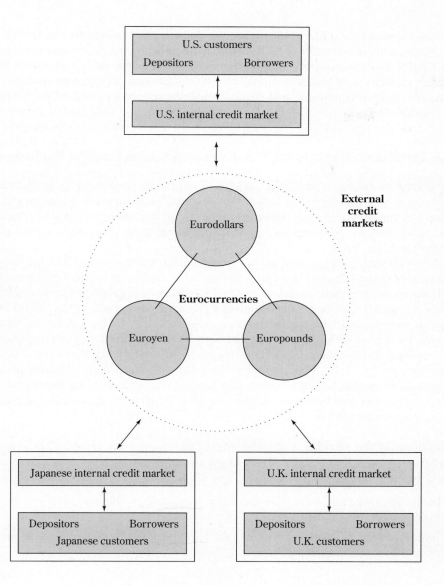

FIGURE 3.1
Linkages between the Credit
and Currency Markets of the
United States, the United
Kingdom, and Japan

Clearing and Settlement Mechanisms for Interbank Transfers

Transfers between international banks are accomplished through a network of telephone lines leased by the **Society for Worldwide Interbank Financial Telecommunications**, called **SWIFT**. Currently, only commercial banks are allowed into the SWIFT network, although the banks in the network number well over a thousand and span the globe. SWIFT ensures low-cost, secure, and error-free transmission of interbank messages and funds transfers.

Within the United States, fund transfers are accomplished through the **Clearing House Interbank Payments System**, or **CHIPS**, which links U.S. banks through a computerized network. Electronic transfers—dollar transactions as well as foreign currency transactions—are entered into CHIPS by member banks. At the end of each day, the CHIPS clearinghouse tallies these transactions, computes each bank's net balance in each currency, and transfers funds between the banks in the proper amounts. This system is extremely efficient, and CHIPS processes several hundred billion dollars of transactions daily.

The Interbank Markets for Eurocurrencies and Foreign Exchange

Functions of the Eurocurrency Markets. The primary function of the Eurocurrency markets, as with any market in deposits and loans, is to bring together savers and borrowers to transfer purchasing power over time. By acting through a financial intermediary, savers with excess funds can invest them profitably with borrowers willing to pay for the use of the funds.

> *The primary function of the Eurocurrency market is to bring together borrowers and savers.*

Although Eurocurrency markets are run alongside national credit markets, they are not subject to the rules that governmental agencies impose on national credit markets. This allows commercial enterprises to avoid interest rate regulations (such as the infamous Regulation Q, which imposed interest rate caps on deposits in the United States until as recently as 1986), reserve requirements, and other barriers to the free flow of capital. Combined with high volume and high liquidity in the Eurocurrency markets, the absence of government restrictions means that Eurocurrency borrowing and lending rates are generally more favorable than domestic borrowing and lending rates. Corporations and financial institutions with access to the Eurocurrency market can typically obtain lower cost funds and/or store funds at higher interest rates than is possible in domestic credit markets.

Functions of the Foreign Exchange Markets. The primary function of the foreign exchange markets is to transfer purchasing power from one currency to another.

> *Currencies are traded in spot and forward currency exchange markets.*

- In the **spot market**, trades are made for immediate (within two business days for most currencies) delivery.
- In the **forward market**, trades are made for future delivery according to an agreed-upon delivery date, exchange rate, and amount.

As we will see in the next chapter, arbitrage keeps spot and forward exchange rates in line with interest rate differentials in this market. When used in combination with the Eurocurrency markets, spot and forward foreign exchange markets allow investors (individuals, institutions, and corporations) to channel capital into its most productive uses regardless of the currency of denomination or the timing of expected future cash flows.

Foreign exchange markets allow speculators (especially those at large international banks) to bet on the direction of changes in currency values. Currency speculation ensures that foreign exchange rates represent a consensus of market participants and provides additional liquidity to the foreign exchange markets.

More important, foreign exchange markets provide a means to hedge foreign exchange risk. **Foreign exchange risk**, or **currency risk**, is the risk of unexpected changes in foreign currency exchange rates. A foreign exchange hedge reduces the consequences of changes in foreign exchange rates. The hedging function of this market has become even more important with the increase in foreign exchange volatility in recent years.

Finally, international portfolio diversification (the topic of Chapter 11) can greatly improve the return/risk performance of investment portfolios. The growing demand for international investments is accomplished through the currency markets.

Efficiency of the Eurocurrency and Foreign Exchange Markets

The performance of a financial market depends on how well the market allocates capital in an economy and on the barriers to capital allocation faced in the market. Three related types of market efficiency are used to describe the performance of financial markets: allocational efficiency, operational efficiency, and informational efficiency.

Allocational Efficiency. **Allocational efficiency** refers to how efficiently a market channels capital toward its most productive uses. This is the basic purpose of any financial market. Eurocurrency and foreign exchange markets do an excellent job of allocating money toward value for currencies with floating exchange rates. Fixed exchange rate systems are less allocationally efficient, because governments intentionally disrupt the flow of funds to meet their fiscal, monetary, and political policy objectives. The extent to which money is reallocated across national borders through the financial markets reveals itself in the balance-of-payments accounts compiled by the International Monetary Fund (as discussed in Chapter 2).

Different nations and different cultures place different values on human behavior. For example, professional basketball players can earn more money playing in the United States than in any other country, but top soccer players are well paid nearly everywhere in the world except the United States. Similarly, nations and cultures place different values on corporate directors and management. As a general rule, corporate officers in the United States are highly paid relative to top management in other industrialized countries. Some have suggested that European managers take their compensation in nonpecuniary forms, such as through corporate perquisites and vacation time. The salaries paid to top managers in emerging markets are rising rapidly, presumably because of a shortage of managerial talent. Value (like beauty) is in the eye of the beholder, and assets are valued differently by people in different countries.

Regardless of what assets are valued in a particular culture, high transaction volumes and freely floating currencies greatly facilitate the reallocation of capital across national boundaries. Active markets for freely floating currencies, such as for the U.S. dollar and the Japanese yen, result in a high degree of allocational efficiency. Markets for less liquid currencies and for currencies with fixed or managed rates are less effective in reallocating capital in an efficient manner.

Operational Efficiency. **Operational efficiency** refers to how large an influence transactions costs and other market frictions have on the operation of a market. Transactions between large international banks in the foreign currency markets have very low transactions costs. Each bank simply debits an account balance in one currency and credits an account balance in another currency; physical currency need not change hands. Because of high volume in these markets, transactions costs as a percent of volume are very low for large interbank transfers.

Allocational efficiency refers to how efficiently a market channels capital toward its most productive uses.

Operational efficiency refers to how large an influence market frictions have on the operation of a market.

Low transaction costs needed

An operationally inefficient capital market runs the risk of being less than efficient in its reallocation of capital. Allocation efficiency requires low and homogeneous transactions costs. High transactions costs restrict the movement of capital to more productive uses. If transactions costs are higher in one national market than in another, then capital tends to flow more freely in the less costly market, perhaps diverting it from otherwise productive uses in countries with higher transactions costs. The interbank markets for spot and forward currency transactions are the most operationally efficient markets on earth, and this high operational efficiency complements the allocational efficiency of these markets.

The external Eurocurrency markets are also both allocationally and operationally efficient. Interest rates are determined by expectations and by the supply and demand for loanable funds to a much greater extent in this market than in the domestic credit markets. Governments are far less likely to be able to manipulate interest rates in the Eurocurrency markets than in their own domestic credit markets.

Informational Efficiency. Informational efficiency refers to whether or not prices reflect "true" value. Foreign exchange markets provide a forum in which market participants can bet on the direction of changes in currency values. Speculators take positions in various currencies and seek to profit by anticipating the direction of changes in currency values. By trying to anticipate the direction of future changes in interest and currency rates, speculators bring new information to the market and help prices in these markets reflect the value of the underlying instruments. In general, speculative activity by well-informed, profit-seeking participants tends to promote the informational efficiency of foreign exchange markets.

INFORMATIONAL EFFICIENCY

Informational efficiency refers to whether or not prices reflect "true" value.

Speculation is widely blamed by government officials for contributing to volatility and serving as a destabilizing influence in currency markets. Whether it is speculators' activity or central bank intervention that is destabilizing is an interesting and debatable point, especially because central banks can and do intervene to temporarily move exchange rates to meet their policy objectives. Through their market making, arbitrage, and speculative activities, international banks ensure that currency values represent a consensus of informed opinion. In this way, they promote liquidity and informational efficiency in the currency markets and ensure that the price of a given currency is the same (within transaction costs) in all locations simultaneously.

EUROCURRENCY MARKET

The Eurocurrency market is an international market in bank deposits and loans residing outside of the domestic country.

3.2 EUROCURRENCY MARKETS

The Eurocurrency market is an international money market in bank deposits and loans residing in banks outside of the domestic country. Eurodollars, for example, are dollar-denominated deposits residing in non-U.S. banks. Eurodollars are generally in the form of variable-rate interest-bearing time deposits with maturities of less than one year. There is an active secondary market for large Eurodollar CDs, which are Eurodollar certificates of deposit with face values of $100,000 and up. These credit markets are operated outside of, or parallel to, national credit markets.

The Eurocurrency market originated in London during the Cold War of the late 1950s. At that time, the Soviet Union held substantial dollar-denominated deposits in U.S. banks. These deposits were used to finance trade with the United States. The

Soviet government was reluctant to leave these deposits in U.S. banks because of fear that the deposits would be frozen or seized for political reasons. Yet they did not want to convert these deposits into other currencies and expose themselves to fluctuations in the value of the dollar. The Soviet government requested that London banks hold dollar-denominated deposits. London bankers were only too happy to oblige, because the dollar-denominated deposits allowed them to make dollar-denominated loans to their customers and solidified their dominance of the international banking industry.

Volume in this market has grown rapidly in the last two decades and is quite large, with well over $2 trillion in Eurodollar contracts outstanding. This is approximately the same as the amount of dollar-denominated deposits at all banks in the United States. Eurodollars account for more than one-half of all Eurocurrency transactions. The majority of trades occur in London, although Eurodollars are also traded in other non-U.S. financial centers of the world, such as Hong Kong, Luxembourg, Paris, Rome, Singapore, and Zurich.

Financial Regulation in the United States

In the United States, fundamental changes in financial regulation were instituted through the Depository Institutions Deregulation and Monetary Control Act of 1980 and a series of subsequent banking acts. The 1980 act instituted a "universal reserve requirement" that all U.S. financial institutions taking deposits set aside reserves on these deposits. Reserve requirements normally range from three to ten percent of the deposit. While reserve requirements help ensure that commercial banks have adequate capital to fulfill their obligations to depositors, reserve requirements also impose an additional cost on domestic deposits and depositors. Prior to the reserve requirement imposed by the 1980 act, commercial banks in the United States sometimes chose to forgo membership in the Federal Reserve System to avoid the burden of reserve requirements. The financial reforms of the 1980s also required that all deposits in the internal market be insured up to $100,000 by the Federal Deposit Insurance Corporation (FDIC) or a related governmental agency. This requirement protects depositors but imposes another hidden cost on domestic deposits.

Prior to the 1980 act, Regulation Q imposed interest rate ceilings on deposits held in financial institutions in the United States. The 1980 act gradually phased out interest rate ceilings on deposits and preempted state "usury ceilings" (or interest rate caps) on some types of loan accounts. Interest rate ceilings are an attempt by the government to control interest rates. As market rates on loans in the United States began to rise above usury ceilings, financial institutions either stopped making loans or restricted loans to those accounts with the best ability to pay. As market rates in the United States rose above deposit rate ceilings in the late 1970s, funds stopped flowing into depository institutions. Small savers in the United States began putting their funds into money market accounts at brokerage houses. Because Regulation Q did not apply to deposits held in foreign bank branches, corporations with large amounts of cash began transferring their funds to the foreign branches of U.S. commercial banks.

Regulators in every country impose their own policy objectives on financial institutions operating in the internal market within their borders. In the United States, truth-in-lending requirements protect borrowers from abuse at the hands of bank lenders. Anti-redlining provisions prohibit lenders from refusing to make loans to a particular

Reserve Requirements ensure stability, impose extra costs.

*. Interest Rate ceilings
. Truth-in-Lending
. Anti-Redlining*

Regulators impose their own policy objectives on financial institutions operating within their borders.

geographical region and ensure that loan applicants are evaluated on their own merit. The federal government also imposes disclosure requirements on financial institutions operating in the United States to ensure that these banks conduct their business in a responsible manner.

Because national governments have no jurisdiction over external markets, each of these regulations is aimed at the internal banking market. And while each of the governmentally imposed regulations has a legitimate goal, in aggregate they raise the cost of doing business in the internal credit market.

An Absence of Government Interference in the Eurocurrency Markets

A distinguishing feature of the Eurocurrency market is the near-total absence of government regulation.

Eurocurrency transactions in the external market fall outside the jurisdiction of any single nation. This results in the Eurocurrency market's most distinctive feature: a near-total absence of outside regulatory interference. In most countries, Eurocurrency transactions in the external market have:

- No reserve requirements
- No interest rate regulations or caps
- No withholding taxes
- No deposit insurance requirements[2]
- No regulations influencing credit allocation decisions
- Less stringent disclosure requirements

With daily volume in the hundreds of billions of dollars and little outside interference, the Eurocurrency market is the most competitive and efficient credit market in the world.

Banks making a market in Eurocurrencies quote **bid rates** at which they will take deposits from other Eurocurrency banks and **offer (or ask) rates** at which they will make loans. Dealer quotes are available on-line from services such as Quotronix and Reuters. About 50 percent of all spot and forward transactions occur through London banks. Conse- quently, the **London Interbank Bid Rate (LIBID)** and the **London Interbank Offer Rate (LIBOR)** are the most frequently quoted rates. LIBID is the bid rate that a Euro- market bank is willing to pay to attract a deposit from another Euromarket bank. LIBOR is the offer rate that a Euromarket bank demands in order to place a deposit at (or, equivalently, make a loan to) another Euromarket bank. LIBID and LIBOR are quoted for all major currencies, including U.S. dollars, yen, deutsche marks, and pounds sterling. The difference between a bank's offer and bid rates for deposits in the Eurocurrency market is called the **interbank spread** and is 1/8 percent for most interbank transactions in major currencies. Because of the absence of withholding taxes on Eurocurrency deposits, most Eurobonds are issued in bearer form to retain the anonymity of the investor, such as a Belgian dentist depositing Swiss francs with a Luxembourg bank.

---

2 Commercial bank deposits in the United States are insured up to $100,000 through the Federal Deposit Insurance Corporation (FDIC).

The market is not entirely free from government interference. In the United States, for example, SEC Rule 144A, which governs private placements, places some restrictions on the activities of U.S. banks engaged in dollar-denominated credit markets. The U.S. government imposes a reserve requirement on dollars redeposited from a foreign bank to a U.S. bank. But for deposits and loans that are not linked to dollars, this external credit market remains essentially unregulated in the United States.

Floating Rate Pricing

In most credit markets, lenders prefer short-term loans, which have lower interest-rate risk and default risk than long-term loans. Borrowers with a preference for long-term loans must pay a premium to attract long-term funds. This supply and demand for loanable funds results in yield curves that are typically upward sloping. Eurocurrency deposits are no different. Borrowers of Eurocurrency typically want long-term loans, and lenders of Eurocurrency prefer to make short-term loans. At least in part because of this imbalance, Eurocurrencies typically have maturities shorter than five years and interest rates tied to a variable-rate base. The short maturity keeps default risk to a minimum. The variable interest rate lowers interest rate risk relative to a fixed-rate contract of comparable maturity. The most common variable-rate base for interest rates in different currencies is LIBOR. Large negotiable Eurocurrency certificates of deposit (CDs more than $100,000 in value) can be bought and sold just like large negotiable CDs in the U.S. market. Fixed rate Eurocurrency deposits and loans and Eurocurrencies with longer maturities than five years (Eurobonds) are also available, but the interbank market conducts most of its transactions in floating rate Eurocurrency contracts with maturities shorter than five years.

Eurocurrency contracts typically have short maturities and floating interest rates

[handwritten margin note: Lenders → want short term LOANS. Borrowers → want Long Term Loans]

Interest Rates in the Domestic Credit and Eurocurrency Markets

The interbank Eurocurrency market is very competitive. The domestic lending rate is greater than LIBOR and the domestic deposit rate is less than LIBID, so the Eurocurrency market pays more interest on deposits and accepts less interest on loans than the domestic market. Figure 3.2 displays the relation between domestic interest rates and Eurocurrency bid and offer rates.

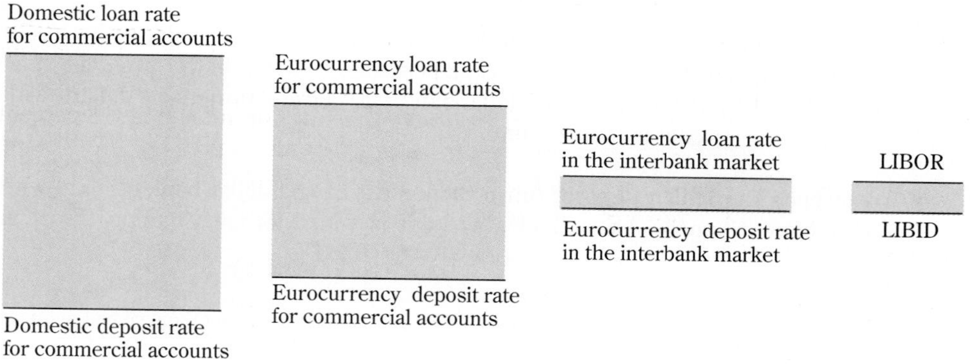

Domestic loan rate
for commercial accounts

Eurocurrency loan rate
for commercial accounts

Eurocurrency loan rate
in the interbank market

LIBOR

Eurocurrency deposit rate
in the interbank market

LIBID

Eurocurrency deposit rate
for commercial accounts

Domestic deposit rate
for commercial accounts

FIGURE 3.2
Spreads in Domestic and
Eurocurrency Credit Markets

· BANKS MAKE $
on Their spread

· BASis
Points

To make a profit, banks purchase funds at low rates and lend them out at high rates. For example, a bank might pay 4 percent per year on the savings account of a depositor and lend these funds out to a small business at 6 percent per year. The 2 percent spread is the source of the bank's profit. For large loans to corporate customers in the external Eurocurrency market, the bank might charge 5.25 percent. For large deposits (greater than $1 million) in the external Eurocurrency market, the bank might be willing to pay 4.75 percent. In this case, the bank's spread with small banks and with nonbank customers falls to one-half percent (5.25 − 4.75). Corporate customers with large enough borrowing needs and good enough credit to be able to borrow in this market can improve on the rates they would face in the domestic market by three-quarters of one percent on both borrowing and lending.

The bank might quote borrowing and lending rates of 4.9475 percent and 5.0625 percent on large short-term transactions with other large international banks in the Eurocurrency market. At these rates, the bank's bid-ask spread (ask price minus bid price) has fallen to 0.115 percent. The bank can afford to quote such a small bid-ask spread to large international banks with high credit quality because of the size of the transaction and the fact that Eurocurrency deposits and loans are floating-rate instruments. Larger bid-ask spreads would be quoted for longer maturities or with banks of lower credit quality.

The interest rate extended to a particular borrower depends on the borrower's credit rating (and, hence, default risk), the size of the borrowing, and market conditions. In September 1995, the U.K. firm BTR placed a loan of $1.1 billion through a loan syndicate composed of Chemical Bank and Chase Manhattan in the United States and Lloyds Bank in the United Kingdom.[3] Interest rate spreads are often quoted in **basis points**, where one basis point is 1/100 of one percent. As of September 1995, the BTR loan had the lowest spread over LIBOR of any corporate loan in history—11 1/2 basis points (0.115 percent). Interest rates on large loans to AAA-rated corporate borrowers are typically made at a minimum of 15–25 basis points (0.15 percent–0.25 percent) over LIBOR.

An Example of a Eurodollar Transaction

Here is a sample sequence of events in the creation of a Eurodollar deposit. Suppose General Motors Corporation (GM) has $10 million set aside to pay an obligation due in three months. GM wants to invest this $10 million principal in a dollar-denominated interest-bearing account for three months. National Bank of Detroit pays 4 percent on three-month CDs in the U.S. domestic market. Amro Bank, a Dutch bank active in the Eurodollar market, is paying a bid rate of 4 1/2 percent on three-month Eurodollar time deposits. Attracted by the higher Eurodollar rate, GM agrees to deposit dollars with Amro Bank at 4 1/2 percent for three months.

1. To accept a Eurodollar deposit, Amro Bank must have a dollar bank account with a U.S. bank. Suppose Amro Bank's account is with Morgan Guaranty Trust in New York.

---

3 Chemical Bank and Chase Manhattan announced a merger in August 1995, but the deal had not been consummated at the time of the BTR offering.

2. General Motors deposits $10 million with Morgan Guaranty for credit to the account of Amro Bank.

3. Amro Bank can now withdraw the funds from its account at Morgan Guaranty. Amro Bank has increased its liabilities by $10 million (the deposit due GM) and has increased its assets by $10 million (the deposit arriving from Morgan Guaranty). Amro bank is now free to loan these funds to another borrower either in Eurodollars or in another currency.

4. Three months later, Amro Bank will transfer $10 million principal plus accrued interest through its account at Morgan Guaranty to whatever account GM designates.

If National Bank of Detroit had received the deposit, the U.S. Federal Reserve would require that a reserve account be set aside. Amro Bank bears no such reserve requirement. Once dollars are received from Morgan Guaranty, Amro Bank is free to loan these funds to anyone willing to pay Amro Bank's Eurodollar loan rate. This absence of reserve requirements lowers Amro Bank's cost of funds and effectively separates the Eurodollar market from the domestic U.S. market for dollar-denominated deposits.

No Reserve requirement w/ the Int'l Bank.

3.3 THE FOREIGN EXCHANGE MARKETS AND FOREIGN EXCHANGE RISK

The foreign exchange market is largely an interbank market that deals in spot and forward foreign currency transactions. The volume of foreign exchange transactions conducted by the world's major commercial banks averages well over $1 trillion per day.[4] For comparison, gross national product (GNP) in the United States during 1995 was about $7 trillion. As shown in Figure 3.3, the major trading centers are located in London, New York, and Tokyo. Active foreign exchange markets are also conducted in Singapore, Hong Kong, Zurich, Frankfurt, and Paris as well as at other regional money centers. The interbank market comprises approximately 75 percent of all foreign exchange transactions. The major banks' remaining business is with retail customers, including corporations and smaller financial institutions. About 60 percent of foreign exchange transactions are in the forward market.

Spot and forward exchange rates are traded in an active interbank market.

Banks making a market in foreign exchange stand ready to quote bid and offer (ask) prices on major currencies. Banks earn their profit by buying foreign currency at their bid price and selling the same currency at a slightly higher offer price. Businesses are the major nonbank participants in the forward market as they exchange cash flows associated with their import/export activities and hedge against losses on future cash flows due to currency fluctuations.

Whenever a bank buys a currency in the foreign currency market, it is simultaneously selling another currency. A bank has a **long position** in a particular currency when it has purchased that currency in the spot or forward market. Conversely, a bank is in a **short position** when it has sold that currency. By aggregating all of its

---

4 Bank for International Settlements, Annual Report, 1995.

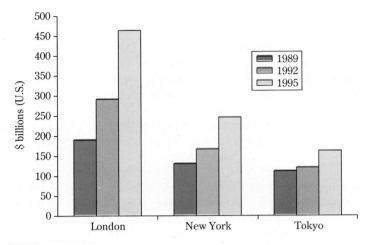

FIGURE 3.3
Major Foreign Exchange
Trading Centers
(Average daily volume in
U.S. $ billions during April
of 1989, 1992, and 1995)

Source: See "London Keeps Forex Supremacy" and "Market Growth Startles Foreign Exchanges" in the *London Financial Times,* September 9, 1995, pages 1 and 4.

currency transactions, the bank can identify its **net position** in each currency and at each forward date.

Spot Exchange Rates and Foreign Exchange Risk

Suppose you are leaving on a vacation on the French Riviera. You have saved $10,000 for the trip, which you booked six months ago. The spot rate of exchange between French francs and U.S. dollars was $S^{FF/\$} = FF5.00/\$$ on the date you booked the trip, so you expected to be able to exchange your dollars for ($10,000)(FF5.00/$) = FF50,000. Of this amount, FF40,000 has already been allocated to transportation and lodging. The remaining FF10,000 was for a planned side trip to Paris.

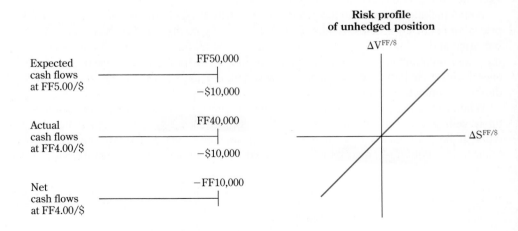

Unfortunately, by the time you arrive in France the spot rate of exchange between French francs and U.S. dollars has changed to $S^{FF/\$}$ = FF4.00/\$. The dollar has **depreciated** relative to the franc or, equivalently, the franc has **appreciated** relative to the dollar. Much to your dismay, you discover that the French franc value of your dollars ($V^{FF/\$}$) has fallen from ($10,000)(FF5.00/\$) = FF50,000 to only ($10,000)(FF4.00/\$) = FF40,000, and you've lost FF10,000 in value. There goes your side trip to Paris.

A **risk profile** of your unhedged $10,000 is shown above. This risk profile shows the gain or loss in the franc value of your $10,000 as a function of changes in the underlying spot rate of exchange, $\Delta S^{FF/\$}$. As the dollar depreciates in value from FF5.00/\$ to FF4.00/\$, you'll be able to buy fewer francs than you expected. A change in the spot exchange rate of $\Delta S^{FF/\$}$ = FF1.00/\$ results in a FF10,000 loss in value. Whenever you hold currency, the value of your holding in other currencies changes as the spot exchange rate changes. This is the most basic of all foreign exchange risk exposures.

EXAMple: Trip to France

Forward Exchange Rates and Foreign Exchange Risk Hedging

In the forward market, trades are made for future delivery at an agreed-upon date and at an agreed-upon price. Let's denote today's price for a forward purchase or sale of currency d (in the denominator) for currency f as $F_t^{f/d} = 1/F_t^{d/f}$. Suppose that when you booked your vacation six months ago you bought FF50,000 forward (and sold dollars forward) at a price of $F_{1/2}^{FF/\$}$ = FF5.00/\$ through your bank. This means that you have agreed to pay $10,000 in exchange for FF50,000 and that the transaction will take place in six months. The size and timing of the cash flows to which you have agreed are shown below. By purchasing francs forward today, you can ensure that your $10,000 savings will buy FF50,000 irrespective of the future spot exchange rate. If the actual spot rate falls to FF4.00/\$, you'll avoid the FF10,000 loss in the value of your savings.

The graph shows the **payoff profile** of this forward contract. If the dollar depreciates to FF4.00/\$ in the next six months (the risk in the unhedged position), you will still be able to purchase FF50,000 for $10,000, and you'll see a FF10,000 *net gain* on the forward contract. On the other hand, if the dollar appreciates to FF6.00/\$ (this would be good news if your original position had been left unhedged), you will be forced

Forward currency contracts can be used to reduce exposure to foreign exchange risk

• FORWARD
  currency
  Contracts
Limit Risk

**Payoff profile
of forward contract**

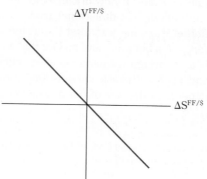

Contractual
cash flows
at FF5.00/\$

FF50,000

−$10,000

Cash flows at
FF4.00/\$ if
left unhedged

FF40,000

−$10,000

Net savings
on forward
contract

FF10,000

After the Plaza Accord in 1985, Japan Air Lines (JAL) entered into a ten-year forward agreement to buy $3.6 billion for ¥666 billion (a price of ¥185/$). At the time of the forward agreement, the spot exchange rate was ¥240/$. By October 1994, the dollar had fallen to ¥100/$. If the contract had been settled in October 1994, Japan's largest airline would have had to pay ¥666 billion for dollars worth only ($3.6 billion)(¥100/$) = ¥360 billion—a foreign exchange loss of ¥306 billion or $3.06 billion. Since entering this agreement, JAL had charged some of this foreign exchange loss against operating profits, but as of October 1994 the extent of the losses had not been reported. In late 1994, the Japanese Ministry of Finance required exchange-listed Japanese companies to disclose unrealized gains or losses from forward currency trading. JAL had a ¥45 billion ($450 million) unrealized loss at that time. JAL spends about ¥80 billion ($800 million) on new airplanes each year, so their total exchange loss on this contract was about half their annual budget for new airplanes.

---

to sell dollars at the lower FF5.00/$ forward rate, and you will forgo the FF1.00/$ gain in the unhedged position.

If your risk profile is positively sloped, then your losses (gains) on this underlying position can be exactly offset by the gains (losses) from a forward contract with a negatively sloped payoff profile. The net result is that regardless of what happens to foreign exchange rates, you will be able to exchange your $10,000 for FF50,000. You have eliminated your exposure to foreign exchange risk with the forward contract and can be assured of an enjoyable springtime in Paris.

• Net result,
eliminate
*   exposure*

3.4 FOREIGN EXCHANGE DEALERS AND THEIR CLIENTS

The Interbank Market: Foreign Exchange Dealers and Brokers

Commercial banks serve as dealers in an active interbank currency market

The bulk of activity in the foreign exchange market is conducted in an interbank wholesale market—a network of large international banks and brokers trading upwards of one million U.S. dollars per trade. The principal function of these banks is to serve as **dealers** making a market in foreign currency exchange. Dealers profit by buying currency at a bid price and selling it at a slightly higher offer price. Banks' primary function is as a foreign exchange dealer; speculation accounts for a small proportion of volume and profit.[5] Bid-ask spreads (ask price minus bid price) in this active global market depend on the size of the transaction, the liquidity and volatility of the currencies being

---

5 Albéric Braas and Charles Bralver find that foreign currency sales, not speculative trades, are the only reliable source of revenues for the currency trading rooms of international banks in "An Analysis of Trading Profits: How Most Trading Rooms Really Make Money," *Journal of Applied Corporate Finance,* Winter 1990, pages 85–90.

traded, and the objectives of the bank quoting exchange rates. Bid-ask spreads on foreign currency can be as low as 20 basis points (or 0.20 percent) for large transactions between major international banks.

As transactions are conducted farther and farther away from the highly liquid interbank wholesale market, transactions costs rise. Transactions costs for travelers exchanging currencies at major international airports can exceed 10 percent. Tourists visiting a resort on the coast of Belgium will find that shopkeepers are more than happy to accept dollars. But beware of the 20 percent additional charge hidden in the exchange rate. One way to get around the exorbitant bid-ask spreads commonly charged by retail outlets on foreign exchange is to purchase merchandise in the local currency using Visa, Mastercard, or American Express. These credit card companies pay the foreign obligation in the local currency and then bill you in your domestic currency at very competitive exchange rates.

Foreign exchange **brokers** also operate in the international currency markets. Whereas dealers take a position in foreign exchange, brokers serve merely as matchmakers and do not put their own money at risk. Brokers actively monitor the exchange rates offered by the major international banks through computerized quotation systems such as Reuters and are able to identify quickly which bank is offering the best rates. Major players, such as central banks and large commercial banks, can conceal their identities, and sometimes their intentions, through the use of foreign exchange brokers. For example, if the German Bundesbank wants to dispose of an accumulated French franc position without signaling its activity to the market, it may choose to use a broker to maintain the Bundesbank's anonymity. In a recent survey of transactions in London, about 30 percent of foreign exchange transactions were conducted through traditional brokers and about 5 percent were conducted through electronic brokers.[6]

Governments

Governments and their central banks can have a pronounced impact on currency exchange rates, especially in the short term, both through their stated intentions and through their market activities.[7] Consider a joint announcement by the French and German central banks that they intend to cooperate to increase the spot exchange rate $S^{DM/FF}$ to stabilize the value of the franc. One way to accomplish this objective in the short term is for both central banks to buy francs and sell deutsche marks. If this joint agreement is a surprise to the market, the $S^{DM/FF}$ rate will probably rise. Individual market participants may react in either of two ways. If market participants think the central banks will be successful in stabilizing the currency exchange rates, the central banks may need to execute only token transactions in the currency markets to signal that they are indeed following through on their intentions. If participants expect the central banks to fail in their attempt to halt the franc's fall, they may try to sell francs (either to the central banks or to speculators betting on a stable rate) before the franc falls any further in value.

Central banks sometimes intervene in the international currency markets

---

6 See "Market Growth Startles Foreign Exchanges," *London Financial Times,* September 9, 1995, page 4.
7 See "Games Central Banks Play with Currencies" by Henry Sender in *Institutional Investor,* Nov. 1985, pages 100–110.

In contrast to the market for large interbank transfers, the market for small interbank transfers (less than ECU10,000) is operationally inefficient. In a study by the European Commission in 1994, banks charged an average of ECU25.4 to make an urgent transfer of ECU100, yet it took an average of 4.15 working days to transfer the funds. Fewer than 1 percent of transfers were accomplished within one working day and more than 15 percent took longer than six working days. The commercial banks and the European Commission are taking a closer look at bank charges for money transfers. Banks see more efficient transfers as a way to increase their presence with small businesses that are increasingly operating across national borders.

Source: "The High Cost of a Small Transfer," *London Financial Times,* Oct. 20, 1994, page 2.

An example can serve to demonstrate the power that governments can exert over financial prices. The price of North Sea crude oil was $22.34 per barrel when Iraq unexpectedly invaded Kuwait on August 2, 1990 (see Figure 3.4). During the ensuing months, oil prices reacted every time the Iraqi leader, Saddam Hussein, made a public announcement about his intentions. When Saddam took a hard-line stance, oil prices jumped in expectation of an oil shortage. When Saddam adopted a conciliatory tone, oil prices dropped as traders hoped for a quick and less painful resolution to the dispute. If Saddam had had better financial advisors, he might have financed his war by buying oil contracts in the forward or futures markets before his hard-line speeches and reversing his position after his conciliatory speeches.

FIGURE 3.4
Oil Prices during the Gulf War

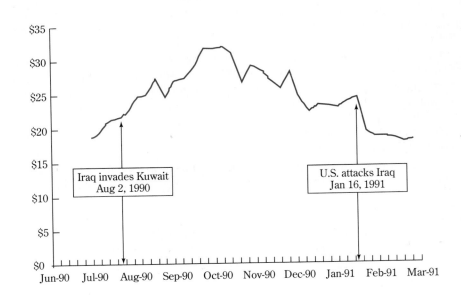

Multinational Corporations

An international bank's biggest and most reliable clientele are multinational corporations. These corporations have a need to exchange currencies in order to conduct their international trade. Multinational corporations often contract to receive and/or pay foreign currencies at future dates, so they are exposed to foreign currency risk. Corporations often hedge these contractual future cash flows through the interbank forward exchange market.

Domestic Banks

Smaller financial institutions also service firms in their domestic markets with a need to exchange currencies for transaction or hedging purposes. For example, a Japanese student attending the University of North Carolina might ask that her local bank cash a yen-denominated check and exchange it for dollars. A local computer retailer might ask the same bank to send a yen-denominated payment to a Japanese semiconductor manufacturer. The North Carolina bank will aggregate these transactions into a net transaction and then use the interbank currency market to execute and settle this transaction. Even though they are not dealers in foreign exchange, these smaller financial institutions can satisfy their clients' needs for foreign currency through the interbank market.

3.5 FOREIGN EXCHANGE RATES AND QUOTATIONS

Two Rules for Dealing with Foreign Exchange

In every market in the world, prices are stated as a price per unit of good or service. When you purchase a bottle of wine in Germany at a price of DM20, the price is quoted as DM20/bottle. The starting wage at a McDonald's franchise in the United States might be quoted as $4.25/hour. This is a natural way to state values, because a higher number in the numerator (given, for example, deutsche marks or dollars) ascribes a higher value to the item being bought or sold in the denominator (a bottle of wine or an hour's wage).

Here's the rub. An exchange of currencies involves two currencies, either of which may arbitrarily be placed in the denominator. As an example, a quote of DM2/$ is equivalent to a quote of $(DM2/\$)^{-1} = \$.5000/DM$. At this rate of exchange, $10 can be exchanged for ($10)(DM2/$) = DM20. If you buy dollars at DM2/$, you are simultaneously selling marks at $.5000/DM, and vice versa.

Either currency may be placed in the denominator of a foreign exchange quote

Because two currencies are involved in every foreign currency exchange, it is essential that you keep track of your currency units. If you don't, you'll often end up multiplying when you should be dividing, and vice versa. This seems simple enough now, but as our discussion of foreign exchange instruments and contracts becomes more complex it will become imperative that you include the currency units wherever they appear in an equation. This is such an important point that it has its own rule:

RULE #1

Always keep track of your currency units.

The next biggest source of confusion in currency trading is in keeping track of which currency is being bought and which currency is being sold. This is called the **currency of reference** or **referent currency**. Buying and selling a foreign currency is like buying and selling any other commodity. If you always think of the currency in the denominator of a foreign exchange quote as the referent currency (that is, the currency being bought or sold), you should always make the correct decision. Each foreign exchange contract is then just like any other commodity. For example, you could substitute "unit" for "deutsche mark" and think of the dollar price as $.5000/unit. You might just as well be buying bottles of wine. Rule #2 will remind of you of this point:

RULE #2

Always think of buying or selling the currency in the *denominator* of a foreign exchange quote.

Here's an example of how it works. Suppose you buy one million deutsche marks at a price of $.5838/DM and then sell one million marks at a price of $.5841/DM. Remember, you are buying and selling deutsche marks—the currency in the denominator. The net result is that you spend ($.5838/DM)(DM1M) = $583,800 to buy one million deutsche marks and then sell them for ($.5841/DM)(DM1M) = $584,100, resulting in a net profit of $300.

Here's an example of what can go wrong. Suppose you are quoted the deutsche mark per dollar rates of ($.5838/DM)$^{-1}$ = DM1.7130/$ and ($.5841/DM)$^{-1}$ = DM1.7120/$. If you try to "buy low and sell high" using these quotes but forget that dollars are now in the denominator, you might buy one million deutsche marks at a price of DM1.7120/$ and then sell them for DM1.7130/$. Your cost is DM1M / (DM1.7120/$) = $584,100. Your payoff in dollars is DM1M / (DM1.7130/$) = $583,800. This results in a net loss of $300. The simplest way to avoid this pitfall is to follow Rule #2 and use the denominator as the referent currency.

Foreign exchange quotations can be easy to understand if these two simple rules are followed. As our analysis becomes more and more complex in the next several chapters, it will become increasingly important to be consistent in your use of these rules. Make your life easy and start now. Make sure that you apply these rules consistently and conscientiously as you practice on the end-of-chapter problems.

European and American Quotes for the U.S. Dollar

European quotes state the foreign currency price of one U.S. dollar

Interbank quotations that include the U.S. dollar are conventionally given in **European terms**, which state the foreign currency price of one U.S. dollar, such as DM1.7125/$ for the deutsche mark. This convention was instituted by New York bankers, and because the U.S. dollar is the most frequently traded currency, it is used worldwide for all dollar quotes except those involving the British pound or the currencies of a few former colonies of the British Commonwealth. The DM1.7125/$ quote could also be called "German terms." It is convenient to a German in that it treats the foreign currency (the U.S. dollar) just like any other commodity. The "buy low and sell high" rule works for a German trading in dollars because the dollar has a low deutsche mark value when it has a low mark price and has a high mark value when it has a high mark price.

United States dollar exchange rates for the British pound sterling, the Australian dollar, the New Zealand dollar, and the Irish punt in the interbank foreign exchange market are quoted as the U.S. dollar price per foreign currency unit, such as $1.4960/£. A quote of the U.S. dollar price per foreign currency unit is called **American terms**. Prior to 1971, one British pound was worth twenty shillings and each shilling was worth twelve pence. The convention of keeping the pound in the denominator was convenient at that time because fractions of a pound were not easily translated into shillings and pence. Even though the British pound is now quoted in decimals, the convention of quoting exchange rates with the pound in the denominator has persisted.

The convention of quoting the U.S. dollar on either European terms or American terms works well for any quote that includes the U.S. dollar. European and American quotes are not possible, however, for transactions that do not include the dollar. For exchange rate quotations that do not include the dollar, a convention based on foreign and domestic (rather than U.S. and non-U.S.) currencies is necessary.

Direct and Indirect Quotes for Foreign Exchange

Banks making a market in foreign exchange quote bid prices at which they are willing to buy another currency and ask or offer prices at which they are willing to sell another currency. Whenever a bank is buying one currency it is simultaneously selling another. For this reason, a bank's bid price for one currency is its offer price for another currency.

The convention in most countries is to use **indirect quotes**, which state the price of a unit of domestic currency in foreign currency terms, such as DM1.7120/$ for a U.S. resident. The currency in the denominator (the dollar in this example) is being bought at the bid price while the currency in the numerator (the mark) is being sold at this price. The indirect quote to a U.S. resident:

DM1.7120/$ BID and DM1.7130/$ ASK

means that the bank is willing to buy dollars (and sell marks) at the DM1.7120/$ price or sell dollars (and buy marks) at the DM1.7130/$ price.

The bank might also quote:

DM1.7130/$ BID and DM1.7120/$ ASK

In this case, the bid price is higher than the offer price. Does this mean that the bank is willing to pay a higher price to buy currency than it is willing to accept when it sells currency? Not at all. By quoting a higher bid price than ask price, the bank is indicating that it is willing to buy marks (in the *numerator*!) at DM1.7130/$ and/or sell marks at the DM1.7120/$ rate. This is of course equivalent to buying dollars at DM1.7120/$ and selling dollars at DM1.7130.

Whenever the bank is buying one currency, it is simultaneously selling another. The rule for determining whether or not the bank is following Rule #2 in its quotation is as follows:

- When the bid quote is lower than the offer quote, the bank is buying and selling the currency in the denominator of the quote.

American quotes state the U.S. dollar price of one unit of foreign currency

Indirect quotes state the foreign currency price of one unit of domestic currency

- When the offer price is lower than bid price, the bank is buying and selling the currency in the numerator.

Note that these indirect quotes to a U.S. resident are equivalent to $(DM1.7120/\$)^{-1} = \$.5841/DM$ and $(DM1.7130/\$)^{-1} = \$.5838/DM$. A German bank quoting these bid and offer prices to a German resident with an indirect quote would state:

$$\$.5838/DM \text{ BID and } \$.5841/DM \text{ ASK}$$

which means that the bank is willing to buy marks (and sell dollars) at 58.38 cents per mark or sell marks (and buy dollars) at 58.41 cents per mark. If asked for the dollar rate, the bank might quote:

$$\$.5841/DM \text{ BID and } \$.5838/DM \text{ ASK}$$

which means that the bank is willing to buy dollars (in the numerator) at the bid price and sell dollars (in the numerator) at the ask price. These quotes are equivalent. In both cases, with indirect quotes the domestic currency is placed in the denominator and the bid price for the domestic currency is less than the offer price for the domestic currency.

As a convenience to domestic customers, banks are also willing to provide **direct quotes**, which state the price of a unit of foreign currency in domestic currency terms. For a domestic resident, this follows Rule #2. As with indirect quotes, the currency in the denominator is being purchased. For a U.S. resident, the direct quote

....
*Direct quotes state the domestic
currency price of one unit of
foreign currency*
....

$$\$.5838/DM \text{ BID and } \$.5841/DM \text{ ASK}$$

means that the bank is willing to buy marks (and sell dollars) at the $\$.5838/DM$ price or sell marks (and buy dollars) at $\$.5841/DM$.

When all of the digits of the bid and offer prices are quoted it is called an **outright quote**, as shown in Table 3.1. Traders in the interbank market use an abbreviated form of the outright quote known as a **points quote**. Using a points quote, the spot rates in Table 3.1 would be stated as "1.7120 to 30." This convention saves time, and because

TABLE 3.1 OUTRIGHT FOREIGN EXCHANGE QUOTATIONS FOR THE GERMAN MARK

	Outright quote supplied to the interbank market (European terms)		Outright quote supplied to the retail market (American terms)		Mid-rates[a] quoted in the financial press	
	Bid	Offer	Bid	Offer	DM/$	$/DM
Spot rate	1.7120	1.7130	.5838	.5841	1.7125	.5839
One month forward	1.7169	1.7179	.5821	.5824	1.7174	.5823
Three months forward	1.7256	1.7267	.5791	.5795	1.7261	.5793
Six months forward	1.7367	1.7379	.5754	.5758	1.7373	.5756

[a] Mid-rates are averages of bid and ask rates.

foreign exchange rates are volatile and quotes are revised on a minute-by-minute basis in the interbank currency market, time is of the essence. Since we are not foreign currency traders, we'll use outright quotes in this book.

3.6 FORWARD PREMIUMS/DISCOUNTS AND CHANGES IN SPOT RATES

Forward premiums and discounts indicate a currency's *nominal* value in the forward market relative to the spot market.[8]

- A currency is trading at a **forward premium** when the nominal value of that currency in the forward market is *higher* than in the spot market.
- A currency is trading at a **forward discount** when the nominal value of that currency in the forward market is *lower* than in the spot market.

A currency is at a forward premium (discount) when its nominal value is higher (lower) in the forward than in the spot market.

As with any calculation involving foreign exchange, it is easiest to keep the referent currency in the denominator of the foreign exchange quote. For foreign currency, this means using direct quotes.

Direct Terms

Forward Premiums and Discounts. Direct quotes make it convenient to think of the domestic currency value of a unit of foreign currency, such as the dollar price of a deutsche mark, $S_0^{\$/DM}$.

- A currency in the *denominator* of a foreign exchange quote is selling at a *forward premium* if the price of the currency in the forward market is *greater than* the price in the spot market.
- A currency in the *denominator* of a foreign exchange quote is selling at a *forward discount* if the price of the currency in the forward market is *less than* the price in the spot market.

Forward premiums and discounts can be expressed as a basis point spread. For a direct quote, if the spot rate is $.5839/DM and the six-month forward rate is $.5754/DM, then the mark is selling at a six-month forward discount of $.0085/DM, or 85 basis points.

Forward premiums and discounts are also quoted as an annualized percentage deviation from the current spot rate. The formula for this calculation is

---

8 This statement is true only for nominal currency values. The impact of inflation on currency values is discussed in Chapters 4 and 5.

$$= \left[\frac{F_t^{d/f} - S_0^{d/f}}{S_0^{d/f}} \right] (n) \qquad (3.1)$$

# of compounding periods/year

where n is the number of compounding periods per year. Multiplying by n translates the periodic forward premium or discount into an annualized rate with n-period compounding. For example, a six-month forward premium or discount is annualized by multiplying the six-month forward premium or discount by n = 2. Similarly, a one-month forward premium or discount is multiplied by n = 12. In the deutsche mark example above, the forward discount is calculated as

$$= \left[\frac{F_t^{d/f} - S_0^{d/f}}{S_0^{d/f}} \right] (n) = \left[\frac{\$.5754/DM - \$.5839/DM}{\$.5839/DM} \right] (2)$$

$$= (-.01456/\text{period})(2\ \text{periods}/\text{year})$$

$$= -0.0291, \text{ or}$$

$$= -2.91\% \text{ per year}$$

The mark is selling at an annualized forward discount of −2.91 percent using direct terms.

Annualized Percentage Changes in Exchange Rates. Calculating percentage changes in foreign exchange rates is similar to calculating forward premiums and discounts. As with any calculation involving foreign exchange, it is easiest to think of the referent currency as the currency in the denominator of a foreign exchange quote. The value of the foreign currency in the denominator of a direct foreign exchange quote changes according to the formula:

PERCENTAGE CHANGE IN FOREIGN CURRENCY VALUE (DIRECT QUOTES)

$$= \left[\frac{\text{Ending rate} - \text{Beginning rate}}{\text{Beginning rate}} \right] \qquad (3.2)$$

Suppose that the spot rate changes from \$.5839/DM to \$.5725/DM over a six-month period. The percentage change in the deutsche mark spot rate using direct quotes for a U.S. resident is

$$\left[\frac{\$.5725/DM - \$.5839/DM}{\$.5839/DM} \right] = -1.95\% \text{ per six months}$$

This is a fall in the value of the mark of 1.95 percent over the six-month period, or −3.9 percent per year on an annualized basis with semiannual compounding.

If the mark falls, the dollar must rise. Rule #2 says that to find the percentage change in the value of the dollar we should first place the dollar in the denominator. The beginning rate is $(\$.5839/DM)^{-1} = DM1.7126/\$$ and the ending rate is $(\$.5725/DM)^{-1} = DM1.7467/\$$. The percentage rise in the value of the dollar (in the denominator) is then:

$$\left[\frac{DM1.7467/\$ - DM1.7126/\$}{DM1.7126/\$} \right] = +1.99\% \text{ per six months}$$

This is a 1.99 percent rise in the value of the dollar over the six month period or +3.98 percent on an annualized basis with semiannual compounding.

This example demonstrates that what the dollar gains, the deutsche mark must give up. Percentage changes in exchange rates are related through the equation

$$(1 + s^{d/f}) = (1 + s^{f/d})^{-1}, \tag{3.3}$$

where $s^{d/f}$ is the percentage change (stated in decimal form) in the spot rate $S^{d/f}$, and $s^{f/d}$ is the percentage change in the foreign per domestic currency spot rate $S^{f/d} = 1/S^{d/f}$. In the example of a 1.95 percent fall in the value of the deutsche mark being offset by a 1.99 percent rise in the value of the dollar, the algebra looks like this:

$$(1 + .0199) = 1.0199$$
$$= 1/.9805$$
$$= (1 - .0195)^{-1}$$

Alternatively, solving for the percentage appreciation of the dollar that corresponds to a 1.95 percent fall in the value of the mark yields:

$$(1 + s^{DM/\$}) = (1 + s^{\$/DM})^{-1}$$
$$= (1 - .0195)^{-1}$$
$$\Rightarrow s^{DM/\$} = 0.199$$

This is 1.99 percent per six months.

Indirect Terms

Forward Premiums and Discounts. Indirect terms put the *domestic* currency in the denominator. This works fine for a foreign investor concerned with the foreign currency price of one unit of domestic currency. But for the domestic investor concerned with the domestic currency price of the foreign currency, it causes all of the usual rules to be reversed. Consider a U.S. resident quoted a spot rate of $(\$.5839/DM)^{-1} = DM1.7126/\$$ and a six-month forward rate of $(\$.5754/DM)^{-1} = DM1.7379/\$$. Using indirect quotes to find the forward premium or discount of the deutsche mark violates Rule #2, because the deutsche mark is in the numerator rather than the denominator. Because the currency of reference to a domestic investor is in the numerator, the direction of premiums and discounts are the opposite of what you might expect.

The rules for finding forward premiums/discounts and percentage changes are for indirect quotes

- A currency in the *numerator* of a foreign exchange quote is selling at a *forward premium* if the price of the currency in the forward market is *less than* the price in the spot market.
- A currency in the *numerator* of a foreign exchange quote is selling at a *forward discount* if the price of the currency in the forward market is *greater than* the price in the spot market.

Stated as an annualized percentage deviation from the current spot rate, the forward premium or discount with indirect rates is computed as

FOREIGN CURRENCY PREMIUM OR DISCOUNT (INDIRECT QUOTES)

$$= \left[\frac{S_0^{f/d} - F_t^{f/d}}{F_t^{f/d}} \right](n) \tag{3.4}$$

where again n is the number of periods per year. A little algebra will show that this is really a disguised version of the same relation in direct quotes. Substituting $S_0^{d/f} = (S_0^{f/d})^{-1}$ and $F_t^{d/f} = (F_t^{f/d})^{-1}$ into equation (3.1) and rearranging:

$$(F_t^{d/f} - S_0^{d/f})/S_0^{d/f} = [(1/F_t^{f/d}) - (1/S_0^{f/d})]/(1/S_0^{f/d})$$
$$= [(S_0^{f/d}/F_t^{f/d}) - (S_0^{f/d}/SS_0^{f/d})]/(S_0^{f/d}/S_0^{f/d})$$
$$= [(S_0^{f/d}/F_t^{f/d}) - 1] = (S_0^{f/d} - F_t^{f/d})/F_t^{f/d}$$

That is, as long as the correct formula is used it doesn't matter whether calculation of forward premiums and discounts is based on direct or indirect quotes.

Consider the example in which the deutsche mark is selling at a forward discount. In direct terms

$$\left[\frac{F_t^{d/f} - S_0^{d/f}}{S_0^{d/f}} \right](n) = \left[\frac{\$.5754/DM - \$.5839/DM}{\$.5839/DM} \right](2)$$
$$= (-.01456/\text{period})(2\,\text{periods/year})$$
$$= -0.0291$$

or −2.91 percent per year with semiannual compounding. This is the same discount as when it is stated in indirect terms:

$$\left[\frac{S_0^{f/d} - F_t^{f/d}}{F_t^{f/d}} \right](n) = \left[\frac{DM1.71262/\$ - DM1.73792/\$}{DM1.73792/\$} \right](n)$$
$$= (-.01456/\text{period})(2\,\text{periods/year})$$
$$= -0.0291$$

or −2.91 percent per year with semiannual compounding. Note that $S_0^{\$/DM} = \$.5839/DM = 1/(DM1.7126/\$) = 1/S_0^{DM/\$}$ and $F_t^{\$/DM} = (\$.5754/DM) = 1/(DM1.7379/\$) = 1/F_t^{DM/\$}$. Regardless of whether direct or indirect quotes are used, the deutsche mark is selling at an annualized forward discount of 2.91 percent to the dollar with semiannual compounding.

Annualized Percentage Changes in Exchange Rates. The formula to compute the annualized percentage change in a spot rate with indirect quotes is

PERCENTAGE CHANGE IN FOREIGN CURRENCY VALUE (INDIRECT QUOTES)

$$= \left[\frac{\text{Beginning rate} - \text{Ending rate}}{\text{Ending rate}} \right] \qquad (3.5)$$

As with forward premiums and discounts on indirect terms, the usual rules are reversed. Using our example of a change from $(\$.5839/DM)^{-1} = DM1.7126/\$$ to $(\$.5725/DM)^{-1} = DM1.7467/\$$, the mark has fallen in value by 1.95 percent over the six-month period

$$\frac{DM1.7126/4 - DM1.7467/\$}{DM1.7467/\$} = -0.0195$$

This of course implies an offsetting increase in the value of the dollar. Using dollars as the currency of reference in the numerator, we get

$$\frac{\$.5839/DM - \$.5725/DM}{\$.5725/DM} = +0.0199$$

Using either the direct or indirect quote formula, the mark fell by 1.95 percent and the dollar rose by 1.99 percent over the six-month period.

A Recommendation

With direct quotes, the "buy low and sell high" rule always make sense. With indirect quotes, the formulas for forward premiums and discounts and for percentage changes in currency exchange rates appear to be backward. There is a simple remedy for keeping things straight—just follow Rule #2:

> Use direct quotes whenever possible, and always think of the currency in the denominator as the currency of reference.

If the currency that you would like to reference is in the numerator, simply place it in the denominator according to $(S^{f/d})^{-1} = S^{d/f}$. Following this convention will help you avoid needless confusion.

Regardless of which formula you use, a currency selling at a forward premium is more valuable in nominal terms in the forward market than in the spot market. Conversely, a currency selling at a forward discount is nominally less valuable in the forward market than in the spot market.

3.7 SUMMARY

We began Chapter 3 with a description of the international activities of commercial banks in large financial centers. The trading rooms of these banks trade Eurocurrencies and spot and forward foreign exchange contracts in an active interbank market.

> *Whenever possible, use direct terms and think of the currency in the denominator as the currency of reference.*

- USE Direct Quotes when possible, "Buy low sell High" Always makes Sense here.

The Eurocurrency markets trade interest rate (deposit and loan) contracts denominated in a single currency but traded outside the borders of the country issuing that currency. The Eurocurrency markets are credit markets that are outside of, or parallel to, the national credit markets. These national and international interest rate markets are linked to each other through the spot and forward foreign exchange markets. In the spot market, trades are made for immediate delivery. In the forward market, trades are made for future delivery at an agreed-upon date.

International banks serve as foreign exchange dealers making a market in foreign exchange and standing ready to quote bid and offer (or ask) prices on major currencies. A bank's bid (offer) price is the price at which the bank is ready to buy (sell) the foreign currency.

The interbank market for foreign exchange is the most active market in the world in terms of value traded. Largely because of this high volume of trade, percentage transactions costs are very small for large interbank trades, making this the most operationally efficient market in the world. Allocational efficiency refers to how efficiently the foreign exchange market allocates capital to its most productive use. Informational efficiency refers to whether prices reflect "true" value. While barriers to the flow of capital are still present, the allocational efficiency of the foreign exchange market has increased with increasing trading volume in the market. While monetary authorities are quick to claim that their currency is misvalued, the jury is still out on the informational efficiency of the foreign exchange markets.

Finally, we presented two very important rules for dealing in foreign exchange.

Rule #1: Always keep track of your currency units.

Rule #2: Always think of buying or selling the currency in the denominator of a foreign exchange quote.

Conscientiously following these rules will help you avoid making careless mistakes when dealing with foreign exchange.

KEY TERMS

Allocational, operational, and informational efficiency

Basis points and basis point spread

Bid and offer (or ask) prices and the interbank spread

Currency appreciation and depreciation

Currency of reference (referent currency)

Currency (foreign exchange) risk hedging and speculation

Direct and indirect quotes

Eurocurrencies (e.g., Eurodollars)

European and American terms

Financial intermediaries

Foreign exchange dealers, brokers, and market makers

Forward premiums and discounts

Internal and external credit markets

LIBID and LIBOR

Long and short currency positions and the net position

Market maker

Outright and points quotes

Risk and payoff profiles

Spot and forward foreign exchange markets

SWIFT and CHIPS

Trading (or dealing) desks

3.1 What is Rule #1 when dealing with foreign exchange? Why is it important?

3.2 What is Rule #2 when dealing with foreign exchange? Why is it important?

3.3 What are the functions of the foreign exchange market?

3.4 Define allocational, operational, and informational efficiency.

3.5 What is a forward premium? A forward discount? Why are forward prices for foreign currency seldom equal to current spot prices?

PROBLEMS

3.1 If exchange rates in 1987 were 200 yen per dollar and 50 U.S. cents per German mark, what was the exchange rate of yen per mark?

3.2 Citicorp quotes French francs on European terms as "FF5.62/$ BID and FF5.87/$ ASK."

a. Which currency is Citicorp buying at the FF5.62/$ bid rate, and which currency is Citicorp selling at the FF5.87/$ offer rate?

b. What are the bid and ask prices in American terms? Which currency is Citicorp buying at these prices and which currency is Citicorp selling?

c. With the foreign currency in the numerator, the "FF5.62/$ BID and FF5.87/$ ASK" quotes are indirect quotes for a U.S. resident. What are the bid and ask prices in direct terms for a U.S. resident? At these prices, which currency is Citicorp buying and which currency is Citicorp selling?

d. If you sell $1,000,000 to Citicorp at their bid price of FF5.62/$ and simultaneously buy $1,000,000 at their offer price of FF5.87/$, how many French francs will you make or lose? What is Citicorp's franc profit or loss on the transaction?

3.3 The following outright quotations are given for the Canadian dollar:

	Bid (C$/U$)	Ask (C$/U$)
Spot rate	1.2340	1.2350
One month forward	1.2345	1.2365
Three months forward	1.2367	1.2382
Six months forward	1.2382	1.2397

Assume you are in the United States. Calculate forward quotes for the Canadian dollar as an annual percentage premium or discount. Would a foreign exchange trader in Canada get a different answer if asked to calculate the annual percentage premium or discount on the U.S. dollar for each forward rate? Why?

3.4 In 1984, the number of German marks required to buy one U.S. dollar was 1.80. In 1987, the U.S. dollar was worth 2.00 marks. By 1992, the dollar was worth 1.50 marks.

a. What was the percentage appreciation or depreciation of the dollar between 1984 and 1987?

b. What was the percentage appreciation or depreciation of the mark between 1984 and 1987? (Hint: Following Rule #2, convert the spot rates to $S^{\$/DM}$.)

c. What was the percentage appreciation or depreciation of the dollar between 1987 and 1992?

d. What was the percentage appreciation or depreciation of the mark between 1987 and 1992?

3.5 Given the following spot and forward quotes, calculate forward premiums on Japanese yen (¥) as (a) a basis point premium or discount, and (b) an annualized percentage premium or discount.

Spot ($/¥)	Forward ($/¥)	Days Forward
0.009057355	0.008968408	30
0.009057355	0.008772945	90
0.009057355	0.008489101	180
0.009057355	0.007920290	360

3.6 The Luxembourg franc (LF) spot rate is LF36.02/$. A 20 percent depreciation of the Luxembourg franc will result in what spot rate? If the Luxembourg franc depreciates by 20 percent, by how much does the dollar appreciate?

3.7 A foreign exchange dealer in Tokyo provides quotes for spot and one-month, three-month, and six-month forward rates. When you ask for current quotations on the Finnish markka (FM) against the dollar over the telephone, you hear: "4.0040 to 200, 120 to 110, 350 to 312, and 680 to 620." This points quote can be stated as an outright quote as follows:

	Bid (FM/$)	Ask (FM/$)
Spot	4.0040	4.0200
One month forward	3.9920	4.0090
Three months forward	3.9690	3.9888
Six months forward	3.9360	3.9580

a. What would you receive in dollars if you sold FM5,000,000 at the current spot rate?
b. What would it cost you in dollars to purchase FM20,000,000 forward three months. When would you make payment?

3.8 You are interested in buying some Swedish krona (SK), which are sold in forward contracts of 30, 90, and 180 days. Current spot, 30-, 60-, and 90-day quotations for the Swedish krona against the dollar are SK7.5050/$ to 150, 100 to 120, 250 to 262, and 540 to 560, respectively.
a. Refer to the points quote conventions in Problem 3.7. Write down the outright quotations for the forward and spot rates on Swedish krona.
b. What would you pay in dollars if you bought SK10,000,000 at the current spot rate?

3.9 Dow Corning is to deliver $1,000,000 of breast implants to the Belgian firm Societé Generale de Belgique (SGB) in one year. The one year forward rate of exchange is BF40/$, and the sale is invoiced in Belgian francs. At the forward rate of exchange, SGB promises to pay Dow ($1M)(BF40/$) = BF40M in one year.
a. Identify Dow's expected future cash flow *in Belgian francs* on a time line.
b. Draw a risk profile for Dow Corning in terms of dollars per Belgian franc.
c. If the actual spot rate in one year is BF25/$ = $.04/BF, how much gain or loss will Dow have if it does not hedge its currency exposure? (Use the current spot exchange rate as the starting point in calculating the gain or loss.)
d. Form a forward market hedge based on the forward price $F_1^{BF/\$}$ = BF40/$. Indicate how the hedge eliminates foreign exchange exposure by identifying the forward contract's cash inflows and outflows on a time line and constructing a payoff profile of the forward contract.

The following article argues that market making, not speculation, is the only reliable source of profit from currency trading rooms. Be aware that many believe that commercial banks do consistently make money speculating in foreign exchange.

Albéric Braas and Charles Bralver, "An Analysis of Trading Profits: How Most Trading Rooms Really Make Money," *Journal of Applied Corporate Finance,* Winter 1990, pages 85–90.

The Foreign Exchange Market Game[9]

This exercise describes a foreign exchange market simulation game that provides a simple and effective vehicle for learning the institutional operation and competitive dynamics of the foreign currency markets. On a practical level, you will learn how to trade with bid and offer quotes and how to manage your foreign exchange position. You will also gain a feel for the market atmosphere and an appreciation of the impact of current events on foreign exchange rates, and you will have the opportunity to explore various trading strategies. The game requires nothing more than paper and pencil and the simple rule to "buy low and sell high."

The game uses a spot foreign exchange market in U.S. dollars and French francs. Operating this two-currency spot market will provide you with enough insight to understand the fundamentals of markets in other currency instruments, including forward, futures, options, swaps, and Eurocurrencies. Trading in these other markets requires knowledge of the different contracts and of international parity conditions (the topic of Chapter 4), but in many other ways trading in these contracts is similar to trading in the spot market.

Market Participants

Keep in mind that whenever you are buying one currency you are simultaneously selling another. In this discussion, French francs (FF) will be used as the currency of denomination and prices will be in dollars. This means that all quotes are dollars per franc. Your instructor may, of course, choose another set of currencies.

Some of you will represent major money-center banks as foreign exchange *dealers*. Dealers are responsible for making a market in foreign currency and must quote bid

---

9 This appendix is based on "A Classroom Exercise to Stimulate the Foreign Exchange Market" by Kirt C. Butler and Chuck C.Y. Kwok, *Journal of Teaching in International Business* Vol. 6, No. 2, 1994, pages 59–73.

and offer prices to anyone inquiring of the bank. A bank is in a long franc position and a short dollar position when it has purchased francs and sold dollars. Conversely, a bank is in a short franc and long dollar position when it has sold francs and purchased dollars. Banks operating with large short or long foreign exchange positions risk big gains or losses as new information enters the market. Dealers will need to record their currency transactions, monitor net franc and dollar exposures, and set bid and offer $/FF rates according to prevailing market conditions.

The remaining students are foreign exchange *traders.* Students performing the trader's function have more flexibility than the dealers in that they need not quote bid and offer prices. Instead, they shop among the foreign exchange dealers (and, if they want, other traders) and attempt to find price differences that provide profit opportunities; that is, they try to "buy low and sell high." Traders can also take speculative positions in the hopes of guessing correctly on the next move in foreign exchange rates. To know their exposure to exchange rate changes, traders must keep track of their net balance in each currency.

Rules and Operation of the Game

The rules of the game are as follows:

1. Your objective is to "buy francs low and sell francs high."
    Follow Rule #2: Always buy or sell the currency in the denominator of a quote.
    Use direct $/FF quotes. (An example is in Figure 3A.1.)

FIGURE 3A.1
Trading Profit in the Foreign Exchange Market

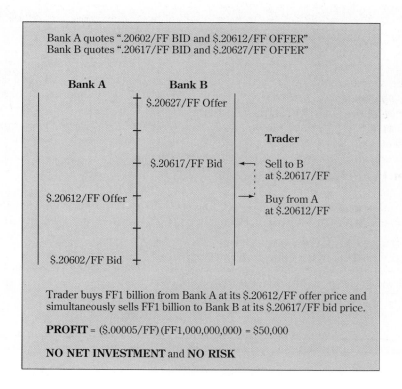

Bank A quotes ".20602/FF BID and $.20612/FF OFFER"
Bank B quotes ".20617/FF BID and $.20627/FF OFFER"

Bank A   **Bank B**

$.20627/FF Offer

Trader

$.20617/FF Bid   ←⌐ Sell to B
                       at $.20617/FF

$.20612/FF Offer   →⌐ Buy from A
                       at $.20612/FF

$.20602/FF Bid

Trader buys FF1 billion from Bank A at its $.20612/FF offer price and simultaneously sells FF1 billion to Bank B at its $.20617/FF bid price.

PROFIT = ($.00005/FF) (FF1,000,000,000) = $50,000

NO NET INVESTMENT and **NO RISK**

	Counterparty	Contracts	Price	Total $/FF	Cumulative FF Balance
NAME _____ DATE _____					
1.					
2.					
3.					
4.					
5.					
6.					
7.					
8.					
9.					
10.					

FINAL CLOSING RATES:
FINAL CLOSING (BALANCING) TRANSACTION:

FIGURE 3A.2
The Foreign Exchange
Ledger

2. One contract is worth FF1,000,000,000. Trade between one and ten contracts at a time (i.e., trade FF1 billion to FF10 billion in increments of FF1 billion).
3. Record each transaction as either a FF purchase or sale on the ledger in Figure 3A.2. A filled-in ledger showing an audit trail of several trades is provided in Figure 3A.3.

FIGURE 3A.3
Record Keeping with the
Foreign Exchange Ledger

NAME _Bank of Cash, Credit, and Industry_____ DATE _October 19, 1996_____

	Counterparty	Contracts	Price	Total $/FF	Cumulative FF Balance
1.	Penn Square	BUY 1	0.22004	−$0.22004	+1
2.	Citicorp	BUY 3	0.22010	−$0.66030	+4
3.	Bk of Tokyo	SELL 2	0.22016	+$0.44032	+2
4.	Bk of Tokyo	SELL 4	0.22020	+$0.88080	−2
5.					
	•				
	•				
	•				

FINAL CLOSING RATES: $.22018/FF BID and $0.22023/FF OFFER
FINAL CLOSING (BALANCING) TRANSACTION:

Closing trade	BUY 2	0.22023	−$0.44046	0
Sum of dollar transactions			+$0.00032/FF	
Times contract size		×	FF1,000,000,000	
Profit (loss)			+$320,000	

4. The maximum allowable bid-offer spread is 1 basis point ($.0001/FF). This means that a dealer quoting a franc bid price of $.20202/FF can quote at most a franc offer price of $.20212/FF.
5. Dealers must stand by their quotes for a minimum of two minutes.

Because of high volatility in currency markets, few traders are willing to go home for the night without closing out their positions. This leads to the following rule:

6. At the closing bell, buy or sell enough French francs at market prices to achieve a zero net franc position.

If you have excess French francs at the end of the game, then sell them to the market at the FF bid rates provided by your instructor. Conversely, if you are short francs, you'll buy francs from the market at the rates provided by your instructor. This final transaction forces your net franc position to zero. The sample ledger provided in Figure 3A.3 demonstrates how this will work.

The International Parity Conditions

Forecasts are all right—so long as you don't use them to predict the future.
Anonymous

OVERVIEW

This chapter describes how the foreign exchange and Eurocurrency markets are linked by market forces through a set of fundamental relationships, or **international parity conditions**. These international parity conditions are summarized in Figure 4.1. In an economist's stylized world in which rational investors transact freely at no cost, these parity conditions relate the forward discount or premium on a currency to the expected future spot rate and to differences in nominal interest rates and/or inflation between the two countries. How closely these parity conditions hold in the real world largely depends on the extent to which capital and real goods market trade barriers restrain the activities of traders from enforcing the law of one price.

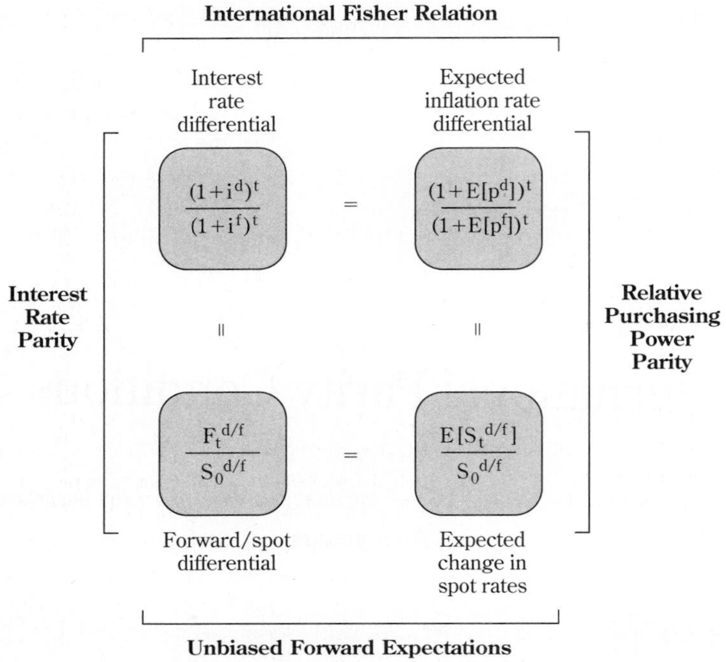

International Fisher Relation

FIGURE 4.1
International Parity
Conditions: Implications
of the Law of One Price

Interest
rate
differential

Expected
inflation rate
differential

$$\frac{(1+i^d)^t}{(1+i^f)^t}$$

$$=$$

$$\frac{(1+E[p^d])^t}{(1+E[p^f])^t}$$

**Interest
Rate
Parity**

$$\parallel$$

$$\parallel$$

**Relative
Purchasing
Power
Parity**

$$\frac{F_t^{d/f}}{S_0^{d/f}}$$

$$=$$

$$\frac{E[S_t^{d/f}]}{S_0^{d/f}}$$

Forward/spot
differential

Expected
change in
spot rates

Unbiased Forward Expectations

4.1 THE LAW OF ONE PRICE

*In the absence of market frictions,
arbitrage ensures that equivalent
assets sell for the same price.*

The law of one price, also known as **purchasing power parity** or PPP, states that

Equivalent assets sell for the same price.

This means that, in the absence of **market frictions** such as transactions costs or other barriers to trade, two identical assets must have the same price wherever they are bought or sold. If purchasing power parity does not hold, then there is an opportunity to simultaneously buy an asset at a low price and sell an identical asset at a high price and lock in an arbitrage profit.

*Riskless arbitrage is a certain
profit with no net investment
and no risk.*

Although the popular press often uses the term "arbitrage" to refer to speculative positions, **pure** or **riskless arbitrage** is more strictly defined as a profitable position obtained with

- No net investment
- No risk

This type of "no money down and no risk" opportunity sounds too good to be true. In the high-stakes game played in the international currency markets, it usually is too good to be true once trading costs are factored into the transaction. Such arbitrage opportunities are quickly exploited and, as market forces drive prices back toward equilibrium, just as quickly disappear.

The law of one price has important implications for international asset pricing. In particular, the phrase "sell for the same price" means that an asset must have the same value regardless of the currency in which value is measured. In the spot foreign exchange market, for instance, the law of one price implies that the spot exchange rate between a domestic and a foreign currency is determined by the current price of an asset in the domestic currency relative to the price of that same asset in the foreign currency.

Arbitrage Profit

When the spot rate is not in equilibrium with the relative prices of foreign and domestic assets, there is the potential for arbitrage profit. As investors buy the low-price asset and simultaneously sell the high-price asset, asset prices and/or currency values are driven back toward equilibrium. If the price difference between the assets cannot be arbitraged because of market frictions (transactions costs, transportation costs, and the like), then the price differential may persist for some time. If the asset being traded is a financial asset with low trading costs, then investors will arbitrage any price difference and prices will respond very quickly.

Let P_t^d denote the price of an asset in the domestic currency at time t and P_t^f denote the price of the same asset or an identical asset in the foreign currency. The time subscript will be dropped when it is unambiguous to do so. If you'd like, you can let d stand for the dollar and f for the franc. The law of one price requires that the value of an asset be the same whether value is measured in the foreign or in the domestic currency. This means that the spot rate of exchange must equate the value of the asset in the foreign currency to the value of the asset in the domestic currency:

$$P_t^d / P_t^f = S_t^{d/f} \qquad (4.1)$$

EQUATIONS TO KNOW ⟵

Equivalently, $P_t^d = (P_t^f)(S_t^{d/f})$.[1] If this equality does not hold within the bounds of transaction costs, then there is an opportunity for an arbitrage profit.

As an example, suppose gold sells for $P^\$ = \$400/oz$ in the United States and $P^{DM} = DM640/oz$ in Germany. In the absence of such market frictions as taxes, transactions costs, and transportation costs, the no-arbitrage condition requires that the value of an ounce of gold in dollars must equal the value of an ounce of gold in deutsche marks. This means that $S^{\$/DM} = P^\$/P^{DM} = (\$400/oz)/(DM640/oz) = \$.6250/DM$. If this relation does not hold, then there is an opportunity to lock in a riskless arbitrage profit in cross-currency gold transactions.

For actively traded financial assets, such as foreign currency and Eurodollar deposits, transactions costs are small in relation to trading volume. Purchasing power parity nearly always holds in these markets, because arbitrage ensures that spot and forward exchange rates and Eurocurrency interest rates are in equilibrium. Transactions

---

[1] Don't forget Rule #1: Always keep track of your currency units. This will ensure that each variable appears in its proper place.

costs are more prominent in markets for real assets. Actively traded real assets for which purchasing power parity is a fairly close approximation include globally traded commodities such as oil, silver, and gold.

The No-Arbitrage Condition

The no-arbitrage condition ensures that purchasing power parity holds within the bounds of transactions costs.

For there to be no arbitrage opportunities, purchasing power parity must hold (within the limits of transactions costs) for identical assets bought or sold simultaneously in two or more locations. This **no-arbitrage condition** is the foundation upon which the law of one price is built. Whether purchasing power parity holds depends in part on the extent to which market frictions restrain market forces (especially arbitrage) from working their magic. Some barriers to the cross-border flow of real and financial assets are generated in the normal course of business as fees are charged for making a market, for providing information, and for delivering an asset. Other barriers are imposed by governmental authorities. These include tariff and nontariff trade barriers; differential taxes, including both tax incentives (subsidies) and disincentives; purchasing policies that give preferential treatment to domestic suppliers; and financial market inflow and outflow controls.

Buying and selling real (or physical) assets, such as commodities and manufactured goods, usually entails higher costs than trading a similar asset in the financial market. As an example, gold is costly to transport because of its weight, but a financial asset representing ownership of gold is easily transferred from one party to another and can be as simple as a piece of paper or a credit in an account. While large amounts of gold are a nuisance to store (imagine a finance professor saying that!), foreign currency can be conveniently "stored" in the Eurocurrency market at competitive market interest rates. Because of this difference between financial and real assets, actively traded financial assets are more likely to conform to the law of one price than similar real assets.

Suppose the spot exchange rate between deutsche marks and dollars is DM1.75/$. If gold costs \$401/oz in dollars and there are no costs of trading currencies, then an arbitrage profit is possible so long as gold can be sold for more than $P^{DM} = P^\$ S^{DM/\$} = (\$401/oz)(DM1.75/\$) = DM701.75/oz.$[2] If gold can be sold for \$399/oz in dollars, then an arbitrage profit is possible so long as the purchase price of gold in deutsche marks is less than $P^{DM} = P^\$ S^{DM/\$} = (\$399/oz)(DM1.75/\$) = DM698.25/oz.$ Arbitrage will thus ensure that a bid-ask quote of "\$399/oz BID and \$401/oz ASK" in dollars will be mirrored by a quote of "DM698.25/oz BID and DM701.75/oz ASK" in marks. Transactions costs must be included in trying to find profit-making opportunities, whether these opportunities are arbitrage or speculative in nature.

Purchasing power parity seldom holds for nontraded assets and cannot be used to compare assets that vary in quality.

The law of one price seldom holds for nontraded assets and cannot be used to compare assets that vary in quality. In such cases, either the asset is not standardized and PPP is not applicable (such as with housing costs in different countries) or there is no easy way to arbitrage price differences between two locations selling the same asset (such as between McDonald's hamburgers selling in London and New York). We'll return to the topic of deviations from purchasing power parity in the next chapter after we have developed the implications of the law of one price for the international currency markets.

---

2 The equality $P^{DM} = P^\$ S^{DM/\$}$ is simply equation (4.1) with d = DM and f = \$.

Riskless arbitrage is a situation in which one can lock in a sure profit with no net investment and no risk. Economist Hal Varian illustrates arbitrage with the following story:

An economics professor and a Yankee farmer were waiting for a bus in New Hampshire. To pass the time, the farmer suggested that they play a game.

"What kind of game would you like to play?" responded the professor.

"Well," said the farmer, "how about this: I'll ask a question, and if you can't answer my question, you give me a dollar. Then you ask me a question and if I can't answer your question, I'll give you a dollar."

"That sounds attractive," said the professor, "but I do have to warn you of something: I'm not just an ordinary person. I'm a professor of economics."

"Oh," replied the farmer, "in that case we should change the rules. Tell you what: If you can't answer my question you still give me a dollar, but if I can't answer yours, I only have to give you fifty cents."

"Yes," said the professor, "that sounds like a fair arrangement."

"Okay," said the farmer. "Here's my question: What goes up the hill on seven legs and down the hill on three legs?"

The professor pondered this riddle for a while and finally replied. "Gosh, I don't know...what does go up the hill on seven legs and down the hill on three legs?"

"Well," said the farmer, "I don't know either. But if you give me your dollar, I'll give you my fifty cents!"

Source: Hal Varian, "The Arbitrage Principle in Financial Economics," *Economic Perspectives* 1, No. 2, Fall 1987.

4.2 INTERNATIONAL PARITY CONDITIONS YOU CAN TRUST

Spot and forward foreign exchange and Eurocurrency contracts are traded in highly liquid financial markets. A market is said to have **liquidity** if traders can buy or sell large quantities of an asset when they want and with low transactions costs. There are few governmental restrictions on currency purchases and sales and transactions costs are very low for large transactions in these markets. Arbitrage between actively traded financial contracts ensures that the international parity conditions that follow hold within the bounds of transactions costs in these markets. These are international parity conditions that you can trust.

Bilateral Exchange Rates and Locational Arbitrage

In the absence of market frictions, the no-arbitrage condition for trade in the spot rates of exchange between two locations A and B is $(S_A^{d/f}) = (S_B^{d/f})$ or, equivalently,

> *Locational arbitrage ensures that bilateral exchange rates are in equilibrium.*

$$(S_B^{d/f})/(S_A^{d/f}) = 1 \qquad (4.2)$$

where the spot rate $S_A^{d/f}$ is offered by Bank A and the spot rate $S_B^{d/f}$ is offered by Bank B. This condition ensures that bilateral exchange rates are in equilibrium.

Suppose that you can buy foreign currency (in the *denominator* of the foreign exchange quote) from Bank A at a price of $S_A^{d/f}$. This of course means that you are selling the domestic currency at this rate. Now suppose that you can sell foreign currency to Bank B (and buy the domestic currency from Bank B) at a price of $S_B^{d/f} = (S_B^{f/d})^{-1}$. If the purchase price $S_A^{d/f}$ is less than the sale price $S_B^{d/f}$, then the bilateral parity condition in equation (4.2) is violated and there is a riskless arbitrage opportunity.

An Example of Locational Arbitrage with Transactions Costs. Consider the example in Figure 4.2. Bank A is quoting "$.5838/DM BID and $.5841/DM ASK" while Bank B is quoting "$.5842/DM BID and $.5845/DM ASK." If you buy one million deutsche marks from Bank A at its $.5841/DM ask price and simultaneously sell one million deutsche marks to Bank B at its $.5842/DM bid price, you can lock in an arbitrage profit of $100 per contract (that is, 0.01 percent of DM1,000,000) with no net investment and no risk. Transactions costs are built into the bid-ask spread, so this $100 profit is free and clear. Because this transaction uses prices from two different banking locations, it is called **locational arbitrage**. The subscripts A and B indicate the two locations.

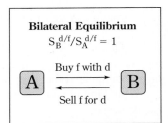

FIGURE 4.2
Arbitrage Profits in the
Foreign Exchange Market

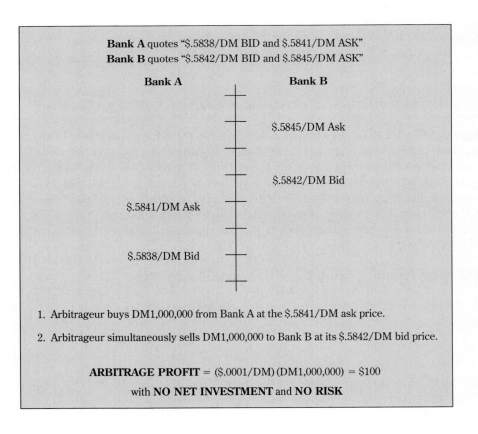

Bank A quotes "$.5838/DM BID and $.5841/DM ASK"
Bank B quotes "$.5842/DM BID and $.5845/DM ASK"

Bank A   Bank B

$.5845/DM Ask

$.5842/DM Bid

$.5841/DM Ask

$.5838/DM Bid

1. Arbitrageur buys DM1,000,000 from Bank A at the $.5841/DM ask price.

2. Arbitrageur simultaneously sells DM1,000,000 to Bank B at its $.5842/DM bid price.

ARBITRAGE PROFIT = ($.0001/DM)(DM1,000,000) = $100

with NO NET INVESTMENT and NO RISK

Here's a complementary way to view the exchange. You are buying from A at $S_A^{\$/DM}$ = \$.5841/DM and selling to B at $S_B^{\$/DM}$ = \$.5842/DM. The ratio in equation (4.2) is $(S_B^{\$/DM})/(S_A^{\$/DM}) \approx 1.0001712 > 1$. Your arbitrage profit is 0.01712% of the transaction amount. A one million deutsche mark transaction results in a profit of (DM1,000,000)(.0001712) = DM171.2, which is worth \$100 at Bank A's ask price of DM1.712/\$ ≈ \$.5841/DM. Of course, if this is a good deal with a one million mark transaction, it is an even better deal with a one billion mark transaction. The larger the trade, the larger the arbitrage profit. Trading one billion marks rather than one million marks in the above transaction would result in a \$100,000 arbitrage profit. If you can find this arbitrage opportunity in the foreign exchange market, you've earned your salary for the day.

With foreign exchange volume often topping \$1 trillion per day, you can bet your bottom dollar (deutsche mark or yen) that there are plenty of arbitrageurs vigilantly monitoring foreign exchange rates. Foreign exchange dealers are just as vigilant in ensuring that their bid and offer quotes are not outside the bounds of other dealers. By convention in the interbank market, banks making a market in foreign exchange can revise their bid and offer prices within one minute of when they are quoted. If a bank's bid or offer quotes do begin to drift outside of the narrow band defined by other dealers' quotes, they quickly find themselves inundated with buy offers for their low-priced currencies and sell offers for their high-priced currencies. Even if banks' quoted rates do not allow arbitrage, the banks offering the lowest offer prices in a currency will attract the bulk of customer purchases in that currency.

The Long and the Short of It. A bank is in a long deutsche mark position and a short dollar position when on balance it has purchased marks and sold dollars. Conversely, a bank is in a short mark and long dollar position when on balance it has sold marks and purchased dollars. Currency balances must be netted out; if a bank has bought DM100 million and sold DM120 million, its net position is short DM20 million. Banks operating with large long or short foreign exchange positions are essentially speculating rather than market-making. If new information enters the market and currency values change unexpectedly, they risk big gains or losses. For this reason, trading desks closely monitor their net foreign exchange positions and attempt to balance their net foreign exchange exposures. This balancing process further ensures that each bank's bid and offer rates are in equilibrium with those of other banks.

A bank is in a long (short) position in a currency when it has purchased (sold) that currency.

Long = Bought
Short = Sold

Cross Rates and Triangular Arbitrage

The direct/indirect quote system discussed in the previous chapter is tied to the domestic currency. The European/American quote system revolves around the U.S. dollar. But if a Japanese trader calls a Swiss foreign exchange dealer and inquires about the German mark and British pound spot rate, $S^{DM/£}$, the Swiss dealer will quote a rate that does not fit under either classification scheme. This exchange rate is called a **currency cross rate** for both the Swiss and the Japanese because it does not involve their domestic currencies. Financial

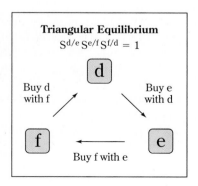

Triangular Equilibrium
$S^{d/e} S^{e/f} S^{f/d} = 1$

newspapers such as the *Wall Street Journal* and the *London Financial Times* publish these bilateral exchange rates in a currency cross rate table like the one in Figure 4.3. Rather than bid and offer prices, currency cross rate tables report the bid-ask midpoint—these rates do not represent actual market transactions.

Suppose you are given cross exchange rates for currencies d, e, and f. The no-arbitrage condition for **triangular arbitrage** in the currency markets is

$$S^{d/e}S^{e/f}S^{f/d} = 1 \qquad (4.3)$$

Triangular arbitrage ensures that currency cross rates are in equilibrium.

Again, remember to follow Rule #1 and keep track of which currencies are in the numerators and which are in the denominators. The reciprocal $(S^{d/e}S^{e/f}S^{f/d})^{-1} = S^{e/d}S^{f/e}S^{d/f} = 1$ holds just as well as equation (4.3). If this condition does not hold within the limits of transactions costs, then there is an opportunity for a riskless profit through triangular arbitrage.

An Example of Triangular Arbitrage. Suppose the following cross rates hold:

$$S^{\$/¥} = \$.00960984/¥$$
$$S^{¥/DM} = ¥60.750/DM$$
$$S^{DM/\$} = DM1.7125/\$$$

EXCHANGE CROSS RATES

May 23		BFr	DKr	FFr	DM	I£	L	Fl	NKr	Es	Pta	SKr	SFr	£	C$	$	Y	Ecu
Belgium	(BFr)	100	18.78	16.47	4.864	2.023	4923	5.441	20.82	499.4	405.2	21.63	3.990	2.088	4.344	3.159	337.2	2.576
Denmark	(DKr)	53.25	10	8.770	2.590	1.077	2621	2.897	11.09	265.9	215.8	11.52	2.125	1.112	2.314	1.682	179.5	1.372
France	(FFr)	60.72	11.40	10	2.953	1.228	2989	3.303	12.64	303.2	246.0	13.13	2.422	1.268	2.638	1.918	204.7	1.564
Germany	(DM)	20.56	3.861	3.386	1	0.416	1012	1.118	4.281	102.7	83.30	4.446	0.820	0.429	0.893	0.649	69.31	0.530
Ireland	(I£)	49.43	9.283	8.141	2.405	1	2433	2.689	10.29	246.9	200.3	10.69	1.972	1.032	2.148	1.561	166.7	1.273
Italy	(L)	2.031	0.381	0.335	0.099	0.041	100.	0.111	0.423	10.14	8.232	0.439	0.081	0.042	0.088	0.064	6.849	0.052
Netherlands	(Fl)	18.38	3.452	3.027	0.894	0.372	904.8	1	3.828	91.79	74.48	3.975	0.733	0.384	0.799	0.581	61.97	0.474
Norway	(NKr)	48.02	9.018	7.909	2.336	0.971	2364	2.613	10	239.8	194.6	10.39	1.916	1.003	2.086	1.517	161.9	1.237
Portugal	(Es)	20.03	3.760	3.298	0.974	0.405	985.8	1.089	4.170	100.	81.15	4.331	0.799	0.418	0.870	0.633	67.52	0.516
Spain	(Pta)	24.68	4.634	4.064	1.200	0.499	1215	1.343	5.139	123.2	100.	5.337	0.985	0.515	1.072	0.779	83.20	0.636
Sweden	(SKr)	46.24	8.682	7.615	2.249	0.935	2276	2.515	9.628	230.9	187.4	10	1.845	0.965	2.009	1.460	155.9	1.191
Switzerland	(SFr)	25.07	4.707	4.128	1.219	0.507	1234	1.364	5.220	125.2	101.6	5.421	1	0.523	1.089	0.792	84.51	0.646
UK	(£)	47.90	8.995	7.889	2.330	0.969	2358	2.606	9.975	239.2	194.1	10.36	1.911	1	2.081	1.513	161.5	1.234
Canada	(C$)	23.02	4.322	3.791	1.120	0.466	1133	1.252	4.793	114.9	93.27	4.978	0.918	0.481	1	0.727	77.61	0.593
US	($)	31.66	5.945	5.214	1.540	0.640	1558	1.722	6.593	158.1	128.3	6.847	1.263	0.661	1.375	1	106.7	0.816
Japan	(Y)	29.66	5.570	4.885	1.443	0.600	1460	1.614	6.176	148.1	120.2	6.415	1.183	0.619	1.289	0.937	100.	0.764
Ecu		38.82	7.289	6.393	1.888	0.785	1911	2.112	8.083	193.8	157.3	8.395	1.549	0.810	1.686	1.226	130.9	1

Danish Kroner, French Franc, Norwegian Kroner, and Swedish Kroner per 10; Belgian Franc, Yen, Escudo, Lira and Peseta per 100.

(Source: *London Financial Times*)

FIGURE 4.3 Key Currency Cross Rates

The product of the spot rates is less than 1:

$$(S^{\$/¥})(S^{¥/DM})(S^{DM/\$}) = (\$.00960984/¥)(¥60.750/DM)(DM1.7125/\$)$$
$$= .999754 < 1$$

Thus, these rates are not in equilibrium, and there is an arbitrage opportunity so long as transactions costs are not prohibitively high. If you play your hand correctly, you can make a riskless arbitrage profit.

Suppose you start with $1 million and simultaneously make the following transactions in a *round turn*—buying and then selling each currency in turn:

Buy ¥ with $:	($1,000,000)/($.00960984/¥)	= ¥104,060,000
Buy DM with ¥:	(¥104,060,000)/(¥60.750/DM)	= DM1,712,922
Buy $ with DM:	(DM1,712,922)/(DM1.7125/$) =	$1,000,246

If you execute these trades simultaneously, you don't really need to put up the initial $1 million. So long as your credit is good, the required payment in each currency is more than covered by the receipt from selling that currency. And since you have no net position, you have no money at risk. You've captured a $246 arbitrage profit with no net investment and no risk.

Now, suppose you go the wrong way on your round turn:

Buy DM with $:	($1,000,000)(DM1.7125/$)	= DM1,712,500
Buy ¥ with DM:	(DM1,712,500)(¥60.750/DM)	= ¥104,034,375
Buy $ with ¥:	(¥104,034,375)($.00960984/¥) =	$999,754

Oops! In this case, you've lost $246. How can you tell which direction to go on your round turn? If you start with dollars, do you buy yen and sell deutsche marks in your round turn? Or, do you sell yen and buy marks? You win if you go the right way. You lose if you go the wrong way. But which way do you go?

Which Way Do You Go? Suppose you have cross rates for three currencies d, e, and f. The no-arbitrage condition is $S^{d/e}S^{e/f}S^{f/d} = 1$. If $S^{d/e}S^{e/f}S^{f/d} < 1$, then triangular arbitrage will force at least one of these spot exchange rates to go up. In this case, you want to buy the currency in the denominator of each spot rate with the corresponding currency in the numerator before arbitrage forces the spot rates to rise. Conversely, if $S^{d/e}S^{e/f}S^{f/d} > 1$ then at least one of the rates $S^{d/e}$, $S^{e/f}$, or $S^{f/d}$ must fall. In this case, you want to sell the currency in the denominator of each spot rate for the currency in the numerator before the spot rates fall in value.

The rule for determining which way to go in triangular arbitrage is:

- If $S^{d/e}S^{e/f}S^{f/d} < 1$ then $S^{d/e}$, $S^{e/f}$, and/or $S^{f/d}$ must rise; *buy* the currency in the denominator with the currency in the numerator of each spot rate.
- If $S^{d/e}S^{e/f}S^{f/d} > 1$ then $S^{d/e}$, $S^{e/f}$, and/or $S^{f/d}$ must fall; *sell* the currency in the denominator for the currency in the numerator of each spot rate.

In our example, $S^{\$/¥}S^{¥/DM}S^{DM/\$} = .999754 < 1$. One or more of these rates must rise, so you should buy the currency in the denominator of each spot rate with the currency in the numerator before the spot rates rise. This means that you should (1) buy yen with dollars at the $S^{\$/¥}$ rate, (2) buy marks with yen at the $S^{¥/DM}$ spot rate, and (3) buy dollars with marks at the $S^{DM/\$}$ rate. In this example, triangular arbitrage is worth doing so long as transactions costs on the round turn are less than about $(1 - S^{\$/¥}S^{¥/DM}S^{DM/\$}) =$ 0.0246% of the transaction amount (that is, $246 on a $1 million round turn).

Here's a complementary way of viewing our example. The inequality

$$(S^{\$/¥}S^{¥/DM}S^{DM/\$}) = 0.999754 < 1$$

can be restated as

$$(S^{\$/¥}S^{¥/DM}S^{DM/\$})^{-1} = (S^{¥/\$}S^{DM/¥}S^{\$/DM}) = 1.000246 > 1$$

This satisfies the second bulleted condition, so we should (1) sell $ for ¥, (2) sell ¥ for DM, and (3) sell DM for $. Of course, whenever you sell the currency in the denominator you are simultaneously buying the currency in the numerator. Viewed in this way, the second bullet is the same prescription as the first. For our example, (1) buy ¥ with $ (or sell $ for ¥), (2) buy DM with ¥ (or sell ¥ for DM), and (3) buy $ with DM (or sell DM for $).

In actuality, all three spot exchange rates (as well as any related bilateral exchange rates) will probably change to bring the currency markets back into equilibrium. Arbitrage activities will continue to push exchange rates in these directions until equilibrium is restored. Including all foreign currencies in a bilateral cross rate table creates a system of simultaneous equations that must be internally consistent within the bounds of transactions costs to preclude arbitrage opportunities. The foreign exchange market is highly competitive, and triangular arbitrage in the foreign currency market is difficult to find and fleeting at best.

Covered Interest Arbitrage and Interest Rate Parity

The law of one price requires that the relation between forward and spot exchange rates be determined by the nominal interest rate differential between the two currencies. This relation is called **interest rate parity**, or IRP. The reason that interest rate parity holds is that each of the prices (forward and spot exchange rates and interest rates) in this relation is an actively traded contract on a standardized and very liquid asset (a unit of currency).

Covered interest arbitrage is the profit-seeking activity that forces interest rate parity to hold. Let nominal interest rates over period t be denoted i_t^f in the foreign currency and i_t^d in the domestic currency. Let $F_t^{d/f}$ be the t-period forward rate traded at time 0 and maturing at time t. The spot exchange rate at time 0 is denoted $S_0^{d/f}$.

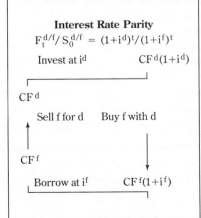

Interest Rate Parity
$$F_t^{d/f}/S_0^{d/f} = (1+i^d)^t/(1+i^f)^t$$

Invest at i^d $CF^d(1+i^d)$

CF^d

Sell f for d   Buy f with d

CF^f

Borrow at i^f $CF^f(1+i^f)$

In locational arbitrage, the subscripts on the exchange rate indicate *location*. In covered interest arbitrage, currency is exchanged at two different points in *time,* so the subscript refers to time rather than to the location of the transaction. As usual, superscripts refer to the currencies being traded in the currency markets or borrowed/invested in the Eurocurrency markets.

Interest rate parity relates the foreign exchange and Eurocurrency markets as follows.

$$\frac{F_t^{d/f}}{S_0^{d/f}} = \frac{(1+i^d)^t}{(1+i^f)^t} \tag{4.4}$$

where i^d and i^f are geometric mean interest rates over the t periods satisfying

$$(1+i^d)^t = (1+i_1^d)(1+i_2^d)...(1+i_t^d) = \prod_{\tau=1}^{t}(1+i_\tau^d)$$

and

$$(1+i^f)^t = (1+i_1^f)(1+i_2^f)...(1+i_t^f) = \prod_{\tau=1}^{t}(1+i_\tau^f).$$

The operator $\prod_{\tau=1}^{t}$ takes the product of the terms on the right-hand side over periods one through t. The term i_τ^d is called an *implied forward rate* because it is implied in forward prices and represents the required return priced as of today (time zero) over a future period τ.

Locational arbitrage takes advantage of price discrepancies between two locations. Triangular arbitrage searches for price disequilibriums among three bilateral cross rates. Through a similar mechanism, covered interest arbitrage takes advantage of interest rate differentials in two currencies that are not fully reflected in spot and forward exchange rates. For major currencies, nominal interest rates are actively traded contracts in the Eurocurrency markets. Likewise, for major currencies there are active markets for spot and forward exchange for maturities of up to five years. For these actively traded contracts in the international currency markets, equation (4.4) holds within the limits of transactions costs. Disequilibrium in this relation would induce arbitrageurs to borrow in one currency, lend in another currency, and hedge the difference in the foreign exchange markets. The threat of covered interest arbitrage forces the foreign exchange and Eurocurrency markets into equilibrium.

Locational arbitrage takes advantage of price discrepancies between 2 locations.

Covered interest arbitrage ensures that the foreign exchange and Eurocurrency markets are in equilibrium.

An Example of Covered Interest Arbitrage. Figure 4.4 presents an example of covered interest arbitrage. While this example ignores bid-ask spreads, it is easy to include transactions costs by using bid and offer quotes when trading each of these contracts. Suppose the following rates hold in U.S. dollars and pounds sterling:

$$S_0^{\$/\pounds} = \$1.25/\pounds \qquad i^\$ = 8.15\%$$
$$F_1^{\$/\pounds} = \$1.20/\pounds \qquad i^\pounds = 11.5625\%$$

$$F_t^{d/f}/S_0^{d/f} = (1 + i^d)^t/(1 + i^f)^t$$

United States

$p^\$ = 5\%$

$r^\$ = 3\%$

$i^\$ = (1 + .03)(1 + .05) - 1 = 8.15\%$

United Kingdom

$p^\pounds = 9.375\%$

$r^\pounds = 2\%$

$i^\pounds = (1.02)(1.09375) - 1$
$\quad\quad = 11.5625\%$

Currency Markets $S_0^{\$/\pounds} = \$1.25/\pounds$
$F_1^{\$/\pounds} = \$1.20/\pounds$

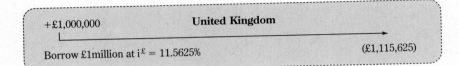

FIGURE 4.4
Covered Interest Arbitrage
and Interest Rate Parity

Interest rate parity does not hold: $(F_1^{\$/\pounds})/(S_0^{\$/\pounds}) = .96 < .969412 \approx (1+i^\$)/(1+i^\pounds)$. Covered interest arbitrage proceeds as follows.

1. Borrow one million pounds in the Eurocurrency market at the prevailing market interest rate of $i^\pounds = 11.5625\%$ for one year. Your obligation will be £1,115,625 in one year.
2. Exchange the one million pounds received from the bank for $1.25 million at the prevailing spot rate. This leaves you with a net dollar cash inflow today and a pound obligation in one year.
3. Invest the $1.25 million in Eurodollars at the market rate of $i^\$ = 8.15\%$/year. Your payoff will be $1,250,000(1.0815) = \$1,351,875$ in one year. The $1.25 million cash outflow gives you a zero net position in both dollars and pounds at time zero. You now have a cash inflow of $1,351,875 and a cash outflow of £1,115,625 in one year.

4. You owe £1,115,625 in one year, based on your Europound loan in step 1. To cover this obligation, sign a one-year forward contract in which you agree to sell $1,338,750 (equal to ($1.2/£)(£1,115,625)) and buy £1,115,625 (equal to $1,338,750/($1.2/£)) at the forward exchange rate of $F_1^{\$/£} = \$1.2/£$.

This transaction exactly offsets your pound liability and leaves you with a net profit of $13,125. The no-arbitrage condition enforced by covered interest arbitrage means that interest rate parity holds within the limits of transactions costs in the nearly frictionless international currency markets.

Which Way Do You Go? We face the same problem here as in triangular arbitrage. Which currency do we borrow and which currency do we lend in order to take advantage of a market disequilibrium? Take another look at the interest rate parity condition from equation (4.4). Suppose $F_t^{d/f}/S_0^{d/f} > (1+i^d)^t/(1+i^f)^t$, so that domestic interest rates are too low and foreign interest rates are too high to justify the forward premium/discount. If the markets are to get back into equilibrium, at least one of these rates must change. Equilibrium could be achieved under either or both of the following scenarios.

- If the ratio $F_t^{d/f}/S_0^{d/f}$ is "too high," then either $F_t^{d/f}$ must fall or $S_0^{d/f}$ must rise.
- If the ratio $(1+i^d)^t/(1+i^f)^t$ is "too low," then either i^d must rise or i^f must fall.

In this example, if you borrow at the domestic rate i^d and lend at the foreign rate i^f while covering your cash flows in the foreign exchange market at the forward rate $F_t^{d/f}$, you'll lock in an arbitrage profit based on the difference in the two ratios. Conversely, if $F_t^{d/f}/S_0^{d/f} < (1+i^d)^t/(1+i^f)^t$, then domestic interest rates are too high and/or foreign interest rates are too low to justify the forward premium/discount. In this case, you want to borrow in the foreign currency and lend in the domestic currency. This suggests the following rules:

- If $F_t^{d/f}/S_0^{d/f} > (1+i^d)^t/(1+i^f)^t$, then borrow i^d, lend i^f, buy $S_0^{d/f}$, and sell $F_t^{d/f}$.
- If $F_t^{d/f}/S_0^{d/f} < (1+i^d)^t/(1+i^f)^t$, then lend i^d, borrow i^f, sell $S_0^{d/f}$, and buy $F_t^{d/f}$.

As with triangular arbitrage, using indirect quotes leads to an equivalent set of rules.

Foreign exchange traders will tell you that relative interest rates determine the forward premium or discount and not vice versa. Forward rates are almost entirely an interest rate play. If there is a disequilibrium, foreign exchange rates are much more likely to change than interest rates in the domestic and foreign credit markets. Nevertheless, these rules send you in the right direction in your search for an arbitrage profit.

Changes in Spot and Forward Foreign Exchange Rates. Over daily sampling intervals, the empirical behavior of spot and forward exchange rates is nearly random with an equal probability of either rising or falling. While there are periods of high and periods of low volatility, your best guess for tomorrow's spot or forward exchange rate is usually today's spot or forward rate.

Covered interest arbitrage ensures that forward premiums are determined by interest rate differentials.

Even though day-to-day changes are random, covered interest arbitrage ensures that the ratio of forward to spot exchange rates is determined by the differential between foreign and domestic interest rates. This means that although day-to-day changes in exchange rates are random, spot and forward rates move up or down by about the same amount each day. As the measurement interval is lengthened to years, the forward rate becomes a better estimate of the future spot rate of exchange. This topic is treated in more depth in Chapter 5.

4.3 LESS RELIABLE INTERNATIONAL PARITY CONDITIONS

In the Eurocurrency and foreign exchange markets, covered interest arbitrage enforces interest rate parity. Covered interest arbitrage is possible because each of the contracts in the relation is an actively traded contract. As we have seen in the previous section, disequilibriums involving contractual cash flows in the international currency markets are quickly forced back into equilibrium through arbitrage activity. Disequilibrium prices on nontraded contracts cannot be so easily arbitraged and can persist for long periods of time.

The international parity conditions in this section relate expected inflation, real rates of return, and expected future spot exchange rates to nominal interest rate differentials and the forward premium or discount. Because there is variability in realized inflation, realized real returns, and realized spot rates, disequilibriums in these international parity conditions cannot be arbitraged away. Nevertheless, the profit-making activities of the many participants in the currency and interest rate markets suggest that these relations are reasonable approximations in the long run.

Relative Purchasing Power Parity

In our discussion of the law of one price, P^d and P^f represented the domestic and foreign prices of a single asset or of two identical assets. Suppose the asset being priced is a standardized basket of consumer goods, such as a consumer price index, rather than a single asset. Let P_t^d and P_t^f represent the prices of these domestic and foreign consumer price indexes at time t.[3] Percentage changes in the consumer price levels over period t are defined as

$$p_t^d = (P_t^d - P_{t-1}^d)/P_{t-1}^d$$

and

$$p_t^f = (P_t^f - P_{t-1}^f)/P_{t-1}^f$$

---

3 In reality, people in different countries consume different goods and services so that these prices reflect different consumption baskets. Because purchasing power parity does not allow us to compare the prices of two different consumption baskets, we need to interpret these equations with a liberal dose of literary license.

Relative to some arbitrarily defined base period t=0, consumer prices at time t depend on inflation during the t intervening periods according to

$$P_t^d = P_0^d \left[\prod_{\tau=1}^{t} (1 + p_\tau^d) \right]$$

and

$$P_t^f = P_0^f \left[\prod_{\tau=1}^{t} (1 + p_\tau^f) \right]$$

where p_τ^d and p_τ^f represent domestic and foreign inflation rates during period τ.

The difference in expected inflation provides an estimate of the expected change in the spot exchange rate. Let $E[P_t^d]$ and $E[P_t^f]$ denote the expected value of the Consumer Price Index at time t in the domestic currency and in the foreign currency, respectively. Then the expected change in the spot exchange rate over t periods is determined by the relative inflationary expectations in the domestic and foreign currencies. Through substitution, we find:

$$E[S_t^{d/f}]/S_0^{d/f} = E[(P_t^d/P_t^f)]/(P_0^d/P_0^f)$$
$$= (E[P_t^d]/E[P_t^f])/(P_0^d/P_0^f)$$
$$= E[(P_t^d]/P_0^d)/(E[P_t^f]/P_0^f)$$
$$= (1 + E[p^d])^t / (1 + E[p^f])^t, \qquad (4.5)$$

where the ratio $(E[P_t]/P_0) = (1+E[p])^t$ is simply one plus the expected geometric mean inflation rate over the next t periods satisfying $(1+E[p])^t = (1+E[p_1])(1+E[p_2])...$ $(1+E[p_t])$. This form of the law of one price is known as **relative purchasing power parity**, or RPPP, and it states that the expected appreciation or depreciation of the spot exchange rate is determined by the mean expected inflation rate over the period. As a special case, if inflation is a known constant in each currency throughout each period, then relative purchasing power parity can be stated as $E[S_t^{d/f}]/S_0^{d/f} = (1+p^d)^t / (1+p^f)^t$.

Relative purchasing power parity ensures that changes in expected future spot exchange rates are determined by inflation differentials.

Because neither expected inflation nor expected future spot rates of exchange are traded contracts, this relationship only holds on average. Over measurement intervals of a few days or even months, spot exchange rates move in nearly a random fashion, and equation (4.5) has low predictive power. In the long run, inflation differences eventually prevail, and exchange rate changes are more highly correlated with inflation differentials.

Figure 4.5 graphs mean annual changes in spot exchange rates against inflation differentials relative to the U.S. dollar for several major currencies over the period 1960–1995. As predicted by RPPP, the dollar tended to rise against currencies with higher inflation, such as the South African rand, the Spanish peseta, and the Italian lira. Conversely, the dollar tended to fall against currencies with lower inflation, such as the Swiss franc, the German deutsche mark, and the Singapore dollar. While it is comforting to know that inflation differentials are eventually reflected in exchange rates, the relation in Figure 4.5 is far from linear. Relative purchasing power parity holds only over the long run and is of little use in predicting day-to-day changes in spot exchange rates.

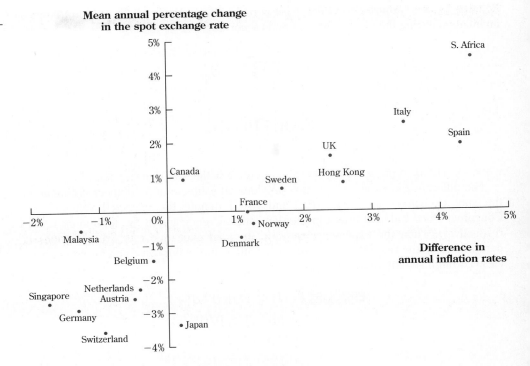

**Mean annual percentage change
in the spot exchange rate**

**Difference in
annual inflation rates**

FIGURE 4.5
Relative Purchasing
Power Parity, 1960–1995

Forward Rates as Unbiased Predictors of Future Spot Rates

> *Forward rates can serve as
> predictors of future
> spot rates.*

Forward rates...

Common sense dictates that forward rates should be unbiased predictors of future spot rates; that is, $F_t^{d/f} = E[S_t^{d/f}]$. This "unbiased expectations" hypothesis is often called **forward parity**. If there is a consistent positive or negative bias in the forward rates, then speculators can buy or sell currencies forward in the hope of capturing a profit on the difference between actual spot rates and the forward contract rate at maturity. The view that forward rates are unbiased predictors of future spot rates can be stated as

$$F_t^{d/f}/S_0^{d/f} = E[S_t^{d/f}]/S_0^{d/f} \tag{4.6}$$

This equation states that forward premiums and discounts are determined by the expected change in the spot rate of exchange.

Because expected future spot rates are not traded contracts, equation (4.6) holds only over the long run. Financial markets cannot foresee the future, and spot and forward exchange rates are quite volatile. For daily exchange rate changes, the best estimate of tomorrow's spot rate (for all but hyperinflationary currencies) is the current spot rate, not the forward rate. As the sampling interval is lengthened, the performance of forward rates as predictors of future spot rates improves. Figure 4.6 plots actual percentage changes in the spot rate $S_t^{£/\$}$ against the percentage forward premium/discount using three-month forward contracts over the period 1986 through 1995. There is very little relation between actual spot exchange rates and forward rates with these three-month

In each of the international parity conditions in this chapter, Rule #1 (keep track of your currency units) is implemented as

numerator to numerator

and

denominator to denominator.

If direct quotes are used, as in

$$E[S_1^{d/f}]/S_0^{d/f} = (1+E[p^d])/(1+E[p^f]) \qquad (4.5)$$

then the domestic currency in the numerator of the spot exchange rates on the left-hand side of equation (4.5) remains in the numerator of the relative inflation rates on the right-hand side. If the spot rates are stated in indirect terms as $S^{f/d}$, then the foreign inflation rate appears in the numerator on the right-hand side:

$$E[S_1^{f/d}]/S_0^{f/d} = (1+E[pf])/(1+E[p^d]) \qquad (4.5a)$$

Follow the rule "numerator to numerator and denominator to denominator" in order to keep track of your currency units.

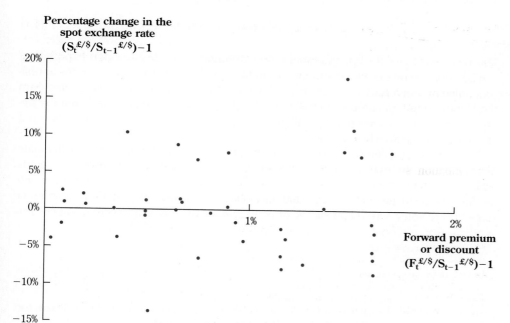

Percentage change in the spot exchange rate $(S_t^{£/\$}/S_{t-1}^{£/\$})-1$

Forward premium or discount $(F_t^{£/\$}/S_{t-1}^{£/\$})-1$

FIGURE 4.6
Forward Rates as Predictors of Future Spot Rates, 1986–1995 (quarterly forward rates $F_t^{£/\$}$ = pound sterling per dollar)

forward contracts. Over shorter forecast horizons, forward exchange rates perform even more poorly as predictors of future spot rates of exchange. Over longer forecast horizons, forward rates perform somewhat better as predictors of future spot rates.[4]

Figure 4.6 also indicates that the variability of actual spot rates along the y-axis is much greater than the variability in forward premia along the x-axis. Forward prices reflect interest rate differentials according to interest rate parity and vary from 0 percent to +2 percent of the spot rate. Actual quarterly changes in spot exchange rates reflect changes in the supply and demand for various currencies and vary from −15 percent to +20 percent. Although forward prices are not good predictors of future spot prices over short forecasting horizons, there are few (if any) good alternatives.

The International Fisher Relation (Fisher Open Hypothesis)

The international Fisher relation relates interest rate differentials to inflation differentials.

The Fisher equation states that nominal interests rates i are related to real (or inflation-adjusted) interest rates r and inflation p according to $(1+i) = (1+r)(1+p)$. Solving this for the nominal interest rate, we get $i = r + p + rp$. The cross product term rp is small if inflation is low, and nominal interest rates are frequently approximated by $i \cong r + p$.

The interest rate parity relation in equation (4.4) includes the ratio $(1+i^d)/(1+i^f)$. Substituting the Fisher equation into the numerator and denominator, we have

$$(1+i^d) / (1+i^f) = [(1+r^d)(1+p^d)] / [(1+r^f)(1+p^f)]$$

If the law of one price holds for real rates of return in two different countries, then $r^d = r^f$ and the real returns r^d and r^f cancel from the right-hand side. Then, in equilibrium with no government intervention, interest rate differentials should reflect inflation differentials according to $(1+i^d)/(1+i^f) = (1+p^d)/(1+p^f)$. Measured over t periods, the relation is

$$(1+i^d)^t / (1+i^f)^t = (1+p^d)^t / (1+p^f)^t. \qquad (4.7)$$

This relation is called the **international Fisher relation**, or the **Fisher open hypothesis**.

Figure 4.7 compares yield differentials on three-month government securities to realized inflation differentials over the corresponding three-month periods using rates from the United Kingdom and the United States for illustration. As you can see from the figure, the relation between realized inflation and nominal interest rate differentials is not very strong for quarterly intervals.

In actuality, real interest rates are not equal across currencies, and they fluctuate over time as well.[5] Figure 4.8 plots yield-to-maturity on one-year Eurocurrencies minus realized inflation over the corresponding one-year period for the U.S. dollar, U.K. pound sterling, German deutsche mark, and Japanese yen during 1987–1995. Real interest rates are not equal across currencies, as evidenced by the 5.5% difference in real returns

---

4 In fact, there are persistent, positively autocorrelated forward premiums in forward exchange rates. However, these premiums are economically small and difficult to predict (see Mark [1988] and Levine [1991]). We'll use equation (4.6) as a reasonable working hypothesis.

5 See Mishkin [1984] for an empirical investigation of several of the international parity conditions, particularly the assumption of a single real rate of interest across currencies.

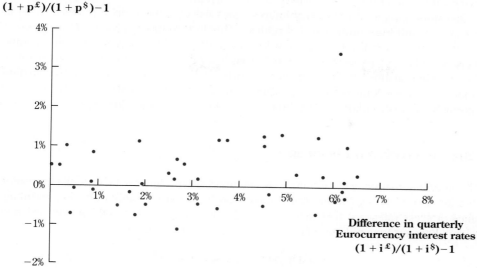

Difference in realized
quarterly inflation
$(1 + p^£)/(1 + p^§) - 1$

Difference in quarterly
Eurocurrency interest rates
$(1 + i^£)/(1 + i^§) - 1$

FIGURE 4.7
International Fisher Relation,
1986–1995 (U.K. pound
sterling versus U.S. dollar.)

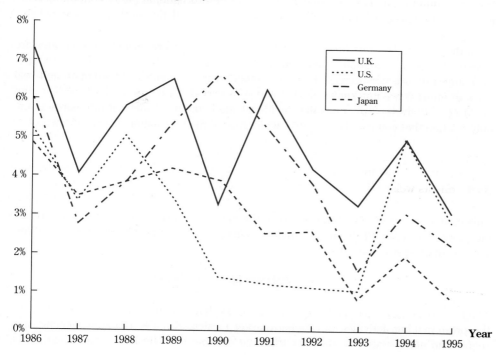

Yield on one-year Eurocurrencies
minus realized inflation during the year

Year

FIGURE 4.8
Real Interest Rates in Four
Currencies, 1986–1995

on U.S. and German government securities as of the end of 1990. There are also wide swings in real interest rates over time in each currency.

Investors attracted to high real interest rates will eventually drive prices upward in currencies with high promised real returns. This in turn drives promised yields downward and pushes real rates back toward equilibrium. Still, at any given point in time there are likely to be fairly substantial cross-border differences in real interest rates. Variation in real interest rates both across currencies and over time means that inflation differentials have little power to explain interest rate differentials. As with the other international parity conditions, equation (4.7) holds only over the long run.

Capital Market Equilibrium

The international parity conditions were summarized in Figure 4.1. Note that the ratios that lie diagonally across the figure must also be equal in equilibrium. For example, since interest rates are tied to the forward premium/discount and the forward premium/discount is a predictor of change in future spot rates, then

$$(1+i^d)^t/(1+i^f)^t = E[S_t^{d/f}]/S_0^{d/f}$$

Similarly, the relation

$$F_t^{d/f}/S_0^{d/f} = (1+p^d)^t/(1+p^f)^t$$

holds in equilibrium. This completes the circuit of international parity conditions relating exchange rates, real and nominal interest rates, and inflation in the international currency markets.

> *Interest rate parity is the only international parity condition that you can trust at all times.*

In the real world, only the contracts for spot and forward rates and interest rates are traded. Expected inflation, expected real returns, and the expected future spot exchange rate are not traded contracts. Actual future spot rates and inflation and real rates of interest are not known at the start of a period. Since the ratios $F_t^{d/f}/S_0^{d/f}$ and $(1+i^d)^t/(1+i^f)^t$ are the only ones that include traded contracts, interest rate parity is the only relation that you can trust to hold at all times in the international currency markets.

4.4 SUMMARY

This chapter develops the implications of the law of one price (also known as purchasing power parity, or PPP) for international currency and Eurocurrency market prices. The law of one price states that

> Equivalent assets sell for the same price.

The law of one price is enforced in the foreign exchange and Eurocurrency markets by the profit-making activities of rational market participants. For riskless positions that require no net investment, riskless arbitrage ensures that the law of one price holds.

Riskless arbitrage ensures that the following international parity conditions in exchange rates and interest rates hold for actively traded financial assets with contractual payoffs:

Purchasing power parity	$P_t^d/P_t^f = S_t^{d/f}$	(4.1)
Bilateral equilibrium	$S_A^{d/f}/S_B^{d/f} = S_B^{f/d}/S_A^{f/d} = 1$	(4.2)
Triangular equilibrium	$S^{d/e}S^{e/f}S^{f/d} = 1$	(4.3)
Interest rate parity	$F_t^{d/f}/S_0^{d/f} = (1+i^d)^t/(1+i^f)^t$	(4.4)

The law of one price has implications for noncontractual prices as well, but only in the long run. International parity conditions that include expectations of future price and exchange rate levels include the following:

Relative PPP	$E[S_t^{d/f}]/S_0^{d/f} = (1+E[p^d])^t/(1+E[p^f])^t$	(4.5)
Unbiased forward expectations	$F_t^{d/f}/S_0^{d/f} = E[S_t^{d/f}]/S_0^{d/f}$	(4.6)
International Fisher relation	$(1+i^d)^t/(1+i^f)^t = (1+E[p^d])^t/(1+E[p^f])^t$	(4.7)

Because they are at least partially based on nontraded contracts, these relations are less reliable than those in equations (4.1) through (4.4).

KEY TERMS

Arbitrage and the no-arbitrage condition
Covered interest arbitrage
Cross rates and triangular arbitrage
Forward parity
Interest rate parity
International Fisher relation (Fisher open hypothesis)

International parity conditions
Liquidity
Locational arbitrage
Market frictions
Purchasing power parity
Relative purchasing power parity

CONCEPTUAL QUESTIONS

4.1 What is the law of one price? What does it say about asset prices?
4.2 Describe riskless arbitrage.
4.3 What is the difference between locational, triangular, and covered interest arbitrage?
4.4 What is relative purchasing power parity?
4.5 How would you arrive at an estimate of a future spot exchange rate between two currencies?
4.6 What does the international Fisher relation say about interest rate and inflation differentials?

PROBLEMS

4.1 Given $S_0^{\$/DM} = \$.6361/DM$ and the 180-day forward rate $F_1^{\$/DM} = \$.6352/DM$, what is the forward premium/discount? Based on the unbiased forward expectations hypothesis, by how much is the deutsche mark expected to appreciate/depreciate over the next 180 days? Provide a forecast of the spot rate of exchange in 180 days.

4.2 The current spot exchange rate is $S_0^{¥/\$}$ = ¥190/$ and the one-year forward rate is $F_1^{¥/\$}$ = ¥210/$. The prime rate in the United States is 15 percent.

a. What should the Japanese prime rate be?

b. Is the dollar trading at a discount or a premium in the forward markets?

4.3 Suppose $S_0^{\$/£}$ = $1.25/£ and the one-year forward rate is $F_1^{\$/£}$ = $1.20/£. The real interest rate on a riskless government security is 2 percent in both England and the United States. The U.S. inflation rate is 5 percent.

a. What is England's inflation rate if the equilibrium relationships hold?

b. What is England's nominal required rate of return on riskless government securities?

4.4 Suppose that for the same basket of goods the time zero price indices in countries D and F are P_0^D = D100 and P_0^F = F1, so that $S_0^{D/F}$ = P_0^D/P_0^F = D100/F. Inflation rates in countries D and F are expected to be 10 percent and 21 percent per period, respectively, over the foreseeable future.

a. What are the expected price levels $E[P_1^D]$ and $E[P_1^F]$ and the expected nominal spot rate of exchange $E[S_1^{D/F}]$ in one period?

b. Looking two years into the future, what are the expected price levels in each country $(E[P_2^D]$ and $E[P_2^F])$?

4.5 A foreign exchange dealer in Tokyo provides quotes for spot and one-month, three-month, and six-month forward rates. When you ask for current quotations on the Finnish markka (FM) against the dollar over the telephone, you hear: "4.0040 to 200, 120 to 110, 350 to 312, and 680 to 620." This points quote can be stated as the following outright quote:

	Bid (FM/$)	Ask (FM/$)
Spot	4.0040	4.0200
One month forward	3.9920	4.0090
Three months forward	3.9690	3.9888
Six months forward	3.9360	3.9580

Here is how points quotes can be translated into outright quotes. The "4.0040 to 200" quote sets the spot rate. The remaining quotes are stated as an increment or decrement from this starting point. If the first number in a pair is greater than the second number, as in "120 to 110," then the currency in the denominator of the quote (the dollar) is selling at a forward discount and the pair should be subtracted from the bid and ask spot rates. The quote "120 to 110" indicates that one-month forward prices are 4.0040 − 0.0120 = 3.9920 bid and 4.0200 − 0.0110 = 4.0090 ask. If the first number in a pair is less than the second number, then the currency in the denominator is selling at a forward premium and the pair should be added to the bid and ask spot rates.

a. In New York, three-month U.S. Treasury bills yield 7 percent per annum. What should be the annualized yield on three-month Finnish government bills? Use the Finnish markka ask quotes for simplicity.

b. Verify your answer to part a. with a hypothetical investment of $10,000,000 for three months in each country. Use only ask quotes for simplicity and ignore other fees, charges, and taxes.

4.6 Swedish krona (SK) are sold in forward contracts of 30, 90, and 180 days. Current spot, 30-, 60-, and 90-day points quotations (refer to Problem 4.5 for a description of this quotation system) for the Swedish krona against the dollar are SK7.5050/$ to 150, 100 to 120, 250 to 262, and 540 to 560, respectively.

a. In New York, the three-month U.S. T-bill rate is 5 percent per annum. What should be the yield on three-month SK government bills? Use ask quotes for simplicity.

b. Verify your answer to part a. by comparing the SK payoff on a three-month investment of SK10,000,000 with the payoff on an equivalent investment in U.S. dollars covered at the forward exchange rate. Use only ask quotes for simplicity and ignore other fees, charges, and taxes.

4.7 Quotes for the U.S. dollar and Thailand baht (Bt) are as follows:

One-year forward contract midpoint	$S^{Bt/\$}$(today)	= Bt24.96/$
Spot contract midpoint	$F^{Bt/\$}$(1 year)	= Bt25.64/$
One-year Eurodollar interest rate	$i^\$$	= 6.125% per year

a. Your newspaper does not quote one-year Eurocurrency interest rates on Thai baht. Make your own estimate of i^{Bt}.

b. Suppose that you can trade at the prices for $S^{Bt/\$}$, $F^{Bt/\$}$ and $i^\$$ given above and that you can also either borrow or lend at a Thai Eurocurrency interest rate of i^{Bt} = 10% per year. Based on a $1,000,000 initial amount, how much profit can you generate through covered interest arbitrage?

SUGGESTED READINGS

These two articles investigate small but persistent deviations from the forward expectations hypothesis.

Ross Levine, "An Empirical Inquiry into the Nature of the Forward Exchange Rate Bias," *Journal of International Economics* 30, No. 3/4 1991, pages 359–370.

Nelson C. Mark, "Time-Varying Betas and Forward Premia in the Pricing of Forward Foreign Exchange Contracts," *Journal of Financial Economics* 22, No. 2, December 1988, pages 335–354.

A general investigation of several of the international parity conditions appears in

Frederic S. Mishkin, "Are Real Interest Rates Equal Across Countries? An Empirical Investigation of International Parity Conditions, " Journal of Finance 39, December 1984, pages 1345–1357.

Continuous Time Finance

Legend has it that many years ago the bankers of the world employed nearsighted men in green accountants' visors and armbands to compound interest continuously (well, perhaps not continuously—let's just say discretely but very often) in the smoky back rooms of commercial banks. But no matter how fast they worked, it proved impossible for these unfortunate lackeys to compound interest on a continuous basis. Eventually, one of these tireless minions discovered that holding period rates of return can be transformed into continuously compounded rates of return with a simple formula. Here's how.

Continuously Compounded Rates of Return

As the number of compounding intervals within a period approaches infinity, returns are said to be *compounded continuously.* At any instant, the rate of return is then called the *instantaneous* rate of return. Henceforth, let's denote continuously compounded rates of return with *italics,* so that i will represent the continuously compounded form of a holding period interest rate i.

Suppose you have an amount V_0 today and you want to know how large this value will be after T periods if it earns a continuously compounded rate of interest i. With continuous compounding, the value of V_0 at time T is given by

$$V_T = V_0\, e^{iT} \tag{4A.1}$$

Conversely, the present value of a future cash flow to be received at time T with continuous compounding is given by

$$V_0 = V_T/e^{iT} = V_T\, e^{-iT} \tag{4A.2}$$

The number e is a constant and is approximately equal to 2.718.

The formula for converting a rate of return i with periodic (for example, annual) compounding into a continuously compounded rate is $i = \ln(1+i)$ where ln is the natural logarithm function with base e. The equation follows from

$$(1 + i) = e^i \Leftrightarrow \ln(1 + i) = \ln(e^i) = i. \qquad (4A.3)$$

For example, the continuously compounded annual rate of return i that is equivalent to an annual rate i = 12.64% with annual compounding is $i = \ln(1 + .1264) = 11.90\%$ per year. That is, $e^{0.1190} = 1.1264$ and $\ln(1.1264) = 0.119$. A 12.64 percent rate of return with annual compounding is equivalent to a 11.9 percent annual return with continuous compounding.

Because the algebra of continuously compounded requires a knowledge of natural logarithms, let's review the properties of the natural logarithm and its inverse function—the exponential function e.

$$\begin{aligned}
e^{\ln(x)} &= \ln(e^x) = x & (4A.4) \\
\ln(AB) &= \ln(A) + \ln(B) & (4A.5) \\
\ln(A/B) &= \ln(A) - \ln(B) & (4A.6) \\
\ln(A^X) &= X \ln(A) & (4A.7)
\end{aligned}$$

These properties make calculating the compound rate of return over a series of continuously compounded rates of return easy, because *continuously compounded rates are additive* rather than multiplicative.

$$\ln[(1+i_1)(1+i_2)...(1+i_T)] = \ln[e^{i_1}e^{i_2}...e^{i_T}] = \ln[e^{(i_1+i_2+...i_T)}]$$
$$= i_1 + i_2 + ... + i_T \qquad (4A.8)$$

Let's try an example. The average rate of return over three periods with annual holding period rates of return (that is, without compounding) of 10 percent, 16 percent, and 12 percent is found with a geometric average as follows:

GEOMETRIC MEAN RETURN WITH PERIODIC COMPOUNDING

$$i_{avg} = [(1.10)(1.16)(1.12)]^{1/3} - 1$$
$$= 0.1264, \text{ or } 12.64\% \text{ per year}$$

An equivalent answer can be found with continuously compounded rates of return:

ARITHMETIC MEAN RETURN WITH CONTINUOUS COMPOUNDING

$$i_{avg} = [\ln(1.10) + \ln(1.12) + \ln(1.16)]/3 = [.0953 + .1133 + .1484]/3$$
$$= 0.1190, \text{ or } 11.9\% \text{ per year}$$
$$\text{compounded continuously}$$

This is equivalent to the $e^{0.1190} = 12.64\%$ average rate of return with annual compounding.

International Parity Conditions in Continuous Time

The international parity conditions in continuous time are a straightforward application of logarithms. Over a single period, the parity conditions are:

$$F_1^{d/f}/S_0^{d/f} = E[S_1^{d/f}]/S_0^{d/f} = (1 + i^d)/(1 + i^f) = (1 + p^d)/(1 + p^f) \qquad (4A.9)$$

Using i to indicate a continuously compounded interest rate and p to indicate a continuously compounded inflation rate, the parity conditions over a single period can be restated as

$$\ln(F_1^{d/f}/S_0^{d/f}) = \ln(E[S_1^{d/f}]/S_0^{d/f}) = i^d - i^f = p^d - p^f \qquad (4A.10)$$

Over t periods, we must apply the rule $\ln(A^X) = X \ln(A)$. Then, the t-period international parity conditions in continuously compounded returns are

$$\ln(F_t^{d/f}/S_0^{d/f}) = \ln(E[S_t^{d/f}]/S_0^{d/f}) = t(i^d - i^f) = t(p^d - p^f) \qquad (4A.11)$$

where the interest and inflation rates are continuously compounded mean rates of return over the t periods.

Empirical tests of the international parity conditions are generally conducted in continuously compounded returns because they are additive and are more likely to satisfy an assumption of linearity. We'll return to continuously compounded returns in the next chapter and again in the chapters on currency options and options on real assets.

Summary

Returns are conveniently stated in their continuously compounded form. Continuously compounded returns are convenient because they are additive rather than multiplicative as with geometric holding period returns. Continuously compounded returns i are related to holding period returns i according to

$$(1 + i) = e^i \Leftrightarrow \ln(1 + i) = \ln(e^i) = i \qquad (4A.3)$$

Over a single period, the international parity conditions can be stated in continuously compounded returns as simply:

$$\ln(F_1^{d/f}/S_0^{d/f}) = \ln(E[S_1^{d/f}]/S_0^{d/f}) = i^d - i^f = p^d - p^f \qquad (4A.12)$$

where i and p represent continuously compounded interest and inflation rates, respectively. In words, the forward premium/discount to the currency spot rate and the expected change in the spot rate are determined by interest rate differentials between the two currencies. If real interest rates are constant across the two currencies, then interest rate differentials are in turn determined by inflation differentials.

4A.1 Suppose you earn a 100 percent return in one period and then lose 50 percent of your value in the next period. Compute your average periodic rate of return over the two periods using geometric holding period returns. Now, compute your average periodic rate of return using continuously compounded returns. Are these equivalent?

4A.2 Suppose P_0^D = D100, P_0^F = F1, and $S_0^{D/F}$ = D100/F. Inflation rates are p^D = 10% and p^F = 21% in holding period returns. Transform these inflation rates to continuously compounded returns and find $E[P_1^D]$, $E[P_1^F]$, $E[S_1^{D/F}]$, $E[P_2^D]$, $E[P_2^F]$ and $E[S_1^{D/F}]$ according to the international parity conditions. (Note that this is a repeat of Problem 4.4 in continuously compounded returns.)

The Nature of Foreign Exchange Risk

There was a story about the quantum theorist Werner Heisenberg on his deathbed,
declaring that he will have two questions for God: why relativity, and why turbulence.
Heisenberg says, "I really think He may have an answer to the first question."

James Gleick, *Chaos*

OVERVIEW

Chapter 4 described how nominal exchange rates change in equilibrium. It did not describe how they change in reality or why changes in exchange rates are important. Multinational finance must necessarily be conducted in the real world of foreign exchange rates and not in the stylized world of the previous chapter.

This chapter covers the following topics:

- The nature of the multinational corporation's exposure to foreign exchange risk
- Why changes in exchange rates are important to international trade and finance
- The difference between *real* and *nominal* changes in exchange rates
- How exchange rates actually behave in the real world
- Approaches to forecasting foreign exchange rates

The material in this chapter is designed to help you recognize and understand what is taking place in the currency markets. This requires an understanding of how changes in foreign exchange rates affect asset values. This understanding is necessary for individual and institutional investors, financial institutions, and multinational corporations to anticipate, manage, and react to changes in foreign exchange rates.

Part 2 Foreign Exchange
and Exchange Rate
Determination

Currency Risk versus Currency Risk Exposure

Before we move on to the ways in which currency fluctuations affect asset values, it is necessary to point out the difference between foreign exchange (or currency) risk and foreign exchange risk exposure.

Risk exists when the future is unknown; that is, whenever actual outcomes can deviate from expected outcomes. With regard to foreign exchange rates, an expected devaluation of a foreign currency by a foreign government does not constitute risk. Risk exists if and only if the actual devaluation can differ from the expectation. Similarly, risk does not exist simply because a promised foreign currency cash inflow is expected to be negatively affected by a depreciation of the foreign currency. Currency risk exists if and only if the actual amount of the appreciation or depreciation is unknown.

Currency risk exposure depends on how much is at risk.

The multinational corporation is exposed to foreign exchange risk when the value of its assets and liabilities can change with unexpected changes in currency values. Exposure to currency risk depends on *how much is at risk*. If an investor's wealth is independent of foreign currency movements (for example, if it is held in cash in the domestic currency), then this investor has no exposure to foreign currency risk. If a U.S. resident has DM150,000 in cash in a German bank, then this individual's exposure to unexpected changes in the spot exchange rate between dollars and deutsche marks is DM150,000. Note that it is natural to denominate foreign currency risk exposure in the foreign currency. If the DM150,000 is converted into $100,000, then the dollar value of this amount is no longer exposed to unexpected changes in the dollar/mark exchange rate.

Monetary versus Nonmonetary Assets and Liabilities

A useful way to categorize the firm's assets and liabilities is according to whether they are monetary (contractual) or nonmonetary (noncontractual) in nature. Consider the balance sheet at the top of Figure 5.1.

Monetary assets and liabilities have contractual payoffs.

Monetary assets and liabilities are assets and liabilities with contractual payoffs, so that the size and timing of promised cash flows are known in advance. The firm's monetary assets include cash and money market securities, accounts receivable, domestic and Eurocurrency deposits, and the cash inflow side of forwards, futures, options, and swap contracts. Monetary liabilities include wages and accounts payable, domestic and Eurocurrency loans, and the cash outflow side of forwards, futures, options, and swap contracts. Monetary contracts may be denominated either in the domestic or in foreign currencies.

Real (nonmonetary) assets and liabilities of the firm are defined as all assets and liabilities that are not monetary. Real assets include the firm's productive technologies and capacities, whether these are physical assets, as in a manufacturing firm, or human assets, as in a service firm. Inventory is also considered a real asset unless it has already been sold or payment has been contractually promised in some way. Returns on real assets are noncontractual and hence uncertain. As we shall see, real assets are exposed

Market Value Balance Sheet

Monetary Assets	Monetary Liabilities
Real Assets	Equity

- Economic exposure   Change in the value of all future cash flows due to unexpected changes in currency exchange rates

  —Transaction exposure   Change in the value of *contractual* future cash flows (*monetary* assets and liabilities) due to unexpected changes in currency exchange rates

  — Operating exposure   Change in the value of *noncontractual* future cash flows (*nonmonetary* assets and liabilities) due to unexpected changes in currency exchange rates

- Translation exposure   Change in financial accounting statements due to unexpected changes in currency exchange rates (also called *accounting exposure*)

FIGURE 5.1
A Taxonomy of Exposures
to Currency Risk

to currency risk regardless of where they are located. For example, the value of both foreign and domestic manufacturing plants depends on the value of exchange rates.

As the residual owner of the firm, common equity is a nonmonetary liability. Other liabilities of the firm are monetary or contractual in nature. These other liabilities include accounts payable, taxes payable, and short- and long-term debt. The market value of common equity is equal to the value of the firm less the value of these other liabilities. In the same way, the cash flows that accrue to equity depend on the nonmonetary cash flows of the firm's real assets and on the net cash flows from the firm's monetary assets and liabilities.

Although each of these asset and liability categories can be exposed to foreign exchange risk, the nature of the risk exposure varies depending on whether the asset or liability is contractual or noncontractual in nature. Since the value of each of these accounts ultimately derives from the expected future cash flows accruing to the account and to the risk of these cash flows, exposure to foreign exchange risk is conventionally defined in terms of the nature of the cash flows.

Economic Exposure to Currency Risk

Economic exposure refers to changes in *all* (monetary and nonmonetary) future cash flows due to unexpected changes in foreign currency exchange rates. Economic exposure includes the impact of unexpected currency changes on contractual (monetary) transactions as well as on the uncertain future cash flows generated by the firm's income-producing real assets. Real changes in foreign exchange rates can cause major

Economic exposure includes transaction exposure and operating exposure.

changes in the value of the multinational corporation's monetary and real cash flows through the firm's economic exposure to real foreign exchange risk. Because economic exposure includes the effect of contractual cash flows exposed to transaction exposure as well as uncertain cash flows arising from future returns to investment, it is a much more general and important exposure than transaction exposure, but also a more difficult risk exposure to estimate. For this reason, managing the multinational's economic exposure to currency risk is an important long-term goal of the multinational financial manager.

Economic exposure to currency risk can be broken down into the net transaction exposure of the firm's monetary assets and liabilities and the operating exposure of the firm's real assets. Since the market value of common equity is simply the value of total (monetary and real) assets minus the value of monetary liabilities, common equity is exposed to currency risk through the exposures of the firm's assets and liabilities.

Transaction exposure refers to the currency risk exposure of monetary assets and liabilities.

Transaction Exposure to Currency Risk. **Transaction exposure** refers to changes in the value of monetary assets and liabilities due to unexpected changes in foreign currency exchange rates; in other words, it is the currency risk exposure of monetary cash flows. Monetary assets and liabilities are assets and liabilities with contractual payoffs, for which the size and timing of promised cash flows are known in advance. Monetary assets and liabilities include cash, marketable securities, accounts receivable, accounts payable, wages and taxes payable, and short- and long-term debt.

Monetary assets and liabilities may be denominated either in the domestic currency or in foreign currencies. Monetary contracts denominated in a foreign currency are fully exposed to changes in the value of that currency. If the functional currency is the domestic currency, then domestic monetary contracts are not directly exposed to foreign currency risk although they are still exposed to domestic purchasing power risk.[1] If monetary assets denominated in a foreign currency are offset by monetary liabilities in the same currency, then the net transaction exposure is equal to **net monetary assets** (monetary assets less monetary liabilities). Managing transaction exposure to currency risk is an important short-term goal of the multinational financial manager.

Operating exposure refers to the currency risk exposure of non-monetary assets and liabilities.

Operating Exposure to Currency Risk. Of more fundamental importance to the stakeholders of the firm (including shareholders, bondholders, employees, and management) is the exposure of real (nonmonetary) assets to foreign exchange risk. The currency risk exposure of nonmonetary cash flows is called **operating exposure**.

Financial managers can reduce the operating exposure of real assets to currency risk through financial market hedges as well as through the location and management of the firm's operations. For example, the manager of the MNC can minimize the MNC's operating exposure by shifting its cross-border sourcing and production decisions to balance cash inflows and outflows in each currency. Managing operating exposure to foreign exchange risk is an important long-term goal of the multinational financial manager.

---

1 This is strictly true only if monetary cash flows are certain. If monetary cash flows are uncertain and payment depends in some way on exchange rates, then domestic monetary contracts are indirectly exposed to currency risk. For instance, a monetary contract might not be paid if an unexpected change in currency values forces a customer out of business.

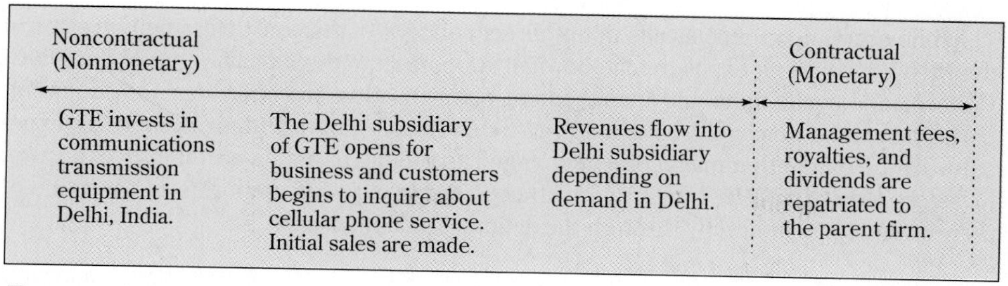

Noncontractual (Nonmonetary)			Contractual (Monetary)
GTE invests in communications transmission equipment in Delhi, India.	The Delhi subsidiary of GTE opens for business and customers begins to inquire about cellular phone service. Initial sales are made.	Revenues flow into Delhi subsidiary depending on demand in Delhi.	Management fees, royalties, and dividends are repatriated to the parent firm.

FIGURE 5.2

An Example of Exposure to Currency Risk: GTE's Investment in Delhi, India

The Spectrum of Monetary/Nonmonetary Cash Flows. Figure 5.2 presents an example of the typical evolution of expected future cash flows from nonmonetary to monetary. Suppose GTE has invested in a cellular phone system for Delhi, India, through a 50 percent–owned subsidiary. The cellular phone system consists of a network of microwave relay stations and switching equipment in the greater Delhi area. At the time of investment, future proceeds from the investment can be estimated but are not known for certain. GTE's real assets—the microwave relay stations and switching equipment—have an operating exposure to currency risk because the dollar value of the proceeds from this investment depends on the exchange rate between rupees and dollars.

As GTE's advertising campaign begins to attract customers, some of these uncertain future proceeds become sales contracts with Delhi residents. Cash flows from these contracts have transaction exposure because the dollar value of these contracts to the parent firm (GTE) depends on the rate of exchange between rupees and dollars.

If GTE has an equity stake in the subsidiary, then GTE has economic exposure to currency risk even after the Delhi subsidiary contractually promises to repatriate dollars to GTE. If the dollar appreciates in value, GTE's promised cash flows will be unaffected because they are denominated in dollars. But GTE's Delhi subsidiary must pay more in rupees to fulfill its dollar obligations. This hurts the value of the Delhi subsidiary and, hence, any equity stake that GTE has in its subsidiary. Once management fees, royalties, and dividends are repatriated in cash dollars to GTE, GTE has no more exposure to currency risk on these payments. Its economic exposure to currency risk remains, however, through its stake in the Delhi subsidiary.

Accounting (Translation) Exposure to Currency Risk

The last and least important exposure to currency risk is **accounting (translation) exposure**. Accounting exposure arises as the parent firm translates the financial accounting statements of its foreign subsidiaries back into its functional currency using the generally accepted accounting principles of the parent country. The parent firm has accounting exposure to the extent that unexpected changes in foreign exchange rates change the parent's financial accounting statements. Since currency exposure may or may not reflect changes in the value of financial cash flows, accounting exposure may or may not reflect changes in the value of the firm's assets.

Accounting exposure may or may not be related to the economic exposure of cash flows and firm value.

While accounting exposure is not of direct concern to the well-diversified investor in the MNC, accounting exposure can be vitally important to the management of the MNC. Performance evaluations and management compensation are often tied to accounting performance, so managers have a strong incentive to minimize their accounting exposure. To the extent that management changes its actions based on accounting exposure, investors also should be concerned with accounting exposure as it affects the value of their investments indirectly through the actions of the managers.

Corporate Views on Currency Risk Exposure

Financial managers are especially concerned with transaction exposure to currency risk

Which form of currency risk exposure is most important? Finance theory has a simple answer. If the objective of the firm is to maximize the value of equity (or perhaps both debt and equity) stakeholders, then hedging of currency risk exposures is only desirable if it affects expected future cash flows or the cost of capital or both.

A survey by Jesswein, Kwok, and Folks polled corporate treasurers and chief financial officers concerning their views on the relative importance of these types of exposures to currency risk.[2] These individuals were asked whether they (1) strongly agreed, (2) agreed, (3) were neutral, (4) disagreed, or (5) strongly disagreed with each of the following statements:

	Mean score of level of agreement
• Managing transaction exposure is important	1.4
• Managing economic exposure is important	1.8
• Managing translation exposure is important	2.4

Mean responses are reported to the right of each question. As is proper, translation (accounting) exposure came in a distant third in importance to transaction and economic exposure.

In the chapters on currency derivatives (futures, options, and swaps) that follow, the principle focus will be on transaction exposure. In the survey by Jesswein, Kwok, and Folks, corporate respondents felt that this was the most important currency risk exposure. The reason why transaction exposure is ranked as more important than the broader category of economic exposure may be that it is easier to measure and manage transaction exposure than it is to measure and manage economic exposure. A more complete discussion of the broader class of economic exposure will have to wait until Parts 4 and 5 of the text.

---

2 Kurt Jesswein, Chuck C.Y. Kwok, and William R. Folks, Jr., "Adoption of Innovative Products in Currency Risk Management: Effects of Management Orientations and Product Characteristics," *Journal of Applied Corporate Finance,* Fall 1995.

An Example of an Exporter's Exposure to Currency Risk

Suppose the Dutch firm Tao Chemical N.V. manufactures GroMane Hair Growth Formula (a generic form of Rogaine) in the Netherlands for sale in the United States at a price of $10 per bottle. The $10 price of GroMane is equivalent to FL20 at the current exchange rate of $S_0^{\$/FL}$ = $.50/FL. Inflation is the same in the United States and the Netherlands, so expected future spot exchange rates are also $E[S_1^{\$/FL}]$ = $.50/FL. Labor expense is Tao's only cost of goods sold (COGS) and is FL10 per bottle. Tao's labor force is local, so labor expense is set in guilders. The production costs of Tao's competitors are similarly fixed in their own local currencies. Corporate income taxes in the Netherlands are 50 percent.

Tao's income statement is shown in U.S. dollars and in Dutch guilders in the "base case" along the left two columns of Table 5.1. Tao expects to sell 2 million bottles per year in perpetuity for an annual after-tax cash flow of $E[CF^{FL}]$ = FL10 million, or $E[CF^\$]$ = $5 million at the current exchange rate. The hurdle rate on investments of this type is $i^\$ = i^{FL}$ = 10 percent in both countries. With perpetual cash flows, the value of Tao Chemical is V^{FL} = (FL10 million) / (0.1) = FL100 million.[3] This is equivalent to $V^\$$ = ($5 million)/(0.1) = $50 million at the $.50/FL exchange rate.

Suppose the guilder unexpectedly depreciates by 20 percent, from $.50/FL to $.40/FL. The guilder is expected to remain at this new level indefinitely. What is the value of Tao after this 20 percent depreciation of the guilder?

Tao's situation with respect to the exchange rate is that of the classic exporter. Tao's cost of goods sold is fixed in Dutch guilders and is unlikely to change as the guilder appreciates or depreciates. In contrast, the price that Tao receives for GroMane is determined in dollars by U.S. consumers. In this situation, a depreciation of the guilder enhances Tao's competitive position relative to its U.S. competition. Pricing strategies that Tao can pursue in response to a depreciation of the guilder include

- Hold the dollar price constant at $10 per bottle (or FL25 per bottle) and try to sell the same quantity in the U.S. market
- Hold the guilder price constant at FL20 per bottle (or $8 per bottle) and try to sell more goods in the U.S. market

If Tao holds its dollar price constant at $10 per bottle, it receives FL25 per bottle at the $.40/FL spot rate as shown in Table 5.1. Because the dollar price is unchanged, Tao's annual sales of 2 million bottles should remain unchanged. The FL25 per bottle price increases Tao's contribution margin to FL15 per bottle, or FL7.50 per bottle after

---

3 The assumption of perpetual cash flows simplifies our algebra. The value V of a perpetual cash flow CF discounted at a constant rate i is simply V = CF/i.

TABLE 5.1 TAO CHEMICAL'S ECONOMIC EXPOSURE: A NAIVE APPROACH

	Base case $0.50/FL		Twenty percent depreciation of the guilder to $0.40/FL					
			Maintain dollar price		Elastic Demand		Inelastic Demand	
			Keep the dollar price and sell the same quantity		Keep the guilder price and sell 50 percent more		Keep the guilder price and sell 10 percent more	
	Cash flows in dollars	Cash flows in guilders	Cash flows in dollars	Cash flows in guilders	Cash flows in dollars	Cash flows in guilders	Cash flows in dollars	Cash flows in guilders
Price per bottle	$10.00	FL20.00	$10.00	FL25.00	$8.00	FL20.00	$8.00	FL20.00
Bottles sold	2,000,000	2,000,000	2,000,000	2,000,000	3,000,000	3,000,000	2,200,000	2,200,000
Revenues	$20,000,000	FL40,000,000	$20,000,000	FL50,000,000	$24,000,000	FL60,000,000	$17,600,000	FL44,000,000
−COGS	−10,000,000	−20,000,000	−8,000,000	−20,000,000	−12,000,000	−30,000,000	−8,800,000	−22,000,000
Before-tax profit	10,000,000	20,000,000	12,000,000	30,000,000	12,000,000	30,000,000	8,800,000	22,000,000
−Tax (at 50%)-	−5,000,000	−10,000,000	−6,000,000	−15,000,000	−6,000,000	−15,000,000	−4,400,000	−11,000,000
Net cash flow	5,000,000	10,000,000	6,000,000	15,000,000	6,000,000	15,000,000	4,400,000	11,000,000
Value of Tao at $i^\$ = i^{FL}$ 10%	$50 million	FL100 million	$60 million	FL150 million	$60 million	FL150 million	$44 million	FL110 million

corporate income taxes. After-tax cash flow is (FL7.50/bottle)(2 million bottles) = FL15 million per year, which is worth FL150 million at the 10 percent discount rate. The guilder value of Tao should increase if it does nothing more than maintain its dollar price for GroMane.

The dollar value of Tao may or may not increase depending on which effect dominates; the increase in contribution margin at the higher guilder sales price or the decrease in the value of the guilder. In this example, the increase in contribution margin dominates and Tao's dollar value increases to $60 million at the $.40/FL exchange rate.

What will happen to Tao's value if it follows the second pricing strategy and holds the guilder price constant? Tao's contribution margin remains the same at FL10 per bottle, but the lower dollar price of $8 per bottle should generate more sales volume. All else equal, the guilder value of Tao should go up. The dollar value may go up or down depending on whether the increase in sales volume is enough to overcome the 20 percent depreciation of the guilder. Whether the dollar value goes up or down depends on the price elasticity of demand for Tao's products.

The Price Elasticity of Demand

The **price elasticity of demand** is defined as the percentage change in quantity sold for a given percentage change in price.

$$\text{Price elasticity of demand} = -(\Delta Q/Q)/(\Delta P/P)$$

If percentage changes in quantity sold are equal to percentage changes in price, then the product has *unit elasticity*. This is a useful starting point, because goods with unit elasticity will see no change in total revenue (= P*Q) with a change in price. What is lost (or gained) in price is exactly offset by a gain (or loss) in quantity sold.

Strictly speaking, unit elasticity holds only for continuously compounded, or infinitesimally small, changes in price and quantity. Larger changes are multiplicative rather than additive. For example, if price decreases by 20 percent, then quantity sold must increase by 25 percent to leave revenue unchanged. Algebraically, this is given by $\text{Rev}_1^{\$} = P_1^{\$} Q_1 = (.80)P_0^{\$} (1.25)Q_0 = P_0^{\$} Q_0 = \text{Rev}_0^{\$}$. For this reason, price elasticity measures the sensitivity of sales volume to (infinitesimally) small changes in price.

Whether the price elasticity of demand is greater or less than one determines whether revenues will decrease or increase in response to a small change in price.

- If the price elasticity of demand is greater than one, then the good is *price elastic*.
- If the price elasticity of demand is less than one, then the good is *price inelastic*.

The beneficial effects of GroMane (or Rogaine) on hair retention are quickly lost and difficult to recover once treatment is suspended. In the short run, GroMane customers will do almost anything to replenish their supply. Whether GroMane is price elastic or price inelastic will depend on whether Tao has other competitors in the United States market. If Tao owns a patent on GroMane and can control supply, demand is likely to be price inelastic. If there are other sources of GroMane in a competitive U.S. market, then demand may be price elastic. The effect of different elasticities on Tao's competitive position is examined below.

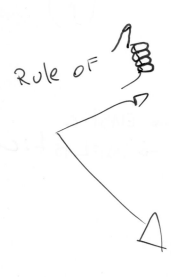

MKTG Lesson→
Price Decrease
needs to Be offset
By a much larger
% sales increase!

Rule of 👍

Back to the Tao Example

The possible consequences of Tao's export pricing choices are shown in the right half of Table 5.1 for elastic demand and for inelastic demand.

Price Elastic Demand. Suppose Tao keeps the guilder price of GroMane unchanged at FL20 per bottle. This reduces the dollar price of GroMane to $8 per bottle at the $.40/FL spot exchange rate. This reduction in the dollar price of GroMane should increase Tao's sales in the United States. The amount of the sales increase depends on the price elasticity of demand.

Suppose the 20 percent decrease in the dollar price of GroMane increases sales volume by 50 percent to 3 million bottles. This increases revenues to (3 million bottles)(FL20/bottle) = FL60 million, but also increases COGS to (3 million bottles)(FL10/bottle) = FL30 million. The net result is a FL15 million annual after-tax cash flow and a FL150 million value for Tao. Tao is again worth $60 million at the $.40/FL spot exchange rate. The dollar value of Tao increases because the additional cash flow on a 50 percent increase in sales volume more than offsets the 20 percent depreciation of the guilder.

Price Inelastic Demand. The columns at the right of Table 5.1 show what can happen when demand is price inelastic. If Tao holds its guilder price fixed at FL20 per bottle (or $8 per bottle) in this example, the increase in sales volume is not sufficient to offset the decrease in contribution margin. Sales volume increases by only 10 percent on a 20 percent fall in price. If price is set at FL20 per bottle rather than the FL25 price from the "maintain dollar price" strategy, revenues fall by 12 percent according to $Rev_1^\$ = P_1^\$ Q_1 = (0.80) P_0^\$ (1.10) Q_0 = (0.88) Rev_0^\$$. Faced with inelastic demand, Tao is better off holding its dollar price fixed at $10 per bottle (or FL25 per bottle).

The Economic Exposure of Importers and Exporters

In summary, the following rules hold for an exporter such as Tao Chemical.[4]

- Exporters tend to gain from a real depreciation of the domestic currency
- Exporters tend to lose from a real appreciation of the domestic currency

Conversely, exporters gain (lose) from a real appreciation (depreciation) of the foreign currency. How much the exporter wins or loses in value depends on the exporter's pricing policies and on the good's price elasticity of demand.

Importers are exposed in the opposite direction. The classic importer buys its goods in foreign markets at prices that are determined in the foreign markets and sells these goods to domestic customers at prices that are determined in the domestic market. This suggests the following rules:

- Importers tend to gain from a real appreciation of the domestic currency
- Importers tend to lose from a real depreciation of the domestic currency

---

4 Exchange rate exposure is discussed in greater detail in Chapter 22.

Conversely, importers gain (lose) from a real depreciation (appreciation) of the foreign currency. Again, the size of the gain or loss depends on the importer's pricing policies and the good's price elasticity of demand.

Note that the above rules are stated in terms of *real*, rather than nominal, changes in currency values. Real changes in currency values refer to changes in nominal currency values that have been inflation-adjusted to remove the effects of foreign and domestic inflation. Real changes in currency values are more important than nominal changes in currency values that arise merely from the inflation difference between two currencies. Real exchange rates are discussed in the next section.

Real rates are more important than Nominal.

5.3 DEVIATIONS FROM PURCHASING POWER PARITY AND THE REAL EXCHANGE RATE

Suppose you invest $100,000 in a one-year certificate of deposit earning 10 percent per year. At the end of the year, you'll have $110,000 in the bank. This sounds great. But what if inflation was also 10 percent during the year. According to the Fisher equation, your real rate of return during the period was

$$r^\$ = (1+i^\$)/(1+p^\$) - 1 = (1.10/1.10) - 1 = 0\%$$

This is not so great. In real or purchasing power terms, you are no better off than at the start of the year. And you are a year older, if not wiser.

A similar phenomenon occurs with changes in foreign exchange rates. If you look only at changes in nominal exchange rates, you miss real changes in purchasing power across currencies. In order to identify real, as opposed to nominal, changes in spot rates of exchange, the effects of inflation need to be backed out.

Real Changes in Purchasing Power

Suppose today's spot rate of exchange between yen and dollars is $S_0^{¥/\$} = ¥100/\$$. Rule #2 from Chapter 3 states that you should think in terms of buying and selling the currency in the denominator, so let's use dollars as our currency of denomination. Expected inflation in Japan is $E[p^¥] = 0$ percent and in the United States is $E[p^\$] = 10$ percent. Relative purchasing power parity (see equation (4.5)) allows us to predict the spot rate that should prevail in one period:

$$E[S_1^{¥/\$}] = S_0^{¥/\$} [(1+E[p^¥])/(1+E[p^\$])] = (¥100/\$)(1.00/1.10) = ¥90.91/\$$$

Suppose that one year later the inflation estimates turn out to be accurate but that the dollar appreciates to $S_1^{¥/\$} = ¥110/\$$. In nominal terms, this is a 10 percent appreciation of the dollar. But relative to the expected spot rate, this represents a 21 percent real (inflation-adjusted) appreciation of the dollar.

$$\frac{\text{Actual} - \text{Expected}}{\text{Expected}} = (¥110/\$ - ¥90.91/\$)/(¥90.91/\$) = 21 \text{ percent}$$

This 21 percent real surprise in the level of the nominal exchange rate is shown in the top panel of Figure 5.3. In this example, the dollar has experienced a 21 percent appreciation in purchasing power relative to the yen. The real exchange rate captures changes in the purchasing power of a currency relative to other currencies by backing out the effects of inflation from changes in nominal exchange rates.

FIGURE 5.3
Deviations from Expected
Future Spot Rates: Changes
in the Real Rate of Exchange

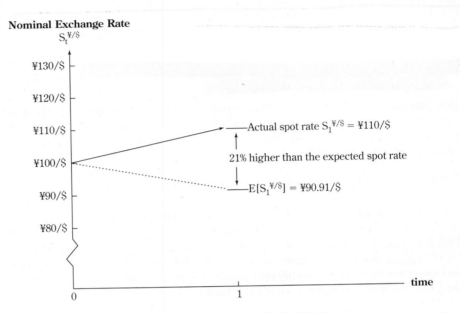

Nominal Exchange Rate
$S_t^{¥/\$}$

¥130/$

¥120/$

¥110/$ — Actual spot rate $S_1^{¥/\$} = ¥110/\$$

21% higher than the expected spot rate

¥100/$

— $E[S_1^{¥/\$}] = ¥90.91/\$$

¥90/$

¥80/$

0   1   time

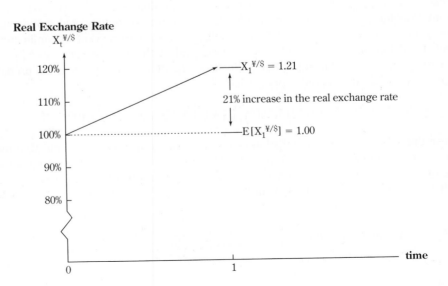

Real Exchange Rate
$X_t^{¥/\$}$

120% — $X_1^{¥/\$} = 1.21$

21% increase in the real exchange rate

110%

100% — $E[X_1^{¥/\$}] = 1.00$

90%

80%

0   1   time

The Real Exchange Rate

In deriving the international parity conditions, we used the law of one price as our guiding principle. This faith is well founded because powerful market forces work to eliminate deviations from purchasing power parity, especially for assets such as gold, oil, and foreign exchange that are actively traded in global markets. As an example, covered interest arbitrage forces foreign exchange rates to reflect interest rate differentials according to interest rate parity (IRP) in the active and relatively frictionless international money markets. But for less actively traded assets, especially those with many barriers to trade such as land and labor, deviations from PPP can and do exist and sometimes persist for several years.

The **real exchange rate** $X_t^{d/f}$ is the nominal exchange rate $S_t^{d/f}$ adjusted for relative changes in the domestic and foreign price levels (that is, adjusted for differential inflation) since an arbitrarily defined base period at time t=0.

$$X_t^{d/f} = \left(\frac{S_t^{d/f}}{S_0^{d/f}} \right) \left[\prod_{\tau=1}^{t} \frac{(1+p_\tau^f)}{(1+p_\tau^d)} \right] \tag{5.1}$$

The real exchange rate provides a measure of change in the relative purchasing power of the two currencies. Dividing the nominal spot rate $S_t^{d/f}$ at time t by the base period spot rate $S_0^{d/f}$ states the real exchange rate as a percentage of the beginning spot rate. The inflation adjustment in the rightmost term of equation (5.1) indicates whether this change in the nominal exchange rate fully reflects the inflation differential between the two currencies during the t periods. If change in the nominal spot rate of exchange exactly offsets the inflation differential, then the real spot rate of exchange will remain at 100 percent of its base period level.

Real changes in currency values reflect changes in the relative purchasing power of two currencies.

A formula for calculating the percentage change in the real exchange rate can be derived from equation (5.1) as follows:

$$x_t^{d/f} = (X_t^{d/f}/X_{t-1}^{d/f}) - 1 = \frac{\left(\frac{S_t^{d/f}}{S_0^{d/f}} \right) \left[\prod_{\tau=1}^{t} \frac{(1+p_\tau^f)}{(1+p_\tau^d)} \right]}{\left(\frac{S_{t-1}^{d/f}}{S_0^{d/f}} \right) \left[\prod_{\tau=1}^{t-1} \frac{(1+p_\tau^f)}{(1+p_\tau^d)} \right]} - 1$$

$$= \left(\frac{S_t^{d/f}}{S_{t-1}^{d/f}} \right) \left[\frac{(1+p_t^f)}{(1+p_t^d)} \right] \left[\frac{\prod_{\tau=1}^{t-1} \frac{(1+p_\tau^f)}{(1+p_\tau^d)}}{\prod_{\tau=1}^{t-1} \frac{(1+p_\tau^f)}{(1+p_\tau^d)}} \right] - 1$$

$$= \left(\frac{S_t^{d/f}}{S_{t-1}^{d/f}} \right) \left[\frac{(1+p_t^f)}{(1+p_t^d)} \right] - 1 \tag{5.2}$$

[handwritten: Formula for calculating real exchange rate]

Spot exchange rates and inflation rates prior to the beginning of period t cancel in equation (5.2), so that percentage changes in real exchange rates depend only on change in the nominal spot rate of exchange and on the relative inflation rates during period t.

It is somewhat misleading to retain the currency units on the symbol for the real exchange rate. The ratio $(S_t^{d/f})/(S_0^{d/f})$ in equation (5.1) captures the level of the time t nominal exchange rate relative to the base period (time zero) nominal exchange rate. The currency units cancel from the numerator and the denominator of this term. The rightmost term measures the relative inflation rates in the two currencies and is also unitless. The resulting measure is a number such as 1.21, representing a 21 percent increase in the real value of the currency in the denominator relative to the base rate at time zero. The currency units are retained in the symbols $X_t^{d/f}$ and $x_t^{d/f}$ to remind us that the real rate is measuring the relative purchasing power of the foreign currency (in the denominator) in terms of the domestic currency (in the numerator).

Let's return to our previous example. The ratio $(S_1^{\yen/\$})/(S_0^{\yen/\$}) = (\yen110/\$)/(\yen100/\$) = 1.10$ indicates that the value of the dollar (in the denominator) increased by 10 percent in nominal terms. This was despite the 10 percent higher realized inflation in dollars: $(1+p^{\$})/(1+p^{\yen}) = 1.10$. Let the beginning-of-period spot rate $S_0^{\yen/\$} = \yen100/\$$ be the base period exchange rate. By definition, the beginning level of the real exchange rate is $X_0^{\yen/\$} = 1.00$. Equations (5.1) and (5.2) yield

$$X_1^{\yen/\$} = [(\yen110/\$)/(\yen100/\$)][(1.10)/(1.00)] = 1.21, \text{ or } 121\% \text{ of the base level}$$

and

$$x_1^{\yen/\$} = [(\yen110/\$)/(\yen100/\$)][(1.10)/(1.00)] - 1 = 0.21,$$

or a real exchange rate that is 21 percent higher than in the base period. The percentage appreciation in the purchasing power of the dollar is 21 percent in this example.

It is most convenient to pick a base period in which the relative purchasing power of the two currencies is close to equilibrium. In this case, PPP holds (approximately) and $S_t^{d/f} \approx P_t^d/P_t^f$. Any base period may be chosen, so the level of the real exchange rate is not as important as change in the real exchange rate. The level of the real exchange rate indicates the purchasing power relative to an arbitrarily defined base period. It is inappropriate to claim, for instance, that a currency is overvalued simply because the level of the real exchange rate is greater than one. It may be that the currency was even more overvalued in the base period and is only slightly less overvalued now. Further, purchasing power parity may hold for some goods and not for others. Change in the real exchange rate merely indicates a real change in the purchasing power of one currency relative to another.

An Exception to Every Rule

Notice that our usual rule for keeping track of the currencies ("numerator to numerator and denominator to denominator") is reversed in equations (5.1) and (5.2). This is because we want to reverse or "back out" the effects of inflation on nominal exchange rates. The formula for real exchange rates is the only exception to the "numerator to numerator and denominator to denominator" rule.

The Real Value of the U.S. Dollar

*Real exchange rates show large
and persistent deviations from
purchasing power parity.*

Figure 5.4 presents the real value of the U.S. dollar against the British pound, the German mark, and the Japanese yen over the period 1970 to 1995. The mean level is set to 100 for each series. Since the dollar is of interest in this figure, the dollar is placed in the denominator of the real exchange rates. If purchasing power parity held at all times, the real value of the dollar would remain at 100 percent of its base value. Figure 5.4 shows that there is quite a bit of variability in the real purchasing power of the dollar relative to other currencies.

The behavior of the dollar during the 1980s is interesting because of the large and persistent deviations from purchasing power parity. The dollar rose in purchasing power terms against all three currencies in the early 1980s, reaching its peak in March 1985. The dollar shares this real exchange rate pattern with most other currencies over the early 1980s. In September 1985 the Group of Ten (in the Plaza Accord) agreed to cooperate in an attempt to bring down the real value of the dollar. It is difficult to tell whether this coalition was successful. The subsequent fall in the value of the dollar may have been caused by more fundamental economic, monetary, and political factors. In fact, the dollar had already begun to fall in purchasing power terms by the spring of 1985. In any case, by the winter of 1987 the dollar had fallen in real terms back to its 1980 value.

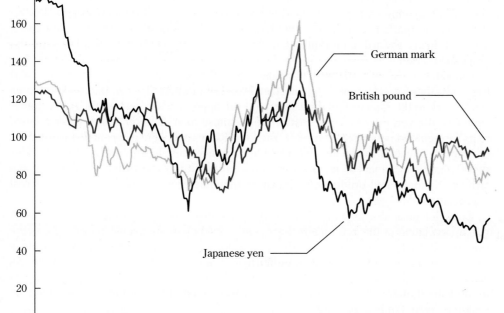

FIGURE 5.4
Real Value of the Dollar,
1970–1995

Mean level = 100 for each series

5.4 THE EFFECT OF CHANGES IN REAL EXCHANGE RATES

If relative purchasing power parity $E[S_1^{d/f}]/S_0^{d/f} = (1+E[p^d])/(1+E[p^f])$ holds, then changes in nominal exchange rates should reflect the difference between foreign and domestic inflation. This implies that nominal foreign exchange rate changes should have little economic significance of their own. In contrast to nominal exchange rate changes, real changes in exchange rates can have a profound impact on a country's international trade. In particular,

- A **real appreciation** of the domestic currency raises the price of domestic goods relative to foreign goods.
- A **real depreciation** of the domestic currency lowers the price of domestic goods relative to foreign goods.

A real appreciation in the value of a currency increases the purchasing power of that currency.

A real appreciation of the domestic currency is both good news and bad news for the domestic economy. A real appreciation of the domestic currency helps domestic customers and the domestic economy because imported goods and raw materials cost less. This helps to hold down inflation. On the other hand, a real appreciation of the domestic currency hurts domestic exporters because their finished products cost more in foreign markets.

When the domestic currency has a high real value, goods and services produced by domestic companies are expensive relative to foreign goods and services in both domestic and foreign markets. The effect on domestic producers is asymmetric—goods and services competing on the world market are hurt more than those competing solely on the domestic market. This shifts resources within the domestic economy from export-oriented firms toward import-oriented firms and firms competing primarily in the domestic market.

Consider the labor expense of a Japanese firm that manufactures goods in Japan and then sells these goods in both Japanese and foreign markets. Two countervailing forces are at work in the Japanese market when the yen appreciates in real terms. A real appreciation of the yen increases the cost of the Japanese manufacturer's local labor relative to its foreign competitors. Conversely, the local labor costs of non-Japanese manufacturers remain constant in the local currency and, hence, cost less in terms of yen. Under these conditions, Japanese factories will find it difficult to export their relatively expensive yen-denominated products, so Japanese manufacturers are typically hurt by a real appreciation of the yen.

Consider instead a Japanese bank looking for investment opportunities overseas. A real appreciation of the yen means that foreign assets look inexpensive to the Japanese investor. If the Japanese bank is in the market for a real estate purchase in California, a real appreciation of the yen makes Californian real estate relatively less expensive. As capital flows out of costly Japanese assets and into relatively cheap (in real terms) assets in the United States, the value of the yen will tend to fall. Equilibrium will eventually be restored, even if only in passing.

Real depreciations in the domestic currency are the flip side of real appreciations. A real depreciation in the domestic currency results in more competitively priced goods in both foreign and domestic markets. This promotes domestic employment. On the downside, a real depreciation in the domestic currency results in higher prices for imported

The law of one price states that equivalent assets sell for the same price. But this law applies only to equivalent assets traded in frictionless markets. It will not hold for assets that vary in quality or that have high transactions costs when they are bought and sold.

The cost of living is an example of a price that varies around the world. Even if you could transport your lifestyle to another location, the cost of maintaining that lifestyle would vary, depending on the cost and availability of local goods and services. Here is the cost of living index for several cities as of June 1, 1995, using New York as the base.

Location	Cost of living index	Inflation	$S^{f/\$}$ as of JUNE 1995
Tokyo, Japan	162.36	0.4%	83.117
Geneva, Switzerland	122.95	1.6%	1.143
Buenos Aires, Argentina	114.37	4.6%	76.602
Frankfurt, Germany	108.82	2.3%	1.383
Hong Kong	107.54	9.6%	7.735
Seoul, Korea	102.82	5.1%	760.524
Beijing, China	102.18	20.7%	8.306
Paris, France	101.82	1.6%	4.874
Singapore	101.11	2.3%	1.390
New York, United States	100	3.1%	1.000
Jeddah, Saudi Arabia	95.68	0.5%	3.750
London, United Kingdom	92.91	3.3%	0.622

Jakarta, Indonesia	89.03	10.0%	2228.920
Warsaw, Poland	85.71	33.1%	2.319
Los Angeles, United States	83.42	3.1%	1.000
Bangkok, Thailand	81.30	5.4%	24.614
Sydney, Australia	80.57	3.9%	1.390
Montreal, Canada	80.01	2.5%	1.371
Kuala Lumpur, Malaysia	79.77	3.3%	2.460
New Delhi, India	78.04	9.7%	31.391
Mexico City, Mexico	77.22	20.4%	6.145
Johannesburg, South Africa	69.65	10.2%	3.668
Caracas, Venezuela	69.27	71.7%	169.779
Prague, Czech Republic	65.93	10.2%	25.943

To obtain an estimate of the current cost relative to New York, adjust the cost of living index as if it were a real exchange rate as follows:

$$\text{Current cost of living} \approx (1995 \text{ cost}) (S_t^{f/\$}/S_0^{f/\$}) [(1+p^\$)/(1+p^f)]^t$$

Use the actual change in the spot rate and realized inflation since June 1995 in this adjustment.

Adapted from "Working Out Where to Live," Richard Donkin, *London Financial Times,* October 20, 1995, page 27.

goods, which increases inflation and erodes living standards. Which of these countervailing forces eventually triumphs determines whether a real depreciation is in aggregate good or bad for the domestic economy.

5.5 THE EMPIRICAL BEHAVIOR OF EXCHANGE RATES

Changes in Nominal Exchange Rates

Now that we have categorized the nature of exposure to foreign exchange risk, it is time to investigate the empirical behavior of foreign exchange rates. A convenient starting point is the process called a **random walk**. In a random walk, instantaneous changes (that is, changes at a particular point in time) have a zero mean and are normally distributed. There is an equal probability of an appreciation or a depreciation in currency value. There is no memory in a random walk, so once a new currency value is established there is again an equal probability of further appreciation or depreciation in the currency.

For daily measurement intervals, both nominal and real exchange rate changes are indeed random with an equal probability of rising or falling. Because of this behavior, the best guess of a future exchange rate is usually today's exchange rate: $E[S_t^{d/f}] = S_{t-1}^{d/f}$ over short forecasting horizons. The current spot rate usually outperforms other nominal exchange rate forecasts for forecasting horizons of up to one year.

As the forecast horizon is lengthened, the correlation between interest and inflation differentials and nominal spot rate changes begins to rise as the international parity conditions begin to exert themselves. Eventually, the forward exchange rate begins to dominate the current spot rate as a predictor of future nominal exchange rates.

Changes in Real Exchange Rates

According to the international parity conditions, real exchange rates should remain constant. Abuaf and Jorion examined changes in the levels of real exchange rates in ten industrialized countries and came to the following conclusions:[5]

- When real exchange rates are sampled either monthly or annually, real exchange rates are autoregressive (that is, they depend on previous levels).
- Disequilibriums in real exchange rates can be substantial in the short run and appear to take about three years to be reduced by half.

Disequilibriums in real exchange rates can last for several years.

The autoregressive nature of real exchange rates is such that they tend to revert to their long-run average. In the short run, there can be substantial deviations from the long-run average.

Persistent deviations from purchasing power parity in real exchange rates can arise from several sources. At the beginning of this chapter, it was pointed out that the economic importance of trade barriers differs across asset classes. Actively traded financial assets have relatively low information and transactions costs and are much more likely to conform to PPP than inactively traded real goods are. PPP holds in its incarnation as interest rate parity so that for actively traded currencies the forward premium or discount is entirely determined by the relative levels of Eurocurrency interest rates.

PPP typically does not hold for commodities such as food and clothing and, hence, does not hold for general price levels. Deviations from PPP represent disequilibriums. After a sufficient length of time has passed, market forces bring market prices and currency values back into equilibrium. In this "disequilibrium" view, frictions in the marketplace cause goods prices to adjust more slowly than financial prices.[6] Deviations from PPP are thus seen as a consequence of differential frictions in the markets for real

---

5 Niso Abuaf and Philippe Jorion, "Purchasing Power Parity in the Long Run," *Journal of Finance* 47, March 1990, pages 157–174.

6 This disequilibrium argument is made in Rudiger Dornbusch's "Expectations and Exchange Rate Dynamics," *Journal of Political Economy,* December 1976, pages 1161–1176.

and financial assets. At issue is why it takes the foreign exchange market several years to regain equilibrium.[7] Persistent deviations from purchasing power parity in real exchange rates are the norm rather than the exception.

Time-Varying Exchange Rate Volatility

Recent empirical investigations into the behavior of exchange rates reject the simplest form of the random walk model. In its place, researchers have modeled exchange rates as a process in which

GARCH

- Exchange rate changes are normally distributed at each point in time
- At each point in time, the variance of exchange rates depends on whether the most recent exchange rate changes have been large or small

A time series exhibiting this behavior is frequently modeled as a **Generalized Autoregressive Conditional Heteroskedasticity (GARCH)** process.[8] The term "generalized autoregressive conditional heteroskedasticity" is simply a statistician's way of saying, "Today's variance depends on the recent history of exchange rate changes." The literal translation is "variance (heteroskedasticity) depends on (is conditional on) previous (autoregressive) variances."

Foreign currency volatility depends on the recent history of exchange rate changes.

The variance of a GARCH(p,q) process at time t is described by the following:[9]

$$\sigma_t^2 = a_0 + \sum_{i=1}^{p} a_i\, \sigma_{t-i}^2 + \sum_{j=1}^{q} b_j\, r_{t-j}^2 \qquad (5.3)$$

where a_0, a_i, and b_j are constants for all i and j,

σ_{t-i}^2 = the exchange rate variance from period t-i for i = 1,...,p,

r_{t-j}^2 = the square of the percentage change in the spot exchange rate during period t−j for j = 1,...,q.

At each point in time, this GARCH process is normally distributed with variance σ_t^2. The variance of this process depends on the recent history of variances σ_{t-i}^2 and squared spot rate changes r_{t-j}^2. The variables p and q identify the maximum number of lags that influence the variance through previous variances and squared spot rate changes. The summation with the j = 1,...,q squared spot rate changes forces the

---

7 There have been several attempts to provide an equilibrium explanation for deviations from PPP. See, for example, Alan C. Stockman, "The Equilibrium Approach to Exchange Rates," *Economic Review,* Federal Reserve Bank of Richmond, March/April 1987, pages 12–30.

8 This phrase is reminiscent of the phrase "supercalifragilistic expiallidocious" from the movie *Mary Poppins.* If you say it fast enough you'll sound either precocious or atrocious, depending on your elocution. Try it and impress your friends. (But practice first!)

9 See Timothy Bollerslev, "Generalized Autoregressive Conditional Heteroskedasticity," *Journal of Econometrics* 31, pages 307–327. Be forewarned, this journal is bedtime reading only for world-class statisticians.

variance at time t to respond to recent changes in the spot rate. The summation with the lagged variances i=1,...,p smooths the process so that it is not overly sensitive to the most recent squared spot rate changes.

The GARCH process includes the random walk model as a special case in which the mean spot rate change is zero and the parameters a_i and b_j are equal to zero at all lags. In this case, the variance σ_t^2 is a constant equal to a_0. Recent empirical studies of nominal exchange rates have rejected the random walk model in favor of a GARCH specification for yearly, monthly, weekly, daily, and intraday sampling intervals. The particular form of GARCH process is not as important as the recognition that exchange rate volatility is autoregressive.

5.6 EXCHANGE RATE FORECASTING

Management of the multinational corporation can react in one of three ways to exchange rate uncertainty. First, they can ignore currency risk in the belief that it is a diversifiable risk and hence is irrelevant to well-diversified shareholders.[10] This response is usually deemed to be unacceptable by management because

1. Managers are not as diversified as investors
2. Managers are exposed to the MNC's total risk rather than just systematic risk

Managers' livelihoods are linked to that of the firm, so their welfare is fully exposed to the corporation's total (rather than systematic) currency risk.

A second alternative is to try to hedge currency risk through the financial markets, perhaps in conjunction with active management of the firm's real assets.[11] This alternative is preferred by management because it reduces a major source of uncertainty that is beyond the control of the firm.

A third alternative is to try to predict the direction of future exchange rates—hedging when exchange rates are expected to turn against the corporation and accepting exposure to currency risk when exchange rates are expected to turn in favor of the corporation. This type of active management of foreign exchange exposure begs the question "Are exchange rates predictable?"

Recall our alternative notions of market efficiency: operational efficiency, allocational efficiency, and informational efficiency. The concept of informational efficiency is particularly important for answering the question "Are exchange rates predictable?" In an **informationally efficient** currency market, currencies are correctly priced. It is not possible to consistently "beat the market" and earn abnormal returns beyond those obtainable by chance on assets of similar risk. The proposition that markets are informationally efficient is called the **efficient market hypothesis**.

---

10 We'll return to this topic in the chapters on international asset pricing and corporate financial risk management.
11 Financial market hedges are examined in Part 3.

There's an old joke that illustrates the efficient market hypothesis. A finance professor and a student are walking down the hall. The professor is expounding on the futility of trying to beat the market when the student spots a $20 bill on the floor. The student exclaims, "Look, there's a $20 bill!" The professor responds "It couldn't be—someone would have picked it up by now."

Although a growing body of evidence suggests that the efficient market hypothesis fits some markets better than others, attempts to forecast short-term changes in exchange rates in the floating-rate era since Bretton Woods have generally failed to beat a naive guess of today's spot exchange rate. Long-run forecasts of nominal exchange rates have difficulty beating the forward exchange rate as predictors of future spot rates of exchange. Given the amount of money, time, and intellectual capital spent by analysts trying to predict exchange rates, the dismal performance of these forecasters suggests that prices in the interbank foreign exchange markets are informationally efficient or, at a minimum, very difficult to predict.

*Changes in currency values
are difficult to predict.*

Market-Based Exchange Rate Forecasts

Two of the international parity conditions provide us with forecasts of future spot rates of exchange based on market prices—either forward exchange rates or an adjustment to current spot rates for the nominal interest rate differential.

- Unbiased forward expectations hypothesis: $E[S_t^{d/f}] = F_t^{d/f}$
- Interest rate parity: $E[S_t^{d/f}] = S_0^{d/f} [(1+i^d)/(1+i^f)]^t$

These two forecasts are equivalent if active currency and Eurocurrency markets allow interest rate parity to be enforced through covered interest arbitrage, so that $F_t^{d/f} = S_0^{d/f} [(1+i^d)/(1+i^f)]^t$. For currencies without active forward markets, a long (short) **synthetic forward position** can be constructed by borrowing in the domestic (foreign) currency, buying the foreign (domestic) currency in the spot market, and then lending in the foreign (domestic) currency. This synthetic forward position takes advantage of the interest rate parity condition in the second bullet. Finally, for less actively traded currencies, a forecast based on inflation differentials has some merit for long horizon forecasts.

A superior forecaster should be able to predict not just change in the nominal exchange rate but change in the real exchange rate as well. The nominal exchange rate is predictable from any of the international parity relations. Real exchange rates, on the other hand, are assumed to be constant across currencies in the international parity relations. Consequently, the international parity conditions are of little help in predicting changes in the real exchange rate. The best that can be said is that real exchange rates will eventually return to their long-run averages.

The beauty of market-based forecasts is that anyone with access to a financial newspaper also has access to these forecasts. Nowadays, real-time forward prices can be retrieved from a variety of sources on the Internet. To add value for their clients, exchange rate forecasters find it necessary to supplement market-based forecasts with one or more of the approaches described below.

*Synthetic
FORWARD
Position*

*Market-based exchange rate
forecasts combine the
international parity conditions
with market prices.*

Persistent Deviations from Forward Parity. According to the international parity conditions, the forward rate should be an unbiased predictor of future spot rates of exchange. This is called the **unbiased expectations hypothesis**, or simply **forward parity**. If there were systematic or persistent deviations from forward parity, then these deviations could be used to improve upon the forward rate as a predictor of future spot rates.

The percentage change in the spot rate during a period is given by $s_t^{d/f} = (S_t^{d/f}/S_{t-1}^{d/f}) - 1$. The forward premium or discount as a percentage of the beginning-of-period spot rate is $FP_t^{d/f} = (F_t^{d/f}/S_{t-1}^{d/f}) - 1$. Forward parity requires that $E[s_t^{d/f}] = FP_t^{d/f}$. A regression test of forward parity can be conducted as follows:

$$s_t^{d/f} = \alpha + \beta \, FP_t^{d/f} + e_t \tag{5.4}$$

Forward parity predicts that the intercept of this regression is zero and that the slope is one; that is, $\alpha = 0$ and $\beta = 1$.

Figure 5.5 plots $s^{\yen/\$}$ against $FP^{\yen/\$}$ for three-month forward exchange rates for the U.S. dollar against the Japanese yen over the period 1986–1995. Forward parity predicts that the differences between actual and predicted spot rates should be evenly distributed around a 45-degree line in Figure 5.5. In fact, estimation of equation (5.4) yields an intercept coefficient of $\alpha = -0.008$ and a slope coefficient of $\beta = -0.002$. The slope is actually in the wrong direction! Froot and Thaler summarize seventy-five empirical studies using a regression like that in equation (5.4) and find a mean slope coefficient of

FIGURE 5.5
One-Month Forward Rates
as Predictors of Future Spot
Rates (1986–1995 yen
per dollar rates)

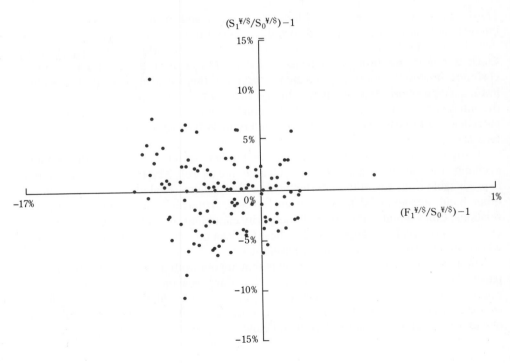

−0.88.[12] Again, the null hypothesis provided by forward parity is that the slope coefficient in equation (5.4) is +1. Clearly, something is wrong.

Figure 5.6 plots the time series of the forecast errors $s_t^{¥/\$} − FP_t^{¥/\$}$. The expected value of these forecast errors is zero, $E[s_t^{¥/\$}] − FP_t^{¥/\$} = 0$. Moreover, for forward parity to hold, the fact that the forward rate was too high in one period should say nothing about whether the forward rate is likely to again be too high (or too low) in the next period. That is, given an overestimation in one period, the prediction error should be of the same sign in the next period about 50 percent of the time. While it is difficult to observe any obvious biases in Figure 5.6, forecast errors are of the same sign as the previous forecast error for 60.5 percent of the observations.[13] More thorough empirical analyses indicate that there are indeed persistent, systematic deviations from forward parity.[14]

Trading Rules Based on Interest Rate Differentials. A similar play is to invest in currencies with high nominal or real interest rates, possibly borrowing in currencies

$(S_1^{¥/\$}−F_1^{¥/\$})/S_0^{¥/\$}$

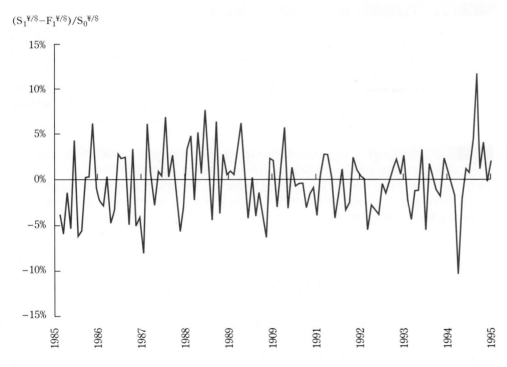

FIGURE 5.6
One-Month Forward Rate Prediction Errors over Time (1986–1995 yen per dollar rates)

12 Kenneth Froot and Richard Thaler, "Anomalies: Foreign Exchange," *Journal of Economic Perspectives* 4, 1990, pages 179–192.

13 This is statistically significant at 5 percent, based on a runs test.

14 For an empirical analysis of the behavior of deviations from forward parity, see Bradford Cornell's "Spot Rates, Forward Rates, and Market Dynamics," *Journal of Political Economy* 5, No. 1, 1977, pages 55–65, and "Spot Rates, Forward Rates, and Exchange Market Efficiency," *Journal of Financial Economics,* December 1976, pages 1161–1176.

with lower nominal or real interest rates to finance the investment. Exchange rates are close to a random walk, so this should yield higher returns at lower costs. This trading rule has been investigated in a variety of ways and by many authors.

Froot and Thaler investigated the payoff on this strategy. Based on a survey of more than seventy-five empirical studies, Froot and Thaler estimated that borrowing for one year in one currency and investing these funds in another currency at a 1 percent higher interest rate yields an expected payoff of 2 percent per year. For example, based on a $1,000 notional amount, this trading strategy has an expected payoff of $20. Unfortunately, the actual return on this strategy is highly variable. Froot and Thaler estimated the standard error of this strategy as 36 percent. Since 68 percent of the normal distribution is within one standard deviation of the mean, there is a 32 percent chance of actual returns being more than $380 ($20+$360) or less than −$340 ($20−$360). The extra expected return does not come without a great deal of risk; the reward/risk ratio of this strategy is very poor. Because transactions costs further reduce returns to this strategy, most investors prefer more conventional investments.

Model-Based Exchange Rate Forecasts

Model-based forecasts of asset prices such as exchange rates can be categorized into two camps: forecasts based on technical analysis and forecasts based on fundamental analysis. Some forecasters religiously use only one of these approaches and forswear the other. Other forecasters combine what they consider to be the best features of each approach. Unfortunately, most studies of the performance of exchange rate forecasting services following these approaches find little evidence of predictive ability.[15]

Technical analysis uses past price patterns to forecast exchange rates.

Technical Analysis. In **technical analysis**, the past history of spot exchange rates is used to predict future exchange rates. Technical trading rules attempt to find repeating patterns in exchange rate series in order to predict the future path of exchange rates. Some market technicians use statistical measures such as autocorrelations or filter rules to identify patterns. Others use heuristic rules of thumb or intuition to try to predict future exchange rates from patterns in the history of exchange rates. Each of these forecasts is based on past exchange rates.

Technical analysts believe that the foreign exchange market is not weak form efficient. A **weak form efficient market** is one in which abnormal profits cannot be earned by trading on information contained in past prices. If exchange rates are a random walk, then there are no recurring patterns in exchange rates. Technical analysts believe that there are patterns in exchange rates and that these patterns allow them to predict future exchange rates.

Spot exchange rate changes do exhibit a slightly positive autocorrelation. Does this mean that technical trading rules yield superior exchange rate forecasts? It is important to distinguish between expected and unexpected changes in the exchange rate. Relative

---

15 See Stephen H. Goodman, "Foreign Exchange Rate Forecasting Techniques: Implications for Business and Policy," *Journal of Finance* 34, 1979, pages 415–427.

purchasing power parity predicts that exchange rate changes will reflect inflation differentials. As inflationary expectations evolve over time, some *apparent* autocorrelation can arise in spot exchange rate changes through positive autocorrelations in expected inflation. This autocorrelation in exchange rates is more apparent than real, because exchange rates reflect the positive autocorrelation in changing inflationary expectations. A positive autocorrelation in spot exchange rate changes is not, in and of itself, sufficient to yield a superior forecast of the *unexpected* component of the exchange rate change.

The level of autocorrelation that is observed in exchange rates also is quite low. The percent of tomorrow's exchange rate change that is explained by today's rate change (as measured by r^2) is typically no more than 5 percent and is quite variable across sample periods. The level of short-term predictability in spot rate changes is wiped out once transactions costs are included.[16]

Fundamental Analysis. Fundamental analysis tries to discern the causes of changes in currency values from economic data. The economic data utilized in a fundamental analysis can include statistics on the balance of payments (for example, the trade balance and the budget deficit/surplus), savings rates, money supply growth, nominal and real interest rate differentials, relative inflation rates, retail sales, industrial production, capacity utilization, and consumer confidence from two or more countries. Fundamental analysis is usually implemented through an econometric model.

Fundamental analysts believe that the foreign exchange market is not semistrong form efficient. Prices in a **semi-strong form efficient market** reflect all publicly available information including past price and volume histories, balance-of-payments data, and other publicly available economic information. Fundamental analysts believe that publicly available information can lead to superior exchange rate forecasts.

Several academic studies have attempted to use such models to forecast exchange rates with only limited success. At least a part of the reason for the poor predictive performance of these models is that in an informationally efficient market, exchange rates react only to *new* information. For example, if the market has already incorporated its expectations regarding inflation into currency values, then only that part of a government inflation report that is *unexpected* will cause a further change in currency values. Without a precise estimate of expected inflation, it is difficult to demonstrate a linkage between unexpected inflation and changes in the spot exchange rate. Further, exchange rates may respond to fundamental variables with a lag or only in the long run. For these reasons, exchange rates do not respond to fundamental information in an easy-to-decipher way.

Fundamental analysis uses
macroeconomic data to
forecast exchange rates.

5.7 SUMMARY

The MNC's exposure to currency risk can be classified as follows:

- **Economic exposure**: Change in the value of *all* future cash flows due to unexpected changes in currency exchange rates
    - **Transaction exposure**: Change in the value of *contractual* future cash flows (that is, cash flows from monetary assets and liabilities) due to unexpected changes in currency exchange rates
    - **Operating exposure**: Change in the value of *noncontractual* future cash flows (that is, cash flows from nonmonetary assets and liabilities) due to unexpected changes in currency exchange rates
- **Translation (accounting) exposure**: Change in financial accounting statements due to unexpected changes in currency exchange rates

Monetary contracts denominated in a foreign currency are fully exposed to foreign currency risk. Monetary contracts denominated in the domestic currency are not directly exposed to currency risk, although they are exposed to domestic purchasing power risk. Because the uncertain cash flows of the firm's real assets depend on foreign exchange rates, real assets are exposed to currency risk regardless of where they are located.

Real exchange rates measure the purchasing power of a currency relative to another currency or currencies. The real exchange rate is defined as

$$X_t^{d/f} = (S_t^{d/f}/S_0^{d/f}) \left[\prod_{\tau=1}^{t} (1+p_\tau^f)/(1+p_\tau^d) \right] \tag{5.1}$$

relative to an arbitrarily chosen base period at $t = 0$. Change in the real exchange rate during period t is calculated as

$$x_t^{d/f} = (S_t^{d/f}/S_{t-1}^{d/f})[(1+p_t^f)/(1+p_t^d)] - 1 \tag{5.2}$$

and does not depend on the base period chosen for calculating the real exchange rates. Changes in the real exchange rate have the following effects:

- A real appreciation of the domestic currency raises the price of domestic goods relative to foreign goods
- A real depreciation of the domestic currency lowers the price of domestic goods relative to foreign goods

Empirical evidence indicates that deviations from PPP can be substantial in the short run and are typically returned to equilibrium only after a period of several years.

The chapter concludes with sections on the empirical behavior of foreign exchange rates and on foreign exchange rate forecasting. Because of their random nature, neither nominal nor real exchange rates are easy to forecast. Both nominal and real exchange rates are close to a random walk over short horizons. Furthermore, exchange rate volatility tends to come in waves. Despite the random nature of exchange rates, real exchange rates can diverge from purchasing power parity for several years at a time. Over longer horizons, real exchange rates tend to revert to their long-run average. Despite the random nature of foreign exchange rates, individuals and corporate financial managers will continue to demand exchange rate forecasts because of the potential for risk reduction and speculative gain. This is one forecast that you can trust.

KEY TERMS

Accounting (translation) exposure

Economic exposure

Efficient market hypothesis

Forward parity

Fundamental analysis

Generalized autoregressive conditional
  heteroskedasticity (GARCH)

Informational efficiency

Monetary and nonmonetary (real) assets
  and liabilities

Net monetary assets

Operating exposure

Price elasticity of demand

Random walk

Real appreciation or depreciation

Real exchange rate

Synthetic forward position

Technical analysis

Transaction exposure

Unbiased expectations hypothesis

CONCEPTUAL QUESTIONS

5.1 What is the difference between currency risk and currency risk exposure?

5.2 What are monetary assets and liabilities? What are nonmonetary assets and liabilities?

5.3 What are the two components of economic exposure to currency risk?

5.4 Under what conditions is accounting exposure to currency risk important to shareholders?

5.5 Will an appreciation of the domestic currency help or hurt a domestic exporter? An importer?

5.6 What does the efficient market hypothesis say about market prices?

5.7 What are real (as opposed to nominal) changes in currency values?

5.8 Are real exchange rates in equilibrium at all times?

5.9 What is the effect of a real appreciation of the domestic currency on the purchasing power of
    domestic residents?

5.10 Describe the behavior of nominal exchange rates.

5.11 Describe the behavior of real exchange rates.

5.12 What methods can be used to forecast future spot rates of exchange?

PROBLEMS

5.1 Suppose $P_0^F = P_0^D = 1$ and $S_0^{D/F} = D100/F$. Inflation in country F and in country D is expected
    to be $p^F = 21\%$ and $p^D = 10\%$, respectively, over the foreseeable future.
    a. What are the expected price levels $E[P_1^F]$ and $E[P_1^D]$ and the expected nominal exchange
       rate $E[S_1^{D/F}]$ in one period?
    b. What is the expected real exchange rate $X_1^{D/F}$ in one period using time zero as a base?
    c. Looking two years into the future, what are the expected price levels in each country
       $(E[P_2^F]$ and $E[P_2^D])$ and the expected real exchange rate $E[X_2^{D/F}]$?

5.2 One year ago, the spot exchange rate between Japanese yen and German marks was $S_{-1}^{¥/DM} = ¥160/DM$. Today, the spot rate is $S_0^{¥/DM} = ¥155/DM$. Inflation during the year was $p^¥ = 2\%$ and $p^{DM} = 3\%$ in Japan and Germany, respectively.

   a. What was the percentage change in the nominal value of the German mark?

   b. One year ago, what nominal exchange rate would you have predicted for today based on the difference in inflation rates?

   c. What was the percentage change in the real exchange rate during the year?

   d. What was the percentage change in the relative purchasing power of the mark?

   e. What was the percentage change in the relative purchasing power of the yen?

5.3 Suppose the U.S. dollar falls against the Dutch guilder from FL1.60/$ to FL1.55/$. Inflation in the Netherlands is the same as in the United States, so this is a real depreciation of the dollar. A U.S. exporter keeps the dollar price of its goods unchanged and sees a 10 percent rise in export sales volume in response to this change in the real value of the dollar.

   a. What is the price elasticity of demand on the U.S. manufacturer's export sales?

   b. If this elasticity remains constant, by how much would export sales change on a 10 percent real depreciation in the value of the dollar?

   c. Given the results in b., what would the dollar change in revenues be in response to a 10 percent real depreciation of the dollar? What would be the change in guilder revenues?

5.4 Suppose you estimate a GARCH model (with p = q = 1) of monthly volatility in the value of the dollar and arrive at the following estimates:

$$\sigma^2_t = 0.08 + (0.20)\sigma^2_{t-1} + (0.30)r^2_{t-1}$$

where the exchange rate variance (σ^2_{t-1}) and the square of the percentage change in the spot exchange rate (r^2_{t-1}) are from the previous period. If $\sigma^2_{t-1} = 5\%$ and $r^2_{t-1} = 25\%$ in a particular period, what is the GARCH estimate of exchange rate volatility?

SUGGESTED READINGS

The components and determinants of economic exposure are discussed in

   John J. Pringle, "A Look at Indirect Foreign Currency Exposure," *Journal of Applied Corporate Finance* 8, No. 3, Fall 1995, pages 75–81.

   John J. Pringle and Robert Connolly, "The Nature and Causes of Foreign Currency Exposure," *Journal of Applied Corporate Finance* 6, No. 3, Fall 1993, pages 61–73.

The behavior of nominal and real exchange rates is discussed in

   Niso Abuaf, "The Nature and Management of Foreign Exchange Risk," *Midland Corporate Finance Journal,* 1986.

   Niso Abuaf and Philippe Jorion, "Purchasing Power Parity in the Long Run," *Journal of Finance* 47, March 1990, pages 157–174.

   Frederic S. Mishkin, "Are Real Interest Rates Equal Across Countries? An Empirical Investigation of International Parity Conditions," *Journal of Finance* 39, December 1984, pages 1345–1357.

The way in which market frictions cause prices to adjust slowly to disequilibrium conditions is discussed in

   Rudiger Dornbusch, "Expectations and Exchange Rate Dynamics," *Journal of Political Economy* 84, December 1976, pages 1161–1176.

The performance of exchange rate forecasts and exchange rate forecasters is discussed in

Kenneth Froot and Richard Thaler, "Anomalies: Foreign Exchange," *Journal of Economic Perspectives* 4, 1990, pages 179–192.

Stephen H. Goodman, "Foreign Exchange Rate Forecasting Techniques: Implications for Business and Policy," *Journal of Finance* 34, No. 2, 1979, pages 415–427.

Richard M. Levich, "Are Forward Rates Unbiased Predictors of Future Spot Rates?" *Columbia Journal of World Business* 14, Winter 1979, pages 39–61.

Richard M. Levich, "On the Efficiency of Markets for Foreign Exchange," in R. Dornbusch and J.A. Frenkel, editors, *International Economic Policy: Theory and Evidence*, Baltimore, MD.: John Hopkins University Press.

Richard J. Sweeney, "Some New Filter Rule Tests: Methods and Results," *Journal of Financial and Quantitative Analysis* 23, 1988, pages, 285–300.

Stephen J. Taylor, "Tests of the Random Walk Hypothesis against a Price Trend Hypothesis," *Journal of Financial and Quantitative Analysis* 17, No. 1, 1982, pages 37–61.

The performance of forward exchange rates as predictors of future spot rates is analyzed in

Ross Levine, "An Empirical Inquiry into the Nature of the Forward Exchange Rate Bias," *Journal of International Economics* 30, No. 3/4, 1991, pages 359–370.

Nelson C. Mark, "On Time-Varying Risk Premia in the Foreign Exchange Market," *Journal of Monetary Economics* 16, No. 1, 1985, pages 3–18.

Nelson C. Mark, "Time-Varying Betas and Forward Premia in the Pricing of Forward Foreign Exchange Contracts," *Journal of Financial Economics* 22, No. 2, December 1988, pages 335–354.

Nelson C. Mark, "Real and Nominal Exchange Rates in the Long Run: An Empirical Investigation," *Journal of International Economics* 28, No. 1/2, 1990, pages 115–136.

Alan C. Stockman, "The Equilibrium Approach to Exchange Rates," *Economic Review* 73, Federal Reserve Bank of Richmond, March/April 1987, pages 12–30.

Real Exchange Rates in Continuous Time

Recall from Appendix 4-A that natural logarithms translate periodic rates of change into continuously compounded rates of change. Continuously compounded rates "linearize" the percentage changes found in holding period returns. Processes that are geometric in holding period returns are linear in instantaneous returns.

As in the previous chapter, *italics* are used to represent a continuously compounded rate of change. The continuously compounded change in the spot rate during period t is $s_t^{d/f} = \ln(1+s_t^{d/f}) = \ln(S_t^{d/f}/S_{t-1}^{d/f}) = \ln(S_t^{d/f}) - \ln(S_{t-1}^{d/f})$. The continuously compounded domestic and foreign inflation rates during period t are $p_t^d = \ln(1+p_t^d)$ and $p_t^f = \ln(1+p_t^f)$, respectively. Translating equation (5.2) into continuously compounded returns, the continuously compounded change in the real exchange rate $x_t^{d/f}$ is

$$
\begin{aligned}
x_t^{d/f} &= \ln(1+x_t^{d/f}) \\
&= \ln[(S_t^{d/f}/S_{t-1}^{d/f})(1+p_t^f)/(1+p_t^d)] \\
&= \ln(S_t^{d/f}) - \ln(S_{t-1}^{d/f}) + \ln(1+p_t^f) - \ln(1+p_t^d)
\end{aligned}
\tag{5A.1}
$$

In continuously compounded returns, change in the real exchange rate is equal to the change in the nominal exchange rate adjusted for the difference in inflation in the two currencies. This formulation of the percentage change in the real exchange rate is used in empirical tests of purchasing power parity.

Consider our example of change in the real exchange rate from earlier in the chapter in which $p_t^{¥} = 0\%$, $p_t^{\$} = 10\%$, $S_{t-1}^{¥/\$} = ¥100/\$$, and $S_t^{¥/\$} = ¥110/\$$. The continuously compounded change in the real rate of exchange during period t is

$$
\begin{aligned}
x_t^{¥/\$} &= \ln(S_t^{¥/\$}) - \ln(S_{t-1}^{¥/\$}) + \ln(1+p_t^{\$}) - \ln(1+p_t^{¥}) \\
&= \ln(¥110/\$) - \ln(¥100/\$) + \ln(1.10) - \ln(1.00) \\
&= (4.70048 - 4.60517) + (0.09531 - 0.00000) \\
&= 0.09531 + 0.09531 \\
&= 0.19062.
\end{aligned}
$$

As in the original example, the real appreciation of the dollar is $e^{0.19062} - 1 = 20$ percent in holding period rate of return.

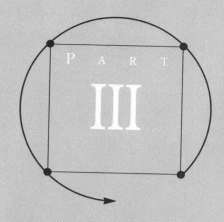

Hedging Currency Risk with Derivative Securities

A man's got to make at least one bet a day, else he could be walking around lucky and never know it.

Jimmy Jones, horse trainer

Derivative securities bear a contractual relationship to an underlying financial price or price index, such as the value of foreign currency. Because the price of a derivative security is derived from that of another asset, derivatives are ideal instruments for hedging exposures to the financial price risk of the underlying asset. Commercial and investment banks and financial exchanges around the world trade derivative securities written on interest rates, foreign exchange rates, and commodity prices.

Chapter 6 begins this part of the book with the reasons for hedging exposure to financial price risk. The remaining chapters are devoted to three derivative instruments: futures, options, and swaps. Although derivative securities can be used for speculation on financial prices, the emphasis in these chapters is on using derivatives to hedge exposure to financial price risk.

The Rationale for Hedging Currency Risk

Human history more and more becomes a race between education and catastrophe.
H.G. Wells

OVERVIEW

Why should the corporation engaged in international operations bother to hedge its exposure to currency risk? On the surface, the answer seems obvious: Hedging creates value by reducing the risk of assets exposed to currency fluctuations. In fact, the conditions under which hedging adds value are not as obvious as one would think. The issue of *why* the multinational corporation should hedge is the topic of this chapter.

In a perfect financial market, financial contracts such as currency forwards, futures, options, and swaps have an expected net present value of zero and are said to be "zero-NPV investments." To add value to the multinational corporation, financial market hedges must either increase the firm's expected future cash flows or reduce the risk of these cash flows in a way that cannot be replicated by individual investors in the firm.

Consider the discounted cash flow approach to firm valuation in which firm value is equal to the present value of expected future cash flows discounted at a rate that reflects the systematic risk of the cash flows. Let CF_t represent the firm's net cash flow at time t and i_t the appropriate risk-adjusted discount rate over the holding period t. Then firm value is determined by

$$V = \sum_{t=1}^{T} [E[CF_t]/(1+i_t)^t] \qquad (6.1)$$

If hedges have no impact on the firm's expected future cash flows or discount rate, then risk hedging also has no impact on firm value. Conversely, if hedging is to add value to the stakeholders of the firm, then hedging must impact either expected future cash flows or the cost of capital or both.

A thorough discussion of whether exposure to currency risk affects the discount rate in the *denominator* of equation (6.1) will have to wait until after the discussion of international asset pricing in Part 4. The net result of that discussion is that hedging currency risk exposure is unlikely to reduce the required return of an investor who is already fully diversified across a broad set of international assets. Hedging currency risk exposure can, however, reduce the required return of an investor who is not internationally diversified.

This chapter shows how hedging against currency risk (or financial price risks in general) can increase expected cash flows in the *numerator* of equation (6.1). The existence of financial market imperfections is a necessary condition for corporate risk hedging to have value. By taking advantage of financial market imperfections, the corporation can create value for investors through their risk-hedging activities.

6.1 A PERFECT MODEL FOR AN IMPERFECT WORLD

It helps to have a starting point for the discussion of the conditions under which corporate risk hedging can add value to the firm. A convenient point of entry is the work of Franco Modigliani and Merton Miller (hereafter referred to as MM).[1] Their landmark article on corporate financial policy set the stage for the development of corporate finance as we know it today. Modigliani and Miller each have won the Nobel Prize in Economics, largely for their work in this area. Their contribution was in identifying conditions under which financial policy (including hedging strategy) does not matter. At the heart of MM's work is their assumption of perfect financial markets. These include

- Frictionless markets
  - No transactions costs: no brokerage fees, bid-ask spreads, or price pressure effects
  - No taxes or other forms of government intervention
  - No costs of financial distress: bankruptcy risk has no impact on cash flows
  - No agency costs: managers attempt to maximize the value of equity
- Equal access to market prices
  - Perfect competition: no single participant can influence market prices
  - No barriers to entry or other constraints on capital flows
- Rational investors: investors perceive more return as good and more risk as bad
- Equal access to costless information: costless access to all public information

1 Franco Modigliani and Merton Miller, "The Cost of Capital, Corporation Finance, and the Theory of Investment," *American Economic Review* 48, June 1958, pages 261–297. The assumptions listed here are similar to those in MM.

In this stylized world, the law of one price holds. Rational investors operating in a perfect financial market will not allow two different prices for identical assets to exist simultaneously, and arbitrage activity will quickly force asset prices to become identical to those of other comparable-risk assets. These assumptions are quite powerful and will be repeated at several points throughout this book.

*The law of one price always holds
in a perfect market.*

Violations of the perfect market assumptions will become important at various points in the text. For example, whether or not everyone has equal access to frictionless markets will be important in the discussion of discount rates in Part 4. Differences in national tax rates will play a key role in the multinational corporation's cross-border investment and financing decisions in Part 5. Capital flow barriers will also be an important determinant of the multinational's financing decisions and will provide the motivation for the discussion of currency swaps as well.

Of particular interest in this chapter is the assumption of frictionless markets. In this chapter, we will develop the implication of the frictionless market assumptions for financial policy, including hedging policy. We'll then investigate what happens as, one by one, we relax the frictionless market assumptions. It will turn out that corporations have

The Group of Thirty Global Derivatives Study Group

The Group of Thirty (G30) established a Global Derivatives Study Group to study the use of derivatives and recommend risk management guidelines. The Group recommends that each dealer and end user of derivatives

- *Determine at the highest level* of policy and decision-making the scope of its involvement in derivatives activities and policies to be applied
- *Value derivatives positions at market*, at least for risk management purposes
- *Quantify its market risk* under adverse market conditions against limits, perform stress simulations, and forecast cash investing and funding needs
- *Assess the credit risk* arising from derivatives activities based on measures of current and potential exposure against credit limits
- *Reduce credit risk by broadening* the use of multiproduct master agreements with close-out provisions and by working with other participants to ensure legal enforceability of derivatives transactions within and across jurisdictions

- *Establish market and credit risk management* functions with clear authority, independent of the dealing function
- *Authorize only professionals* with the requisite skills and experience to transact and manage the risks, as well as to process, report, control, and audit derivatives activites.
- *Establish management information systems* sophisticated enough to measure, manage, and report the risks of derivatives activities in a timely and precise manner.
- *Voluntarily adopt accounting and disclosure* practices for international harmonization and greater transparency, pending the arrival of international standards

While most of these points are common sense, the consequences of not following these dictums can be severe. The recent derivatives-related failures of Barings Bank and Orange County in California can be directly traced to a failure to enforce one or more of these guidelines.

Source: The Group of 30 (G30) Global Derivatives Study Group, *Derivatives: Practices and Principles* (1993).

an incentive to hedge foreign exchange risk when faced with differential taxes or tax rates, costs of financial distress, and/or agency costs afflicting the various stakeholders in the firm.

6.2 When Hedging Adds Value

The Corporation's Financial Policy

Equal access to perfect financial markets has an important consequence—*individual investors can replicate any financial action that the firm can take.* For example, investors can create "homemade leverage" if additional financial leverage is desirable by borrowing in the financial markets and investing the proceeds in common stock. Similarly, if investors want to hedge a particular financial price risk such as currency risk, then costless "homemade hedging" through the financial markets is possible.

Because of equal access to perfect financial markets, the firm's financial policies and strategies become irrelevant—investors can always create "homemade" financial transactions that are equivalent to anything the firm can create. The value of a firm is then solely determined by the value of expected future *investment* cash flows. This is Miller and Modigliani's famous **irrelevance proposition**:

If financial markets are perfect, then corporate financial policy is irrelevant.

MM's assumptions are obviously a poor description of the real world. MM's analysis intentionally assumes away much that is interesting in the real world. Yet, by starting from this point, we can identify conditions that are necessary for financial policy to have value. By establishing the case in which financial policy does not matter, MM allow the discussion of real-world financial policy to focus on how real-world market imperfections influence firm value and, hence, corporate financial policy.

Let's restate MM's irrelevance proposition in its converse form:

If financial policy is to increase firm value, then it must either increase the firm's expected future cash flows or decrease the discount rate in a way that cannot be replicated by individual investors.

If corporate financial policy is to have value, then at least one of the perfect market assumptions cannot hold. A firm's financial policies are important to firm valuation only if they affect cash flows or the discount rate through a change in taxes, transaction costs, bankruptcy costs, agency costs, information costs, or greater access to capital markets. Miller and Modigliani's irrelevance proposition is summarized in Figure 6.1.

1. Frictionless markets	No transactions costs
	No taxes
	No costs of financial distress
	No agency costs
2. Equal access to market prices	Perfect competition
	No barriers to entry
3. Rational investors	More return is good and more risk is bad
4. Equal access to costless information	Instantaneous and costless access to all public information

Miller and Modigliani's (MM) Irrelevance Proposition

- If financial markets are perfect, then corporate financial policy is irrelevant.
- If financial policy is to increase firm value, then it must either increase the firm's expected future cash flows or decrease the discount rate in a way that cannot be replicated by individual investors.

MM's Irrelevance Proposition for Corporate Risk Hedging

- If financial markets are perfect, then corporate hedging policy has no value.
- If corporate hedging policy is to increase firm value, then it must either increase the firm's expected future cash flows or decrease the discount rate in a way that cannot be replicated by individual investors.

FIGURE 6.1
The Perfect Market
Assumptions and
Their Implications

The Multinational Corporation's Hedging Policy

Corporate risk hedging is a subset of the firm's overall financial strategy, so MM's basic argument applies to multinational corporation's risk-hedging policy as well. With regard to corporate risk hedging, Miller and Modigliani's proposition can be restated as follows:

> If financial markets are perfect, then corporate hedging policy has no value.

The rationale is as follows. If individual investors can already costlessly recreate corporate hedges through "homemade hedging" in the financial marketplace, then corporate risk hedging cannot add value to the firm or to investors. That is, corporations are unable to engage in hedging activities that investors cannot already construct for themselves.

If risk hedging has no value in a perfect financial market, then a necessary condition for hedging to have value is that financial markets be imperfect. Let's restate the hedging irrelevance proposition in its converse form.

> If corporate hedging policy is to increase firm value, then it must either increase the firm's expected future cash flows or decrease the discount rate in a way that cannot be replicated by individual investors.

This means that if corporate hedging policy is to have value, then at least one of the MM assumptions cannot hold. The hedging irrelevance proposition is summarized in Figure 6.1.

*Market imperfections are greater
across national boundaries than
within national boundaries.*

The validity of MM's irrelevance proposition depends on the nature and degree of market imperfections. The greater the market imperfections, the more likely it is that hedging has value. The firm can create value for its stakeholders by reducing frictions, such as expected tax payments and bankruptcy costs, through risk hedging.

Market imperfections are greater across national boundaries than within national boundaries. Because of this, multinationals are well positioned not only to reduce risk through international asset and liability diversification but also to exploit cross-border differences in taxes and capital costs. The impact of financial market imperfections on the value of firm asset and liabilities is correspondingly greater for multinational corporations than for firms that are primarily domestic.

The remainder of this chapter discusses three market imperfections that affect the corporation's hedging policy and risk management strategies including

- Tax schedule convexity
- Costs of financial distress
- Stakeholder game playing

Market imperfections in these areas create incentives to hedge on the part of one or more of the firm's stakeholders—stockholders, bondholders, management, and/or employees. The value that can be added by hedging financial price risk depends on the extent of tax schedule convexity, the likelihood and costs of financial distress, and the extent of agency conflicts between management and other stakeholders.[2]

6.3 CONVEXITY IN THE TAX SCHEDULE

*Tax schedules are convex when
effective tax rates are greater
at high levels of income.*

Tax schedules are said to be **convex** when the effective tax rate is greater at high levels of taxable income than at low levels of taxable income. In the presence of a convex tax schedule, corporations can reduce their expected tax payment by reducing the variability of investment outcomes. Two major factors contribute to convexity in national tax schedules: (1) progressive taxation and (2) tax preference items.[3]

Progressive Taxation

Progressive taxation is a tax system in which larger taxable incomes receive a higher tax rate. Most nations have progressive taxes on individual income. For example, tax rates of more than 100 percent on individual income have at times been imposed on very high incomes in socialist countries, such as Sweden. National taxes on corporate income are usually progressive only over a narrow range of taxable incomes.

---

2 See "On the Determinants of Corporate Hedging" by Deanna R. Nance, Clifford W. Smith, Jr., and Charles W. Smithson, *Journal of Finance* 48, 1993, pages 267–284.

3 Tax schedule convexity is discussed by Jerold L. Zimmerman, "Taxes and Firm Size," *Journal of Accounting and Economics,* August 1983, pages 119–149 and by P.J. Wilkie, "Corporate Average Effective Tax Rates and Inferences about Relative Tax Preferences," *Journal of American Taxation,* Fall 1986, pages 75–88.

In the United Kingdom, income up to £250,000 was taxed at 15 percent during 1993. Income in excess of £250,000 was taxed at a rate of 35 percent. Suppose the taxable income of Cricket International, a U.K.-based multinational corporation, will be either £0 or £500,000 with equal probability (that is, a 50 percent probability of each) and that the variability of taxable income arises entirely from variability in the pound value of the U.S. dollar.

If the multinational corporation does not hedge its currency risk, its situation is as in the solid lines in Figure 6.2. If Cricket's taxable income is zero, then its tax bill is also zero. If Cricket's taxable income is £500,000, then it pays $(.15)(£250,000) = £37,500$ on the first £250,000 of income and an additional $(.35)(£250,000) = £87,500$ on the next £250,000 of income. Total taxes on £500,000 of taxable income are then £37,500 + £87,500 = £125,000. The expected tax payment is then $(\frac{1}{2})(£0) + (\frac{1}{2})(£125,000) = £62,500$.

If Cricket can hedge its currency risk and lock in taxable income of $(\frac{1}{2})(£0) + (\frac{1}{2})(£500,000) = £250,000$ for certain, then Cricket will also lock in a tax payment of $(.15)(£250,000) = £37,500$ for certain. This is £25,000 less than the expected tax payment of £62,500 on the unhedged taxable income. In essence, Cricket is avoiding the 50 percent probability of having to pay an additional 20 percent tax rate (35 percent versus

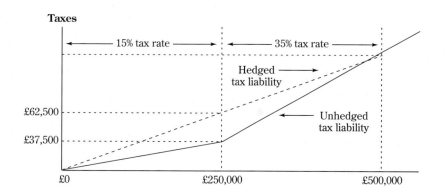

FIGURE 6.2
A Progressive Corporate
Tax Schedule

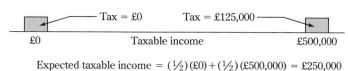

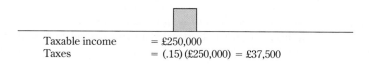

15 percent) on the second £250,000 of taxable income; that is, $(\frac{1}{2})(.20)(£250,000)$ = £25,000. This £25,000 reduction in the expected tax liability is a 10 percent savings in taxes based on the £250,000 level of expected income.

In reality, currency risk cannot be completely eliminated unless Cricket's cash flows are entirely contractual and business risk is zero. Most firms' taxable income is based on at least some noncontractual cash flows, so most firms cannot reduce the variability of taxable income to zero through hedging. Further, because tax progressivity is usually slight at higher levels of taxable income, the potential for creating value through corporate risk hedging is not usually as large as in this example. Nevertheless, risk hedging can create significant tax savings in some circumstances.

As another example, the *alternative minimum tax (AMT) rules* in the United States can result in tax schedule convexity and relatively high marginal tax rates for corporations subject to the AMT rules. The AMT rules in effect give the government an option to claim additional taxable income of the firm. Option values are positively related to variability in the price of the underlying asset. To minimize the value of the government's option on taxable income, corporations want to minimize the variability of taxable income. By minimizing the variability of taxable income through hedging, multinationals can reduce the probability of the government's AMT being invoked, and thereby forcing the corporation to pay higher taxes at the AMT rates.

Tax Preference Items

Tax preference items are items such as tax loss carryforwards and carrybacks and investment tax credits that are used to shield corporate taxable income from taxes. Tax-loss *carryforwards* and *carrybacks* lose present value because they are carried forward or backward at historical cost. To maximize the present value of tax shields from operating losses, the deductions should be taken as soon as possible. *Investment tax credits* can only be used if the firm shows an operating profit. If there is some chance that the firm will show a loss if it is unhedged, then hedging can sometimes lock in a profit and ensure that the corporation can use the investment tax credit. Since the most valuable tax preference items are used first, the effective tax rate rises as less valuable tax preference items are used. This results in a convex tax schedule.

Figure 6.3 shows an example of how tax-loss carryforwards result in a convex tax schedule. In Figure 6.3, a U.S. exporter is selling to consumers in Finland. The components of taxable income are shown in the exporter's income statement at the top of the figure. Expenses ($1,000,000 per year) are in dollars while revenues (FM5,000,000) are in Finnish markkas, so the U.S. exporter is exposed to currency risk. Suppose the spot rate will be either $.1500/FM or $.2500/FM with equal probability. The subsidiary's expected taxable income is $(\frac{1}{2})($250,000) + (\frac{1}{2})(-$250,000)$ = $0.

Convexity in the tax schedule arises because gains are taxed immediately at a rate of T_C = 50 percent while losses are carried forward until a gain is realized. Refer to the diagram at the bottom of Figure 6.3. Tax on an operating profit of $250,000 is $125,000 payable immediately. In the event of a $250,000 operating loss, the most favorable outcome is for the tax shield on the loss to be recaptured in the year following the loss. If one-year discount bonds yield $i_B^\$$ = 25 percent in the United States, then the present value of the tax shield received in one year on an operating loss of $250,000 is only $($250,000)(.5)/(1.25)$ = $100,000. The net result is that while gains are taxed at 50

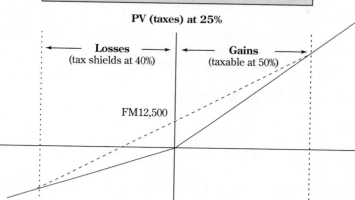

A U.S. Exporter's Income Statement

FM Revenues	FM5,000,000	FM5,000,000
Spot rate $S^{\$/FM}$	$.1500/FM	$.2500/FM
$ Revenues	$750,000	$1,250,000
Operating Expense	$1,000,000	$1,000,000
Taxable Income	− $250,000	+$250,000

PV (taxes) at 25%

←— **Losses** —→   ←— **Gains** —→
(tax shields at 40%)   (taxable at 50%)

FM12,500

−FM250,000   FM0   +FM250,000

Taxable income

Unhedged tax liability

PV(Tax) = −FM100,000   Tax = FM125,000

−FM250,000   FM250,000

Expected taxable income = $(\tfrac{1}{2})(-\text{FM}250{,}000)+(\tfrac{1}{2})(+\text{FM}250{,}000)=\text{FM}0$
Expected PV(taxes)   = $(\tfrac{1}{2})(-\text{FM}100{,}000)+(\tfrac{1}{2})(+\text{FM}125{,}000)=\text{FM}12{,}500$

Hedged tax liability

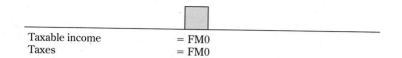

Taxable income	= FM0
Taxes	= FM0

FIGURE 6.3
A Tax Preference Item:
Tax-Loss Carryforwards

percent, losses that are recouped in the following year yield tax shields of only
$(0.50)/(1.25) = 0.40$ or 40 percent in present value terms. The expected tax payment on
a present value basis is then $E[\text{PV(taxes)}] = (\tfrac{1}{2})(\$125{,}000) - (\tfrac{1}{2})(\$100{,}000) = \$125{,}000$.

In general, losses that are offset by gains t periods into the future generate tax
shields at a rate of $T_C/(1+i_B)^t$, where i_B is the firm's before-tax cost of debt. Tax
schedule convexity is greatest when interest rates are high and when several years pass
before tax-loss carryforwards are captured. If the subsidiary is able to reduce the
currency-induced variability of taxable income through currency hedging, then it can

increase the value of the firm. This reduction in taxes payable accrues primarily to the equity stakeholders.

6.4 COSTS OF FINANCIAL DISTRESS

Costs of financial distress come in two forms—direct and indirect. **Direct costs of financial distress** can be directly observed during bankruptcy proceedings. They include attorney and court fees for settling the various claimants' priority of claim on any remaining assets in bankruptcy liquidation or reorganization. More difficult to classify and measure are the various **indirect costs of financial distress**: lost sales, the costs of lost credibility in the goods and capital markets, and various forms of stakeholder gamesmanship that accompany financial distress.

Equity as a Call Option on Firm Value

Equity can be viewed as a call option on firm value.

The effect of direct costs of financial distress on corporate financial policy is easiest to illustrate by viewing the equity claim as a form of call option on firm value. A **call option** is an option to buy an underlying asset at a predetermined price and on a predetermined date (called the *expiration date* of the option). Suppose debt is given a promised claim (called the *exercise price* of the option) on the assets of the firm. Equity

FIGURE 6.4
The Equity Call Option on Firm Value

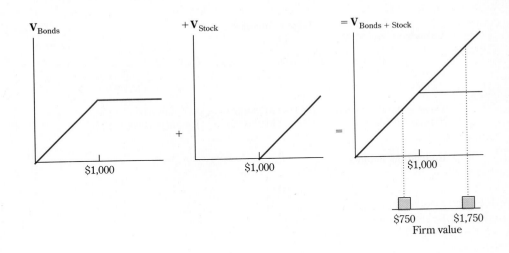

Unhedged	$E[V_{BONDS}] =$	$(\frac{1}{2})(\$750) + (\frac{1}{2})(\$1,000) =$	$\$875$
	$+E[V_{STOCK}] =$	$(\frac{1}{2})(\$0) + (\frac{1}{2})(\$750) =$	$\$375$
	$E[V_{FIRM}] =$	$(\frac{1}{2})(\$750) + (\frac{1}{2})(\$1,750) =$	$\$1,250$
Hedged	$E[V_{BONDS}]$		$= \$1,000$
	$+E[V_{STOCK}]$		$= \$250$
	$E[V_{FIRM}]$		$= \$1,250$

holds a claim on any residual value after the debt has been paid its promised amount. In the event of bankruptcy, the value of the firm's assets goes first to paying off the bondholders. Any remaining value goes to equity. The positions of debt and equity are shown in Figure 6.4 in the absence of costs of financial distress.

Viewed in this way, equity holds a call option on the value of the firm's assets. If the firm's assets are worth more than that promised to debtholders, then equity will exercise its option to buy the assets of the firm from the debtholders at the exercise price. If firm assets are worth less than the promised claim, equity will not exercise its option and debt receives 100 percent of the value of the firm. In this case, debt would receive less than its promised claim.

Suppose that the firm has promised to pay bondholders $1,000 in one period and that the assets of the firm will be worth either $750 or $1,750 at that time depending on the value of the firm's foreign currency cash flows. If these events are equally likely, then the expected value of the firm is

$$E[V_{FIRM}] = (\tfrac{1}{2})(\$750) + (\tfrac{1}{2})(\$1,750) = \$1,250$$

Suppose further that there are no costs of financial distress and that in one year the assets of the firm will be split between debt and equity according to their claims on the firm. The two possible outcomes are shown in Figure 6.4. If the firm is worth $750, then equity will not exercise its option to buy the firm back from the bondholders at a price of $1,000. In this case, equity receives nothing and debt receives the $750 value of the firm (rather than its promised claim of $1,000). If the firm is worth $1,750, then equity will exercise its call option and pay the bondholders their promised claim of $1,000. In this case, equity retains the residual $750 value after paying off the bondholders their $1,000 claim. In this example, the $1,250 expected value of the firm is split between debt and equity according to

$$E[V_{BONDS}] = (\tfrac{1}{2})(\$750) + (\tfrac{1}{2})(\$1,000) = \$875$$

and

$$E[V_{STOCK}] = (\tfrac{1}{2})(\$0) + (\tfrac{1}{2})(\$750) = \$375$$

Thus, $E[V_{FIRM}] = E[V_{BONDS}] + E[V_{STOCK}] = \$875 + \$375 = \$1,250$.

Suppose hedging can completely eliminate foreign exchange risk and lock in a firm value of $(\tfrac{1}{2})(\$750) + (\tfrac{1}{2})(\$1,750) = \$1,250$ with certainty (see Figure 6.4). The total cash flow generated by the firm has not changed. There is still $1,250 to share between debt and equity. However, the distribution of this cash flow between debt and equity does change. In this example, equity is worth $125 more when the firm's cash flows are left unhedged than when they are hedged ($375 versus $250). The value of debt increases by a corresponding amount from $875 to $1,000 when currency risk is hedged.

This example illustrates an interesting property of options:[4]

Option values increase with an increase in the volatility of the underlying asset.

[handwritten margin note: Option values increase w/ the increase in volatility of underlying asset.]

4 We shall return to the topic of volatility and option valuation in Chapters 8 and 17.

A decrease in the variability of firm value is good news for debt and bad news for the equity call option, other things held constant. What debt gains, equity must give up. In this example, the net effect of hedging was a $125 increase in the value of debt and a corresponding $125 decrease in the value of the equity call option. Viewing equity as holding a call option on the value of the firm will prove useful as we add direct and indirect costs of financial distress in the following two sections.

Direct Costs of Financial Distress

The equity call option example is extended to include direct costs of financial distress in Figure 6.5. Suppose direct bankruptcy costs of $500 will be incurred if the company defaults on its debt obligation. If firm assets are worth $750 at the end of the period, then direct bankruptcy costs absorb $500 and debtholders receive the remaining $250. If the firm is worth $1,750, then debt receives its promised payment of $1,000 and equity receives the remaining $750. The expected value of the firm net of bankruptcy costs is

$$E[V_{FIRM}] = (\tfrac{1}{2})(\$250) + (\tfrac{1}{2})(\$1,750) = \$1,000$$

This is split between debt and equity according to

FIGURE 6.5
The Equity Option with
Direct Bankruptcy Costs

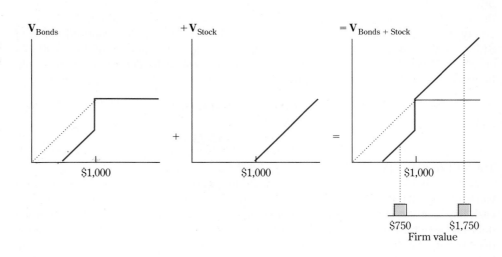

Unhedged	$E[V_{BONDS}] = (\tfrac{1}{2})(\$250) + (\tfrac{1}{2})(\$1,000)$	$= \$625$
	$+E[V_{STOCK}] = (\tfrac{1}{2})(\$0) + (\tfrac{1}{2})(\$750)$	$= \$375$
	$E[V_{FIRM}] = (\tfrac{1}{2})(\$250) + (\tfrac{1}{2})(\$1,750)$	$= \$1,000$

Hedged	$E[V_{BONDS}]$	$= \$1,000$
	$+E[V_{STOCK}]$	$= \$250$
	$E[V_{FIRM}]$	$= \$1,250$

$$E[V_{BONDS}] = (\tfrac{1}{2})(\$250) + (\tfrac{1}{2})(\$1,000) = \$625$$

and

$$E[V_{STOCK}] = (\tfrac{1}{2})(\$0) + (\tfrac{1}{2})(\$750) = \$375$$

Thus, $E[V_{FIRM}] = E[V_{BONDS}] + E[V_{STOCK}] = \$625 + \$375 = \$1,000$.

The firm can reduce its expected bankruptcy costs by hedging its currency risk. As before, if hedging can eliminate currency risk and lock in a firm value of $1,250 with certainty, then bonds always receive their promised payment of $1,000 and stock receives the $250 residual value. The $500 direct bankruptcy cost can be avoided entirely. By hedging its currency risk, this firm can avoid the deadweight direct costs of financial distress.

Who benefits from this reduction in expected bankruptcy costs through hedging? Because debtholders have first claim on corporate assets, corporate hedging of business risk helps debtholders first and may or may not help equityholders. In our example, the value of corporate debt increased by $375 (from $625 to $1,000). In contrast, the $250 value of the equity in the hedged alternative is $125 less than the $375 value of the equity in the unhedged alternative. The $375 increase in debt value comes from two sources: (1) the $(\tfrac{1}{2})(\$0) + (\tfrac{1}{2})(\$500) = \$250$ reduction in expected bankruptcy costs and (2) a $125 transfer in value from the equity to the debt.

The reason that equity lost value in this example is best understood by viewing equity as a call option on the assets of the firm. Option values are positively related to both the level and the variability of the asset returns underlying the option. The $250 increase in the value of firm assets net of bankruptcy costs is good news for both debt and equity. The decrease in the variability of firm assets is bad news for equity but good news for debt. In this particular example, the net effect is a $125 decrease in the value of the equity call option.

Does this mean that it is not in the best interests of equity to hedge currency risk? Not necessarily. Both debt and equity stakeholders can observe the behavior of other firms in bankruptcy and can formulate expectations of the probability of bankruptcy and the direct and indirect costs associated with bankruptcy. Both bondholders and stockholders will price their claims on the firm based on these expectations. As the expected costs of financial distress rise, the interest rate charged by debtholders also increases to compensate for the additional risk of their investment. If the variability of investment outcomes can be reduced through hedging, then debt funds can be raised at lower cost and with fewer restrictions in the debt covenants. With lower and less restrictive financial costs, more value can be left over for equity. Whether equity ultimately wins or loses through corporate hedging depends on whether the debt goes up more or less in value than the savings in expected bankruptcy costs.

Indirect Costs of Financial Distress

Indirect costs of financial distress are far more important to corporate hedging decisions than are direct costs. The effects of indirect costs are also more subtle than the effects of direct costs of financial distress. In particular, financial distress impacts the firm's customers and suppliers as well as debtholders, equityholders, and management. This means that indirect costs of financial distress influence the activities of the firm not just in bankruptcy but prior to bankruptcy as well. Financial distress impacts the firm's operations in several ways:

Indirect costs

Lost credibility

- Lost credibility
  - Lower revenues
  - Higher operating costs
  - Higher financial costs
- Stakeholder gamesmanship

The net result of lower sales and higher operating and financing costs is lower expected future cash flows and a lower firm value. Stakeholder gamesmanship arises from conflicts of interest among debt, equity, and management.

The Costs of Lost Credibility. Firms often find it more difficult to sell their products once rumors of an impending collapse hit the newspapers. This is especially true of firms selling products for which quality and after-sale service are important marketing tools. Customers shopping for quality items will be reluctant to purchase from a local vendor in the midst of a bankruptcy sale. The customer knows that the remaining products will be those that were not already purchased by other customers. The quality of the remaining goods is questionable, and once the firm is out of business, there will be no recourse for the customer unhappy with the quality of the goods. Going-out-of-business sales attract lowball prices precisely because customers know that the firm going out of business is unlikely to have better offers.

Foreign customers are in an even worse position when it comes to getting an exporter's quality merchandise. A multinational corporation in financial distress is most likely to take care of its home market first and foremost. If the company's output varies in quality, the foreign markets are more likely to get the lower quality goods. Consequently, foreign consumers can be even more sensitive to rumors of financial distress than domestic customers. Offsetting this natural tendency is the fact that foreign consumers may not be as informed as domestic consumers about the company's financial situation.

Firms in financial distress also find it more difficult to purchase materials and labor to run their operations. Suppliers tend to put more effort into providing quality parts and prompt service to repeat customers. Firms in financial distress can find themselves receiving other firms' rejected goods. Employees also demand their compensation in cash and may be unwilling to work toward the long-run betterment of the firm.

As with quality goods, foreign suppliers are especially sensitive to the financial situation of their business partners. Suppliers that ordinarily sell on credit terms such as "30 days, same as cash" or "2/10, net 60" (i.e., 2 percent discount if paid in ten days, otherwise due in sixty days) demand that firms in financial distress pay their bills COD (cash on delivery) or finance their sales through bank letters of credit that guarantee payment to the supplier. A financial intermediary, such as a commercial bank, is able to provide two services: (1) it can reduce the perceived default risk of the payment to the supplier and (2) it can price this risk and pass the cost along to the purchaser in the form of a fee. These activities allow the purchaser and the supplier to concentrate on their core business activities.

Conflicts of Interest between Debt and Equity. It is during difficult times that the struggle for the firm's assets is most contentious, and gamesmanship becomes a big part of the conduct of debt and equity stakeholders. Debt wants to hold onto the value

Stakeholder gamesmanship

Debt vs. Equity

of its claim on firm assets. Equity, on the other hand, wants to increase the value of the equity call option, even if this is at the expense of debtholders. The two most popular games that equity plays during financial distress involve

- An incentive to underinvest in new projects
- An incentive to take large risks

2 most popular games

Underinvestment occurs when equity refuses to invest additional capital into positive-NPV investments during financial distress. Why should equity invest more funds (even in positive-NPV investments) if debt gets the first claim on any new funds generated by the project? On the contrary, equity has an incentive to pull out any funds that it can before liquidation, perhaps as an extra cash dividend. This is another instance in which the protective covenants on bonds (in particular, a limitation on dividends) can be important to the bondholders. Debt can reduce the probability of equity and/or management playing games with the funds that they have loaned to the firm through their bond covenants.

Underinvestment

In financial distress, equity also has a preference for the firm to take on large risks in order to increase the value of the equity call option. As we shall see in Chapter 8, the value of an option increases with an increase in the volatility of the underlying asset. By taking on risky projects, equity can increase the variability of investment outcomes. This increases the value of equity's call option on firm value. In some cases, equity may even want to take on negative-NPV projects if equity value increases despite the decrease in firm value from the negative-NPV investment. In this case, debtholders bear the brunt of both the negative-NPV project and the value transfer to the equity call option from increased volatility in the value of the firm. Protective covenants are specifically written to prevent this sort of gamesmanship on the part of equity. This incentive was clearly at work in some of the more notorious bank failures in the United States during the 1970s and 1980s.

TAKE LARGE risks

An Example with Both Direct and Indirect Costs of Financial Distress. Consider the previous example. Suppose that indirect costs of financial distress cause a $250 downward shift in the distribution of firm value. This means that the value of firm assets will be either $500 or $1,500 with equal probability in one year. If direct bankruptcy costs still total $500, then the positions of debt and equity are as shown in Figure 6.6. Without hedging, the expected value of the firm is

$$E[V_{FIRM}] = (\$0) + (\frac{1}{2})(\$1,500) = \$750$$

This is split between debt and equity according to

$$E[V_{BONDS}] = (\frac{1}{2})(\$0) + (\frac{1}{2})(\$1,000) = \$500$$
$$E[V_{STOCK}] = (\frac{1}{2})(\$0) + (\frac{1}{2})(\$500) = \$250$$

In this example, both debt and equity suffer from the direct and indirect costs of financial distress.

If the firm hedges its currency risk and locks in a firm value of $1,000, direct costs of financial distress can be avoided and bondholders receive their promised payment of $1,000 with certainty. Unfortunately, stockholders receive nothing. This is similar to

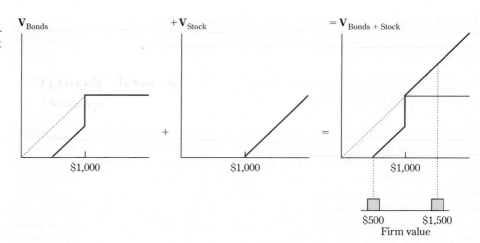

$$V_{\text{Bonds}} \qquad +V_{\text{Stock}} \qquad =V_{\text{Bonds + Stock}}$$

$1,000 $1,000 $1,000

$500 $1,500
Firm value

Unhedged		$E[V_{\text{BONDS}}]$	=	$(\tfrac{1}{2})(\$0)$	+	$(\tfrac{1}{2})(\$1,000)$	= $500
		$+E[V_{\text{STOCK}}]$	=	$(\tfrac{1}{2})(\$0)$	+	$(\tfrac{1}{2})(\$500)$	= $250
		$E[V_{\text{FIRM}}]$	=	$(\tfrac{1}{2})(\$0)$	+	$(\tfrac{1}{2})(\$1,500)$	= $750

Hedged	$E[V_{\text{BONDS}}]$ = $1,000
(with indirect costs)	$+E[V_{\text{STOCK}}]$ = $0
	$E[V_{\text{FIRM}}]$ = $1,000

Hedged	$E[V_{\text{BONDS}}]$ = $1,000
(without indirect costs)	$+E[V_{\text{STOCK}}]$ = $250
	$E[V_{\text{FIRM}}]$ = $1,250

FIGURE 6.6
The Equity Option with
Direct and Indirect
Bankruptcy Costs

the situation with direct costs except that firm value has been shifted to the left by the $250 indirect cost of financial distress.

Suppose the firm can avoid the indirect costs of financial distress through its risk management policies. Perhaps hedging reduces the perceived risk of the firm and improves its credibility in the marketplace. If indirect costs can be eliminated entirely, then the distribution of firm value reverts to its original level—either $750 or $1,750 with equal probability. Hedged, this results in firm value of $1,250 with certainty as in the original example. Debt receives its promised payment of $1,000 and equity receives $250 with certainty. Comparing the unhedged situation with both direct and indirect costs (at the top of Figure 6.6) to the hedged situation with no costs of financial distress (at the bottom of Figure 6.4), the expected value of equity is unchanged and debt holders are unambiguously better off. In practice, debt should be willing to accept a smaller return in the hedged firm than in the unhedged firm. Because of this lower cost of debt, equity can also win by hedging risk.

A Summary of Costs of Financial Distress

Here is a summary of the lessons in this section:

- Hedging can increase the expected cash flows available to debt and equity by reducing the direct and indirect costs of financial distress.
- Hedging reduces the required return of debtholders and, hence, the cost of capital to the firm.
- Equity may or may not benefit from risk hedging depending on whether the increase in firm value is more or less than the value transfer to the debt from the reduction in risk.

In practice, equity may or may not choose to hedge currency risk depending on whether the benefit accruing to equity from avoiding the costs of financial distress is more or less than the transfer in value to the debt from reduction in the variability of outcomes.

6.5 AGENCY COSTS

In MM's perfect world, the firm's optimal investment criterion is simple: Accept all positive-NPV projects. This decision rule maximizes the value of both debt and equity stakeholders in the firm. Conflicts of interest that can arise between debt and equity when financial markets are not perfect are the subject of the previous section.

In this section we'll focus on the built-in conflict of interest between managers and other stakeholders. As in the conflict between debt and equity, conflicts between managers and other stakeholders are especially prevalent when financial distress is threatening the health of the enterprise. In this circumstance, the "accept all positive-NPV projects" rule can act against the interests of debt, equity, and/or management. This is especially true when a firm is in financial distress.

Conflicts of Interest between Managers and Other Stakeholders

Management is hired to run the firm, but management typically has objectives that are different than those of other stakeholders in the firm. This leads to agency conflicts as managers act nominally as agents for the firm's stakeholders but, in actuality, in their own best interests. These interests are sometimes in conflict with those of other stakeholders. These agency conflicts give rise to **agency costs** as other stakeholders try to ensure that managers do no act against their interests.

Top managers are seldom as diversified as other stakeholders, especially equity stakeholders. The top managers' livelihoods are intimately tied to the health of the company. In contrast, equity stakeholders typically have a variety of ownership interests spread across a broad spectrum of companies and industries. This means that managers are concerned with the total risk of the company whereas equityholders are more concerned with systematic risk (the contribution of the MNC to the risk of their portfolios). Managers thus have an incentive to hedge against currency risk even if these are not systematic risks. Hedging reduces the variability of the MNC's total cash flow and thus reduces the managers' exposure to currency risk.

Agency costs

Conflicts Between stakeholders and managers

At the end of 1994, London's Barings Bank was one of the world's most venerable and respected merchant banks. In its distinguished 233-year history it had frequently been involved in affairs of state. It had bankrolled kings, wars, business magnates, and the Louisiana Purchase for the U.S. government. Its owners and top management boasted five hereditary peerages.

Barings Bank collapsed over the weekend of February 23 and 24, 1995. Nick Leeson, a modestly educated twenty-eight-year-old trader based in Singapore, had accumulated massive positions in Nikkei index futures trading on the Singapore International Monetary Exchange (SIMEX) and Osaka futures exchanges. When the market moved against him, Leeson doubled his bets in the futures and options markets in the hopes of a market turnaround. On February 25, 1995, Barings announced that it had lost $1.4 billion on these contracts—more than three times Barings' book equity. The Bank of England then placed Barings into bankruptcy proceedings.

Most investment banks closely monitor their traders' market exposures and separate the trading and accounting/settlement functions. Barings had placed Leeson in charge of both trading and settlement in the Singapore office and had then failed to monitor Leeson's trading activities. This recipe for disaster allowed Leeson to hide the size of Barings' exposure from top management back in London, even though the size of Barings' exposure was common knowledge on the Osaka and Singapore exchanges.

Leeson was trading as an agent of Barings. When Leeson's trades went sour, Barings' failure to monitor his activities allowed him to violate this principal/agent relationship. Had Leeson acted properly as an agent of Barings, he would have closed his position early and probably would have only lost his job. Instead, he gambled everything on an unlikely market turnaround. If Leeson's gamble had paid off, chances are he would have been lauded by his colleagues as a financial genius. Instead, he received a six-and-one-half year sentence from a Singapore court of justice.

It is during financial distress that the principal/agent relationship is most prone to trouble. The fact that Leeson was speculating rather than hedging served to reinforce the chasm between the incentives of the agent (Leeson) and of the principal (Barings' owners). Without proper monitoring, Leeson was free to run amok and, ultimately, to lead Barings to ruin.

The U.S. General Accounting Office (GAO) issued a report on derivatives trading in May 1994. The report called operational risk the biggest threat to the financial system from derivatives trading. The report defined *operational risk* as the risk of loss resulting from inadequate systems, management failure, faulty controls, fraud, or human error. The Barings/Leeson affair confirmed the wisdom of the GAO's report in a horrific way.

Compiled from news reports

Even if management attempted to act in the best interests of equity, legal and institutional barriers ensure a conflict of interest between managers and equity holders. In countries with market-based economies, management is hired by a board of directors representing various stakeholders in the firm. Requirements concerning the composition of the board vary across countries. In the United States, the board is elected by shareholders, although debtholders and labor unions sometimes negotiate for representation on the board. Chrysler Corporation is an example of a U.S. firm with labor representation on its board. Labor union representation was negotiated in 1983 while Chrysler was in the throes of financial distress. Even though management is indirectly controlled by shareholders through the board of directors in the United States, court case law holds that management is answerable to *all* stakeholders of the firm.

Required representation on the board for labor and other nonequity stakeholders is common in many countries around the world. For example, workers in large publicly held German firms (called *Aktiengesellschaft* and abbreviated AG) hold a proportion of seats on the *Aufsichtsrat,* the German equivalent of the Board of Directors. The firm's bankers also are usually are represented on the *Aufsichtsrat* als. Indeed, the *Aufsichtsrat* was established in Germany during the 1800s to give debtholders a voice in the conduct of the firm.[5] The goal of requiring that these nonequity stakeholders be represented on the board is to ensure that managers act in the best interests of all stakeholders and not just in the interests of equityholders. No matter what the composition of the board of directors, management will nevertheless have objectives that are at odds with those of the firm's other stakeholders.

Management's Incentive to Hedge

Management of Transaction Exposure. Because their performance is usually based on unit performance, unit managers have an incentive to hedge their unit's transaction exposure to currency risk. This is true even if the corporation as a whole is hedged against transaction exposure. Consider a firm based in the United States with two lines of business. An export division buys jewelry in Santa Fe, New Mexico, and sells it in Paris, France. The industry convention is for payment in six months. Contracts are denominated in French francs. A typical transaction in this division is as follows:

The import division of the company buys Parisian fashions in France and sells these items to rich tourists in Santa Fe. Again, sales are invoiced in francs. A typical transaction in this division is as follows:

These two transactions net to zero, so the firm and its investors have no need to pay the deadweight costs of hedging each division's exposure to the franc/dollar spot rate.

The divisional managers do have an incentive to hedge. Divisional managers can reduce the variability of divisional performance by hedging against changes in the franc/dollar spot rate. If both managers hedge, there is no gain from hedging the firm's zero net position in francs. The cost of the hedges is a deadweight loss to equity. If only one manager hedges, there is a deadweight loss from the cost of the hedge as well as a new exposure to currency risk from the hedge.

---

5 Bradford Cornell and Alan Shapiro make a similar point with regard to U.S. law in "Corporate Stakeholders and Corporate Finance," *Financial Management* 16, No. 1, 1987, pages 5–14.

Management of Translation Exposure. Because management is usually judged on accounting performance rather than on financial (cash flow) performance, managers also prefer to hedge their accounting (translation) exposure to currency risk. This is so even if the exposure is purely accounting based and there is no element of economic (transaction or operating) exposure at all. By reducing the variability of accounting income, managers can reduce the variability of their performance evaluations.

Reducing Agency Costs by Aligning the Incentives of Managers and Shareholders. If a contract could be designed that aligned the objectives of managers and equity holders, managers would have no need to hedge against transaction or accounting exposure. In the absence of such an optimal contract, management has an incentive to hedge. If hedging also reduces the costs of agency conflicts between managers and shareholders, then it may actually increase the value of the firm to shareholders by aligning management's incentives with those of shareholders.[6] Managers' actions will then be consistent with shareholders' preferences. Whether this is the lowest cost or most effective way to align the incentives of managers with those of other stakeholders is an open question.

6.6 The Hedging Decision

The decision of whether to hedge and how much to hedge must be made on a case-by-case basis. Although the need to hedge is greater for smaller, less-diversified, and riskier firms, the costs of hedging are also greater for these firms. For example, there are large economies of scale in direct bankruptcy costs, so small firms experience larger direct costs as a percent of assets than large firms do.[7] Unfortunately for small firms, there are also large economies of scale in the cost of most financial hedges. Bid-ask spreads on forward, option, and swap contracts traded through commercial or investment banks are much narrower for larger transactions, so firms attempting to hedge small amounts can face large percentage transaction costs. In contrast to the large economies of scale on these contracts, exchange-traded options and futures contracts have a fixed cost per contract; costs are proportional to the number of contracts traded.

6.7 Summary and Conclusions

This chapter provides the rationale for hedging currency risk. The perfect market assumptions were introduced as a way of identifying conditions under which hedging policy matters. Perfect financial markets have the following properties:

- Frictionless: no transactions costs, taxes, agency conflicts, or costs of financial distress
- Equal access to market prices: no barriers to entry into perfectly competitive markets

---

6 Raj Aggarwal makes this point in "Management of Accounting Exposure to Currency Changes: Role and Evidence of Agency Costs," *Managerial Finance* 17, No. 4, 1991, pages 10–22.

7 See Jerold B. Warner, "Bankruptcy Costs: Some Evidence," *Journal of Finance* 32, No. 2, May 1977, pages 337–347.

J.P. Morgan and RiskMetrics™

Growth in the futures, options, and swaps markets during the 1980s was truly phenomenal. Unfortunately, as derivative instruments became a part of the financial manager's toolkit, losses related to derivatives trading correspondingly increased. The early 1990s saw a rising call by industry watchdogs and policy makers, such as the Bank for International Settlements, for standards and consistency in measuring and reporting risks related to derivative products.

In October 1994, the United States investment banking firm J.P. Morgan announced that it would allow free and open access to a central component of its internal system for measuring financial risks. The system—RiskMetrics—provides users with daily data on three hundred financial prices including interest rates, exchange rates, and equity indices in fifteen markets. The system estimates volatilities in each index and calculates more than 100,000 correlations between indices. It is designed to assist users in assessing their exposure to the financial price risks tracked by the system. J.P. Morgan's stated objective in providing access to the system is to promote greater transparency of financial price risks so that financial managers can concentrate on developing informed risk management strategies rather than simply collecting data on financial prices. If RiskMetrics becomes widely adopted as the industry standard risk management tool, J.P. Morgan stands to gain from increased derivatives business from new and existing customers.

Computers and statistical analysis are central to measurement, management, and control of the risks that come with derivative use. Nevertheless, statistical analysis cannot replace good judgment. As J.P. Morgan's publication *Introduction to RiskMetrics* states in bold print on page 1: "We remind our readers that no amount of sophisticated analytics will replace experience and professional judgment in managing risks."

RiskMetrics is a registered trademark of J.P. Morgan and Company.

Internet users can access J.P. Morgan's Web site at http://www.jpmorgan.com.

- Rational investors: more return is good and more risk is bad
- Equal and costless access to all public information

If hedging policy (indeed, any financial policy) is to have value, then one or more of these perfect market assumptions cannot hold. This leads to the following rule:

> If corporate hedging policy is to increase firm value, then it must either increase the firm's expected future cash flows or decrease the discount rate in a way that cannot be replicated by individual investors.

The importance of currency risk exposure depends on the presence of one or more market imperfections. Particularly important imperfections with respect to the firm's hedging policies are:

- Convex tax schedules with different tax rates at different levels of taxable income
- Costs of financial distress (both direct and indirect)
- Agency costs

Important imperfections w/ respect to a Firm's Hedging policy.

Hedging can create value for shareholders (indeed, for all stakeholders) by reducing taxes, costs of financial distress, or agency costs.

KEY TERMS

Agency costs
Convex tax schedule
Direct versus indirect costs of financial distress
Irrelevance proposition
Progressive taxation
Tax preference items

CONCEPTUAL QUESTIONS

6.1 Describe the conditions that can lead to tax schedule convexity.
6.2 Define financial distress. Give examples of direct and indirect costs of financial distress.
6.3 What is an agency conflict? How can agency costs be reduced?

PROBLEMS

6.1 Suppose corporate income up to one million rand is taxed at a 20 percent rate in South Africa. Income over one million rand is taxed at 40 percent. The taxable income of Widget International (a multinational corporation based in South Africa) will be either R500,000 or R1,500,000 with equal probability. This variability arises entirely from variation in the value of the rand against the Dutch guilder.
   a. Draw a graph similar to Figure 6.2 depicting tax schedule convexity in South Africa.
   b. What is Widget's expected tax liability if it does not hedge its currency risk?
   c. Draw a line in your graph between R500,000 and R1,500,000. What is Widget's expected tax liability (and hence its after-tax income) if it is able to completely hedge its currency risk exposure and lock in taxable income of R1,000,000 with certainty?
   d. In what way does hedging have value for Widget International?
6.2 Gidget International is domiciled in the Land of Make-Believe. The local currency is called the Goodwill (abbreviated G). Gidget will own assets worth either G6,000 or G16,000 this year (with equal probability), depending on the value of the local currency on world currency markets. Gidget has a promised payment to debt of G10,000 due in one year. Although there are no taxes in the Land of Make-Believe, there are lawyers (this isn't a perfect world, after all). If Gidget cannot meet its debt obligations, legal fees will impose direct bankruptcy costs of G2,000 as the firm is divided amongst its creditors.
   a. How much will the debt and equity owners receive asset values of G16,000 and of G6,000?
   b. Draw the value of debt and of equity as a function of the value of firm assets as in Figure 6.5.
   c. How can hedging increase the value of Gidget International in the presence of direct bankruptcy costs? Who wins—debt? equity? or both?
6.3 Refer to Problem 6.2. Suppose that, in the absence of risk hedging, the indirect costs of financial distress shift sales downward and result in an asset value of either G14,000 or G4,000 with equal probability. How much will each stakeholder receive at each of these values?
   a. Draw the value of debt and of equity as a function of firm value as in Figure 6.6.
   b. Can hedging increase the value of Gidget International in the presence of both direct and indirect costs of financial distress? Who wins—debt? equity? or both?

A thorough and readable survey of financial risk management, including the rationale for hedging financial price risks, appears in

Clifford W. Smith, Jr., Charles W. Smithson, and D. Sykes Wilford, *Managing Financial Risk,* 1990 by Ballinger Publishing Company.

Imperfections that contribute to the incentive of corporate stakeholders to hedge currency risk are discussed in the following articles

J. McDonald, "The Mochiai Effect: Japanese Corporate Cross-Holdings," *Journal of Portfolio Management* 18, Fall 1989.

Franco Modigliani and Merton Miller, "The Cost of Capital, Corporation Finance, and the Theory of Investment," *American Economic Review* 48, June 1958, pages 261–297.

Deanna R. Nance, Clifford W. Smith, Jr., and Charles W. Smithson, "On the Determinants of Corporate Hedging," *Journal of Finance* 48, 1993, pages 267–284.

Jerold L. Zimmerman, "Taxes and Firm Size," *Journal of Accounting and Economics* 5, August 1983, pages 119–149.

P.J. Wilkie, "Corporate Average Effective Tax Rates and Inferences about Relative Tax Preferences," *Journal of American Taxation,* Fall 1986, pages 75–88.

Bradford Cornell and Alan Shapiro, "Corporate Stakeholders and Corporate Finance," *Financial Management* 16, No. 1, 1987, pages 5–14.

Raj Aggarwal, "Management of Accounting Exposure to Currency Changes: Role and Evidence of Agency Costs," *Managerial Finance* 17, No. 4, 1991, pages 10–22.

Jerold B. Warner, "Bankruptcy Costs: Some Evidence," *Journal of Finance* 32, No. 2, May 1977, pages 337–347.

Corporate risk management practices are surveyed and critically discussed in

Kurt Jesswein, Chuck C.Y. Kwok, and William R. Folks, Jr., "What New Currency Risk Products Are Companies Using and Why?" *Journal of Applied Corporate Finance* 8, No. 3, Fall 1995, pages 115–124.

"Bank of America Roundtable on Derivatives and Corporate Risk Management," moderated by Robert McKnew, *Journal of Applied Corporate Finance* 8, No. 3, Fall 1995, pages 58–74.

The fall of Barings Bank and financial management practices that might have prevented the collapse are described in

James Brickley, Clifford Smith, and Jerold Zimmerman, "The Economics of Organizational Architecture," *Journal of Applied Corporate Finance* 8, No. 2, Summer 1995, pages 115–124.

Currency Futures and Futures Markets

Everything has been thought of before, but the problem is to think of it again.
Johann W. von Goethe (1749–1832)

OVERVIEW

Futures contracts that trade on organized exchanges throughout the world have become a major force in the marketplace in recent years. If your risk exposure is large and your risk profile can be approximately matched by a standardized futures contract traded on a futures exchange, this futures contract can be cheaper than the customized forward contracts traded in the interbank market.

Futures contracts are very similar in function to forward contracts. As with a forward contract, a **foreign currency futures contract** is a commitment to exchange a specified amount of one currency for a specified amount of another currency at a specified time in the future. Whereas forward contracts are traded in an interbank market and are customized to fit the particular needs of each client, futures contracts are highly standardized and are traded on organized futures exchanges. Standardization means that futures contracts come in only a limited number of currencies, expiration dates, and transaction amounts. While this promotes liquidity in the futures market, it comes at the price of flexibility. For a corporate treasurer, the choice of forward or futures contract depends on this trade-off between flexibility and liquidity and on the particular needs and objectives of the user. Futures contracts can be used by speculators betting on future currency values, but they are more commonly used by hedgers attempting to reduce exposure to a financial price risk, such as currency, interest rate, or commodity price risk.

7.1 THE EVOLUTION OF FINANCIAL FUTURES EXCHANGES

Spot and forward markets for agricultural products, metals, and raw materials have been around as long as recorded history. Futures contracts are a relative newcomer to the scene, first appearing as the *lettre de faire* in medieval times. Organized exchanges for trading commodity futures contracts grew up somewhat later. One of the first known futures exchanges serviced the rice market at Osaka, Japan, in the early 1700s. This market bore many similarities to present-day futures markets. Rice futures contracts were standardized according to weight and quality, had a specified contract life, and were traded through a futures exchange clearinghouse.[1]

In the United States, the Chicago Board of Trade (CBOT) began trading spot and forward contracts on agricultural produce in 1848. Agricultural futures contracts were introduced on the CBOT during the 1860s. Another Chicago futures exchange, the Chicago Mercantile Exchange (CME), began trading currency futures contracts in 1972 in response to the dramatic increase in currency risk following the collapse of the Bretton Woods Agreement in 1971.[2] Table 7.1 ranks the world's top ten futures and options exchanges by trading volume in the first half of 1995.[3]

Financial futures exchanges today trade both currency futures and interest rate futures and are often, but not always, associated with a commodity futures exchange. Financial futures are nearly identical in operation to commodity futures—the only difference is in the deliverable asset. The most active financial futures markets are conducted at

- The International Monetary Market (IMM)
  (a subsidiary of the Chicago Mercantile Exchange)
- The Philadelphia Board of Trade (PBOT)
  (a subsidiary of the Philadelphia Stock Exchange)
- The Bolsa Mercadorias & de Futuros (BM&F) in Brazil
- The London International Financial Futures Exchange (LIFFE)
- The Marché à Terme des Instruments Financiers (MATIF)
- The Singapore International Monetary Exchange (SIMEX)
- The Tokyo International Financial Futures Exchange (TIFFE)
  (a subsidiary of the Tokyo Stock Exchange)

Each of these exchanges trades a variety of foreign currency futures contracts, typically based on price quotations in their local currency. For example, the CME uses U.S. dollar prices for futures contracts on Australian dollars, British pounds, Canadian dollars, German marks, French francs, Japanese yen, Swiss francs, and European Currency Units (ECUs). Since 1985, the SIMEX has traded CME Eurodollar, pound, mark, and

While commodity futures have been around for centuries, currency futures only began trading on the CME in 1972.

Commodity and currency futures

---

1 Chicago Board of Trade, *Commodity Trading Manual*, 1985, Chicago Board of Trade, Chicago, Illinois.

2 CME price information can be obtained from the Chicago Merc's home page on the World Wide Web at http://www.cme.com/.

3 Options and currency options markets are the topic of Chapter 8.

TABLE 7.1 TOP TEN FUTURES AND OPTIONS EXCHANGES, JANUARY–JUNE 1995

Exchange	Volume Jan–Jun 1995	Volume Jan–Jun 1994
Chicago Board of Trade (CBOT), United States	109.7	121.7
Chicago Mercantile Exchange (CME), United States	103.9	106.5
Bolsa Mercadorias & de Futuros (BM&F), Brazil	71.7	39.1
London International Financial Futures Exchange (LIFFE), United Kingdom	68.9	84.8
New York Mercantile Exchange (NYME), United States	39.2	40.9
Marché à Terme des Instruments Financiers (MATIF), France	36.6	57.0
London Metals Exchange (LME), United Kingdom	24.3	22.8
Deutsche Termin Bourse (DTB), Germany	23.6	23.4
Tokyo International Financial Futures Exchange (TIFFE), Japan	23.0	21.2
Meff Renta, Spain	19.3	18.2

Source: Futures Industry Association statistics quoted in "Slow but Steady Convergence," *London Financial Times,* November 16, 1995, page II. Volume figures are not directly comparable across exchanges because contract sizes and the methods for counting options volumes vary by exchange.

yen futures contracts through a cooperative link with the CME. This provides nearly twenty-four-hour trading of CME currency futures. Currency futures are traded in lesser volumes at several other national and regional exchanges, such as the MidAmerica Commodities Exchange, the New Zealand Futures Exchange, and the Stockholm Options Market. Table 7.2 lists the most popular financial futures contracts based on the number of contracts traded during the first six months of 1995. Figure 7.1 shows the growth of futures and options trading around the world.

On both major U.S. exchanges, futures contracts expire on the Monday before the third Wednesday of each contract month. The previous Friday is the last day of trade. Contract sizes vary somewhat on the world's futures exchanges. For example, one deutsche mark futures contract is equivalent to DM125,000 on the CME and DM62,500

TABLE 7.2 TOP FINANCIAL FUTURES CONTRACTS, JANUARY–JUNE 1995

Contract	Exchange	Number of contracts
Eurodollar	Chicago Mercantile Exchange (CME), United States	56,390,314
U.S. T-bond	Chicago Board of Trade (CBOT), United States	47,399,398
U.S. dollar	Bolsa Mercadorias & de Futuros (BM&F), Brazil	38,485,237
3-month Euroyen	Tokyo International Financial Futures Exchange (TIFFE), Japan	22,824,920
Notionnel	Marché à Terme des Instruments Financiers (MATIF), France	17,534,956
German Bund	London International Financial Futures Exchange (LIFFE), United Kingdom	16,805,994
Interest rate	Bolsa Mercadorias & de Futuros (BM&F), Brazil	14,538,804
S&P 500	Chicago Board Options Exchange (CBOE), United States	14,491,774
3-month Euromark	London International Financial Futures Exchange (LIFFE), United Kingdom	14,453,815

Source: "Alliances with a Future," London Financial Times, September 7, 1995, page 11.

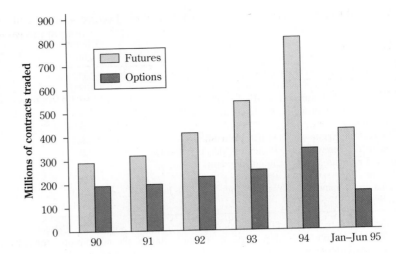

FIGURE 7.1
The Growth of Exchange-
Traded Derivatives

Source: "Alliances with a Future," London Financial Times, September 7, 1995,
page 11.

on the PBOT. Japanese yen futures on the CME have a contract price of ¥12,500,000
and a PBOT contract price of ¥6,250,000. CME currency futures expire in March, June,
September, or December.

Use of a standardized contract promotes liquidity and marketability of these instruments but reduces their flexibility relative to forward contracts. If the amount of the
futures contract does not divide evenly into your underlying exposure or if it matures on
a different day from your underlying exposure, then futures contracts will not permit a
perfect hedge of your currency risk exposure.

*standardized
contracts*

7.2 OPERATION OF FUTURES MARKETS

Looking good, Billy Ray! Feeling good, Louis![4]

An interesting scene involving the futures market for frozen concentrated orange juice
is in the movie *Trading Places.* Eddie Murphy plays a down-and-out black man named
Billy Ray who runs small-time scams for a living. Dan Akroyd plays a rich, privileged
white man named Louis who trades commodity futures on behalf of a pair of brothers
named Duke. The Duke brothers make a one-dollar bet over which of these men—
Louis (Dan Akroyd) or Billy Ray (Eddie Murphy)—would prosper if their fortunes were
reversed. To wit: Is it heredity or environment that makes the man? In an amusing
social experiment, the Dukes hire Billy Ray and fire Louis. Louis and Billy Ray eventually discover the Dukes' ruse and join forces to seek their revenge.

In the movie, the futures market is concerned over the effect of the cold winter on
the orange harvest. A U.S. Department of Agriculture (USDA) report on the status of
the orange juice crop finds that the winter was not as bad as expected. The Dukes conspire to steal the report before it becomes public. Louis and Billy Ray intercept the

---

4 Excerpts from Trading Places © by Paramount Pictures. All rights reserved. Used with permission.

report and send the Duke brothers a false report stating that the winter's toll was worse than expected. Trading on the floor of the exchange on the morning of the report, Louis and Billy Ray play out the following scene:

9:00 a.m.	Frozen Concentrated Orange Juice (FCOJ) futures open at $102. The Dukes, thinking the orange harvest will be small, buy FCOJ futures in anticipation of a price rise. Observing the Dukes' behavior, many other traders follow their lead and buy futures contracts. Louis and Billy Ray are only too happy to oblige and sell as many contracts as they can as the price rises to $142.
10:00 a.m.	The USDA report is read over the television:
	"The cold winter has apparently not affected the orange harvest."
	While Louis and Billy Ray are short the orange juice futures contract, most traders (especially the Dukes) are long. Panic selling sets in and the price starts to fall. Louis and Billy Ray have closed out their position by the time the price hits $29. With an initial margin of 2 percent, Louis and Billy Ray have earned up to ($142−$29)/(.02)($29) = 19,483% on their investment in FCOJ futures. When the Duke brothers' margin call comes in at $394 million, they are bankrupt.

"Looking good, Billy Ray! Feeling good, Louis!"

Forces Moving the Futures Markets

This amusing scene faithfully represents two powerful forces moving the market:

- *Public information*—Information is only valuable when it differs from expectations. A statement that "The winter was bad" conveys no information to the market if the market already knew the winter was bad. The statement "The winter was worse than expected" conveys much information that is relevant to the value of oranges and frozen orange juice futures contracts.
- *Private information*—The value of private information is clearly portrayed. Private information (if it is accurate!) can let investors buy before the price rises and sell before the price falls.

Although entertaining, this fanciful futures market scene is highly unlikely for at least one reason—the price movements of the FCOJ futures contract are greatly exaggerated. Movement in true price from $102 to $142 and then back to $29 is highly unlikely, and trading would be halted in any case once true price moved out of a 1 percent price limit surrounding the opening price. Based on an opening price of $102, a one percent daily price limit would limit movement up or down by $1.02. This trading delay would have given the Duke brothers and the rest of the market a chance to incorporate information in the USDA's report on the orange juice harvest in a more leisurely, and hopefully more reasoned, manner.

7.3 Futures Contracts

Forward Contracts and Default Risk

The major problem with forward contracts is that the forward contract is a pure credit instrument; whichever way the price of the spot rate of exchange moves, one party has an incentive to default. Consider a forward contract at a rate of $.5754/DM. If the deutsche mark appreciates to $.5800/DM on the expiration date, then whoever has agreed to sell the foreign currency at the forward rate of $.5754/DM has an incentive to default. If the deutsche mark depreciates to $.5700/DM, then the party obliged to buy the foreign currency at the forward rate of $.5754/DM has an incentive to default.

The Futures Contract Solution

Futures contracts provide a remedy for the default risk inherent in forward contracts through the following conventions (see Figure 7.2):

- An exchange clearinghouse takes one side of every transaction.
- Futures contracts are marked to market on a daily basis.
- An initial margin and a maintenance margin are required.

The slogan of the Chicago Board of Trade Clearing Corporation is "A Party to Every Trade." With the exchange clearinghouse on the other side of every transaction, players in the futures market are assured daily settlement of their contract by the clearinghouse. The exchange insures itself against loss through a performance bond called a **margin requirement** and by settling any changes in the value of a contract on a daily basis, or **marking to market**. This means that at any given time both the trader and the clearinghouse face at most one day's risk in the futures contract. The clearinghouse reduces its risk by requiring that for every futures contract bought another one is sold. This leaves the clearinghouse with a zero net position.

While margin accounts on both futures and stocks serve to protect the interests of the broker, margin accounts on futures perform this function in a somewhat different way. A margin account on a share of stock allows an equity investor to borrow from the brokerage house in order to buy stock. A maintenance margin serves as a down payment on the price of the stock, with the difference between the price of the stock and the maintenance margin being borrowed from the broker. The borrower must pay back the broker when the stock position is liquidated. On a futures contract, the maintenance margin is not a down payment on a loan; rather, it is a performance bond guaranteeing that the futures holder will make required payments as the contract is marked to market each day.

Suppose a DM125,000 futures contract is purchased at a price of $.6281/DM on the Chicago Mercantile Exchange. An initial margin must be put up by the purchaser, although no dollars are actually spent on deutsche marks upon purchase of the contract. If the futures price rises to $.6291/DM by the close of trading on the following day, then the clearinghouse adds ($.0010/DM)(DM125,000) = $125 to the purchaser's margin account. If the contract price falls back to $.6281 on the next day, $125 is transferred

	Forwards	**Futures**
Location	Interbank	Exchange floor
Maturity	Negotiated	CME contracts expire on the Monday before the third Wednesday of the month; last trading day is the previous Friday; seller chooses when to make delivery during the delivery month.
Amount	Negotiated	DM125,000 on the CME and DM62,500 on the PBOT. "Open interest" = # of contracts.
Fees	Bid-ask	Commissions charged per "round turn" (usually about $30 per contract on the CME).
Counterparty	Bank	Exchange clearinghouse.
Collateral	Negotiated	Purchaser must deposit an initial margin (bank letter of credit, T-bills, cash, etc.); contract is then marked to market daily; an initial margin and a maintenance margin ensure daily payment.
Settlement	Nearly all	Fewer than 5 percent settled by physical delivery; most positions are closed early by buying the opposite forward position. Open interest is then netted out.
Trading hours	24 hours	Only during exchange hours (there are some exceptions: Singapore's SIMEX trades CME contracts through the Reuters-owned Globex trading system while the CME is closed).

CME stands for Chicago Mercantile Exchange
PBOT stands for Philadelphia Board of Trade
SIMEX stands for Singapore International Monetary Exchange

FIGURE 7.2
Forwards versus CME
Futures Contracts

• marking to market Reduces exposure

from the customer's margin account to the clearinghouse. This daily marking to market ensures that the clearinghouse's exposure to currency price risk is at most one day.

Maintenance margins for futures contracts are determined by the exchanges and vary by contract and by exchange. Contract specifications (especially margin requirements and daily price limits) are frequently revised by the exchanges. As an example of how margin works on a futures contract, suppose the maintenance margin is $1,500 for a DM futures contract on the CME. The minimum dollar price tick of one basis point (0.01 percent) is worth $.0001/DM times DM125,000/contract, or $12.50 per contract. The maximum price move before a price limit is reached is one hundred basis points (1 percent) or $1,250 per contract. Since contracts are marked to market on a daily basis and the $1,500 maintenance margin is greater than the daily price limit of $1,250, the clearinghouse can always recoup one-day variations (up to the price limit) in the futures contract. If an investor cannot meet a margin call, the exchange clearinghouse cancels the contract and offsets its position in the futures market on the following day. Because average daily volatility is much less than the one hundred basis point price limit, the maintenance margin is usually more than enough to cover the financial price risk in the futures contract.

Don't be fooled by this price limit. Just because the prices at which a futures contract is traded are artificially limited to a narrow band around the previous day's close does not mean that true prices can't exceed these bounds. If true price moves more than the price limit in a single day, default risk exists on the difference. Fortunately, since the exchange clearinghouse is on the other side of every transaction, the holder of a futures contract can rest assured that payment will be received. The futures exchange clearinghouse can further lay off its credit risk by requiring that futures trades come through a brokerage house called a **futures commission merchant** rather than an end customer. If the end customer defaults on the forward obligation, it is the broker rather than the clearinghouse that bears the consequences.

REAL PRICES CAUSE some RISK

Price Limits

There was a story of a farmer who, tired of the fluctuations in temperature that occur from one day to the next and the effects on his crops, decided to eliminate the problem by having his thermometer altered so that it could move no more than five degrees in either direction from the previous day's reading.

From *Investments* by William F. Sharpe, Prentice-Hall, Inc., 3d ed., page 534.

A Futures Contract as a Portfolio of One-Day Forward Contracts

Because of daily marking to market, a futures contract is a package of renewable one-day forward contracts.

Because futures are marked to market each day, a futures contract can be viewed as a bundle of consecutive one-day forward contracts. Each day, the previous day's forward contract is replaced by a new one-day forward contract with a delivery price equal to the closing (or settlement) price from the previous day's contract. At the end of each day, the previous day's forward contract is settled and a new one-day forward contract is formed. The purchaser of a futures contract buys the entire package. A three-month futures contract, for instance, contains ninety renewable one-day forward contracts. The futures exchange clearinghouse renews the contract daily until expiration, so long as the maintenance margin is satisfied. On the investor's side of the futures contract, an offsetting transaction can be made at any time to cancel the position.

Forward and futures contracts are equivalent once they are adjusted for differences in contract terms and liquidity. Indeed, the difference between a futures and a forward contract is operational rather than valuational in that it depends on the contracts themselves (the deliverable asset, settlement procedures, maturity dates and amounts, and so on) and not on prices.[5] As with forward contracts, the expected return on a futures

---

5 See Kenneth R. French, "A Comparison of Futures and Forward Prices," *Journal of Financial Economics* 12, No. 3, November 1983; also John C. Cox, Jonathan E. Ingersoll, Jr., and Stephen A. Ross, "The Relation Between Forward and Futures Prices," *Journal of Financial Economics* 9, No.4, 1981.

contract is determined by relative interest rates in the two currencies according to interest rate parity:

$$F_t^{d/f} = S_0^{d/f} \, [(1+i^d)/(1+i^f)]^t$$

(7.1)

expected Return on A FUTURES contract.

Rather than receiving a lump sum settlement at expiration, as in a forward contract, in a futures contract the changes in currency value are settled daily via the mark-to-market convention. As the expiration date approaches, the futures price converges to the spot price. At expiration, the net of all daily settlements on a futures contract is equal to the gain on a forward contract with a contract price equal to the initial spot rate of exchange.

As with forward contracts, futures contracts do not allow you to hedge against *real* changes in the foreign exchange rate. If inflation in the foreign country is more than expected, for example, the forward rate won't buy as much purchasing power as you expected. In general, currency forward and futures contracts can eliminate currency risk but not inflation or interest rate risk within an individual currency.

← Don't eliminate inflation and interest rate risk

7.4 FORWARD VERSUS FUTURES MARKET HEDGES

Both futures and forward prices are determined according to interest rate parity. Suppose we denote futures and forward prices for a foreign currency f (in the denominator) in terms of the domestic currency d (in the numerator) at time t for exchange at time T as $Fut_{t,T}^{d/f}$ and $F_{t,T}^{d/f}$, respectively. At expiration, both futures and forward prices converge to spot prices because $Fut_{t,T}^{d/f} = F_{t,T}^{d/f} = S_t^{d/f} \, [(1+i^d)/(1+i^f)]^{T-t} \rightarrow S_T^{d/f}$ as t→T. The rest of this section compares futures and forward market hedges of currency risk.

Exposure to Currency Risk and Currency Risk Profiles

Osborne Distributing is a U.S. firm that buys Japanese VCRs and distributes them to a chain of German retail stores. It is now the third Friday in December. Osborne has promised to pay its Japanese supplier ¥12,500,000 on the third Friday in March (which also happens to be the expiration date of a CME futures contract). The German retailer has promised to pay Osborne DM250,000 on the same date. Osborne's expected cash flows are

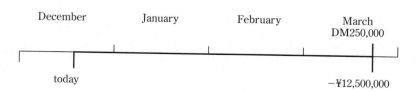

Osborne is short yen and long deutsche marks three months forward. Osborne's yen and deutsche mark risk profiles are shown below.

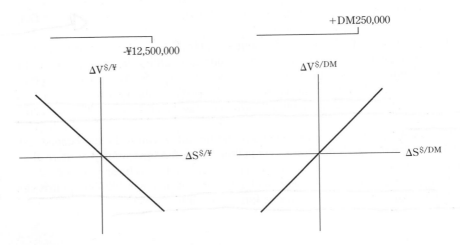

Depending on the volatility of $/¥ and $/DM spot rates of exchange, Osborne may be spending some sleepless nights between now and March.

Forward Market Hedges

Osborne can hedge these risk exposures in the forward market by buying ¥12,500,000 forward and selling DM250,000 forward. Suppose forward rates are equal to current spot rates such that $S_0^{\$/¥} = F_{0,T}^{\$/¥} = \$.00800/¥$ and $S_0^{\$/DM} = F_{0,T}^{\$/DM} = \$.4000/DM$. Buying yen forward is equivalent to selling (¥12,500,000) ($.00800/¥) = $100,000. Selling deutsche marks forward is equivalent to buying (DM250,000) ($.4000/DM) = $100,000. These forward contracts lock in the following cash flows and payoff profiles:

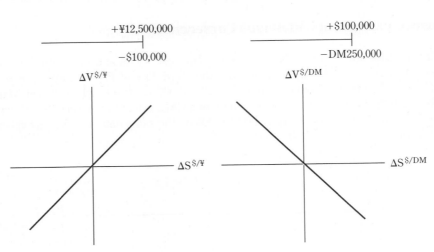

*FORWARD
MARKET
HEDGE

In this example, the $100,000 cash outflow of the long yen position exactly offsets the $100,000 cash inflow of the short deutsche mark position. When combined with Osborne's underlying short yen and long mark positions, these transactions exactly neutralize Osborne's exposures to yen and deutsche mark currency risks.

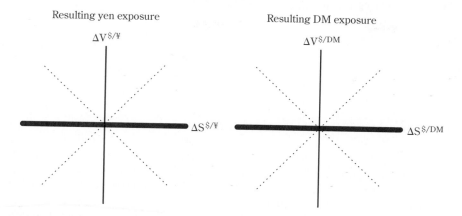

Osborne can now sleep soundly at night.

Futures Market Hedges

Because these cash flows are an integer multiple of the standard CME futures contract and occur on a CME futures contract expiration date, these exposures can be hedged exactly in the futures market. To hedge against currency risk, Osborne needs to go long yen and short deutsche marks. For Osborne's risk exposures, this means buying one CME three-month yen futures contract (and simultaneously selling dollars) worth ¥12,500,000 and selling two CME three-month deutsche mark futures contracts (and simultaneously buying dollars) worth $2*(DM125,000) = DM250,000$. Once this is done, cash inflows (outflows) in each currency are exactly offset by cash outflows (inflows), and there is no net exposure to foreign currency risk in either currency.

Forwards versus Futures: Vive la différence

The biggest operational difference between futures contracts and forward contracts is that the futures contract is marked to market daily. Changes in the underlying spot rate of exchange are settled daily in the futures contract, whereas they are settled at maturity in the forward contract.

Suppose the current yen spot rate is $S_0^{\$/¥} = \$.010000/¥$ and that 180-day Eurocurrency interest rates are $i^{\$} = 4.03\%$ and $i^{¥} = 1.00\%$. Today's futures and forward prices for exchange in one six-month period are given by interest rate parity:

$$\text{Fut}_{0,1}^{\$/¥} = F_{0,T}^{\$/¥} = S_0^{\$/¥}[(1+i^{\$})/(1+i^{¥})]^{T-t}$$
$$= (\$.010000/¥)[(1.0403)/(1.0100)]^1$$
$$= \$.010300/¥. \tag{7.2}$$

The yen must sell at a forward premium because Eurodollar interest rates are greater than Euroyen interest rates.

The biggest operational difference between forward and futures contracts is in the daily marking to market.

Suppose actual spot rates rise by $.000005/¥ per day over each of the next 180 days to $S_1^{\$/¥}$ = ($.010000/¥)+($.000005/¥)(180) = $.010900/¥. This is a 9 percent increase over the current spot rate of $.010000/¥. The purchaser of a yen forward contract would pay $F_1^{\$/¥}$ = $.010300/¥ at expiration for yen worth $.010900/¥ in the spot market for a net gain of $.000600/¥ at expiration.

Settlement of a forward contract at expiration
(Profit = $S_1^{\$/¥} - F_1^{\$/¥}$)

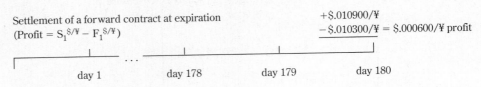

This is a 6 percent profit on each yen purchased.

In contrast, the futures contract is settled one day at a time. According to interest rate parity, the spot price is expected to rise by approximately ($.0003/¥)/(180 days) = $.0000016/¥ per day. If in fact it rises by ($.0009/¥)/(180 days) = $.000005/¥ per day, there is a net gain at each daily settlement of ($.000600/¥)/(180 days) = $.0000003/¥. Accumulated over 180 days, this equals a 6 percent gain. At expiration, the accumulated gain on the futures contract is the same as the gain on the forward contract. The difference is that the gain is received one day at a time.

Daily settlement of a futures contract

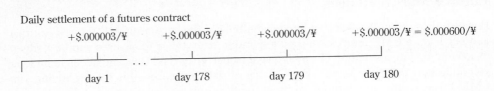

In the more general case in which exchange rates fluctuate randomly over time, the net gain at the expiration of the forward contract still equals the sum of the daily settlements on a comparable futures contract. Figure 7.3 shows spot and futures prices that begin at $S_0^{\$/¥}$ = $.010000/¥ and $Fut_{0,1}^{\$/¥}$ = $.0103000/¥ and then fluctuate randomly toward a spot price at expiration of $S_T^{\$/¥}$ = $.010900/¥. As in the previous example, day-to-day changes in the futures price are settled daily through the margin account as the contract is marked to market. At the end of the contract, the futures price will have converged to the spot price. Since the beginning and ending points are the same as in the previous example, the sum of the payments to or from each customer's margin account over the life of the futures contract must equal the gain or loss at expiration on a comparable forward contract. The size and timing of the cash flows from the futures contract depend on the time path of the futures price, but the net gain or loss is the same as the forward contract. This is the reason why futures and forwards are near substitutes and share the same payoff profile.

Standardized or Customized: Which Do You Choose?

The size, timing, and currency underlying a forward contract are negotiated between a commercial bank and its client. This means that the transaction exposure of a foreign currency cash inflow or outflow can be matched exactly with a forward contract. If the

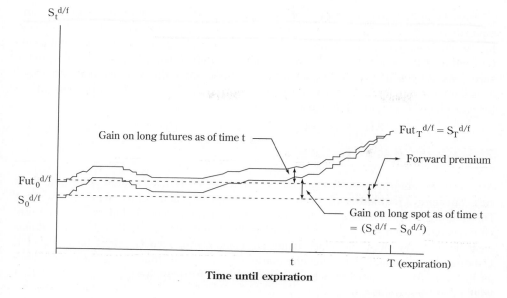

$S_t^{d/f}$

Gain on long futures as of time t

$Fut_T^{d/f} = S_T^{d/f}$

Forward premium

$Fut_0^{d/f}$
$S_0^{d/f}$

Gain on long spot as of time t
$= (S_t^{d/f} - S_0^{d/f})$

t   T (expiration)

Time until expiration

FIGURE 7.3
Futures and Spot Price
Convergence

size and timing of the foreign currency cash flow are exactly offset by a forward contract, the forward contract is a perfect hedge against currency risk.

Futures contracts provide a perfect hedge against currency risk only when the expected future transaction falls on the same day and is in an integer multiple of a futures contract. To the extent that the amount or timing of expected future cash flows do not match the standardized exchange-traded futures contracts, futures will be an imperfect hedge of currency risk. The size mismatch is usually not a problem for large transactions. The maturity mismatch can be important, however, because exchange-traded futures contracts typically expire only every three months.

Exchange-traded futures contracts have standardized terms and usually do not provide a perfect hedge.

Seat Prices on the CME

Because the Chicago Mercantile Exchange began life as an agricultural futures exchange, seat holders from the agricultural futures pits have traditionally held the most voting power on internal governance issues at the CME. Today, financial futures are the more robust segment of the market. CME Eurodollar interest rate futures contracts are the most actively traded futures contract in the world. The major users of financial futures are large banks and multinational corporations. These participants are increasingly integrating their derivatives and risk management trading strategies and using the financial futures markets to hedge their portfolios of derivative securities. Competition for seats on the floor of the CME has bid up seat prices in the Eurodollar trading pit to nearly $1 million.

Forward and futures contracts cannot be compared on cost alone unless the size and maturity of the forward and futures positions are identical. In this case, the standardized futures contract traded on a futures exchange will typically be less expensive than a customized forward contract traded through an international bank. If the underlying exposure does not exactly match that of a futures contract, then the benefits of a more exact fit using a forward contract must be weighed against the higher transaction cost (in the form of a bid-ask spread) of the forward contract.

7.5 CROSS-RATE HEDGES

When there is a currency mismatch, a futures hedge is called a cross-hedge.

Multinational enterprises with cash flows in multiple currencies should determine their **net currency exposure** in each currency and at each future date. If Osborne Distributing hedges using CME futures contracts denominated in dollars, as in the previous example, then the dollar cash flow on the yen contract exactly offsets the dollar cash flow on the deutsche mark contract. Total hedging costs might be reduced if Osborne buys yen and sells deutsche marks directly rather than going through dollars as in the CME futures contracts. This **cross-rate futures hedge** (or **cross-hedge**) wouldn't involve dollars.

Suppose Osborne can trade a ¥/DM futures contract on the CME.[6] Triangular arbitrage will ensure that cross rates are in equilibrium, so that $S^{¥/DM} = (S^{¥/\$})(S^{\$/DM})$. The ¥/DM spot exchange rate must be $S^{¥/DM} = (\$.00800/¥)^{-1}(\$.4000/DM) = ¥50/DM$. At this spot rate, each contract is worth $(¥50/DM)(DM125,000) = ¥6,250,000$. If Osborne sells two ¥/DM cross-rate futures contracts, then Osborne's exposure in marks is $2*(DM125,000) = DM250,000$ short. The offsetting exposure in yen is $2*(¥6,250,000) = ¥12,500,000$ long. Osborne can completely hedge its risk exposure with this contract. The commission charged on two cross-rate CME futures contracts will be less than the commission charged on three CME futures contracts (one $/¥ and two $/DM contracts) when going through dollars.

Osborne should shop around in order to hedge currency exposure most effectively and at the least cost. For example, Osborne could consider trading ¥/DM futures contracts on the Tokyo International Financial Futures Exchange (TIFFE). Osborne faces several obstacles to trading this contract in Japan. Osborne would need to have established a relation with a brokerage house that is authorized to trade futures contracts on the TIFFE. Foreign customers are often charged a higher commission than domestic customers are charged, especially if the foreign customer does not have an established relation with a Japanese futures commission merchant. If Osborne has a Japanese subsidiary, a cross-rate hedge on the Tokyo exchange may be less expensive than multiple contracts on the CME. Finally, for this particular transaction, the size of the ¥/DM cross-rate futures contract traded in Tokyo might not match the size and timing of Osborne's underlying exposure.

---

6 Both the Tokyo and Frankfurt futures exchanges trade ¥/DM futures contracts. The CME traded a ¥/DM cross-rate futures contract with a contract size of DM125,000 and priced in Japanese yen until early 1993. The CME contract was dropped because of low volume.

Forward contracts hedge foreign currency cash flows one to one when the forward contract matches the size, timing, and currency of the underlying exposure. Futures hedges also provide a perfect hedge against currency risk when the amount of a transaction that is exposed to currency risk is an even multiple of a futures contract and matures on the same date as a futures contract in the same currency. Unfortunately, exchange-traded futures contracts come in only a limited number of contract sizes, maturities, and currencies. Unlike forward contracts, exchange-traded futures contracts cannot be tailored to meet the unique needs of each hedger. A classification of futures hedges as a function of the maturity and currency of the underlying currency exposure is presented in Figure 7.4.

[handwritten margin note: Futures can't be exactly tailored to meet unique needs]

Maturity Mismatches and Delta-Hedges

A futures hedge is called a **delta-hedge** when there is a mismatch between the maturity (but not the currency) of a futures contract and the underlying exposure. When there is a maturity mismatch, a futures hedge is unlikely to provide a perfect hedge against currency risk.

[handwritten margin note: "Delta-Hedge"]

When there is a maturity mismatch, a futures hedge is called a delta-hedge.

Hedge (hedge ratio estimation)		Currency	
		Exact match	Mismatch
Maturity	Exact match	Perfect hedge $(s_t^{d/f} = \alpha + \beta s_t^{d/f} + e)$ (so that $\alpha = 0$ and $\beta = 1$)	Cross-hedge $(s_t^{d/f_1} = \alpha + \beta s_t^{d/f_2} + e)$
	Mismatch	Delta-hedge $(s_t^{d/f} = \alpha + \beta \, fut_t^{d/f} + e)$	Delta-cross-hedge $(s_t^{d/f_1} = \alpha + \beta \, fut_t^{d/f_2} + e)$

FIGURE 7.4
A Classification of Futures Hedges

Key:
$s_t^{d/f} = (S_t^{d/f} - S_{t-1}^{d/f})/S_{t-1}^{d/f}$
$fut_t^{d/f} = (Fut_t^{d/f} - Fut_{t-1}^{d/f})/Fut_{t-1}^{d/f}$
d = domestic currency
f_1 = currency in which the underlying exposure is denominated
f_2 = currency used to hedge against the underlying exposure
f = foreign currency when $f_1 = f_2$

Suppose that today is Friday, March 13, (time 0) and that Hackett Machinery Company has a DM10 million obligation coming due on Friday, October 26. There are 227 days between March 13 and October 26, so with annual compounding this is t = (227/365) of one year. The nearest CME deutsche mark futures contracts mature on Friday, September 11, and on Friday, December 16. This maturity mismatch is shown below:

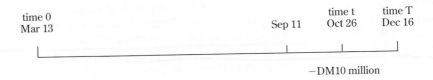

A hedge with the futures contract that expires on September 11 only hedges against currency risk through that date. Hackett remains exposed to changes in currency values from the end of the contract through October 26. In contrast, the December futures contract can provide a hedge against currency risk through October 26 and can then be sold on that date. December 16 is 278 days after March 13, so the time until expiration of the December contract is T = (278/365) of one year.

Suppose the spot exchange rate is $S_0^{\$/DM}$ = $.6010/DM on March 13. Annual interest rates in the United States and Germany are $i^\$$ = 6.24% and i^{DM} = 4.04%, respectively. According to interest rate parity, the forward price for exchange on October 26 is

$$F_{0,t}^{\$/DM} = S_0^{\$/DM} [(1+i^\$)/(1+i^{DM})]^t \qquad (7.3)$$
$$= (\$.6010/DM)[(1.0624)/(1.0404)]^{(227/365)} \cong \$.6089/DM$$

Hackett can form a perfect hedge with a long forward contract for delivery of DM10 million on October 26 in exchange for ($.6089/DM)(DM10,000,000) = $6,089,000. As we shall see below, the futures hedge using the December 16 futures contract is not quite as precise.

The Basis Risk of a Delta-Hedge

In a futures hedge, the underlying position is settled in the spot market and the futures position is settled at the futures price. Although futures prices converge to spot prices at expiration, prior to expiration there is a risk that nominal interest rates will change in one or both currencies. If interest rates change unexpectedly, the forward premium or discount will also change unexpectedly through interest rate parity.

The relative interest rate differential is often approximated by the simple difference in nominal interest rates $(i^d - i^f)$. This difference is called the **basis**. The basis changes as interest rate levels in the two currencies rise and fall unexpectedly. The risk of unexpected change in the relationship between the futures prices and spot prices is called **basis risk**. When there is a maturity mismatch between the futures contract and the underlying currency exposure, basis risk makes a futures hedge slightly riskier than a forward hedge.

Using the Hackett Machinery Company example, here is how basis is determined and how it can change prior to expiration. As with a forward contract, the price of the

Basis is the difference between nominal interest rates in two currencies.

[handwritten notes in margin: Basis = Difference in nominal i. · Basis Risk →]

March 13 DM futures contract for December delivery (that is, at time T in 278 days) is determined by interest rate parity.

$$Fut_{0,T}^{\$/DM} = S_0^{\$/DM} [(1+i^\$)/(1+i^{DM})]^T$$
$$= (\$.6010/DM)[(1.0624)/(1.0404)]^{(278/365)} \cong \$.6107/DM. \quad (7.4)$$

When this price is set on March 13, the expectation is that on October 26 the spot price will not have risen by the full amount. The expectation of the October 26 spot price is the same as the price for forward delivery on that date.

$$F_{0,t}^{\$/DM} = E[S_{0,t}^{\$/DM}] = S_0^{\$/DM} [(1+i^\$)/(1+i^{DM})]^t$$
$$= (\$.6010/DM)[(1.0624)/(1.0404)]^{(227/365)} \cong \$.6089/DM. \quad (7.5)$$

This expectation will hold only if the ratio of interest rates, $(1+i^\$)/(1+i^{DM})$ = $(1.0624)/(1.0404)$ = 1.02115, remains constant. This ratio is the "basis" for changes in futures prices over time.

The convergence of futures prices to the spot price at expiration is almost linear over time, so the basis $i^\$ - i^{DM}$ = 6.24% − 4.04% = 2.20% is often used in lieu of the precise relation in equation (7.5). Using this approximation to the ratio in equation (7.5), the spot price on October 26 is predicted to be (0.0220)(227/365) = 0.0137, or 1.37% above the March spot price. This suggests an October spot price of (\$.6010/DM)(1.0137) = \$.6092/DM, which is fairly close to the forward price of \$.6089/DM from equation (7.5).

As of October 26, there are still fifty-one days remaining on the December futures contract. The December futures contract provides a perfect hedge of Hackett's October 26 exposure so long as the basis of 2.20 percent does not change. If the basis changes, then the futures hedge is imperfect and there will be some variability in the hedged payoffs. Figure 7.5 gives an example of basis risk using three scenarios.

Scenario #1. Scenario #1 represents the market expectation. In this scenario, the interest rates i\$ and iDM do not change and the spot rate on October 26 turns out to be the \$.6089/DM rate predicted by equation (7.5). On October 26, the futures price for December delivery is based on the prevailing spot exchange rate of \$.6089/DM, the basis of 2.20 percent per year, and the (T2t) = (2782227) = 51 days remaining on the futures contract:

Basis risk is the risk of unexpected change in the relationship between spot prices and futures prices.

$$Fut_{t,T}^{\$/DM} = S_t^{\$/DM} [(1+i^\$)/(1+i^{DM})]^{T-t}$$
$$= (\$.6089/DM)[(1.0624)/(1.0404)]^{(51/365)} \cong \$.6107/DM$$

This is the same price as in equation (7.4). In this scenario, the gains (losses) on the long futures position and on the short underlying spot position are as follows:

Profit on futures: $(Fut_{t,T}^{\$/DM} - Fut_{0,T}^{\$/DM})$ = (\$.6107/DM−\$.6107/DM) = +\$0/DM

Profit (loss) on underlying short position in the spot currency:

$$-(S_t^{\$/DM} - E[S_t^{\$/DM}]) = -(\$.6089/DM - \$.6089/DM) = -\$0/DM$$

In this scenario, there is no net gain or loss on the combined position.

time 0	time t	time T
Mar 13	Oct 26	Dec 16

Profit on long DM futures position: $(\text{Fut}_{t,T}^{\$/DM} - \text{Fut}_{0,T}^{\$/DM})$

Unexpected profit on short DM spot position: $-(S_t^{\$/DM} - E[S_t^{\$/DM}])$

Time zero: $S_0^{\$/DM} = \$.6010/DM$ $\quad i^\$ = 6.24\%$ $\quad i^{DM} = 4.04\%$

$\Rightarrow \text{Fut}_{0,T}^{\$/DM} = S_0^{\$/DM}[(1 + i^\$)/(1 + i^{DM})]^T$

$= (\$.6010/DM)\,[(1.0624)/(1.0404)]^{(278/365)} \cong \$.6107/DM$

- -

Scenario #1: $S_t^{\$/DM} = \$.6089/DM$ $\quad i^\$ = 6.24\%$ $\quad i^{DM} = 4.04\%$

$\text{Fut}_{t,T}^{\$/DM} = (\$.6089/DM)\,[(1.0624)/(1.0404)]^{(51/365)} \cong \$.6107/DM$

Profit on futures:	$+ (\$.6107/DM - \$.6107/DM)$	$+ \$.0000/DM$
Profit on spot:	$- (\$.6089/DM - \$.6089/DM)$	$- \$.0000/DM$
Net gain		$- \$.0000/DM$

Scenario #2: $S_t^{\$/DM} = \$.6255/DM$ $\quad i^\$ = 6.24\%$ $\quad i^{DM} = 4.54\%$

$\text{Fut}_{t,T}^{\$/DM} = (\$.6255/DM)\,[(1.0624)/(1.0454)]^{(51/365)} \cong \$.6269/DM$

Profit on futures:	$+ (\$.6269/DM - \$.6107/DM)$	$+\$.0162/DM$
Profit on spot:	$- (\$.6255/DM - \$.6089/DM)$	$-\$.0166/DM$
Net gain		$-\$.0004/DM$

Scenario #3: $S_t^{\$/DM} = \$.5774/DM$ $\quad i^\$ = 6.74\%$ $\quad i^{DM} = 4.04\%$

$\text{Fut}_{t,T}^{\$/DM} = (\$.5774/DM)\,[(1.0674)/(1.0404)]^{(51/365)} \cong \$.5795/DM$

Profit on futures:	$+ (\$.5795/DM - \$.6107/DM)$	$-\$.0312/DM$
Profit on spot:	$- (\$.5774/DM - \$.6089/DM)$	$+\$.0315/DM$
Net gain		$+\$.0003/DM$

FIGURE 7.5
An Example of a
Futures Hedge

Scenario #2. In Scenario #2 the DM rises in value to St$/DM = \$.6255/DM$ on October 26 in response to a rise in the short-term German interest rate to iDM = 4.54%. At this higher German interest rate, the October futures price for December delivery is

$$\text{Fut}_{t,T}^{\$/DM} = S_t^{\$/DM}\,[(1+i^\$)/(1+i^{DM})]^{T-t}$$
$$= (\$.6255/DM)\,[(1.0624)/(1.0454)]^{(51/365)} \cong \$.6269/DM.$$

The gains (losses) on the futures and spot positions are now as follows:

Profit on futures: $(\text{Fut}_{t,T}^{\$/DM} - \text{Fut}_{0,T}^{\$/DM}) = (\$.6269/DM - \$.6107/DM) = +\$.0162/DM$

Profit (loss) on underlying short position in the spot currency:

$$-(S_t^{\$/DM} - E[S_t^{\$/DM}]) = -(\$.6255/DM - \$.6089/DM) = -\$.0166/DM$$

Metallgesellschaft A.G. is a large multinational corporation based in Germany with interests in engineering, metals, and mining. In 1991, Metallgesellschaft's U.S. subsidiary MG Refining and Marketing (MGRM) nearly drove Metallgesellschaft into bankruptcy through an ill-fated hedging strategy in crude oil futures. MGRM had arranged long-term contracts to supply U.S. retailers with gasoline, heating oil, and jet fuel. These long-term contracts were of three types: (1) "firm-fixed" (fixed rate) contracts that guaranteed a set price over the life of the contract, (2) "firm-flexible" (variable-rate) contracts with prices that fluctuated with spot oil prices, and (3) "guaranteed margin" contracts that pegged the price of refined oil products to the prices paid by local competitors. Through these contracts, MGRM had assumed much of the oil price risk of its customers.

To hedge the risk of these delivery obligations, MGRM formed a "rolling stack" of long positions in crude oil futures contracts of the nearest maturity. Each month, the long position was rolled over into the next month's con-

tract. MGRM used a one-to-one hedging strategy in which long-term obligations were hedged dollar for dollar with positions in near-term crude oil futures contracts.

While the intent of this hedging strategy was well intentioned, the mismatch between the long-term delivery obligations and the short-term long positions in oil futures created havoc for MGRM. Fluctuations in the price of near-term futures contracts resulted in wildly fluctuating short-term cash flow needs that did not match the maturity of MGRM's long-term delivery contracts. Metallgesellschaft nearly went bankrupt in 1991 as a result of the cash flow drain on the parent from the maturity mismatch in this hedge. Metallgesellschaft's experience is a reminder that the timing of the cash flows in a financial hedge must match the timing of the cash flows in the underlying exposure.

* Metallgesellschaft's difficulties with its crude oil futures hedges are described in a series of articles in the *Journal of Applied Corporate Finance* 8, No. 1, Spring 1995. See the Suggested Readings at the end of the chapter.

The net position is then $+\$.0162/\text{DM} - \$.0166/\text{DM} = -\$.0004/\text{DM}$, or $-\$4,000$ based on the DM10 million underlying positions. This loss arises because of a change in the German interest rate and not because of change in the spot exchange rate.[7]

Scenario #3. In Scenario #3 the DM spot rate falls to $S_t^{\$/\text{DM}} = \$.5774/\text{DM}$ in response to a rise in dollar interest rates to $i^\$ = 6.74\%$. German interest rates remain unchanged at $i^{\text{DM}} = 4.04\%$. The October futures price for December delivery is

• DM FALLS
in VALUE
to $S_t^{\$/DM}$

$$\text{Fut}_{t,T}^{\$/\text{DM}} = S_t^{\$/\text{DM}} [(1+i^\$)/(1+i^{\text{DM}})]^{T-t}$$
$$= (\$.5774/\text{DM})[(1.0674)/(1.0404)]^{(51/365)} \cong \$.5795/\text{DM}$$

In this instance, the profit (loss) on the two positions are as follows:

Profit on futures: $(\text{Fut}_{t,T}^{\$/\text{DM}} - \text{Fut}_{0,T}^{\$/\text{DM}}) = (\$.5795/\text{DM} - \$.6107/\text{DM}) = -\$.0312/\text{DM}$

---

7 Try Problem 7.6 at the end of the chapter if you are unconvinced that it is basis risk and not the spot rate change that is the source of risk in a futures hedge.

Profit (loss) on underlying short position in the spot currency:

$$-(S_t^{\$/DM}-E[S_t^{\$/DM}]) = -(\$.5774/DM-\$.6089/DM) = +\$.0315/DM$$

The net gain is $(-\$.0312/DM + \$.0315/DM) = +\$.0003/DM$, or \$3,000 based on the DM10 million short and long positions. Again, it is basis risk that spoils the futures hedge.

Hackett's unhedged short DM position is exposed to considerable currency risk. If the range of spot rates is from \$.5774/DM to \$.6255/DM as in scenarios #2 and #3, then the range of dollar obligations is \$481,000 (from −\$5,774,000 to −\$6,255,000) on the DM10 million underlying exposure in the spot market. This risk arises from *variability in the level of the exchange rate*. A forward contract can reduce the variability of the hedged position to zero. The futures hedge does almost as well, producing a \$7,000 range of outcomes (from −\$4,000 to +\$3,000). The remaining risk in the futures hedge arises from *variability in the basis*—the risk that interest rates in one or both currencies will change unexpectedly. The futures hedge transforms the nature of Hackett's currency risk exposure from a bet on exchange rate levels to a bet on the difference between domestic and foreign interest rates.

Futures Hedging Using the Hedge Ratio

The Forward Hedge. The **hedge ratio** N_F^* of a forward or futures position is defined as

$$N_F^* = \text{Amount in forward position/Amount exposed to currency risk} \qquad (7.6)$$

In a perfect forward hedge, the forward contract is the same size as the underlying exposure. A forward contract provides a perfect hedge because gains (losses) on the underlying position are exactly offset by losses (gains) on the forward position. The optimal hedge ratio is thus $N_F^* = -1$ where the minus sign indicates that the forward position is opposite (short) the underlying exposure.

The Futures Hedge. As with forward contracts, most of the change in the value of a futures contract is derived from change in the underlying spot rate of exchange. However, because the futures contract is exposed to basis risk, there is not a one-to-one relation between spot prices and futures prices. For this reason, futures contracts do not generally provide perfect hedges against currency exposure. However, futures contracts *can* provide very good hedges, because basis risk is small relative to currency risk.

The relation between changes in spot and futures prices can be viewed as a regression line:

$$s_t^{\$/DM} = \alpha + \beta\, fut_t^{\$/DM} + e_t \qquad (7.7)$$

where $s_t^{d/f} = (S_t^{d/f} - S_{t-1}^{d/f})/S_{t-1}^{d/f}$ and $fut_t^{d/f} = (Fut_t^{d/f} - Fut_{t-1}^{d/f})/Fut_{t-1}^{d/f}$ are percentage changes in spot and futures prices during period t. In the Hackett example above, this regression should be estimated using futures contracts that mature in $7\frac{1}{2}$ months (for example, from March through October). The regression then provides an estimate of how well changes in futures prices predict changes in spot prices over maturities of $7\frac{1}{2}$ months.

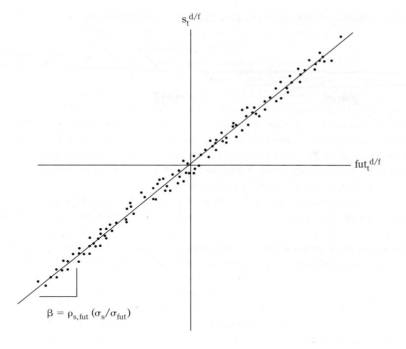

$$\beta = \rho_{s,fut}\,(\sigma_s/\sigma_{fut})$$

FIGURE 7.6
Linear Regression
and the Hedge Ratio

The regression in equation (7.7) is shown graphically in Figure 7.6. Since both spot and futures prices are close to a random walk, the expectation of both $fut_t^{\$/DM}$ and $s_t^{\$/DM}$ is zero and the intercept term α in this regression is usually ignored. As in any regression, the slope β in equation (7.7) is equal to

$$\beta = \sigma_{s,fut}/\sigma_{fut}^2 = \rho_{s,fut}\,(\sigma_s/\sigma_{fut}) \tag{7.8}$$

This slope (β) measures changes in futures prices relative to changes in spot prices. The error term e captures any variation in spot rate changes $s_t^{\$/DM}$ that is unrelated to futures price changes $fut_t^{\$/DM}$.

If the historical relation between spot prices and futures prices is a reasonable approximation of the expected future relation, then this regression can be used to estimate the number of futures contracts that will minimize the variance of the hedged position. Let N_S be the size of the underlying exposure to currency risk. Let N_{Fut} represent the amount of currency to be bought or sold in the futures market to offset the underlying exposure. The optimal amount to put into futures to minimize the risk of the futures hedge is

$$N_{Fut}^* = \text{Amount in futures contracts/Amount exposed to currency risk} \tag{7.9}$$
$$= -\beta$$

In this context, the hedge ratio provides the optimal amount in the futures hedge per unit of value exposed to currency risk. A futures hedge formed in this fashion is called a **delta-hedge** because it minimizes the variance (the Δ or delta) of the hedged position.[8]

DELTA Hedge
Δ minimizes the variance

---

8 Ederington [1979] develops the properties of the delta-hedge ratio in "The Hedging Performance of the New Futures Markets," *Journal of Finance* 34, No.1, 1979, pages 157–170.

....

*Hedge quality is measured
by r-square in regression
equation (7.7).*

....

- Hedge Quality
  $= r^2$)
  = % variation
  ↑ r^2 = Good, Low Risk
  ↓ r^2 = High Risk

Hedge quality is measured by the r-square of the regression in equation (7.7). The r^2 (or *coefficient of determination*) is bounded by $0 \le r^2 \le 1$ and measures the percentage of the variation in $s_t^{\$/DM}$ that is explained by variation in $fut_t^{\$/DM}$. A high r^2 indicates low basis risk and a high-quality delta-hedge. A low r^2 means that basis risk is high relative to the underlying currency risk.

The regression in equation (7.7) is designed to estimate basis risk over the maturity of a proposed hedge. Unfortunately, it is difficult to construct a sample of futures prices of constant maturity t. In the example above, this would be a $7\frac{1}{2}$-month maturity. Exchange-traded futures expire only every three months, and the futures prices on any single contract converge to the spot rate at maturity. Fortunately, interest rate parity determines both the forward price and the futures price for a given maturity. It is much easier to construct a sample of forward prices of constant maturity than a sample of futures prices of constant maturity, so the hedge ratio is conventionally estimated from the relation of forward price changes to spot rate changes over the desired maturity.

An Example of a Delta-Hedge. Suppose the regression in equation (7.7) yields a regression coefficient of $\beta = 1.025$. The futures hedge should then consist of:

$$N_{Fut}^* = \text{Amount in futures contracts/Amount exposed} = -\beta$$

$$\Rightarrow \text{Amount in futures contracts} = (-\beta)(\text{Amount exposed})$$

For Hackett's underlying DM10 million short exposure, this requires a long position of

$$\begin{aligned} \text{Amount in futures contract} &= (-1.025)(-DM10,000,000) \\ &= DM10,250,000 \end{aligned}$$

Instead of forming a "naive" hedge with a DM10 million long position in December futures, the variability in the hedged position can be minimized with DM10,250,000 of December futures. On the CME, this would be worth (DM10,250,000)/(DM125,000/contract) = 82 futures contracts.

- Delta-Cross-Hedge
  when
  Both currency
  & maturity
  mismatches
  exist

....

*When both maturity and currency
are mismatched, a futures hedge
is called a delta-cross-hedge.*

....

Cross-Hedges and Delta-Cross-Hedges

A **delta-cross-hedge** is used when there are both a maturity mismatch and a currency mismatch between the underlying currency transaction and the futures contract used to hedge against currency risk. The regression in equation (7.7) must be modified for a delta-cross-hedge to include both basis risk from the maturity mismatch as well as currency cross-rate risk from the currency mismatch. The general form of the regression equation for estimating the optimal hedge ratio of a delta-cross-hedge is:

$$s_t^{d/f_1} = \alpha + \beta \, fut_t^{d/f_2} + e_t \tag{7.10}$$

for an underlying transaction exposure in currency f_1 and a futures hedge in currency f_2. The interpretation of the slope coefficient as the optimal hedge ratio is the same as in equation (7.9); that is, buy futures contracts according to the ratio $N_{fut}^* = -\beta$.

A cross-hedge is a special case of the delta-cross-hedge. As discussed earlier, in a cross-hedge there is a currency mismatch but not a maturity mismatch. The optimal hedge ratio of a cross-hedge is estimated from

$$s_t^{d/f_1} = \alpha + \beta \, s_t^{d/f_2} + e_t \qquad (7.11)$$

• Cross-Hedge =
   currency mismatch
        NO
   maturity mismatch.

This is identical to equation (7.10) except that fut_t^{d/f_2} is replaced by s_t^{d/f_2}. Spot rate changes s_t^{d/f_2} can be substituted for fut_t^{d/f_2} because futures prices converge to spot prices at maturity, and the maturity of the futures contract is the same as that of the underlying transaction exposure in the spot market.

If futures are not available in the currency that you wish to hedge, a cross-hedge using a futures contract on a currency that is closely related to the desired currency can at least partially hedge against currency risk. As an example, a U.S.-based MNC can hedge a Dutch guilder obligation with a long deutsche mark futures contract, because the value of the guilder is closely related to that of the mark. For a DM hedge of a Dutch guilder obligation, the spot exposure is in guilders and the futures exposure is marks. Hence, the regression should include guilder spot rate changes and DM futures price changes:

$$s_t^{\$/FL} = \alpha + \beta \, fut_t^{\$/DM} + e_t \qquad (7.12)$$

The quality of this cross-rate futures hedge is only as good as the correlation between the guilder and the mark. If futures contracts in guilders are unavailable, however, the DM futures hedge can reduce exposure to the value of the guilder.

When both the maturity and the currency match that of the underlying obligation, equation (7.10) reduces to

$$s_t^{d/f} = \alpha + \beta \, s_t^{d/f} + e_t \qquad (7.13)$$

Since the correlation of $s_t^{d/f}$ with itself is +1, this is a perfect hedge ($r^2 = 1$) and the optimal hedge ratio is $N_{Fut}^{*} = -\beta = -1$. In this circumstance, the futures hedge is equivalent to a forward market hedge, and currency risk can be completely eliminated.

7.7 SUMMARY

Forward contracts are pure credit instruments and are therefore subject to default risk. Futures contracts reduce the risk of default relative to forward contracts through the following conventions:

Futures Contracts ?

• An exchange clearinghouse takes one side of every transaction.
• An initial and a maintenance margin are required.
• Futures contracts are marked to market on a daily basis.

Because they are marked to market daily, futures contracts are essentially a bundle of consecutive one-day forward contracts. This means that they are functionally equivalent

Choice between Futures and Forwards

to forward contracts and, aside from contractual differences, are priced in the same way. Whereas forward contracts can form perfect hedges against transaction exposure, futures hedges are imperfect when there is a mismatch between the size, maturity, and/or currency of the underlying exposure and of the futures contract used to hedge the exposure. The choice between a forward or a futures contract depends on the cost of each contract and on how closely the underlying risk profile is to that of a standardized futures contract.

A delta-hedge is used when the timing of the transaction exposed to currency risk is not the same as the maturity of available futures contracts. While a delta-hedge can eliminate currency risk, it cannot eliminate basis risk—the risk that the relation of futures prices to spot prices will change. This is because spot and futures prices do not move in unison when there are changes in the basis—the difference in nominal interest rates between the foreign and domestic currencies. The hedge ratio of a delta-hedge can be estimated from

• Hedge Ratio

$$s_t^{d/f} = \alpha + \beta \, fut_t^{d/f} + e_t \qquad (7.7)$$

where $s_t^{d/f} = (S_t^{d/f}/S_{t-1}^{d/f}) - 1$ and $fut_t^{d/f} = (Fut_t^{d/f}/Fut_{t-1}^{d/f}) - 1$ are percentage changes in spot and futures prices, respectively. The hedge ratio

$$N_{Fut}^* = \text{Amount in futures contracts/Amount exposed} = -\beta \qquad (7.9)$$

minimizes the risk of the hedged position.

Similarly, futures do not provide a perfect hedge when there is a currency mismatch. A futures hedge using a currency that is closely related to the exposed currency is called a cross-hedge. For an underlying exposure in foreign currency f_1 and a futures hedge using currency f_2, the hedge ratio is estimated from the regression

• cross-hedge: Using a closely related currency to the one not offered

$$s_t^{d/f_1} = \alpha + \beta \, s_t^{d/f_2} + e_t \qquad (7.11)$$

where d is the hedger's domestic currency of reference.

A futures hedge for which there is both a currency mismatch and a maturity mismatch is called a delta-cross-hedge. This is the most general form of equations (7.7) and (7.11):

• Δ-Cross-Hedge

$$s_t^{d/f_1} = \alpha + \beta \, fut_t^{d/f_2} + e_t \qquad (7.10)$$

If the underlying exposure and the futures contracts are in the same currency, then $f_1 = f_2 = f$, and the hedge is a delta-hedge. If there is a maturity match but a currency mismatch, then $fut_t^{d/f_2} = s_t^{d/f_2}$ and the hedge is a cross-hedge. If there are both a maturity and a currency match, then a futures hedge is equivalent to a forward market hedge and the futures hedge can completely eliminate currency risk so long as the underlying transaction exposure is an even increment of the futures contract size.

Basis	Futures contract
Basis risk	Hedge quality
Cross-rate futures hedge (cross-hedge)	Hedge ratio
Delta-cross-hedge	Margin requirement
Delta-hedge	Marking to market
Futures commission merchant	Net currency exposure

CONCEPTUAL QUESTIONS

7.1 How do currency forward and futures contracts differ with respect to maturity, settlement, and the size and timing of cash flows?

7.2 What is the primary role of the exchange clearinghouse?

7.3 Draw and explain the payoff profile associated with a currency futures contract.

7.4 What is a delta-hedge? a cross-hedge? a delta-cross-hedge?

7.5 What is the basis? What is basis risk?

7.6 How do you measure the quality of a futures hedge?

PROBLEMS

7.1 On September 11, a U.S.-based multinational corporation expects to receive DM3,000,000 from a German customer. The current spot exchange rate is $0.5950/DM. The transfer will occur on December 10. The current DM futures price for December delivery is $0.6075/DM. The size of the CME futures contract is DM125,000. How many DM futures contracts should the U.S. multinational buy or sell to hedge this forward obligation? What is the multinational's net profit (or loss) on December 10 in the hedged position if the spot rate on that date is $0.5900/DM?

7.2 Snow White Manufacturing makes snowmobiles, some of which it sells to Japan for recreation in the wilderness of the northern islands. Snow White is expecting a payment of ¥9 million in six months.
a. Draw a time line illustrating the transaction.
b. Draw a payoff profile for this project with $/¥ on the axes.
c. Suppose Snow White takes out a forward contract to hedge this transaction. Describe this contract.
d. If Snow White takes out a futures contract instead of a forward contract, describe the advantages/disadvantages to Snow White.

7.3 Suppose that at time zero the spot rate equals the ninety-day forward rate at $S^{\$/DM} = F^{\$/DM} = \$0.65/DM$. Assume that the spot rate increases by $0.0002/DM each day over the ensuing ninety days. You buy marks in both the forward and futures markets. Draw a time line for each contract showing the cash inflows/outflows arising from the daily change in the spot rate.

7.4 Suppose Cotton Bolls, Inc., does business with companies in France and Germany. Cotton Bolls expects to pay FF500,000 and receive DM125,000 on the Friday before the third Wednesday of April. Forward rates for that date are $F^{\$/FF} = \$0.1625/FF$ and $F^{\$/DM} = \$0.65/DM$.
a. Show time lines illustrating each transaction.
b. How would Cotton Bolls hedge these transactions with $/FF and $/DM futures contracts?
c. Suppose the forward rate for DM and FF is DM0.2500/FF. Describe a cross-hedge that would accomplish the same objective as the two hedges in part b.

7.5 You work for Texas Instruments and are considering ways to hedge a 10 billion Belgian franc obligation due in six months. Your currency of reference is the U.S. dollar. The current spot exchange rate is $S_0^{\$/BF} = \$.025/BF$ (or $S_0^{BF/\$} = BF 40/\$$).

a. The futures exchange in Brussels trades BF/$ contracts that expire in seven months with a contract size of $50,000. Based on the regression $s_t^{\$/BF} = \alpha + \beta \, fut_t^{\$/BF} + e$, you estimate $\beta = 1.025$. The r^2 of the regression is .98. How many BF/$ futures contracts should you buy to minimize the risk of your hedged position?

b. A merchant bank is willing to sell a deutsche mark futures contract in any amount with a maturity on the date that your obligation is due in six months. Based on the regression $s_t^{\$/BF} = \alpha + \beta \, s_t^{\$/DM} + e$, you estimate $\beta = 1.04$. The r^2 of the regression is .89. How many DM/$ futures contracts should you buy to minimize the risk of your hedged position?

c. The Deutsche Termin Bourse in Frankfurt trades DM/$ futures contracts that expire in seven months and have a contract size of $50,000. Based on the regression $s_t^{\$/BF} = \alpha + \beta \, fut_t^{\$/DM} + e$, you estimate $\beta = 1.05$. The r^2 of this regression is .86. How many DM/$ futures contracts should you buy to minimize the risk of your hedged position?

d. Which of these futures market hedges provides the best quality?

7.6 Refer to Figure 7.5. It is now March 13 and the current spot exchange rate is $.6010/DM. You have a DM10 million obligation due on October 26. The nearest DM futures contract expires on December 16. Interest rates are 6.24 percent in the U.S. and 4.04 percent in Germany.

a. Suppose the spot exchange rate on October 26 is $.6089/DM. Fill in the three scenarios in Figure 7.5 assuming (1) $i^\$ = 6.24\%$ and $i^{DM} = 4.04\%$, (2) $i^\$ = 6.24\%$ and $i^{DM} = 4.54\%$, and (3) $i^\$ = 6.74\%$ and $i^{DM} = 4.04\%$.

b. Suppose interest rates do not change (so that $i^\$ = 6.24\%$ and $i^{DM} = 4.04\%$) but that the spot exchange rate does change. Fill in the three scenarios in Figure 7.5 assuming (1) $S_t^{\$/DM} = \$.6089/DM$, (2) $S_t^{\$/DM} = \$.6255/DM$, and (3) $S_t^{\$/DM} = \$.5774/DM$.

SUGGESTED READINGS

Excellent comparisons of futures and forward contracts appear in

John C. Cox, Jonathan E. Ingersol, Jr., and Stephen A. Ross, "The Relation Between Forward and Futures Prices," *Journal of Financial Economics* 9, No 4, 1981, pages 321-346.

Kenneth R. French, "A Comparison of Futures and Forward Prices," *Journal of Financial Economics* 12, No. 3, November 1983, pages 311–342.

A thorough coverage of currency and interest rate futures contracts appears in

Edward W. Schwarz, Joanne H. Hill, and Thomas Schneeweis, *Financial Futures: Fundamentals, Strategies, and Applications,* 1986, Irwin Publishing.

An easy-to-read introduction to forwards, futures, swaps, and options appears in

Charles W. Smithson, "A LEGO Approach to Financial Engineering: An Introduction to Forwards, Futures, Swaps, and Options," *Midland Corporate Finance Journal* 4, No. 4, Winter 1987, pages 16–28.

A discussion of appropriate and inappropriate hedging strategies surrounding Metallgesellschaft's crude oil futures hedges appears in the following articles from the *Journal of Applied Corporate Finance* 8, No. 1, Spring 1995

Franklin R. Edwards and Michael S. Canter, "The Collapse of Metallgesellschaft: Unhedgeable Risks, Poor Hedging Strategy, or Just Bad Luck?"

Antonio S. Mello and John E. Parsons, "Maturity Structure of a Hedge Matters: Lessons from the Metallgesellschaft Debacle"

Christopher L. Culp and Merton H. Miller, "Hedging in the Theory of Corporate Finance: A Reply to Our Critics"

along with

Christopher L. Culp and Merton H. Miller, "Metallgesellschaft and the Economics of Synthetic Storage," *Journal of Applied Corporate Finance* 7, No. 4, Winter 1994, pages 62–76.

CHAPTER

8

Currency Options and Options Markets

There are two times in a man's life when he should not speculate:
when he can't afford it and when he can.

Mark Twain

OVERVIEW

For both speculators and hedgers, forward and futures contracts share a common short-coming—what is gained on one side of the contract price is lost on the other. Speculators convinced that a currency will fall in value and hedgers insuring against a fall in a currency value sometimes want an instrument with a one-sided payoff. Currency options provide speculators and hedgers with such an instrument.

Many other contractual and noncontractual assets have optionlike characteristics. For example, Eurodollar floating rate notes (FRNs) are contractual agreements that are sometimes sold with a *cap* or a *floor* on the interest rate. The firm also encounters many different types of options through its investment and financing activities. Some are explicitly attached to corporate securities. These include call options on corporate bonds, which allow the firm to call (or repurchase) the bonds at a prearranged price. Another option allows investors in convertible bonds to convert the bonds into common stock at a prearranged conversion price. Other forms of options are more subtly hidden in the firm's investments. These include the option to expand, suspend, or abandon an investment project. Assets with optionlike qualities do not always come with red tags identifying the options.

Options are derivative securities in that their value is derived from the value of some underlying asset. For currency options, the underlying asset is the spot rate of exchange between two currencies. As spot exchange rates change, so do option values written on the spot exchange rate. In this chapter we rely on a few simple graphs to develop the intuition behind option valuation and its use in hedging financial price risks. The technical details of option valuation are presented in the appendix to this chapter.

8.1 What Is an Option?

An option refers to a choice. If your instructor offers you the option of taking the final examination a week late, it is your choice whether to exercise this option. Once the option is offered, it is the instructor's obligation to fulfill the contract. If one side of the agreement has the option, the other side has an obligation.

In an option contract, one side has the option and the other side has an obligation to perform.

The difference between an option and a forward (or futures) contract comes down to choice. Foreign currency options are like foreign currency forward contracts in that they allow two parties to exchange currencies according to a prearranged date, amount, and rate of exchange. In a forward contract, both sides have an obligation to perform. In an option contract, one side has the option of forcing the exchange while the other side has an obligation to perform if the option holder exercises the option. This is the fundamental difference between options and forward obligations.

Types of Foreign Currency Options

There are two types of options—calls and puts.

- A foreign currency **call option** is the right to *buy* the underlying currency at a specified price and on a specified date.
- A foreign currency **put option** is the right to *sell* the underlying currency at a specified price and on a specified date.

If you sell (or "write") a foreign currency call option, the buyer of the option has the right to buy one currency with another currency at the contract's **exercise price**, or **striking price**. The option writer has the obligation to sell the stated amount of foreign currency to the option holder. A foreign currency put option holder has the right to sell a specified amount of foreign currency at the exercise price. A foreign currency put option writer has the obligation to buy the foreign currency from the put option holder should the option be exercised.

Markets in Currency Options

Exchange-Traded Currency Options. Currency options were first traded on an organized exchange in 1983 at the Philadelphia Stock Exchange. Today, the two biggest options exchanges in the United States are conducted at

- The International Monetary Market (IMM) of the Chicago Mercantile Exchange (CME)
- The Philadelphia Stock Exchange (PSE)

These exchanges trade standardized contracts on major currencies and are the most liquid foreign currency options markets in the United States. Currency options exchanges operate at the European Options Exchange in Amsterdam, the Montreal Stock Exchange, and several other exchanges around the world. Figure 8.1 shows how to read PSE and CME options quotations in the *Wall Street Journal*.

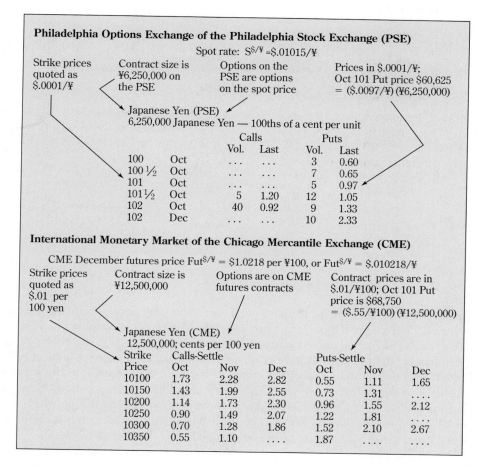

Philadelphia Options Exchange of the Philadelphia Stock Exchange (PSE)

Spot rate: $S^{\$/¥} = \$.01015/¥$

Strike prices quoted as $.0001/¥

Contract size is ¥6,250,000 on the PSE

Options on the PSE are options on the spot price

Prices in $.0001/¥; Oct 101 Put price $60,625 = ($.0097/¥) (¥6,250,000)

Japanese Yen (PSE)
6,250,000 Japanese Yen — 100ths of a cent per unit

		Calls		Puts	
		Vol.	Last	Vol.	Last
100	Oct	...	...	3	0.60
100 ½	Oct	...	...	7	0.65
101	Oct	...	...	5	0.97
101½	Oct	5	1.20	12	1.05
102	Oct	40	0.92	9	1.33
102	Dec	...	...	10	2.33

International Monetary Market of the Chicago Mercantile Exchange (CME)

CME December futures price $Fut^{\$/¥} = \$1.0218$ per ¥100, or $Fut^{\$/¥} = \$.010218/¥$

Strike prices quoted as $.01 per 100 yen

Contract size is ¥12,500,000

Options are on CME futures contracts

Contract prices are in $.01/¥100; Oct 101 Put price is $68,750 = ($.55/¥100) (¥12,500,000)

Japanese Yen (CME)
12,500,000; cents per 100 yen

Strike Price	Calls-Settle			Puts-Settle		
	Oct	Nov	Dec	Oct	Nov	Dec
10100	1.73	2.28	2.82	0.55	1.11	1.65
10150	1.43	1.99	2.55	0.73	1.31	....
10200	1.14	1.73	2.30	0.96	1.55	2.12
10250	0.90	1.49	2.07	1.22	1.81	....
10300	0.70	1.28	1.86	1.52	2.10	2.67
10350	0.55	1.10	....	1.87	....	....

FIGURE 8.1
Currency Option Prices Reported in the *Wall Street Journal.*

The underlying asset or *deliverable instrument* of the option is the currency being bought or sold.[1] PSE contracts are settled in spot foreign currency. The deliverable instrument of the CME futures option contract is the nearest CME currency futures contract that expires one week after the expiration of the option contract. As we shall see in a later section, options on spot and futures prices are identical in their ability to hedge foreign exchange risk because (1) spot and futures prices move in unison and (2) spot and futures price volatilities are nearly the same.

Several terms and conditions are either explicitly or implicitly identified in a foreign currency option quote, such as a "British pound Dec 145 call" option traded on the

Options on currency spot and on currency futures prices are identical in their ability to hedge currency risk.

---

1 This is the *currency of reference* of Chapter 3. Following Rule #2, it is most convenient to keep this currency in the denominator of a foreign exchange quote.

"British pound Dec 145 call" (European-style) on the PSE	
"British pound Dec 1450 put" on the CME	
Type of option	Call option on the Philadelphia Stock Exchange (PSE) Put option on the Chicago Mercantile Exchange (CME)
Underlying asset	British pound sterling on both exchanges
Expiration date	Third Wednesday in December on both exchanges
Exercise price	$1.45/£ spot rate on the PSE $1.45/£ futures price on the CME
Rule for exercise	European options are exercisable only at expiration American options are exercisable anytime until expiration
Pounds/contract	£31,250 on the PSE £62,500 on the CME
Other	Margin requirements, taxes, etc.

FIGURE 8.2
Currency Option Quotations

Philadelphia exchange or a "British pound Oct 1450 put" option from the Chicago Mercantile Exchange. These terms are listed in Figure 8.2. Consider the PSE call option. Each PSE pound currency option contract is worth £31,250. The holder of this option has the right to buy £31,250 British pounds sterling at an exercise price of $K^{\$/£} = \$1.45/£$ on the expiration date of the contract. We'll use $K^{d/f}$ to indicate the exercise price in domestic currency per foreign currency unit. PSE currency options expire on the Saturday before the third Wednesday of the month, so the last day on which they can be traded is the previous Friday. The third Wednesday of the month is the settlement date on which the exercise price is exchanged.

The Philadelphia exchange contract is a **European option**, exercisable only at expiration. A single contract on the PSE is worth £31,250, so the holder of this option will pay £31,250($1.45/£) = $45,312.50 and receive £31,250 upon exercise. Some currency options are **American options**, which are exercisable anytime until expiration. Holders of American options are usually better off if they leave the options unexercised rather than exercise early.[2] If they do not want to hold these options, then they should sell to someone who does want to hold them. Because the early exercise option in an American call option contract is seldom exercised, European and American foreign currency call options are nearly equivalent in a freely floating exchange rate system.

Over-the-Counter Currency Options. An active over-the-counter (OTC) market in currency options is operated by commercial and investment banks in the world's financial centers. Although exchange-traded currency options are standardized contracts,

European options are exercisable only at expiration.

Exchange-traded options are standardized contracts. Over-the-counter options are customized to the needs of individual customers.

---

2 The option to exercise an American put option early is valuable when the future value of exercising early and investing the exercise price at the risk-free rate of interest is greater than the expected value of the put option at expiration. Under conditions encountered in practice, the early exercise option is usually not valuable. We'll leave this topic to a specialized course in option pricing.

OTC currency options are customized to fit the needs of the banks' wholesale and retail customers. In this market, expiration dates and contract amounts are specified by the bank's customers, and prices and fees are then negotiated.

Retail clients include corporations and financial institutions exposed to currency risk. These clients typically value the right to exercise a currency option and do not want the obligation from writing option contracts. International commercial and investment banks making a market in currency options are typically the writers of currency options. This asymmetry between the buyers and sellers of option contracts is not seen in forward and futures markets in foreign exchange.

There is also an active wholesale market between major international banks. This market is used by banks to hedge, or reinsure, the currency risk exposures in their assets and liabilities. All of the bank's assets and liabilities are in general exposed to currency risk, but the most exchange-rate sensitive are the bank's portfolios of currency forwards, currency options, and currency swaps.

8.2 OPTION PAYOFF PROFILES

A Zero-Sum Game

Currency Call Options. The left-hand graph below plots the dollar value of a purchased (or long) pound sterling call option as a function of the spot rate of exchange between dollars and pounds at expiration. The time subscript T on the call option value and on the spot exchange rate are reminders that these values are at expiration.

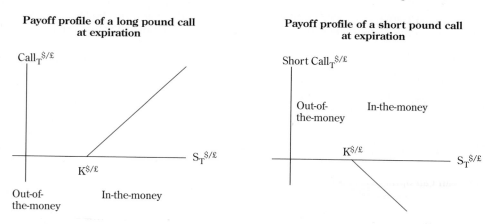

Payoff profile of a long pound call at expiration

Payoff profile of a short pound call at expiration

The deliverable instrument is the pound. A call option for which the spot rate of exchange is below the exercise price is called **out-of-the-money**. In this case, it is cheaper to buy pounds in the spot market than at the exercise price of $1.45/£. If the spot rate closes above the exercise price, the call option is **in-the-money**. Suppose the spot rate at expiration is $1.50/£ on a £125,000 CME option. The option holder has the right to call the option and buy pounds sterling at a price of $1.45/£ from the option writer. The option holder can then sell this £125,000 in the spot market at $1.50/£ for a five-cents-per-pound profit, or (£125,000) ($.05/£) = $6,250.

The right-hand graph plots the call option value from the perspective of the writer of the option. This contract is a zero-sum game; any value gained by the option holder is a loss to the option writer, so the payoff profile of the short call is the mirror image of the long call.

Currency Put Options. The graphs below plot the dollar value of a long and of a short pound sterling put option at expiration.

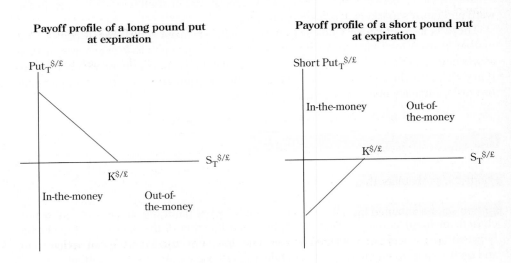

| Payoff profile of a long pound put at expiration | Payoff profile of a short pound put at expiration |

Put options

Put options are options to *sell* the underlying asset (in this case, the pound), so these options are in-the-money when the exercise price is greater than the underlying currency price. If the exercise price on a £125,000 CME currency put option is $1.45/£, then the option holder will exercise the option at expiration whenever the underlying spot exchange rate is below $1.45/£. For example, if the spot rate at expiration is $1.40/£, then the option holder can buy £125,000 in the spot market for $1.40/£ and simultaneously exercise the option to sell £125,000 to the option writer for $1.45/£, for a net profit of (£125,000)($.05/£) = $6,250. As shown in the right-hand graph, any gain in value to the option holder is a loss to the option writer.

Hedging with Options

Consider the financial manager of a U.S. firm anticipating a £31,250 cash inflow on December 13, which happens to be a Friday on which PSE currency options expire. Suppose the forward rate on this date is $1.50/£. If left unhedged, the dollar value of this payment will depend on the spot rate of exchange prevailing on the expiration date. The financial manager can eliminate foreign exchange risk by selling £31,250 pounds and buying dollars forward at the forward rate with an expiration date on Friday, December 13. The size and timing of the expected future cash flow is identical to that of the pound futures contract, so a futures market hedge will probably be even less expensive than a forward hedge. With either a forward or a futures contract, downside risks as well as upside gains are reduced or eliminated.

With an option hedge, the payoff profile is asymmetric. An option expiring out-of-the-money has no value regardless of how little or how far it is out-of-the-money. In contrast, an option expiring in-the-money has more value the more in-the-money it is. In this way, the financial manager hedging a £31,250 expected future cash inflow with an at-the-money long pound put option will be compensated for any fall in the value of the pound below the exercise price $K^{\$/£}$. If the spot exchange rate rises above $K^{\$/£}$, however, the corporation will capture the full benefit of the higher pound exchange rate on its underlying exposure without any loss from the put option contract. Because of the characteristic shape of an option's payoff profile, foreign currency options are used as a form of _disaster hedge_ against unfavorable changes in the value of a currency. When used to hedge currency risk, foreign currency options let the option holder participate in gains on one side of the exercise price while limiting losses on the other side of the exercise price.

DiSASter Hedge.

8.3 PROFIT AND LOSS ON FOREIGN CURRENCY OPTIONS

The option holder cannot get this option for free. The option writer (the seller of the option) will demand a premium for writing the option, and this premium will depend on both the probability that the option will expire in-the-money and the writer's expected losses should the option expire in-the-money. Some idea of the effect of this option premium can be obtained by superimposing the cost of the option on the payoff profile.

A premium is charged FOR options SerViCES

Profit and Loss on a Foreign Currency Call Option at Expiration

Consider a "DM Dec 6400 call" selling on the Chicago Mercantile Exchange at a price of $.0120/DM. This has an exercise price of $.64/DM and expires on the third Wednesday in December. The deliverable instrument of a CME currency option is the corresponding CME futures contract. Each deutsche mark option contract on the CME is worth DM125,000. At an exercise price of $.64/DM, this costs ($.64/DM) (DM125,000) = $80,000 to exercise. At a price of $.0120/DM, this option costs ($.0120/DM) (DM125,000) = $1,500 to purchase.

The value of this option at the expiration of the contract depends on the difference between the futures price and the exercise price. The profit or loss at expiration is shown in Figure 8.3 at several possible exchange rates. This graph combines the option value at expiration with the initial cost of the option. For example, if the actual futures price is $.652/DM at expiration, then selling DM125,000 in the futures market will yield $81,500, which will just cover the $80,000 exercise price and the original $1,500 purchase price of the option. The writer of this call option will see the mirror image of this profit diagram. This is a zero-sum game between the option writer and the option holder. The option holder gains (and the holder loses) whenever the futures price closes above $.652/DM. The option writer gains whenever the futures price closes below $.652/DM.

Profit and Loss on a Foreign Currency Put Option at Expiration

Profit and loss positions as a function of closing futures prices are shown in Figure 8.4 for a foreign currency put option. Consider a CME "DM Dec 6400 put" selling at

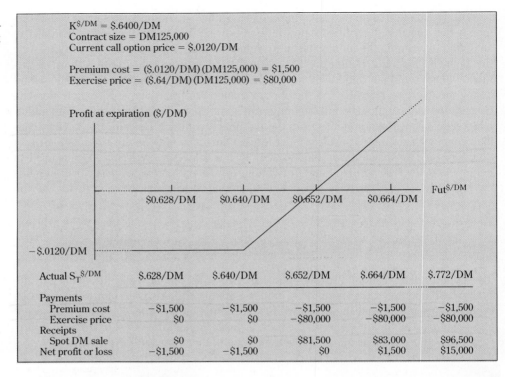

FIGURE 8.3
Profit/Loss on a
Call Option at Expiration

FIGURE 8.4
Profit/Loss on a
Put Option at Expiration

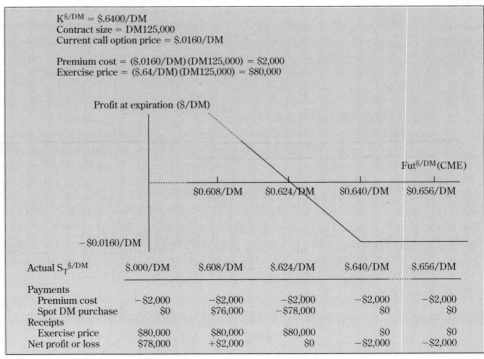

$.0160/DM. At this price, one DM125,000 contract costs ($.0160/DM)(DM125,000) = $2,000. The cost of exercise is again $80,000 at the $.6400/DM exercise price.

The payoff to the writer of this put option is the mirror image of the option holder's payoff. The option holder gains at expiration when the exchange rate closes at any price below $.6240/DM. The option writer gains at expiration whenever the exchange rate closes above $.6240/DM. Again, the gain to the option holder is equal to the option writer's loss—currency options are a zero-sum game.

8.4 AT-THE-MONEY OPTIONS

Suppose a currency option is **at-the-money**, which means that the exercise price is equal to the current exchange rate. If exchange rates are a random walk, then this is also equal to the expected rate of exchange on the expiration date. As in previous chapters, we can center the origin of these graphs on the exercise price in order to look at changes in option value as a function of changes in the underlying rate of exchange. This view is presented below for a long and a short call option on British pounds sterling.

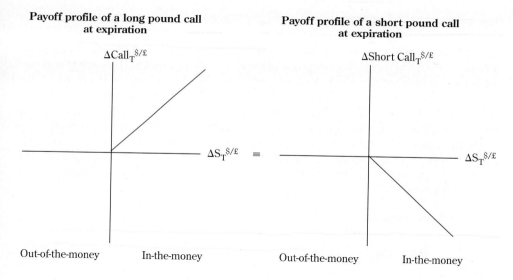

The deliverable instrument is the pound, so pounds are kept in the denominator, and all prices of this underlying currency are stated in terms of dollars. Stating change in option value as a function of change in the underlying rate of exchange transforms option payoff profiles into the same format as the one we have used for forward and futures contracts and for underlying risk exposures.

A Call by Any Other Name

Remember that whenever you are buying pounds at the spot rate $S^{\$/£}$ you are simultaneously selling dollars at the spot rate $S^{£/\$}$. For this reason, an option to buy pounds at a price of $K^{\$/£}$ is the same contract as an option to sell dollars at $K^{£/\$}$. That is, *a call option*

> A call option to buy one currency is equivalent to a put option to sell the other currency.

to buy pounds sterling is equivalent to a put option to sell dollars. The payoff profiles of a pound call and its counterpart, the dollar put, are shown below.

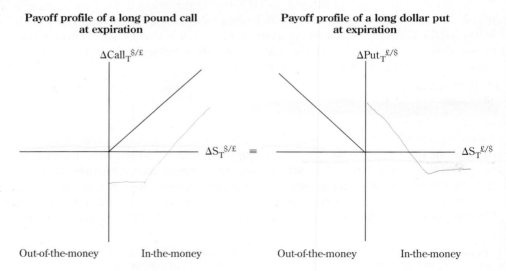

Payoff profile of a long pound call at expiration

$\Delta \text{Call}_T^{\$/\pounds}$

$\Delta S_T^{\$/\pounds}$

Out-of-the-money   In-the-money

Payoff profile of a long dollar put at expiration

$\Delta \text{Put}_T^{\pounds/\$}$

$\Delta S_T^{\pounds/\$}$

Out-of-the-money   In-the-money

Prices in these two figures are related through the relation $P^{\$/\pounds} = (P^{\pounds/\$})^{-1}$, which states that the dollar price of a pound is the reciprocal of the pound price of a dollar. This option is in-the-money when the spot rate $S^{\$/\pounds}$ is above the exercise price $K^{\$/\pounds}$ or, equivalently, when the spot rate $S^{\pounds/\$}$ is below the exercise price $K^{\pounds/\$}$. Since a call option to buy pounds with dollars is equivalent to a put option to sell dollars for pounds, these payoff profiles are equivalent. In this sense, a foreign currency option is simultaneously both a put and a call.

On the other side of the contract, the option writer has an obligation to sell pounds and buy dollars. From the option writer's perspective, an obligation to sell pounds for dollars is equivalent to an obligation to buy dollars with pounds. These identical payoffs are shown below.

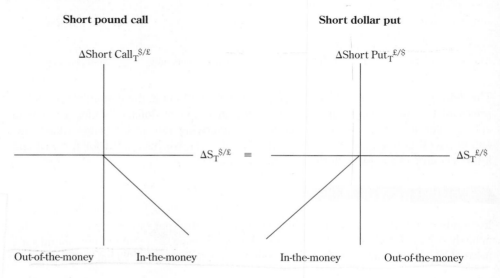

Short pound call

$\Delta \text{Short Call}_T^{\$/\pounds}$

$\Delta S_T^{\$/\pounds}$

Out-of-the-money   In-the-money

Short dollar put

$\Delta \text{Short Put}_T^{\pounds/\$}$

$\Delta S_T^{\pounds/\$}$

In-the-money   Out-of-the-money

Shakespeare said that "A rose by any other name would smell as sweet." This is true for currency options as well. An in-the-money pound call is just as sweet as an in-the-money dollar put.

A Forward by Any Other Name

Suppose we purchase an at-the-money call option on pounds sterling and simultaneously sell an at-the-money put option on pounds with the same expiration date. The payoff profiles of these positions at expiration can be combined into a single payoff profile.

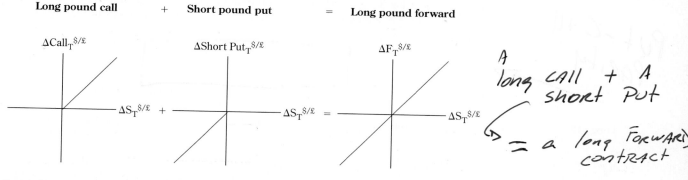

Long pound call   +   **Short pound put**   =   **Long pound forward**

Does this graph look familiar? It should. A combination of a long pound call and a short pound put forms a payoff profile that is identical to a long forward contract on pounds sterling. If you want to construct a "synthetic" foreign currency forward contract, just combine a long call with a short put on the same currency with exercise prices equal to the forward rate of exchange.

A forward position is equivalent to a long call and a short put on the underlying asset.

Suppose you have a pound cash inflow so that your dollar-per-pound risk profile is positively sloped as in the long pound forward contract. You want to hedge this risk profile with a negatively sloped payoff profile. You know that selling pounds forward will do the job. As an alternative, consider selling an at-the-money call option on dollars while simultaneously buying an at-the-money put option on pounds. The combined payoff profile is shown below.

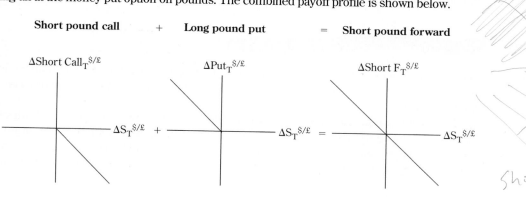

Short pound call   +   **Long pound put**   =   **Short pound forward**

If the value of the pound falls, the long pound put pays off by allowing you to sell pounds at the exercise price and offset the loss in the underlying position. If the value of the pound rises, gains in the underlying position offset losses on the short pound call. In either case, changes in the value of the underlying position are exactly offset by changes in the values of the option contracts.

A Forward by Any Other Name: The Case of Put-Call Parity

....

Put-call parity relates call and put values to the value of a forward contract.

....

The discussion in the previous section showed that the risk profile of a forward contract arising from changes in the value of an exchange rate is exactly replicated in the payoff profile of a combination of a long at-the-money call and a short at-the-money put. To talk about the *value* (rather than changes in the value) of a long call and a short put, we need to adjust for the exercise price. The general case is called "put-call parity," and it relates the value of a long call, a short put, the exercise price, and the forward price.[3] At expiration, put-call parity states that

$$\text{Call}_T^{d/f} - \text{Put}_T^{d/f} + K^{d/f} = F_T^{d/f} \tag{8.1}$$

The put-call relation at expiration of the option is shown graphically below.

The rightmost graph is a 45-degree line from the origin because the forward price converges to the spot price at expiration. Note that an option holder pays the exercise price on a call option (an option to buy) and receives the exercise price on a put option (an option to sell).

8.5 COMBINATIONS OF OPTIONS

When you understand how to draw these option payoff profiles at expiration, it is easy to combine two or more option positions. Simply snap together the appropriate building blocks.

Here's an example. In early 1995, a rogue trader named Nick Leeson drove Barings Bank into bankruptcy through unauthorized speculation in Nikkei stock index futures on the Singapore and Osaka stock exchanges. Leeson began Barings' descent toward bankruptcy by selling option *straddles* on the Nikkei index at a time when volatility on

---

3 The general case of put-call parity prior to expiration is presented in Appendix 8-A.

the Nikkei index was low. A long option straddle is a combination of a long call and a long put on the same underlying asset and with the same exercise price. Leeson took the short position by simultaneously selling calls and puts on the Nikkei index. The pay-off profiles on a long straddle and on a short straddle on the Nikkei index look like this:

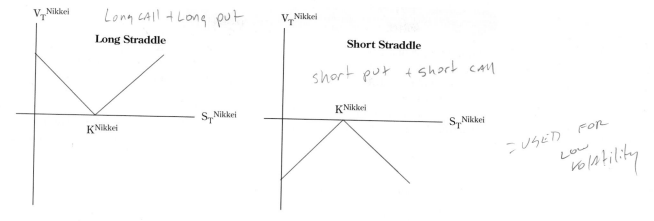

Including the proceeds from the sale of the call and the put, the profit/loss diagram on the short straddle position at expiration looks like this:

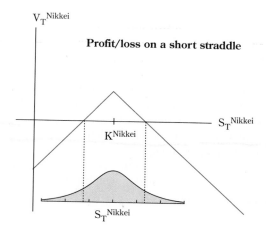

The probability distribution of the Nikkei index at expiration appears below the profit/loss diagram.

Essentially, Leeson placed a bet on the volatility of the Nikkei index over the life of the option. In option parlance, Leeson "sold volatility." As long as the Nikkei index did not vary too much, Leeson would have won. Leeson would have had a winning position if the end-of-period Nikkei index had fallen between the two points at which the profit/loss pyramid crosses the x-axis. Leeson would have lost if the Nikkei index had fallen too low or had risen too high. Volatility on the Nikkei index was low at the time Leeson sold this position, so the proceeds from the sale were small (and Leeson's gamble was large) relative to what would have been received on this position in a high volatility market. As it turned out, the Nikkei index fell below the profitable range. Leeson attempted to recoup his losses by buying futures on the Nikkei index in the hopes of a recovery that, to Barings' regret, never occurred.

8.6 DETERMINANTS OF OPTION VALUES

Combining graphs in this way provides a simple yet powerful tool for understanding the risks and potential payoffs of even the most arcane option positions. Option payoff profiles can make even the most complex option positions seem transparent. Yet these graphs only give option values at expiration. This section presents the determinants of American option values prior to expiration.

Currency option values are a function of the six variables shown below. The impact on the price of an American currency call or put option when each of the determinants is increased (while holding the other determinants constant) is as follows.[4]

Option value determinant		Call$^{d/f}$	Put$^{d/f}$
1. Underlying exchange rate	$S^{d/f}$ or $Fut^{d/f}$	+	−
2. Exercise price	$K^{d/f}$	−	+
3. Riskless rate of interest in currency d	i^d	+	−
4. Riskless rate of interest in currency f	i^f	−	+
5. Time to expiration	T	+	+
6. Volatility in the underlying exchange rate	σ	+	+

With the exception of volatility, each of these determinants is readily observable for currency options quoted on major exchanges. The exercise price and expiration date are stated in the option contract. The underlying (spot or futures) exchange rate and the foreign and domestic interest rates are quoted in the financial press. For publicly traded options, the option value itself is also quoted in the newspaper. The only item that is not directly observable is the volatility of the underlying exchange rate. Volatility turns out to be an extremely important input into option valuation.

The rest of this section discusses two sources of value in options: the *intrinsic value* if exercised immediately and the *time value,* which reflects the value of waiting until expiration before exercising the option.

With the exception of volatility, the determinants of option values are observable in the financial press.

• voLAtiLity

Option Value at Expiration and the Intrinsic Value of an Option

Intrinsic vALue

The intrinsic value of an option is the value of the option if it is exercised today.

The **intrinsic value** of an option is the value of the option if it is exercised today. The intrinsic value of a currency option depends only on the difference between the underlying exchange rate and the exercise price and on whether the option is a call or a put. Consider the currency call and put options presented below.

---

4 These relations also hold for European options with one exception; European put options may decrease in value at more distant expiration dates depending on the values of the other option parameters.

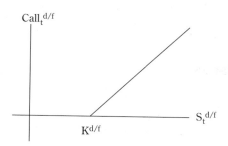

Call option value when exercised

$\text{Call}_t^{d/f}$

$S_t^{d/f}$

$K^{d/f}$

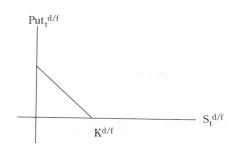

Put option value when exercised

$\text{Put}_t^{d/f}$

$S_t^{d/f}$

$K^{d/f}$

If a call or a put option is out-of-the-money, its intrinsic value is zero. If an option is in-the-money, its intrinsic value depends on the difference between the exercise price and the value of the underlying asset. Call and put option values at exercise on the spot exchange rate are determined by the following:

option values @ exercise

- Call option value when exercised = Max $[(S_t^{d/f} - K^{d/f}), 0]$.
- Put option value when exercised = Max $[(K^{d/f} - S_t^{d/f}), 0]$.

These are the intrinsic values of the call and put options, respectively. Every graph that has appeared up to this point in the chapter has been a graph of intrinsic value.

As the underlying asset value moves away from the exercise price, option values follow a one-way path. Currency call option holders gain when the underlying exchange rate rises above the exercise price, but cannot lose more than the option premium as the underlying exchange rate falls below the exercise price. Put option holders gain as the underlying exchange rate falls below the exercise price, but lose at most the option premium as the exchange rate rises. It is this asymmetry that gives options their unique function as a disaster hedge.

Option Valuation Prior to Expiration and the Time Value of an Option

Time Value

The **time value** of an option is the difference between the market value of an option and its intrinsic value if exercised immediately. In addition to depending on the exchange rate and the exercise price, the time value of an option also depends on (1) the volatility of the underlying exchange rate and (2) the time to expiration of the option.[5] Variability in the underlying (spot or futures) exchange rate at expiration determines how far in-the-money or out-of-the-money a currency option is likely to expire. Time to expiration has an effect that is similar to volatility: for a given exchange rate volatility, having more time until expiration results in more variable exchange rates at expiration. The general rules for American options are as follows.

Time value is the difference between market value and intrinsic value.

- As exchange rate volatility increases, the values of both American call and put options increase.
- As the time to expiration increases, the values of both American call and put options increase.

General Rules For American Options

---

5 Changes in foreign and domestic interest rates also affect option values. See Appendix 8-A.

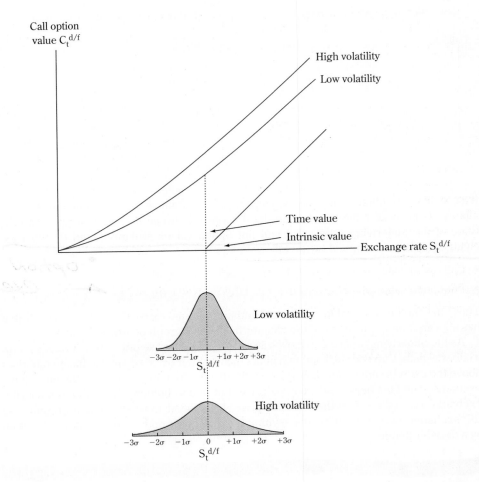

FIGURE 8.5
Option Value = Intrinsic
Value + Time Value

That is, American option values are greater if volatility in the underlying asset (the exchange rate for currency options) increases or if the time to expiration is longer. These two influences on the time value of a call option are illustrated in Figure 8.5.

Consider the payoffs to a dollar call and a dollar put option, each with an exercise price of $K^{¥/\$} = ¥100/\$$. Suppose the spot rate at expiration will be either ¥90.484/\$ or ¥110.517/\$.[6] Payoffs to these options are as follows:

	Closing spot exchange rate $S_T^{¥/\$}$	
	¥90.484/\$	¥110.517/\$
Value of a call	¥0/\$	¥10.517/\$
Value of a put	¥9.516/\$	¥0/\$

---

6 These spot prices correspond to ±10 percent *in continuously compounded returns* from the current spot rate of $S^{¥/\$} = ¥100/\$$: $(¥100/\$)e^{-.10} = ¥90.484/\$$ and $(¥100/\$)e^{+.10} = ¥110.517/\$$. Continuously compounded returns are discussed in Appendix 4-A. A brief review appears in the next section.

Suppose the volatility of the spot rate increases such that the spot rate at expiration can be as low as ¥81.873/$ or as high as ¥122.140/$.[7] The values of a dollar call and a dollar put at these spot rates and with an exercise price of ¥100/$ are as follows:

	Closing spot exchange rate $S_T^{¥/\$}$	
	¥81.873/$	¥122.140/$
Yen value of a dollar call	¥0/$	¥22.140/$
Yen value of a dollar put	¥18.127/$	¥0/$

Because option holders continue to gain on one side of the exercise price but do not suffer continued losses on the other side of the exercise price, options become more valuable as the end-of-period exchange rate distribution becomes more dispersed. For this reason, prior to expiration more good things than bad can happen to an option value. This result is easy to see for an at-the-money call option, but the general result also holds for puts and calls that are not at-the-money.

Let's do this same exercise graphically. Consider the two deep-out-of-the-money call options shown below. At the exercise of a currency option, only that portion of the distribution of the underlying exchange rate that expires in-the-money has value. The deep-out-of-the-money call option in the left graph has little value because there is little likelihood of the spot rate climbing above the exercise price. As the variability of end-of-period exchange rates increases, there is an increasing probability that the spot rate will close above the exercise price. This is shown in the right graph.

Spot exchange rate volatility and out-of-the-money call option value

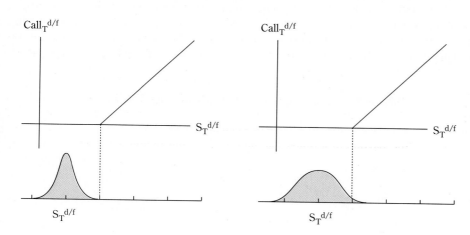

The next two graphs depict an at-the-money call option. This call option also gains from increases in volatility. An at-the-money call option gains if the spot rate closes

---

7 These closing spot rates correspond to ±20 percent *in continuously compounded returns:*
(¥100/$)e$^{-.20}$ = ¥81.873/$ and (¥100/$)e$^{+.20}$ = ¥122.140/$.

farther above the exercise price but does not lose if the spot rate closes farther below
the exercise price. As the variability of end-of-period exchange rates increases (the right
graph), the distribution falls farther in-the-money (as well as farther out-of-the-money),
and the option is more valuable.

Spot exchange rate volatility and at-the-money call option value

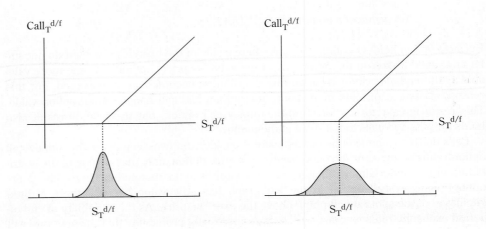

Options gain in value from
variability in the distribution
of end-of-period spot rates.

The same general principle holds for in-the-money call options, although the reasons
are not as obvious as for out-of-the-money and at-the-money call options. One way to
look at the two in-the-money call options below is to note that the portion of the distribution that falls out-of-the-money has no value no matter how far out-of-the-money the spot
rate falls. On the other hand, as the spot rate increases the call option continues to
increase in value.

Spot exchange rate volatility and in-the-money call option value

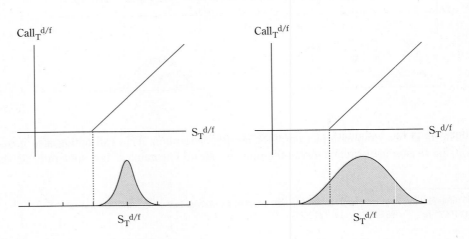

We won't go through these graphs for put options, but the same rule holds true—put options gain more in value from exchange rate decreases than they lose in value from increases of the same magnitude. The general rule is that currency options gain from increasing variability in the distribution of end-of-period exchange rates regardless of whether the option starts out-of-the-money, near-the-money, or in-the-money. In turn, variability in the distribution of end-of-period exchange rates depends on exchange rate volatility and on the time to expiration of the option.

8.7 EXCHANGE RATE VOLATILITY REVISITED (ADVANCED)

The empirical behavior of exchange rates is best performed in continuously compounded returns, so let's start this section with a brief review. If you find the algebra to be intimidating, try to follow the intuition behind the algebra. If necessary, skip the numeric examples altogether. You don't really need the algebra of continuous compounding to follow the discussion of exchange rate volatility.

A Refresher on Continuously Compounded Returns

Continuously compounded returns are conventionally assumed to be independently and identically distributed (iid) as normal with mean μ and variance σ^2, or $N(\mu, \sigma^2)$. The parameter σ^2 is the "instantaneous" variance and is usually assumed to be a constant. Keep in mind that these are assumptions of convenience rather than an entirely accurate characterization of returns. The reason for assuming normality is that the normal distribution has convenient statistical properties. Whether or not returns are independently and identically distributed as normal is an empirical question that we will look at shortly. For now, let's develop the statistical properties of iid normal distributions.

The term "identically" in the phrase "independently and identically distributed" implies that returns are drawn from the same distribution at every instant of time. Returns are assumed to be normally distributed, so they are drawn from the same normal distribution at every instant. The term "independently" means that the return realized at each instant of time does not depend on previous returns. Together, the assumptions of independent and identically distributed returns imply that the return series is **stationary**.[8] In a stationary series, the process generating returns is identical at every instant of time. A snapshot of the return distribution at one instant yields the same snapshot as at every other instant.

In a stationary time series, the process generating returns is identical at every instant of time.

In an iid normal time series, return variance increases linearly with time. That is, the end-of-period variance after T periods is T times the instantaneous variance:

$$\sigma_T^2 = T \, \sigma^2 \qquad (8.2)$$

where σ^2 is the instantaneous variance measured over a single period and σ_T^2 is the volatility measured over T periods. This implies $\sigma_T = (\sqrt{T}) \sigma$, so the standard deviation

---

8 In fact, this is an assumption of *strong-form* stationarity. There are less stringent (weak-form) stationarity assumptions. In this text we'll stick to the strong-form variety.

2 ways to measure volatility

increases with the square root of time. In the section on option value determinants, an increase in either volatility or in time to expiration serves to increase option values. Equation (8.2) identifies the manner in which volatility σ and time to expiration T interact to increase the variability of the end-of-period return distribution σ_T.

Volatility can be estimated in several ways. The two most prominent methods are called historical volatility and implied volatility. Historical volatility is a backward-looking measure that captures observed variations over the recent past in the hope that recent history will repeat itself. Implied volatility is a forward-looking measure that uses current option prices to estimate volatility in the underlying asset. Because it is based on current prices, implied volatility reflects the expectations of participants in the options markets. We'll look at historical and implied volatility next and some examples of how they are used.

implied - vs - Historical

Historical Volatility

Historical volatility is the actual volatility realized over some historical period.

Historical volatility is the actual volatility realized over some historical period. Historical volatility can be estimated by calculating the observed variance of continuously compounded returns r_t sampled over T periods:

$$\sigma^2 = (1/\text{T}) \, \Sigma_t \, (r_t - \mu)^2 \qquad (8.3)$$

As an example, suppose the standard deviation of continuously compounded changes in the yen/dollar spot rate is estimated from equation (8.3) to be $\sigma = 0.00645 = 0.645\%$ per trading day over the 252 trading (or business) days in a particular calendar year. Assuming zero volatility on nontrading days, such as weekends and holidays, the annual standard deviation of continuously compounded changes in the exchange rate is then $\sigma = (\sqrt{\text{T}}) \sigma_T = (\sqrt{252}) (0.00645) = 0.1024 = 10.24\%$ per year. If exchange rates are normally distributed, plus or minus one standard deviation results in plus or minus 10.24 percent per year in normally distributed continuously compounded returns.

Suppose the spot rate of exchange is currently $S^{¥/\$} = ¥130/\$$. Plus two standard deviations of 10.24 percent in continuously compounded returns is simply $(2)(0.1024) = 0.2048$, or 20.48 percent in continuously compounded returns. As a periodic rate of change over t periods, the rate of change is $R = e^{2\sigma\sqrt{t}} - 1 = e^{+0.2048} - 1 = 22.73\%$. Two standard deviations above the ¥130/\$ spot rate is thus $(¥130/\$)(1.2273) = ¥159.55/\$$. In periodic returns, this is a 22.73 percent increase in the spot rate. Similarly, two standard deviations below the spot rate is $(1+R)S^{¥/\$} = e^{2(-0.1024)}(¥130/\$) = (0.8148)(¥130/\$) = ¥105.93/\$$. This is equivalent to a $(1 - 0.8148) = 18.52\%$ decrease in the spot rate. About 95 percent of the normal distribution falls within two standard deviations of the mean, so there is a 95 percent chance that the actual spot rate of exchange in one year will fall between ¥105.93/\$ and ¥159.55/\$.

As a check, let's back out the continuously compounded changes in exchange rates that are implied by a change in the spot from ¥130/\$ to either ¥105.93/\$ or ¥159.55/\$. If the spot rate moves from ¥130/\$ to ¥159.55/\$, the percentage change is $(¥159.55/\$)/(¥130/\$) - 1 = 0.2273 = 22.73\%$. In continuously compounded returns, this is (sure enough) equal to $\ln(1.2273) = 0.2048$, or 20.48 percent. Similarly, ln((¥105.93/$)/(¥130/$)) = −0.2048, or −20.48 percent in continuously compounded returns.

Here's another useful fact about exchange rate volatility: Exchange rate volatility measured in continuously compounded returns does not depend on the currency of reference. To verify this claim, let's perform the same calculations using $/¥ quotes. The yen/dollar exchange rates convert into dollar/yen spot rates according to $S^{\$/¥} = 1/S^{¥/\$}$:

Exchange rate volatility measured in continuously compounded returns does not depend on the currency of reference.

$$1/(¥159.55/\$) = \$0.0062676/¥$$
$$1/(¥130.00/\$) = \$0.0076923/¥$$
$$1/(¥105.93/\$) = \$0.0094402/¥$$

A 22.73 percent dollar appreciation from ¥130/$ to ¥159.55/$ is equivalent to a 19.52 percent yen depreciation from $0.0076923/¥ to $0.0062676/¥. A 19.52 percent dollar depreciation from ¥130.00/$ to ¥105.93/$ is the same as a 22.73 percent yen appreciation from $0.0076923/¥ to $0.0094402/¥. Alternatively,

$$\ln[(\$0.0062676/¥)/(\$0.0076923/¥)] = \ln(0.8148) = -0.2048$$

and

$$\ln[(\$0.0094402/¥)/(\$0.0076923/¥)] = \ln(1.2273) = 0.2048$$

Sure enough, these represent 20.48 percent changes in continuously compounded returns.

Implied Volatility

There are six determinants of a currency option value: (1) the spot rate of exchange $S^{d/f}$, (2) the exercise price $K^{d/f}$, (3) the risk-free rate i^d in the domestic currency, (4) the risk-free rate i^f in the foreign currency, (5) time to expiration T, and (6) the volatility of the underlying asset σ. For publicly traded options, five of the six determinants, as well as the option value itself, can be found in the local press.[9] The only determinant that is not directly observable is the volatility of the underlying asset. Suppose you know the equation specifying how option values are related to these six variables. Then, given five of the six inputs and the option price, the value of the single unknown determinant (that is, exchange rate volatility) can be found by trial-and-error.[10] Volatility estimated in this way is called **implied volatility**, because it is implied by the option price and the other option value determinants.

Six determinants of implied volatility

Implied volatility is the volatility that is implied by the option price.

---

9 Some time ago a student of mine was reading the sports pages in class. When asked why he wasn't reading the financial section, he replied, "If you had as much money riding on sporting events as I do, you'd consider the sports pages to be your financial pages too."

10 Closed-form solutions that provide approximations to implied volatility have been found by a number of authors, including M.A.J. Bharadia, N. Christofides, and G.R. Salkin, "A Quadratic Method for the Calculation of Implied Volatility Using the Garman-Kohlhagen Model," *Financial Analysts Journal* 52, March/April 1996, pages 61–66.

As an example, consider a "December DM 73 call" trading on the Philadelphia exchange. Suppose the following values are known:

Value of call option	$Call^{\$/DM}$	=	$.0102/DM
Price of underlying asset	$S^{\$/DM}$	=	$.7020/DM
Exercise price	$K^{\$/DM}$	=	$.7300/DM
Domestic riskless rate	i^d	=	4%
Foreign riskless rate	i^f	=	0%
Time to expiration	T	=	$2\frac{1}{2}$ months
Volatility of the spot rate	σ	=	?

A currency option pricing model is given in Appendix 8-A. Solving it for the standard deviation of the spot exchange rate $S^{\$/DM}$ yields an implied volatility of 0.148, or 14.8 percent per year. This is the only standard deviation that (when combined with the five other inputs) results in an option value of $.0102/DM.

A Cautionary Note on Implied Volatilities

Let's look at another quote, a "December DM 63 call" on the Philadelphia exchange. Suppose the following prices can be found in the *Wall Street Journal:*

Value of call option	$Call^{\$/DM}$	=	$.0710/DM
Price of underlying asset	$S^{\$/DM}$	=	$.7020/DM
Exercise price	$K^{\$/DM}$	=	$.6300/DM
Domestic riskless rate	i^d	=	4%
Foreign riskless rate	i^f	=	0%
Time to expiration	T	=	$2\frac{1}{2}$ months
Volatility of the spot rate	σ	=	?

Both options are based on the December spot rate, so the implied volatility of this option should be the same as that of the previous option. However, trying to find an implied volatility based on these prices is futile. There is no value for volatility that will yield a call price of $.0710/DM. What's wrong?

The *Wall Street Journal* reports prices from the last trade. The call option's time of last trade may or may not correspond to the time of last trade of the exchange rate underlying the option. Suppose the last time this option traded on the Philadelphia exchange was at noon, at which time the spot rate was $.6900/DM. The implied volatility at that instant is determined from the following:

Value of call option	Call$^{\$/DM}$	=	$.0710/DM
Price of underlying asset	S$^{\$/DM}$	=	$.6900/DM
Exercise price	K$^{\$/DM}$	=	$.6300/DM
Domestic riskless rate	i^d	=	4%
Foreign riskless rate	i^f	=	0%
Time to expiration	T	=	$2\frac{1}{2}$ months
Volatility of the spot rate	σ	=	?

The implied volatility in this example is 22.4 percent per year. There was no solution to the previous example because the end-of-day exchange rate was used to price an option that last traded at noon. <u>This example suggests a general result: Beware of prices in thinly traded markets</u>. In this example, we were comparing apples and oranges. Or perhaps more precisely, we were comparing the size of apples at two different times of the growing season.

Beware of prices in thinly traded markets.

Volatility and Probability of Exercise

Let's go back to the example of a December DM 73 call on the PSE.

Value of call option	Call$^{\$/DM}$	=	$.0102/DM
Price of underlying asset	S$^{\$/DM}$	=	$.7020/DM
Exercise price	K$^{\$/DM}$	=	$.7300/DM
Domestic riskless rate	i^d	=	4%
Foreign riskless rate	i^f	=	0%
Time to expiration	T	=	$2\frac{1}{2}$ months
Volatility of the spot rate	σ	=	14.87 per year

What is the probability of this option being in-the-money on the expiration date in December? The spot rate would have to go from $S_0^{\$/DM}$ = $.7020/DM to $S_T^{\$/DM}$ = $.73/DM for a continuously compounded change of $\ln(1+R)$ = $\ln[(\$.73/DM)/(\$.7020/DM)]$ = 0.039, or 3.9 percent. The standard deviation over 2.5 months is σ_T = $(\sqrt{T})\,\sigma$ = $(2.5/12)^{1/2}(.148)$ = .0676, or 6.76 percent per $2\frac{1}{2}$ months. The change in the underlying exchange rate must be $(0.039)/0.067$ = 0.58, or 58 percent of one standard deviation above the current spot rate. The probability mass of the normal distribution above $.58\sigma$ is about 0.40. Thus, there is about a 40 percent chance of this option expiring in-the-money.

EXAMPLE

Time-Varying Volatility

Recall that empirical investigations of exchange rate behavior reject the simple random walk model. Instead, researchers have found that exchange rates can be described as having **generalized autoregressive conditional heteroskedasticity (GARCH)**:[11]

- At each point in time instantaneous returns are normally distributed.
- The instantaneous variance at each point in time depends on whether exchange rate changes in the recent past have been large or small.

The fact that foreign exchange volatility is not a constant means that option pricing models that assume stationary price changes (such as the binomial and the Black-Scholes models found in Appendix 8-A) are misspecified for currency options. An implied volatility is actually a time-weighted average of the instantaneous volatilities prevailing over the life of the option. For this reason, implied volatilities obtained from traded option values may not represent the instantaneous volatility at any point in time during the life of the option. As an example, during turbulent periods in the foreign exchange markets implied volatilities are sometimes as large as 30 percent per year. A 30 percent implied volatility on a three-month option might represent a 40 percent volatility over the first month and a 10 percent volatility over the following two months. Because of time-varying volatility, foreign exchange volatilities estimated from option pricing models are at best imprecise estimates of current and expected future exchange rate volatility.

> *Foreign exchange volatility varies over time.*

8.8 SUMMARY

An option represents a choice. Holders of options can exercise those options at their discretion. Sellers (or writers) of options have an obligation to perform at the option of the option holders.

Currency options are useful for hedging and for speculation because, in contrast to forward and futures contracts, their payoffs are asymmetric. This asymmetry allows currency options to serve as a disaster hedge against unfavorable changes in the value of a currency or to bet on the direction or volatility of foreign exchange rates.

Options can be categorized along several dimensions. The most important is whether the option is a call or a put.

- A call option is the right to *buy* the underlying asset.
- A put option is the right to *sell* the underlying asset.

With foreign exchange, whenever you buy one currency you simultaneously sell another. For this reason, a call option on one currency is simultaneously a put option on another currency.

Option values can be decomposed as follows:

$$\text{Option value} = \text{Intrinsic value} + \text{Time value}$$

---

11 A more complete discussion of the GARCH model appears in Chapter 5.

The intrinsic value of a currency option is its value if it is exercised immediately. Intrinsic value depends on the difference between the underlying exchange rate and the exercise price. The time value of a currency option comes from the possibility that currency values will move further in-the-money and the intrinsic value of the option will increase prior to expiration of the option.

There are six determinants of a currency option value: (1) the value of the underlying exchange rate, (2) the exercise price of the option, (3) the riskless rate in the domestic currency, (4) the riskless rate in the foreign currency, (5) the time to expiration on the option, and (6) the volatility of the underlying exchange rate. With the exception of volatility, each of these determinants is readily observable for currency options quoted on major exchanges. The most important determinant—and the only one that cannot be found in the financial section of a newspaper—is the volatility of the underlying exchange rate.

There are two ways to estimate the volatility of exchange rates. Historical volatility is calculated from the time series of exchange rate changes. Implied volatility is the exchange rate volatility that is implied by the value of an option given the other determinants of option value.

KEY TERMS

American option

At-the-money option

Call option

European option

Exercise price

Generalized autoregressive conditional heteroskedasticity (GARCH)

Historical volatility

Implied volatility

In-the-money option

Intrinsic value

Out-of-the-money option

Put option

Stationarity

Striking price

Time value

CONCEPTUAL QUESTIONS

8.1 What is the difference between a call option and a put option?

8.2 What are the differences between exchange-traded and over-the-counter currency options?

8.3 In what sense is a currency call option also a currency put option?

8.4 In what sense is a currency forward contract a combination of a put and a call?

8.5 What are the six determinants of a currency option value?

8.6 What determines the intrinsic value of an option? What determines time value of an option?

8.7 In what ways can you estimate currency volatility?

PROBLEMS

8.1 Suppose the yen value of a dollar is ¥100/$ and that it has an equal probability of moving to either ¥90.484/$ or ¥110.517/$ in one period. To what continuously compounded rates of return do these changes correspond?

8.2 Suppose the spot rate is ¥105/$ and there is an equal chance that it will fall to ¥70.38/$ or rise to ¥156.64/$. To what continuously compounded rates of return do these changes correspond?

8.3 Using one year (252 trading days) of historical data, you have estimated a daily standard deviation of .00742 = 0.742% for the $S^{\$/DM}$ exchange rate.

a. What is the annual standard deviation of the $S^{\$/DM}$ exchange rate if exchange rate changes are independently and identically distributed as normal?

b. Suppose the current spot rate of exchange is DM1.40/\$. Find the exchange rates that are plus or minus two standard deviations from this rate after one year based on the annual volatility in part a.

c. Verify that the volatility of the \$/DM rate is equal to the volatility of the DM/\$ rate by (1) translating your $\pm 2\sigma$ and $S^{\$/DM}$ rates into DM/\$ rates and (2) finding the annual standard deviation implied by these rates from $r = \ln(S^{DM/\$}/S^{DM/\$})$.

d. Verify that volatility is the same whether in direct or indirect quotes by repeating part b in direct terms and comparing your answers (i.e., $\pm 2\sigma$) to those in b.

8.4 Section 8.6 used graphs to show how volatility affects the time value of out-of-the-money, at-the-money, and in-the-money call options. Use similar graphs to show how volatility affects the time value of out-of-the-money, at-the-money, and in-the-money put options.

8.5 Construct an option position (that is, some combination of calls and/or puts) with the same risk profile ($\Delta Call^{\$/DM}$ versus $\Delta S^{\$/DM}$) as a forward contract to buy DM at a forward price of $F_1^{\$/DM} = \$0.75/DM$. Use both words and graphs and be sure to

a. Label the axes

b. Identify the asset underlying the option(s)

c. Indicate whether each option is a put or a call

d. Indicate whether you are buying or selling the option, and

e. Indicate the option(s) exercise price

8.6 Suppose you believe that the market has underestimated the volatility of the yen/dollar exchange rate. You are not sure whether the dollar will rise or fall in value, only that it will probably rise or fall by a larger amount than expected by other market participants. Consider forming a "purchased straddle" by combining a purchased dollar call and a purchased dollar put with the same exercise price $K^{\yen/\$}$ and expiration date. Diagram the payoff profile of this position at expiration.

8.7 You head the currency trading desk at Bearings Bank in London. As the middleman in a deal between the U.K. and Danish governments, you have just paid £1,000,000 to the U.K. government and have been promised DKr8,4386,000 from the Danish government in three months. All else constant, you wouldn't mind leaving this short krone position open. However, elections next month in Denmark may close the possibility of Denmark joining the European Union. If this happens, you expect the krone to drop on world markets. As a hedge, you are considering purchasing a krone put option with an exercise price of DKr8.4500/£ that sells for DKr0.1464/£.

a. Fill in the put option values at expiration in the following table.

Spot rate at expiration (DKr/£):	8.00	8.40	8.42	8.44	8.46	8.48
Put value at expiration (DKr/£):						

b. Draw the payoff profile for this short krone put option at expiration. Label your axes and plot each of the points from part a.

c. Draw a profit/loss graph for this short put at expiration. Refer to the long put in Figure 8.4 for reference.

The Black-Scholes Option Pricing Model (see Appendix 8-A) was first introduced in
   Fischer Black and Myron Scholes, "The Pricing of Options and Corporate Liabilities," *Journal of Political Economy* 81, May–June 1973, pages 637–659.

Fischer Black modified the original model to value options on futures in
   Fischer Black, "The Pricing of Commodity Options," *Journal of Financial Economics* 3, No. 1/2, 1976, pages 167–179.

The option pricing model was modified for currency options in
   Nahum Biger and John Hull, "The Valuation of Currency Options," *Financial Management* 12, Spring 1983, pages 24–28.

   Mark Garman and Steve W. Kohlhagen, "Foreign Currency Option Values," *Journal of International Money and Finance* 2, No. 3, 1983, pages 231–237.

   Jimmy E. Hilliard, Jeff Madura, and Alan L. Tucker, "Currency Options Pricing with Stochastic Domestic and Foreign Interest Rates," *Journal of Financial and Quantitative Analysis* 26, No. 2, June 1991, pages 139–151.

A good review of the performance of foreign currency option pricing models appears in
   James Bodurtha and Georges Courtadon, "Efficiency Tests of the Foreign Currency Options Market," *Journal of Finance* 41, March 1986, pages 151–161.

The practical aspects of currency option use are discussed in
   Fischer Black, "How to Use the Holes in Black-Scholes," *Journal of Applied Corporate Finance* 1, No. 4, 1989, pages 67–73.

   Ian H. Giddy, "Uses and Abuses of Currency Options," *Journal of Applied Corporate Finance* 8, No. 3, Fall 1995, pages 49–57.

Discussions of option values under stochastic volatility appear in
   John C. Hull and Alan White, "The Pricing of Options on Assets with Stochastic Volatilities," *Journal of Finance* 42, No. 2, 1987, pages 281–300.

   James B. Wiggins, "Option Values Under Stochastic Volatility: Theory and Empirical Estimates," *Journal of Financial Economics* 19, No. 2, 1987, pages 351–372.

Currency Option Valuation

Option valuation involves the mathematics of stochastic processes. The term **stochastic** means "random," and the study of stochastic processes is essentially a study of randomness. Study of stochastic processes has revolutionized asset valuation since its introduction in the early 1970s. Although the mathematics of stochastic processes can be intimidating, the good news is that it doesn't take a rocket scientist to use options to hedge financial price risks, such as currency risk, using the option payoff profiles in the body of this chapter.

The option pricing models in this appendix will help those with an interest in options to develop a deeper understanding of how option prices move with the value of the underlying asset.

8A.1 THE BINOMIAL OPTION PRICING MODEL

In the body of the chapter we concentrated on option values at expiration. To value options prior to expiration, we need to develop an option pricing model. The simplest way to do this is with the binomial pricing model.

Recall from Appendix 4-A that continuously compounded returns r are related to holding period returns R according to the relation

$$r = \ln(1+R) \text{ or } R = e^r - 1 \tag{8A.1}$$

For example, if the yen/dollar spot rate appreciates from ¥100/$ to ¥110.517/$, then the holding period rate of change of R = 10.517% is equivalent to a continuously compounded change of $r = \ln(1+R) = \ln(1.10517) = 0.10 = 10\%$. Conversely, if the spot rate depreciates by a continuously compounded 10 percent from an initial price of ¥100/$, then the holding period rate of change of $e^{-.10} - 1 = -0.09516 = -9.516\%$ will result in an end-of-period spot rate of ¥90.484/$.

Binomial Option Payoffs

The Binomial Option Pricing Model begins with the simplest possible (nontrivial) circumstance in which there are only two possible outcomes in the underlying exchange rate. To illustrate, let's take the perspective of a Japanese resident purchasing a call option to buy U.S. dollars in one period on the Tokyo Stock Exchange. The currency of reference is the U.S. dollar, so we'll keep dollars in the denominator. For convenience, the option contract size is assumed to be one dollar. The option is exercisable in one period with an exercise price equal to the expected future spot exchange rate of $E[S_1^{¥/\$}] = K^{¥/\$} = ¥100/\$$. The current spot rate is also ¥100/\$.

Suppose that the exchange rate at expiration of the option in one period will be either ¥90.484/\$ or ¥110.517/\$ with equal probability. The payoff on this foreign currency call option will be zero if the exchange rate closes out-of-the-money at ¥90.484/\$. An option holder would be better off buying dollars in the spot market at ¥90.484/\$ than at the exercise price of ¥100/\$, so the option will remain unexercised at expiration. If the spot rate closes at ¥110.517/\$, a call option holder can exercise the option to buy dollars from the option writer at the ¥100/\$ exercise price and then sell dollars in the foreign exchange market at the market rate of ¥110.517/\$. The payoff at expiration on this call option position is $(S_1^{¥/\$} - K^{¥/\$}) = (¥110.517/\$ - ¥100/\$) = ¥10.517/\$$. These alternatives are depicted graphically below.

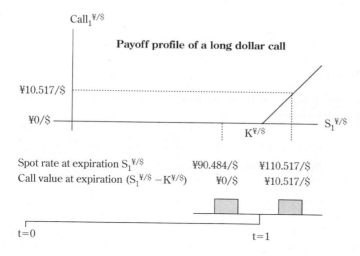

To value this option prior to expiration, let's replicate the call option payoffs with money market instruments and then find the value of this position in the money market.

"Buy a Dollar and Borrow Yen"

Compare this payoff profile with that of buying one dollar today at the current spot rate of ¥100/\$ and borrowing (¥90.484)/1.05 = ¥86.175 from a bank at the 5 percent Japanese rate of interest. The yen value of the dollar will fluctuate depending on the spot exchange rate $S^{¥/\$}$. In contrast, the yen value of the loan repayment is $-¥90.484$ regardless of the spot rate of exchange. In sum, the "buy a dollar and borrow yen" strategy replicates the call option payoff. This is represented graphically below.

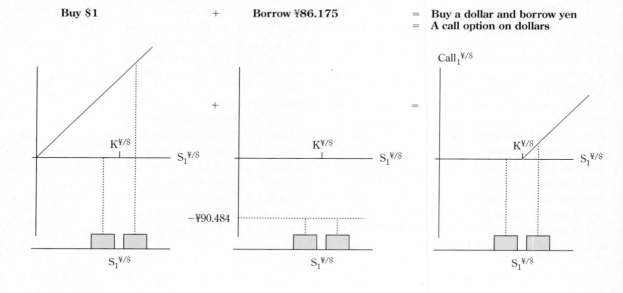

Algebraically, the payoffs on these strategies as a function of the end-of-period spot exchange rate are as follows:

Closing spot rate $S_1^{¥/\$}$	¥90.484/$	¥110.517/$
Yen value of dollar	¥90.484	¥110.517
Loan repayment	$-¥90.484$	$-¥90.484$
Net payoff	¥0	¥20.033

These values represent the spread of possible values in the "buy a dollar and borrow yen" strategy, given the two possible outcomes in the spot exchange rate. The value of this position at today's ¥100/$ spot exchange rate is as follows:

Value of "buy a dollar and borrow yen"
= present value of a "buy $1 and borrow ¥86.175"
= ¥100 − ¥86.175 bank loan
= ¥13.825

Since this money market strategy is a multiple of the call option strategy, we should be able to value the call option prior to expiration by scaling down the "buy a dollar and borrow yen" strategy until the payoffs on the two strategies are equal.

Using the Hedge Ratio to Value Currency Options

The option's **hedge ratio or option delta** indicates the number of call options required to replicate the payoff from buying one unit (in this case, one dollar) of the underlying asset.[12]

$$\text{Option delta} = \frac{\text{Spread of possible option prices}}{\text{Spread of possible underlying asset values}}$$

$$= \text{number of call options required to replicate}$$
$$\text{one unit of the underlying asset}$$

For our example, this is equal to $(¥10.517)/(¥20.033) = 0.52498$ call options per dollar. The payoff on the dollar call option is 52.498% of the value of the "buy a dollar and borrow yen" strategy regardless of the future spot rate of exchange, so the value of the call must be 52.498% of the value of the "buy a dollar and borrow yen" strategy.

Instead of buying $1, suppose you buy $0.52498 and borrow $(¥86.175)(0.52498) = ¥45.240$ at the 5 percent yen interest rate.[13] In one period, you'll owe $¥45.240(1.05) = ¥47.502$ on the loan. Your payoff on the "buy $0.52498" strategy will be 52.498 percent of the "buy a dollar" strategy; that is, either ¥47.502 or ¥58.019 with equal probability. Your net payoff on this money market position will be as follows:

Closing spot rate $S_1^{¥/\$}$	¥90.484/$	¥110.517/$		
Yen value of dollar	¥47.502	¥58.019	=	(¥110.517)(0.52498)
Loan repayment	−¥47.502	−¥47.502	=	(¥90.484)(0.52498)
Net payoff	¥0	¥10.517		

The payoff to the call option strategy is now identical to the payoff from buying $0.52498 and borrowing ¥45.240 at 5 percent and paying off ¥47.502 in one period. Since the payoffs are identical, arbitrage will ensure that the value of this "buy $0.52498 and borrow yen" strategy is equal to the "buy a dollar call option" strategy.[14]

Value of a one-dollar call option
  = 52.498% of the value of a "buy $1 and borrow ¥86.175" strategy
  = Value of "buy $0.52498 and borrow ¥45.240"
  = $(¥100)(0.52498) - (¥86.175)(0.52498)$
  = $¥52.498 - ¥45.240$
  = $¥7.2578.$

---

12 This hedge ratio is similar in spirit to the delta-hedge of Chapter 7. Both hedge ratios identify the ratio (hedged amount)/(exposed amount) that minimizes variability in the hedged position.

13 Since we're making up the rules as we go, let's assume that call options are "infinitely divisible"; that is, you can split them up into as many pieces as desired. If you don't like this assumption, you can multiply all contracts and prices by 10,000 and achieve a similar result.

14 If you are still uncomfortable with the assumption of infinite divisibility, compare the payoffs to buying call options on $10,000 versus buying $5249.80 and borrowing ¥452,400 at 5 percent. The larger the transaction, the less we have to worry about an asset's divisibility.

Voilà! You've valued your first call option. If payoffs are binomially distributed, the payoffs to a foreign currency call option can be replicated by borrowing the domestic currency and buying the foreign currency according to the proportion in the hedge ratio.

A General Case of the Binomial Model

In the example above, there are only two possible outcomes for the end-of-period spot exchange rate. It turns out that the Binomial Option Pricing Model is easily extended to an arbitrary number of outcomes by allowing the exchange rate to *bifurcate* (or split) several times in succession. Suppose the underlying exchange rate diverges from ¥100/$ by ±1 percent twice in succession. After the first split, the exchange rate is either (¥100/$)$e^{\pm.01}$ = ¥99.005 or ¥101.005/$ with equal probability.

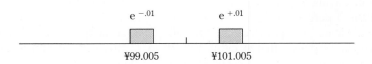

As these outcomes diverge by an additional ±1 percent, there are three possible outcomes: ¥98.020/$ with 25 percent probability, ¥100/$ with 50 percent probability, and ¥102.020/$ with a 25 percent probability.

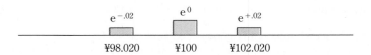

These outcomes correspond to −2 percent, 0 percent, and +2 percent in continuously compounded returns. Another round of ±1 percent changes results in ±3 percent (each with 1/8 probability) and ±1 percent (each with 3/8 probability) as follows:

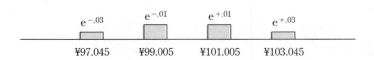

The next bifurcation results in five possible outcomes, and so on. This type of repetitive bifurcation is summarized in a tree diagram below:

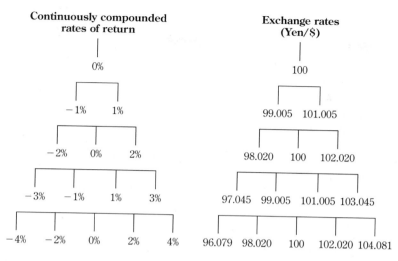

If the probabilities and distances of up and down movements are equal at each bifurcation, then the continuously compounded end-of-period rate of return approaches the normal distribution as the number of bifurcations increases. In fact, for more than eight bifurcations (leading to $2^8 = 256$ possible price paths), the distribution of end-of-period rate of return is virtually indistinguishable from the normal distribution.

The binomial model can be generalized by allowing the process generating up movements and down movements to bifurcate over shorter and shorter intervals. The binomially distributed up-and-down movements are halved each time the interval is halved. As an example, the standard deviation created by eight yen/dollar exchange rate bifurcations of ±1 percent each is 3.75 percent, or ¥3.75/\$.[15] In the limit, the distribution of continuously compounded exchange rates approaches the normal distribution. The binomial model is then equivalent to the currency option pricing model presented in the next section.

8A.2 CURRENCY OPTION PRICING

A Starting Point: The Black-Scholes Option Pricing Model

In 1973, Fischer Black and Myron Scholes borrowed a model from fluid dynamics (a branch of engineering) to create a formula for the value of a European option on a share of non-dividend-paying stock.[16] The key assumption in the Black-Scholes Option Pricing

---

15 You might try verifying this standard deviation on a spreadsheet. Allow the ¥100/\$ exchange rate to vary by ±1 percent successively over eight periods and calculate the standard deviation of the resulting exchange rate distribution.

16 An interesting account of the solution to the option pricing problem appears in Fischer Black's "How We Came Up with the Option Formula," *Journal of Portfolio Management* 15, No. 2, 1989, pages 4–8.

Model (OPM) was that continuously compounded stock returns are normally distributed with constant mean and variance. The Black-Scholes formula for the value of a European call option on a share of non-dividend-paying stock is

$$\text{Call} = P \cdot N(d_1) - e^{-iT} \cdot K \cdot N(d_2) \qquad (8A.2)$$

where Call = the value of a call option on a share of stock
P = the current share price
K = the exercise price of the call option
i = the riskless rate of interest in continuously compounded returns
σ = the instantaneous standard deviation of annual return on the stock
T = the time to expiration of the option expressed as a fraction of one year
d_1 = [ln (P/K) + (i + ($\sigma^2/2$))T] / ($\sigma\sqrt{T}$)
d_2 = ($d_1 - \sigma\sqrt{T}$)
$N(\cdot)$ = the standard normal cumulative distribution function.

The value of a put option on a share of stock can be found from put-call parity.

$$\text{Call} - \text{Put} + e^{-iT} \cdot K = P \qquad \Leftrightarrow \qquad \text{Put} = \text{Call} - P + e^{-iT} \cdot K \qquad (8A.3)$$

The term $e^{-iT} = 1/(1+i)^T$ discounts the exercise price back to the present at the riskless rate of interest. As in the binomial model, this equation is enforced through riskless arbitrage with a replicating portfolio, and the appropriate discount rate is the riskless rate of interest.

Here is the intuition behind the Black-Scholes formula. At expiration, time value is equal to zero and call option value is composed entirely of intrinsic value:

$$\text{Call}_T = \text{Max} [0, P_T - K]$$

Prior to expiration, the actual closing price is a random variable that will not be known until expiration. To value a call option prior to expiration, we need to find the expected value of $[P_T - K]$ given the option expires in-the-money (that is, given $P_T > K$). In the Black-Scholes formula, $N(d_1)$ is the probability that the call option will expire in-the-money. This probability is shown in the graph below.

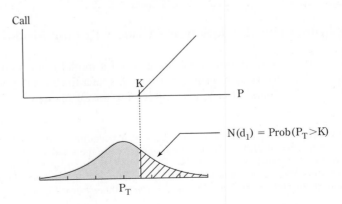

While the option pricing formulas presented in this appendix work well in most instances, you should be aware of their limitations:

1. The most important input in any option pricing formula is volatility. Volatility is also the only input that cannot be read directly out of a financial newspaper. Regardless of how sophisticated the option pricing model is, option values are only as reliable as the volatility estimate.

2. The formulas assume that continuously compounded returns are normally distributed and stationary over time. Empirical studies have found that returns to most assets (including exchange rates) are **leptokurtic**, with more probability around the mean and in the tails and less probability in the shoulders relative to the normal distribution. Assets also have volatilities that vary over time. These differences between the Black-Scholes assumptions and actual asset returns result in Black-Scholes option values that are inaccurate or even biased.

3. While these formulas are for European options, many exchange-traded and OTC options are American options. The early-exercise feature of American options makes them worth slightly more than European options at the same exercise price.

See Fischer Black, "How to Use the Holes in Black-Scholes," *Journal of Applied Corporate Finance* 1, No. 4, 1989, pages 67–73.

The term $P \cdot N(d_1)$ in equation (8A.2) is the expected value of share price at expiration, given $P_T > K$. Similarly, $K \cdot N(d_2)$ is the expected value of the exercise price at expiration, given $P_T > K$. The e^{-iT} term in equation (8A.2) discounts the exercise price that the call option holder must pay back to the present at the riskless rate of interest. Option value is thus the present value of the option's expected value at expiration.

An Extension of the Black-Scholes OPM to Currency Options

Biger and Hull [1983] applied the Black-Scholes framework to European currency options by replacing stock prices with exchange rates and assuming constant interest rates in the foreign and domestic currencies.[17] Biger and Hull's European currency option pricing formula can be stated either in terms of spot exchange rates or in terms of forward exchange rates:

$$\text{Call}^{d/f} = e^{-i^d T} [F_t^{d/f} \cdot N(d_1) - K^{d/f} \cdot N(d_2)] \qquad (8A.4)$$
$$\Leftrightarrow \quad \text{Call}^{d/f} = e^{-i^f T} [S^{d/f} \cdot N(d_1)] - e^{-i^d T} [K^{d/f} \cdot N(d_2)] \qquad (8A.5)$$

---

17 For a solution with stochastic foreign and domestic interest rates, see Hillier, Madura, and Tucker, "Currency Options Pricing with Stochastic Domestic and Foreign Interest Rates," *Journal of Financial and Quantitative Analysis* 26, No. 2, June 1991, pages 139–151.

where $\text{Call}^{d/f}$ = the value of a call option on one unit of foreign currency

$\quad S^{d/f}$ = today's spot exchange rate

$\quad F_T^{d/f}$ = today's forward exchange rate for delivery at time T

$\quad K^{d/f}$ = the exercise price on one unit of foreign currency

$\quad i^d$ = the riskless domestic interest rate in continuously compounded returns

$\quad i^f$ = the riskless foreign interest rate in continuously compounded returns

$\quad \sigma$ = the instantaneous standard deviation of the exchange rate per year

$\quad T$ = the time to expiration of the option expressed as a fraction of one year

$\quad d_1$ = $[\ln (S^{d/f}/K^{d/f}) + (i^d - i^f + (\sigma^2/2))T]/(\sigma\sqrt{T})$

$\quad d_2$ = $(d_1 - \sigma\sqrt{T})$

$\quad N(\cdot)$ = the standard normal cumulative distribution function.

Equations (8A.4) and (8A.5) are related through interest rate parity, which states (in continuously compounded returns) that $F_T^{d/f} = S_0^{d/f}\, e^{+i^d T}\, e^{-i^f T}$. The value of a put option on foreign currency is found from put-call parity:

$$\text{Put}^{d/f} = \text{Call}^{d/f} + (K^{d/f} - F_T^{d/f})\cdot e^{-i^d T} \qquad (8A.6)$$

$$\Leftrightarrow \qquad \text{Put}^{d/f} = \text{Call}^{d/f} - e^{-i^f T}\cdot S^{d/f} + e^{-i^d T}\cdot K^{d/f} \qquad (8A.7)$$

where interest rate parity again ensures that $F_T^{d/f} = S_0^{d/f}\cdot e^{+i^d T}\cdot e^{-i^f T}$.

As in the Black-Scholes OPM, $N(d_1)$ is the probability of a call option expiring in-the-money. Because a put option with the same exercise price is in-the-money whenever a call is out-of-the-money and vice versa, the probability of a put option expiring in-the-money is $1-N(d_1)$. $N(d_1)$ is also equal to the hedge ratio—the number of call options required to replicate the payoff from buying one unit of foreign currency. Because the probability of a put being exercised is 1 minus the probability of a call being exercised, the hedge ratio for a put option is equal to $1-N(d_1)$.

The International Monetary Market of the Chicago Mercantile Exchange, as well as many other options exchanges around the world, trades options on futures rather than options on spot exchange rates. The volatilities of futures and spot prices are equal (except for basis risk) and futures prices converge to spot prices at expiration, so the differences between options on futures and options on spot exchange rates are minor.[18] Equation (8A.4) works with futures prices as well as with forward exchange rates.

Solution of the option pricing problem proved to be a turning point in the evolution of modern finance. The OPM set the stage for the subsequent introduction and growth of options trading on a variety of assets, including stocks, bonds, commodities, interest rates, and exchange rates. Unfortunately for practitioners, the OPM also made a course in stochastic processes a required part of doctoral programs in finance.

KEY TERMS

hedge ratio (option delta)

leptokurtic

stochastic (random)

---

18 For an adaptation of the Black-Scholes model to options on futures, see Fischer Black's "The Pricing of Commodity Options," *Journal of Financial Economics* 3, No. 1/2, 1976, pages 167–179.

8A.1 What is the value of a European call option on U.S. dollars with an exercise price of ¥100/$ and a maturity date six months from now if the current spot rate of exchange is ¥80/$ and the risk-free rate in both Japan and the United States is 5 percent? You have estimated the instantaneous standard deviation of the yen/dollar exchange rate as 10 percent per year based on the variability of past currency movements.

8A.2 Suppose that in problem 8A.1 the currency markets are undergoing a period of unusually high volatility. If the true standard deviation of the yen/dollar spot rate is 20 percent, by how much have you under- or overestimated the value of the dollar call option?

8A.3 Consider the following "December Yen 84 call" on the Philadelphia exchange.

Current call price	$.000118/¥
Price of underlying asset	$.008345/¥
Exercise price	$.008400/¥
Riskless rate in dollars	4%
Riskless rate in yen	4%
Time to expiration	2½ months

What is the volatility of the dollar-per-yen exchange rate implied by the currency option pricing model?

8A.4 As head of currency trading at Ball Bearings Bank in London, you need to price a series of options of various maturity on Danish kroner. The current spot rate is $S_0^{DKr/£}$ = DKr8.4528/£. Riskless interest rates in the United Kingdom and in Denmark are 1.74 percent and 1.30 percent per three months, respectively. Instantaneous volatility on the pound/krone spot rate is 5 percent per three months. The international parity conditions hold.

a. Assume an exercise price of $K^{DKr/£}$ = DKr8.5000/£. Fill in the following table based on the international parity conditions and the currency option pricing formulas in equations (8A.5) and (8A.7).

	Maturities			
	1 month	3 months	6 months	1 year
Forward rate (DKr/£)				
Call option value				
Put option value				

b. Repeat part a. using the currency option pricing formula in equation (8A.4) and (8A.6).

c. Draw a payoff profile that includes all five call options on the same graph.

d. Draw a payoff profile that includes all five put options on the same graph.

8A.5 Rather than varying the maturity of the options as in Problem 8A.4, let's vary the exercise price. Fill in the following table assuming a three-month time to expiration and the information from Problem 8A.4.

	Exercise prices (DKr/£)			
	8.200	8.400	8.600	8.800
Call option value				
Put option value				

CHAPTER 9

Currency Swaps and Swaps Markets

Derivatives are something like energy; dangerous if mishandled, but bearing the potential to do good.

Arthur Levitt, Chairman of the SEC
(Congressional testimony—January 5, 1995)

OVERVIEW

A **currency swap** is a contractual agreement to exchange a principal amount of two different currencies and, after a prearranged length of time, to give back the original principal. Interest payments in each currency also typically are swapped during the life of the agreement. As an example, suppose British Petroleum issues pound sterling debt to finance a new oil refinery servicing the United States at the same time that Ford Motor Corporation issues dollar debt to finance a new manufacturing plant serving the United Kingdom and Western Europe. The operating cash flows of each foreign subsidiary are in the foreign currency, but interest expenses are in the domestic currencies of the parent companies. The financial performance of each foreign subsidiary will then depend on future exchange rates, so each firm is exposed to currency risk. If the two parent corporations agree to exchange their domestic-currency debt for foreign-currency debt, the exposure of each foreign subsidiary to exchange rate fluctuations can be reduced. This is an example of a currency swap.

If the principal amounts are in the same currency, the swap is called an **interest rate swap**. In an interest rate swap, the principal amount is called **notional principal** because it is used only to calculate interest payments and is not exchanged. Only the **difference check** between the two interest payments is exchanged. As an example, suppose that both IBM and Boeing Corporation have five-year $100 million bond issues outstanding and that IBM's debt bears a fixed rate of 9 percent while Boeing's carries a floating rate pegged to the ninety-day Treasury bill rate. Further, suppose that IBM is concerned over the shortening life cycle of its product line and does not want to be

[handwritten margin note: FIXED-FOR-FLOATING interest RATE swap example → Boeing-IBM]

locked into fixed interest payments. Meanwhile, Boeing has just secured a long-term government contract for a guaranteed number of planes at a fixed price, so it prefers to exchange its existing floating rate for fixed rate debt. If IBM and Boeing agree to pay each other's interest payments, they can effectively swap their debt obligations without having to refund and then reissue their existing debt. This is an example of a fixed-for-floating interest rate swap.

Like forwards, futures, and options contracts, swaps are a form of **derivative security** that is exposed to financial price risk. Although forwards, futures, and options are relatively short-term financial instruments, swaps usually involve long-term exposures to financial price risks. As an example, currency risk can be cost-effectively hedged on currency futures and options exchanges for maturities of up to one year and, at slightly greater cost, for up to five years in the currency forward markets. But beyond a few years, forward contracts are either nonexistent or high cost for even actively traded currencies. Swaps provide a cost-effective vehicle for quickly changing the exposure of a corporation, financial institution, or investment fund to long-term financial price risk.

Swap contracts evolved out of a financial arrangement called a *parallel loan* that was developed in the United Kingdom during the 1970s. This chapter begins with a description of parallel loans so you will understand how today's swap contracts came to possess their current structure.

———————————●———————————

9.1 PARALLEL LOANS: NECESSITY IS THE MOTHER OF INVENTION

Throughout the 1970s, the United Kingdom imposed a tax on cross-border currency transactions involving pounds sterling as a way of slowing the flow of pounds out of the country. This made it expensive for British-based multinationals to transfer funds to and from their foreign subsidiaries and for foreign multinationals to transfer funds to and from their British subsidiaries. These firms had a need for a legal funding method that circumvented the pound sterling tax. In the process of achieving this goal, a new funding instrument was created that turned out to possess several unanticipated benefits.

The MNC can fund foreign operations by borrowing funds directly in the foreign country.

One alternative for multinational corporations with the need to fund foreign operations is to borrow funds directly in the foreign country. This is especially attractive when the foreign country has a well-developed capital market and the multinational is well known in the foreign country. Debt raised in a foreign country to finance foreign operations is a *natural hedge* in that interest payments are deducted from revenues in the functional currency of the subsidiary. Keeping as many cash inflows and outflows as possible in the local currency shields the subsidiary from foreign exchange risk. The livelihood of the foreign subsidiary then depends on its operating performance and not on changes in foreign exchange rates over which it has no control.

[handwritten margin note: shield from foreign exchange risk →]

Consider the U.S. branch (BP^{US}) of British Petroleum (BP). Suppose BP^{US} is financed with pound sterling debt and equity capital but operates domestically in the U.S. market. The functional currency of BP is pounds sterling, so we'll keep the U.S. dollar in the denominator of the exchange rate and consider changes in the pound value of BP^{US}. The currencies in BP^{US}'s income statement and the risk profile shared by BP^{US} and its parent BP are shown below.

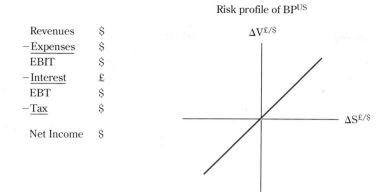

Risk profile of BP^{US}

Revenues	$
− Expenses	$
EBIT	$
− Interest	£
EBT	$
− Tax	$
Net Income	$

Both the parent and the subsidiary face foreign exchange risk because the operating cash inflows are in a different currency from the financial cash outflows. As the value of the dollar appreciates relative to the pound, debt denominated in pounds becomes less of a burden on the U.S. subsidiary. If the dollar depreciates, however, U.S. dollar cash inflows may be unable to cover the pound-denominated interest payments.

A U.S. multinational with a U.K. subsidiary faces a similar exposure in the opposite direction.[1] Ford Motor Company operates a manufacturing and assembly plant in Coventry, England (Ford^{UK}). Both BP and Ford have an incentive to fund their foreign operations with debt denominated in the foreign currency because that is the currency in which their other revenues and costs are denominated. In the presence of a U.K. tax on cross-border pound sterling transactions, both multinationals also have an incentive to fund their foreign subsidiaries without running afoul of the U.K. tax. This means ensuring that no pounds cross the United Kingdom's borders. But how can these multinational corporations fund their foreign operations without sending funds across the United Kingdom's borders?

Alternative #1: Borrow Foreign Currency in the Foreign Market

One alternative is for each multinational to fund its foreign operations with debt raised directly in the foreign country. In this alternative, BP^{US} borrows dollars in the U.S. debt market and Ford^{UK} borrows pounds in the U.K. market. Suppose borrowing costs for fixed rate debt in the United States and in the United Kingdom are as follows:

---

1 This example ignores the fact that if the pound falls in value the prices of the U.S. subsidiary's products will become more competitive on world markets. Whether this long-term impact overcomes the short-term impact of the more expensive dollar interest costs depends in part on the price elasticity of demand for the foreign subsidiary's products. This form of exposure to currency risk is called *economic exposure*, and is discussed in Chapter 5.

	Borrower	
Country	BP	Ford
U.K.	5%	7%
U.S.	8%	6%

In this example, each multinational has a comparative advantage borrowing in its domestic market, where the firms have established reputations and the information costs faced by lenders are low.

Suppose the foreign subsidiary of each multinational borrows multiyear fixed rate debt in the foreign market. BP^{US} borrows an amount $X^\$$ from Citicorp in the United States to fund its U.S. operations. $Ford^{UK}$ borrows an amount $X^\pounds$ from Hongkong and Shanghai Banking Corporation (HSBC) in the United Kingdom to fund its U.K. operations. This situation is as shown below.

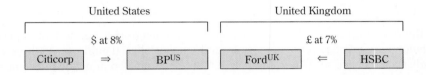

The resulting expected future cash flows can be shown on a time line as follows:

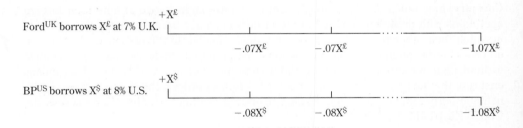

Foreign firms face a disadvantage relative to domestic firms when borrowing in the domestic market. Of course, each parent could borrow in its domestic credit market and then lend the funds to its subsidiary. But each firm would then have to pay the U.K. tax on cross-border pound transactions.

Alternative #2: A Parallel Loan

In a **parallel loan**, the MNC borrows in its own currency where it enjoys a *relative advantage* in borrowing costs and then trades this debt for the foreign currency debt of a foreign counterparty. This combines the advantages of low domestic borrowing rates with foreign-source financing of the foreign subsidiaries. One possible parallel loan arrangement is summarized below.

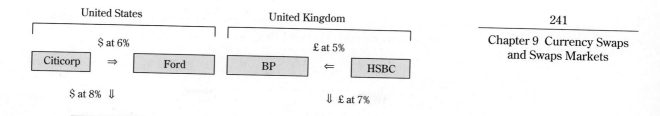

In this example, each parent borrows domestic currency at its domestic borrowing cost. These funds are then loaned to the subsidiary of the foreign parent at the rate that the subsidiary would have had to pay in the domestic market.

The U.S. Perspective. From Ford's perspective, expected cash flows over the next several years look like this:

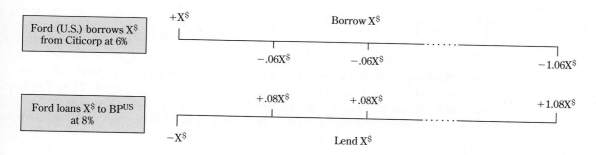

The timing of these payments can be contractually set so that they precisely overlap. Similarly, the principal amount can be set equal in each contract so that $X^\$ = X^\pounds S^{\$/\pounds}$. The net cash flow of Ford in the United States is then

The U.S. parent earns 2 percent of the face amount $X^\$$ per year in interest expense. If both loans are riskless, then this is a pure arbitrage profit with no net investment and no risk. It is important to note that BP^{US} is not averse to this loan because the 8 percent cost is the same rate that it would have paid had it borrowed dollars directly in the U.S. market.

Parallel loans can provide a cost savings to both counterparties

The U.K. Perspective. The situation of British Petroleum in the United Kingdom is the flip side of that of Ford in the United States. British Petroleum borrows a face amount $X^£ = X^\$ S^{£/\$}$ at 5 percent in the United Kingdom and then loans this to Ford^{UK} at seven percent, earning 2 percent of $X^£$ per year on the deal.

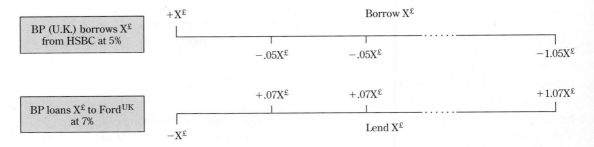

As before, the 2 percent difference in the cost of debt accrues to the parent firm.

Again, this does not hurt the foreign subsidiary of the counterparty because the 7 percent cost of debt is the same as Ford^{UK} would have paid without the parallel loan agreement. Both foreign subsidiaries are no worse off, the parent firms BP and Ford have each earned 2 percent per year on the face value of the loans—and no funds have crossed a national border.

9.2 Pros and Cons of Parallel Loans

Benefits of Parallel Loans

Parallel loans allowed MNCs to acquire low-cost financing in foreign countries

This parallel loan arrangement has several advantages. First, it legally circumvents the U.K. tax on cross-border pound transactions. Neither the original principal nor the interest checks need to cross a border. The pounds raised by BP can be sent directly to Ford^{UK} within the United Kingdom, just as dollars raised by Ford can be sent directly to BP^{US} within the United States. The interest payments can be made in the currency in which they are earned by each foreign subsidiary. Second, the parallel loans allow each multinational to borrow in its home market, where it enjoys low relative borrowing costs. Third, the parallel loans allow each foreign subsidiary to be financed with low-cost foreign-source debt, which reduces the currency risk exposure of the foreign subsidiaries and of the domestic parents. Finally, the parallel loans allow the parent firms to access new capital markets, which can further reduce their overall cost of capital. These benefits are especially valuable for multinational corporations with foreign exchange exposure in many currencies.

Problems with Parallel Loans

Despite the advantages of parallel loans, in the early days they were difficult and costly to arrange. Investment bankers had to arrange for two or more parties in different countries (often on different continents) to sing the same tune despite the existence of different sets of sheet music. Three drawbacks of the parallel loan arrangement are default risk, the balance sheet impact, and search costs.

Parallel loans suffer from high default risk and search costs and must be capitalized on the balance sheet.

Default Risk. Each loan in a parallel loan arrangement is a separate agreement, so if one party defaults it does not release the other party from its obligation. One remedy for this problem is to link the loans in a separate agreement defining the **rights of set-off** should one party default on its obligation. Because these rights of set-off are not linked in a single document to the parallel loans, settlement of disputes arising from one party's default is not foolproof. Often, the issue is jurisdiction. Because the two sides of the parallel loan are executed in different countries, the agreement defining the rights of set-off must be binding in both countries, in which case both countries can claim jurisdiction. In which country are disputes to be adjudicated? There is no simple solution to the jurisdiction problem when contracts are signed separately in different countries.

Balance Sheet Impact. Because the parallel loans are two separate contracts (actually, three contracts if you count the rights of set-off agreement), parallel loans must appear on both sides of the consolidated balance sheet for accounting, tax, and regulatory purposes. On the liability side of the balance sheet, this raises the book value debt-to-equity ratio of the parent firm. For example, if debt and equity are each worth $5 million, then the debt-to-equity ratio is one-to-one. If an additional asset and an offsetting liability worth $5 million are added through a parallel loan, then the apparent debt-to-equity ratio rises to two-to-one. Even though this additional debt is effectively canceled by the parallel loan on the asset side of the balance sheet, the higher perceived level of financial leverage can impair the ability of the parent firm to raise additional debt.

Search Costs. Each domestic firm must be matched with a foreign firm with the opposite funding need. When parallel loans were first used, there was not an active market for these kinds of transactions. In the absence of an active market, search costs were high. In the early days of swaps, investment banks served as brokers rather than dealers, putting none of their own money at risk and simply acting as matchmakers. This resulted in slow growth in the early market for parallel loans.

9.3 SWAPS TO THE RESCUE

The remedy to these problems was to package the parallel loans in a single legal agreement called a **swap contract**. A swap contract identifies the currencies of denomination and the amount and timing of all future cash inflows and outflows. The swap contract releases each party from its obligation should the other party default on its obligation. By binding the rights of set-off into a single contract along with the two loans, the swap contract neatly avoids many of the vexing legal issues surrounding default in parallel loans. Because the entire package is covered by a single legal agreement, in the event of

Currency swaps provide a remedy for the problems of parallel loans.

default the nondefaulting party can simply stop making interest payments on its side of the contract and, if necessary, seek compensation in court.

Accounting and regulatory conventions in most countries treat swaps as off–balance sheet transactions that appear in the footnotes to financial statements. The reason is that the swap contract includes both loans in a single contract, so neither loan needs to appear on the balance sheet. The swap's impact is felt through interest expense on the income statement and, in the case of currency swaps, through foreign currency transactions. Because neither side of the swap is capitalized on the balance sheet, the appearance of high debt levels is avoided.

As the benefits of swap contracts were recognized after their introduction in the 1970s, volume in the swap market grew by leaps and bounds. In 1981, Salomon Brothers engineered a currency swap between the World Bank and International Business Machines that, because of the stature of the participants, served to legitimize the swap contract. By the early to middle 1980s, investment banks (particularly Salomon Brothers) were nurturing an increasingly active market in currency and interest rate swaps. These early swaps were customized, low-volume, high-margin deals. As volume and liquidity grew, international investment and commercial banks began serving as swap dealers and not just as brokers, and the market turned into a high-volume, low-margin business. As swap dealers began making a market in swaps, search costs were greatly reduced, thus eliminating the last of the three problems with parallel loans. Today, commercial banks have the lead over investment banks as the major dealers in the market using standardized swap contracts that follow conventions set forth by the *International Swap Dealers Association*.

9.4 SWAPS AS PORTFOLIOS OF FORWARD CONTRACTS

You've taken a fast-track job as a junior analyst with Merck & Co. It's your first day on the job and Judy Lewent, Merck's CFO, brings you into her office to discuss the currency exposure of Merck's operations. You only get one chance to make a first impression, and you are anxious to demonstrate that your time at school was well spent.

Lewent: Please step into my office. I want to get your opinion on a persistent problem that we face here at Merck. We have sales in more than 140 countries worldwide. Yet 70 percent of our research and development expenses, the bulk of our production expenses, and most of our interest expenses are in dollars. Our dividends are also paid in dollars. I'm particularly concerned about our exposure to the currencies of countries in the European Union. A high percentage of our sales come from these countries, yet our operating expenses are largely in dollars. What do you suggest?

(Okay—now what was it that you studied in school? Think fast! Ah, yes. A currency swap might be just the thing. Stepping into the breach, you suggest a dollar-for-DM currency swap.)

You: Well, we might consider a currency swap for deutsche marks. The currencies in the European Exchange Rate Mechanism all float fairly closely with the D-mark. We could swap our dollar debt for D-mark debt on the same amount of principal and thereby convert some of our dollar expenses to D-mark expenses. Our counterparty would pay the dollar interest payments on our debt and we would pay the D-mark interest payment on a comparable amount of D-mark debt. This would form a natural hedge against revenues denominated in D-marks and other currencies of the European Union.

Lewent: Who do you propose as a counterparty?

You: This should be a fairly standard financial transaction, so I'd suggest an international bank making a market in currency swaps. I have a classmate in the swap department at Bankers Trust. I'm sure she could give us a quote.

Lewent: Bankers Trust? Their swap department has been in the news quite a bit lately. What if they default on their side of the deal and are unable to pay our dollar interest payments?

You: We'd stop paying them as soon as they stopped paying us. At most, we'd be out six months' interest on the notional principal.

Lewent: Wrong. We'd be out six months' interest plus one junior analyst.

How do you respond? What is the default risk of a swap contract?

Judy Lewent's question is most easily answered by comparing the swap contract to a futures contract. Futures contracts are nothing more than a bundle of consecutive one-day forward contracts in which changes in wealth due to changes in exchange rates are marked to market daily. Swaps are also a bundle of forward contracts. But instead of being laid end-to-end as consecutive one-day forward contracts, a swap is a bundle of *simultaneous* (rather than consecutive) forward contracts, each with a different maturity date.

> *A swap is a portfolio of simultaneous forward contracts, each with a different maturity date.*

Suppose a domestic firm borrows an amount X^d in a T-period nonamortizing loan with periodic (fixed or floating rate) interest payments $C_t^d = i_t^d X^d$ throughout the life of the loan.

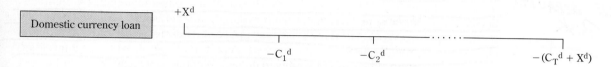

If the company has a need to hedge revenues from a foreign subsidiary, it can swap this domestic currency loan for a foreign currency loan of equal value ($X^d = X^f S^{d/f}$) paying interest payments $C_t^f = i_t^f X^f$. If the principal being received is set equal to the principal being paid, there is no reason to exchange the principal amounts, and the principal is called notional principal. Rather than exchange the full amount of the interest payments, only the difference check need be exchanged. This difference check is equal to

$(C_t^d - C_t^f S^{d/f})$ after translating the foreign currency interest payment into domestic currency. From the perspective of the domestic firm, the net cash flows look like this:

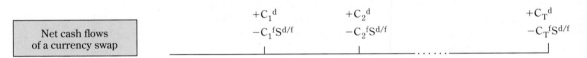

| Net cash flows of a currency swap | | | |

$$+C_1^d \quad\quad +C_2^d \quad\quad\quad +C_T^d$$
$$-C_1^f S^{d/f} \quad -C_2^f S^{d/f} \quad -C_T^f S^{d/f}$$

This cash-flow pattern is equivalent to a portfolio of T forward contracts each with a different maturity.

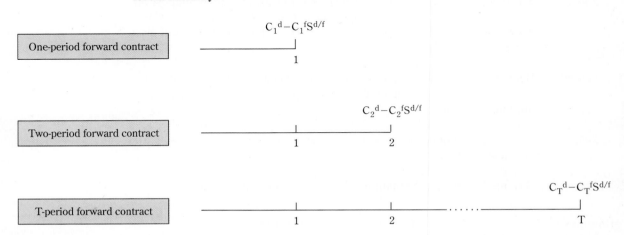

One-period forward contract

$$C_1^d - C_1^f S^{d/f}$$
$$1$$

Two-period forward contract

$$C_2^d - C_2^f S^{d/f}$$
$$1 \quad\quad 2$$

T-period forward contract

$$C_T^d - C_T^f S^{d/f}$$
$$1 \quad\quad 2 \quad\quad T$$

Swaps are essentially bundles of forward contracts of different maturities. Judy Lewent's concern is at least partially justified because swap contracts, like forward contracts, are subject to default risk. But although the risk and consequences of default are somewhat more than in a comparable futures contract, they are far less than for straight debt because of the rights of set-off built into the swap contract.

A futures contract reduces default risk relative to a forward contract by (1) requiring a margin, (2) having an exchange clearinghouse as the counterparty, and (3) marking to market daily. Swaps can also be evaluated along these three dimensions. First, swaps do not generally require a performance bond, such as a margin requirement, and this tends to give swaps slightly more default risk than comparable futures contracts. Second, a commercial or investment bank making a market in the swap will generally be the counterparty, and to the extent that the bank is more prone to default than a clearinghouse, this tends to slightly increase default risk. Third, whereas futures are marked to market daily, swaps are essentially marked to market each time an interest payment is due. Because the performance period between payments is longer (typically six months) than the daily performance period of a comparable futures contract, swaps are more risky than futures contracts. The default risk of a swap contract falls somewhere between the risk of a comparable futures contract (which is negligible) and the risk of the forward contract with the longest maturity in the bundle of forward contracts that make up the swap.

Swaps are far less risky than straight debt because if one side defaults the other side is released from its obligations as well. Further, the entire principal is not at risk as it is in a loan because of the exchange of actual or notional principals at the beginning and at the end of the contract. The interest payments are less at risk than in straight debt because the difference check depends on the difference between the rates rather than on the level of one of the interest rates. For these reasons, swaps are far less risky than comparable straight debt.[2]

9.5 TYPES OF SWAP CONTRACTS AND SWAP PRICING

Financial engineering is a buzzword on Wall Street that aptly describes the "name of the game" in investment banking. The rapid pace of financial innovation in the creation (or engineering) of new financial products to meet both old and new financing needs is truly extraordinary. This high rate of technological change is both a blessing and a curse for multinational financial managers. The blessing is that access to capital markets is far greater today than at any time in history. The curse is that it is difficult to keep abreast of the innovations in new financial products. Without a thorough understanding of the benefits and risks of financial contracting, value can easily be destroyed rather than created. Innovation is especially prominent in the market for swaps. Fortunately, financial products that at first appear to be new and curious contracts are in most cases new versions of established contracts.

Currency and interest rate swaps are by far the most frequently traded swap contracts. Many variations of the basic swap product can be created through combinations of *plain vanilla* versions of currency and interest rate swaps. This section describes several of the more common forms of swap contracts, including detailed discussions of currency and interest rate swaps.

Currency Swaps

The most common form of currency swap is the **currency coupon swap**, a fixed-for-floating rate nonamortizing currency swap traded primarily through international commercial banks. In a nonamortizing loan the entire principal is repaid at maturity and only interest is paid during the life of the loan. Currency swaps also come with amortizing loans in which periodic payments spread the principal repayment throughout the life of the loans. Currency swaps can be structured as fixed-for-fixed, fixed-for-floating, or floating-for-floating swaps of either the nonamortizing or amortizing variety.

Swap dealers quote **indication pricing schedules** for actively traded currency swaps. A dealer such as Citicorp might quote the following schedule for nonamortizing

most common

The most common currency swap is a fixed-for-floating rate currency coupon swap.

- A FIXED - FOR - Floating rate, nonamortized currency swap
- Entire principal repaid @ maturity and only interest is paid during the life of the loan.

---

2 Robert Litzenberger presents a detailed discussion of the default risk of swaps along with applicable portions of the U.S. bankruptcy code in "Swaps: Plain and Fanciful," *Journal of Finance* 47, No. 3, July 1992, pages 831–850.

fixed-for-floating (LIBOR) deutsche mark/dollar currency coupon swaps with semiannual ("sa") interest payments on maturities of from two to five years:

Currency Coupon Swap
Indication Pricing Schedule (DM/$)

Maturity	Midrate (in DMs)
2 years	6.12% sa
3 years	6.38% sa
4 years	6.52% sa
5 years	6.68% sa

Deduct 5 bps if the bank is paying a fixed rate.
Add 5 bps if the bank is receiving a fixed rate.
All quotes are against six-month dollar LIBOR flat.

The fixed-rate side of the swap pays the quoted midrate plus (when the bank is receiving the fixed rate) or minus (when the bank is paying the fixed rate) five basis points (5 bps). As an example, if the bank receives the fixed rate payments, it receives two semiannual payments of $(6.73\%)/2 = 3.365\%$ of the notional principal. The annualized yield on this amount is calculated from

$$\text{Annualized yield} = [1 + (i/N)]^N - 1$$

where N is the number of compounding periods per year and i is the total interest paid per year. With semiannual payments of 3.365 percent, the annualized yield to Citicorp on the fixed rate payments is $(1.03365)^2 - 1 = 0.06842$, or 6.842 percent. In receiving ten more basis points than it pays on the fixed rate side, Citicorp earns a bid-ask spread of ten basis points by buying funds low (five basis points below the fixed midrate) and selling funds high (five basis points above the fixed midrate).

The floating rate side of the swap has semiannual interest payments at the six-month LIBOR rate. By setting the floating rate side of each swap at LIBOR flat, the swap bank has zero net exposure to LIBOR so long as the bank's swap book is in balance—that is, the bank's net exposure in each currency is zero.

A Note on Bond Pricing Conventions. Before looking at an example of how to use this pricing schedule, we need to take care of one technical detail. Conventions for quoting bond yields vary across national bond markets. In the United States, Treasury notes and bonds are conventionally quoted as a semiannual **bond equivalent yield** (BEY) that assumes a 365-day year and semiannual interest payments. Floating-rate Eurocurrencies such as those pegged to LIBOR are quoted as a **money market yield** (MMY) based on a 360-day year and semiannual coupons. This difference means that a 10 percent money market yield is not equivalent to a 10 percent bond equivalent yield. The relation between the two is

$$MMY = BEY(360/365)$$

or, equivalently,

$$BEY = MMY(365/360)$$

For example, a 10 percent per year bond equivalent yield on a U.S. Treasury bond is the same as a $0.10(360/365) = 0.09863$ or 9.863 percent per year money market yield on a Eurodollar deposit pegged to LIBOR. This transformation will help you compare yields on Eurocurrency contracts with those on U.S. Treasury bonds.

Example: The Swap Bank Receives the Fixed Rate. America, Inc. (AI) has $50 million of five-year debt at a floating rate of six-month ($) LIBOR + 125 bps. AI wants fixed-rate deutsche mark debt to fund its German operations. Citicorp agrees to pay AI's floating-rate dollar debt in exchange for a fixed-rate deutsche mark payment from AI. Suppose the spot exchange rate is $S^{\$/DM} = \$.6667/DM$. At this spot rate, $50 million is equal in value to DM75 million.

Citicorp receives fixed-rate deutsche mark interest payments at a rate of 6.68% + 5 bps = 6.73% (quoted as a bond equivalent yield) on the principal amount. Citicorp pays the floating six-month LIBOR Eurodollar rate (quoted as a money market yield). Cash transactions proceed as follows:

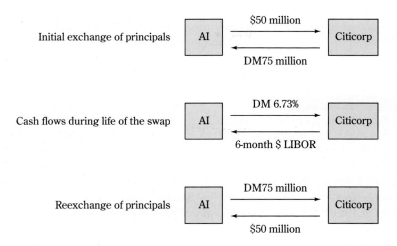

AI's original cost of debt was 125 basis points over the LIBOR Eurodollar rate. Citicorp only pays LIBOR flat, so AI still must pay this premium. After converting the 125 floating rate basis points to a bond equivalent yield, AI's net cost of fixed rate deutsche mark funds is $0.0673 + 0.0125(365/360) \approx 0.0800$, or 8.00 percent.

Example: The Swap Bank Pays the Fixed Rate. Expert Systems A.G. (ES) has DM75 million of five-year fixed rate debt with a 7.68 percent bond equivalent yield.[3] ES

---

3 A.G., or *Aktiengesellschaft,* are large, publicly traded German corporations.

wants floating-rate dollar debt to fund its U.S. operations. Citicorp agrees to pay ES's fixed-rate deutsche mark debt in exchange for a floating-rate dollar payment. At the spot rate of $S^{\$/DM} = \$.6667/DM$, the DM75 million debt is equivalent to $50 million.

Citicorp pays the fixed rate deutsche mark debt at 6.68% − 5 bps = 6.63%. Citicorp receives the floating-rate dollar debt at six-month LIBOR flat. Transactions during the life of the swap proceed as follows:

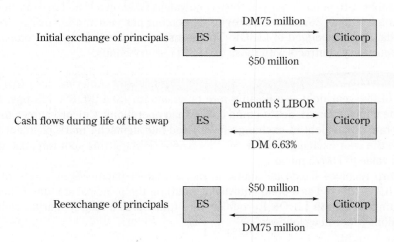

Citicorp's net cost of floating rate funds is the six-month LIBOR Eurodollar rate. The difference between ES's fixed rate pound outflows and inflows is 0.0768 − 0.0663 = 0.0105, or 105 basis points. After converting this to a money market yield, ES's net cost of floating rate Eurodollar funds is LIBOR + (105 bps)(360/365) ≈ LIBOR + 104 bps.

The Swap Bank's Gains. From Citicorp's perspective, the AI and ES swaps offset one another. On the floating-rate side, Citicorp is paying the six-month LIBOR dollar interest rate to AI on $50 million principal and receiving the six-month LIBOR dollar rate from ES on $50 million principal. Aside from transactions costs from within Citicorp, these transactions net out to zero over the life of the swap. On the fixed-rate side, Citicorp is paying 6.63 percent semiannually in deutsche marks and receiving 6.73 percent semiannually on the same principal amount. This leaves a bid-ask profit of ten basis points on every deutsche mark of notional principal.

Interest Rate Swaps

An interest rate swap is a variant of the currency swap in which both loans are denominated in the same currency. Since the principal on both loans of the swap are in the same currency, the principal is notional and needn't be exchanged. The notional principal is used only to calculate interest payments. Only the difference check between the interest payments is exchanged when interest payments are due.

Coupon Swap

The most common interest rate swaps are fixed-for-floating coupon swaps and floating-for-floating basis swaps.

The most common forms of interest rate swaps are the coupon swap and the floating-for-floating basis swap. A **coupon swap** is a fixed-for-floating swap that pairs fixed-rate debt with floating-rate debt pegged to an interest rate index, such as six-month LIBOR. A **basis swap** pairs floating-rate debt pegged to two different interest rate indexes, such as six-month LIBOR and the U.S. thirty-day T-bill rate. Interest rate swaps come in maturities of one to fifteen years.

Let's consider an indication pricing schedule for a fixed-for-floating coupon swap, the most common form of interest rate swap. Citicorp might quote prices as follows:

Coupon Swap
Indication Pricing Schedule

Maturity	Bank Pays Fixed Rate	Bank Receives Fixed Rate	Current TN Rate
2 years	2 yr TN sa + 19bps	2 yr TN sa + 40bps	7.05%
3 years	3 yr TN sa + 24bps	3 yr TN sa + 47bps	7.42%
4 years	4 yr TN sa + 28bps	4 yr TN sa + 53bps	7.85%
5 years	5 yr TN sa + 33bps	5 yr TN sa + 60bps	7.92%

This schedule assumes nonamortizing debt and semiannual rates (sa). All quotes are against six-month dollar LIBOR flat. TN = U.S. Treasury note rate.

Example: The Swap Bank Pays the Fixed Rate. Skittish Co. has $50 million of five-year debt with a bond equivalent yield of 9 percent compounded semiannually. This is 1.08 percent over the current five-year T-note yield of 7.92 percent. Skittish prefers floating-rate debt, but its current fixed-rate debt is widely held and would be costly to repurchase. Besides, Skittish's investment banker, Salomon Brothers, quotes a rate of LIBOR + 100 bps on a new debt issue. This is higher than Skittish believes is appropriate given Skittish's credit rating. Skittish is looking for a less costly source of floating-rate debt.

Citicorp agrees to a fixed-for-floating swap with Skittish. According to the indication pricing schedule, Citicorp will pay Skittish a fixed-rate five-year note with semiannual compounding at 33 basis points over the five-year T-note rate. With the T-note at 7.92 percent, this means a bond equivalent yield of 0.0792 + 0.0033 = 0.0825, or 8.25 percent with semiannual compounding, for an annualized yield of $[1+(0.0825/2)]^2-1= 0.0842$, or 8.42 percent. Skittish will pay Citicorp a floating rate five-year note at LIBOR with semiannual payments.

On the original loan, Skittish was paying 9 percent fixed. After the swap, Skittish receives 8.25 percent fixed from Citicorp and pays LIBOR floating to Citicorp. The difference between Skittish's 9 percent fixed-rate payments and 8.25 percent fixed-rate receipts leaves a net cost of 75 basis points on the fixed-rate side. Stating this as a money market yield, Skittish's net cost on the fixed-rate side is (75 bps) (360/365) ≈ 74 basis points. Skittish's net cost of floating rate funds is then LIBOR + 74 bps in money market yield. This is 26 basis points below the LIBOR + 100 bps rate quoted by Salomon Brothers on new debt.

Example: The Swap Bank Receives the Fixed Rate. Trendy Co. has $50 million of five-year debt with a cost of six-month LIBOR + 125 bps in money market yield. Trendy prefers fixed rate debt, but issues of similar risk are yielding 9.90 percent in bond equivalent yield. Citicorp comes to the rescue again with an agreement to pay Trendy a floating rate in exchange for a fixed-rate payment from Trendy. According to the indication pricing schedule, Citicorp pays Trendy the six-month LIBOR rate and Trendy pays Citicorp the five-year T-note rate + 60 bps for a semiannually compounded bond equivalent yield of $0.0792 + 0.0060 = 0.0852$, or 8.52 percent. Trendy's cost of floating rate funds is $0.0852 + (0.0125)(365/360) = 0.0979$, or 9.79 percent in bond equivalent yield. This is a savings of 11 bps over the 9.90 percent funding available in the market.

The Swap Bank's Gains. From Citicorp's perspective, the interest rate swap with Trendy offsets the interest rate swap with Skittish. Citicorp earns ($50 million) (60 bps − 33 bps) ≈ $135,000 per year in semiannually compounded money market yield on the notional principal of $50 million. Because each of the fixed-rate contracts pays semiannual interest payments over five years, Citicorp is fully hedged (and makes a profit) on the fixed-rate side. The floating-rate side of each swap is against six-month LIBOR flat, so Citicorp is also fully hedged on the floating-rate side.

Other Types of Swaps and Swap Combinations

Chapter 1 introduced the term "financial price risk" and described three important types of financial prices—currency exchange rates, interest rates, and commodity prices. Not surprisingly, swap contracts are traded on each of these financial prices. Swap contracts can be traded, in principal, on any asset. Although there is some standardization of contracts in the most liquid segments of the currency and interest rate swap markets, customized swap contracts are written on a wide variety of other assets and in a wide variety of combinations.

Combinations of Swaps. Interest rate and currency swaps can be combined to form new financial products. For example, a currency coupon swap in which the domestic rate is fixed and the foreign rate is floating can be combined with an interest rate swap in the foreign currency to create a *fixed-for-fixed currency swap*. If the fixed-rate side of a currency coupon swap is combined with the fixed-rate side of a fixed-for-floating interest rate swap in the domestic currency, the net result is a *floating-for-floating currency swap*. Interest rate and currency swaps can be combined in this way to transform the nature of the firm's exposures quickly and at low cost.

Commodity Swaps. Just as swaps are traded on currencies and interest rates, **commodity swaps** are used to hedge against commodity price risks. Commodity swaps are traded against many commodities, including oil, gold, and pork bellies. The first commodity swaps were engineered by Chase Manhattan Bank in 1986. Commodity swaps can be based either on two different commodities or on the same commodity. (Indeed, the currency swap can be thought of as a subset of the commodity swap in which the commodities underlying each contract are currencies.) When the commodities are the same, commodity swaps typically take the form of a floating-for-fixed swap in which one party makes periodic payments at a fixed per-unit price for a given quantity of some commodity while the other party makes periodic payments at a floating rate

The regional managers of a multinational corporation have an incentive to hedge against currency risk in order to reduce the variability of their divisional performance. But hedges are not costless, and one division's risk exposures may be offset by risk exposures elsewhere in the company. By "netting" risk exposures across the entire company, corporate headquarters can take an integrated approach to the management of currency risk. Duplicate or offsetting hedges can then be avoided and financing costs minimized.

Consider how Ford Motor Company manages its currency risk exposure. As a multinational automobile manufacturer with production and sales in many countries throughout the world, Ford is exposed to significant currency risk. Ford recently instituted a program (*Ford 2000*) to integrate its regional operations into a single unit called Ford Automotive Operations. This division is responsible for managing and coordinating Ford's manufacturing operations in North America, Europe, Asia-Pacific, and Latin America.

One of the advantages of being a multinational corporation is that Ford's operating exposure to currency risk is lower than that of a pure exporter. Operating exposure to currency risk is managed by establishing manufacturing operations in each of the regions in which Ford does business. Manufacturing operations in each region are then used to support sales in that same region.

Nevertheless, the individual regions can and do face significant currency risks. With its regional operations consolidated under one roof, Ford can more easily match these regional currency exposures internally. After matching exposures within the firm, Corporate Treasury then manages Ford's *net transaction exposure* in the financial markets. By offsetting exposures internally before going to the financial markets, Ford minimizes its external hedging costs and maximizes the effectiveness of its hedging strategies.

Source: Complied by author from conversations with Ford executives.

---

pegged to the spot commodity price. In this case, the principal is notional and there need be no exchange of principal. Commodity swaps across two different commodities can be structured as fixed-for-fixed, fixed-for-floating, or floating-for-floating swaps. In this case, the commodities could be exchanged but the difference in spot prices is usually settled in cash. This minimizes the transactions costs associated with the swap.

Debt-for-Equity Swaps. Mrs. Bear and Mr. Bull are portfolio managers for two different families of mutual funds. Mrs. Bear has $100 million invested in a well-diversified portfolio of stocks that is highly correlated with the S&P 500 and wants to get into ten-year T-bonds for one year. Mr. Bull has a $100 million portfolio of ten-year T-bonds and wishes to get into stocks for one year. Unfortunately for Mr. Bull and Mrs. Bear, it is expensive to sell an entire portfolio and then reinvest the proceeds in a new asset class.

In this circumstance, opposites attract. Mr. Bull and Mrs. Bear could form a **debt-for-equity swap** in which Mrs. Bear pays Mr. Bull the S&P 500 return on a $100 million notional principal and Mr. Bull pays Mrs. Bear the interest payments from his $100 million portfolio of ten-year T-bonds. This swap could be engineered with a one-year term. With a single swap transaction, Mr. Bull and Mrs. Bear can replicate the payoffs of their desired positions and avoid the transactions costs of buying and selling (and, after one year, selling and then buying) individual assets. This type of debt-for-equity swap was introduced in 1989 by Bankers Trust.[4]

A number of combinations and variations of this debt-for-equity swap are possible. The plain vanilla fixed-for-S&P 500 equity swap could be combined with a fixed-for-floating interest rate swap to create a floating-for-S&P 500 swap. The T-bond position could be swapped against the Nikkei 225 on the Japanese market rather than the S&P 500. An S&P 500 position could be swapped for another equity portfolio, such as the Nikkei 225 or a small-capitalization index on the U.S. market. These swaps allow large investors such as mutual funds and pension funds the luxury of changing their asset allocation decisions without suffering the transactions costs of buying and selling individual assets.

Swaptions. A **swaption** is a swap with one or more options attached. The fixed-rate side of a swaption usually has the option and the floating-rate side the obligation, because the floating-rate side (for example, LIBOR) adjusts to changing market conditions and has less need for an option. The most common forms of swaptions include *mirror-image swaptions* (the fixed-rate receiver has the option to cancel), *right-to-terminate swaptions* (the fixed-rate payer has the option to cancel), and *extendible swaptions* (the fixed-rate side has the right to extend the contract life). The option component of each of these swaps is like an option on the underlying fixed-rate bond and is priced accordingly.

9.6 Hedging the Swap Bank's Financial Risk Exposure

Indication pricing schedules must be revised frequently to reflect changes in market pricing and to correct imbalances in the bank's swap portfolio, or **swap book**. Swap banks hedge their net swap positions in their swap books either internally, within the bank, or in external financial markets using the interbank spot, forward, futures, options, and bond markets. Once the swap bank finds an offsetting position, as Citicorp was able to do in the currency and interest rate swap examples above, the swap bank can offset its positions on the two swaps. It is then hedged against the financial price risk underlying the swap.

Mismatches in the bank's swap book can arise across a number of dimensions, including currencies, maturities, and money market instruments. For example, if the bank is paying funds on swaps pegged to six-month LIBOR and receiving funds on swaps pegged to one-month T-bills, the swap bank has a maturity mismatch as well as basis risk between LIBOR and T-Bill rates. By constantly monitoring the swap bank's net position across currencies, fixed-versus-floating interest rates, and floating interest rate exposures at all forward dates, management can ensure that the bank is not caught by surprise by large changes in these financial prices.

Constant monitoring needed...

---

4 Another type of swap, the *LDC debt-equity swap* or *debt swap,* allows investors to trade the external debt obligations of less-developed countries (LDCs) for currency or for equity positions in government-owned companies based in those same countries. Don't confuse these LDC debt swaps with the debt-for-equity swap of Mr. Bull and Mrs. Bear.

9.7 THE BENEFITS OF SWAPS TO THE MULTINATIONAL CORPORATION

Swaps provide corporations with a great deal of flexibility in their financing choices. In particular, swaps allow corporations to transform the nature of their obligations at very low cost and without having to repurchase and then reissue those obligations. They also allow the corporation to separate the form of debt offered to the market from the form of debt preferred by the corporation and ultimately paid to the market.

Swaps provide the multinational corporation with a great deal of flexibility in its choice of financing.

Consider the example of the parallel loans in section 9.2. Each parent wanted to issue foreign-currency debt but was prohibited from doing so directly by the high interest rate demanded by foreign suppliers of debt capital. Swap contracts allow firms to separate the currency of denomination on their original debt offering from the currency of denomination on their ultimate obligation. If the domestic market is willing to pay a higher price for the debt of domestic corporations than for the debt of foreign corporations, then domestic firms can issue domestic currency debt where its comparative borrowing advantage is greatest and then swap into foreign currency debt through a swap contract. This allows corporations to seek funds from their lowest cost sources and then swap back into the form of debt desired.

If there were no barriers to issuing debt in whatever market offered the highest price, price differences between markets would disappear and swaps would be no better than other financing alternatives. In fact, there are still significant barriers to capital flows between markets—transaction and information costs, differential taxes and regulations across markets, and legal restrictions on foreign currency transactions. Swaps are valuable financing vehicles because they allow corporations to arbitrage across these differences and thereby reduce their cost of capital. They also provide firms with flexibility in transforming the nature of their debt obligations.

Barriers to Capital Flow necessitate Swaps

9.8 SUMMARY

Currency swaps are patterned after parallel loan agreements in which two firms borrow in their home markets and then loan the funds to each other's foreign subsidiaries. Parallel loans allow parent firms with foreign subsidiaries to indirectly obtain foreign-currency debt financing for their foreign subsidiaries at low-cost foreign-currency rates despite facing higher borrowing costs in foreign debt markets. Shortcomings that make parallel loans less-than-ideal vehicles for cross-border financing include

- Difficulties in adjudicating disputes between parties to the parallel loan
- The requirement to capitalize parallel loans and place them on the balance sheet as an asset and an offsetting liability, thus inflating debt-to-equity ratios
- High search costs in finding firms with parallel funding needs

Parallel Loan Risks:

Packaging the parallel loans into a single swap contract remedies all three of these problems.

- Because one party can cancel the agreement if the other party does not fulfill its obligation, default risk is greatly reduced.

Swaps Fix the Risks

- Swaps are foreign currency transactions that are reported in the financial statements only in footnotes.
- Search costs are reduced as volume expands.

Swaps are in essence a bundle of forward contracts of different maturities, so they are subject to default risk. Although the consequences of default are somewhat more than in a comparable portfolio of futures, they are far less than for a straight debt instrument. The reason for this lower default risk is because the rights of set-off specify that if one side defaults on its payments the other side is released from its obligations as well. The exchange of principals further reduces the counterparties' risk exposures.

Swaps are valuable financing vehicles for multinational corporations because they allow corporations to arbitrage across domestic and international credit markets and to reduce their cost of capital by financing in the lowest-cost market. Swaps are especially useful for transforming long-maturity debt obligations that are not easily refinanced directly in the long-term debt markets.

KEY TERMS

Basis swap	Financial engineering
Bond equivalent versus money market yields	Indication pricing schedules
Commodity swaps	Interest rate swap
Coupon swap	Notional principal
Currency coupon swap	Parallel loan
Currency swap	Rights of set-off
Debt-for-equity swap	Swap book
Derivative securities	Swap contract
Difference check	Swaption

CONCEPTUAL QUESTIONS

9.1 What is a parallel loan arrangement? What are its advantages and disadvantages?
9.2 How can a currency swap remedy the problems of parallel loans?
9.3 How are swaps related to forward contracts?
9.4 What is a currency coupon swap?
9.5 What is a coupon swap?
9.6 What is the difference between a bond equivalent yield and a money market yield?

PROBLEMS

9.1 Sunflower International can borrow in the United States at 5 percent and in Italy at 8 percent. Rosa Internationale can borrow in Italy at 7 percent and in the United States at 9 percent.
   a. Draw a time line showing percentages for interest payments (e.g., 8 percent) and principal (e.g., 100 percent) assuming that each borrows in the foreign currency for three years with annual nonamortizing interest payments.

b. Now assume that the two companies perform a parallel loan and that Sunflower charges Rosa 9 percent on dollars and that Rosa charges Sunflower 8 percent interest on lire. Draw a time line illustrating this.

c. What are Sunflower's net borrowing costs in lire?

d. What are Rosa's net borrowing costs in dollars?

9.2 The Little Prince Co. (LP) has $100 million of two-year fixed-rate debt with a bond equivalent yield of 8.25 percent compounded semiannually. Given the nature of LP's assets and, hence, its financing needs, LP would prefer to have floating-rate debt. The market is asking LIBOR + 100 bps. How could an investment banker help LP achieve its objective with a swap contract?

9.3 Consider the following indication pricing schedule for currency coupon swaps of yen and pounds sterling:

Currency Coupon Swap
Indication Pricing Schedule (¥/£)

Maturity	Midrate (in £)
2 years	5.93% sa
3 years	6.18% sa
4 years	6.30% sa
5 years	6.41% sa

Deduct 5 bps if the bank is paying a fixed rate.
Add 5 bps if the bank is receiving a fixed rate.
All quotes are against six-month pounds sterling LIBOR flat.

Just like U.S. Treasury securities, bonds in Japan and in the United Kingdom are quoted as a bond equivalent yield.

a. Japan, Inc. (JI) has three-year yen debt at a floating-rate money market yield of six-month (¥) LIBOR + 105 bps. JI wants fixed-rate pound sterling debt to fund its U.K. operations. Describe JI's yen-for-pound currency coupon swap.

b. British Dog, Ltd. (BD) has three-year fixed rate pound debt at a bond equivalent yield of 7.45 percent. BD wants floating-rate yen debt to fund its expansion into Japan. Describe BD's pound-for-yen currency coupon swap.

c. What does the swap bank gain from these transactions?

SUGGESTED READINGS

The most comprehensive and easily understood textbook references on swaps are

John F. Marshall and Kenneth R. Kapner, *The Swaps Market,* 2d ed., 1993, Kolb Publishing Company.

Clifford W. Smith, Jr., Charles W. Smithson, and Lee M. Wakeman, *Managing Financial Risk,* 1995, Irwin Publishing Company.

Interesting review articles in the academic literature include

Charles W. Smithson, "A LEGO Approach to Financial Engineering: An Introduction to Forwards, Futures, Swaps, and Options," *Midland Corporate Finance Journal* 4, Winter 1987, pages 16–24.

Clifford W. Smith, Jr., Charles W. Smithson, and Lee M. Wakeman, "The Evolving Market for Swaps," *Midland Corporate Finance Journal* 3, No. 4, Winter 1986, pages 20–32.

Clifford W. Smith, Jr., Charles W. Smithson, and Lee M. Wakeman, "The Market for Interest Rate Swaps," *Financial Management* 17, No. 4, Winter 1988, pages 34–44.

A presentation of the (zero net) gains to swaps in a perfect market appears in

Stewart M. Turnbull, "Swaps: A Zero-Sum Game," *Financial Management* 16, No. 1, Spring 1987, pages 15–21.

Robert Litzenberger's 1992 Presidential Address to the American Finance Association discusses motivations for swap transactions in imperfect markets

Robert H. Litzenberger, "Swaps: Plain and Fanciful," *Journal of Finance* 47, No. 3, July 1992, pages 831–850.

On commodity and equity swaps, see

John F. Marshall, E.H. Sorensen, and Alan L. Tucker, "Equity Derivatives: The Plain Vanilla Equity Swap and Its Variants," *Journal of Financial Engineering* 10, No. 2, September 1992, pages 219–241.

S. Hansell, "Is the World Ready for Synthetic Equity?" *Institutional Investor,* August 1990, pages 54–62.

J. Lewis, "Oil Price Jitters? Try Energy Swaps," *Institutional Investor,* December 1990, pages 206–208.

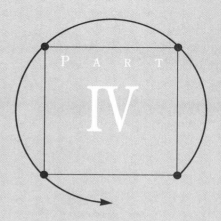

International Capital Markets and Portfolio Investment

How fair is a garden amid the toils and passions of existence?
Benjamin Disraeli

Part 4 discusses several national markets for debt and equity capital and describes the most prominent differences among these markets. Multinational corporations are increasingly raising capital in international markets. Investment portfolios are also becoming increasingly diversified internationally, so individual investors also care about the behavior of prices in international capital markets.

Chapter 10 begins this part of the book with a survey of the international capital markets. Chapter 11 introduces the algebra of portfolio diversification and applies this algebra to international assets. Chapter 12 extends the discussion of international portfolio diversification, applying it to international asset pricing and the diversifiability of currency risk. Chapter 13 concludes this part of the book with a discussion of international portfolio management.

A Tour of the World's Capital Markets

We are so small between the stars—so large against the sky.
Leonard Cohen

OVERVIEW

A wide variety of debt, equity, and hybrid debt-equity securities trade in the world's capital markets. Most trade in domestic markets, but a growing volume and variety of securities are traded in international markets. This chapter begins our journey through the world's capital markets by surveying the many forms and venues in which debt and equity capital are traded.

10.1 CAPITAL MARKETS VERSUS MONEY MARKETS

Financial markets are markets for financial, as opposed to real, assets and liabilities. A useful way to categorize financial markets is according to maturity. **Money markets** are markets for financial assets and liabilities of short maturity, usually considered to be less than one year. The market for Eurocurrency deposits and loans is an example of a money market. **Capital markets** are markets for financial assets and liabilities with maturity greater than one year. These markets include long-term government and corporate bonds as well as common and preferred stock. Common stock is the ultimate long-term asset; it possesses a potentially infinite lifetime. Table 10.1 lists the world's

Financial markets are categorized into money markets and capital markets.

money markets:
< one year
capital mkts:
> one year

TABLE 10.1 The World's Largest Capital Markets

Rank	Stock Markets[a]	$ billions	Rank	Government Bonds[b]	$ billions
1.	United States	4,936	1.	United States	2,112
2.	Japan	2,847	2.	Japan	1,224
3.	United Kingdom	1,091	3.	Germany	652
4.	Germany	402	4.	United Kingdom	650
5.	France	371	5.	France	442
6.	Switzerland	329	6.	Italy	365
7.	Netherlands	232	7.	Netherlands	214
8.	Hong Kong	213	8.	Canada	179
9.	Canada	171	9.	Belgium	169
10.	Australia	169	10.	Spain	145
11.	South Africa	140	11.	Sweden	111
12.	Italy	140	12.	Denmark	102
13.	Sweden	129	13.	Australia	60
14.	Malaysia	116	14.	Austria	52
15.	Spain	116	15.	Switzerland	30
16.	Belgium	80	16.	Finland	25
17.	Singapore	64	17.	Ireland	21
18.	Denmark	39	18.	Norway	15
19.	Mexico	39	19.	Portugal	14
20.	Finland	30	20.	New Zealand	11
20.	Norway	25			
21.	New Zealand	22			
22.	Ireland	19			
23.	Austria	19			
	Rest of the world	64		Rest of the world	n/a
	Total world value	11,801		Total world value	6,592

[a] Financial Times —Actuaries World Stock Market Indices (December 1995)
[b] Salomon Brothers Fixed Income Government Bond Indices (December 1995)

largest public stock and government bond markets. Figures 10.1 and 10.2 display the largest national markets as a percentage of the world market.

For many other financial assets the difference between short-term and long-term is an arbitrary distinction. In the domestic bond market, a thirty-year Treasury bond is classified as a long-term financial asset and is traded in the capital market at the time of its issue. But when a Treasury bond is three months from expiration, it is technically classified as a short-term instrument and is priced by market participants in the same way that three-month Treasury bills are priced. In the forward currency markets, the technical language used in a thirty-day forward currency contract is virtually indistinguishable from that of a five-year forward currency contract. The market for five-year forward contracts is less liquid and has higher bid-ask spreads, but otherwise it is not much different from the market for thirty-day forward contracts.

Liquidity refers to the ease with which you can exchange an asset for another asset of equal value.

The primary difference between short- and long-term versions of a particular financial asset is in the liquidity of the asset. **Liquidity** refers to the ease with which you can exchange an asset for another asset of equal value. Consider the floating-rate Eurocurrency market. There is an active Eurocurrency market for major currencies for maturities of one year or less. At longer maturities, liquidity in the Eurocurrency markets dries up even for the most actively traded currencies. There is very little market for Eurodollar

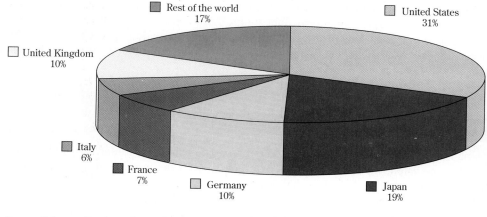

FIGURE 10.1
The World's Major
Government Bond Markets

Source: Salomon Brothers Government Bond Indicies (December 1995)

deposits and loans with maturities greater than two years, and most other currencies have no market beyond one year. Similarly, although there are forward markets for major currencies in maturities up to ten years, liquidity is poor and bid-ask spreads are high at distant forward dates. Covered interest arbitrage is quite effective at enforcing interest rate parity over short maturities, but it is much less effective at enforcing interest rate parity over long maturities because of poor liquidity in the long-term forward currency market and the absence of a Eurocurrency market at longer maturities.

Despite the apparently arbitrary classification of financial assets and liabilities according to maturity, the distinction is important because investors and financial managers use these markets in different ways. For example, investors in the bond markets have strong maturity preferences (called "preferred habitats") as they match the maturities of their assets to those of their liabilities. Commercial banks tend to lend in the short- and intermediate-term markets to offset their short- and intermediate-term

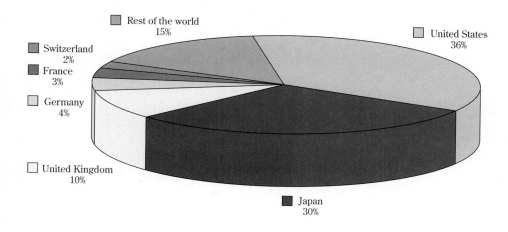

FIGURE 10.2
The World's Major
Stock Markets

Source: Financial Times–Actuaries World Stock Market Indices (December 1995)

liabilities. Insurance companies and pension funds tend to lend in the long-term market to counterbalance their long-term obligations. Furthermore, the distinction between capital and money markets is often encoded in national regulations governing securities issues. For these reasons, the distinction between capital and money markets is important.

10.2 INTERNATIONAL DEBT MARKETS

Debt markets can be categorized along three dimensions: (1) intermediated versus nonintermediated, (2) internal versus external, and (3) domestic versus international. These dimensions and their relations to each other are shown in Figure 10.3. The rest of this section describes each of these bond characteristics and then gives an example of a domestic bond and of two types of international bonds (foreign bonds and Eurobonds).

Commercial Banks as Financial Intermediaries

Funds can be moved from savers to borrowers either through a financial intermediary such as a commercial bank or directly through a securities market. For this reason, debt markets can be classified according to whether or not a financial intermediary stands between borrowers and savers (see Figure 10.3).

Financial intermediation is the process whereby a financial institution stands between savers and borrowers.

- In an **intermediated debt market**, a financial institution, such as a commercial bank, channels loanable funds from individual and corporate savers to borrowers.
- In a **nonintermediated or direct debt market**, large borrowers, such as governments and large corporations, appeal directly to savers for debt capital through the securities markets without using a financial institution as intermediary.

Nearly all borrowers—individuals, businesses, governments, and supranational institutions, such as the World Bank—use financial intermediaries to some extent. Nations differ

FIGURE 10.3
Bond Market Taxonomy
from a U.S. Perspective

	Domestic Bonds	International	
		Foreign Bonds	Eurobonds
Direct (public or private)	GMAC zr15 (NYSE)	AirExp 6s03 (OTC, U.S.)	FNMA 7.40 04 (OTC, non-U.S.)
Intermediated	Domestic bank loans to a domestic firm	Domestic bank loans to a foreign firm	Foreign bank loans to a foreign affiliate of a domestic firm
	Internal		External

Rank	Bank	Country of Origin	Percent of Business Outside Country of Origin			Assets ($ billion)
			1994	1993	1992	
1.	Standard Chartered	United Kingdom	70.2	70.1	66.1	53.5
2.	Credit Suisse Holding	Switzerland	66.4	64.2	65.0	298.6
3.	HSBC Holdings	United Kingdom	62.3	60.6	56.9	314.9
4.	Union Bank of Switzerland	Switzerland	62.2	64.2	60.2	248.9
5.	ABN-AMRO	Netherland	61.0	39.8	37.0	290.8
6.	Bank of China	China	55.0	46.3	46.3	217.6
7.	Credit Lyonnais	France	53.6	50.5	46.4	327.9
8.	Banque Indosuez	France	51.0	54.0	51.0	76.3
9.	Société Générale	France	50.2	51.0	49.9	278.0
10.	J.P. Morgan	United States	49.5	45.2	41.9	154.9
11.	Bankers Trust	United States	48.3	45.8	42.8	97.0
12.	Paribas	France	48.2	52.8	46.4	242.2
13.	National Westminster	United Kingdom	47.3	50.3	44.4	247.3
14.	Swiss Bank Corporation	Switzerland	47.1	53.3	55.5	161.8
15.	Citicorp	United States	45.6	48.7	44.7	250.5
16.	Banque Nationale de Paris	France	43.0	44.3	45.6	271.6
17.	Deutsche Bank	Germany	43.0	36.9	n/a	368.3
18.	Bank of Tokyo	Japan	42.1	n/a	28.4	271.2
19.	National Australia Bank	Australia	42.0	42.7	47.6	81.2
20.	ANZ Banking Group	Australia	40.0	38.7	37.8	65.8
21.	Republic New York Corp.	United States	38.9	31.9	40.8	41.1
22.	Bank of Montreal	Canada	38.0	35.9	38.6	99.6
23.	Scotiabank	Canada	37.0	41.2	43.5	94.7
24.	Sumitomo Trust & Banking	Japan	35.3	n/a	n/a	168.6
25.	Banca Commerciale Italiana	Italy	35.0	30.5	40.9	92.6

Source: *The Banker* (a *Financial Times* magazine), February 1995, page 70.

on the extent to which intermediated debt is supplemented through the securities markets.

Commercial banks develop a need to "go global" as they follow their customers into foreign markets. These banks usually develop a complete line of financial services to facilitate the overseas trade of their customers. In addition to commercial credit, commercial banks provide a variety of ancillary financial services including market making in spot and forward currency, invoicing, collection, and trade financing through letters of credit, banker's acceptances, and forfaiting (purchasing medium-term receivables at a discount from face value). International banks are increasingly moving into interest rate and currency risk management services and international cash management services.

Table 10.2 ranks the world's largest banks by the percentage of their business conducted outside their country of incorporation. These globally diversified banks differ from domestic banks in the proportion of their business conducted with other banks and with commercial enterprises domiciled in other countries. HSBC Holdings (Hongkong and Shanghai Banking Corporation) is an example of a commercial bank that has grown into an international competitor through its trade financing services. Incorporated in Hong Kong until 1992, HSBC grew during the nineteenth and twentieth centuries with the growth of trade between the United Kingdom and Asia with Hong Kong as the conduit. In 1991, HSBC conducted 81.9 percent of its business outside of

TABLE 10.3   THE GROWTH IN INTERNATIONAL BANKING

Country	1969		1978		1986	
	% of assets	# of banks	% of assets	# of banks	% of assets	# of banks
Australia	2.0	6	1.4	7	1.0	4
Belgium	1.1	4	2.5	6	2.0	7
Canada	4.6	7	3.2	7	2.5	6
France	4.2	9	9.2	15	7.7	12
Italy	8.0	21	6.5	23	5.4	18
Japan	16.0	46	24.1	58	34.2	62
Netherlands	1.7	5	3.1	6	2.3	5
Spain	1.6	7	2.4	12	1.8	10
Sweden	1.2	5	1.3	5	1.0	5
Switzerland	2.3	6	2.9	7	2.6	6
United Kingdom	7.1	15	4.3	8	4.6	9
United States	35.8	98	17.0	56	15.0	59
West Germany	7.7	25	13.6	35	9.6	32

Source: L.G. Goldberg and G.A. Hanweck, "Growth of the world's 300 largest banking organizations by country," *Journal of Banking and Finance,* February 1991, pages 207–223.

Hong Kong, including about 45 percent of its business in the United Kingdom. HSBC incorporated in the United Kingdom during 1992 to avoid the political uncertainty of operating under Chinese rule beginning in July 1997. HSBC also consolidated its U.K. affiliate Midland Bank at that time. As a newly incorporated U.K. bank, HSBC's percent of business overseas dropped from 81.9 percent in 1991 to 56.9 percent in 1992.

Table 10.3 documents the evolution of international banking activities in thirteen industrialized countries. Two trends stand out in this table. First, as Japan has grown as an export nation, the international banking activities of Japanese banks such as Fuji Bank and Sumitomo Bank have grown as well. Second, commercial banks in the United States have lost business to their overseas competitors during the last thirty years. This is largely because of a U.S. banking law called Regulation Q that constrained the expansion of U.S. banks both across state lines and internationally until the late 1970s. As can be seen in the table, the international banking activities of U.S. corporations had largely shifted to overseas banks by 1978. The pace at which U.S. banks lost business to their overseas competitors slowed considerably after bank deregulation in the late 1970s and early 1980s freed U.S. banks to compete on an international scale.

Bonds issued directly to the public through investment bankers fall under the nonintermediated debt category. The United States leads the list of government bond markets (see Table 10.1 and Figure 10.1) by a wide margin because the United States government is the world's largest single borrower. The size of national corporate bond markets generally follows the ranking of government bond markets in Table 10.1. The U.S. corporate bond market is the world's largest corporate bond market. Large U.S.-based corporations correspondingly rely more heavily on the public debt market than do their counterparts in other countries, although publicly traded bonds also play a major role in the financing of corporations in the United Kingdom.

In most other countries, commercial banks assume a more prominent role in allocating debt and equity capital. For example, corporations in Germany and Japan are much more likely to raise debt capital through commercial banks than through public bond markets, despite the active equity markets in these countries. Corporate relations with the lead banker or bankers are much closer in Germany and Japan than in the United States and the United Kingdom. Another factor tying German and Japanese companies more closely to their bankers is that commercial banks are allowed to own stock for their own account in these countries.[1] In many countries, including Germany and Japan, commercial banks also serve as investment bankers in public debt and equity offerings. As we shall see in a later section, cross-border differences in banking relations have a profound impact on the incentives and controls placed on management in different countries.

Internal and External Debt Markets

The fact that bonds can be issued in other than the functional currency of the borrower suggests another way that debt markets can be categorized (see Figure 10.3).

- Debt placed in an **internal market** is denominated in the currency of a host country and placed within that country.
- Debt placed in an **external market** is placed outside the borders of the country issuing the currency.

Government regulation and intervention are nearly absent in the short-term external Eurocurrency market. Internal markets for long-term debt capital are monitored and regulated by local authorities. Government influence in the external Eurobond markets is a little less direct than in internal markets but no less important. Government regulation of the internal and external bond markets is discussed in the following section.

Domestic and International Bonds

Debt issues can be further categorized according to whether they are sold into the domestic or the international markets (again, see Figure 10.3).

International bonds are traded outside the country of the issuer.

- **Domestic bonds** are issued and traded within the internal market of a single country and are denominated in the currency of that country.
- **International bonds** are traded outside the country of the issuer. International bonds come in two varieties:
  - **Foreign bonds** are issued in a domestic market by a foreign borrower, denominated in domestic currency, marketed to domestic residents, and regulated by the domestic authorities.
  - **Eurobonds** are denominated in one or more currencies but are traded in external markets outside the borders of the countries issuing those currencies.

---

1 In the United States, the Glass-Steagall Act prohibits commercial banks from participating in investment banking activities and from owning stock (except in trust accounts for their clients).

TABLE 10.4 NEW INTERNATIONAL BOND ISSUES LISTED IN THE *FINANCIAL TIMES* (FRIDAY, MAY 10, 1995)

Borrower	Amount m.	Coupon %	Price	Maturity	Fees %	Spread bp	Book-runner
US DOLLARS							
AECAMT 1996-1, Class A(a)‡	867.5	(a1,l)	(a1)R	May 2001	0.30R	(a1) (6¼%–01)	Merrill Lynch International
Philip Electronics	250	7.00	99.276R	Jun 2001	0.325R	+52(6¼%–01)	HSBC Markets
Den Danske Bank(b)‡	200	(b1)	99.886R	Jun 2006	0.45R	–	Salomon Brothers Intl
CNCP Intl Finance(c)‡	150	(c1)	99.87R	May 2001	0.25R	–	JP Morgan Securities
AC International Finance	110	8.125#	99.417R	Nov 2001	0.75R	+173(6¼%–01)	JP Morgan Securities
Lebanese Republic(d,s)	100	9.125	99.82R	Jul 2000	1.00R	+295(6⅛%–00)	Paribas Capital Markets
UBS Finance(e,s)	100	6.00	98.80R	Dec 1999	0.1875R	−1(5%–99)	UBS
Business Dev Bank of Canada	100	6.375	99.783R	May 1999	0.1875R	+3(6⅜%–99)	M Stanley/Tokyo-Mitsubishi
Banco Bozano(f)	75	10.375#	99.82R	May 2004	0.875R	+395(6⅜%–99)	Barclays de Zoete Wedd
D-MARKS							
Commonwealth Bank of Australia	300	5.375	99.658R	Jun 2001	0.25R	+32(5⅛%-00)	Banque Paribas (Deutsch)
SGZ Bank Ireland‡	300	(g)	99.535	Jun 2001	0.20	–	HSBC Trinkaus/Merrill Lynch
SWISS FRANCS							
Mita Industrial★	80	4.25	100.80	May 2001	1.50	–	Sakura Bank (Schweiz)
CANADIAN DOLLARS							
Province of Manitoba(s)	150	7.00	100.00R	Sep 1999	0.225R	+10(7¾%-99)	CIBC Wood Gundy
AUSTRALIAN DOLLARS							
World Bank(l)★	250	7.65#	99.72	Jun 1999	0.80	–	Yamaichi Intl (Europe)
Toronto Dominion Bank, London	100	8.125	100.785	May 1998	1.25	–	Toronto Dominion Bank
PESETAS							
LW Rentenbank(h)	10bn	(h1)	101.121	Jun 2006	1.625	–	BNA/BNP España
Komuninvest	10bn	8.65	101.269	Jun 2001	1.625	–	BSN/NatWest/Nikko España

Final terms, non-callable unless stated. Yield spread (over govt bond) at launch supplied by lead manager. ★Unlisted. ‡Floating-rate note. #Semi-annual coupon. R: fixed re-offer price; fees shown at re-offer level. a) American Express Credit Account Master Trust. Legal Maturity: 15/12/03. Monthly coupons. a1) Priced later: T's +35–37bp area. a2) Class B: $57.5m, 15/5/01, +50–52bp. b) Callable from Jun 2003 at par. b1) 6-mth Libor +37½bp to Jun 2003, then +187½bp. c) Callable from May 1999 at par. c1) 3-mth Libor +20bp. d) Fungible with $300m. No accrued. e) $200m launched 29/4/96 increased to $300m. f) Callable & puttable on 23/5/99 at 99½% & 01 at 99¾%. g) 3-mth Libor flat. h) Callble on 10/6/99 at par. h1) 9% to 10/6/99, then 9¾%. l) Long 1st coupon. s) Short 1st coupon.

Borrowers that are well known internationally sometimes find that their financing costs are lower in foreign bond markets or in the external Eurobond market than in their own domestic bond market. These opportunities arise because of disequilibriums in the international parity conditions, such as a difference in real interest costs between two currencies. Most borrowers, however, find that their borrowing costs are lower for domestic bond issues than for international bond issues because of the high information costs in international markets. Borrowers in the international bond markets include major multinational corporations, such as General Motors and British Petroleum; national governments, such as the United States and Japan; government agencies, such as the Federal National Mortgage Association (abbreviated FNMA and referred to as "Fannie Mae"); and supranational organizations, such as the World Bank. The London *Financial Times* publishes a weekly "New International Bond Issues" article that lists major foreign and Eurobond issues. The May 10, 1995, listing appears in Table 10.4.

Domestic Bonds and National Bond Markets. The most prominent bonds selling in national bond markets are domestic bonds. Because they are issued and traded in an internal market, domestic bonds are regulated by the domestic government and are traded according to the institutional conventions of the domestic bond market. The "GMAC zr 15" listed as a domestic bond in Figure 10.3 is a zero-coupon (deep discount) dollar-denominated bond issued by General Motors Acceptance Corporation, maturing in the year 2015, and traded on the New York Stock Exchange. This is a domestic, internal, direct issue under the authority of the U.S. Securities and Exchange Commission.

Domestic bonds are preferred by domestic investors because the borrowers are usually well-known domestic firms or the domestic government. Since information costs are lower within a single country than across national borders, domestic borrowers often get better prices for bonds issued domestically than for bonds issued outside of the home country. Higher bond prices in the domestic market lead to lower capital costs in the domestic market for the typical borrower.[2]

Bond market price and yield quotation conventions, governmental registration and disclosure requirements, and withholding taxes differ from country to country. Some of the differences in bond-trading conventions are listed in Table 10.5. In the United States, government bonds are traded in an over-the-counter market through commercial and investment banks. Corporate bonds are traded over-the-counter by commercial banks as well as on the New York Stock Exchange. In other national markets, the publicly traded bonds of major corporations are exchange-listed on the nation's exchange(s), traded over-the-counter by commercial and investment banks, or both.

Corporate and government bonds in the United States and Japan are generally issued in **registered form** and pay semiannual interest. In countries requiring that bonds be issued in registered form, each issuer maintains a record of the owners of its bonds. Registration facilitates the calculation and payment of accrued interest, but it also imposes a record-keeping burden on bond issuers.

---

2 Financial opportunities arising from differences in borrowing costs between foreign and domestic issuers in a single internal market are discussed in Chapter 9.

TABLE 10.5 CHARACTERISTICS OF THE MAJOR NATIONAL BOND MARKETS

Type of Bond	Ownership	Coupons	Price Quote	Withholding Tax under Tax Treaty with the United States
Domestic				
Canada	Registered	Semiannual	Actual/365	15%
Japan	Registered	Semiannual	Actual/365	10%
France	Bearer	Annual	Actual/365	0–10%
Germany	Bearer	Annual	30/360	0%
Switzerland	Bearer	Semiannual	30/360	5%
United Kingdom	Bearer	Semiannual	Actual/365	0%
United States	Registered	Semiannual	30/360 (corporate bonds)	–
			Actual/365 (Treasury bonds)	–
Eurobond				
Fixed-rate bonds	Bearer	Annual	30/360	–
Floating-rate notes (FRNs)	Bearer	Quarterly or semiannual	Actual/360	–

Bearer bonds retain the anonymity of the owner.

The convention in many West European countries is to use **bearer bonds**. Bearer bonds are not registered and can be redeemed by the holder. The principle advantage of bearer bonds is that they retain the anonymity of the bondholder. This can be very important to some investors. The bearer is assumed to be the legal owner of the bond, so bondholders must ensure that they do not lose the bonds or the bond coupons. Because it is inconvenient to present bond coupons for payment of interest, bearer bonds are usually issued with annual coupons.

The price-plus-accrued-interest method is by far the most common bond price quotation system for domestic bonds. The advantage of buying and selling bonds with accrued interest is that bond prices do not fall on the ex-payment date (that is, on the day after a coupon interest payment is made). This makes it easier to compare prices and yields across bonds with different coupons and payment dates. Domestic bonds that do not conform to this convention and are quoted with coupons attached include U.K. government bonds ("gilts") of more than five-year maturity and some convertible and index-linked bonds. These bonds fall in price on the ex-payment date in much the same way that common stock prices fall on ex-dividend dates.

Markets also differ in the conventions used for quoting bond prices and yields. In the United States, Treasury notes and bonds are quoted as a **bond equivalent yield** ("Actual/365" in Table 10.5) assuming a 365-day year and semiannual coupon payments. Market prices on Treasury notes and bonds are quoted assuming interest accrues to the bondholder on a daily basis according to the actual number of days that have passed since the most recent coupon interest payment. Consider a Treasury bond with a 10 percent coupon. This bond pays 5 percent semiannually on June 30 and on December 31. If it is now the morning of February 6, then 36 days (January 1 through February 5) have elapsed since the last coupon interest payment. The price on this bond is quoted assuming the current bondholder is entitled to $0.05(36/182.5) \approx 0.00986$, or 0.986 percent of the principal as accrued interest.

U.S. corporate bonds are quoted as a **money market yield** that assumes a 360-day year with thirty-day months. Under the thirty-day convention, no interest accrues on the thirty-first of any month. A U.S. corporate bond paying 10 percent interest on a semiannual basis would be quoted on February 6 assuming the bondholder is entitled to thirty days of accrued interest from January plus five days of accrued interest from February for 0.05(35/180) ≈ 0.00972, or 0.972 percent of the principal as accrued interest. Accrued interest through the end of January would be 0.05(30/180) ≈ 0.00833, or 0.833 percent of the principal since no interest accrues on January 31. The last day of February receives the last several days' worth of interest from February. Three days' worth of interest is received on the twenty-eighth of February when this is the last day of the month.

Bond yield quotations in the United States assume semiannual compounding for both government and corporate bonds. For example, a 10 percent bond that pays 5 percent interest semiannually is quoted in the United States as paying 10 percent, which means 10 percent compounded semiannually. Bond dealers in Europe do not follow the U.S. convention of quoting annual yields with semiannual compounding. European bond dealers quote a 10 percent coupon paid semiannually (that is, 5 percent semiannually) as an **effective annual yield** of $(1.05)^2 - 1 = 0.1025$, or 10.25 percent. This is the actuarially correct yield calculation.

Trading conventions in other bond markets can be arcane. Bond yields in Japan are quoted according to a simple interest calculation that amortizes the bond's premium or discount to par value over the life of the bond as follows:

$$\text{Yield} = \left(\text{Coupon rate} + \frac{100\% - \text{Price}}{\text{Years to maturity}} \right) \left(\frac{100\%}{\text{Price}} \right) \qquad (10.1)$$

A Fool and His Money Are Quickly Parted

— PYRAMID scheme

Russia and other countries of the former Soviet Union are in the process of transforming their economics from state-controlled communism to free-market capitalism. During 1994, Russian investors hit a large pothole on the road to a market economy. Share prices in MMM, at one time the country's largest investment company, fell from a high of 105,600 rubles (about $50) to less than 1,000 rubles.

MMM's "investments" were nothing more than an advertising campaign promising returns of more than 1000 percent to investors. As investors in the United States and other developed markets have discovered, there is no easy money. It turns out that early investors (the ones earning the 1000 percent returns) were being paid with the proceeds of later share sales. When this pyramid scheme finally collapsed in 1994, trading in MMM shares was suspended and MMM's president, Sergei Mavrodi, was arrested for tax evasion. In a demonstration that markets have little memory, Mavrodi was subsequently elected to represent his native Moscow in the Russian parliament.

Pyramid schemes are often called "Ponzi schemes" after an infamous pyramid scheme run by Charles Ponzi in Boston during the 1920s. Pyramid schemes such as MMM's are common in emerging markets as investors learn the pitfalls of the free-market system. A similar scandal called "Caritas" duped Romanian investors in 1993. However, investors in emerging economies are by no means the only ones vulnerable to these get-rich-quick schemes. Every market economy sees its share. At least four Ponzi schemes of $10 million or more collapsed during 1994 in the United States. These are hard lessons in the free-market principle of caveat emptor—let the buyer beware.

For example, a bond selling in the United States with a 10 percent coupon and semi-annual payments (that is, 5 percent semiannually) with two years until maturity and selling at 80 percent of par value would be quoted in Japan as selling at a yield of $[0.10+(1.00-0.80)/2](1.00/0.80) = 0.25$, or 25 percent. The effective semiannual yield-to-maturity for this bond would be the solution to

$$80 = \frac{5}{(1+i)^1} + \frac{5}{(1+i)^2} + \frac{5}{(1+i)^3} + \frac{105}{(1+i)^4}$$

or i = 11.518 percent. The effective annual yield is then $(1.11518)^2 - 1 = 0.24363$, or 24.363 percent. In Europe, the convention is to quote this effective annual yield as the yield-to-maturity. In the United States, this bond would be quoted with a bond equivalent yield of $(2)(0.11518) = 0.23036$, or 23.036 percent compounded semiannually.

Because of these institutional differences in bond market conventions, caveat emptor (let the buyer beware) applies whenever unfamiliar bonds are bought or sold.

Foreign Bonds: When in Rome, Do As the Romans Do. Foreign bonds are issued by a foreign borrower but traded in another country's internal market and denominated in the local currency. Foreign bonds are issued in the local currency to make the bonds attractive to local residents. Foreign bonds are regulated by the domestic authorities of the country within which the bonds are issued and traded. Bond trading conventions on foreign bonds typically conform to the local conventions rather than those of the borrower. Foreign bonds are known as Yankee bonds in the United States, as bulldog bonds in the United Kingdom, and as samurai bonds in Japan. By far the greatest value of foreign bonds is traded in Switzerland (the reason for this is discussed in the section on Eurobonds), followed by the United States and then Japan.

Foreign bonds are traded and denominated in another country's internal market and currency.

The "AirExp 6s03" listed in the direct-internal-foreign bond category of Figure 10.3 is a dollar-denominated Yankee bond issued in the United States by the U.K.-based airline Air Express. This bond is sold over-the-counter through commercial and investment banks in the United States, pays a 6 percent semiannual coupon, and matures in 2003. This is a foreign bond issued in the U.S. internal market by a foreign borrower through a direct placement.

For a foreign borrower to attract debt capital at competitive prices, the foreign bond issuer should be well known in the host country. The World Bank has more than fifteen dollar-denominated bond issues outstanding with maturities ranging from one to fifteen years. Foreign bonds traded on the New York Stock Exchange are issued by familiar names such as Amoco Canada, Air Express, Atari, Greyhound, Roadmaster, Storer Broadcasting, Time Warner, and Viacom. Less familiar names are forced to issue their bonds in the over-the-counter market, typically at lower prices and higher yields.

Eurobonds are issued and traded in the external bond market.

Eurobonds: Necessity is the Mother of Invention. The second type of international bond is the Eurobond. Eurobonds are issued and traded in the external bond market. The "FNMA 7.40 04" bond issue in the Eurobond category of Figure 10.3 is a dollar-denominated bond issued by the Federal National Mortgage Association with a 7.4 percent annual coupon and a maturity date in 2004. This Eurobond is issued directly to non-U.S. investors (in this case, by a U.S. borrower) in an external, public debt market.

As with many financial innovations, the Eurobond market was born and matured as borrowers and investors sought ways to circumvent government restrictions on cross-border capital flows. Governments constrain capital flows for a number of economic and political reasons. Constraints on capital outflows are designed to protect the balance of payments from excessive capital outflows and to preserve the scarce long-term capital supplied by domestic savers. Constraints on capital inflows are designed to protect domestic businesses from foreign competition.

Two governmentally imposed barriers gave birth to the Eurobond market. In 1963, the United States levied an *interest equalization tax* on interest paid to U.S. investors by foreign borrowers. This put a tariff on non-U.S. borrowers attempting to issue foreign bonds in the U.S. market. Foreign bonds were not subject to interest withholding taxes within the United States, but the income tax on U.S. residents investing in foreign bonds made foreign bonds a costly way for foreign firms to raise dollar debt capital. Rather than go directly to the U.S. market, foreign borrowers began to issue dollar-denominated bonds in countries other than the United States. The interest equalization tax lasted until 1974, but by that time the Eurodollar bond market was firmly established.

The second barrier was an interest withholding tax on domestic U.S. bonds that was imposed through 1984. The interest withholding tax made it inconvenient for foreign investors to own dollar-denominated bonds. The Eurobond market was an attractive alternative for foreign investors wishing to avoid the interest withholding tax. When the United States dropped the withholding tax requirement on domestic bonds in 1984, the Eurodollar bond market and the domestic U.S. bond market became close substitutes for foreign investors.

Shareholder and Bondholder Registration in Russia

Russia has instituted an ambitious privatization program in its efforts to convert to a market-based economy. Despite its best efforts, the level of direct foreign investment in Russian industry is minuscule. The European Bank for Reconstruction and Development (EBRD) estimates that Russia received $2 billion in direct foreign investment over the period 1990–1993. This is only about $7 per capita compared with $214 per capita in Hungary and $59 per capita in the Czech Republic. Total direct foreign investment grew to about $2 billion in 1994 but still lagged direct foreign investment into other countries of the former Soviet Union.*

One barrier to foreign portfolio investment is Russia's share registration system. According to Russian law, factory managers are legally responsible for maintaining the shareholder and bondholder registers in Russia. The Western financial press has reported several abuses of this system in which unwanted owners have been deleted from the ownership register by managers wishing to rid themselves of outside control. The potential for fraud and abuse will persist in Russia as long as there is no independent stewardship of the ownership register.

Deficiencies and uncertainties in the laws governing business transactions and private property are currently the biggest obstacles to foreign investment in Russia and the other countries of the former Soviet Union.

* These figures are from "Full potential is still untapped" in a *London Financial Times* survey of Russia, April 10, 1995, page IV. Also see Peter Marber's "Banking the Bear: Financial Marketization in Russia," *Columbia Journal of World Business* 24, No. 4, Winter 1994, pages 30–41.

In the United States, the Securities Exchange Act of 1934 required that all new public securities issues be registered with the Securities and Exchange Commission (SEC). The SEC is responsible for ensuring that the registration statements accompanying the debt or equity issue disclose all material information about the issuer. There are no registration or disclosure requirements on private placements. The SEC has allowed a similar exemption on the Eurobonds of U.S. issuers that satisfy the SEC's criteria for private placement. This has helped to make Eurodollar bonds issued by U.S. firms competitive with those issued by foreign firms.

Once the benefits of Eurodollar bonds became apparent to governmental and corporate borrowers and to the international investment banking community, Eurobonds denominated in other currencies soon followed. Presently, several thousand Eurobond issues trade in a fairly active secondary market. The most common Eurobond currencies are the U.S. dollar, the British pound sterling, the deutsche mark, the Japanese yen, and the European Currency Unit (ECU). The ECU is a weighted average of the currencies in the European exchange rate mechanism (ERM). Eurobonds denominated in ECU are often issued by companies residing in European Union countries that do not have active Eurobond markets in their own currencies. These countries include Italy, Spain, Portugal, Belgium, and the Netherlands.

The Swiss franc is notably absent from the list of popular Eurobond currencies. The Banque Nationale Suisse (the Swiss central bank) does not allow Swiss banks or foreign banks with Swiss branches to trade Eurobonds denominated in Swiss francs. This has effectively closed the Eurobond market to Swiss franc issues. Instead, Switzerland has facilitated the access of foreign borrowers to the Swiss franc foreign bond market through streamlined registration procedures and easy access to this highly liquid market. The Swiss foreign bond market trades more foreign bonds than any other national bond market because it substitutes for the nonexistent Swiss franc Eurobond market.

Eurobond dealers are members of the *Association of International Bond Dealers* (AIBD). The AIBD is a self-regulated industry group based in Zurich. No commissions are charged in the Eurobond market; dealers make their profit through the bid-ask spread. Transactions in the secondary Eurobond market are conventionally settled within seven days. About two-thirds of all secondary market Eurobond transactions are cleared through *Euroclear,* which is operated by Morgan Stanley out of Brussels. The remaining Eurobond transactions are cleared through *Cedel,* which is based in Luxembourg and operated by the member banks of the AIBD. Exchange listing is often required by the home governments of the firms issuing Eurobonds. Luxembourg is a convenient site for clearing operations because many Eurobonds are listed on the Luxembourg exchange to satisfy the listing requirement.

Global Bonds

A global bond trades in the Eurobond market as well as in one or more internal markets.

A **global bond** is a bond that trades in the Eurobond market as well as in one or more national bond markets. To appeal to a global investor base, borrowers must be large and AAA-rated and must borrow in actively traded currencies. The World Bank was the first to issue a global bond, with a series of dollar-denominated issues in the late 1980s. Global bonds are usually denominated in dollars because the dollar bond market has the most liquidity.

To appeal to domestic U.S. investors, global dollar bonds have semiannual coupons and are sold in registered form. Recall that most fixed-rate Eurodollar bonds have annual coupons and are sold in bearer form. Euromarket investors are willing to buy registered bonds with semiannual coupons in the Eurobond market as long as there is adequate liquidity.

Matsushita Electric Industrial Company was the first corporate borrower to tap the global bond market. In 1992, Matsushita issued $1 billion of ten-year fixed-rate bonds at $7\frac{1}{4}$ percent or 41 basis points higher than the rate on ten-year U.S. Treasuries. Matsushita's original allocation was 40 percent to the domestic U.S. bond market, 40 percent to Europe, and 20 percent to the Asia/Pacific region. These bonds now sell in both the domestic U.S. bond market and in the Eurobond market, so this initial allocation no longer constrains where these bonds are bought and sold.

Equity-Linked Eurobonds

Many Eurobonds are sold with an equity option. Equity options typically come in one of two forms: convertible debt or debt with warrants. These equity-linked bonds are designed to be attractive to two clienteles by offering two elements of return. The bond provides a return that is attractive to fixed-income investors. The equity option supplies a "kicker" that appeals to investors wanting to take a more speculative gamble on the equity.

Convertible bonds are bonds with a conversion feature that allows the holder to convert the bond into common stock on or prior to a conversion date and at a prespecified conversion price. If the stock price rises above the conversion price, the equity option is in-the-money, and the convertible bond can be converted into common stock. The conversion option cannot be detached from the underlying bond. Convertible bonds provide individuals and institutional investors an equity option while promising a fixed return on the bond portion of the instrument.

Convertible bonds can be used as a back door into the equity markets of countries that do not allow foreign ownership or allow only limited foreign ownership of their companies. For example, non-Korean ownership of Korean equities is allowed only through one of the Korea Funds that are sold on stock exchanges around the world (including the London and New York exchanges). A Korea Fund is a closed-end mutual fund invested in large Korean companies. The Korean equities that are owned by these funds are strictly regulated by the Korean government. Because of limited supply, these funds can sell at substantial premiums to the net asset value of the underlying assets. Indirect participation in the Korean equity market can be accomplished by purchasing the convertible Eurobonds of Korean companies.

Warrants are long-term options to buy stock in the issuing company at a prespecified exercise price. The exercise date is usually several years in the future. Warrants are usually detachable so that the option can sell separately from the bond. Warrants often find their way back to the home market of the issuing company if that country does not allow stock option trading on its exchanges. Most Eurobonds issued by Japanese companies come with detachable warrants for this reason.

A Brief Tour of the World's Major Stock Exchanges

Table 10.1 presents a list of the world's largest national stock markets. Figure 10.2 displays these national market capitalizations as a percentage of the world stock market capitalization. The United States equity market is the largest, with a total market value of $4.936 trillion at the end of 1995. Japan is second at $2.847 trillion and the United Kingdom is third at $1.091 trillion.

Figure 10.4 displays stock returns earned in several geographic regions of the world since 1970. The economies of Western Europe, the United States and Canada were already at a high level of development by 1970, so these developed economies have been unable to match the phenomenal growth of the economies in Southeast Asia and the Far East. This is reflected in the higher rates of return earned in these fast-growing regions.

North America. The largest stock market in North America is the New York Stock Exchange (NYSE). The American Stock Exchange (AMEX) is a distant second in trading value and value traded among the U.S. exchanges operating out of a single location. The National Association of Securities Dealers Automated Quotation System (NASDAQ) operates an automated National Market System (NMS) in large stocks and a less liquid non-NMS market in smaller companies. The NASDAQ recently surpassed the New York Stock Exchange in trading volume, although the value of companies listed on the two NASDAQ systems is still smaller than the value of stocks traded by the NYSE.

FIGURE 10.4
Stock Returns around the World (December 1969 level = 100)

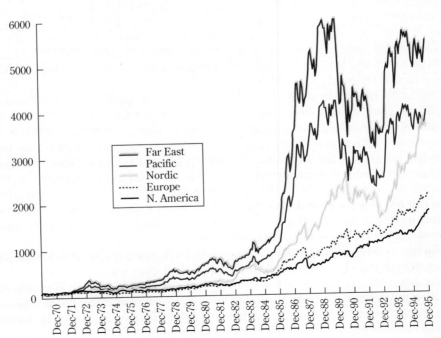

Source: Morgan Stanley Capital International

The value of the Japanese stock market is easy to overestimate because of share cross-holdings between Japanese companies. These cross-holdings are concentrated in six *keiretsu*—networks of companies linked through share ownership and through customer/supplier relations. Debt ratios in these companies are not always as they appear.

Consider the two firms below in the absence of corporate cross-holdings:

Ownership structure *without* corporate cross-holdings

Firm A			
Real assets	100	Debt	50
		Equity	50
Total assets	100	Total liabilities	100

Firm B			
Real assets	100	Debt	50
		Equity	50
Total assets	100	Total liabilities	100

The combined market value of these firms without corporate cross-holdings is simply 100+100=200, the sum of the real asset values. Suppose that these companies exchange common stock nominally worth 50. The new balance sheets look like this:

Ownership structure *with* corporate cross-holdings

Firm A			
Real assets	100	Debt	50
Shares in B	50	Equity	100
Total assets	150	Total liabilities	150

Firm B			
Real assets	100	Debt	50
Shares in A	50	Equity	100
Total assets	150	Total liabilities	150

With cross-holdings, the apparent value of these companies is equal to 150+150=300. But 50+50=100 of this value is not based on any real assets and is purely illusory. The value of the real assets in these two companies is still only 200. In this way, the market value of common stock is overstated in countries with high levels of corporate cross-holdings.

Note that the debt ratios of these companies are understated when equity cross-holdings are present. The asset-based debt ratios of these companies are $D/V = 50/100 = 50$ percent as in the balance sheets without cross-holdings. With corporate cross-holdings, the apparent debt ratio is only $D/V = 50/150 = 33$ percent. Corporate equity cross-holdings cause observed debt ratios to understate the true level of financial leverage.

Regional exchanges, such as the Pacific Stock Exchange and the Philadelphia Stock Exchange, trade lesser volumes, primarily in the shares of regional companies.

Japan, Southeast Asia, and the Far East. The largest stock exchange in Japan is the Tokyo Stock Exchange (TSE) in the "eastern capital" of Tokyo. The value of stocks listed on the Osaka Stock Exchange near the "western capital" of Kyoto is surpassed only by the Tokyo and New York exchanges.[3] The value of stocks traded in Japan surpassed the value of stocks traded on the New York Stock Exchange in the late 1980s, according to Morgan Stanley Capital International, but then fell behind the NYSE during a crash in Japanese share prices in 1990 and 1991. The aftershocks of this stock

---

3 "Tokyo" and "Kyoto" translate literally as "eastern capital" and "western capital," respectively.

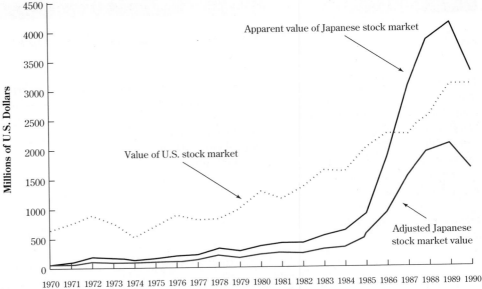

FIGURE 10.5
Value of Japanese Stock
Market Adjusted for
Corporate Cross-Holdings,
1970–1990

Source: Kenneth R. French and James M. Poterba, "Were Japanese Stock Prices too High?" *Journal of Financial Economics* 29, No. 2, 1991, pages 337-363.

market collapse are still being felt in Japanese politics and consumer confidence, as well as in their industrial and financial institutions.

The size of the Japanese equity market relative to the U.S. equity market is overstated in Table 10.1 for two reasons. First, the stock exchanges at Tokyo and Osaka account for the vast majority of Japanese share value; the value of stocks traded on the Japanese over-the-counter market is very small. The NASDAQ market in the United States is not included in Table 10.1, and it accounts for a large and increasing share of U.S. equities. The second reason that the Japanese market value in Table 10.1 overstates the value of the Japanese stock market is because of large corporate cross-holdings in Japan. Figure 10.5 presents one estimate of the value of the Japanese stock market after adjusting for corporate cross-holdings.

The fastest-growing stock markets in the world are located in southeast Asia and include the "little dragons" or "tiger economies" of Korea, Vietnam, Thailand, Taiwan, Malaysia, Indonesia, and Hong Kong. Along with companies from Mexico, companies from these countries dominate the list of top emerging market companies in Table 10.6.

Companies in the smaller Asian national and regional markets have not had access to the Japanese equity markets because of cross-border capital controls imposed by the Japanese government. These capital controls were relaxed only as recently as 1994. The number of foreign companies listed on the Tokyo Stock Exchange actually fell from 125 during Tokyo's heyday in 1990 to about 90 stocks by 1995 as large multinational corporations delisted their shares from the exchange. The value of foreign shares traded on the Tokyo Stock Exchange is only about 10 percent of what it was in 1990. The relative lack of competition from the large markets at Tokyo and Osaka has given the smaller Asian stock markets room to grow.

The apparent value of the Japanese stock market is exaggerated by the large share cross-holdings of Japanese corporations

TABLE 10.6 TOP THIRTY EMERGING-MARKET COMPANIES: MARKET CAPITALIZATION AS OF JUNE 30, 1994

Rank	Company	Country	$ billions
1.	Telefonos de Mexico (Telmex)	Mexico	30
2.	Korea Electric Power	Korea	20
3.	Tenaga Nasional	Malaysia	17
4.	Cathay Life Insurance	Taiwan	15
5.	Telekom Malaysia	Malaysia	15
6.	Electrobras	Brazil	11
7.	Telebras	Brazil	11
8.	Hua Nan Bank	Taiwan	9
9.	Grupo Financiero Banacci	Mexico	9
10.	YPF	Argentina	9
11.	Grupo Carso	Mexico	8
12.	First Bank	Taiwan	8
13.	Petrobras	Mexico	8
14.	Grupo Televisa	Mexico	8
15.	Cifra	Mexico	8
16.	Pohang Iron and Steel	South Korea	8
17.	Chang Hwa Bank	Taiwan	7
18.	Bangkok Bank	Thailand	7
19.	Telecomasia	Thailand	7
20.	Telefonica de Argentina	Argentina	7
21.	Cemex	Mexico	7
22.	China Steel	Taiwan	6
23.	Samsung Electronics	South Korea	6
24.	Malayan Bank	Malaysia	6
25.	Resorts World	Malaysia	6
26.	Endesa	Chile	6
27.	San Miguel	Philippines	5
28.	Genting	Malaysia	5
29.	Siam Cement	Thailand	5
30.	Telecommunicacoes de Sao Paulo	Brazil	5

Source: Morgan Stanley Capital International as reported in *The Economist*, July 16–22, 1994, page 102.

Hong Kong trades the largest number of foreign stocks of any Asian market, although many foreign companies are delisting from the Hong Kong exchange in anticipation of the 1997 transfer of power from the British to the Chinese. Hong Kong also trades the shares of a number of companies based in mainland China. The performance of these *H-shares*—Chinese enterprises listed in Hong Kong—has been (and most likely will continue to be) highly erratic as shareholders respond to changing economic and tax proclamations on the part of Chinese governmental authorities. For example, Hong Kong's *Hang Seng China Enterprises Index* of H-shares fell from over 2,000 in December 1994 to 685 on November 16, 1995, as the Chinese government removed several tax advantages available to shares listed in Hong Kong.

Europe. Europe has more than forty stock markets, but these are smaller than the largest markets in the United States and Japan. The largest stock market in Europe is the London Stock Exchange (LSE). The LSE plays a special role in international finance because of London's place as a major international center for currency and

The LSE plays a special role in international finance because of London's position in currency and Eurocurrency trading.

Eurocurrency trading. The next largest markets are the Frankfurt Stock Exchange in Germany and the Paris Bourse in France. There are several other prominent regional exchanges, most notably in Switzerland at Zurich, Geneva, and Basel.

The London Stock Exchange and other European markets actively compete for share trading in both foreign and domestic stocks. Share trading tends to gravitate toward the most liquid and operationally efficient market. Sometimes this is the LSE, sometimes it is a local or regional exchange, and sometimes shares are dually listed on the LSE and on one or more other exchanges.

Other Markets. The Bombay Stock Market in India is a fairly well developed capital market, although foreign access to the market has been restricted for many years by the Indian government. Around seven thousand companies are listed in India. About three thousand of these are traded regularly. The Bombay Stock Exchange trades almost 70 percent of the value of the country's total stock transactions. Foreign portfolio investment in the Indian market was prohibited by the Indian government until September of 1992, when up to 24 percent of the equity in individual Indian companies was opened to registered foreign institutional investors. The largest Indian companies were quick to take advantage of the relaxed limit on foreign institutional ownership, with a large number of foreign stock offerings (usually in the form of global depository receipts) following the 1992 revision in the government's stance on foreign portfolio investment.

Stock markets on the African, South American, and Asian continents are, with few exceptions, still in their infancy. The Johannesburg Stock Market in South Africa is by far the largest stock market on the African continent. The second largest African stock market is the Casablanca Stock Exchange in Morocco, with a market value of only about $5 billion. With the exception of the active stock market in Mexico City, Central American and South American stock markets are also relatively small. Stock markets are gradually being established and nurtured in the former republics of the Soviet Union as these nations switch from centrally planned to market-based economies. Although these stock markets have small capitalizations, they can be crucial to the economic development of these nations.

Stock Exchange Regulation, Ownership, and Operation

The regulation, ownership, and management of stock exchanges around the world reflect each nation's financial system. Ownership (private or public) and primary regulatory responsibility (governmental or self-regulated) are listed in Table 10.7 for the ten largest stock exchanges.

Stock exchanges can be classified according to which of the following is the predominant regulatory and operational force in the marketplace:

- The national government (as in France)
- Commercial banks (as in Germany)
- Private enterprise (as in the United Kingdom and the United States)

Whether the government, the banks, or private enterprise takes the lead in a particular national stock market influences many aspects of daily economic life: the nature of

TABLE 10.7 INSTITUTIONAL ARRANGEMENTS IN THE WORLD'S TEN LARGEST EQUITY MARKETS[a]

Country / City	Major Stock Market Indexes	Owner-ship[b]	Primary Regulator[c]	Auction Mechanism[b]	Official Specialists[b]	Automated Quotations[c]	Automated Executions[c]	Forward Trading[c]	Settlement Period[c]	Transactions Costs[d] (fees, spreads, and taxes)
Canada / Toronto	Toronto Stock Exchange (TSE) 300	n/a	Gov't & self	Continuous	Yes	Yes	Yes	No	n/a	n/a
France / Paris	CAC 40, CAC General (200)	Public	Gov't	Mixed	Yes	Yes	Yes	Yes	Monthly and daily	0.40%
Germany / Frankfurt	DAX 100, Commerzbank (60)	Public	Self	Continuous	Yes	No	No	No	2 business days	0.45%
Hong Kong / Hong Kong	Hang Seng (33)	Private	Gov't	Continuous	No	Yes	No	No	n/a	0.70%
Italy / Milan	Banca Commerziale (200)	Public	Gov't	Mixed	No	No	No	Yes	Monthly	0.50%
Japan / Tokyo	Tokyo Stock Exchange 300 & 1000, Nikkei/Dow Jones Average (225)	Public	Gov't & self	Continuous	Yes	Yes	Yes	No	4 business days	0.80%
Netherlands / Amsterdam	ANP-CBS General (50)	Private	Self	Continuous	Yes	No	No	No	10 business days	0.40%
Switzerland / Zurich	Société de Banque Suisse (90)	Private	Gov't	Mixed	No	Yes	No	Yes	3 business days	0.50%
United Kingdom / London	Financial Times Ordinaires (30), FTSE (100), FT All Shares (750)	Private	Self	Continuous	No	Yes	Yes	Yes	Biweekly	0.85%
United States / New York	NYSE Composite (1800), Dow Jones Industrials (30)	Private	Gov't & self	Continuous	Yes	Yes	Yes	No	5 business days	0.30%

a The approximate number of stocks in each index is given in parentheses when it is not evident from the name of the index.
b Source: Richard Roll, "The International Crash of October 1987," *Financial Analysts Journal* 44, No. 5, 1988, pages 19–35.
c Source: *The Capital Market Effects of International Accounting Diversity*, Frederick D.S. Choi and Richard M. Levich, 1990, Richard D. Irwin Publishing Company, pages 110–111.
d Source: *International Investments*, Bruno Solnik, 1996, Addison-Wesley Publishing Company, page 198.

securities regulation and the operation of public debt and equity markets, the disclosure requirements for public securities issues, whether the predominant form of financing is through public or private markets or both, and corporate governance, including managerial control of the corporation.

The Public Stock Exchange. An example of a financial system dominated by the national government is the system in France. The French government regulates and operates the Paris Bourse (stock exchange). The framework for the French system was established during the reign of the emperor Napoléon I. Napoléon established a strong central government that was intimately involved in the regulation and operation of daily business life. Financial markets in France and in countries influenced by French culture and history (including Italy, Spain, and Belgium) reflect this predilection for government regulation of business life. Securities brokers in France are registered agents of the French government. Until 1989, brokers had a monopoly on share trading and received commissions that were fixed by the French Ministry of Finance. Membership on the Paris Bourse is gradually being opened up to commercial banks.

The Paris Bourse is an example of a public stock exchange operated by a national government.

The strong role of the government is seen in other areas of French business life. When François Mitterrand was elected French President on a Socialist platform in 1981, many French companies were **nationalized**, and ownership was transferred to the French government. Large and well-known companies that were at least partially nationalized include Compagnie Générale d'Electricité (telecommunications and energy), Rhône-Poulenc (pharmaceuticals), Société Nationale Elf Aquitaine (petrochemicals), and Credit Lyonnais (commercial banking). Public ownership and management of these firms proved cumbersome and unresponsive to market forces. A 1986 law set in motion a series of **privatizations** in the late 1980s that transferred ownership of nationalized companies back to the private sector. Privatization of French industry continues to this day.

The Frankfurt Stock Exchange is an example of a bankers' stock exchange.

The Bankers' Stock Exchange. In other countries, such as Germany, commercial banks have played the dominant role in business life. German financiers have played a central role in the growth of German trade and industry at least since the Middle Ages. While German banks are now predominantly publicly held corporations rather than family-owned financial empires, they have retained their central position in German business life.

Commercial banks in Germany provide many financial services beyond simply supplying commercial credit. German banks are allowed to own stock, and they also serve as securities brokers and investment bankers in the German financial system. Because they are both lenders and equity owners, commercial banks exert a much stronger influence over German corporate life than banks in France do. Indeed, the structure of the German supervisory board (the Aufsichtsrat) was established to ensure bankers a formal role in the operation and management of their corporate constituency. The supervisory body of the Frankfurt Stock Exchange, called the Borsenvorstand or "exchange supervisor," is composed of bankers and their representatives.

The Private Stock Exchange. Corporations in the United States and the United Kingdom rely more on the public debt and equity markets and less on commercial banks than corporations in Germany and Japan do. Stock and bond markets in the United States and the United Kingdom are privately owned (rather than government owned) and rely more heavily on self-regulation than do their counterparts in France and Japan.

The Glass-Steagall Banking Act of 1933 prohibited U.S. banks from owning stock (except in trust accounts for their clients) and from investment banking activities. Because they provide only debt capital, banks in the United States and the United Kingdom have a much smaller voice in the affairs of their corporate clients. Since bank deregulation in the 1980s, entrants such as Sears Financial and General Motors Acceptance Corporation increasingly are competing in the traditional markets of commercial banks. As traditional barriers to banking activities erode, Glass-Steagall is coming under increasing scrutiny by regulators and legislators.

Other countries have hybrids of public, private, and bankers' stock exchange systems. For example, financial markets in Hong Kong reflect that city's history in their unique mixture of British-led banks and Chinese trading houses. Belgium has a mix of Germanic and French institutions reflecting the two cultures residing within a single border: the French-speaking Walloons and the Flemings of Germanic descent.

Stock markets in the United States and the United Kingdom are owned and operated by private investors.

Global Equity Offerings in the Telecommunications Industry

Telecommunications are vitally important to the economic vitality of every nation. For this reason, national governments historically have been heavily involved in promoting and regulating telecommunications within their national borders. In recent years, there has been a flood of privatizations in the telecommunications industry as governments sell their interests in state-owned telecommunications operators in an effort to stimulate competition and promote service. Many of these privatizations have been *global equity offerings* sold in the international equity markets.

In the fast-growing markets of Southeast Asia and the Pacific Rim, governments have struggled to keep up with the huge demand for new capital to finance telecommunications infrastructure development and expansion. This has resulted in many formerly state-owned telecommunications operators being privatized and sold to the international markets.

In Western Europe, privatization has been given an extra push by a European Union plan to open up most EU markets to competition by January 1, 1998. Because most European telecoms have been majority-owned by European national governments, this has created a series of privatizations and a glut of equity offerings on international markets. More than $30 billion worth of European telecom stock offerings was scheduled to be issued during 1996.* The EU's hope is that the sluggish state telecom monopolies will be transformed into an aggressive batch of European "Baby Bells" that will quickly open new markets and achieve greater operating efficiencies. European telecom offerings in 1995 included Italy's STET, Spain's Telefonica de España, and the Netherlands' KPN. Deutsche Telekom raised about $10 billion from international markets during 1996.

* "Getting a Line on Europe's Telecom Free-for-All," *Business Week,* June 19, 1995.

Institutional Differences in Stock Exchange Operations

Table 10.7 lists some of the institutional conventions used in the operation of the world's major stock exchanges. This section discusses only a few of the many institutional differences in share trading systems.

Price Determination: Continuous Quotations versus Periodic Call Auctions.

*Stock trading systems can be
continuous quotation or
periodic call or both.*

The two most common methods for setting prices are a continuous quotation system and a periodic call auction. In a **continuous quotation system**, buy and sell orders are matched as they arrive with market makers assuring liquidity in individual shares. The market making function may be provided by a single individual as on the NYSE (the NYSE specialist has a monopoly on trading in particular shares) or through dealers (called "jobbers" on the London Stock Exchange) competing with each other and quoting bid and ask prices. On computerized trading systems, sometimes only the high bid and low offer of the competing dealers are reported.

The Paris Bourse is an example of a market with a **periodic call auction** for less actively traded shares. A continuous market is conducted for frequently traded shares on the Paris Bourse. Less actively traded stocks are auctioned at regular intervals throughout the day. Call auctions on the Paris Bourse are determined through a closed bid system in which all unfilled buy and sell orders are submitted to an exchange representative. The representative sets the price to accommodate the most orders and equate supply with demand. Trading is conducted after this price fixing as brokers attempt to match any remaining buy and sell orders. Other exchanges use an open outcry system. In Zurich, stocks are called for trading twice a day and may not be traded at other times. On some exchanges (including the NYSE), opening prices are determined through call auctions after which continuous trading takes place.

Spot and Forward Stock Market Transactions.

*Stock market transactions are
settled either on a spot or a
forward basis.*

The most common share trading procedure is on a spot basis (or cash basis), with transactions settled within a few days of trade. This is the procedure used on all of the U.S., German, and Japanese exchanges. An alternative trading procedure is on a forward basis (or futures basis), with transactions being settled on a specified future date. Germany and Japan prohibit forward and futures trading of stocks, so only cash markets exist in these countries. London, Paris, and Zurich have some form of forward stock market. Forward trades are settled biweekly in London and at the end of the month in Paris. Zurich allows more remote forward settlement dates. Stock exchanges that trade on a forward basis also trade on a spot basis or provide some mechanism for customers demanding cash transactions.

Like forward currency transactions, forward stock transactions are a form of credit instrument. Delivery is made either in stock (in a short stock trade) or in cash (in a long stock trade) on a specified future delivery date. The difference between the spot and forward price for a share of stock reflects the rate of interest (that is, the time value of money) in that currency. To ensure settlement, some form of deposit is usually required on forward stock transactions.

Some markets (including the U.S. markets) allow margin trading—buying stock on borrowed money—as another form of stock purchase on credit. The margin account is low risk to the broker because it is secured by stock, so margin rates can approach the level of short-term government interest rates. (And this is quite a bit less than the rates on a new car loan!)

International Differences in Regulations Governing Securities Issues

This section reviews the regulations governing securities issues in the two largest capital markets—the United States and Japan.

Securities Regulation in the United States. In the United States, the Securities Exchange Act of 1933 governs new securities issues and the Securities Exchange Act of 1934 governs trade in outstanding securities. Companies issuing debt or equity securities to the public in amounts greater than $1.5 million are required to prepare and file a **registration statement** with the U.S. Securities and Exchange Commission (SEC) that fully discloses all relevant information and includes a financial history of the company, the state of existing businesses, and how the funds raised through the public offering are to be used. Once the registration statement is filed with the SEC, there is a waiting period of twenty days while the SEC reviews the accuracy and completeness of the registration statement. The issue is priced and sold after the waiting period.

The SEC's registration procedure must be followed for all securities issues with two exceptions:

- Loans maturing within nine months
- Private placements

These two exceptions to the U.S. registration requirements classify financial markets along two dimensions: (1) according to maturity and (2) according to whether the issue is made to the public or to a small group of private investors.

The first exception to the SEC's registration requirement explicitly recognizes the difference between money market and capital market securities. This exception is the reason why commercial paper in the United States is offered with maturities of nine months or less. Corporate securities issues of less than nine months must be accompanied by a brief **offering statement** rather than the full-fledged registration statement.

The second exception treats private placements separately from public securities issues. Whether a firm issues securities to the public or to private entities has an enormous influence on the types of public disclosures that must be made and the type of control exerted by outside stakeholders in the firm. In the United States, **private placements** as defined by the Securities Act of 1933 conform to all five of the following conditions:

- Sold to large and sophisticated investors
- Sold to only a few investors
- Investors must have access to information like that in a registration statement
- Investors are capable of sustaining losses
- Investors purchase the securities for their own investment portfolios and not for resale

Securities issues in foreign markets usually include a local representative in the investment banking syndicate.

Securities issues satisfying these conditions are presumably placed with informed investors able to obtain accurate information on the issuer and to judge the merits of the investment for themselves.

If an offering does not conform to all five of these criteria, then it is a **public securities offering** and falls under the jurisdiction of the SEC. The U.S. securities laws require complete and accurate disclosure of all relevant information for public securities issues to ensure that investors are not fooled by exaggerated claims or outrageous promises. The securities laws do not ensure that an investment will meet its promised or expected return. Instead, the securities laws attempt to ensure that investors have enough information to judge the merits of a proposed investment for themselves.

Public debt and equity securities issues are organized by a **lead manager** (called a "book runner" in the United Kingdom) and perhaps one or more *comanagers* to share the risk. These securities issues are marketed by a **syndicate** (or selling group) that must be familiar with the market(s) into which the placement will be made. A securities issue placed into the dollar market by a U.S. or non-U.S. issuer should include a U.S. investment banker, such as Goldman Sachs or Merrill Lynch, in the investment banking syndicate. Similarly, an issue denominated in pounds and sold by a U.K. or non-U.K. issuer should include a United Kingdom investment banker, such as S.G. Warburg, in the syndicate.

Securities Regulation in Japan. New public issues in Japan must be approved by the Japanese Ministry of Finance (MOF). The waiting period in Japan is somewhat longer than in the United States, occasionally lasting several months. As in the United States, the issue is priced and sold after the waiting period. The Japanese government takes a much more active role in determining which Japanese companies are allowed to issue securities to the Japanese market. In addition to regulating which companies are allowed to issue securities, the MOF also regulates securities trading within Japan.

The Japanese version of the U.S.'s Glass-Steagall Act was dismantled in early 1995, and commercial banks were allowed to enter the investment banking and securities trading industries. Consistent with the spirit of Glass-Steagall, commercial and investment banking operations are to be kept strictly separate. Initially, five banks (Dai-Ichi Kangyo, Fuji, Sanwa, Sakura, and Mitsubishi) won approval to compete in the securities industry. Sumitomo Bank failed to win approval for its proposed investment banking subsidiary. The reason that the MOF refused Sumitomo's request was that the proposed name, Sumigin (a contraction of the characters for Sumitomo Bank), gave the appearance of linking Sumitomo's commercial and investment banking interests (the Japanese character for *gin* means "bank"). This is one example of the Japanese government's strict regulatory control over securities issuance and trading.

International Stock Exchange Listings

Domestic residents and their domestic stock markets often feel they have an obligation (if not a divine right) to conduct the bulk of trade in domestic stocks. When domestic companies have foreign owners, domestic residents feel they have less control over market forces, stock prices, local employment decisions, and ownership in their domestic industries. Indeed, many countries impose restrictions on foreign ownership of domestic assets.

With the increasing integration of the world's capital markets, national markets can no longer claim a monopoly on trade in their own national stocks. For example, company shares from all across the nations of the Middle East are traded in Riyadh, Saudi Arabia. Share trading in companies from all across Europe has migrated toward the London Stock Exchange because of the high liquidity found in the City (as London is called by its financial community). Exchanges on the continent have fought back through innovation in trading rules and mechanisms. Trade in Germany is migrating away from the eight smaller exchanges toward the Frankfurt Stock Exchange, which conducts three-fourths of the trading volume in Germany. To remain viable, the smaller regional exchanges in Germany, such as those in Düsseldorf and Munich, are forming alliances with the Frankfurt exchange. Falling volume on the Tokyo Stock Exchange since the 1991 stock market crash in Japan has prompted an exodus of foreign listings from the Tokyo exchange to regional exchanges in other southeast Asian countries, particularly to the exchange in Hong Kong. This exodus, along with a growing demand for Japanese listings from companies based in mainland China, forced the Tokyo Stock Exchange to relax its rules governing foreign listings in 1994.

Stock exchanges in the United States are under intense competition from foreign exchanges in the trading of both U.S. and foreign shares. U.S. exchanges are disadvantaged by the SEC's disclosure and registration requirements, particularly the rule that foreign companies must prepare financial statements according to U.S. Generally Accepted Accounting Principles (GAAP).[4] This requirement is intended to protect U.S. investors against false or misleading information. Foreign companies counter that the accounting conventions of their home countries provide enough information to investors and report it within the cultural context in which it occurs. The cost of translating financial statements into U.S. GAAP can be prohibitive. Largely because of this impediment to foreign listing on U.S. exchanges, there has been no growth in the *number* of foreign shares traded on U.S. exchanges since the SEC's registration requirement was extended to the NASDAQ exchange in 1983. This is despite the fact that the *value* of foreign shares held by U.S. residents has tripled since the mid-1980s.

Competition between national stock markets is increasing and will continue to increase as barriers to cross-border portfolio investment erode.

National stock markets can no longer claim a monopoly on trade in their own local stocks.

The Trend toward Capital Market Integration

Even though each national securities market retains its own unique character, national markets are converging in a number of ways. The most visible change is in the way that trading information is processed and disseminated. Trades and prices in the major securities markets are now tracked by computer and relayed around the globe to other markets nearly instantaneously via satellite. Governments increasingly are relaxing barriers such as differential taxes and outright restrictions on cross-border financial transactions. In this brave new world, computer and telecommunications technologies have forged the segmented national markets of the early twentieth century into an increasingly integrated network of financial markets.

---

4 See Franklin R. Edwards, "Listing of Foreign Securities on U.S. Exchanges," *Journal of Applied Corporate Finance* 5, No. 4, Winter 1993, pages 29–36.

10.4 SUMMARY

Financial securities can be broken down along two dimensions

- Maturity
- Public versus private placements

Money market instruments are short-term debt instruments, such as Eurodollar deposits and commercial paper. Capital market instruments are long-term instruments and include stocks, government and corporate bonds, and long-term warrants.

The debt market can be broken down along three additional dimensions.

- Intermediated versus nonintermediated (direct placement) debt
- Internal versus external market debt
- Domestic versus international market debt

Intermediated debt is placed through a financial intermediary, such as a commercial bank. Direct placement debt issues are nonintermediated and are issued either directly to the public or privately to a small group of informed investors. Internal market debt is denominated in the currency of a host country, traded within that country, and regulated by that country. Eurobonds are an external market debt instrument that is denominated in one or more currencies but placed outside the borders of the countries issuing those currencies. In contrast to Eurodollar deposits and loans, governments do exert indirect control over the Eurobond market in their currency through regulations on financial intermediaries operating within their borders. Domestic bonds are issued and traded within the internal market of a single country and are denominated in the currency of that country, whereas international bonds are traded outside the country of the issuer. International bonds are of two types: (1) Eurobonds are traded in the external market and (2) foreign bonds are issued by a foreign borrower in a domestic internal market, denominated in the domestic currency, and regulated by the domestic authorities. In most countries around the world, the most active secondary markets for domestic and international debt instruments are conducted through commercial banks.

Equity ownership in the world's publicly traded firms is either listed on a stock exchange or is unlisted and trades on a less informal basis. The largest equity markets are in the United States, Japan, and England, respectively. There are many institutional differences in the regulation and operation of stock exchanges around the world. Despite these regulatory and institutional differences between stock exchanges, corporations are finding it easier to raise capital in other countries' capital markets. Well-known corporations are finding that they can appeal directly to foreign investors through depository receipts and multiple exchange listings. Investors find that they are facing fewer barriers to investment in foreign equities. Capital market integration can be expected to continue as barriers to cross-border capital investment fall.

Bond equivalent yield

Continuous quotation versus periodic call
auction

Convertible bonds

Domestic bonds

Effective annual yield

Eurobonds

Financial markets

Foreign bonds

Global bonds

Intermediated versus non-intermediated debt
markets

International bonds

Internal markets versus external markets

Lead manager and the syndicate (or selling
group)

Liquidity

Money market yield

Money markets versus capital markets

Nationalization versus privatization

Offering statement

Private placement versus public securities
offering

Registered versus bearer bonds

Registration statement

Warrants

CONCEPTUAL QUESTIONS

10.1 What is the difference between a money market and a capital market?

10.2 Define liquidity.

10.3 What is the difference between an intermediated and a nonintermediated financial market?

10.4 What is the difference between an internal and an external market?

10.5 What are the characteristics of a domestic bond? an international bond? a foreign bond? a
Eurobond? a global bond?

10.6 What are the benefits and drawbacks of offering securities in bearer form relative to registered form?

10.7 What is an equity-linked Eurobond?

10.8 What is the difference between a public bourse, a bankers' bourse, and a private stock
exchange.

10.9 What is the difference between a continuous quotation system and a periodic call auction?

10.10 What is the difference between a spot and a forward stock market?

PROBLEMS

10.1 In a bond market using a "30/360" price quotation convention, how many days' worth of
accrued interest would fall on July 31?

10.2 In a bond market using an "actual/365" price quotation convention, how many days worth of
accrued interest would fall on July 31 if interest payments fall on June 30 and December 31?

10.3 In a bond market using a "30/360" price quotation convention, how many days worth of
accrued interest would fall on February 29 during a leap year?

10.4 It is the year 2000 and there are two years remaining until maturity on Matsushita Electric
Industrial Company's ten-year global bonds issued with a coupon of $7\frac{1}{4}$ percent in 1992. The
bonds pay a semiannual coupon of $(7\frac{1}{4}$ percent$)/2) = 3\frac{5}{8}$ percent. These bonds are nonamortizing, so they pay only interest until maturity, at which time they repay 100 percent of the
principal amount. Matsushita's bonds are selling at par.

    a. What is the promised yield to maturity on this bond using the U.S. bond equivalent yield
calculation?

b. What is the promised yield to maturity on this bond using the German effective annual yield calculation?

c. What is the promised yield to maturity on this bond using the Japanese bond yield calculation?

10.5 Refer to Matsushita's global bonds from Problem 10.4. Suppose the bonds are selling at 101 percent of par value.

a. What is the promised yield to maturity on this bond using the U.S. bond equivalent yield calculation?

b. What is the promised yield to maturity on this bond using the German effective annual yield calculation?

c. What is the promised yield to maturity on this bond using the Japanese bond yield calculation?

SUGGESTED READINGS

Possible reasons for the 1990 stock market crash in Japan are investigated in
Kenneth R. French and James M. Poterba, "Were Japanese Stock Prices Too High?" *Journal of Financial Economics* 29, 1991, No. 2, pages 337–363.

Barriers facing foreign securities listings in U.S. markets are chronicled in
Franklin R. Edwards, "Listing of Foreign Securities on U.S. Exchanges," *Journal of Applied Corporate Finance* 5, No. 4, Winter 1993, pages 29–36.

International Portfolio Diversification

Oh, what a world! What a world....
The Wicked Witch of the West in *The Wizard of Oz*

OVERVIEW

Foreign debt and equity investments have great appeal for investors, portfolio managers, and multinational corporations. The primary appeal of foreign investments lies in their potential for higher returns. While much of the world's wealth resides in developed countries, such as the United States, Japan, and the countries of Western Europe, developing economies are much more likely to experience higher-than-average economic growth. This can lead to higher expected returns in foreign markets, especially those emerging markets with high growth potential.

Another source of appeal is foreign investments' potential for lowering the risk of an investment portfolio. National economies do not move in unison, and stock and bond returns vary widely across national markets. Diversifying across international markets can greatly reduce portfolio risk because of the relatively low correlation between national debt and equity market indexes. As barriers to trade in these markets progressively fall, international portfolio diversification is increasingly attractive to individual investors and fund managers.

Let's begin the discussion of portfolio diversification and asset pricing with the **perfect financial market assumptions** that were introduced in Chapter 6. These conditions allow us to develop the algebra of portfolio theory in a highly stylized setting. In the last section of this chapter, we'll see how real-world **market imperfections** influence international financial markets and asset prices as these assumptions are relaxed.

The perfect financial market assumptions are as follows:

- Frictionless markets
  - No transaction costs: No brokerage fees, bid-ask spreads, or price pressure effects
  - No taxes or other forms of government intervention
  - No costs of financial distress: Bankruptcy risk has no impact on cash flows
  - No agency costs: Managers attempt to maximize the value of equity
- Equal access to market prices
  - Perfect competition: No single participant can influence market prices
  - No barriers to entry or other constraints on capital flows
- Rational investors: Investors perceive more return as good and more risk as bad
- Equal access to costless information: Costless access to all public information

In perfect markets, rational investors have equal access to information and to market prices in a frictionless market.

In an earlier chapter three forms of market efficiency were introduced: operational efficiency, allocational efficiency, and informational efficiency. The assumption of frictionless markets is an assumption of **operational efficiency** in the financial markets. This assumption means that there are no drains on funds as they are shifted from one use to another. This does not mean that there are no opportunity costs in reallocating funds. Assets selling in perfect financial markets still have a competitively priced opportunity cost or required return depending on their risk.

The last three assumptions (perfect competition, rational investors, equal access to costless information) are sufficient to ensure informationally efficient markets. Prices in an **informationally efficient** market fully and instantaneously reflect all relevant information. Informational efficiency does not require frictionless markets and operational efficiency. In the foreign exchange market, for example, prices could fully reflect information despite the existence of transactions costs. A bid-ask spread on currency transactions would simply preclude costless arbitrage, although currencies could still be correctly priced within the bounds of transactions costs. Similarly, efficient stock and bond markets could be informationally efficient despite relatively high transactions costs on foreign stock and bond transactions.

The joint assumptions of operational efficiency and informational efficiency ensure that financial markets are also **allocationally efficient**. In an allocationally efficient market, prices are determined in such a way that savings are optimally allocated to productive investments.

Of course, these conditions intentionally omit much that is interesting (but problematic) in the real world. The assumption of frictionless markets is perhaps the worst of the lot. Try to envision a frictionless world. In a world with no government regulations there would be no need for regulators, bank auditors, or attorneys. With no taxes there would be no need for tax collectors. With equal access to market prices and no transaction costs there would be no need for financial intermediaries such as banks and brokers, nor any market for finance graduates. And with costless information there would be no need for finance professors or for this text.[1]

The perfect financial market conditions are violated even in the most operationally efficient markets. Transaction and information costs are even more pronounced in the financial markets of emerging nations and in trades between national markets. Nevertheless, these simplifying assumptions allow us to begin looking at international asset pricing in a world in which all market participants have equal and costless access to capital market information and market prices.

11.2 THE ALGEBRA OF PORTFOLIO DIVERSIFICATION

In 1990, Harry Markowitz and William Sharpe were awarded the Nobel Prize in economics for their work in asset pricing and portfolio theory.[2] The insight at the heart of their work is quite simple. Markowitz and Sharpe pointed out that the characteristics of assets that matter to investors depend on whether the assets are held as part of a portfolio or in isolation. In Markowitz and Sharpe's framework, investors are concerned only with the expected return and risk of their portfolio of assets, not with the return on any single asset in their portfolio. When an asset is held in a portfolio, the characteristics that are important to investors are the asset's contributions to the expected return and risk of the portfolio. To fully appreciate the implications of this insight for asset prices in a global marketplace, we first need to develop a little algebra.

The risk of an asset depends on its contribution to portfolio risk and not on its risk when held in isolation.

The Mean-Variance Framework

So far, we've assumed only that capital markets conform to the perfect market assumptions. To further simplify the algebra, let's add two more assumptions:

- End-of-period nominal returns are normally distributed.
- Investors want more nominal return and less risk in their functional currency.

The normal distribution is completely described by its mean and standard deviation (or variance). Faced with nominal asset returns that are normally distributed, rational investors want to maximize expected nominal returns and minimize the standard deviation of nominal returns on their investments.[3]

---

1 With regard to this stylized world, the author agrees with the Wicked Witch of the West from *The Wizard of Oz:* "Oh, what a world! What a world!"

2 Merton Miller shared the 1990 Nobel Prize in economics with Markowitz and Sharpe. Miller's work is discussed in Chapter 20.

3 An assumption of quadratic utility of wealth, $U(W) = a + bW + cW^2$, also results in investors who care only about the mean and variance of expected future returns. So that we do not have to deal with the form of investors' preferences for wealth, we'll stick to an assumption of normally distributed asset returns.

Like the perfect market conditions, these assumptions are invoked more for convenience than for the way in which they represent the real world. We know, for instance, that domestic stock prices are not normally distributed; they are leptokurtic (or "fat-tailed" relative to the normal distribution) and skewed, with large negative returns being more probable than large positive returns. Because exchange rate changes are also leptokurtic, returns on foreign stocks and bonds are even less normal than those of domestic assets. Changes in exchange rate volatility over time result in even greater deviations from normal on foreign assets. Finally, investors with obligations in more than one currency want returns in more than one currency. Nevertheless, an assumption of normally distributed returns in a single functional currency is a convenient starting point in a discussion of portfolio diversification because it greatly simplifies the algebra of portfolio diversification and captures most of what is important to investors.

The Expected Return on a Portfolio

Portfolio expected return is a weighted average of expected returns on the assets in the portfolio.

The expected return on a portfolio of assets, $E[R_P]$, is a simple weighted average of the expected returns on the individual assets in the portfolio. Let X_A represent the weight (or proportion of wealth) devoted to asset A and X_B the weight of B. The expected return on a portfolio made up of assets A and B is

$$E[R_P] = X_A E[R_A] + X_B E[R_B] \qquad (11.1)$$

such that $X_A + X_B = 1$, the total wealth invested in the portfolio. Similarly, the expected return on a portfolio of i=1,...,N assets is a linear function of the expected returns $E[R_i]$ on the individual assets in the portfolio and on the weight given to each of the assets:

$$E[R_P] = \Sigma_i X_i E[R_i] \qquad (11.2)$$

where the portfolio weights sum to one; $\Sigma_i X_i = 1$. If **short selling** (that is, selling an asset that you do not own) is not allowed, then each weight is constrained to $0 \leq X_i \leq 1$.

Table 11.1 and Figure 11.1 present the historical performance of several international equity market indexes. Suppose investments in American and Japanese equities have return distributions as in Table 11.1.[4] If history were to repeat itself, then the mean return would be 11.5 percent on American equities and 21.9 percent on Japanese equities. Of course, history is unlikely to repeat itself in precisely this way. We'll use these numbers as expected returns for convenience and not as indicators of future returns. Applying equation (11.1), the expected return on an equally weighted (that is, $X_A = X_J = \frac{1}{2}$) portfolio of American and Japanese equities is $E[R_P] = (\frac{1}{2})(0.115)+(\frac{1}{2})(0.219) = 0.167$, or 16.7 percent.

---

4 Although the term "American" should properly refer to all of the Americas (North, South, and Central), it is used here for simplicity of discussion to refer to equities in the United States.

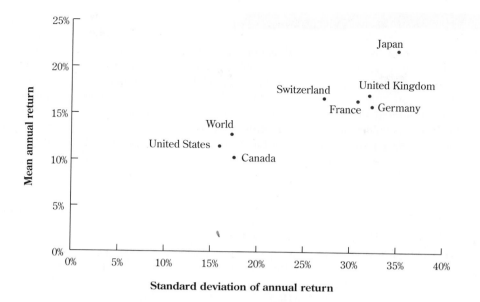

FIGURE 11.1
Historical Market
Performance, 1970–1994

TABLE 11.1 ANNUAL INTERNATIONAL STOCK AND BOND RETURNS TO U.S. INVESTORS, 1970–1994[a]

Stock Returns

| | Mean (%) | Stdev (%) | β_W | SI | Correlation Coefficients | | | | | | |
					CN	FR	DM	JP	SW	UK	US
Canada	10.3	17.4	0.66	.138							
France	16.5	30.7	1.23	.280	.533						
Germany	16.0	32.3	0.97	.250	.193	.700					
Japan	21.9	35.1	1.43	.399	.409	.452	.319				
Switzerland	16.7	27.1	1.00	.325	.353	.715	.907	.359			
United Kingdom	17.1	31.9	1.28	.288	.428	.460	.392	.262	.568		
United States	11.5	15.8	0.76	.228	.618	.490	.386	.334	.505	.616	
World	12.7	17.1	1.00	.281	.652	.687	.516	.698	.631	.686	.818

Bond Returns

| | Mean (%) | Stdev (%) | β_W | SI | Correlation Coefficients | | | | | | |
					CN	FR	DM	JP	SW	UK	US
Canada	9.3	10.2	0.15	.135							
France	12.2	14.5	0.33	.297	.201						
Germany	13.5	13.6	0.02	.414	.154	.651					
Japan	14.8	15.9	0.37	.432	−.009	.511	.524				
Switzerland	12.4	15.2	0.03	.296	−.132	.609	.869	.641			
United Kingdom	12.3	22.5	0.44	.194	.180	.334	.363	.609	.365		
United States	9.4	11.7	0.24	.132	.852	.442	.394	.110	.105	.164	
World	10.8	10.8	0.28	.269	.506	.687	.726	.765	.629	.652	.633

[a] Based on Morgan Stanley's *Capital International Perspectives.* "Mean" and "Stdev" represent the mean (μ_i) and standard deviation (σ_i) of annual return, respectively. Sharpe's Performance Index SI = $(\mu_i - \mu_F)/\sigma_i$ is based on annual data using the mean annual return on U.S. T-bills ($\mu_F = 7.9\%$), where μ_i represents the mean and σ_i the standard deviation of return to asset i. Beta, β_i, is measured against monthly changes in the world stock market portfolio.

Part 4 International Capital
Markets and Portfolio
Investment

*Portfolio risk is measured by
the variance or standard
deviation of return.*

If an asset's returns are distributed as normal $N(\mu,\sigma^2)$, then its return distribution can be completely described by its mean and variance of return. Since the percentage-squared ($\%^2$) units of variance are not the same as the units on expected return, risk is often more conveniently stated as the standard deviation of return, $(\sigma^2)^{1/2} = \sigma$, which is in units of percent (%). Before we calculate the standard deviation, however, we must first find a formula for the variance of return on a portfolio.

The formula for the variance of return, $Var(R_P) = \sigma_P{}^2$, on a portfolio of two assets A and B can be developed by substituting for $R_P = X_A R_A + X_B R_B$ (such that $X_A + X_B = 1$) as follows:

$$Var(R_P) = Var(X_A R_A + X_B R_B)$$
$$= Var(X_A R_A) + Var(X_B R_B) + 2Cov(X_A R_A, X_B R_B)$$

where Cov(...) is a covariance term. Because the weights X_A and X_B are constants, these terms can be brought out of the variance and covariance terms as follows:

$$Var(R_P) = X_A{}^2 Var(R_A) + X_B{}^2 Var(R_B) + 2X_A X_B Cov(R_A, R_B)$$
$$= X_A{}^2 \sigma_A{}^2 + X_B{}^2 \sigma_B{}^2 + 2X_A X_B \sigma_{AB} \tag{11.3}$$

where $\sigma_{AB} = Cov(R_A, R_B)$ is the **covariance** of returns between assets A and B. The covariance term can alternatively be stated in terms of the **correlation** ρ_{AB} between the returns to assets A and B:

$$\sigma_{AB} = \sigma_A \sigma_B \rho_{AB} \quad \Leftrightarrow \quad \rho_{AB} = \sigma_{AB}/\sigma_A \sigma_B$$

The correlation coefficient is simply the covariance scaled by the standard deviations of returns to assets A and B. Dividing the percentage-squared units of covariance by the product of two standard deviations (each with units in percent) results in a unitless correlation measure bounded on the interval $-1 \le \rho_{AB} \le +1$.

Correlation and covariance measure how closely two assets move together. They are important measures because:

The extent to which risk is reduced by portfolio diversification depends on how highly the individual assets in the portfolio are correlated.

---

*The extent to which risk is
reduced by diversification depends
upon the correlation between
individual assets in a portfolio.*

If the correlation between assets is equal to one, then diversifying across assets is ineffective in reducing portfolio risk. If the correlation is less than one, then diversifying across assets results in portfolio risk that is less than a simple average of the variances of the individual assets in the portfolio.

For illustration, let's calculate the standard deviation of an equally weighted portfolio of American (A) and Japanese (J) equities using the standard deviations $\sigma_A = 15.8\%$ and $\sigma_J = 35.1\%$ from Table 11.1. To demonstrate the impact that correlation has on portfolio risk, we'll perform this calculation under three assumptions: (1) a perfect positive correlation ($\rho_{AJ} = +1$), (2) a perfect negative correlation ($\rho_{AJ} = -1$), and (3) the historically observed correlation of ρ_{AJ} = .334 between American and Japanese equities from Table 11.1. Remember, the expected return on an equal-weighted portfolio of American and Japanese equities is $E[R_P]$ = (½)(0.115)+(½)(0.219) = 0.167, or 16.7 percent, regardless of the correlation of return between these assets.

Case 1: Perfect Positive Correlation. If returns in two markets are perfectly positively correlated (ρ_{AJ} = +1), then the standard deviation of portfolio return reduces to

$$\sigma_P = (X_A^2\sigma_A^2 + X_J^2\sigma_J^2 + 2X_AX_J\rho_{AJ}\sigma_A\sigma_J)^{1/2}$$
$$= (X_A^2\sigma_A^2 + X_J^2\sigma_J^2 + 2X_AX_J\sigma_A\sigma_J)^{1/2}$$
$$= [(X_A\sigma_A + X_J\sigma_J)^2]^{1/2}$$
$$= X_A\sigma_A + X_J\sigma_J$$

The standard deviation of return on an equal-weighted portfolio of the American and Japanese stocks from Table 11.1 is then

$$\sigma_P = [(½)^2(0.158)^2 + (½)^2(0.351)^2 + 2(½)(½)(0.158)(0.351)]^{1/2}$$
$$= (0.064770)^{1/2}$$
$$= 0.2545, \text{ or } 25.45 \text{ percent}$$

When ρ_{AJ} = +1, portfolio standard deviation is a simple weighted average of the individual standard deviations. Combining assets A and J in different proportions results in a straight line that runs between points A and J, as shown in Figure 11.2. Both the expected return and the standard deviation of return on the portfolio change linearly as wealth is shifted from one asset to another. In this case, there are no risk reduction benefits from portfolio diversification.

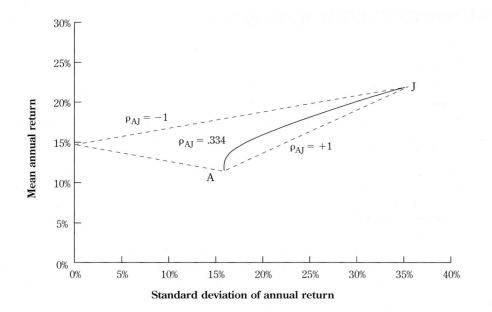

FIGURE 11.2
Portfolio Diversification and the Correlation Coefficient

Case 2: Perfect Negative Correlation. If these two markets are perfectly negatively correlated ($\rho_{AJ} = -1$), then the standard deviation of portfolio return is

$$\sigma_P = (X_A^2\sigma_A^2 + X_J^2\sigma_J^2 + 2X_AX_J\rho_{AJ}\sigma_A\sigma_J)^{1/2}$$
$$= (X_A^2\sigma_A^2 + X_J^2\sigma_J^2 - 2X_AX_J\sigma_A\sigma_J)^{1/2}$$
$$= [(X_A\sigma_A - X_J\sigma_J)^2]^{1/2}$$
$$= X_A\sigma_A - X_J\sigma_J$$

The risk reduction benefits of portfolio diversification are at their greatest when two
assets are perfectly negatively correlated. If $\rho_{AJ} = -1$ for the American and Japanese
equities of Table 11.1, then the standard deviation of an equal-weighted portfolio is
equal to

$$\sigma_P = [(1/2)^2(0.158)^2 + (1/2)^2 (0.351)^2 - 2(1/2)(1/2)(0.158)(0.351)]^{1/2}$$
$$= (0.009312)^{1/2}$$
$$= 0.0965, \text{ or } 9.65 \text{ percent}$$

In fact, with a judicious choice of portfolio weights, the losses on one asset can
be exactly offset by gains on the other asset when $\rho_{AJ} = -1$. In this example, if you
pick $X_A = (0.351)/(0.158+0.351) = 0.690$ and $X_J = (0.158)/(0.158+0.351) = 1 - X_A =
0.310$, portfolio risk falls to $\sigma_P = 0$ and losses (or gains) on A are exactly offset by
gains (or losses) on J.[5] Expected return on this portfolio is $E[R_P] = (0.69)(0.0115) +
(0.31)(0.219) = 0.147$, so you can capture a riskless return of 14.7 percent as illustrated
in Figure 11.2. Progressively varying the portfolio weights from $X_A = 100\%$ to $X_J =
100\%$ defines a straight line that begins at point A, bounces off the vertical axis, and
continues to point J. If $\rho_{AJ} = -1$, any portfolio along this line can be achieved.

Case 3: A Realistic Correlation between -1 and $+1$. Most correlations between
international stock markets range between .3 and .9. Substituting $\sigma_{AJ} = \rho_{AJ}\sigma_A\sigma_J$
into equation (11.3), the equation for the standard deviation of a portfolio of assets
A and J is

$$\sigma_P = (X_A^2\sigma_A^2 + X_J^2\sigma_J^2 + 2X_AX_J\rho_{AJ}\sigma_A\sigma_J)^{1/2}$$

Using the historically observed correlation of .334 between American and Japanese
stock returns in Table 11.1, the standard deviation of an equal-weighted portfolio is

$$\sigma_P = [(1/2)^2(0.158)^2 + (1/2)^2 (0.351)^2 + 2(1/2)(1/2)(0.334)(0.158)(0.351)]^{1/2}$$
$$= (0.046303)^{1/2}$$
$$= 0.215, \text{ or } 21.5 \text{ percent}$$

---

5 As an exercise, verify that $\sigma_P = 0$ using these weights and equation (11.3).

This is less than halfway between the standard deviation of return on American (σ_A = 15.8%) and Japanese (σ_J= 35.1%) equities. By varying the proportion of wealth invested in each asset, investors can obtain any point (that is, any portfolio) along the curved line from A to J in Figure 11.2. Although a correlation of ρ_{AB} = .334 does not yield the same reduction in risk as a perfect negative correlation, it does provide a noticeable improvement in portfolio risk over the straight line between A and J corresponding to ρ_{AB} = 1. Again, the general rule is: The less the correlation between two assets, the greater the potential for risk reduction through portfolio diversification.

Portfolios of Many Securities

The variance of a portfolio with N securities is calculated as a weighted average of the N^2 cells in the variance-covariance matrix.

$$
\begin{aligned}
\mathrm{Var}(R_P) &= \sigma_P^2 \\
&= \Sigma_i \Sigma_j X_i X_j \sigma_{ij} \\
&= \Sigma_i X_i^2 \sigma_i^2 + \Sigma_i \Sigma_j X_i X_j \sigma_{ij} \\
&\quad\quad\quad\quad\quad\; {\scriptstyle i \neq j}
\end{aligned}
\tag{11.4}
$$

where the weights sum to one ($\Sigma_i X_i$ = 1) across the N assets in the portfolio. The double summation $\Sigma_i \Sigma_j X_i X_j \sigma_{ij}$ has a total of N^2 terms including N variance terms along the diagonal of the covariance matrix and $N^2 - N$ covariance terms in the off-diagonal elements.

As an example, suppose we extract the variance-covariance matrix of a three-asset portfolio of American, British, and Japanese stocks from Table 11.1. Each term in the variance-covariance matrix is calculated as $\sigma_{ij} = \rho_{ij}\, \sigma_i \sigma_j$.

	United States	United Kingdom	Japan
United States	0.0250	0.0310	0.0185
United Kingdom	0.0310	0.1018	0.0293
Japan	0.0185	0.0293	0.1232

The variance-covariance matrix of this three-asset portfolio has N^2 = 9 cells including N = 3 variances along the (shaded) diagonal and $N^2 - N$ = 6 covariances in the off-diagonal (unshaded) cells. The diagonal cells represent national return variances because $\sigma_{ii} = \sigma_i^2$ for i = j. For example, the middle cell is the variance of British equity returns: σ_B^2 = $(0.319)^2$ = 0.1018. The off-diagonal covariances $\sigma_{ij} = \rho_{ij}\sigma_i\sigma_j$ are symmetric around the diagonal for i ≠ j. For example, the covariance of the American and British equity markets is σ_{AB} = $\rho_{AB}\sigma_A\sigma_B$ = (0.616)(0.158)(0.319) = 0.0310. An equal-weighted portfolio of all three equity indices has a return variance of σ_P^2 = $(1/3)^2[(0.0250) + (0.1018) + (0.1232)] + 2(1/3)^2[(0.0310) + (0.0185) + (0.0293)]$ = 0.0453. The standard deviation of return is σ_P = $(0.0453)^{1/2}$ = 0.213, or 21.3 percent.

As the number of assets held in a portfolio increases, the covariance terms begin to dominate the portfolio variance calculation. Because N of the N^2 cells in the variance-covariance matrix are variance terms, the ratio of variance cells to total cells is $N/N^2 = 1/N$. For N=2, there are N=2 variance terms and $N^2 - N = 4 - 2 = 2$ covariance terms, so one-half of the cells in the variance-covariance matrix are variances. For N=3, one-third of the ($N^2 = 9$) cells are variances, and two-thirds of the cells are covariances ($N^2 - N = 6$). For N = 100, only 1 percent of the ($N^2 = 10,000$) cells in the variance-covariance matrix are variances, and 99 percent ($N^2 - N = 10,000 - 100 = 9,900$) are covariances. To summarize:

> As the number of assets held in a portfolio increases, the variance of return on the portfolio becomes more dependent on the covariances between the individual securities and less dependent on the variances of the individual securities.

This is the large-portfolio analog of our statement "the extent to which risk is reduced by portfolio diversification depends on how highly the individual assets in the portfolio are correlated." In a large portfolio, portfolio variance depends on the covariances between the individual assets and not on the individual asset variances.

This has an interesting consequence for the risk of an asset when it is held as a part of a portfolio. If an investor is concerned with the risk of his or her total portfolio, then the characteristic of an individual asset that matters is the asset's return covariance with other assets in the portfolio and not its return variance.

> The risk of an individual asset when it is held in a portfolio with a large number of securities depends on its return covariance with other securities in the portfolio and not on its return variance.

This concept is the key to understanding the benefits of international portfolio diversification. It is also central to what should be included in (and excluded from) an international asset pricing model.

Of course, an investor can't pick the correlation between two assets. This is determined in the capital markets. But through judicious selection of assets with high expected returns and low correlations, the benefits of risk reduction through portfolio diversification can be obtained with a minimum number of assets and without sacrificing expected return.

11.3 MEAN-VARIANCE EFFICIENCY

The popular press often claims that investor behavior is driven by "fear and greed." Portfolio theory is also based on these two fundamental human motives. If asset returns are distributed as normal, then investors' objective is to maximize the expected return and minimize the standard deviation of return in their portfolios. Investors want to be as far up and to the left as possible in Figure 11.2. When an asset has higher mean return

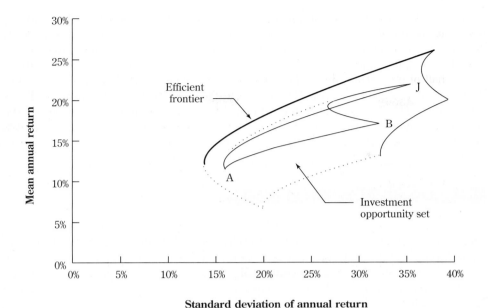

Standard deviation of annual return

FIGURE 11.3
Mean-Variance Efficiency

at a given level of risk (or, lower risk at a given level of return), it is said to be **mean-variance efficient** relative to another asset.[6]

Consider what happens when assets are combined to form a portfolio. Let's start with the American and Japanese assets as in Figure 11.2. Given a correlation of ρ_{AJ} = .334, an investor can reach any point along a curved line from A to J by varying the weight assigned to each asset. As additional assets are added to the set of possible investments, these new assets can be combined with A, with J, or with any combination of A and J.

Suppose there is an asset B (for British) with $E[R_B]$ = 17.1%, σ_B = 31.9%, and correlations ρ_{AB} = .616 and ρ_{BJ} = .262. Combining assets A and J in various weights results in a curved line between A and J, as shown in Figure 11.3. Combining B with J allows an investor to achieve any point along a curved line between B and J. Asset B can also be combined with portfolios of A and J. The dotted line that falls between lines AJ and BJ represents mean-variance efficient combinations of A, B, and J.

As additional assets (such as other national stock market indices) are added to the set of possible investments, additional possibilities can be added to the graph. These additional assets are likely to move the set of possible investments even farther up and to the left. By examining the set of all possible combinations of the N assets in this market, investors can identify the **investment opportunity set** bounded by the outside border in Figure 11.3.

Mean-variance efficient assets have higher mean returns than other assets at a given level of risk.

6 Don't confuse mean-variance efficiency with market efficiency. Mean-variance efficiency refers to the return/risk performance of an individual asset or portfolio. Market efficiency refers to how well the market performs its operational, informational, and/or allocational functions.

When investors come to the financial marketplace, this investment opportunity set provides the menu of choices from which they must select. As in any decision, once investors have identified the available alternatives they must choose from these alternatives based on their personal preferences. This choice depends on the investor's level of risk aversion; that is, how much risk the investor is willing to accept in order to capture a given level of expected return. Investors want the most return at the least risk. These sought-after portfolios lie along the **efficient frontier**, the upper left border of the investment opportunity set in Figure 11.3. These portfolios are efficient in a return/risk (or mean-variance) sense in that they provide the most return for a given level of risk or, alternatively, the least risk at a given level of expected return.

Measuring Mean-Variance Efficiency

The Sharpe index is a measure of excess return per unit of risk.

If an investor is concerned with portfolio risk and return, then a straightforward way to measure a portfolio's *ex post* (after-the-fact) return/risk performance is to divide the portfolio's excess return (return in excess of the risk-free rate R_F) by its standard deviation of return. Called the **Sharpe index (SI)**, this performance measure is appropriate when comparing the realized returns to investors whose entire wealth is invested in one asset or another.

$$\text{Sharpe index (SI)} = (R_P - R_F)/\sigma_P$$

Sharpe's performance index is reported in Table 11.1 for several national stock and bond indexes. These indexes use dollar returns from a U.S. investor's perspective, so the mean U.S. T-bill rate of 7.9 percent is used as the risk-free rate. The national stock market index with the smallest standard deviation is that of the United States. The relatively low standard deviation of 15.8 percent reflects the diversified industrial base in the United States. The relatively low mean return (11.5 percent) in the United States resulted in only a mediocre return/risk performance of 0.228, or 0.228 percent in excess return (that is, above the risk-free rate) for every 1.0 percent in standard deviation of return. Japanese stocks saw the highest standard deviation of return (35.1 percent), yet enjoyed the highest Sharpe performance index (0.399) among the stock indexes because of the high mean return (21.9 percent) during the period. The highest return/risk performance according to Sharpe's index was for an investment in Japanese bonds.

Systematic versus Unsystematic Risk

The portion of an individual asset's risk that cannot be diversified away by holding the asset in a large portfolio is called **systematic risk**. Systematic risk is also called *nondiversifiable risk* or *market risk* because it is a risk that is shared by all assets in the market. Systematic risks arise through market-wide events, such as real economic growth, a rise in government spending, and changing investor sentiment regarding asset values.

The portion of an individual asset's risk that can be diversified away by holding a portfolio with many securities is called **unsystematic risk**. Other terms for unsystematic risk are *nonmarket risk* and *diversifiable risk*. If the asset is a share of stock in a company, then that part of total risk that is diversifiable is also called *company-specific risk*.

Unsystematic risks include labor strikes, changes in top management, company-specific sales fluctuations, and any other events that are unique to a single company.

The total risk (or variance) of an asset's returns can be decomposed into systematic and unsystematic risk.

$$\text{Total Risk} = \text{Systematic Risk} + \text{Unsystematic Risk}$$

Unsystematic risk is unrelated to market returns and can be eliminated through portfolio diversification.

In Chapter 12, we will see that only systematic risk matters to well-diversified investors. Unsystematic risk can be diversified away in a large portfolio, so it is not priced in the marketplace.

The relative proportion of systematic and unsystematic risk in an individual asset's returns depends on the asset's correlations or covariances with other assets in the portfolio. If an asset's return is highly correlated with the returns on other assets, then total risk will be largely composed of systematic risk. If an asset's returns have relatively low correlations with returns on other assets in the portfolio, then the algebra of portfolio diversification results in a relatively large proportion of unsystematic risk and a smaller proportion of systematic risk.

Portfolio Theory and Hedging with Derivative Securities

The algebra of portfolio diversification applies to all financial securities, including the derivative securities (forwards, futures, options, and swaps) discussed in Parts 2 and 3 of the text. Consider a U.S. resident with an expected cash outflow of 50,000 French francs (FF) payable in six months. The spot rate of exchange is $S^{\$/FF}$ = $.20/FF, so at current rates the franc cash outflow will cost (FF50,000) ($.20/FF) = $10,000. If the spot rate goes to $S^{\$/FF}$ = $.25/FF, then FF50,000 will cost $12,500. For every $.05/FF change in the dollar value of the French franc, there is a (FF50,000) (–$.05/FF) = –$2,500 change in the value of the unhedged position. The unhedged obligation is exposed to currency risk as shown in the risk profile at left.

The payoff profile of a forward contract to buy francs and sell dollars is shown in the middle figure. In isolation, this forward contract is just as risky as the original position.

The risk exposures of both the original position and the forward contract are derived from the underlying spot exchange rate. However, the exposures to the underlying exchange rate are in opposite directions. Denote the unhedged position as U and the forward market hedge as H. The correlation between unhedged and hedged returns is ρ_{UH} = −1. Although their exposures to currency risk are in opposite directions, the return variabilities of the original position and of the forward contract are identical. Suppose the standard deviation of both the underlying position and of the forward contract are equal to σ_U = σ_H = σ. If we put portfolio weight X = ½ (= X_U = X_H) into each contract, then the standard deviation of portfolio return is σ_P = $(X_U^2\sigma_U^2 + X_H^2\sigma_H^2 + 2X_UX_H\rho_{UH}\sigma_U\sigma_H)^{1/2}$ = $(X_U^2\sigma_U^2 + X_H^2\sigma_H^2 - 2X_UX_H\sigma_U\sigma_H)^{1/2}$ = $X\sigma - X\sigma$ = 0. When combined with the underlying position, the forward contract results in the riskless profile at the right, which is fully hedged against currency risk.

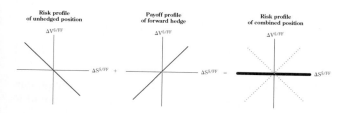

Risk profile of unhedged position — $\Delta V^{\$/FF}$ — $\Delta S^{\$/FF}$ + Payoff profile of forward hedge — $\Delta V^{\$/FF}$ — $\Delta S^{\$/FF}$ = Risk profile of combined position — $\Delta V^{\$/FF}$ — $\Delta S^{\$/FF}$

11.4 THE BENEFITS OF INTERNATIONAL PORTFOLIO DIVERSIFICATION

The risk-reduction benefits of international portfolio diversification arise from two sources. First, because many national economies are dominated by only a few industries, many foreign markets retain a distinctive national character. For this reason, many foreign stock markets are only loosely linked to other national stock markets. It is easy to find examples of national stock markets with firms concentrated in a few key industries. Scandinavian economies are dominated by fishing. The economies of Saudi Arabia and its Persian Gulf neighbors are dominated by oil and construction companies. The Brazilian economy is dominated by its abundant natural resources. The Korean economy is dominated by a few manufacturing industries. Stock markets in each of these countries reflect the local economy.

The second reason that returns to foreign investment differ from those of comparable domestic investments is because of the influence of foreign exchange rates. From a domestic U.S. investor's perspective, the return on a foreign investment derives partly from the foreign market return in the local currency and partly from the change in the spot rate of exchange. Suppose the Paris Bourse appreciates 21 percent but that the franc depreciates by 10 percent. The total return to a domestic U.S. investor in the French market is $(1.21)/(1.10) - 1 = 0.10$, or 10 percent. The 21 percent rise in the Bourse is offset by a 10 percent fall in the dollar value of the franc, and U.S. investors see only a 10 percent rise in the dollar value of the French market. Because the correlation between exchange rates and national market returns is very low, dollar-denominated returns on foreign investments are further isolated from returns in U.S. markets.

Returns on Foreign Investments

Here's how these two sources of return can be decomposed using the **law of one price**. Let the foreign currency price of the foreign asset at time t be given by P_t^f. The domestic currency price of the foreign asset P_t^d is

$$P_t^d = P_t^f S_t^{d/f} \tag{11.5}$$

This is simply the price of the foreign asset in the foreign currency translated back into the domestic currency at the spot exchange rate. For example, if the French franc value of an asset is FF500 and the spot exchange rate is \$.20/FF, then according to the law of one price the value of the asset in dollars is $P_t^d = P_t^f S_t^{d/f} = (FF500)(\$.20/FF) = \$100$. Let the percentage change in the spot exchange rate over period t, $s^{d/f}$, be stated as

$$1 + s^{d/f} = S_t^{d/f}/S_{t-1}^{d/f} \tag{11.6}$$

where the time index on $s^{d/f}$ is dropped for notational convenience. Let the foreign currency and domestic currency returns on the foreign asset over period t be denoted R^f and R^d, respectively. The domestic currency return on the foreign asset is then

---

Handwritten margin notes (left):

Example
- Return on mexican stock exchange = +30%.
- Peso has fallen against the $ = -20%

Return on your investment in the last year, in $ =

$R^\$ = R^P + S^{\$/P} + R^P S^{\$/P}$

$= (.30) + (-.20) + (.30)(-.20)$

$= .10 + (-.06)$

$= .04$

$R^\$ = 4\%$,

Example: Japanese
Return = -20% in won
Yen fell -20% in relation to the won

$\therefore 1 + S^{\$/w} = \dfrac{1}{1 + s^{w/\$}}$

$1 + S^{\$/w} = \dfrac{1}{1 - .2}$

$1 + S^{\$/w} = 1.25$

$S^{\$/w} = 25\%$

Handwritten (bottom right):

$R^\$ = (-.20) + (.25) + (-.20)(.25)$

$= \emptyset$

$$R^d = \frac{P_t^d}{P_{t-1}^d} - 1 = \frac{P_t^f S_t^{d/f}}{P_{t-1}^f S_{t-1}^{d/f}} - 1 = (P_t^f / P_{t-1}^f)(S_t^{d/f}/S_{t-1}^{d/f}) - 1$$

$$= (1 + R^f)(1 + s^{d/f}) - 1$$

$$= R^f + s^{d/f} + R^f s^{d/f} \qquad (11.7)$$

The domestic currency return on a foreign asset arises from foreign market returns, from changes in spot exchange rates, and from the interaction of foreign market returns with the exchange rate.

Expected Return on a Foreign Asset

The expected return on a foreign asset is given by

$$E[R^d] = E[R^f] + E[s^{d/f}] + E[R^f s^{d/f}] \qquad (11.8)$$

Equation (11.8) states that the expected domestic currency return on a foreign asset is composed of the expected return in the foreign currency, the expected change in the spot rate, and the expectation of the cross-product.[7]
   The algebra of equations (11.7) and (11.8) is much like that of the Fisher equation, which relates nominal interest rates i to real rates r and inflation p according to $1+i = (1+r)(1+p) \Rightarrow i = r+p+rp$. If the real interest rate is 1 percent and inflation is 10 percent, then the nominal interest rate is $i = r+p+rp = 0.01+0.10+(0.01)(0.10) = 0.111$, or 11.1 percent. Similarly, if the foreign market goes up $R^f = 1\%$ in the foreign currency and the spot foreign currency value rises by $s^{d/f} = 10\%$, then the domestic currency return on the foreign asset is $0.01+0.10+(0.01)(0.10) = 0.111$, or 11.1 percent.

Variance of Return on a Foreign Asset

The variance of return on the foreign asset in the domestic currency, $Var(R^d)$, can be obtained from equation (11.4). Consider a return R composed of three parts, A, B, and C, such that $R = A + B + C$. The general case for the variance of a random variable $R = A + B + C$ is

$$Var(R) = Var(A) + Var(B) + Var(C) + 2Cov(A,B) + 2Cov(B,C) + 2Cov(A,C)$$

---

7 In continuously compounded returns, the continuously compounded return on a foreign asset in the domestic currency is $R^d = \ln(1+R^d) = \ln[(1+R^f)(1+s^{d/f})] = \ln(1+R^f)+\ln(1+s^{d/f}) = R^f + s^{d/f}$, where R^f and $s^{d/f}$ are the continuously compounded foreign asset return and change in the spot exchange rate, respectively. Continuous compounding eliminates the cross-product term, so that $E[R^d] = E[R^f] + E[s^{d/f}]$.

In the portfolio setting with investments of $R = X_A R_A + X_B R_B + X_C R_C$, the A, B, and C represent the weighted returns: $A = X_A R_A$, $B = X_B R_B$, and $C = X_C R_C$. Two properties of a constant X times a random variable R are useful in this context. These properties are

$$\text{Var}(XR) = X^2\,\text{Var}(R) \quad \text{and} \quad \text{Cov}(X_A R_A, X_B R_B) = X_A X_B \text{Cov}(R_A, R_B)$$

The return variance on a three-asset portfolio is then given by

$$\text{Var}(R) = X_A{}^2\,\text{Var}(R_A) + X_B{}^2\,\text{Var}(R_B) + X_C{}^2\,\text{Var}(R_C)$$
$$+\,2 X_A X_B \text{Cov}(R_A, R_B) + 2 X_A X_C \text{Cov}(R_A, R_C) + 2 X_B X_C \text{Cov}(R_B, R_C).$$

Similarly, the variance of $R^d = R^f + s^{d/f} + R^f\,s^{d/f}$ is given by

$$\text{Var}(R^d) = \text{Var}(R^f) + \text{Var}(s^{d/f}) + \text{Var}(R^f s^{d/f}) + 2\text{Cov}(R^f, s^{d/f}) \tag{11.9}$$

where the covariance terms $2\text{Cov}(R^f, R^f s^{d/f})$ and $2\text{Cov}(s^{d/f}, R^f s^{d/f})$ equal zero and fall out of the equation.[8] Equation (11.9) states that volatility in the spot exchange rate contributes to the risk of foreign investments through exchange rate volatility itself and through the interaction of exchange rates with foreign market returns. Before we tackle the more difficult case of risky foreign currency cash flows, let's first consider the case of riskless foreign currency cash flows.

Riskless Foreign Currency Cash Flows. Suppose you are a U.S. multinational corporation and are promised a riskless cash flow of FF50,000 from the French government in six months. The spot and six-month forward exchange rates are both $S^{\$/FF} = F^{\$/FF} = \$.2000/FF$. This unhedged cash flow is fully exposed to changes in the $S^{\$/FF}$ spot rate of exchange, as shown below.

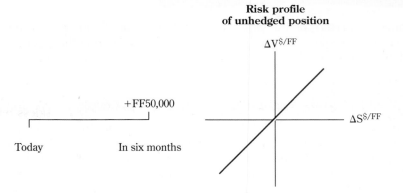

**Risk profile
of unhedged position**

$\Delta V^{\$/FF}$

+FF50,000

Today   In six months

$\Delta S^{\$/FF}$

---

8 After scaling by the random variable that is common to both terms, the covariances $\text{Cov}(R^f, R^f s^{d/f}) = (R^f)^2\text{Cov}(1, s^{d/f})$ and $\text{Cov}(s^{d/f}, R^f s^{d/f}) = (s^{d/f})^2\,\text{Cov}(1, R^f)$ are equal to the covariance of a random variable with a constant and therefore zero.

For every $.01/FF change in the value of the franc there is a ($.01/FF)(FF50,000) = $500 change in the value of the unhedged position. For example, if the value of the franc falls to $S^{\$/FF} = \$.1900/FF$ then this FF50,000 cash flow will convert to only $9,500 rather than the $10,000 expected value.

This is both good news and bad news for riskless cash flows denominated in francs. The bad news is that the value of the cash flow in dollars depends on the spot exchange rate. The good news is that the dollar value of the foreign currency cash flow depends only on the spot exchange rate. Because the French franc payment is guaranteed by the French government, it has a constant nominal return R^{FF}. This means that $Var(R^{FF}) = 0$, $Cov(R^{FF}, s^{\$/FF}) = 0$, and $Var(R^{FF}s^{\$/FF}) = 0$. Variability of return in dollars on this riskless franc cash flow then reduces to

$$Var(R^{\$}) = Var(R^{FF}) + Var(s^{\$/FF}) + Var(R^{FF}s^{\$/FF}) + 2Cov(R^{FF}, s^{\$/FF})$$
$$= 0 + Var(s^{\$/FF}) + 0 + 0$$
$$= Var(s^{\$/FF})$$

For riskless foreign cash flows, the only source of variability in domestic nominal return is exchange rate volatility itself.

To hedge against unanticipated changes in the spot rate, you should sell FF50,000 forward in exchange for $(FF50,000)(\$.2000/FF) = \$10,000$ at the forward exchange rate $F^{\$/FF} = \$.2000/FF$.

Sell French francs forward

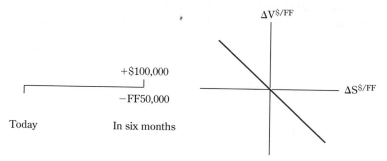

The riskless franc cash flow can be converted into a riskless dollar cash flow in this way. But is this "riskless" dollar cash flow truly riskless?

As a general rule, both domestic and foreign cash flows (even riskless ones) are exposed to purchasing power (or inflation) risk. In real terms, the purchasing power of a nominal cash flow to be received in the future depends on whether domestic inflation is as expected. In the example above, the real future value of the nominally riskless $10,000 cash flow may be more or less than $10,000 in six months depending on realized inflation over the period. Hedging foreign currency risk does not completely eliminate risk. It merely substitutes exposure to domestic purchasing power (inflation) risk for exposure to currency risk.

To hedge against domestic purchasing power risk, contracts must be signed in real, not nominal, terms. This means pegging all contracts to an appropriate inflation index,

Hedging

....

Hedging an exposure to currency risk merely substitutes domestic purchasing power risk for foreign exchange risk.

....

such as the Consumer Price Index (CPI). This hedges against domestic purchasing power risk to the extent that changes in the CPI approximate changes in the inflation actually faced by the hedger. Contracts pegged to an inflation index are common in high-inflation countries. An approximation to this hedge can be obtained using contracts with rates that float according to the level of interest rates. To the extent that nominal interest rate changes reflect only changes in inflation and not changes in the real rate of return, floating-rate contracts hedge against purchasing power risk.

Risky Foreign Currency Cash Flows. As firms extend their planning horizons farther and farther into the future, cash flows become more and more uncertain. As an example, suppose a U.S. multinational exports "Made in the U.S.A." personal computers to France through a French partner. While the actual level of sales in France will depend in large part on the firm's pricing decisions, there are many other factors affecting sales—the product itself, its promotion, and its distribution channels—so the actual level of sales in France is uncertain.

Risky foreign currency cash flows are exposed to each of the terms in equation (11.9). As with riskless cash flows, the dollar value of French franc cash flows depends on the level of exchange rates, so the exchange rate term $\text{Var}(s^{\$/FF})$ contributes to dollar return variability. And, because the actual return earned on the investment in francs is uncertain, the term $\text{Var}(R^{FF}) > 0$ also contributes to dollar return variability. Finally, the last two terms of equation (11.9) capture the interaction between the random variables R^{FF} and $s^{\$/FF}$.

Risky foreign currency cash flows are exposed to changes in foreign market returns and in currency values.

Exchange rate changes $s^{\$/FF}$ and foreign currency returns R^{FF} interact through the $\text{Cov}(R^{FF}, s^{\$/FF})$ and $\text{Var}(R^{FF}s^{\$/FF})$ terms because the actual level of sales and profits in France will depend on the value of the French franc. This is easiest to see if we consider two alternatives for pricing the computers in France. Pricing the computers in *francs* may make it easier to forecast the French franc return R^{FF}, but the dollar value of these sales will then depend on the exchange rate. Pricing the computers in *dollars* can remove uncertainty over the exchange rate faced by the U.S. multinational, but sales in France will then fall (rise) as the value of the dollar goes up (down). This influences the French franc returns R^{FF}. Risky foreign currency cash flows cannot be perfectly hedged against foreign exchange risk when the interaction terms are nonzero.

Financial Contracts in High-Inflation Countries

The convention in many high-inflation countries is to link financial contracts to a local price index. For example, Brazilian inflation is often high and always volatile. For this reason, the Brazilian government constructs consumer and producer price indices for various sectors of the economy. Brazilian financial contracts, such as savings deposits and bank loans, are then indexed to one of these price indexes. Pegging financial contracts to a representative inflation index can greatly reduce exposure to inflation risk for both borrowers and lenders.

The top half of Table 11.2 presents a breakdown of U.S. dollar returns according to equation (11.9) for various foreign stock investments over the period 1970–1994. The variance of foreign stock market returns to U.S. investors arose primarily from return variance in the local stock market $Var(R^f)$ and to a lesser extent from the variance in exchange rates $Var(s^{\$/f})$. With the exception of Canada and Japan, the contribution of the covariance term is nearly zero. The contribution of the cross-product term $Var(R^f s^{\$/f})$ was zero (within rounding error) for dollar returns to each country index. The dominant risk in each of these national equity markets was return variability in the national market itself and not the variability of foreign exchange rates.

In contrast to foreign stock market investments, the variance of foreign bond investments, shown in the lower half of Table 11.2, was dominated by exchange rates and exchange rate volatility. The contribution of exchange rate volatility is nearly always greater than that of the volatility of bond returns in the local currency. The only exceptions are Canada and the United Kingdom, which have relatively low currency volatility against the dollar and interest rate markets that are closely linked to those of the dollar. The relatively large influence of exchange rates on the variance of dollar returns on foreign bond investments suggests that it may be useful to hedge these investments against currency risk. We'll return to the issue of hedging foreign investments against currency risk in the next two chapters.

TABLE 11.2 DECOMPOSITION OF U.S. DOLLAR RETURN VARIANCE ON FOREIGN INVESTMENTS, 1970–1994

Stocks[a]	$Var(R^f)$	+	$Var(s^{\$/f})$	+	$2Cov(R^f, s^{\$/f})$	+	$Var(R^f s^{\$/f})$	=	$Var(R^\$)$
Canada	94.20%		5.19%		0.46%		0.14%		100.00%
France	84.94%		14.06%		−1.11%		2.10%		100.00%
Germany	86.07%		16.17%		−5.90%		3.66%		100.00%
Japan	83.86%		12.01%		3.22%		0.91%		100.00%
Switzerland	80.00%		23.31%		−6.29%		2.99%		100.00%
United Kingdom	90.12%		11.54%		−3.61%		1.95%		100.00%

Bonds[b]	$Var(R^f)$	+	$Var(s^{\$/f})$	+	$2Cov(R^f, s^{\$/f})$	+	$Var(R^f s^{\$/f})$	=	$Var(R^\$)$
Canada	87.75%		14.90%		−2.93%		0.27%		100.00%
France	49.11%		56.57%		−7.28%		1.60%		100.00%
Germany	38.68%		75.18%		−14.83%		0.97%		100.00%
Japan	32.52%		77.14%		−10.60%		0.93%		100.00%
Switzerland	25.27%		84.04%		−9.78%		0.47%		100.00%
United Kingdom	71.50%		34.94%		−7.96%		1.52%		100.00%

[a] Based on monthly stock returns from Morgan Stanley's *Capital International Perspectives* over the period from January 1970 through December 1994.
[b] Based on monthly long-term government bond returns from Ibbotson Associates over the period from January 1970 through June 1994.

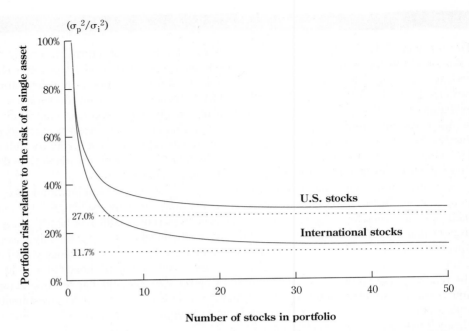

FIGURE 11.4
Risk Reduction through
International Diversification

Adapted from Bruno Solnik, "Why Not Diversify Internationally Rather Than Domestically?"
Reprinted with permission, from *Financial Analysts Journal*, July/August 1974, pages 48–54.
Copyright 1974, The Financial Analysts Federation, Charlottesville, VA. All rights reserved.

Diversifying with International Equity Investments

*Systematic risk falls as
portfolios are diversified across
national borders.*

Reduce Risk
Through
diversification

Bruno Solnik was the first to formally quantify the risk reduction benefits of international diversification.[9] Solnik estimates that the proportion of systematic risk to total risk (that is, return variance) for a typical stock in the U.S. market is about 27 percent. This means that about 73 percent of the total risk of an individual U.S. stock can be eliminated through diversification within a large U.S. portfolio. The remaining element of risk is common to all stocks and reflects general macroeconomic developments in the U.S. domestic stock market.

Figure 11.4 presents Solnik's estimate of the additional gain possible from international equity diversification for a U.S. resident. As the opportunity set is expanded from domestic U.S. stocks to a globally diversified equity portfolio, the systematic risk portion of the portfolio falls to 11.7 percent of the average variance of an individual security. This is less than half of the level of systematic risk in a fully diversified domestic U.S. equity portfolio.

The benefits of international diversification are greatest for residents of those countries with the least diversified economies. Even for residents of countries with diversified economies, such as the United States, the risk reduction benefits of international portfolio investment are still substantial.

---

9 Bruno Solnik, "Why Not Diversify Internationally Rather Than Domestically?" *Financial Analysts Journal* 30, No. 2, 1974, pages 48–54.

TABLE 11.3 ANNUAL RETURNS TO NATIONAL STOCK MARKETS, 1970–1994

	Principal exchange	Local returns Mean	Local returns Stdev	Dollar returns Mean	Dollar returns Stdev	Correlations vs U.S.	Correlations vs World	Beta vs World
Australia	Sydney	14.33	27.67	12.59	27.07	.700	.788	1.276
Austria	Vienna	11.64	31.49	17.19	41.54	.413	.399	0.735
Belgium	Brussels	15.25	23.35	17.35	24.26	.465	.634	0.868
Canada	Toronto	11.40	16.71	10.46	17.17	.630	.678	0.664
Denmark	Copenhagen	17.63	35.81	17.74	31.30	.421	.422	0.885
France	Paris	15.01	27.65	15.76	30.74	.587	.705	1.142
Germany	Frankfurt	10.69	26.64	14.99	31.69	.532	.585	0.913
Hong Kong	Hong Kong	33.94	53.09	32.79	53.25	.560	.608	1.889
Ireland	Dublin	4.52	17.79	3.12	18.27	.221	.328	0.341
Italy	Milan	14.98	36.85	11.98	41.70	.445	.614	1.324
Korea	Seoul	n/a	n/a	n/a	n/a	n/a	n/a	n/a
Japan	Tokyo	14.77	30.24	22.08	36.57	.363	.610	1.080
Mexico	Mexico City	40.71	78.35	8.81	39.30	.166	.496	2.275
Netherlands	Amsterdam	14.43	22.71	17.32	19.50	.725	.665	0.884
New Zealand	Wellington	3.09	15.44	1.51	20.73	.219	.267	0.242
Norway	Oslo	19.88	48.54	21.10	51.56	.120	.114	0.325
Singapore/Malaysia		19.42	50.36	22.51	50.76	.440	.504	1.487
Spain	Madrid	13.85	28.65	12.35	33.38	.221	.530	0.890
Sweden	Stockholm	20.21	29.32	17.99	25.22	.397	.493	0.846
Switzerland	Zurich	10.12	24.36	15.34	25.93	.722	.677	0.966
Taiwan	Taipei	n/a	n/a	n/a	n/a	n/a	n/a	n/a
United Kingdom	London	18.90	34.69	16.99	32.10	.636	.582	1.182
United States	New York	11.63	15.79	11.63	15.79	1.00	.816	0.755
World		12.87	17.08	12.87	17.08	.816	1.00	1.000

Based on annual returns from Morgan Stanley's *Capital International Perspectives* (MSCI) from January 1970 through October 1994. (Annual returns for 1994 are calculated from January through October.) Statistics for Ireland and New Zealand are based on 1988–1994. Morgan Stanley began reporting separate indices for Singapore and Malaysia (Kuala Lumpur) and for Korea and Taiwan in 1993.

To capture really big returns, of course, means taking really big risks. Table 11.3 presents annual return statistics on the national stock markets followed by Morgan Stanley. The countries with the highest mean returns also tend to have the highest standard deviation of return, whether measured in local currency or in dollars. The stocks of smaller countries are often concentrated in a few industries, so they are less diversified than the major stock markets. These countries usually have more volatile economic and political climates as well. The good news is that the returns to stocks in emerging markets usually have a low correlation with stock returns in developed markets.[10]

Diversifying with International Bond Investments

Diversification into foreign bond markets can substantially reduce the risk of an internationally diversified bond portfolio. In Table 11.1, the average pairwise correlation between national stock indices is .48 while it is only .38 between national bond indices. This low correlation means that the potential for risk reduction through international

---

10 This was pointed out by Vihang R. Errunza in "Gains from Portfolio Diversification into Less Developed Countries," *Journal of International Business Studies* 8, Fall–Winter 1977, pages 83–99.

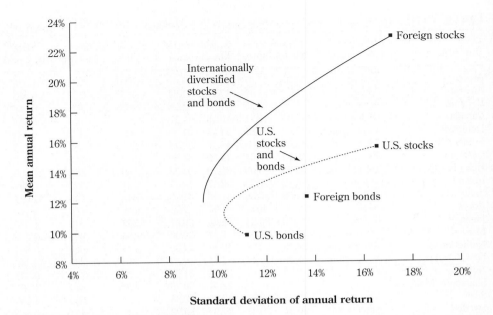

FIGURE 11.5
Efficiency Gains through
International Stock and
Bond Diversification

Adapted from "Asset Allocation with Hedged and Unhedged Foreign Stocks and Bonds" by
Philippe Jorion, *Journal of Portfolio Management*, Summer 1989, pages 49–54. Reprinted with permission.

portfolio diversification with bonds is often even greater than with stocks.[11] For U.S.
investors, foreign bonds have had the additional benefit of higher mean returns as well.

The prices of fixed-rate bonds are determined by the level of interest rates in the
local economy. Changes in interest rates are in turn determined by changes in inflation
and in real required returns. Although stock values also vary with inflation and with real
required returns, there is a much bigger company-specific component to stock returns
than to bond returns.

Currency risk is a much larger percentage of total variance for bonds than for stocks.
For example, exchange rate volatility accounts for 77.14 percent of the variance on a
Japanese bond portfolio in Table 11.2 whereas it accounts for only 12.01 percent of the
variance on a Japanese stock portfolio. This means that hedging the currency risk of an
international bond portfolio can be an important source of risk reduction. Fixed-rate
bonds have contractual payoffs that are simple to hedge against currency risk using currency forwards, futures, options. and swaps.

Diversifying with International Stocks and Bonds

When combined with stocks, bonds can further improve the return-risk efficiency of a
globally diversified portfolio. Figure 11.5 presents Philippe Jorion's estimate of the gains
from international stock and bond diversification from the perspective of a U.S.

---

11 See Haim Levy and Zvi Lerman, "The Benefits of International Diversification in Bonds," *Financial
Analysts Journal* 44, September/October 1988, pages 56–64.

investor.[12] This figure shows that investing in foreign stocks can improve the return-risk performance of a portfolio of stocks. Similarly, investing in foreign bonds can improve the return-risk performance of a bond portfolio. Because the returns on (foreign and domestic) stocks and bonds have low correlations, further gains can be obtained by combining stocks and bonds in an internationally diversified portfolio. Although past performance is no guarantee of future results, it is clear that portfolio performance can be improved through diversification into foreign stocks and bonds.

11.6 BARRIERS TO INTERNATIONAL PORTFOLIO DIVERSIFICATION

Obtaining the risk reduction (and possibly higher return) benefits of international portfolio diversification sounds great in theory. But what are the impediments to forming an internationally diversified portfolio? This section describes how financial market imperfections impede foreign investment and the free flow of capital across national borders. These market imperfections are becoming less important as time goes on and both developed and developing nations open their markets to foreign capital. Nevertheless, financial market imperfections can still present formidable obstacles to international portfolio diversification.

Market imperfections impede the free flow of capital across national borders.

Market Frictions

Government Controls. Ever since (and probably before) King Hammurabi tried and failed to freeze prices in ancient Babylonia, governments have been only too willing to impose price controls to achieve their fiscal and monetary policy objectives. Price freezes treat the symptom and not the cause of inflation, and they are unlikely to have much of an effect unless accompanied by fundamental changes in other fiscal and monetary policies, such as government spending and growth of the money supply. Artificially freezing prices when true prices are rising disables the normal price-discovery function of the marketplace and creates excess demand and a shortage of supply at the frozen price levels. Because the price mechanism is prohibited from balancing demand with supply, in the short run price freezes result in rationing, shortages, hoarding, and other suboptimal behaviors on the part of consumers and producers. In the long run, either black markets arise for the controlled goods and services or consumers find substitutes for the price-controlled assets.

gov't Controls

Governments often try to stabilize cross-border financial flows through foreign exchange controls. The most extreme barrier to cross-border financial flows arises when a government prohibits the conversion of its currency into other currencies. A less extreme form of this barrier occurs when a government mandates that currencies be exchanged at an official rate determined by the government rather than at exchange rates determined in a competitive financial marketplace. Such fixed exchange rate

Governments often try to stabilize cross-border financial flows through foreign exchange controls.

12 Philippe Jorion, "Asset Allocation with Hedged and Unhedged Foreign Stocks and Bonds," *Journal of Portfolio Management* 15, Summer 1989, pages 49–54.

regimes (discussed in Chapter 2) can have lasting and profound effects on foreign trade, economic development, and the distribution of income and wealth within the country. If domestic currency prices are set below market rates, then the high price of imports and the excess demand by foreign investors for domestic goods and assets fuel domestic inflation. If domestic currency values are set above market prices, then imports look cheap, capital flows out of the country, and domestic production and employment suffer. Efforts to control cross-border financial flows through exchange rates can be at least partially successful in the short run. In the long run, high transaction volume and high volatility in the foreign exchange markets make it difficult for governments to arbitrarily impose their own exchange rates on the currency markets.

Governments try to selectively control capital inflows and outflows by requiring that particular types of cross-border transactions be conducted at official rates that vary from market rates. Rather than pegging all transactions to a single rate, selective currency controls target key industries or sectors of the economy. Selective controls can be used to encourage some types of foreign transactions and discourage others. For example, the foreign investment transactions of domestic residents may be conducted at official rates that make it relatively expensive to invest abroad. Special exchange rates on foreign transactions have been implemented through the *dollar premium* in the United Kingdom, the *franc financier* in Belgium, the *devise titre* in France, and the *interest equalization tax* in the United States.

Another common form of capital flow constraint is a prohibition or limitation on foreign investment by domestic residents, on domestic investment by foreign residents, or both. These are called capital inflow and capital outflow controls. The Finnish market provides an example.[13] Under Finnish law in the 1980s, foreign investors were allowed to own up to 20 percent of the assets of any Finnish company. These shares were called *unrestricted shares* and could be owned by anyone regardless of residency or citizenship. The remaining 80 percent of shares carried a stamp indicating that they were *restricted shares* and could be owned only by Finnish investors. For foreign investors wishing to diversify into the Finnish stock market, unrestricted shares were the only direct way to gain access to the Finnish market. This two-tier structure resulted in restricted and unrestricted shares selling at vastly different prices. From January 1984 through June 1985, unrestricted shares sold at premiums over restricted share prices of 2 percent to 63 percent.

Another way that countries restrict access to their financial markets through capital inflow and outflow controls is by prohibiting foreign investors from owning domestic shares except through closed-end country funds (CECFs). CECFs are closed-end mutual funds invested in the assets (typically common stocks) of a country. By identifying which companies may be held in the fund and by limiting the number of shares owned by the fund, governments can control foreign access to their domestic capital markets. Because CECFs provide investors with access to otherwise restricted markets, CECFs often trade at substantial premiums to their net asset values in the home market. We will return to the subject of CECFs in Chapter 13.

---

13 The structure of the Finnish market is described by Pekka T. Hietala in "Asset Pricing in Partially Segmented Markets: Evidence from the Finnish Market," *Journal of Finance* 44, No. 3, July 1989, pages 697–718. Finland removed its currency controls and its restrictions against foreign ownership of Finnish companies with the Finnish Securities Act of 1989.

Taxes. If all nations shared the same tax laws, then there would be no international dimension to tax planning. Because there are wide cross-country differences in the definition and taxation of income and assets, multinational tax planning occupies a central role in the conduct of international business.

TAXES

Despite national differences in tax rates on real and financial assets, there are similarities in the tax treatment of foreign operations by different countries. This is largely because of model international treaties such as the *Model Treaty of the Organization for Economic Cooperation and Development.* Among other objectives, international tax treaties are intended to eliminate double taxation of gains received from foreign operations or investment. Double taxation can be avoided by (1) assigning various forms of taxable gains to a single tax jurisdiction or (2) by allowing a tax deduction or credit for foreign taxes paid.

Taxes are imposed on three types of events:

- Capital gain realizations
- Dividend and interest income distributions
- Financial transactions.

Capital gains taxes on foreign investments are the most straightforward. Capital gains are taxed by the investor's home government in the same way that domestic capital gains are taxed. Because capital gains are difficult to monitor and are not taxed until realized, there are typically no withholding taxes on capital gains.

A tax on a financial transaction is often called a *stamp tax.* Transactions taxes can be proportional to the amount of the transaction. For example, in Switzerland there is a federal stamp tax equal to 0.09 percent of the transaction amount. In some other European countries, the tax is applied as a value-added tax based on the size of the broker's commission. Still other countries charge a flat fee per transaction.

On dividend and interest income the game gets interesting. Countries often impose a *withholding tax* on interest and/or dividends paid in their currency and within their borders. This means that foreigners may be taxed twice—once in the country from which income is paid and once in the country in which it is received.

During the mid-1980s many countries (including the United States, France, and Germany) eliminated withholding taxes on foreign bond investments in their domestic markets as a way to keep domestic credit markets competitive with Eurobond markets. In some countries, elimination of withholding taxes on interest income has resulted in a great deal of income going unreported. For example, the Bundesrechnungshof (the German tax authority) estimated in the late 1980s that 65 percent to 70 percent of all interest received by West German residents was not being reported.[14] In some cases, tax avoidance by local residents has prompted the reinstitution of withholding taxes and/or increased penalties for noncompliance.

---

14 Wolf Bay and Richard Stehle report this statistic in "Elimination of the Double Taxation of Dividends: Is the German Experience Relevant for the U.S.A?" University of Augsburg (Germany) Working Paper, 1992.

Withholding taxes on dividend distributions are the norm in most countries. The most common dividend withholding tax rate is 15 percent, although the rate varies from zero in Hong Kong to higher than 50 percent in Mexico. Withholding taxes on foreign shares are typically claimed as a tax deduction or credit by taxable investors in their home country up to the amount of the home country tax liability. There is an opportunity cost on dividend withholdings, because no interest is earned on funds from the time they are withheld by the foreign government until the time they are claimed as a tax credit, but this opportunity cost is the same for both foreign and domestic investments. Nontaxable investors, such as pension funds, may suffer a loss if taxes are withheld, although the size of the loss is usually small. For example, unrecoverable withholding taxes of 15 percent on a stock with a dividend yield of 2 percent result in a maximum loss of $(0.15)(0.02) = 0.003$, or 0.03 percent.

The diversity of tax regimes and tax rates across countries is the driving force behind multinational tax planning. Whenever tax rates differ, there is an opportunity to engage in tax arbitrage (usually a form of locational arbitrage) between the two countries or, at the very least, to shift assets, liabilities, and the size, timing, and form of cash flows in ways that minimize taxes. The effects of international taxation differences on the activities of multinational corporations are discussed in Part 5 of this text.

Transactions Costs. Transactions costs on international investments are charged in many explicit and implicit ways, including trading commissions, fees, and bid-ask spreads. Transactions costs are sometimes set by the government or by an agency representing brokers, but the worldwide trend has been toward negotiated commissions. Commissions were deregulated on the New York Stock Exchange in 1974 and on the London Stock Exchange in 1986. One way to measure the extent of a particular market's development is as an inverse function of the size of its trading costs. In the United States, transactions costs can be as low as 0.1 percent for large transactions in actively traded stocks. In less developed financial markets, direct trading costs on stocks often exceed 1 percent.

In countries where transactions costs are negotiable, transactions costs fall as trade sizes rise. This means that small investors do not have access to prices in the international financial markets in the same way as large international banks, corporations, and mutual funds. In these markets, small investors may need to put their wealth into mutual funds to get competitive prices at low transactions costs. Management fees are incurred through the funds, but the reduction in transactions costs on foreign investments is usually worth the price of admission.

Unequal Access to Market Prices

In perfectly competitive financial markets, the required returns on financial assets reflect the costs and risks of investment. Perfect competition requires a large number of rational buyers and sellers each trading for personal profit. A large number of buyers and sellers ensures that no single competitor can influence asset prices. Consequently, competitors have equal access to market prices in a perfectly competitive financial market.

In fact, wealth is not distributed equally across the world's inhabitants. The gap between the haves and the have-nots is large, and asset prices are occasionally manipulated in international markets. The most powerful manipulators are governments, large corporations, securities industry insiders, and wealthy individuals. This section discusses the influence of governments on stock prices. Be aware, however, that corporate insiders and wealthy individuals also occasionally influence market prices.

Governments exert a powerful influence on asset prices through their fiscal and monetary policies. Governments influence prices either by changing the supply of an asset (such as a currency) or by changing their demand for an asset. On the supply side, governments influence domestic interest rates and currency values through their monetary policies. Cartels such as the Organization of Petroleum Exporting Countries (OPEC) can influence oil prices by expanding or restricting the production of oil. Investors spend a great deal of time and money trying to anticipate (and even influence) the actions of governments around the world.

Governments occasionally intervene on the demand side of international financial markets as well. For example, governments often try to support stock prices following stock market crashes. When the Kuwait Stock Exchange lost more than fifty percent of its value during a single month in 1983, the Kuwaiti government intervened and bought shares in Kuwaiti companies in an effort to support prices. Similarly, when equity values in Japan plummeted in January 1990, the Japanese government responded by supplying below-market loans to Japanese businesses and financial institutions in an effort to prop up the economy.

As a general rule, the lower the liquidity and market capitalization of an asset the more likely it is that price can be affected by a single buyer's or seller's actions. **Liquidity** is the ability to buy or sell an asset quickly and at a fair price. Assets trading in smaller markets, such as the stock and bond markets of developing countries, are usually less liquid than similar assets trading in larger markets. Liquidity also appears to be a function of transaction volume. In illiquid markets, price movements can appear "sticky" because of low transaction volume.

A comparison of the stock markets in Kuwait and Saudi Arabia provides an example of how market structure can affect liquidity, transaction volume, and the price discovery process.[15] Despite similar economies, politics, climates, and cultures, Kuwait and Saudi Arabia had adopted quite different stock market structures prior to the Iraqi invasion of Kuwait in 1989. In response to the 1983 stock market crash in Kuwait, stock trading in Kuwait had been modernized with trading regulations similar to those in the United States and a computerized trading system at a central stock exchange. Stock trading in Saudi Arabia continued with a costly, antiquated, manual trading system conducted through twelve Saudi banks. Not surprisingly, stock market liquidity and transaction volume were much higher in Kuwait than in Saudi Arabia during this time, despite the smaller market capitalization and size of the Kuwaiti market. Stock price movements in Kuwait were similar to those of over-the-counter (OTC) stocks in the United States, but prices in the Saudi market behaved erratically.

Another barrier to investing in foreign assets is that in many nations a large proportion of wealth is either owned by the government or concentrated in the hands of a few

---

15 See Kirt Butler and S.K. Malaikah, "Efficiency and Inefficiency in Thinly Traded Stock Markets: Kuwait and Saudi Arabia," *Journal of Banking and Finance,* February 1992, pages 197–210.

*Investor
        Behavior*

individuals. For example, local economies in Mexico are often dominated by a single family. Assets held by governments or in private hands are illiquid, and direct portfolio investment in these assets can be difficult and costly.

Investor Irrationality

The perfect market conditions listed at the beginning of this chapter include an assumption that rational investors seek to maximize the expected return and minimize the risk of their investments, where return is measured in their functional currency. Rational investors price assets with a dispassionate eye toward their expected returns and risks. Psychological factors in foreign investing, such as fear of the unknown, do not enter into valuation except insofar as they affect perceived risks and returns and the cost of acquiring additional information about foreign investments.

A growing body of literature in finance and economics does not assume rationality on the part of some or all investors. This *behavioral finance* approach to asset valuation results in prices that are not necessarily semi–strong form efficient (that is, correctly priced based on all relevant publicly available information). The nature and extent of market inefficiencies continue to be among the most actively investigated areas of finance, especially for international assets.

Unequal Access to Information

The assumption of equal access to information belies the fact that language serves as a very real barrier to the flow of information across (and sometimes within) national boundaries. The first order of business when dealing with potential customers, suppliers, or partners from foreign lands is finding a common language. Yet even with a common language, information is difficult to convey and can change in the telling. The statement "Let's meet for lunch at 2:00" can take on vastly different meanings in different cultural settings. In Frankfurt, Germany, it means "Let's meet precisely at 2:00—no earlier and no later." In Mexico City it might mean "Let's meet sometime between 2:00 and 2:30."

Cross-cultural differences become even more interesting when financial and accounting disclosure practices are concerned. There are two potential types of differences in financial statements. First, accounting measurement can be quite different across countries. For example, the items included in the definition of income can be quite different. Even an analyst fluent in the language is likely to have difficulty interpreting financial statements from another country because of differences in accounting measurement. Second, there are substantial differences in national accounting disclosure practices, particularly between industrially developed countries and less developed countries. By 1980, most industrialized nations had instituted disclosure requirements. Disclosure conventions in developing countries are usually far less extensive and reliable.

11.7 HOME ASSET BIAS

Investors exhibit home asset bias and favor local stocks.

Portfolio theory tells us that rational investors should invest in an internationally diversified portfolio of assets. Portfolio weights on each asset should be the same for all investors—all investors should hold the market value weight of each asset in their port-

TABLE 11.4   HOME BIAS IN EQUITY PORTFOLIOS AS OF DECEMBER 1987

	Market capitalization as a percentage of total	Percentage of equity portfolio held in domestic equities
France	2.6	64.4
Germany	3.2	75.4
Italy	1.9	91.0
Japan	43.7	86.7
Spain	1.1	94.2
Sweden	0.8	100.0
United Kingdom	10.3	78.5
United States	36.4	98.0

Source: Ian Cooper and Evi Kaplanis, "Home Bias in Equity Portfolios, Inflation Hedging, and International Capital Market Equilibrium," *Review of Financial Studies* 7, No. 1, Spring 1994, pages 45–60. Used by permission of Oxford University Press.

folios. Despite the compelling logic of portfolio theory, few investors fully diversify their portfolios across national borders. Instead, investors tend to overinvest in assets based in their own country. This tendency is called **home asset bias** (or home bias).

Table 11.4 presents the home bias in the equity portfolios of investors in several developed countries as of 1987. Investors in Western Europe have more of a cultural tradition of international diversification as reflected in their lesser degree of home bias. Investors in the United States are among the least diversified internationally, with a very high percentage of their equity portfolios held in domestic U.S. equities. This is in part because the investment opportunities of U.S. investors in the large and diversified U.S. market are greater than the opportunities of investors in Western Europe in their local markets. Nevertheless, as of 1987 U.S. investors held only 2 percent of their equity investments in foreign stocks. This percentage is only slightly higher today.

What could account for this strong home bias in equity portfolios? Two explanations for why investors are not more internationally diversified have been studied in the literature on home asset bias:

- The costs of international diversification
- The ability of a domestic stock portfolio to hedge domestic inflation risk

First, market imperfections are clearly at work. Cross-border capital flow constraints, transactions costs, differential taxes, and other market frictions impede the cross-border flow of capital. These costs encourage home bias by reducing the net return on foreign investments. It is also more difficult to gain access to information from foreign markets and to interpret this information. However, the relatively high turnover on foreign equity investments relative to turnover on domestic equity markets suggests that transactions costs alone are an unlikely explanation for home asset bias.[16]

The second explanation involves international asset pricing. Investors in different countries consume different bundles of goods, so investors are exposed to inflation risk

---

16 See Linda L. Tesar and Ingrid M. Werner, "Home Bias and High Turnover," *Journal of International Money and Finance* 14, No. 4, 1995, pages 467–492.

in their own domestic currency. Investors prefer to hold domestic equities if these equities serve as a hedge against inflation risk in the domestic currency.[17] Ian Cooper and Evi Kaplanis examine each of these explanations and find that, at best, each is only a partial explanation for the observed home bias.[18] A more satisfactory explanation will have to await further research on the home bias puzzle.

11.8 Summary

This chapter began by stating the perfect financial market assumptions: (1) frictionless markets (no taxes, transactions costs, costs of financial distress, or agency costs), (2) equal access to market prices (perfect competition and no barriers to trade), (3) rational investors, and (4) equal access to costless information. We then added an assumption that investors care only about the mean and variance of nominal returns in their functional currency. These abstractions from reality allowed us to consider the algebra of portfolio diversification in a stylized world in which everyone has equal access to costless information and market prices.

According to the algebra of portfolio diversification, the expected return and variance of a portfolio are given by

$$E[R_P] = \Sigma_i X_i E[R_i] \tag{11.2}$$

and

$$Var(R_P) = \sigma_P^2$$
$$= \Sigma_i \Sigma_j X_i X_j \sigma_{ij}$$
$$= \Sigma_i X_i^2 \sigma_i^2 + \Sigma_i \Sigma_j X_i X_j \sigma_{ij} \tag{11.4}$$
$$i \neq j$$

This has three implications for portfolio risk and return:

- The extent to which risk is reduced by portfolio diversification depends on how highly the individual assets in the portfolio are correlated.
- As the number of assets held in a portfolio increases, the variance of return on the portfolio becomes more dependent on the covariances between the individual securities and less dependent on the variances of the individual securities.
- The risk of an individual asset when it is held in a portfolio with a large number of securities depends on its return covariance with other securities in the portfolio and not on its return variance.

17 See Michael Adler and Bernard Dumas, "International Portfolio Choice and Corporation Finance: A Synthesis," *Journal of Finance* 38, June 1983, pages 925–984.
18 Ian Cooper and Evi Kaplanis, "Home Bias in Equity Portfolio, Inflation Hedging, and International Capital Market Equilibrium," *Review of Financial Studies* 7, No. 1, Spring 1994, pages 45–60.

The total risk of an asset can be decomposed into systematic and unsystematic components. Systematic risks are related to risks in other stocks and cannot be diversified away in a large portfolio. Unsystematic risks are unrelated to risks in other stocks and are diversifiable in a large portfolio.

Returns on foreign investments are given by

$$R^d = R^f + s^{d/f} + R^f s^{d/f} \tag{11.7}$$

This has expected return

$$E[R^d] = E[R^f] + E[s^{d/f}] + E[R^f s^{d/f}] \tag{11.8}$$

and variance

$$\text{Var}(R^d) = \text{Var}(R^f) + \text{Var}(s^{d/f}) + \text{Var}(R^f s^{d/f}) + 2\text{Cov}(R^f, s^{d/f}) \tag{11.9}$$

Hedging foreign currency risk does not completely eliminate risk. As a general rule, both domestic and foreign cash flows are exposed to purchasing power risk. Hedging against currency risk merely substitutes exposure to domestic purchasing power risk for exposure to foreign currency risk.

KEY TERMS

Covariance and correlation
Efficient frontier
Home asset bias
Law of one price
Liquidity
Mean-variance efficiency
Operational, informational, and allocational
   market efficiency

Opportunity set
Perfect financial market assumptions
Sharpe index (SI)
Short selling
Systematic versus unsystematic risk

CONCEPTUAL QUESTIONS

11.1 What is a perfect market?

11.2 What is operational efficiency in a financial market? informational efficiency? allocational efficiency?

11.3 How is portfolio risk measured? What determines portfolio risk?

11.4 What happens to portfolio risk as the number of assets in the portfolio increases?

11.5 What happens to the relevant risk measure for an individual asset when it is held in a large portfolio rather than in isolation?

11.6 In words, what does the Sharpe index measure?

11.7 Name two synonyms for "systematic risk."

11.8 Name two synonyms for "unsystematic risk."

11.9 Is international diversification effective in reducing portfolio risk?

11.10 Describe several of the barriers to international portfolio diversification.

PROBLEMS

11.1 Based on the historical returns in Table 11.1, calculate the mean and standard deviation of return in dollars for an equally weighted portfolio of French and German stocks. Calculate the Sharpe index for this portfolio using the historical rate of 7.9 percent on U.S. T-bills as the risk-free rate.

11.2 Based on the historical returns in Table 11.1, calculate the mean and standard deviation of return in dollars for an equally weighted portfolio of German and Japanese stocks. Calculate the Sharpe index for this portfolio using the historical rate of 7.9 percent on U.S. T-bills as the risk-free rate.

11.3 The correlation between dollar returns to the MSCI world stock and bond market indices listed in Table 11.1 is .444. Calculate the expected return and standard deviation of return in dollars to an equally weighted portfolio of stocks and bonds. Calculate the Sharpe index for this portfolio using the historical rate of 7.9 percent on U.S. T-bills as the risk-free rate.

11.4 Based on the historical returns in Table 11.1, calculate the expected return and standard deviation of return in dollars to an equally weighted portfolio of U.S., U.K., and Japanese stocks. Calculate the Sharpe index for this portfolio using the historical rate of 7.9 percent on U.S. T-bills as the risk-free rate.

11.5 Suppose you calculated a Sharpe index for every security in the world over the most recent year. Are any of these securities likely to exhibit performance (measured as excess return per unit of risk) that is superior to that of the world market portfolio?

11.6 The Philippine stock market in Makati rises 12 percent in Philippine pesos (P). During the same period, the Philippine peso rises from $.0425/P to $.0440/P against the U.S. dollar. By how much does the Philippine stock market rise in U.S. dollars?

11.7 What is the variance of return on the Philippine stock market to a U.S. investor if $Var(R^P, s^{\$/P}) = Cov(R^P, s^{\$/P}) = 0$, $Var(R^P) = 24.8\%$, and $Var(s^{\$/P}) = 32.7\%$?

SUGGESTED READINGS

The algebra of international portfolio diversification and asset pricing is developed in
Michael Adler and Bernard Dumas, "International Portfolio Choice and Corporation Finance: A Synthesis," *Journal of Finance* 38, June 1983, pages 925–984.

Articles that make a case for international portfolio diversification include
Bruno Solnik, "Why Not Diversify Internationally Rather Than Domestically?" *Financial Analysts Journal* 30, No. 2, 1974, pages 48–54.

Vihang R. Errunza, "Gains from Portfolio Diversification into Less Developed Countries," *Journal of International Business Studies* 8, Fall–Winter 1977, pages 83–99.

Haim Levy and Zvi Lerman, "The Benefits of International Diversification in Bonds," *Financial Analysts Journal* 44, September/October 1988, pages 56–64.

Philippe Jorion, "Asset Allocation with Hedged and Unhedged Foreign Stocks and Bonds," *Journal of Portfolio Management* 15, Summer 1989, pages 49–54.

Studies that investigate the impact of market imperfections on asset prices include
Catherine Bonser-Neal, Greggory Brauer, Robert Neal, and Simon Wheatley, "International Investment Restrictions and Closed-End Country Fund Prices," *Journal of Finance* 45, No. 2, 1990, pages 523–548.

Kirt C. Butler and S.K. Malaikah, "Efficiency and Inefficiency in Thinly Traded Stock Markets: Kuwait and Saudi Arabia," *Journal of Banking and Finance,* February 1992, pages 197–210.

Cheol S. Eun and S. Janakiramanan, "A Model of International Asset Pricing with a Constraint on the Foreign Equity Ownership," *Journal of Finance* 41, No. 4, 1986, pages 897–913.

Pekka T. Hietala, "Asset Pricing in Partially Segmented Markets: Evidence from the Finnish Market," *Journal of Finance* 44, No. 3, July 1989, pages 697–718.

Bertrand Jacquillat and Bruno H. Solnik "Multinationals Are Poor Tools for International Diversification," *Journal of Portfolio Management,* Winter 1978, pages 8–12.

Home asset bias is investigated in the following articles

Ian Cooper and Evi Kaplanis, "Home Bias in Equity Portfolios, Inflation Hedging, and International Capital Market Equilibrium," *Review of Financial Studies* 7, No. 1, Spring 1994, pages 45–60.

Ian Cooper and Evi Kaplanis, "Home Bias in Equity Portfolios and the Cost of Capital for Multinational Firms," *Journal of Applied Corporate Finance* 8, No. 3, Fall 1995, pages 95–102.

Linda L. Tesar and Ingrid M. Werner, "Home Bias and High Turnover," *Journal of International Money and Finance* 14, No. 4, 1995, pages 467–492.

International Asset Pricing

Though this be madness, yet there is method in it.
William Shakespeare

OVERVIEW

In perfect financial markets and with a few additional assumptions (to be discussed shortly), the algebra of Chapter 11 leads to the traditional Capital Asset Pricing Model (CAPM). To be useful in pricing international assets, asset pricing models such as the CAPM must be extended to a multicurrency setting. Chapter 12 makes this extension and then discusses several points relating to currency risk measurement and exposure.

12.1 THE TRADITIONAL CAPITAL ASSET PRICING MODEL

Before we move on to the international version of the CAPM, we need to complete the development of the traditional version. Up to this point, we've assumed that

- Financial markets conform to the perfect financial market conditions
  - Frictionless markets
  - Perfect competition
  - Rational investors
  - Equal access to costless information
- Nominal returns are normally distributed
- Investors want more nominal return and less risk in their functional currency

Two additional assumptions are necessary to complete the traditional version of the CAPM. The first is an assumption that all investors have the same expectations.

- Investors have homogeneous expectations regarding next period's expected returns and risks

In a world in which all investors have the same expectations, every investor faces the same investment opportunity set in Figure 12.1. An assumption of homogeneous expectations may seem especially out of place in a book founded on differences among the people of the world, but it is necessary for the traditional version of the CAPM.

The second assumption implicitly assumes away bankruptcy costs and other costs of financial distress.

- Everyone can borrow and lend at the riskless rate of interest R_F

The risk-free asset is represented by point F in Figure 12.1. The rate R_F is a risk-free rate of interest at which any party in the market can borrow and lend. Returns to this riskless asset are certain, so $\sigma_F = 0$. Certain returns to the risk-free asset also mean that the covariance of the risk-free asset with any risky asset A is zero, so $\sigma_{F,A} = 0$. The standard deviation of a portfolio of the risk-free asset F and any risky asset A has a particularly simple form: $\sigma_P^2 = X_F^2 \sigma_F^2 + 2X_F X_A \sigma_{F,A} + X_A^2 \sigma_A^2 = X_A^2 \sigma_A^2$, so that $\sigma_P = X_A \sigma_A$. The standard deviation of a combination of assets A and F is proportional to the percentage invested in the risky asset A.

The capital market line describes the most efficient combination of risky and riskless assets.

The most mean-variance efficient combination of the risk-free asset F with a risky asset occurs when asset F is combined with the asset that lies along a line tangent to the efficient frontier. This line is called the **capital market line** and goes through the point M in Figure 12.1. Along this tangency line, investors achieve the highest level of

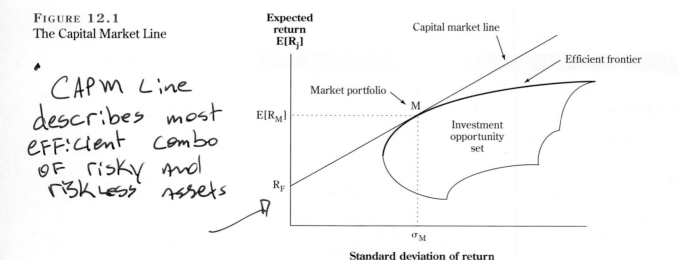

FIGURE 12.1
The Capital Market Line

CAPM Line describes most efficient combo of risky and riskless assets

expected return per unit of risk; that is, the "biggest bang for the buck." There is a single tangency point, so portfolio M *must* be a portfolio of all assets in the opportunity set weighted according to their market values. Point M is called the **market portfolio**. Under the assumptions of the CAPM, each investor choosing to invest in a risky asset will hold this portfolio.

Systematic versus Unsystematic Risks

The market portfolio includes a little (or a lot, depending on its market value) of every asset in the market. Because each investor will choose to hold this portfolio, the **systematic risk** (also called *nondiversifiable* or *market risk*) of an individual asset can be measured by how its returns covary with those of the market portfolio. This allows us to shift the focus from capital market equilibrium as depicted in Figure 12.1 to the expected return and risk of a single asset in the market portfolio as shown in Figure 12.2.

Systematic (Nondiversifiable) Risk and the Security Market Line. Assets are correctly priced in efficient financial markets, so the expected net present value of any financial investment is zero. This means that the expected return on each asset must be equal to that asset's required return. In the CAPM, this required return is given by the **security market line (SML)**. The equation of the SML is

The security market line describes the relation between systematic risk and required return.

Security MKT
Line

$$R_j = R_F + \beta_j (E[R_M] - R_F) \qquad (12.1)$$

The SML is graphed in Figure 12.2. This relation states that the required return on an individual asset is equal to the risk-free rate R_F plus a risk premium appropriate for

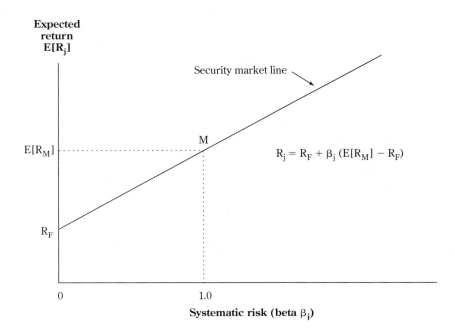

Expected
return
$E[R_j]$

Security market line

M

$E[R_M]$

$R_j = R_F + \beta_j (E[R_M] - R_F)$

R_F

0   1.0

Systematic risk (beta β_j)

FIGURE 12.2
The Security Market Line

$$R_j = \alpha_j + \beta_j R_M + e_j \quad \Leftrightarrow \quad R_j - \mu_j = \beta_j F_M + e_j,$$

$$\text{where } F_M = R_M - \mu_M$$

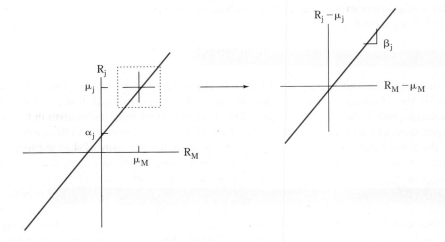

FIGURE 12.3
Beta As a Regression
Coefficient

the systematic risk of the asset. The risk premium is the product of the **market risk premium** (that is, the risk premium on an average stock, $E[R_M] - R_F$) and the firm's systematic risk, or **beta** (β_j). Beta is a measure of systemic risk and reflects the sensitivity of an asset's price to changes in the value of the market portfolio. Systematic risks arise through marketwide events, such as real economic growth or changing investor sentiment regarding asset values. Systematic risks cannot be diversified away by holding assets in portfolios.

Risk-adjusted investment performance is measured by the difference between actual return and expected return from equation (12.1):

$$e_j = R_j - E[R_j] = R_j - [(R_F + \beta_j(R_M - R_F)] \tag{12.2}$$

where R_j is the observed return to asset j and $E[R_j]$ is the expected (and required) return from the SML. Using the current T-bill rate as R_F and the observed excess return of the market portfolio over the risk-free rate ($R_M - R_F$), the residual return e_j measures risk-adjusted performance. Because the expectation of e_j is zero, abnormal (positive or negative) investment performance is measured by the difference of e_j from zero.[1]

Beta is estimated by regressing security return on the return of a proxy for the market index using the regression equation,

$$R_j = \alpha_j + \beta_j R_M + e_j \tag{12.3}$$

This equation is depicted in the left graph of Figure 12.3. It is called the **market model** because of its regression of an individual stock's returns on market index returns. The

---

1 A t-test comparison of means is used as a test of statistical significance.

slope coefficient β_j captures that part of the variation in an individual stock that is linearly related to the market return.

As with any regression coefficient, beta can be restated as a correlation coefficient scaled by the standard deviations of R_j and R_M.

$$\beta_j = \rho_{j,M} \, (\sigma_j / \sigma_M) \qquad (12.4)$$

In this way, beta measures the asset's sensitivity to returns on the market portfolio; that is, the systematic risk of the asset. The beta of the market itself is $\beta_M = \rho_{M,M} (\sigma_M / \sigma_M) = 1$ and the beta of the risk-free asset is zero ($\rho_{F,M}(\sigma_F/\sigma_M) = 0$). Firms with betas greater than one have more systematic risk than the average firm in the market. These stocks tend to perform better than the average when the overall market is up and worse than the average when the market is down. Another way of stating this is that firms with betas greater than one are more sensitive to changes in the market index than the average firm. Conversely, firms with betas less than one have less systematic risk than the average.

Unsystematic (Diversifiable) Risk. The residual term e_j captures all return variation in R_j that is unrelated to the market portfolio. The residual term captures that portion of individual security risk that can be diversified away by holding the security in a portfolio with many securities. Such risk is called **unsystematic risk**. It is also called *nonmarket* or *diversifiable risk*. If returns are normally distributed, then the residual term is also distributed as normal with zero mean ($E[e_j] = 0$), and it is uncorrelated with other securities ($\text{Cov}(e_i,e_j) = 0$ for $i \neq j$) and with the market portfolio ($\text{Cov}(e_j,R_M) = 0$). If the asset is a share of stock in a company, then the portion of risk that is diversifiable is also called *company-specific risk*. Unsystematic risks include labor strikes, changes in top management, company-specific sales fluctuations, and any other events that are unique to a single company.

An important source of risk on a foreign investment is **political risk**—the risk of unexpected political events in a host country affecting the value of an investment. Many types of political risk are *country-specific*. To assess the importance of a country-specific risk, investors weigh the probability of an adverse country-specific event by the consequences of that event. Political risks that have a low probability but that are catastrophic in nature include the risk of expropriation. **Expropriation** occurs when a government seizes foreign assets within its borders. When the Ayatollah Khomeini seized power from the Shah of Iran, the Iranian government expropriated U.S. assets within Iran. The U.S. government responded by freezing Iranian assets within the United States.

A political risk of particular importance to multinational corporations is the risk of unexpected changes in the operating environment, such as the risk of an unexpected change in tax laws and regulations. This type of political risk is much more common than catastrophic events, such as expropriation. The consequences of unexpected changes in the operating environment can be nearly as profound as those of expropriation. The uncertain operating environments in the republics of the former Soviet Union and in the People's Republic of China have kept many multinational corporations from investing in these potentially lucrative markets.

To the extent that country-specific political risks can be diversified away by holding country-specific investments within a globally diversified portfolio, these risks are

Market model beta measures an asset's sensitivity to changes in the market.

Country-specific political risk is diversifiable and, hence, does not affect required return.

unsystematic and, hence, should not be reflected in the required return from the security market line. The theoretically correct way to handle country-specific political risks is to incorporate them into the expected future cash flows from investment. Despite the divesifiability of country-specific political risk, managers in multinational corporations often prefer to reflect country-specific political risks in the returns required on investment in high-risk countries. Corporate managers derive a large proportion of their wealth from current employment, so they have a major stake in the survival of the company. Because of this lack of diversification, managers have an incentive to protect themselves against country-specific political risks even if these risks can be diversified away by shareholders. Requiring high hurdle rates on risky foreign investment is one way that managers can protect themselves.

Roll's Critique of the CAPM

The intuition behind the CAPM is simple—higher risks demand higher returns. This intuition suggests that there should be a strong cross-sectional relation between ex post mean return and beta. In fact, if a mean-variance efficient market index is used as the performance benchmark, then the algebra of the CAPM requires that beta and only beta explains mean return. There is no systematic portion of return left to be explained by any variable other than beta.

Empirical tests often find no relation between mean returns and betas.

Unfortunately for proponents of the CAPM, empirical tests commonly find *no* relation between mean returns and betas. For example, Eugene Fama and Kenneth French find that "the relation between market beta and average return is flat, even when beta is the only explanatory variable."[2] Fama and French do find that other variables, such as firm size and the ratio of market to book value of assets, play a statistically significant role in explaining mean returns. This is a curious and unsettling finding for the CAPM. If beta is unrelated to mean return, then it makes no sense to use beta in cost of capital estimation, in the construction of investment portfolios, or in measuring investment performance.

The heart of the problem was identified by Richard Roll and is often called *Roll's Critique* of the CAPM.[3] In theory, the CAPM market portfolio is a value-weighted index of all assets, including frequently traded assets, such as stocks and bonds; less frequently traded assets, such as real estate; and nontraded assets, such as human capital. In practice, a proxy for the market portfolio must be constructed from assets with observable returns, such as a stock market index. Roll made the following observations:

- If performance is measured relative to an index that is ex post efficient, then from the algebra of the CAPM no security will have abnormal performance when measured as a departure from the security market line.

- If performance is measured relative to an index that is ex post inefficient, then *any* ranking of portfolio performance is possible depending on which inefficient market index has been chosen as the standard for comparison.

---

2 Eugene F. Fama and Kenneth R. French, "The Cross-Section of Expected Stock Returns," *Journal of Finance* 67, June 1992, pages 427–466.

3 Richard Roll, "A Critique of the Asset Pricing Theory's Tests," *Journal of Financial Economics* 4, March 1977, pages 129–176.

Mean-variance efficiency is a little like pregnancy. Just as you can't be a little pregnant, a market index is either efficient or it is not. Because investors around the world are not fully diversified internationally, no single world market portfolio is held by all investors. In this setting, investors choose to hold portfolios that are not mean-variance efficient. And because the market index held by investors is not mean-variance efficient, performance evaluation based on risk-adjusting asset returns according to the beta of the asset is suspect.

In a more recent article, Professor Roll and his coauthor and business partner Stephen Ross investigated how far off the efficient frontier an index must be to produce a set of true betas that have no relation to true expected returns.[4] Roll and Ross found that market index proxies lying only a small distance inside the efficient frontier can produce betas that are unrelated to mean return. They concluded that "the almost pathological knife-edged nature of the expected return-beta OLS cross-sectional relation…is a shaky base for modern finance." Roll's Critique was originally aimed at the traditional single-currency CAPM. Because of real and perceived barriers to cross-border portfolio investment, it turns out to be even more devastating for the multicurrency version of the CAPM developed in the next section.

12.2 THE INTERNATIONAL ASSET PRICING MODEL

International Asset Pricing in a Perfect World

The differences between nations are what distinguish one nation from another. Imagine a world in which everyone speaks French, has the same consumption preferences for wine and other goods, shares the same production technologies in farming and manufacturing, pays taxes according to French tax laws, follows French civil and criminal law, and uses the French franc as currency. For all intents and purposes, everyone in this world would be French.

National sovereignty manifests itself in many ways that affect international trade and commerce. In the Ricardian model of international trade in the appendix to Chapter 2, nations were distinguished by their production technologies; countries had comparative production advantages in different goods. Other international trade models allow consumption preferences to differ across national borders. Market imperfections also create distinctive national clienteles. These imperfections include distinctive national tax rates and tax systems, quotas, tariffs, restrictions on cross-border investment, and other capital flow barriers.

An important difference between nations is in the currency they use for transactions and as a store of value. From this perspective, a nation can be defined as a set of individuals sharing the same functional currency or, more precisely, using the same price index in deflating expected returns. Some sovereign nations do not choose to use a currency of their own. Notable examples include the Vatican (Italian lira), Liechtenstein (Swiss franc), and Monaco (French franc). National identity in these sovereign nations is strongly linked to that of the nation whose currency they use.

---

4 Roll and Ross manage a family of mutual funds.

Int'l Asset Pricing model

....

*In the IAPM, investors hold
a world market portfolio and
a hedge portfolio.*

....

One way to generalize the CAPM to accommodate the fact that investors have different functional currencies is to create a world in which the international parity conditions always hold.[5] In addition to the assumptions of the traditional CAPM, two more conditions are necessary to ensure that the international parity conditions hold:

- Investors have the same consumption basket, so inflation is measured against the same benchmark in every country.
- Purchasing power parity holds, so prices and real interest rates are the same in every country and for every individual.

If the international parity conditions hold, then changes in exchange rates simply mirror inflation differentials. In this world, the exchange rate is nothing more than a device for translating between currencies and holds no real power over investors.

Once these conditions are imposed, extension of the CAPM to a world of many functional currencies is straightforward. The resulting model is called the **International Asset Pricing Model (IAPM)**. Just as in the traditional CAPM, all investors hold their funds at risk in a single, mean-variance efficient market portfolio. In the IAPM, the market portfolio is a *world* market portfolio comprised of *all* assets weighted according to their market values at prevailing exchange rates. In the IAPM, investors also hold a currency-specific **hedge portfolio** that serves a role similar to that of the risk-free asset in the traditional CAPM.[6] This hedge portfolio consists of domestic and foreign bonds and is held for two reasons:

- As a store of value (like the risk-free asset in the traditional CAPM)
- To hedge the currency risk of the market portfolio

If inflation is a constant in each currency, then the hedge portfolio held by each investor reduces to the investor's home-currency risk-free asset as in the CAPM.[7]

Roll's Critique and the IAPM

....

*Roll's Critique also applies to
the international version
of the CAPM.*

....

Roll's Critique is particularly devastating for the IAPM. Identification of an efficient portfolio is difficult enough in the domestic setting. In the presence of home asset bias or barriers to international portfolio diversification or both, there is no unique market portfolio for all investors. Despite the gradual deterioration of barriers to international investment, the impediments to holding the world market portfolio clearly still outnumber the impediments to holding one's domestic market portfolio. Restrictions on cross-border investment, differential taxes between countries, high and differential transactions costs, information costs, and unobservable returns on privately held assets

---

5 Grauer, Litzenberger, and Stehle [1976] were the first to construct such a world. More complete models appear in Solnik [1981] and Stulz [1981]. Adler and Dumas [1983] and Dumas [1993] present thorough reviews of the international version of the CAPM.
6 We'll return to the notion of hedge portfolios in Chapter 13.
7 See Adler and Dumas [1983], page 947.

mean that the world market portfolio is more of a pedagogical ideal and less of an operational tool. Roll's Critique simply tells us that we need to look elsewhere for meaningful measures of systematic risk and for an explanation of why mean returns differ across assets.

The fact that a particular market index proxy is not mean-variance efficient does not mean that market indices have no use. Although inefficient indices are unlikely to yield meaningful measures of systematic risk, an index does provide a performance benchmark for the assets included in the index. Roll and Ross commented on the role of market indices as follows:[8]

> Despite these problems with the (Capital Asset Pricing) Model, market value weighted index proxies are of considerable interest in their own right because they reflect averages of investor holdings. Whether or not such indices produce betas that are cross-sectionally related to average returns, their own returns serve as a benchmark for investment comparisons. Beating or trailing a value-weighted index has become the most widely accepted criterion of investment performance.

National market indices, such as the S&P 500 and Tokyo's Nikkei 225, provide performance benchmarks for these national markets. Industry indices, such as the Dow Jones Utilities Index, provide performance benchmarks for investments in these industries. The *Wall Street Journal* reports performance across the entire world, by region (Americas, Europe, and Asia/Pacific), and for individual industries, including consumer goods, energy, financial, and technology. Global, regional, and industry indices provide valuable performance benchmarks for investments in these asset classes.

Integrated versus Segmented Capital Markets

In practice, the market portfolio is usually proxied by a domestic stock portfolio. For example, the *ValueLine Investment Survey* reports betas measured with weekly returns over a five-year window against the value-weighted New York Stock Exchange (NYSE) Composite Index. Other information services calculate and report betas relative to other domestic market indices. In light of Roll's critique of the CAPM, why should these services use a proxy for the domestic market index that is known to be mean-variance inefficient?

The assumptions of the IAPM are sufficient to ensure that financial markets (including national stock and bond markets, spot and forward currency markets, and Eurocurrency markets) are integrated. In an **integrated financial market**, there are no barriers to financial flows, and purchasing power parity holds across equivalent assets wherever they are traded. Equilibrium prices are established across all markets, so required returns on assets of the same risk are the same in all locations. Because markets are integrated in the IAPM, everyone is fully diversified across asset classes. Any assets put at risk are placed in the world market portfolio, and this optimal world market portfolio

Purchasing power parity holds in an integrated financial market.

8 Richard R. Roll and Stephen A. Ross, "On the Cross-Sectional Relation between Expected Returns and Betas," *Journal of Finance* 49, March 1994, pages 101–121.

is shared by investors in every country. Risk-averse investors will hold a hedge portfolio that includes riskless domestic bills.

In theory, the world market portfolio is a fully diversified set of international assets— stocks, bonds, bills, derivatives, real estate, human capital, and so on. The systematic risk of an asset in an integrated financial market reflects the asset's sensitivity to changes in the value of the world market portfolio. Industry and national market indices are of importance only in that they reflect the sensitivity of the industry or national market to changes in the value of the world market portfolio.

By way of contrast, suppose national markets were completely **segmented** from one another (either by capital flow restrictions or by investor choice) so that prices were set independently in each national market. In that case, purchasing power parity would not hold across national markets even though it might hold within each national market. Investors in each national market would choose to hold their national market portfolio because the world market portfolio would be unattractive or unavailable to them. The systematic risk of each asset would then depend on its sensitivity to national market movements and not on its sensitivity to world market movements.

Home asset bias is an indication of a segmented financial market.

The reality of present-day financial markets lies somewhere between these two extremes.[9] Investors exhibit a strong **home asset bias**, favoring their own domestic market portfolio rather than choosing to be fully diversified internationally. For example, less than 5 percent of pension assets in the United States are invested in foreign markets despite the fact that more than 60 percent of the world's publicly traded assets reside outside the United States. Pension assets in smaller, less diversified economies also exhibit home asset bias, although to a lesser extent. This is prima facie evidence that markets are not fully integrated. The extent of market segmentation varies across national and international markets as well as over time.

12.3 ARBITRAGE PRICING THEORY

Arbitrage Pricing Theory assumes a linear relation between required return and one or more systematic risk factors.

The CAPM and IAPM have great intuitive and practical appeal because they suggest a simple measure of systematic risk (beta) and a simple linear relation (the security market line) between systematic risk and expected return. The major shortcomings of these asset pricing models involve their testability and the fact that beta is not related ex post to mean return. A finding of no relation between beta and ex post mean return is not surprising given (1) the sensitivity of tests of the CAPM and IAPM to the market portfolio proxy and (2) the fact that there is not a single world market portfolio held by all investors.

The **Arbitrage Pricing Theory (APT)** of Stephen Ross offers a potential remedy to these shortcomings.[10] Like the CAPM, the APT assumes a linear relation between risk and expected return. A security's risk in the CAPM depends on its sensitivity to changes in the value of the market portfolio. The APT takes a more general view of the

Arbitrage
Pricing
Theory.

---

9 A technical treatment of the integration/segmentation debate and of how markets evolve over time appears in Geert Bekaert and Campbell R. Harvey, "Time-Varying World Market Integration," *Journal of Finance* 50, No. 2, June 1995, pages 403–444.

10 Stephen A. Ross, "The Arbitrage Theory of Asset Pricing," *Journal of Economic Theory* 13, December 1976, pages 341–360.

types of risks that might be priced in the market. In the APT, a security's rate of return is a linear function of K systematic risk factors:

$$R_j = \mu_j + \beta_{1j}F_1 + \ldots + \beta_{Kj}F_K + e_j \tag{12.5}$$

where
R_j = the random rate of return on asset j,
μ_j = the mean or expected return on asset j,
β_{kj} = the sensitivity of asset j's return to factor k where k=1,...,K,
F_k = systematic risk factor k,
e_j = a random error or noise term specific to asset j.

The APT is based on the idea that the actual return on an individual security is composed of an expected part and an unexpected part. The expected return $E[R_j]$ is common to all assets. The unexpected part of the return contains a systematic risk component $(\Sigma_k \beta_{kj}F_k)$ and an unsystematic risk component e_j. The systematic factors F_k are risks that affect a large number of assets. The systematic risk and, hence, the return of an individual security j depend on the K systematic risk factors F_k as well as the asset's sensitivities β_{kj} to those factors.

As in the CAPM and IAPM, unsystematic risk $Var(e_j)$ is specific to a single asset and depends on such firm-specific events as management changes, company research and development breakthroughs, labor strife, retainment or retirement of key personnel, and so on. The APT's unsystematic or firm-specific error e_j is unrelated to the systematic risk factors as well as to other firms' error terms, so that $E[e_j] = Cov(e_i,e_j) = 0$ for i≠j.

The major drawback of the APT is that the factors that might be priced in the market are not identified a priori by the model. In the CAPM, the one and only systematic risk factor is the market portfolio return. This is the major appeal of the CAPM. In the APT, the systematic risk factors must be either empirically identified from the data (for example, with factor analysis) or independently identified through another asset pricing theory in order to guide the search for factors that might be priced in the market. The rest of this chapter examines several alternative factor models.

The One-Factor Market Model

A prominent special case of the APT is the **one-factor market model**. Figure 12.3 presents this model in graphical form. This is the same market model that was used in equation (12.3) to estimate beta in the CAPM, although it will be developed in a little more detail here. The model is as follows:

$$R_j = \alpha_j + \beta_j R_M + e_j \tag{12.3}$$

The expectation of this equation is $E[R_j] = \alpha_j + \beta_j E[R_M]$. Substituting observed means μ_j and μ_M for the expectations and subtracting the resulting equation $(\mu_j = \alpha_j + \beta_j\mu_M)$ from the one-factor market model in equation (12.3) results in a one-factor market model in *excess return form:*

$$R_j - \mu_j = (\alpha_j + \beta_j R_M + e_j) - (\alpha_j + \beta_j \mu_M)$$
$$= \beta_j (R_M - \mu_M) + e_j$$

or

$$R_j = \mu_j + \beta_j F_M + e_j \qquad (12.6)$$

The systematic risk factor in this model is the difference between actual market index returns and the mean market return: $F_M = R_M - \mu_M$. Equation (12.6) is the APT equivalent of the one-factor (CAPM) market model in equation (12.3). The measure of systematic risk, $\beta_j = \rho_{j,M} (\sigma_j / \sigma_M)$, captures the sensitivity or exposure of security return to unexpected changes in the market index.

Haven't We Seen This Before?

We have seen equation (12.6) before in another guise. Suppose in one month you are to receive a French franc payment of FF1,000 that should be worth (FF1,000)($0.2000/FF) = $200 at the expected spot exchange rate $E[S^{\$/FF}] = \$0.2000$. The value of the French franc is graphed against the value of the spot exchange rate in the left-hand graph below. Unexpected changes in the dollar value of the franc are graphed against unexpected changes in the spot rate $s^{\$/FF}$ in the rightmost graph below.

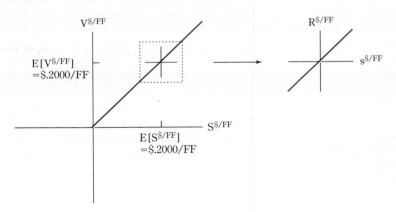

The FF1,000 cash flow is fully exposed to currency risk, so an unexpected change of 1 percent in the spot rate to $0.2020/FF results in a proportionate 1 percent increase in the dollar value of the foreign currency cash flow.

In a similar fashion, the regression $R_j = \alpha_j + \beta_j R_M + e_j$ in equation (12.3) captures the exposure of an individual security to fluctuations in the market factor. Adjusting R_j and R_M for their mean values as in Figure 12.3 results in the same transformation that was used for currency exposure in the graph above. First, plot the return on asset j against the return on the market portfolio. Centering a new graph on the point (μ_j, μ_M) results in an excess return version of the original market model as shown in Figure 12.3. The systematic risk (beta) component captures the exposure of security return to unexpected market index returns in the same way that the currency risk profile captured changes in the value of a foreign currency cash flow to changes in an underlying spot exchange rate.

There are two differences between the currency risk profile of a derivative security (such as a forward contract) and the market model regression:

- In the currency risk profile of a derivative security, there is a one-to-one correspondence between changes in the value of the spot rate of exchange and changes in the value of the underlying position. Because the value of the foreign currency cash flow is *derived from* the underlying spot rate, the line has a 45-degree slope and β_j is equal to one. The slope of the market model regression can be more or less than one.
- In the currency risk profile there is no variation around the line. Equation (12.6) allows some variability around the regression line. In formal terms, in the currency risk profile there is no unsystematic risk and $Var(e_j) = 0$, but in the market model regression there is unsystematic risk and $Var(e_j) > 0$.

If points lie closely around the regression line in Figure 12.3, then there is a high correlation and, hence, a strong relation between $R^{\$/FF}$ and $s^{\$/FF}$. A low correlation means that points are relatively more spread out around the regression line. A zero correlation means that returns to security j are unrelated to market index returns. If $\rho_{j,M} = 1$, then $Var(e_j) = 0$ and the regression line in equation (12.6) captures all of the variation in R_j arising from variations in R_M. If there is not a linear correspondence between returns to asset j and to the market so that $-1 < \rho_{j,M} < 1$, then $Var(e_j) > 0$ and unexpected changes in the market return cannot be hedged exactly.

Five Macroeconomic Factors Associated with Domestic Stock Returns

The best-known application of the APT is Chen, Roll, and Ross's [1986] study of U.S. stocks. Through a simple discounted cash flow model, Chen, Roll, and Ross identified five pervasive factors that a priori should be priced in the stock market as sources of systematic risk. These macroeconomic factors (F_k) are

Unlike the CAPM, the APT does not identify the factors that matter to the market.

F_1: industrial production
F_2: expected inflation
F_3: unexpected inflation
F_4: risk premia required by investors on risky investments
F_5: the term structure of interest rates

Chen, Roll, and Ross used the difference between corporate and government bond yields to proxy for the risk premia that investors require on risky assets, and the difference between long-term and short-term government bond yields as a measure of the term structure of interest rates.

Chen, Roll, and Ross then estimated the APT model in equation (12.5) as:[11]

$$R_j = \mu_j + \beta_{1j}F_1 + \beta_{2j}F_2 + \beta_{3j}F_3 + \beta_{4j}F_4 + \beta_{5j}F_5 + e_j \qquad (12.7)$$

---

11 Each of these factors is constructed so that $E[F_k] = 0$. Subtracting the mean return μ_j from both sides of equation (12.7) results in $R_j - \mu_j = \beta_{1j}F_1 + \beta_{2j}F_2 + \beta_{3j}F_3 + \beta_{4j}F_4 + \beta_{5j}F_5 + e_j$. This is the regression equivalent to the "$\Delta V^{d/f}$ versus $\Delta S^{d/f}$" framework of previous chapters. Equation (12.7) "centers" the regression on the origin just as the "$\Delta V^{d/f}$ versus $\Delta S^{d/f}$" framework "centered" the relation on the origin.

Although Chen, Roll, and Ross did not report overall regression results, the coefficients on each of the five factors were in general statistically significant. The influence of these fundamental economic factors was especially strong for the industrial production, risk premium, and term structure indices. Moreover, when market portfolio indices were included along with the economic factors, the market indices were found to have insignificant coefficients, but the importance of the five economic factors remained largely undiminished. Chen, Roll, and Ross concluded that although the stock market factor is significantly related to individual stock returns, the explanatory power of the market factor is largely a statistical artifact—a consequence of the fact that all stocks are exposed to systematic economic risks that underlie returns to the market portfolio. The stock market factor does not explain intertemporal movements in individual stocks or cross-sectional differences in mean returns once these five economic variables have been priced.

The Relative Importance of Industry, National, and International Factors

Bruno Solnik and Arlei de Freitas [1988] studied 279 stocks trading in sixteen national stock markets over the period 1972–1984.[12] Solnik and de Freitas used world, national, and industry stock market indices in the following regressions:

$$R_j = \alpha_j + \beta_{Hj} R_H + e_j \tag{12.8a}$$
$$R_j = \alpha_j + \beta_{Wj} R_W + e_j \tag{12.8b}$$
$$R_j = \alpha_j + \beta_{Ij} R_I + e_j \tag{12.8c}$$

where
R_j = returns to stock j in stock j's home currency
R_H = returns to the national market ("home") index in stock j's home currency
R_W = returns to the world market index in stock j's home currency
R_I = returns to an industry index in stock j's home currency
β_{ij} = asset j's sensitivities (or betas) to home, world, and industry indices
α_j and e_j = regression intercept and error term for stock j

The percent of the variation in R_j that is "explained by" variation in each index in these regressions is called the **coefficient of determination**, or **R-square**. With a single independent variable, R-square equals the square of the correlation between the dependent (R_j) and independent (R_H, R_W, or R_I) variable.

The average R-square across the 279 firms in Solnik and de Freitas's sample was 0.42 for regression equation (12.8a), indicating that 42 percent of the variation in the individual stock returns was explained by variation in that firm's national market index. On average, only 18 percent of individual stock variance was explained by variation in the world market portfolio in equation (12.8b). When both the world and the national market indices were included in a multiple regression, the R-square was increased to only 0.44. The coefficients β_{Hj} on the domestic market index in this multiple regression were

---

12 Bruno Solnik and Arlei de Freitas, "International Factors of Stock Price Behavior" in S. Khoury and A. Ghosh (eds.) *Recent Developments in International Finance and Banking*, Vol. 2, Lexington Books, Lexington, Mass., 1988.

generally not much different than in the regressions that included only the national market index. In contrast, the coefficients β_{Wj} on the world market index R_W generally were not significantly different from zero in the multiple regression that included the domestic market index. This suggests that the information in the world market index is largely subsumed by the national market indices.[13]

Solnik and de Freitas also investigated whether industry indices that cross national borders in equation (12.8c) explain individual stock returns. The average R-square for this regression was 0.23. This is greater than the 0.18 R-square for the world market index but much less than the 0.42 R-square for the national market index. Combining industry with national market indices resulted in an R-square of 0.48, a statistically significant increase over the 0.42 R-square of the national market index alone.

Based on this evidence, Solnik and de Freitas reached the following conclusions:

- The national market index dominates the world market index and cross-national industry indices in explaining domestic stock returns.
- Cross-national industry indices also play a role in explaining international stock returns.

The national market index dominates industry and world market factors in explaining stock returns.

These findings are not necessarily inconsistent with either the CAPM or the IAPM. Nothing in the CAPM or the IAPM prevents individual securities from being more highly correlated with industry indices and/or national market indices than with the value-weighted world market index. Indeed, other studies have found that a large portion of national stock market returns are explained by the industries that dominate a nation's economy.[14] Solnik and de Freitas's study merely illustrates the relative importance of industry, national, and international factors in individual stock returns.

12.4 THE CURRENCY RISK FACTOR IN STOCK RETURNS

Portfolio Theory and the Irrelevance of Hedging in a Perfect World

In a perfect capital market, portfolio theory tells us that the firm cannot do anything through diversification that investors cannot already do for themselves. Foreign exchange risk is company-specific, so it should be diversifiable and therefore irrelevant to firm valuation. From the shareholders' point of view, hedging a risk that is not priced by the market is a waste of managers' time and shareholders' money.

Hedging does not add value to the firm in a perfect capital market.

Here's a simple example that illustrates how foreign exchange risks may be irrelevant to a globally diversified investor. Consider two companies, L and S. Each company resides in the United States and considers the U.S. dollar to be its functional currency. Company S has promised to make a payment of DM100,000 to Company L in one year.

---

13 The same conclusion was reached by Manoj Gupta and Joseph Finnerty using more elaborate statistical techniques in "The Currency Risk Factor in International Equity Pricing," *Review of Quantitative Finance and Accounting* 2, No. 3, 1992, pages 245–257.

14 For example, see Richard Roll, "Industrial Structure and the Comparative Behavior of International Stock Market Indices," *Journal of Finance* 47, No. 1, March 1992, pages 3–42.

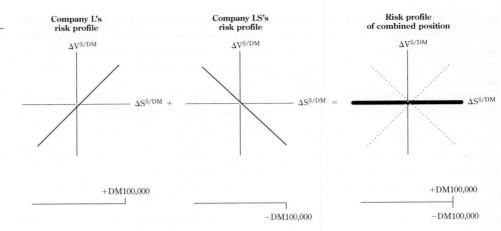

FIGURE 12.4
The Diversifiability of
Currency Risk Exposure

Company L is *long* the deutsche mark (and short the dollar) while Company S is *short* the mark (and long the dollar). The risk profile of each company with respect to the deutsche mark is shown in Figure 12.4.

A well-diversified U.S.-based investor owning shares in each company faces *no net foreign exchange risk*. Changes in the value of Company L in response to changes in the spot rate $S^{\$/DM}$ are exactly offset by changes in the value of Company S. To a well-diversified investor owning shares in each company, foreign exchange risks such as these are diversifiable and result in the risk profile shown at the right in Figure 12.4. In a globally integrated marketplace, foreign exchange risks such as this should not be priced. If the managers of either firm hedge these risks, any hedging costs incurred will be a net out-of-pocket cost to shareholders with no reduction in shareholders' portfolio risk.

Measuring Currency Risk Exposure

Like other factors, exposure to currency risk can be measured in a regression framework:

$$R_j^{\$} = \alpha_j^{\$} + \beta_j^{FF} s^{\$/FF} + e_j^{\$} \tag{12.9}$$

where $\quad R_j^{FF}$ = return on a French asset j in francs

$\qquad s^{\$/FF}$ = percentage change in the dollar/franc spot exchange rate $S^{\$/FF}$

$\qquad R^{\$} = (1+R^{FF})(1+s^{\$/FF}) - 1$

$\qquad$ = dollar-denominated return on the French asset j

In its APT form, equation (12.9) becomes

$$\begin{aligned} R_j^{\$} &= \mu_j^{\$} + \beta_j^{FF} (s^{\$/FF} - \mu_s) + e_j^{\$} \\ &= \mu_j^{\$} + \beta_j^{FF} s^{\$/FF} + e_j^{\$} \end{aligned} \tag{12.10}$$

If spot exchange rates are a random walk, then the mean change in the spot exchange rate (μ_s) is zero. This is why the mean exchange rate change does not appear in equation (12.10); that is, $(s^{\$/FF} - \mu_s) = s^{\$/FF}$ for $\mu_s = 0$. The unexpected change in the spot rate is simply $s^{\$/FF}$.

These regression equations decompose the variability of dollar-denominated returns on the French asset into the part associated with exchange rate changes (measured by the coefficient β_j^{FF}) and the part that is unrelated to currency movements (that is, $e_j^\$$). Because foreign currency returns R_j^{FF} are also exposed to currency risk (that is, $\text{Cov}(R_j^{FF}, s^{\$/FF}) \neq 0$), the French franc exposure coefficient β_j^{FF} depends in general on both spot rate changes and changes in the value of the French asset in francs.[15] The error term $e_j^\$$ is denominated in dollars and includes all sources of variability that are unrelated to currency fluctuations, such that $\text{Cov}(e_j^\$, s^{\$/FF}) = 0$. The expectation of the error term is, of course, $E[e_j^\$] = 0$.

Currency risk hedging cannot, in general, completely eliminate risk. Rather, currency risk hedging merely removes that part of the variation in $R_j^\$$ that is linearly related to changes in the spot exchange rate $s^{\$/FF}$. The remaining uncertainty is independent of the exchange rate. In this way, currency risk hedging substitutes exposure to domestic purchasing power risk for exposure to foreign currency risk.

Is Exchange Rate Risk Priced in Financial Markets?

Although the APT provides no guidance on whether currency risk should be priced in the financial marketplace, it does allow us to test whether currency risk *is* priced in the financial markets.

Solnik and de Freitas estimated the one-factor model in equation (12.9) for their sample of 279 international firms.[16] The average R-square in their regression is 0.01, indicating that only about 1 percent of the variation in domestic-currency returns is explained by variation in the spot rate of exchange. If stock returns are independent of exchange rate changes, then currency risk is not a systematic risk factor in the APT and, hence, is not priced in the stock market. In other words, hedging currency risk cannot affect the systematic risk of the multinational corporation.

In a more rigorous multifactor analysis of currency risk, Philippe Jorion added an exchange rate factor to the domestic market index factor:[17]

$$R_j^\$ = \mu_j^\$ + \beta_{1j}(R_M^\$ - \mu_M^\$) + \beta_{2j}^{FF} s^{\$/FF} + e_j^\$. \qquad (12.11)$$

Jorion also added an exchange rate factor to the five economic factors identified by Chen, Roll, and Ross [1986] and listed in equation (12.7):

$$R_j^\$ = \mu_j^\$ + \beta_{1j} F_1^\$ + \beta_{2j} F_2^\$ + \beta_{3j} F_3^\$ + \beta_{4j} F_4^\$ + \beta_{5j} F_5^\$ + \beta_{6j}^{FF} s^{\$/FF} + e_j^\$ \qquad (12.12)$$

The $ superscripts indicate that changes in the five factors and returns to security j are denominated in dollars. Using relatively powerful statistical techniques, Jorion came to the same conclusion as Solnik and de Freitas—the exchange rate factor is subsumed into the market index in equation (12.11) and into the five economic factors in equation

---

15 The joint dependence of domestic-currency returns on changes in spot and foreign-currency prices comes from $\text{Var}(R^\$) = \text{Var}(R^{FF}) + \text{Var}(s^{\$/FF}) + 2\text{Cov}(R^{FF}, s^{\$/FF}) + \text{Var}(R^{FF} s^{\$/FF})$ as in equation (11.9).
16 Bruno Solnik and Arlei de Freitas, "International Factors."
17 Philippe Jorion, "The Pricing of Exchange Rate Risk in the Stock Market," *Journal of Financial and Quantitative Analysis* 26, September 1991, pages 363–376.

$$R_j^d = \mu_j^d + \beta_j^f \, (s^{d/f}) + e_j^d$$

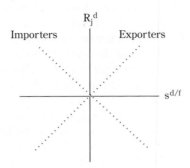

FIGURE 12.5
The Currency Risk Exposure
of Importers and Exporters

(12.12). Jorion concluded that exchange rate risk is diversifiable and is not priced in aggregate in the stock market.[18]

Despite this conclusion, Jorion found considerable cross-sectional variation in the exchange rate exposure of individual firms and industries. Exporters, such as mining and machinery firms, tended to benefit from a depreciation of the dollar. Importers, such as textile and apparel firms, tended to benefit from an appreciation of the dollar. In a related study, Jorion found that the magnitude of the coefficient on the exchange rate factor was positively related to the percentage of foreign operations for a sample of U.S. multinationals.[19] A stylized characterization of the currency risk exposure of exporters and importers appears in Figure 12.5.

Consider the currency risk exposure of a domestic automaker, such as General Motors Corporation in the United States. GM's manufacturing facilities are predominantly in the United States, so its production costs are predominantly in dollars. However, GM exports a large number of U.S.-produced cars outside the United States. When the dollar appreciates against foreign currencies, GM's production costs rise relative to those of its competitors outside the United States. Conversely, when the dollar depreciates, GM's production costs fall relative to those of non-U.S. automakers. This allows GM to either lower its prices and sell more cars or earn higher profits per car or both. Hence, the value of an exporter such as GM is negatively related to the value of the dollar or, as in Figure 12.5, positively related to foreign currency values.

Importers, such as U.S. textile and apparel firms, are more likely to benefit from a real appreciation of the dollar. A dollar appreciation means that foreign products enjoy a cost advantage relative to domestic goods. Twenty-five percent of the world's cotton production comes from China and another 10 percent comes from Pakistan. A U.S. importer of cotton apparel from these countries benefits from an appreciation of the

Despite firm-specific variation in currency exposure, currency risk is not an important source of systematic risk.

---

18 This remains an area of active debate in the literature. For an opposing view, see Eun and Resnick [1988] or Dumas and Solnik [1995]. Cheung, Kwan, and Lee [1995] find weak evidence that exchange rate risk is priced in the Canadian market, perhaps from mild segmentation of the Canadian market.
19 Philippe Jorion, "The Exchange-Rate Exposure of U.S. Multinationals," *Journal of Business* 63, No. 3, 1990, pages 331–346.

dollar because it costs fewer dollars to purchase these foreign inputs. This in turn results in higher profit margins on U.S. sales. As the dollar depreciates, these foreign inputs cost more in dollars. This leads to no increase in prices to U.S. consumers (and, hence, lower profit margins on sales), to price increases (and lower sales), or to some combination of the two. In any case, the value of an importer is positively related to the value of the domestic currency or, as in Figure 12.5, negatively related to foreign currency values.

12.5 CURRENCY RISK EXPOSURE AND MNC HEDGING ACTIVITIES

Academic inquiry into whether exchange rate risk is priced by financial markets is still in its infancy. Nevertheless, we can make some statements about the exposure of firms to currency risk and about whether shareholders and/or management should hedge their exposure to currency risk.

The Shareholders' Perspective

Preliminary evidence suggests that *currency risk is diversifiable* in a large portfolio; thus, it is not priced in the stock market. Nevertheless, individual firms engaged in foreign operations are likely to be exposed to significant currency risk, although this risk is likely to be unsystematic from the perspective of diversified investors in the firm. Even if currency risk is a diversifiable risk that does not affect the required returns of investors, investors will prefer that managers hedge currency risk if the firm's *expected future cash flows* can be increased through hedging. Hedging can increase expected future cash flows by reducing costs of financial distress, taxes, or agency costs.[20]

The Managers' Perspective

In contrast to other stakeholders, managers have a huge incentive to hedge against currency risks. A manager's livelihood depends on the health and continued existence of the company. Managers are overinvested in the firm and are unable to fully diversify their wealth. Further, the performance evaluation and compensation of a divisional manager is tied to divisional performance. The performance assessment of divisional managers can be sensitive to exchange rate fluctuations. In these circumstances, managers have an incentive to hedge against currency risk exposure even though it may not benefit investors.

Managers have a huge incentive to hedge against currency risks.

Corporate Hedging Activities

Firms can change the currency risk exposure of the company through off-balance-sheet hedging transactions in the financial markets. For example, even though the *operations* of a U.S. exporter may be hurt by a real appreciation of the dollar, the exporter can

---

20 This is the subject of Chapter 6.

mitigate this operating risk through the use of currency forward, futures, option, or swap hedges. Hedging activities use the financial markets to transform the *net currency exposure* of the firm. Unfortunately for the outside observer, corporate hedging activities are not generally observable by the financial markets until they are disclosed in the financial statements. Even then, only a portion of the firm's hedging activities are typically reported. Although the financial markets cannot observe all of the hedging activities of the firm, the currency risk exposure revealed by stock price movements is the market's best guess of the net currency exposure of the firm; that is, net of any additional hedging that the firm has contracted in the financial markets.

12.6 SUMMARY

Assumptions necessary to develop the Capital Asset Pricing Model (CAPM) are: (1) perfect financial markets (frictionless, competitive, equal access to information), (2) normally distributed nominal returns, (3) rational investors (more return is good and risk is bad), (4) homogeneous expectations, and (5) equal access to the risk-free rate R_F. These assumptions allowed us to complete our development of the Capital Asset Pricing Model. The fundamental result of this model is the security market line (SML):

$$R_j = R_F + \beta_j \left(E[R_M] - R_F \right) \tag{12.1}$$

which states that the required return on an asset j is a linear combination of the expected market risk premium and the asset's sensitivity to changes in market returns. Beta, $\beta_j = \rho_{j,M} \left(\sigma_j / \sigma_M \right)$, is a measure of the sensitivity of security j's returns to market returns and is estimated with the market model regression equation:

$$R_j = \alpha_j + \beta_j R_M + e_j \tag{12.3}$$

Richard Roll [1976] pointed out a critical weakness of the CAPM. If performance is measured relative to an ex post efficient market index, then beta is the only measure of systematic risk. The algebra of the CAPM ensures that measuring performance relative to an ex post efficient index results in all assets falling on the security market line; there is then no possible room for abnormal performance. On the other hand, measuring performance against an ex post inefficient index yields nearly no information regarding risk-adjusted return; any ranking of investment performance is possible.

The next step in our development of an international pricing model was to extend the CAPM to a multicurrency setting. Two additional assumptions were necessary: (1) Investors in each country have the same consumption basket and (2) purchasing power parity holds. This ensures that the international parity conditions hold. The resulting model is called the International Asset Pricing Model, or IAPM. Roll's Critique is just as relevant for this model, because world market portfolios are even more difficult to construct than domestic market portfolios. Indeed, investors tend to overinvest in their domestic portfolios relative to what the IAPM would suggest. Not surprisingly, stock price movements are more closely related to changes in their own national stock market than to changes in the world stock index.

Stephen Ross's [1976] Arbitrage Pricing Theory (APT) offers a partial remedy to Roll's Critique. In this model, security returns are assumed to be a linear function of K systematic risk factors F_k:

$$R_j = \mu_j + \beta_{1j}F_1 + \ldots + \beta_{Kj}F_K + e_j \qquad (12.5)$$

where μ_j is the expected return on asset j, the β_{kj} are the asset's sensitivities to the K factors, and e_j is firm-specific random error. Chen, Roll, and Ross [1986] identified and tested five systematic risk factors: (1) industrial production, (2) expected inflation, (3) unexpected inflation, (4) risk premia, and (5) the term structure of interest rates.

The chapter concluded with an investigation of the currency risk factor in stock returns. Jorion [1991] added exchange rates to Chen, Roll, and Ross's [1986] five APT risk factors:

$$R_j^{\$} = \mu_j + \beta_{1j}F_1^{\$} + \beta_{2j}F_2^{\$} + \beta_{3j}F_3^{\$} + \beta_{4j}F_4^{\$} + \beta_{5j}F_5^{\$} + \beta_{6j}^{FF}s^{\$/FF} + e_j^{\$}. \qquad (12.12)$$

Jorion found that foreign currency exchange rates had no power to explain security returns beyond what was already included in these five economic factors. Jorion found the same result when an exchange rate factor was added to the domestic market portfolio.

$$R_j^{\$} = \mu_j^{\$} + \beta_{1j}(R_M^{\$} - \mu_M^{\$}) + \beta_{2j}^{FF}s^{\$/FF} + e_j^{\$}. \qquad (12.11)$$

The conclusion is that exchange rate risk is not priced in the stock market. Nevertheless, there is considerable variation in the currency exposure of individual firms. Exporting firms tend to benefit from a depreciation of the domestic currency, and importing firms tend to benefit from an appreciation of the domestic currency.

Although diversified shareholders will not want managers to hedge unsystematic currency risk unless it increases the firm's expected future cash flows, managers themselves are undiversified and have an incentive to hedge whenever their performance or compensation is exposed to currency risk.

KEY TERMS

Arbitrage Pricing Theory (APT)
Beta (β)
Capital Asset Pricing Model (CAPM)
Capital market line
Expropriation
Hedge portfolio
Home asset bias
Integrated financial market
International Asset Pricing Model (IAPM)
Market model (one-factor market model)

Systematic versus unsystematic risk
Market portfolio
Market risk premium
Political risk
R-square (the coefficient of determination)
Security market line (SML)
Segmented market
Systematic versus unsystematic risk

CONCEPTUAL QUESTIONS

12.1 What is the capital market line? Why is it important?

12.2 What is the security market line? Why is it important?

12.3 What is beta? Why is it important?

12.4 Does political risk affect required returns?

12.5 What is Roll's Critique of the CAPM? Does it apply to the IAPM? Does it apply to APT?

12.6 What assumptions must be added to the traditional CAPM to derive the international version of the CAPM?

12.7 What is the hedge portfolio in the international version of the CAPM?

12.8 What is the difference between an integrated and a segmented capital market?

12.9 What is home asset bias?

12.10 What is the APT? In what ways is it both better and worse than the IAPM?

12.11 What five APT factors did Chen, Roll, and Ross identify in their study of the U.S. stock market?

12.12 Are individual stock returns more closely related to returns on the world market portfolio, on the domestic market portfolio, or on an industry portfolio?

12.13 Can hedging add value to the firm in a perfect capital market? Why or why not?

12.14 Are individual stocks exposed to currency risk? Does currency risk affect required returns?

PROBLEMS

12.1 If the risk-free rate is 8 percent, beta is 1.5, and the market risk premium is 8.5 percent, what is the required return on equity according to the CAPM?

12.2 The correlation between returns to Daimler-Benz (DB) and to the Morgan Stanley Capital International (MSCI) German stock index is .44. The standard deviations of monthly returns to DB stock and to the German index are 10.5 percent and 4.6 percent, respectively.

a. What is the beta of DB relative to the German domestic stock index?

b. If the risk-free rate in Germany is 5 percent and the market risk premium on the German index is 6 percent, what is the required return on DB stock?

c. The correlation between the MSCI German and world stock indices is .516. The standard deviation of monthly returns on the German and world stock indices are 4.6 percent and 17.1 percent respectively. What is the beta of the German stock index?

d. Given the answers to a. through c., what is the beta of DB stock relative to the world stock market index? (Note that all securities and market indices are assumed to lie along the security market line.)

e. Given the answers to a. through d., what is the correlation between DB stock and the MSCI world stock market index?

12.3 As a security analyst for the London branch of Merrill Lynch, you have identified the following factors and factor sensitivities for British Petroleum (BP):

$$E[R] = \mu + \beta_{Prod} F_{Prod} + \beta_{Oil} F_{Oil} + \beta_{Spot} F_{Spot}$$

Factors and factor sensitivities are as follows:

Factors		Betas
F_{Prod}:	change in world industrial production	$\beta_{Prod} = +1.50$
F_{Oil}:	change in crude oil prices	$\beta_{Oil} = -0.80$
F_{Spot}:	change in the value of the pound against a basket of currencies with which BP trades (measured by s£/f)	$\beta_{Spot} = +0.01$

[handwritten margin notes:]

= .08 + (1.5)(.085)
= .2075

a) $\beta = (.44)\left(\frac{.105}{.046}\right) = 1$

b) $R = .05 + (.1)(.06) = .11$

$\beta = (.516)\frac{.046}{.171} = .139$ 13.88%·.05

c) $\beta = .139$

$\beta = \left(\frac{.105}{.171}\right).139 = .614$

d) $\beta = .139$

e) corr $= \beta_{DB,world}\left(\dfrac{\sigma_{DB}}{\sigma_{world}}\right)$

BP's expected return if all factors are equal to their expectation is $\mu = 14\%$.

    a. All else constant, are BP's shares likely to go up or down if world industrial production increases? with an increase in crude oil prices? with an increase in the value of the pound?

    b. What is the expected return on BP stock in a year when world industrial production is 2 percent above the expectation, oil prices rise unexpectedly by 10 percent, and the spot rate $S^{£/f}$ goes down by 5 percent?

    c. If BP stock rises by 4 percent during this period, by how much does BP over- or underperform its expectation?

12.4   Assume that the expected return of security j is generated by the CAPM as follows:

$$E[R_j] = R_F + \beta_j(E[R_M] - R_F)$$

The k-factor model with a risk-free asset is given by

$$E[R_j] = R_F + \beta_{1j}F_1 + \beta_{2j}F_2 + \dots + \beta_{kj}F_k$$

Prove that if the k factors are appropriately priced, the APT is consistent with the CAPM.

SUGGESTED READINGS

The International Capital Asset Pricing Model (IAPM) is developed, tested, and reviewed in the following articles:

    Michael Adler and Bernard Dumas, "International Portfolio Choice and Corporation Finance: A Synthesis," *Journal of Finance* 38, June 1983, pages 925–984.

    Bernard Dumas, "Partial- vs. General-Equilibrium Models of the International Capital Market," *National Bureau of Economic Research,* Working Paper No. 4446, September 1993.

    Frederick L. Grauer, Robert H. Litzenberger and Richard E. Stehle, "Sharing Rules and Equilibrium in an International Market under Uncertainty," *Journal of Financial Economics* 4, No. 3, 1976, pages 233–256.

    Rene Stulz, "A Model of International Asset Pricing," *Journal of Financial Economics* 9, No. 4, 1981, pages 383–406.

Arbitrage Pricing Theory (APT) was introduced and applied in the following articles:

    Nai-Fu Chen, Richard Roll, and Stephen A. Ross, "Economic Forces and the Stock Market," *Journal of Business* 59, July 1986, pages 383–404.

    Richard Roll and Stephen A. Ross, "The Arbitrage Pricing Theory Approach to Strategic Portfolio Planning," *Financial Analysts Journal* 40, May/June 1984, pages 14–26.

    Stephen A. Ross, "The Arbitrage Theory of Asset Pricing," *Journal of Economic Theory* 13, December 1976, pages 341–360.

Arbitrage Pricing Theory is applied to international assets in the following:

    Michael Adler and Bernard Dumas, "Exposure to Currency Risk: Definition and Measurement," *Financial Management* 13, Summer 1984, pages 41–50.

    Geert Bekaert and Campbell R. Harvey, "Time-Varying World Market Integration," *Journal of Finance* 50, No. 2, June 1995, pages 403–444.

    C. Sherman Cheung, Clarence C.Y. Kwan, and Jason Lee, "The Pricing of Exchange Rate Risk and Stock Market Segmentation: The Canadian Case," *Review of Quantitative Finance and Accounting* 5, No. 4, 1995, pages 393–402.

Bernard Dumas and Bruno Solnik, "The World Price of Foreign Exchange Risk," *Journal of Finance* 50, No. 2, June 1995, pages 445–479.

Cheol S. Eun and Bruce G. Resnick, "Exchange Rate Uncertainty, Forward Contracts, and International Portfolio Selection," *Journal of Finance* 43, No. 1, March 1988, pages 197–215.

Manoj Gupta and Joseph Finnerty, "The Currency Risk Factor in International Equity Pricing," *Review of Quantitative Finance and Accounting* 2, No. 3, 1992, pages 245–257.

Shinsuki Ikeda, "Arbitrage Asset Pricing with Exchange Risk," *Journal of Finance* 46, No. 1, 1991, pages 447–456.

Philippe Jorion, "The Exchange-Rate Exposure of U.S. Multinationals," *Journal of Business* 63, No. 3, 1990, pages 331–346.

Philippe Jorion, "The Pricing of Exchange Rate Risk in the Stock Market," *Journal of Financial and Quantitative Analysis* 26, September 1991, pages 363–376.

Richard Roll, "Industrial Structure and the Comparative Behavior of International Stock Market Indices," *Journal of Finance* 47, No. 1, March 1992, pages 3–42.

Bruno Solnik, "International Arbitrage Pricing Theory," *Journal of Finance* 38, No. 2, 1983, pages 449–459.

Bruno Solnik and Arlei de Freitas, "International Factors of Stock Price Behavior" in S. Khoury and A. Ghosh (eds.) *Recent Developments in International Finance and Banking,* Vol. 2, Lexington Books, Lexington, Mass., 1988, pages 259–276.

The cross-sectional relation between betas and mean returns is discussed in

Richard Roll, "A Critique of the Asset Pricing Theory's Tests," *Journal of Financial Economics* 4, March 1977, pages 129–176.

Eugene F. Fama and Kenneth R. French, "The Cross-Section of Expected Stock Returns," *Journal of Finance* 67, June 1992, pages 427–466.

Richard Roll and Stephen A. Ross, "On the Cross-Sectional Relation between Expected Returns and Betas," *Journal of Finance* 49, March 1994, pages 101–121.

Managing an International Investment Portfolio

If a man takes no thought about what is distant, he will find sorrow close at hand.
Confucius (551–479 B.C.)

OVERVIEW

Why diversify an investment portfolio internationally? First, international diversification results in lower portfolio risk because of the relatively low correlation between national stock market returns. Second, although much of the world's wealth resides in developed countries such as the United States and Japan, developing economies are more likely to experience above-average economic growth. For these reasons, investors in search of higher returns and/or lower portfolio risk are increasingly investing in foreign markets as information costs and transaction costs fall.

Many roads lead to Rome—and there are many alternatives for investing in foreign securities. This chapter begins with a review of the alternatives for diversifying an investment portfolio internationally. The rest of the chapter focuses on the theoretical and practical issues of managing an internationally diversified investment portfolio.

———————————●———————————

13.1 VEHICLES FOR OVERCOMING CAPITAL FLOW BARRIERS

Chapter 11 lists the barriers to international portfolio diversification. How can these barriers be overcome? Investment portfolios can be diversified internationally through investment in multinational corporations, through direct purchase of foreign securities in the domestic or in the foreign market, and through professionally managed mutual funds. Each of these alternatives is described below along with some more exotic forms of entry into foreign securities markets.

Invest in Domestic-Based Multinational Corporations

An easily accessible alternative for investors in countries with developed capital markets is to invest in domestic firms that do business internationally. Numerous large multinational corporations based in the United States boast a large percentage of sales from foreign operations. For example, about half of 3M Corporation's (Minnesota Mining and Manufacturing) sales have been from outside the United States during the 1990s. Buying stock in multinational corporations is potentially an even more effective diversification vehicle for residents of smaller countries. For example, more than 90 percent of the revenues of the Dutch firms Royal Dutch Petroleum (Shell Oil), Unilever, and Phillips come from outside the Netherlands. The Swiss giants Nestle, Ciba-Geigy, and Sandoz similarly derive the bulk of their revenues from outside Switzerland.

The diversification benefits of a multinational corporation depend on the type of foreign operations conducted by the multinational. Consider 3M Corporation. Although about one-half of 3M Corporation's revenues come from outside the United States, the majority of 3M's manufacturing capacity is in the United States. Consequently, 3M export sales and costs are tied to the value of the dollar in the same way that sales of other domestic U.S. firms are tied to the dollar. This begs the question: Are U.S. multinational corporations effective vehicles for achieving international portfolio diversification?

The test of whether a multinational corporation provides international diversification benefits ultimately rests on whether its share price moves with the domestic stock market or with foreign markets. As it turns out, the stock returns of U.S. multinational corporations are much more closely related to the U.S. stock market than to foreign markets. For example, the correlation coefficient between the S&P 500 market index and a portfolio of the fifty largest U.S. multinationals is higher than .9. This provides little if any international portfolio diversification benefit. For this reason, investing in domestic multinational corporations may not be as effective as direct ownership of foreign assets for achieving international portfolio diversification.[1]

MNC share prices move with the home market, so MNCs do not provide the same diversification benefits as direct investment in foreign shares.

Invest in Individual Foreign Securities

Investors may invest in foreign debt and equity securities directly in the financial markets. The costs and benefits of this direct route to international portfolio diversification

---

[1] See Bertrand Jacquillat and Bruno Solnik, "Multinationals Are Poor Tools for International Diversification," *Journal of Portfolio Management* 4, Winter 1978, pages 8–12.

depend on the particular foreign assets chosen for investment and on the vehicles used to gain access to these foreign assets. The rest of this section describes several ways that foreign securities can be purchased by domestic investors.

Direct Purchase in the Foreign Market. The most straightforward way to diversify a portfolio internationally is to buy foreign securities directly in the foreign market. Unfortunately for the small investor, it is usually more difficult to obtain and interpret information on foreign firms than on domestic firms. There are other impediments besides the obvious language barrier to direct purchase in the foreign market. For instance, firms in foreign countries follow different accounting conventions, so the components leading to net income in one country may or may not be included in net income in another country. Additional burdens arise because of the necessity of dealing with foreign tax laws (such as withholding taxes on dividends) and the inconvenience of receiving dividends and capital gains in the foreign currency. Finally, commissions on foreign transactions are often higher than on domestic transactions. These high information costs and transactions costs can be formidable hurdles to international portfolio diversification through direct purchase of foreign securities.

Direct Purchase in the Domestic Market. Borrowers (governments, corporations, and individuals) want to attract capital at the least cost. This means selling securities where they bring the best price. A growing number of corporations are tapping the well-developed stock markets in North America, Europe, and Southeast Asia in their pursuit of low-cost capital. Similarly, the global bond markets are increasingly being used to satisfy the borrowing needs of national governments, multinational corporations, and transnational agencies such as the IMF and the World Bank.

A non-U.S. company can list its shares on a U.S. exchange in two ways:

- American shares
- American depository receipts (ADRs)

American shares are shares of a foreign corporation issued directly to U.S. investors through a transfer agent in accordance with SEC regulations. American shares are denominated in the currency of the issuing company, so dividends and capital gains are also received in the foreign currency. Because they are still denominated in the foreign currency, American shares can be an inconvenient way for small investors to achieve international diversification. Managers of large portfolios can exchange foreign currency into domestic currency at low cost, so American shares can be a low-cost way for institutional investors to achieve international diversification. Some institutional investors find that stocks are more liquid when they are traded in their home market than when they are traded outside of the home market. For U.S. investors, the convenience of American shares should be weighed against their lower liquidity in the U.S. market.

The biggest obstacle to conducting trade in American shares is that they pay dividends and are traded in the foreign currency. An easy way around this is for the foreign company to use a domestic broker to create a derivative security called a **depository receipt**. In the United States, these are known as *American depository receipts* (ADRs).

Depository receipts are denominated in the domestic currency and trade on a domestic exchange just as any other domestic share does.

To issue an ADR, a foreign company employs a U.S. investment banker to purchase a block of shares in the foreign company. The investment banker then issues dollar-denominated stock certificates called ADRs to the U.S. public with the foreign shares as collateral. The underlying asset is a portfolio of foreign shares held by a domestic trustee. Dividends are converted into the domestic currency and distributed by the trustee directly to investors. Like the foreign shares, U.S. owners of ADRs are exposed to currency risk because foreign share prices are translated into domestic share prices at prevailing exchange rates.

Depository receipts are a derivative security with share prices depending on the value of the foreign shares in the foreign currency and the prevailing spot exchange rate. When transactions costs and capital flow barriers between the domestic and foreign markets are small, arbitrage ensures that the law of one price holds and the value of a depository receipt is the value in the foreign currency translated back into the domestic currency at the prevailing exchange rate: $P^d = (P^f)(S^{d/f})$. Depository receipts can sell at slight premiums or discounts to their foreign market value, especially if there are large transactions costs or capital flow barriers between the domestic and foreign markets.

More than four hundred firms from nearly thirty countries list their ADRs on the New York, American, and NASDAQ stock exchanges. Approximately one-half of these are Canadian firms. The United Kingdom is the next most common country represented on U.S. exchanges, with more than fifty firms listed. Well-known foreign companies trading on the NYSE include the Royal Dutch/Shell Group (Netherlands), Daimler-Benz (Germany), British Petroleum (U.K.), and Matsushita Electric (Japan). Foreign listings (either in foreign shares or as depository receipts) are also common on the London, Tokyo, and Hong Kong stock exchanges.

Mutual Funds Specializing in Foreign Securities

The small investor trying to select individual foreign stocks faces formidable transactions and information costs. Information costs are higher on foreign investment because of geographic and cultural distances, including differences in language, accounting and tax systems, and disclosure conventions. Transactions costs further inhibit international diversification. Transactions and information costs as a percentage of total assets under management can be reduced by concentrating funds from many small investors in the hands of one or a few professional portfolio managers.

Open-End and Closed-End Mutual Funds. Mutual funds are called **open-end funds** if the amount of money under management grows/shrinks as investors buy/sell the fund. In **closed-end funds** the amount of funds under management is fixed, and ownership in the funds is bought and sold in the market like a depository receipt. Mutual funds as an investment class are most popular in the United States, although their popularity is increasing in other countries. Mutual funds are called "unit trusts" in the U.K. and "sicavs" in France.

Many global, regional, and country funds are available to investors in the United States and around the world, as are a variety of sector or industry funds. Many of the larger funds are *index funds* that follow a passive buy-and-hold strategy in an attempt to mimic an equity index, such as the Nikkei 225 or German DAX. Many international funds are actively managed, either through security selection (stock picking) or through asset allocation (that is, by shifting funds across international borders and/or asset classes in the hope of hitting the winners).

In the United States, many families of mutual funds provide specialized country, regional, and global funds. For example, the NYSE-listed Templeton family includes the following funds:

- Templeton China Fund (mainland China)
- Templeton Dragon Fund (Southeast Asia)
- Templeton Emerging Markets Fund
- Templeton Market Fund (largely U.S. equities)
- Templeton Income Fund (largely U.S. blue-chip stocks)
- Templeton Global Government Fund (government securities around the world)
- Templeton Global Fund (global equities)
- Templeton Opportunities Fund (small-cap stocks)

Each of the large brokerage firms maintains a selection of country, sector, regional, and/or globally diversified funds, although these are sometimes closed-end rather than open-end funds.

Closed-End Country Funds. **Closed-end country funds** (CECFs) invest in assets (typically shares of stock) from a single country. Many emerging markets have CECFs

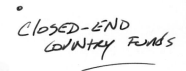

Debt of Developing Countries

Commercial banks made huge loans to the governments of developing nations to fund infrastructure development and foreign aid during the 1960s and 1970s. By the 1980s, nearly all of these loans had soured and commercial banks were faced with the unpleasant task of writing down the value of their loan portfolios. The largest losses were suffered on loans to Mexico, Brazil, and Argentina. For example, Citibank set aside $3 billion in 1987 as a reserve after Brazil ceased making interest payments on its debt. Although smaller in magnitude, percentage losses were even larger on loans to smaller countries, such as Cuba, Nicaragua, and the Sudan. The debt of these countries is referred to as *exotics* by commercial and merchant bankers.

Exotics are traded by commercial and merchant banks at a discount to face value. Institutional investors, such as hedge funds willing to tolerate large risks and illiquidity, can occasionally pick up exotics at bargain-basement prices and capture huge returns. Equally likely, of course, are huge losses. Exotics fluctuate in value with political events within the country. For example, Sudanese debt went from 0.5 percent of face value in 1993 to 6 percent of face value in 1994 (a return of 500 percent) on rumors of a debt-reduction deal. Prices fell back down to 1.5 percent of face value when the deal fell through.

trading on the NYSE and other major exchanges around the world. Countries with closed-end country funds trading on the NYSE include Brazil (two funds), Germany (two funds), Italy, India (two funds), Korea (two funds), Mexico (two funds), Malaysia, South Africa (ASA), Spain, Switzerland (Swiss Helvetica Fund), Taiwan, Thailand (two funds), and the United Kingdom. The American Stock Exchange trades CECFs specializing in Australia (First Australian Fund) and Canada (Central Fund of Canada).

Many governments in emerging markets allow limited access to their capital markets through CECFs. Governments impose restrictions on capital flows into and out of their countries as a way of controlling and protecting their capital markets. When there are capital *outflow* restrictions, investors in the country can find it difficult to invest in the assets of other countries. When there are capital *inflow* restrictions, investors from outside the country must search for other vehicles for entry into the market. Closed-end country funds provide a convenient way for small investors to gain access to foreign markets and can serve as building blocks in an internationally diversified portfolio.

The value of a closed-end country fund can diverge from its underlying **net asset value (NAV)** because the fund shares sell in the domestic market, whereas the underlying assets sell in the foreign market. With portfolio investment barriers, arbitrage between the markets is not possible. Consequently, CECF shares can trade in the domestic market at a substantial premium (or discount) to their net asset value in the foreign market. As capital flows between the domestic and foreign markets are liberalized, arbitrage between the markets becomes possible and CECF premiums tend to disappear.[2]

Two explanations have been offered as to why CECFs sometimes sell at substantial premiums to their net asset values:

- Portfolio maximization in the presence of investment restrictions
- Investor sentiment

Neither of these alone is a complete explanation of the CECF premium puzzle. Rather, elements of each appear to be at work.

The portfolio maximization school has approached the problem as a classic portfolio maximization problem in which rational investors with homogeneous expectations attempt to maximize the mean-variance efficiency of their portfolios. The effect of ownership restrictions on the actions of foreign and domestic investors is then derived using the same methods used to derive the standard capital asset pricing model. As an example, Cheol Eun and S. Janakiramanan developed an international asset pricing model in which an investment restriction on domestic ownership of foreign assets results in closed-end country fund premiums.[3] Bonser-Neal, Brauer, Neal, and Wheatley

Net-Asset value

CECFs often trade at a premium to NAV when there are limits on foreign ownership.

---

2 Domestic closed-end funds often sell at slight discounts to NAV. CECFs that have been open-ended and the CECFs of countries that have no restrictions on foreign investment also tend to sell at or slightly below net asset value. A comprehensive review of the literature appears in "Closed-End Fund Discounts and Premiums" by Michael S. Rozeff, *Pacific-Basin Capital Markets Research* II, 1991, pages 503–522.

3 Cheol Eun and S. Janakiramanan, "A Model of International Asset Pricing with a Constraint on the Foreign Equity Ownership," *Journal of Finance* 41, No. 4, 1986, pages 897–914.

found empirical evidence consistent with Eun and Janakiramanan's model using a cross-sectional test of the relation between announcements of changes in CECF ownership restrictions and changes in CECF share prices.[4]

The investor sentiment school of thought does not assume rationality, choosing instead to emphasize heterogeneity in investor expectations and allowing for potential inefficiencies in asset pricing. Charles Lee, Andrei Schleifer, and Richard Thaler [1991] observed that the principal owners of closed-end funds are small investors. They argued that the sentiment of these domestic investors should systematically affect the prices of (foreign and domestic) closed-end funds selling in the domestic market.[5] These authors assumed:

- Rational institutional investors with unbiased expectations of the expected future return and risk of the CECF

- Irrational individual investors with heterogeneous expectations

If domestic individual investors are more bullish on foreign stocks than their foreign counterparts, they can bid up the price of CECF shares relative to net asset values. According to this view, premiums/discounts reflect the differential between domestic and foreign sentiment regarding the assets underlying the closed-end country fund. Changes in the expectations of domestic individual investors regarding foreign stocks relative to domestic stocks result in changes in CECF premiums/discounts that are common to all closed-end country funds.

Consistent with this story, Bodurtha, Kim, and Lee found that[6]

- CECF premiums/discounts move together

- Domestic closed-end fund premium/discount changes are not correlated with U.S. market returns, whereas closed-end country fund changes are positively correlated with U.S. market returns

- Changes in NAV are strongly positively correlated with foreign market returns but are not correlated with domestic market returns

Because CECF shares trading in a domestic market are more highly correlated with other domestic stocks than they are with their own foreign-market net asset values, CECFs tend to be poor vehicles for international portfolio diversification.[7] The anticipated diversification benefits of entry into restricted foreign markets may not be realized because CECFs move more with the domestic market than with the foreign market.

---

4 Catherine Bonser-Neal, Greggory Brauer, Robert Neal, and Simon Wheatley, "International Investment Restrictions and Closed-End Country Fund Prices," *Journal of Finance* 45, No. 2, 1990, pages 523–548.

5 Charles Lee, Andrei Schleifer, and Richard Thaler, "Investment Sentiment and the Closed-End Fund Puzzle," *Journal of Finance* 46, No. 1, 1991, page 75–110.

6 James N. Bodurrha, Dong-Soon Kim, and Charles Lee, "Closed-End Country Funds and U.S. Market Sentiment," *Review of Financial Studies* 8, Fall 1995.

7 See Warren Bailey and Joseph Lim, "Evaluating the Diversification Benefits of the New Country Funds," *Journal of Portfolio Management* 18, Spring 1992, pages 74–80.

....

*Hedge funds are private
investment partnerships with a
general manager and a small
number of limited partners.*

....

Hedge Funds

Hedge funds are private investment partnerships with a general manager and a small number of limited partners. A typical hedge fund pays the general partner a 1 percent management fee and 20 percent of any profits. Given this lucrative compensation package, it is not surprising that the top money winners on Wall Street are hedge fund managers. George Soros of Soros Fund Management earned $1.1 billion in fees in 1993—as much as the 1993 earnings of McDonald's Corporation![8]

Hedge funds first became popular in the U.S. during the 1950s. The first hedge funds hedged by selling equities short. Today, hedge funds invest in a wide array of assets, from low-risk government bonds to high-risk emerging markets. There are upwards of one thousand hedge funds in the United States with about $100 billion under management. These funds can wield trading power that is many times that amount through their use of leverage and derivative market transactions. Hedge funds are also becoming popular in Europe, with more than one hundred hedge funds currently in operation. The total of funds under management by European partnerships is less than $20 billion, so European hedge funds do not wield the same market power as their counterparts in the United States.[9] Several major U.S. hedge funds have set up operations in London and Paris to facilitate their trades in Europe.

The principal investors in hedge funds are large pension funds and well-heeled investors that can afford to put up the partnership fee—often as high as a $1 million minimum investment—and commit to a minimum investment period of several years. (If you have to ask how much it costs, you can't afford it.) Because they are organized as partnerships, invested funds are illiquid. In the United States, hedge funds are not regulated by the SEC so long as there are fewer than one hundred partners and each partner passes the SEC's accreditation process (individuals must have a net worth of $1 million or income of $200,000 in the year prior to investment). This is in contrast to mutual funds, which are heavily regulated by the SEC. Hedge funds are the target of frequent criticism in the popular press because of the lucrative compensation packages paid to management, the fact that they are unregulated, and the huge speculative positions taken by some of the more aggressive funds.

Hedge funds range from very low risk to very high risk depending on the investment objectives and trading strategies of fund managers. Hedge fund managers have wide latitude in the positions that they take and often use specialized trading strategies such as borrowing on margin, short selling, and derivative market transactions. *MAR Hedge,* a newsletter that follows the industry, categorizes hedge fund strategies as (1) arbitrage, (2) emerging markets, (3) market-neutral (indexed), (4) opportunistic, (5) short selling (the traditional favorite), (6) small cap, (7) special situations, (8) value, and (9) yield-curve arbitrage.[10] There are also funds of funds—hedge fund partnerships that diversify across other hedge funds. Clearly, not all hedge funds are created equal.

---

8 "The Wall Street 100," Stephen Taub and David Carey, *Financial World,* July 5, 1994, pages 30–40.
9 "In Pursuit of Absolute Return," Stephanie Cooke, *Euromoney,* August 1994, pages 45–48.
10 "So, What are Hedge Funds?" *Euromoney,* April 1994, pages 29–33.

Equity-Linked Eurobonds. Eurobonds are increasingly being offered with equity options attached. These equity options come in the form of **convertibles** and bonds with **warrants**. Convertible Eurobonds allow bondholders to participate in a company's good fortune via an equity option while providing a minimum promised return from the bond component of the convertible bond. If the share price rises above the conversion price specified in the bond covenants, convertible bonds can be traded for equity. Institutional investors that are prohibited from owning equity find convertible bonds to be a convenient way to indirectly participate in the equity market. The convertibility feature cannot be separated from the underlying bond.

Equity-linked Eurobonds include convertible bonds and bonds with warrants.

Warrants are equity options that can be separated from the underlying Eurobond. This allows the debt and equity components of the offering to appeal to different clienteles. Often the equity component finds its way back to investors in the country from which the bond originated. For example, the Japanese Ministry of Finance does not allow options on common stock to be traded on Japanese markets. Many Japanese firms have issued Eurobonds with detachable warrants. These warrants are often purchased by Japanese investors as an indirect way to hold options on Japanese equities.

Foreign Market Index Futures, Swaps, and Options Contracts. Investments in foreign stock indices can be obtained with **stock index futures**.[11] Index futures are cost-effective for short investment horizons because individual stocks need not be purchased in the foreign market. Futures contracts are available on more than fifteen national market indices. For example, the London Stock Exchange trades futures contracts on several national market indices, including the French CAC-40, the German DAX, the Nikkei 225, and the S&P 500. Like currency futures, stock index futures are marked to market daily. Futures exchanges require an initial margin of 5 percent to 10 percent of the face value of the contract depending on the volatility of the national stock index and the exchange on which the futures contract is traded.

Futures, options, and swaps are available on country stock indices.

A number of **index options** contracts also are traded on national stock indices. In the United States, the Chicago Board of Trade lists both near-term and long-term options (called "leaps") on a Mexican stock index. The American Stock Exchange lists short-term options on Mexican and Japanese indices and long-term options on the Hong Kong stock index. The Japanese Ministry of Finance does not allow option trading of any kind on Japanese exchanges, so stock index options are not available in Japan. Options are highly levered investments, so index options are not good tools for international diversification. Instead, they should be used for hedging against, or speculating on, sudden changes in a particular national market.

A **stock index swap** is also possible if a counterparty can be found that wants to swap into or out of a foreign market for a period of time. For example, a long position in a foreign market index could be swapped for a short position in a domestic (or another foreign market) stock index. This would be a stock-for-stock swap. An investor wanting to swap into a long position in the foreign market index also could construct

---

11 For details see Philippe Jorion and Leonid Roisenberg, "Synthetic International Diversification: The Case for Diversifying with Stock Index Futures," *Journal of Portfolio Management* 19, Winter 1993, pages 65-74.

a debt-for-equity swap with a short position in foreign bonds (perhaps hedging the foreign bond investment in the spot and forward currency markets), a short position in domestic bonds, or any other position that a counterparty might accept. The major disadvantage of a stock index swap is that it can be difficult and costly to find a counterparty with the opposite investment preferences. Unlike exchange-traded stock index futures and options, swaps on national stock indices must be individually arranged through an investment banker.

13.2 PORTFOLIO MANAGEMENT STYLES

Mutual funds describe their investment objectives and strategies in the fund **prospectus**. The prospectus identifies whether the fund primarily invests in stocks, bonds, derivatives, real estate, or some combination of assets. The prospectus also describes the investment philosophy (active or passive) of the fund. The prospectus sets limits on the proportions of various assets held in the fund. The prospectus also states whether the fund engages in financial market transactions (forward, futures, options, and swap contracts) to reduce exposure of the fund to financial price risks or to take advantage of speculative opportunities. Finally, the prospectus provides information on past and expected future commission charges incurred in managing the assets of the fund.

Asset Allocation Policy and Investment Philosophy

Asset allocation policy refers to the target weights given to various asset classes in an investment portfolio.

Asset allocation policy refers to the target weights given to various asset classes in an investment portfolio. The fund's asset allocation policy is the most important decision made by the fund management. For example, Nobel Prize winner William Sharpe estimates that 90 percent of a portfolio's return is determined by the asset allocation decision.[12] Mutual funds' asset allocation policies also largely determine how they are marketed to the public.

Once a fund's asset allocation policy is determined, the fund's managers must decide on an investment philosophy. **Investment philosophy** refers to the investment approach—active or passive—pursued by the fund and its managers. Individual investors tend to migrate toward either a passive buy-and-hold approach or a more active investment approach. Mutual funds cluster into active or passive funds to appeal to these two distinct investor clienteles. Investment philosophy is an important marketing tool in targeting one or the other of these two investor clienteles.

The advantages of a passive buy-and-hold approach to portfolio management are that it is less costly to implement and, for the investor without better-than-average skill, less risky than an actively managed portfolio invested in similar assets. The disadvantage of the passive approach is that returns are likely to be no better (and yet not much worse) than returns on benchmark portfolios of comparable risk.

Successful active management holds out the promise of higher portfolio return and, by avoiding those assets that fall in value, lower portfolio risk as well. For an actively

---

12 William F. Sharpe, "Asset Allocation: Management Style and Performance Measurement," *Journal of Portfolio Management* 18, No. 2, 1992, pages 7–19.

managed portfolio, long-run asset allocation refers to the average proportion of each asset class in the portfolio over the long run. The extent to which a particular portfolio manager diverges from these long-run target weights is a reflection of the manager's investment philosophy. Aggressively managed funds can diverge quite a bit from target weights. Less aggressively managed funds "tilt" the portfolio away from the long-run weights to a lesser degree. For a passively managed fund, asset allocation refers to the weights on each asset class that the fund tries to maintain at all times.

Passive Fund Management

The logic of passive fund management comes from the algebra of portfolio diversification and the literature on market efficiency. The efficient markets hypothesis suggests that financial markets are informationally efficient. Active fund management in such a market is futile because consistently successful market timing or security selection is not possible. If national and international financial markets are perfect and efficient and asset returns are normally distributed, then the world market portfolio should be mean-variance efficient. An internationally diversified mutual fund that holds individual assets according to their market value weight in the world market portfolio should provide better return-risk performance over the long run than any other portfolio.

Following this logic, passively managed global funds are often diversified both across countries and across asset classes to exploit the ability of portfolio diversification to improve return-risk performance. Fund managers use the low correlation between national markets to achieve mean-variance efficient returns given the investment objectives of the fund. Many passively managed funds are index funds that try to hold the same proportion of stocks as a major market index. The most commonly tracked global indices are

- The MSCI World Index (Morgan Stanley Capital International)
- The FT/S&P Actuaries World Index (a joint product of London Financial Times Ltd., Goldman Sachs & Co., and Standard and Poor's)

The most widely tracked bond index is Salomon Brothers' International Bond Index. Each of these indices weight assets according to their market capitalization.

Many investors prefer to build up their portfolios by using index funds as building blocks. To appeal to this clientele, index funds also specialize in particular countries, regions, or industries. Although individual investors may either passively or actively manage these portfolios of index funds, the funds themselves try to replicate the performance of a particular index. Regional and national funds are often set up to track the regional or country indices published by Morgan Stanley or FT/S&P Actuaries. Commonly tracked national indices include the NYSE Composite and the S&P 500 in the United States, Tokyo's Nikkei 225, Frankfurt's DAX, Paris's CAC 40, Hong Kong's Hang Seng, and London's FTSE ("Footsie") thirty- and one hundred-stock indices. The *Wall Street Journal* (Dow Jones, Inc.) also publishes a cross-section of globally diversified industry indices in the consumer products, energy, financial, industrial, materials, and technology industries.

Passively managed funds often try to track a particular market index.

• •
*Active strategies include market
timing and security selection.*
• •

Active Fund Management

Actively managed funds follow one or both of the following investment strategies:

• Active asset allocation (or market timing) strategies in which funds are shifted between asset classes in anticipation of market events
• Active security selection (for example, stock picking) strategies that selectively invest in securities (such as stocks or bonds) that are underpriced by the marketplace and avoid (or short sell) those securities that are overpriced by the marketplace

Each of these active investment strategies presumes an ability to anticipate next period's returns and then shift funds accordingly.

Active Asset Allocation Strategies. National economies seldom move in phase with each other, and stock returns vary widely across national markets in both the short run and the long run. The lure of potentially higher returns and lower portfolio risk entices many investors into diverging from passive international diversification into a **market timing** strategy of shifting among asset classes. Successful market timing strategies rely on correctly predicting which asset classes will appreciate during the coming period. By allocating funds into the right assets at the right time, successful market timing can increase expected returns and reduce portfolio risk.

Unfortunately for market timers without timing skill, randomly shifting between assets results in higher portfolio risk than a buy-and-hold strategy at the same level of expected return.[13] With transactions costs, timing strategies executed without timing skill result in lower expected returns as well. The existence of this return-risk penalty for ineffective market timing means that investors without timing skill are better off with a buy-and-hold strategy than with an active timing strategy.

The penalty for ineffective market timing is the flip side of portfolio diversification. Consider Figure 13.1, which shows the set of portfolios attainable by combining MSCI's U.S. and U.K. stock market indices over the period 1971–1993. A portfolio of U.S. and U.K. stocks benefits from the low correlation between these markets, as indicated by the line bowed to the left in Figure 13.1. The line to the right in Figure 13.1 shows the expected return and standard deviation of return for a market timer randomly switching between U.S. and U.K. stocks. Whereas the mixer benefits from low correlations across assets, the timer chooses to forgo these diversification benefits. Market timers without timing skill suffer a penalty relative to the buy-and-hold investor in the form of higher portfolio risk. Butler, Domian, and Simonds estimated that a market timer randomly switching between U.S. and Japanese stocks faces 26 percent more standard deviation of return than a comparable buy-and-hold investor at the same level of expected return. This is indicated in Figure 13.1 as the "Market timer's penalty."[14]

---

13 See William F. Sharpe, "Are Gains Likely from Market Timing?" *Financial Analysts Journal* 31, No. 2, 1975, pages 60–69.
14 Kirt Butler, Dale Domian, and Richard Simonds, "International Portfolio Diversification and the Magnitude of the Market Timer's Penalty," *Journal of International Financial Management and Accounting* 6, Winter 1995, pages 193–206.

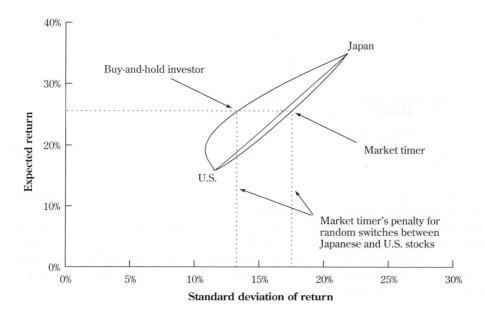

FIGURE 13.1
Portfolio Diversification and
the Market Timer's Penalty
Based on MSCI's U.S. and
Japanese Stock Market
Indices, 1970–1995

Evidence on the market timing performance of mutual funds is mixed. Some studies have found empirical evidence of timing ability on the part of individual funds (for example, Stanley Kon [1983] and Chen-Few Lee and Shafigur Rahman [1990]), but others have failed to find evidence of timing ability (for example, Roy Henriksson [1984] and Robert Cumby and Jack Glen [1990]). Indeed, even if some fund managers are able to consistently outperform a buy-and-hold strategy, it may be difficult to identify these superior market timers with any degree of statistical precision. Even well-known portfolio managers have achieved average annual returns only slightly higher than competing benchmark portfolios.

Active Security Selection. Managers following an active **security selection** strategy attempt to identify individual securities that are underpriced relative to other securities in a national market, relative to other firms in an industry, or relative to other firms in a particular national market and industry.

As an example of an international stock selection strategy, Capaul, Rowley, and Sharpe compared the returns to *value stocks* (stocks with low price/book ratios) to those of *growth stocks* (stocks with high price/book ratios) in France, Germany, Japan, Switzerland, the United Kingdom, and the United States.[15] Value stocks outperformed growth stocks in each country during their 1981–1992 sample period according to several measures. Across their entire sample, return-risk performance according to the Sharpe index = $(R_P - R_F)/\sigma_P$ was .46 for value stocks and only .21 for growth stocks.

---

15 See Carlo Capaul, Ian Rowley and William F. Sharpe, "International Value and Growth Stock Returns," *Financial Analysts Journal* 49, January–February 1993, pages 27–36.

This translated into a 1.88 percent difference in return on value stocks over growth stocks at the same level of portfolio risk.

To identify underpriced securities, active security selection strategies require information along a number of dimensions.

- Macroeconomic information on economic activity, cross-border trade flows, interest rates, and exchange rates
- Industry-specific information on the prospects and obstacles facing particular industries
- Company-specific information on investment alternatives, potential strategic alliances, and new product development

Needless to say, it is much more difficult to acquire this information in a global village than in one's local village. Company-specific information in particular can be difficult to obtain and interpret. Successful investing in international markets (whether through active security selection, market timing, or passive investing) also requires familiarity with the cross-border differences that exist in financial measurement and disclosure. Because of their importance in international investing, the next section is devoted to these differences.

13.3 CROSS-BORDER FINANCIAL STATEMENT ANALYSIS

Getting information on foreign firms can be difficult because of differences in language, accounting measurement, and financial reporting requirements.

One of the more imposing barriers to successful international investing is in obtaining and interpreting information on foreign firms. The most obvious barrier is language. Yet learning the local idiom can be a problem even for investors that share a common language. For example, to an American the term "stock" refers to common equity. In the United Kingdom, the term refers to an inventory of unsold goods. In the United States, firms with large amounts of debt in their capital structures are said to be "highly levered." In the United Kingdom, this is referred to as "gearing." This is enough to make you want to table the entire issue of international accounting diversity.[16]

Language barriers can be overcome with the help of an interpreter familiar with the business culture and accounting conventions of the foreign country. More difficult to overcome are cross-country differences in accounting conventions that spring from each country's unique history; legal, tax, and institutional structures; political system; and cultural environment. *Legalistic* accounting systems are found in countries with so-called *code law* legal systems. France and Germany use a legalistic system of accounting. Business laws in these countries are a list of "thou shalts" that define proper corporate behavior.[17] In a legalistic accounting system, the state mandates accounting rules and conventions to ensure a procedurally consistent application of accounting across all legal entities in the country. Because the state is setting the standards, the principal focus is on ensuring that taxes are assessed consistently across companies. The accounting focus in these countries is on the legal rather than the economic entity.

---

16 Here we go again. To an American, the term "table" means to "discontinue discussion" of a topic. To a Brit, it means to "put it on the table" and open the topic for discussion. What a bloody mess.

17 It has been said that the only things that aren't forbidden in Germany are required.

The United States and the United Kingdom follow a *nonlegalistic* accounting system that views the corporation as an economic rather than a legal entity. Nonlegalistic accounting systems are associated with so-called *common law* countries in which laws are a list of "thou shalt nots" that define the limits of legal activity. In a nonlegalistic accounting system, management has much more discretion to tailor the accounting assumptions and procedures to fit the particular business circumstance so long as its decisions are within accepted norms.

The rest of this section examines international differences in the measurement and disclosure of financial information. This is not intended to be a comprehensive guide to cross-border financial statement analysis. It is only intended to make you aware of some of the difficulties encountered by financial analysts on their voyages into the financial accounting conventions of other countries.

International Differences in Financial Accounting Measurement

Cross-country financial statement analysis is difficult because of cross-country differences in the measurement of accounting income. Table 13.1 lists some of the major areas of disagreement in the national accounting systems of the United States, the United Kingdom, Germany, and Japan. Cross-country differences show up in the construction of nearly every financial account, but differences are especially large in the accounting treatments of goodwill, discretionary reserves, pensions, and inflation.

Goodwill. Goodwill is created when one firm acquires or merges with another firm. Mergers and acquisitions are designed to achieve *synergies*—additional value above and beyond the preacquisition value of the acquired firm. In most countries, the takeover premium is called **goodwill**, and it is either expensed immediately or put on the balance sheet and amortized. Japan allows merging firms to expense this difference immediately through the income statement. Other countries recognize that the acquiring firm has

TABLE 13.1 CROSS-BORDER DIFFERENCES IN ACCOUNTING CONVENTIONS

	United States	United Kingdom	Japan	Germany
Goodwill[a]				
Option to expense immediately	No	No	Depends	No
Option to charge to equity	No	Yes	No	Yes
Amortization period	40 years (maximum)	Rare	5 years (maximum)	5 years
Tax deductibility of amortization	No	No	Yes	Yes
Discretionary reserves[b]	No	No	Yes	Yes
Pension accounting[a]				
Actuarial assumptions	Mgmt's estimate	Actuary's estimate	Set by law	Set by law
Future compensation levels	Mgmt's estimate	Actuary's estimate	Set by law	Not included
Inflation accounting[a]	Historical cost supplemented with inflation cost information	Combination of historical cost and inflation cost information	Historical cost	Historical cost

[a] Arthur Andersen and Co., Coopers and Lybrand, Deloitte and Touche, Ernst and Young, KPMG Peat Markick, and Price Waterhouse, *Survey of International Accounting Practices,* 1991, page 3.
[b] Larry Sundby and Bradley Schwieger, "EC, EZ?" *Journal of Accountancy* 173, No. 3, 1992, pages 71–76.

(presumably) purchased something of value and recognize this value as an increase in an asset account or a decrease in a liability account. In the United States, goodwill appears as a new asset account on the balance sheet. In contrast, firms in the United Kingdom and Germany deduct the takeover premium from equity rather than adding it as an asset. Goodwill is usually amortized once it is on the balance sheet, but the amortization period varies across countries. Some countries (including Japan and Germany) allow amortization expense to be deducted from taxable income, but other countries (including the United Kingdom and the United States) do not.

Discretionary Reserves. In the United States, after-tax earnings are either paid out as dividends or reinvested as accumulated retained earnings in a common equity account. Many other countries allow discretionary reserve accounts that can be used to "smooth" reported earnings. **Discretionary reserve accounts** are used to temporarily store excess earnings during good times, and they can be drawn upon during bad times to boost reported earnings. Note that the use of discretionary reserves does not change cash flow unless there are additional tax consequences or changes in the firm's investment or financial policies. Comparative financial statement analysis is more difficult when there are cross-border differences in the existence or use of discretionary reserve accounts.

Pension Liabilities. Cross-country accounting differences in the recognition of future **pension liabilities** results in differences in reported earnings even when there are no differences in the future pension liabilities themselves.

Pension plans in the United States are sponsored by the employer. As shown in Table 13.1, management has some discretion over the actuarial assumptions used in determining the value of future pension obligations. *Defined benefit plans* promise the employee a defined benefit at retirement, often based on salary and years of service. In a *defined contribution plan* the employer and perhaps also the employee contribute into an account that accumulates pension benefits. Because the contributions to a defined contribution plan are easier to measure than the size and timing of the future benefit in a defined benefit plan, there are material differences in pension accounting even within the U.S. accounting system.

Pension plans outside the United States tend to be sponsored by the government rather than by private industry. In these countries, the government usually sets much more rigid standards for recognition of future pension liabilities. Since passage of *Statement of Financial Accounting Standards #106* (SFAS #106), corporations in the United States must also recognize postretirement liabilities other than pensions. Pension standards in the United States recognize higher pension liabilities than most other countries, which results in lower reported income in the United States even when there are no differences in actual pension liabilities.

Inflation Accounting. Countries with low inflation typically do not adjust for inflation; they state balance sheet and income statement items at their historical cost. During the late 1970s, both the United States (in SFAS #33, "Financial Reporting and Changing Prices") and the United Kingdom (in *Statement of Standard Accounting Practice #16*, "Current Cost Accounting") required that inflation-adjusted information be provided along with historical cost information in response to double-digit inflation. Each country later made these disclosures voluntary rather than mandatory as inflation was brought under control during the early and middle 1980s. Most major U.S. and U.K. corporations continue to provide inflation cost accounting information along with their standard financial statements. Accounting standards in Germany and Japan have not had to respond to high inflation, because inflation has been low in these countries since World War II.

Unfortunately, historical cost information is quickly distorted by high inflation. *International Accounting Standards Committee Statement #29* ("Financial Reporting in Hyperinflationary Economies") recommends that the financial statements of companies or subsidiaries in hyperinflationary countries be restated to reflect the year-end purchasing power of the currency. The analyst performing cross-border comparative financial statement analysis must be aware of the conventions used for inflation accounting in each country and of the history of inflation in each country.

An Example of the Hazards in Cross-Border Financial Statement Analysis.

Suppose that you work in commercial credit for Citicorp and have just received your dream assignment—a one-year posting in Citicorp's London branch. This should be a lark, you think. Your first assignment is to review a proposed loan to a microbrewery in Chelsea called Brown Bog Brewery. Brown Bog provides you with the following current accounts:

Cash	£20,000		
Accounts receivable	£40,000	Wages payable	£40,000
Inventory	£40,000	Taxes payable	£20,000
Total current assets	£100,000	Total current liabilities	£60,000

As a seasoned loan officer, you quickly calculate a *current ratio* to measure Brown Bog's liquidity.

Brown Bog (U.K. accounting): current ratio = current assets / current liabilities
= £100,000 / £60,000 = 1.67

But wait. Is this high or low? By whose standards should you judge this measure of liquidity?

Fortunately, you remember that you performed a credit analysis last year on a similar U.S. microbrewery called Red Dog Brewery. You retrieve Red Dog's loan analysis from your library of floppy disks. Here are the U.S. microbrewery's current accounts:

Cash	$60,000	Bank overdrafts	$30,000
Accounts receivable	$60,000	Wages payable	$60,000
Inventory	$60,000	Taxes payable	$30,000
Total current assets	$180,000	Total current liabilities	$120,000

You calculate Red Dog's ratio.

Red Dog (U.S. accounting): current ratio = current assets / current liabilities
= $180,000 / $120,000 = 1.5

The U.K. firm appears to be more liquid than its U.S. counterpart. You might as well make the loan, right?[18]

The U.K. follows the *Statements of Standard Accounting Practice* (SSAP), which do not always coincide with the *generally accepted accounting principles* (GAAP) promulgated through the *Statement of Financial Accounting Standards* (SFAS) of the United States. In fact, the United States and the United Kingdom do not share a common accounting definition of cash. According to U.S. GAAP, "cash" is defined as cash, demand deposits, and highly liquid investments. In the United Kingdom, "cash" is defined as cash, demand deposits, and highly liquid investments *less bank overdrafts*. For comparability, you restate Red Dog's current accounts after adjusting for the U.K. definition of cash.

Cash (less overdrafts)	$30,000		
Accounts receivable	$60,000	Wages payable	$60,000
Inventory	$60,000	Taxes payable	$30,000
Total current assets	$150,000	Total current liabilities	$90,000

Under this convention, Red Dog's current ratio is exactly the same as Brown Bog's.

Red Dog (U.K. accounting): current ratio = current assets / current liabilities
= $150,000 / $90,000 = 1.67

After adjusting for this accounting difference, the current ratio of Red Dog is identical to that of Brown Bog.

The definition of cash would seem to be the *least* ambiguous of the financial accounts. If cross-border differences in the definition of cash can make such a big difference, just think what the United Kingdom's accounting conventions are doing to your U.S.-based notions of inventory, wages payable, and taxes payable! Maybe this assignment to London won't be the lark that you had envisioned. Off you go to the pub to drown your misery with a pint of Brown Bog ale.

In fact, cross-border financial statement analysis must go beyond mere differences in national accounting measurement systems. A substantial country-specific element affects financial ratios even after adjusting for differences in accounting definitions. For example, many U.K. pubs have exclusive arrangements with a single U.K. brewer. This can lead to different credit terms because the U.K. brewer provides more flexible credit terms to its exclusive outlets. This, in turn, inflates Brown Bog's receivables relative to similar U.S. breweries.

The accounting systems of the United Kingdom and the United States are about as similar as any in the world. Yet we have seen that adjusting for U.K.-U.S. differences in accounting measurement and business culture can be subtle and pervasive. Even more caution should be exercised when comparing the financial statements of companies from dissimilar accounting measurement systems or business cultures.

---

18 If you are from the United Kingdom, you'll have to reverse the perspective in this example. Assume that you have been assigned to the U.S. branch of Standard Chartered Bank in (pick a U.S. city) and have been asked to review Red Dog's loan application. From the U.S. perspective, Red Dog appears to lack liquidity.

MNC Responses to the Need for Financial Information. The multinational corporation can respond in one of four ways to a demand on the part of foreign stakeholders for financial accounting information:

- Do nothing. Small companies that have few dealings with the outside world have neither the need nor the resources to prepare supplementary financial statements.

- Prepare convenience translations. Under this alternative, the firm translates the names of the financial accounts into another language but does not change the accounting conventions used to construct the accounts. Large U.S. multinational corporations seldom go beyond preparing convenience translations for foreign investors, relying instead on the foreign investor to understand and interpret the financial statements according to U.S. GAAP.

- Restate selected items using a different set of accounting principles. The firm can also restate selected financial items (for example, shareholders' equity) according to the accounting conventions of a foreign country or international accounting standard.

- Prepare a second set of financial statements using a different set of accounting principles. The firm can restate all financial statements according to the accounting conventions of a foreign country or international accounting standard. Japanese multinationals frequently prepare secondary financial statements in English and according to U.S. GAAP. European MNCs often choose to report to nonresident investors according to the accounting conventions of the *International Accounting Standards Committee* (IASC), an international organization devoted to harmonizing accounting standards. As a practical matter, IASC standards are very similar to U.S. GAAP.

The response chosen by a particular firm reflects the importance of international investors in its financing activities.

International Differences in Financial Disclosure Requirements. International differences in the market for corporate control are reflected in differences in public disclosure requirements. Public disclosure requirements are most common in economies with active public markets, the United States and the United Kingdom in particular. In many developing countries the majority of funds are still raised privately through banks, wealthy investors, and the government. In these countries, there are likely to be few public disclosure requirements.

Public stock and bond markets facilitate the transfer of wealth between investors and promote the allocational efficiency of financial flows within the financial sector. Although many countries now have liquid public markets for equity securities, bond markets are seldom as developed as those in the United States. Even in those countries with well-established national stock markets, such as Japan, Germany, and the United Kingdom, bond markets tend to lag those of the United States in terms of trading volume, liquidity, and market capitalization (or value).

The biggest impediment to a listing on a U.S. exchange for a non-U.S. firm is the SEC's requirement that foreign firms follow U.S. disclosure requirements and report

TABLE 13.2 CONFORMANCE WITH OECD DISCLOSURE REQUIREMENTS[a]

Country	Operating results (industrial & financial firms)			Intra-firm pricing (industrial firms only)		
	Full	Partial	None	Full	Partial	None
Germany	0	19	0	0	0	15
Japan	2	21	0	2	0	17
United Kingdom	19	6	0	6	0	14
United States	34	19	0	29	0	18

Source: OECD, "Disclosure of Information by Multinational Enterprises," document by the Working Group on Accounting Standards, No. 6, 1989.

[a] See Stephen Prowse, "Corporate Governance in an International Perspective," Bank for International Settlements Economic Papers, No. 41, July 1994.

their financial statements according to U.S. GAAP. Many non-U.S. multinational corporations gladly accept the additional burden of U.S. accounting and disclosure requirements in order to obtain access to the deep liquidity of the U.S. markets. Financial statements prepared according to U.S. accounting rules help these firms market their shares to U.S. investors. As mentioned earlier, large Japanese multinational corporations routinely prepare financial statements in English and according to U.S. GAAP as a convenience to their U.S. and other international investors. Some large foreign firms avoid the U.S. equity markets rather than subject themselves to the scrutiny brought by public financial disclosure.

A study by the *Organization for Economic Cooperation and Development* (OECD) reveals some interesting international differences in the public information disclosures of multinational firms. The OECD maintains a set of recommended disclosure requirements as a standard against which to compare actual disclosure in various countries. Table 13.2 reports the extent to which a sample of firms complied with these standards. Clearly, information disclosure is greatest in the United States and the United Kingdom. It should be noted that commercial banks are more important stakeholders in Germany and Japan than in the United States and the United Kingdom and that the lead bankers have access to reports of firms' financial performances through the monitoring activities of their commercial credit groups. Consequently, the need for public disclosure requirements is less in these countries than in the United States and the United Kingdom.

13.4 THE SHIFTING SANDS OF PORTFOLIO ANALYSIS

Inputs to Portfolio Analysis

Quantitative inputs to portfolio analysis include expected returns, variances, and covariances. For both active and passive asset allocation strategies, these inputs include national (stock and bond) markets, industry indices, or both. For active security selection, these inputs must be at the firm level.

Consider the expected return and variance of return on a diversified portfolio of international securities. Investors and fund managers must estimate portfolio return and risk with the following equations.

$$E[R_P] = \Sigma_i X_i E[R_i] \tag{13.1}$$

$$Var(R_P) = \sigma_P^2 = \Sigma_i X_i^2 \sigma_i^2 + \underset{i \neq j}{\Sigma_i \Sigma_j} X_i X_j \sigma_{ij} \tag{13.2}$$

Chapter 11 provided historical measures of expected return $E[R_i] = \mu_i$, standard deviation of return σ_j, and cross-market correlation ρ_{ij} for the major national market indices.

The fund manager's estimate of future portfolio return and risk will only be as good as the inputs to portfolio analysis. If the expected returns or standard deviations of national market indices change, or if the correlations between national market indices change, then historical estimates will not accurately predict the distribution of future returns. For this reason, disclaimers such as "past returns are no guarantee of future performance" appear prominently in mutual fund prospectuses. There ain't no such thing as easy money.

Time-Varying Expected Returns, Volatilities, and Covariances

A growing body of evidence indicates that the expected returns and volatilities of U.S. stocks and bonds vary over time and that these variations are related to the business cycle.[19] The expected returns and volatilities of U.S. stocks and bonds vary as follows:

- The volatility of today's return depends on the volatility of returns in the recent past
- Expected return and volatility are positively related

The expected returns and volatilities of international stock and bond investments behave in a similar fashion. Exchange rates also move in predictable ways over time.[20] The predictability of time-varying expected returns and volatilities may allow active asset allocation strategies to outperform passive buy-and-hold strategies despite the return-risk penalty for active market timing.[21]

Expected returns and volatilities vary over time and are related to business cycles.

Figure 13.2 plots monthly returns to Morgan Stanley's (MSCI) German, Japanese, and U.S. stock indices over the period January 1970 to June 1995. Note that these are local currency (not dollar) returns. The international stock market crash of October 1987 appears as a large downward spike in each market. October 1987 was the largest monthly drop in all but the Japanese market, which suffered even larger losses during several months in 1990. Each market had periods of high volatility and periods of low volatility. Although the empirical evidence is just beginning to accumulate, it appears

---

19 Classic references include Keim and Stambaugh [1986], Campbell [1987], and Fama and French [1989].

20 Richard T. Baillie and Tim Bollerslev, "Common Stochastic Trends in a System of Exchange Rates," *Journal of Finance* 44, No. 1, March 1989, pages 167–182.

21 Robert C. Klemkosky and Rakesh Bharati, "Time-Varying Expected Returns and Asset Allocation," *Journal of Portfolio Management* 21, Summer 1995, pages 80–87.

Part 4 International Capital
Markets and Portfolio
Investment

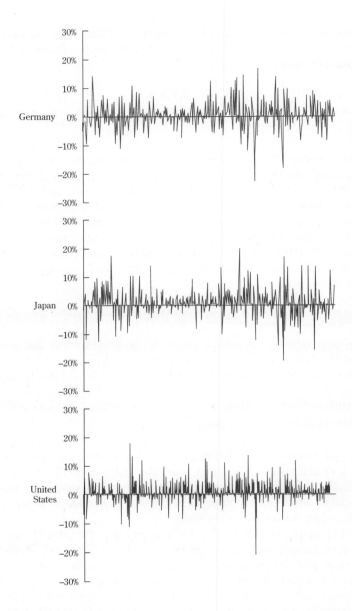

FIGURE 13.2
Volatility of National Stock
Markets in Local Currency
Returns, 1970–1995

that expected returns also vary across national markets. Stock returns and volatility also flow between national markets as the sun travels around the world.[22] Instability in expected returns and volatilities across national indices make the portfolio manager's job more difficult, but also more interesting.

---

22 See Weng-Ling Lin, Robert F. Engle, and Takatoshi Ito, "Do Bulls and Bears Move Across Borders? International Transmission of Stock Returns and Volatility, *Review of Financial Studies* 7, Fall 1994, pages 507–538.

Figure 13.3 plots sixty-month rolling correlations between each of several national stock market indices and the U.S. stock market using the MSCI indices. Each point on the graph is a correlation between a national market index and the U.S. market calculated with the returns from the previous sixty months. Canadian stocks have the highest correlation with the U.S. stock market (around .8) because of the geographic proximity and market overlap of the United States and Canada. Germany and Japan have the lowest correlations because of their greater geographic distance from the U.S. market and the relatively low intersection between the European, Asian, and North American markets.

The risk reduction benefits of international portfolio diversification cannot be precisely estimated using historical data.

What is most striking about these rolling correlations is their instability. The German market has a correlation that varies from a low near zero in 1980 to a high above .6 in 1992. The instability of the correlation between national stock markets means that it is difficult to predict the risk reduction effects of portfolio diversification. Portfolio weights based on historic correlations may or may not turn out to provide the same risk reduction benefits in the future.

All is not lost, however. Clearly the Canadian market has a higher correlation with the U.S. market than Germany, Japan, or the United Kingdom does. Just as clearly, the German and Japanese stock markets are likely to provide more diversification benefits than the Canadian market to a U.S. investor because of their lower correlation with the U.S. market. Instability in the correlation coefficients between the United States and other national markets simply serves to caution us that the *future* risk reduction benefits of international portfolio diversification cannot be precisely estimated using historical data.

The International Stock Market Crash of October 1987. Consider the international stock market crash of October 1987 depicted in Figure 13.4. Stock markets

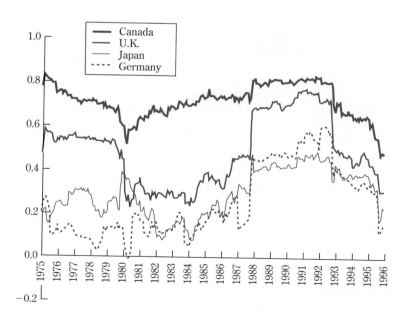

FIGURE 13.3
Sixty-Month Rolling
Correlations with the
U.S. Stock Market

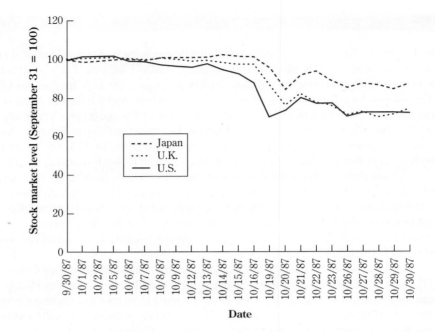

FIGURE 13.4
National Stock Market
Indices during the Crash
of October 1987

worldwide dropped precipitously following the weekend of October 17–18, with local currency losses ranging from 16.3 percent in Italy to 45.8 percent in Hong Kong. Richard Roll found that the size of each market's movement during the crash was largely explained by that market's beta (systematic risk) relative to a world market portfolio.[23] Recall that the beta of a national market i is calculated from $R_i = \alpha_i + \beta_i R_M + e_i$. This is nothing but a scaled correlation coefficient, $\beta_i = \rho_{i,M} (\sigma_i / \sigma_M)$, where $\rho_{i,M}$ is the correlation between the national and world market indices and σ_i and σ_M are the standard deviations of the national and of the world markets, respectively. Roll found that national markets with higher betas measured against a world market index tended to fall further than markets with low betas during the month of the crash.

Pundits around the world tended to look for local reasons for the stock market crash. In the United States, the crash was blamed on everything from a perceived change in Federal Reserve policy to a shift in U.S. investor sentiment. (Quite a shift!) Similarly parochial explanations were seen in other countries, with local politicians as common scapegoats. Regardless of the cause, the common movement among national stock markets during October 1987 was remarkable. The crash of 1987 was a truly international event.

The aftereffects of the crash of 1987 will be seen in stock market data for decades to come. Evidence of the crash appears in Figure 13.3 as an upward shift in the correlations of each of the national stocks with the U.S. stock market beginning in October 1987 and continuing for sixty months. Once October 1987 falls off the tail end of the

23 See Richard Roll, "The International Crash of October 1987," *Financial Analysts Journal* 44, No. 5, 1988, pages 19–35.

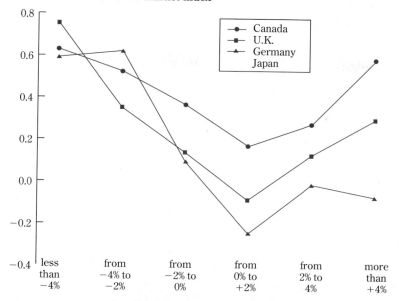

Correlation of the U.S. stock market with the world stock market index

Legend:
- Canada
- U.K.
- Germany
- Japan

Y-axis: 0.8, 0.6, 0.4, 0.2, 0.0, −0.2, −0.4

X-axis (World stock market return category): less than −4%, from −4% to −2%, from −2% to 0%, from 0% to +2%, from 2% to 4%, more than +4%

FIGURE 13.5
Sixty-Month Rolling
Correlations with the
U.S. Stock Market,
October 1987 Deleted

sixty-month rolling correlations, cross-market correlations return to near their former levels. Figure 13.5 presents sixty-month rolling correlations after deleting October 1987. These rolling correlations do not exhibit the upward jump visible in Figure 13.3.

Higher Correlations During Volatile Periods. Figures 13.3 and 13.5 suggest that national stock markets moved together to a greater degree than usual during the crash of 1987. This turns out to be generally true. Correlations between national markets tend to increase when market volatility increases.[24]

Suppose we categorize monthly returns in the U.S., Canadian, U.K., German, and Japanese stock markets according to the return on the world stock market index during that month. Returns on these five markets during those months in which the MSCI world index fell more than 4 percent are placed in one category. A second category includes those months in which the world stock market portfolio fell by 2 percent to 4 percent. A third category includes months in which the world index fell by 0 percent to 2 percent. The process is continued for categories of 0 percent to +2 percent, +2 percent to +4 percent, and greater than 4 percent.

Figure 13.6 displays the correlations of each national market index with the U.S. market within each of the return categories. Correlations between the U.S. and foreign markets are higher when the volatility of the world market is high. This is reflected in the

Correlations between national markets tend to increase when market volatility increases.

24 This observation appears in Odier and Solnik [1993]. The real economic causes of correlation instability are investigated in Erb, Harvey, and Viskanta [1994].

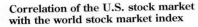

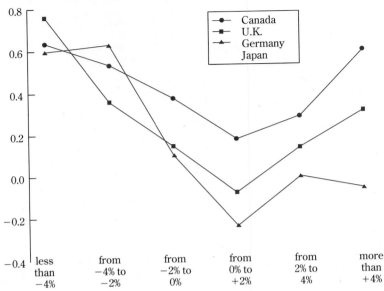

FIGURE 13.6
When It Rains, It Pours

dip in the middle and the rising tails at each end of Figure 13.6. Further, cross-country correlations are greater during large drops in the world market than during large rises.

As the saying goes, "When it rains, it pours." Cross-market correlations increase just when low cross-market correlations are most needed—when returns around the world are large and negative. While the "portfolio insurance" provided by international portfolio diversification is still valuable, the benefits of international diversification in stocks are somewhat less during volatile market conditions than during normal times.

13.5 PORTFOLIO HEDGING STRATEGIES

In Chapter 12, we found that changes in currency values are largely unrelated to changes in both the world stock market index and the national stock market indices. This suggests that we should be able to improve the return-risk efficiency of an internationally diversified portfolio of stocks and bonds by hedging the additional layer of currency risk on foreign investments.

Currency Risk and the IAPM. In the international asset pricing model (IAPM), each investor's optimal portfolio consists of positions in the world market portfolio, domestic and foreign bonds, and a currency-specific **hedge portfolio** used to strip foreign bonds of their currency risk. All investors hold individual stocks in proportion to their market value weights in a globally diversified equity portfolio. The composition of the hedge portfolio depends on the investor's functional currency.

Martin Zweig is a well-known money manager, market timer, newsletter writer, and a frequent guest on the TV program *Wall Street Week*. He posed the following question:* What real return would you expect for the stock market of a country that, over the course of 120 years, rises from a backwater nation of little consequence to a position as the foremost economic and military power in the world? Clearly, Dr. Zweig has the United States in mind.

Jeremy Siegel reconstructed U.S. debt and equity market returns over the last two centuries of U.S. capital market history. Siegel found that the mean equity risk premium over T-bills has been only 6 percent over the last

120 years of U.S. capital market history (as well as about 6 percent during each sixty-year subperiod) despite the phenomenal economic and geopolitical ascendance of the United States during this 120-year period. Capital markets in many other countries did even worse. For example, capital markets in Germany (twice) and Japan (once) lost nearly 100 percent of their value at some point during this period. These national market experiences should caution us against excessive optimism regarding the likely returns to foreign investment.

* Address at his alma mater, Michigan State University, on February 4, 1994.

Like the CAPM, the IAPM is a one-period model. In a one-period world, interest rate parity tells us that an investment in a riskless foreign bond is equivalent to a combination of a riskless domestic bond along with a long forward position in the foreign currency:

Foreign bond	Domestic bond in the foreign currency	Long forward position in foreign currency f
$+X^f$	$+X^d$	$+X^f$
	$=$	$+$	$-X^d$

Mean-variance efficient portfolios are combinations of foreign and domestic stocks and bonds hedged against currency risk.

The Benefits of Hedging Currency Risk in an International Investment Portfolio.

In practice, there are many ways to construct a hedge portfolio. One alternative is to hedge the entire amount of funds exposed to currency risk.[25] Figure 13.7 presents Philippe Jorion's estimate of the additional benefit from hedging 100 percent of the currency risk of the world market portfolio.[26] The leftmost line represents the

---

25 Another popular alternative is to construct a minimum-variance hedge using a form of the hedge ratio presented in Chapter 7. A discussion appears in Michael Adler and Philippe Jorion's "Universal Currency Hedges for Global Portfolios," *Journal of Portfolio Management* 18, Summer 1992, pages 28–35.
26 Philippe Jorion, "Asset Allocation with Hedged and Unhedged Foreign Stocks and Bonds," *Journal of Portfolio Management* 15, Summer 1989, pages 49–54.

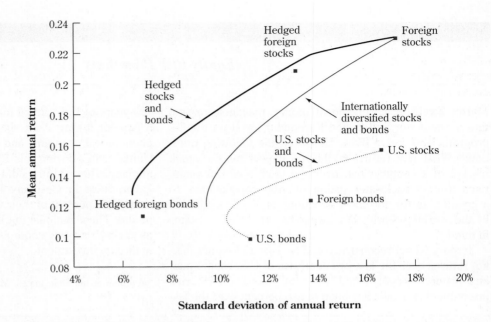

FIGURE 13.7
The Benefits of Hedging
Currency Risk

Adapted from "Asset Allocation with Hedged and Unhedged Foreign Stocks and Bonds" by Philippe Jorion, *Journal of Portfolio Management,* Summer 1989, pages 49–54. Reprinted with permission.

return-risk performance possible by hedging the currency risk of the combined stock-bond portfolio. To obtain Figure 13.7, Jorion uses a rolling one-month forward hedge of the full amount of the investment in each foreign currency. With a one-month rolling foreign currency hedge, the amount invested in each foreign market is sold forward at the start of each month with a one-month forward contract. As Figure 13.7 shows, the potential gains in return-risk efficiency from hedging the currency risk in an internationally diversified portfolio can be substantial.

13.6 SUMMARY

This chapter began by describing several ways to diversify into international stocks and bonds. These include

- Invest in domestic multinational corporations
- Invest in foreign securities in the foreign market
- Invest in foreign securities in the domestic market
  - American shares
  - American depository receipts (ADRs)
  - Mutual funds
  - Private investment partnerships (hedge funds)

Open-ended mutual funds provide excellent vehicles for international diversification (at least in those countries without capital inflow restrictions) at low cost. For U.S. investors willing to buy individual companies, American shares and ADRs provide substantial international diversification benefits, although at slightly higher cost than open-end mutual funds invested in foreign assets. The entry fee into hedge funds is high, so these are only available to wealthy investors. International diversification through closed-end country funds (a form of mutual fund) and through multinational corporations is also possible, although these vehicles provide fewer diversification benefits than direct investment in foreign securities. Investors choosing closed-end country funds for foreign investment may face an implicit transaction cost in the form of large premiums to net asset values.

We then looked at passive and active portfolio management styles and how they are implemented on a global scale. The inputs to portfolio analysis include expected returns, variances, and covariances. Returns on international investments are difficult to predict because of randomness in foreign market returns and in currency exchange rates. Combined with the changing expected returns and variances of national market indices and instability in cross-market covariances, the short-term investor faces a difficult challenge. These quantities are more stable over the long term, making it easier for the long-term investor to take advantage of international portfolio diversification.

Finally, we examined the gains in return-risk efficiency that can be obtained by hedging the currency risk of foreign investments. Reducing the currency risk of an internationally diversified portfolio can greatly reduce the variability of return without a corresponding decrease in expected return.

KEY TERMS

American shares
Asset allocation policy
Closed-end funds (including closed-end
   country funds)
Convertible bonds
Depository receipts (including American
   depository receipts, or ADRs)
Discretionary reserves
Goodwill
Hedge funds
Hedge portfolio
Index options

Investment philosophy
Market timing
Net asset value (NAV)
Open-end funds
Pension liabilities
Prospectus
Security selection
Stock index futures
Stock index swaps
Warrants

CONCEPTUAL QUESTIONS

13.1 List the various ways in which you might invest in foreign securities.

13.2 Do MNCs provide international portfolio diversification benefits? If so, do they provide the same diversification benefits as direct ownership of companies located in the countries in which the MNC does business?

13.3 What is the difference between a passive and an active investment philosophy?

13.4 What makes cross-border financial statement analysis difficult?

13.5 What is the difference between a legalistic and a nonlegalistic approach to accounting? In what countries are each of these systems found?

13.6 What alternatives does a multinational corporation have when investors in a foreign country demand accounting and financial information?

13.7 You are planning for retirement and must decide on the inputs to use in your asset allocation decision. Knowing the benefits of international portfolio diversification, you want to include foreign stocks and bonds in your final portfolio. What statistics should you collect on the world's major national debt and equity markets? Can you trust that the future will be like the past?

13.8 Which benefits more from currency hedging—a portfolio of international stocks or a portfolio of international bonds?

PROBLEMS

13.1 Frau Gatti's beginning-of-year account balances with her Zurich bank are shown below. (Note the Swiss convention of switching the commas and periods in decimal values. For example, "one thousand shares" is written "1.000 shares" and "twelve and three-tenths percent" is written "12,3 percent" in this statement.)

Gnomes of Zurich Bank—Account of Frau Gatti   1 Jan., 199x

Security (dividend yield or interest rate)	Number of shares or par value	Local price (local)	Capital amount (local)	Dividends or accrued interest (local)	Spot rate (SF/f)	Capital amount (SF)	Div or accr int (SF)	Market value (SF)	Sub-totals %
Equities									
Daimler Benz (1,6%)	1.000 shs	692	DM692.000	DM11.072	SF0,836/DM	SF578.512	SF9.256	SF587.768	12,3
Mazda Motors (0,0%)	50.000 shs	380	¥19.000.000	¥0	SF0,01315/¥	SF249.850	SF0	SF249.850	5,2
General Motors (2,4%)	2.000 shs	52½	$105.000	$2,520	SF1,168/$	SF122.640	SF2.943	SF125.583	2,6
Bonds									
French Govt ECU (6% 2004)	ECU1.000.000	89.00	ECU890.000	ECU60.000	SF1,550/ECU	SF1.379.500	SF93.000	SF1.472.500	30,8
German Govt (6.875% 2005)	DM1.000.000	100.95	DM1.009.500	DM68.750	SF0,836/DM	SF843.942	SF57.475	SF901.417	18,9
U.S. Govt (6.5% 2005)	$1.000.000	102.08	$1.020.800	$65.000	SF1,168/$	SF1.192.294	SF75.920	SF1.268.214	26,6
Cash									
Swiss Francs (1,5%)	SF168.000		SF168.000	SF2,520		SF168.000	SF2.520	SF170.520	3,6
Total						SF4.534.738	SF241.115	SF4.775.853	100,0

Beginning cash balance	SF168.000	
Deduct divs & accrued int (SF)		(SF241.115)
Add to cash balance (SF)	+SF241.115	
Ending cash (SF)	SF409.115	

Given the end-of-year figures below, compute the returns that Frau Gatti has earned on her various investments including dividends and accrued interest. Note that the Swiss money market interest rate has fallen to 1.4% per year.

Security (dividend yield or interest rate)	Number of shares or par value	Local price (local)	Capital amount (local)	Dividends or accrued interest (local)	Spot rate (SF/f)	Capital amount (SF)	Div or accr int (SF)	Market value (SF)	Sub-totals %
Equities									
Daimler Benz (1,6%)	1.000 shs	704			SF0,842/DM				
Mazda Motors (0,0%)	50.000 shs	372			SF0,01152/¥				
General Motors (2,4%)	2.000 shs	58¼			SF1,204/$				
Bonds									
French Govt ECU (6% 2004)	ECU1.000.000	90.20			SF1,560/ECU				
German Govt (6.875% 2005)	DM1.000.000	101.05			SF0,842/DM				
U.S. Govt (6.5% 2005)	$1.000.000	102.42			SF1,204/$				
Cash									
Swiss Francs (1,5%)	SF409.115		SF409.115						
Total									

Beginning cash balance	SF409.115								
Deduct divs & accrued int (SF)									
Add to cash balance (SF)	+SF					(SF)			
Ending cash (SF)	SF								

13.2 You are a U.S.-based investor evaluating a closed-end country fund called Korea Foods. Korea Foods' sole assets are the following three investments in South Korea:

	Share price (Millions of won)	Portfolio weight
Chop Chae Corporation	8,000	½
Bulgogi Business Machines, Inc.	4,000	¼
Yuk Gae Jong International Corp.	8,000	¼

The current spot rate is W800/$ and the fund sells in the United States for $11 per share. There are one million shares outstanding.

a. What is the net asset value (NAV) of this fund in South Korean won?
b. What is the NAV in U.S. dollars?
c. Is this a good investment?

SUGGESTED READINGS

The easiest-to-read references in this list are from *Financial Analysts Journal* and the *Journal of Portfolio Management*. Articles in the *Review of Financial Studies, Journal of Finance,* and *Journal of Financial Economics* can be difficult but are worth the additional effort.

Articles that examine various investment vehicles for diversifying internationally include
    Warren Bailey and Joseph Lim, "Evaluating the Diversification Benefits of the New Country Funds," *Journal of Portfolio Management* 18, Spring 1992, pages 74–80.

Robert E. Cumby and Jack D. Glen, "Evaluating the Performance of International Mutual Funds," *Journal of Finance* 45, June 1990, pages 497–521.

William G. Droms and David A. Walker, "Investment Performance of International Mutual Funds," *Journal of Financial Research* 17, No. 1, Spring 1994, pages 73–96.

Cheol S. Eun, Richard Kolodny, and Bruce G. Resnick, "U.S.-Based International Mutual Funds: A Performance Evaluation," *Journal of Portfolio Management* 17, Spring 1991, pages 88–94.

Bertrand Jacquillat and Bruno Solnik, "Multinationals Are Poor Tools for International Diversification," *Journal of Portfolio Management,* Winter 1978, pages 8–12.

Philippe Jorion and Leonid Roisenberg, "Synthetic International Diversification: The Case for Diversifying with Stock Index Futures," *Journal of Portfolio Management* 19, Winter 1993, pages 65–74.

Articles that investigate the causes of closed-end country fund (CECF) premiums to net asset value include

James N. Bodurtha, Dong-Soon Kim, and Charles Lee, "Closed-End Country Funds and U.S. Market Sentiment," *Review of Financial Studies* 8, No. 3, Fall 1995.

Catherine Bonser-Neal, Greggory Brauer, Robert Neal, and Simon Wheatley, "International Investment Restrictions and Closed-End Country Fund Prices," *Journal of Finance* 45, No. 2, 1990, pages 523–548.

Cheol Eun and S. Janakiramanan, "A Model of International Asset Pricing with a Constraint on the Foreign Equity Ownership," *Journal of Finance* 41, No. 4, 1986, pages 897–914.

Charles Lee, Andrei Schleifer, and Richard Thaler, "Investor Sentiment and the Closed-End Fund Puzzle," *Journal of Finance* 46, No. 1, 1991, pages 75–110.

Articles that review the performance of market timing and security selection across domestic and/or international markets include

Kirt C. Butler, Dale L. Domian, and Richard R. Simonds, "International Portfolio Diversification and the Magnitude of the Market Timer's Penalty," *Journal of International Financial Management and Accounting* 6, Winter 1995, pages 193–206.

Carlo Capaul, Ian Rowley, and William F. Sharpe, "International Value and Growth Stock Returns," *Financial Analysts Journal* 49, January–February 1993, pages 27–36.

Roy D. Henriksson, "Market Timing and Mutual Fund Performance: An Empirical Investigation," *Journal of Business* 57, No. 1, 1984, pages 73–96.

Stanley J. Kon, "The Market-Timing Performance of Mutual Fund Managers," *Journal of Business* 56, No. 3, 1983, pages 323–347.

Cheng-Few Lee and Shafiqur Rahman, "Market Timing, Selectivity, and Mutual Fund Performance: An Empirical Investigation," *Journal of Business* 63, No. 2, 1990, pages 261–278.

William F. Sharpe, "Are Gains Likely from Market Timing?" *Financial Analysts Journal* 31, No. 2, 1975, pages 60–69.

William F. Sharpe, "Asset Allocation: Management Style and Performance Measurement," *Journal of Portfolio Management* 18, No. 2, 1992, pages 7–19.

The difficulties of cross-border financial statement analysis are discussed in

Ray Ball, "Making Accounting More International: Why, How, and How Far Will It Go?" *Journal of Applied Corporate Finance* 8, No. 3, Fall 1995, pages 19–29.

Frederick D.S. Choi, Hisaaki Hino, Sang Kee Min, San Oh Nam, Junichi Ujiie, and Arthur I. Stonehill, "Analyzing Foreign Financial Statements: The Use and Misuse of International Ratio

Analysis," *Journal of International Business Studies,* Spring/Summer 1983, pages 113–131.

Kenneth R. French and James M. Poterba, "Were Japanese Stock Prices Too High?" *Journal of Financial Economics* 29, No. 2, 1991, pages 337–364.

The literature on time-varying expected returns, volatilities, and covariances and on the international transmission of stock market prices tends to be rather technical. The most accessible articles appear in the *Journal of Portfolio Management* or *Financial Analysts Journal.*

Richard T. Baillie and Tim Bollerslev, "Common Stochastic Trends in a System of Exchange Rates," *Journal of Finance* 44, No. 1, March 1989, pages 167–182.

Geert Bekaert and Campbell R. Harvey, "Time-Varying World Market Integration," *Journal of Finance* 50, No. 2, June 1995, pages 403–444.

John Y. Campbell, "Stock Returns and the Term Structure," *Journal of Financial Economics* 18, No. 2, 1987, pages 373–400.

Claude B. Erb, Campbell R. Harvey, and Tadas E. Viskanta, "Forecasting International Equity Correlations," *Financial Analysts Journal* 50, November–December 1994, pages 32–45.

Eugene F. Fama and Kenneth R. French, "Business Conditions and Expected Returns on Stocks and Bonds," *Journal of Financial Economics* 25, No. 1, 1989, pages 23–50.

Donald B. Keim and Robert F. Stambaugh, "Predicting Returns in the Stock and Bond Markets," *Journal of Financial Economics* 17, No. 2, 1986, pages 357–390.

Robert C. Klemkosky and Rakesh Bharati, "Time-Varying Expected Returns and Asset Allocation," *Journal of Portfolio Management,* Summer 1995, pages 80–87.

Weng-Ling Lin, Robert F. Engle, and Takatoshi Ito, "Do Bulls and Bears Move Across Borders? International Transmission of Stock Returns and Volatility," *Review of Financial Studies* 7, No. 3, Fall 1994, pages 507–538.

Richard Roll, "The International Crash of October 1987," *Financial Analysts Journal* 44, No. 5, 1988, pages 19–35.

Israel Shaked, "International Equity Markets and the Investment Horizon," *Journal of Portfolio Management* 11, Winter 1985, pages 80–84.

Jeremy J. Siegel, "The Equity Premium: Stock and Bond Returns Since 1802," *Financial Analysts Journal* 48, January/February 1992, pages 28–38.

Jeremy J. Siegel, "The Real Rate of Interest from 1800–1990," *Journal of Monetary Economics* 29, April 1992, pages 227–252.

Jack W. Wilson and Charles P. Jones "A Comparison of Annual Common Stock Returns: 1871–1925 with 1926–1985," *Journal of Business* 60, No. 2, 1987, pages 239–258.

Articles that discuss currency hedging of internationally diversified portfolios include

Michael Adler and Philippe Jorion, "Universal Currency Hedges for Global Portfolios," *Journal of Portfolio Management* 18, Summer 1992, pages 28–35.

Fischer Black, "Universal Hedging: Optimizing Currency Risk and Reward in International Equity Portfolios," *Financial Analysts Journal* 45, No. 4, 1989, pages 16–22.

Jack D. Glen and Philippe Jorion, "Currency Hedging for International Portfolios," *Journal of Finance* 48, December 1993, pages 1865–1887.

Philippe Jorion, "Asset Allocation with Hedged and Unhedged Foreign Stocks and Bonds," *Journal of Portfolio Management* 15, Summer 1989, pages 49–54.

Patrick Odier and Bruno Solnik, "Lessons for International Asset Allocation," *Financial Analysts Journal* 49, March–April 1993, pages 63–77.

Articles that discuss the problems and potentials of portfolio investment in selected regions or countries include

Marek Lorinc, "Investing in Financial Markets of East and Central Europe," *Columbia Journal of World Trade* 30, No. 1, Spring 1995, pages 88–111.

Peter Marber, "Banking the Bear: Financial Marketization in Russia," *Columbia Journal of World Trade* 29, No. 4, Winter 1994, pages 30–41.

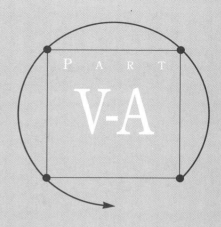

Multinational Corporate Finance

The Environment of Multinational Corporate Finance

Do the thing you fear the most, and the death of fear is certain.
Ralph Waldo Emerson

The two chapters in Part 5A of the book survey the environment of international business with special emphasis on the cultural, social, political, and economic differences among peoples of the world. These differences create natural advantages for local firms in providing goods and services to their local markets. The successful multinational corporation must overcome these obstacles and bring something to local markets that local firms cannot bring. This also requires that the successful multinational financial manager be able to execute the firm's business strategies across a variety of cultures.

Chapter 14 categorizes the competitive advantages that the multinational corporation enjoys over local firms according to the *eclectic paradigm,* borrowed from the international business literature. Chapter 15 discusses the ways in which the multinational corporation can gain access to, and then maintain, competitive advantages over local firms. These two chapters set the stage for the more technical material on the multinational corporation's investment and financing decisions that makes up the remainder of the book.

14

The Multinational Corporation: Opportunities, Costs, and Risks

There is nothing more difficult to take in hand, more perilous to conduct, or more uncertain in its success, than to take the lead in the introduction of a new order of things.

Niccolò Machiavelli, *The Prince*

OVERVIEW

Why are some manufactured goods and services successfully exported while other products and services sell only in local markets? Why do some multinational corporations prefer to export while others build overseas manufacturing facilities and invest directly in the foreign market? When are franchising and licensing preferred to exporting or foreign direct investment as a means of market entry?

No single theory of the multinational firm explains all of the many forms of cross-border trade. This is largely because the multinational operations of business enterprises are so diverse. This diversity is both a blessing and a curse for efforts to impose some order on a discussion of the opportunities and threats facing the multinational firm. Although no single theory of the multinational firm has emerged, we know many of the characteristics associated with success in the global marketplace.

These characteristics are identified in the *eclectic paradigm,* which is discussed in the first section of this chapter. The eclectic paradigm attempts to categorize the factors that contribute to the multinational corporation's advantage over domestic firms. At the heart of these competitive advantages are imperfections in the markets for factors of production, final products, or both. The eclectic paradigm recognizes that international activities are situation-specific—what works at one time or place and for a particular firm may or may not work in another circumstance. According to the eclectic paradigm, the multinational corporation's advantages accrue from ownership of proprietary assets, from access to advantageous geographic locations, or from an ability to supply goods and services to customers and markets that would otherwise go unsatisfied.

An understanding of the sources of the multinational's competitive advantage can provide insight into how multinationals create and preserve value through their foreign operations. This understanding can in turn guide multinational financial managers' searches for positive-NPV investments and help them sustain these advantages despite the costs and risks of operating in unfamiliar business environments.

Multinational corporations face many risks in the conduct of foreign operations. Besides the inconvenience of dealing with more than one currency and the ordinary business and financial risks faced by domestic firms, multinational corporations face three new risks.

- Currency risk: The risk that currency values will change unexpectedly
- Political risk: The risk of an unexpected change in the political or regulatory environment
- Cultural risk: Risks arising from dealing with an unfamiliar culture

Currency, political, and cultural risk are the three most important forms of **country risk**—the risk of conducting business in a particular foreign country. Most of the rest of this book deals with currency risk in one form or another. After introducing the theory of the multinational corporation, this chapter discusses political risk and cultural risk in sections 14.2 and 14.3, respectively.

————————————————●————————————————

14.1 THE ECLECTIC PARADIGM: THE WHY, WHERE, AND HOW OF INTERNATIONAL BUSINESS

The major difficulty in creating a comprehensive theory of the multinational firm is in the diversity of situations in which cross-border trade can flourish. What works for one company or country may or may not work in another. Firms in one country or industry may prosper while others languish. The mode of market entry also takes myriad forms. Cross-border trade can take the form of exporting in one situation, foreign direct investment in another, and franchising in yet another. Fitting all of these situations into a single theoretical framework is a formidable task.

The most ambitious attempt to synthesize the elements that make for success in the international marketplace is the **eclectic paradigm** proposed by John Dunning.[1] The eclectic paradigm attempts to characterize the breadth, depth, and form of multinational business activity by focusing on three types of advantages benefiting multinational firms: ownership-specific advantages, location-specific advantages, and internalization

———————————————————————————

1 A thorough exposition of the eclectic theory of the multinational firm appears in Dunning's *Multinational Enterprises and the Global Economy*, Addison-Wesley, 1993.

advantages. According to the eclectic paradigm, the most successful multinational firms will be those that

- Have the most pronounced ownership-specific (O) advantages from owning proprietary assets, such as brand names, patents, copyrights, proprietary technology or technological processes, and marketing and management expertise
- Have privileged access to location-specific (L) advantages such as abundant natural or manufactured resources, low taxes or wage costs, and high labor productivity
- Can most successfully exploit their O-advantages and L-advantages through market internalization (I) advantages, that is, advantages from circumventing or exploiting market failures

The particular way in which a multinational exploits its advantages depends on the particular circumstance and on the multinational's endowment of each of these advantages.

Ownership Advantages: The Why of Multinational Operations

Local firms have an inherent advantage over nonresident firms in local markets. Local firms are more familiar with consumer preferences and with production, marketing, and distribution of goods in the local marketplace. Local governments and the local populace are often unsympathetic (indeed, can be downright hostile) to foreign firms attempting to gain entry into local markets.

Goods and factor inputs market imperfections are preconditions for foreign direct investment.

If multinationals operated in perfectly competitive markets they would have no advantage over local firms. Thus, for the multinational corporation to have an advantage over local firms it must bring something to the marketplace that local firms cannot. This requires that there exist one or more imperfections in the markets for real goods, factor inputs, and/or capital. The observation that market imperfections are preconditions for foreign direct investment was made by Stephen Hymer in his 1960 doctoral dissertation at the Massachusetts Institute of Technology.[2] According to Hymer's view, the multinational must have a competitive advantage either in generating higher returns on investment or in securing funds at a lower cost.

Consider the discounted cash flow approach to firm valuation in which the value of an asset is equal to the present value of expected future cash flows discounted at a rate that reflects the systematic risk of the cash flows:

$$V_j = \Sigma_t \left[\frac{E[CF_{jt}]}{(1+i_{jt})^t} \right] \qquad (14.1)$$

CF_{jt} is firm j's net cash flow at time t and i_{jt} is the appropriate risk-adjusted discount rate over the period from today through time t. To create value, the multinational must be able to generate higher cash flows in the numerator (through higher sales or lower operating cost) and/or a lower discount rate in the denominator through its

---

2 Stephen Hymer's work was published as *The International Operations of National Firms: A Study of Direct Foreign Investment,* MIT Press, Cambridge, Mass., 1976.

multinational operations than through its domestic operations as well as relative to local firms. If it cannot, then it has no business trying to compete in the international marketplace. This requires some sort of imperfection in the markets for real assets in the numerator or financial assets in the denominator of equation (14.1). Because of imperfections in the real goods markets, multinationals are able to act as monopolists or oligopolists and are able to earn monopoly rents from their assets.

Hymer's observation is important because it focuses attention away from the classical economists' assumption of perfect competition toward a more realistic world in which market imperfections bestow competitive advantages on some firms and not on others. Hymer pointed out that the basis for the multinational's advantage over local firms lies in firm-specific advantages that come in the form of property rights or intangible assets (patents, trademarks, organizational and marketing expertise, production technology and management) and the general organizational abilities of employees in each of the MNC's functional areas of business (finance, marketing, management, and so on).[3] The eclectic paradigm refers to these as **ownership-specific advantages** (O-advantages) and holds that they can lead to many different forms of multinational activity, including exporting, licensing, franchising, various forms of strategic alliance, and foreign direct investment in manufacturing capacity.

O-advantages are firm-specific, difficult to copy, and easily transferred.

Richard Caves extended Hymer's analysis by noting that for O-advantages to lead to foreign direct investment these advantages must be firm-specific, difficult to copy, and easy to transfer to foreign affiliates.[4] Without control of the source of its advantage, the multinational corporation risks losing its advantage to foreign competitors or even to its own foreign partners should they eventually obtain independence from the multinational. O-advantages of this sort are found in industries dominated by large investments in research and development, especially where the fruits of R&D can be protected through enforceable patents, control of production processes, and trade secrets. Specialized knowledge and large R&D investments are formidable barriers to entry in these industries.

The pharmaceutical industry is an example of an industry in which advantages are firm-specific, difficult to copy, and easy to transfer to foreign affiliates. Consider Merck & Co., one of the world's largest manufacturers of prescription pharmaceuticals. At the heart of Merck's success are its research laboratories. Merck spends heavily on research and new product development. Demand for pharmaceutical drugs is highest in developed economies and, fortunately for Merck, most of these economies have well-developed patent enforcement policies. By obtaining patents on the products it discovers, Merck retains monopoly power for a period of time in its markets. Patent protection in the United States lasts for seventeen years. Although getting approval from the Food and Drug Administration in the United States can take several years, regulatory approval takes considerably less time in most other countries. Once the details of the production technology are established, it is relatively easy to transfer pharmaceutical technology to foreign affiliates. Not surprisingly, Merck manufactures a good deal of its pharmaceutical drugs through affiliates in foreign countries.

Many of the advantages of ownership stem directly from ownership itself and do not require multinationality. Patent protection, for example, is provided by the governments

---

3 Stephen Hymer, *International Operations of National Firms.*
4 Richard E. Caves, "International Corporations: The Industrial Economics of Foreign Investment," *Economica,* February 1971, pages 1–27.

of most developed countries to both foreign and domestic firms. Similarly, technological superiority can be a huge barrier to entry for both domestic and foreign competitors. Oil companies owning the rights to oil fields enjoy an ownership advantage in oil production over oil companies that merely distribute petroleum, and companies owning a well-known chain of gas stations enjoy an ownership advantage in distribution. These O-advantages are often not related to multinationality per se, although they are in the form of economies of scale and are therefore related to firm size.

The advantages of ownership also accrue to firms purely because of their multinationality. Multinationality provides firms with flexibility in production, sourcing, and sales. Multinationality allows firms to take advantage of location-specific differences in labor and raw material costs, capital costs, information technology, tax rates, and production and marketing expertise. Cross-border diversification also can provide an advantage to the multinational relative to purely domestic firms if investors are prohibited or restricted (perhaps by information or transactions costs) from diversifying internationally. Finally, experience in different markets confers on the multinational corporation a more comprehensive knowledge of the types of activities and products that sell in different markets around the world and of how to adapt its O-advantages to new circumstances.

Whether the advantages of ownership come from intangible assets or property rights or from multinationality itself, ownership-specific advantages provide the *why* of multinational business activity. As in Hymer's explanation of foreign direct investment, ownership-specific advantages rely on natural or man-made market imperfections for their sustenance. Without some sort of ownership advantage, multinational firms do not enjoy an advantage over local firms. The task for the multinational corporation is to sustain these O-advantages in its current markets and to leverage existing advantages into new O-advantages through its management of human and capital resources.

Hymer provided us with the *why* of multinational operations. However, the observation that market imperfections are necessary for the multinational to have an advantage over local firms does little to explain the *how* of multinational operations. That is, how do firms operationalize their competitive advantages and why do they organize their multinational activities in particular ways? Why do some firms export while others establish overseas manufacturing plants? Similarly, Hymer's observation does little to explain the *where* of multinational operations. That is, why do multinationals choose to license their technology in one location and invest directly in foreign manufacturing facilities in another location? A partial answer to these questions is provided in the next two sections.[5]

Location-Specific Advantages: The Where of Multinational Operations

Advantages that are available only or primarily in a single location are termed **location-specific advantages** (L-advantages). L-advantages include natural resources, resources created by the local economy, high labor productivity and low real wage costs, transportation and communication systems, governmental investment incentives, preferential

L-advantages are specific to a particular location.

5 The *when* of multinational operations is discussed in Chapter 17. See Pietra Rivoli and Eugene Solario, "Foreign Direct Investment and Investment under Uncertainty," *Journal of International Business Studies* 27, No. 2, 1996, pages 335–357, for an analysis of real options in the context of the eclectic paradigm.

tax treatments, and the work ethic of the local labor force. Multinational corporations that have diversified their operations across a number of geographic regions have greater access to L-advantages than single-country companies have. This allows them to shift resources at lower cost in response to changes in location-specific advantages.

Local governments sometimes confer a location's advantages on one or more "favored sons" in return for political or financial favors. More commonly, the L-advantages are available to the highest bidder. This means that L-advantages by themselves are not sufficient to give the multinational corporation a competitive advantage over its competitors unless other competitors, including local competitors, cannot gain access to the advantages of the location. To justify foreign direct investment, the multinational corporation must be better than local firms at exploiting the advantages of a particular location. This requires that the multinational corporation be better at internalizing the potential of the firm's O- and L-advantages.

Market Internalization Advantages:
The How of Multinational Operations

Peter Buckley and Mark Casson, among others, point out that ownership-specific advantages by themselves are not sufficient to ensure the multinational success over local firms.[6] If local firms can purchase O-advantages at competitive prices from another company, then they can compete directly with foreign multinationals. Unless ownership-specific advantages are preserved in some way, local firms will eventually be able to replicate the advantages of the multinational corporation. Similarly, as local firms grow and prosper, they too can begin to access capital on an international scale and reap the benefits of economies of scale. To ensure a continuing source of value, the multinational must be able to preserve its O-advantages in a way that cannot be replicated by local firms.

I-advantages allow the MNC to exploit the failure of an arms-length market to efficiently accomplish a task.

The ability of a multinational to realize and sustain a potential advantage depends on many factors, including the nature of the industry, the countries in which the multinational is competing, and the business culture of the multinational corporation. Thus, technology-intensive products generally enjoy more sustainable O-advantages than low-technology products do because they are more costly to replicate. Similarly, it may be easier to sustain an O-advantage in a developing economy than in a developed economy because of the ease with which other competitors can replicate the multinational's products. On the other hand, it may be more difficult to sustain an O-advantage in a developing economy if patents are not enforced. Cooperation among business partners (as in Japan, for example) may be the most effective organizational form in some situations, but competition among suppliers (such as in the United States) may be a more effective organizational form in another situation. The way in which a particular O-advantage is pursued is thus a function of the cultural context in which it occurs.

To incorporate the effect of differences in the business culture on the ability of the multinational firm to realize potential advantages, the eclectic paradigm posits a class of

6 Peter J. Buckley and Mark Casson, *The Future of the Multinational Enterprise,* Macmillan, London, 1976.

advantages called **market internalization advantages** (I-advantages). I-advantages allow the multinational corporation to internalize or exploit the failure of an arms-length market to efficiently accomplish a task. The market internalization literature has its beginnings in the work of Richard Coase in the 1930s.[7] Coase viewed the firm as the nexus of a set of contracts between the various stakeholders in the firm, broadly defined to include debt, equity, managers, employees, suppliers, customers, and the government. I-advantages accrue to firms that find more value by realizing their O-advantages through contracts within the firm rather than through the external marketplace; that is, they "internalize" the market for a particular product. The corporation should establish its own internal product markets when the net benefits of organizing production within the firm outweigh those of organizing production externally. This circumstance is called **market failure** because it represents a failure of the financial markets to complete the production of a particular product.

Internal markets within the firm can increase gains and reduce costs along a number of dimensions relative to contracting directly in the financial markets. Internalizing a product market can help the multinational corporation maintain its monopolistic or oligopolistic position relative to local firms. Internalization can help the multinational capture and retain scale economies in both individual and interdependent operations. Internalization can help a firm control supplies and suppliers and thereby protect the quality of its products. Internalization can allow a multinational corporation to diversify into markets that are closed to portfolio investment. For example, a partnership between an Iranian firm and Conoco to develop an Iranian oil field might be permissible, whereas direct investment by Conoco may be prohibited by both the U.S. and Iranian governments. Internalization can reduce search and information costs, negotiation costs, the costs of dispute settlement, and conflicts of interest. Finally, internalization allows the multinational corporation to take advantage of cross-border differences in tax systems and tax rates through transfer prices and other internal tax-planning strategies that are not available to other participants in the financial markets.

14.2 POLITICAL RISK

Political risk is the risk that a sovereign host government will unexpectedly change the rules of the game under which businesses operate. If change can be anticipated, then it is not truly risk. For this reason, political risk is based on *unexpected* change in the business environment of the host country or in the political relations of the host country to other governments. If a corporation knows with certainty that a foreign income tax rate is to be increased from 10 percent to 30 percent, then this is not risk. The higher tax rate will reduce future profitability, but by knowing the new tax rules in advance the firm can incorporate these new tax rules into its investment, financial, and tax planning decisions. The multinational corporation faces political risk only if there is a chance (as there always is) of a sovereign government changing the rules in a way that cannot be anticipated by the managers of the multinational corporation.

Political risk is the risk that a sovereign host government will unexpectedly change the rules of the game.

---

7 Richard H. Coase, "The Nature of the Firm," *Economica* 4, November, 1937, pages 386–405.

Sources of Political Risk

The objectives of governments and of multinational corporations are frequently in conflict. Governments are responsible to the individual people living in their country and to their national society as a whole. Corporations are responsible to stockholders, bondholders and other creditors, employers, suppliers, and customers. Many of these stakeholders live in the multinational corporation's domestic country and not in the foreign countries in which the multinational corporation conducts its business. Even if the constituencies of national governments and the corporation were one and the same, the political and corporate leaders representing these constituencies operate in different political arenas and respond to their constituencies in different ways. It is not surprising that governments and multinational corporations come into conflict over economic, political, environmental, and social policies.

Stephen Kobrin identifies two dimensions of political risk:[8]

- *Macro risks* affect all foreign firms in a host country
- *Micro risks* are specific to an industry, company, or project

Examples of macro risks faced by multinational corporations include unexpected changes in the host country's monetary and fiscal policies, tax rates, capital controls, and bankruptcy and ownership laws. Unexpected changes in each of these affect a broad cross-section of society as well as all firms doing business in the country.

Examples of micro risks include unexpected changes in foreign trade policy, environmental laws and regulations, tax rules, and regulations on the use of foreign labor. For example, most governments keep fairly tight controls on foreign labor working within the country. Employers attempting to bring foreign labor into a host country usually must demonstrate that the imported laborers are not displacing domestic workers. To the extent that a multinational corporation uses imported labor, such as expatriate managers from the home office, changes in immigration policies can adversely affect the multinational corporation relative to its local competitors.

Types of Political Risk

Expropriation Risk. Mao Tse-tung wrote that "political power grows out of the barrel of a gun."[9] Indeed, the most extreme form of political risk is **expropriation** in which a foreign government seizes the assets of a firm. This often occurs following revolutions, such as in Iran in the 1970s, as the new regime attempts to throw out the foreign infidels and make a fresh start.

From a conceptual standpoint, expropriation risk is relatively easy to handle. Nobody likes having their assets seized, but you can plan ahead if you know that this is a possi-

---

8 Stephen J. Kobrin, "Political Risks: A Review and Reconsideration," *Journal of International Business Studies,* Spring–Summer 1979, pages 67–80.
9 Mao Tse-tung (1893–1976), *Selected Works of Mao Tse-tung,* 1965, Vol. I, Foreign Language Press, Peking, page 28.

bility. Chapter 16 presents a formal way to incorporate expropriation risk into a capital budgeting analysis. In practice, expropriation is a messy affair that involves disruptions in worldwide operations in the short term and litigation through the international courts in the long term.

Risk of Disruptions in Operations. Expropriation is the most extreme form of political risk, but political risk comes in many more subtle forms that can disrupt the local and even worldwide operations of the multinational corporation. Asset seizures make the newspaper headlines, but disruptions in operations are far more prevalent than disruptions in ownership and can be devastating to the operations of the multinational corporation. Governments impose burdens on multinational companies through tariffs, "local content" regulations that require a certain percentage of the final product to be manufactured locally, limitations on the use of expatriate workers, and changes in taxes and the regulatory environment within the host country. In the absence of change in the business environment, each of these disruptions is a cost of foreign operations. The multinational corporation is exposed to political risk when there can be *unexpected* changes in the business environment of the host country within which the multinational corporation must operate.

Political risk affects the operations of the MNC.

Foreign firms operating within the United States are not immune to political risk. The U.S. Congress tinkers with the U.S. tax code about every four years. Both foreign and domestic firms are subjected to periodic changes in the U.S. regulatory environment as well. Both foreign and domestic firms face political risk as these environmental regulations evolve. These types of disruptions in operations occur in every country as governments implement their fiscal, monetary and political agendas.

As an example, in 1977 the state of California adopted an unusual unitary tax system for companies operating within the state. Under the unitary method, tax is calculated on a company's worldwide income instead of only on income earned in the state. At the time California adopted the unitary tax, several multinational corporations either postponed or canceled planned investments in the state because of the perceived increase in costs and risks. To continue to attract out-of-state capital, California subsequently allowed foreign multinationals to choose to be taxed according to the unitary method or on income earned within the United States.

Barclays Bank of the United Kingdom and Colgate-Palmolive of the United States challenged the unitary tax in U.S. courts on the grounds that it discriminates against foreign (Barclays) and out-of-state (Colgate-Palmolive) commerce. In June 1994 the U.S. Supreme Court upheld the constitutionality of California's unitary tax, declaring that the tax did not infringe on Congress's right to "regulate commerce with foreign nations, and among the several states."

Protectionism. Foreign firms often must overcome distrust and resentment in the local community. Some products (such as Parisian fashions and U.S. cigarettes) do command a certain romantic cachet among select foreign clienteles, but in most cases homegrown products and services are strongly preferred by local residents. Foreign firms exporting to the U.S. market face "buy American" sentiment from individuals, government officials, labor unions, and other special interest groups. Similarly, Germans

Protectionist governments erect import tariffs, quotas, or regulations that discriminate against foreign businesses.

prefer German beer, French prefer French wine, and Japanese prefer Japanese rice. This economic manifestation of nationalism is called **protectionism** when it is codified in a nation's business laws and tax code.

Even when foreign competition is not expressly restricted by the local government, it can be difficult to gain entry to foreign markets. For example, investment securities have historically been sold to individuals in Japan through networks of agents visiting investors in their homes. This institutional structure began to change when the Japanese stock market collapsed in January 1990. Nevertheless, a non-Japanese securities firm trying to establish such a network from scratch in Japan faces a formidable task. Japanese securities firms enjoy a natural competitive advantage in doing business in Japan because of this subtle form of nationalistic protectionism.

MNCs must protect their intellectual property rights.

Risk of Losing Intellectual Property Rights. Another example of political risk lies in the multinational's potential loss of intellectual property rights to competitors or even to former business partners. **Intellectual property rights** are patents, copyrights, and proprietary technologies and processes that are the basis of the multinational corporation's competitive advantage over local firms. Corporations protect intellectual property in their home markets through copyrights, patents, and trade secrets. To the extent that foreign governments allow local firms to steal the intellectual property rights of MNCs, the MNC is exposed to foreign political risk that it does not face in its domestic market.

Multinational firms operating in developed countries can take precautions to protect themselves against loss or theft of their technological knowledge. Foremost among these protections is the patent process. Unfortunately for the multinational corporation based in a developed country such as the United States, intellectual property rights are seldom respected in developing countries. Multinational firms operating in developing countries run the risk of losing ownership of their production technologies to their foreign affiliates and/or competitors. For example, businesses in developing countries sometimes form joint ventures with high-technology firms with the intent of obtaining proprietary production technologies. If the multinational corporation does not exercise vigilance in the transfer and management of its technology, it can find itself competing against former partners in foreign markets and even in its own domestic market.

Assessing Political Risk

A variety of services provide assessments of country political risk. Many of these combine political risk assessment with an overall assessment of the business climate in a country. For example, Ernst & Young (a U.S.-based accounting and consulting firm) publishes a country risk ranking that rates investors' perceptions of emerging markets based on the following categories.

- Business opportunities: the size and structure of the domestic market and attitudes toward foreign investment
- Political risk: stability of a government and its market-oriented policies
- Credit rating: external debt and attitude of international financial markets

TABLE 14.1 RANKINGS[a] FOR CENTRAL AND EASTERN EUROPEAN COUNTRIES

Country	Business Opportunities	Political Risk	Credit Rating	Status of Economy	Stability	Business Infrastructure	Total
Czech Republic	2	1	1	3	1	2	10
Poland	1	2	2	3	2	2	12
Hungary	3	2	2	3	2	2	14
Slovenia	4	2	2	3	2	2	15
Estonia	4	2	3	3	2	2	16
Latvia	4	2	3	3	2	3	17
Lithuania	4	2	3	3	2	4	18
Bulgaria	3	3	4	3	3	3	19
Kazakhstan	2	3	3	4	3	4	19
Romania	2	3	4	3	3	4	19
Russia	1	4	4	3	5	3	20
Slovakia	4	3	3	4	3	3	20
Belarus	3	3	4	4	3	4	21
Uzbekistan	3	4	3	4	3	4	21
Ukraine	2	4	5	4	4	3	22
Croatia	4	4	4	4	3	4	23
Albania	4	4	4	4	4	4	24
Kyrgyztan	4	4	4	4	4	4	24
Moldova	4	4	4	4	4	4	24
Armenia	4	4	5	4	4	5	26
Azerbaijan	3	5	4	5	5	4	26
Turkmenistan	5	4	5	5	4	4	27
Georgia	5	4	5	5	4	5	28
Former Yugoslavia[b]	5	5	5	5	5	5	30
Macedonia[b]	5	5	5	5	5	5	30
Tajikistan	5	5	5	5	5	5	30

[a] 1 = best ranking, 5 = worst rating

[b] Until the political situation has been resolved, the status for investment in the former Yugoslavia and Macedonia cannot be determined. Countries are rated on the basis of inward investors' perception of the emerging markets, based on the following categories: business opportunities = size and structure of domestic market and attitudes towards foreign investment; political risk = stability of government and market-oriented policies; credit rating = external debt and attitude of international financial markets; status of local economy = domestic economic performance; stability = overall political and economic stability; business infrastructure = legal framework, professional services, telecommunications, and distribution.

Source: Ernst & Young, *Market Profiles,* April 1995, as reported in the *London Financial Times,* October 23, 1995, page 3.

• Status of local economy: domestic economic performance

• Stability: overall political and economic stability

• Business infrastructure: legal framework, professional services, telecommunications and distribution

Ernst & Young's March 1995 rankings for Central and Eastern European countries appear in Table 14.1.

Political Risk Insurance

Some political risks are insurable. The risks of currency inconvertibility (that is, not being able to freely convert or exchange the currency), asset expropriation, war, revolution, and insurrection arising from political events are insurable through governmental agencies and private insurers. Companies based in the United States can obtain insurance against these political risks through a U.S. government agency called the Overseas Private Investment Corporation (OPIC) as well as through private insurers such as Lloyd's of London and the American International Group (AIG). By diversifying across countries, these insurers spread political risks in individual countries across their entire portfolio.

The costs of political risk insurance can be high. Annual insurance premiums through private insurers can be as high as 10 percent of the amount of the investment in high-risk countries. Insurance premiums through OPIC are generally less than through private insurers. The premiums of private insurers vary widely, so it makes sense to shop around.

The attractiveness of political risk insurance depends on the diversification of the company being insured. Multinational corporations that are diversified in their revenues, operating expenses, and financial expenses across a large number of countries and currencies are, in essence, self-insuring. Less-diversified companies, especially those with a major proportion of their operations located in a single foreign country, have a much greater incentive to purchase political risk insurance.

14.3 CULTURAL RISKS

An English aristocrat once said, "The only trouble with going abroad is that you have to leave home to do it." True enough. **Cultural risks** and their attendant costs arise because the management and employees of the multinational corporation must deal with unfamiliar business cultures and popular cultures as they seek to extend the firm's ownership-specific advantages into new goods and factor markets.

Cultural risks arise as the MNC deals with new cultures.

This section describes several types of cross-cultural differences and alerts you to some of the more common pitfalls in dealing with foreign cultures. Be forewarned that cultural differences come in many subtle variations—only a few examples are covered here.[10] So, at the risk of oversimplifying, here's a list of cultural costs and risks that are encountered by the multinational corporation.

Differences in the Business Environment

One way to categorize differences in national business environments is along the traditional functional areas of business: marketing, distribution, personnel management, law, accounting, taxes, and finance. The examples in this section are illustrative of the costs and risks of international business, but they are not intended to be exhaustive or mutually exclusive.

---

10 A good reference on cultural risks in international business is *The Cultural Environment of International Business* by Vern Terpstra and Kenneth David, 1991, South-Western College Publishing Co., Cincinnati, Ohio.

Marketing Differences. International marketers must modify their marketing strategies for each new culture. The annals of international business are replete with anecdotes of marketing blunders.[11] One anecdote has General Motors Corporation attempting to sell their Chevrolet Nova under its original name when it was first marketed in Puerto Rico. Literally translated, *no va* means "it goes not." GM renamed the car Caribe for sale in Latin American countries. Another anecdote has Coca-Cola advertising in China with a set of Chinese characters that sounded like "Coca-Cola" but translated as "bite the wax tadpole." Coke's advertising slogan "Coke adds life" was literally translated as "Coke brings you back from the dead." True to its multinational nature, Coca-Cola was quick to spot these problems and modify its Chinese advertising program.[12]

Marketing difficulties only begin with these errors in language translation. Far more subtle are the many *nonverbal* differences between cultures. For example, Walt Disney owns and operates the world's most successful theme parks. At the heart of the success of Disneyland in California and Disney World in Florida is Disney's appeal to the entire family. Disney tried to retain this American-style family orientation when it opened its EuroDisney theme park outside of Paris in the late 1980s. When it opened, EuroDisney was beset by a long succession of obstacles, including overoptimistic revenue forecasts, labor strife, and political and popular opposition. As if these obstacles were not enough, EuroDisney decided to follow its practice in the United States and refused to sell alcoholic beverages at the theme park. This unfortunately ensured that no self-respecting Frenchman would visit the park ("No wine with dinner? Sacre bleu!"). Fortunately for Disney, its equity stake had been kept to a minimum by bringing in a variety of European debt and equity investors in a complex project financing arrangement. Disney's reputation did take a beating, along with several classes of foreign investors and the reputation of the French government of François Mitterrand.

A foreign venture that does not respect the language, culture, and sensibilities of the local peoples is destined for trouble. Multinationals and their managers must learn new social behaviors and political systems, including what types of corporate behavior are punished, what types of behavior are merely tolerated, and what types of behavior can lead to fruitful partnerships with the local residents and their government.

Differences in Distribution Channels. A prolonged stay in a foreign country inevitably means shopping for groceries in the local community. This can be an enjoyable experience because it allows the shopper to catch the "flavor" of the local population. An observant shopper will detect many regional differences in the way foods are distributed. People in most major U.S. cities are accustomed to large grocery store chains that offer a wide selection of food and nonfood items. These regional and national chains keep expenses low through economies of scale and create value for their stakeholders by internalizing the market for food distribution.

In many other parts of the world, groceries are sold in locally owned and operated mom-and-pop stores. Large discount stores are seen as impersonal and are not trusted by shoppers. The source of the local store owners' advantage lies in their continuing

---

11 David Ricks has compiled an amusing assortment of anecdotes in *Big Business Blunders: Mistakes in Multinational Marketing,* 1983, Irwin Publishing, Homewood, Illinois.

12 Terpstra and David, *Cultural Environment.*

relations with members of the local community. Because of these cultural differences in shopping habits, size may be seen as an advantage in one country and as a disadvantage in another country. This is just one example of a distribution channel that exhibits great variation around the world.

Differences in Personnel Management. In many cases, multinationals must adapt their organizational structures to accommodate the types of employees they will employ in their foreign operations. Personnel management policies that work in one culture may not work in another. In other cases, personnel policies developed at home can be successfully exported.

Japanese businesses have achieved huge international successes since World War II. This success has led to a rapid succession of theories contrasting Japanese and American personnel management practices. Although this revolving door of theories makes it appear as if the field of organizational behavior suffers from a "theory du jour" syndrome, these are sincere efforts at combining the best practices of each business culture into a more efficient and productive corporate culture.

Differences in Legal, Accounting, and Tax Systems. Multinational financial managers must learn new and unfamiliar tax laws and tax systems, legal conventions, and business procedures to be successful in foreign countries. As an example, governments in developing countries often offer tax benefits in the form of reduced tax rates and/or

---

What Time Is It?

Mexico City, February 12, 1997, 11:55 a.m.: You are a New Yorker working for AT&T on a satellite communications deal with Telmex, the huge Mexican telecommunications conglomerate. You have scheduled lunch with Miguel Rodriguez, your chief Telmex contact, for noon at a fashionable restaurant in the city. Conscious of the potential size and importance of the Mexican telecommunications market and of your part in the venture, you arrive early and secure a table.

12:20 p.m.: Twenty minutes have passed since your arrival and still no sign of Miguel. Could he have been caught in one of Mexico City's infamous traffic jams? Should you try to contact him on your cellular phone? The waiter doesn't seem concerned that you haven't begun to order. Should you order food for the two of you? Oh, dear.

12:35 p.m.: It has been more than half an hour! Now you are really concerned. Your imagination starts to run away

with you. Perhaps the deal has fallen through? No, you're just panicky. Perhaps he was overcome by smog? The delay is beginning to irritate you. You resolve to contact Miguel by phone—and just at that moment he strolls calmly into the restaurant. Greeting you as if nothing is out of the ordinary, he takes a seat at your table and inquires how you have been. Doesn't he realize what an inconvenience he has caused?

You and Miguel are suffering from a cultural difference in the perception of time. People in some cultures schedule their everyday activities with a great deal of precision. This orientation is characteristic of Germans, Swiss, Dutch, and most North Americans. In contrast, people from Latin cultures such as Italy, Spain, and most South American countries do not feel compelled to schedule their days so precisely. The next time you set up a luncheon appointment with Miguel, be sure to ask whether he is using "New York time" or "Mexico City time."

tax holidays as an incentive for foreign direct investment. Negotiating these tax benefits and ensuring that they are not revoked subsequent to investment can be a delicate and time-consuming job for top management.

Differences in Financial Practices. Financial practices also vary across countries. The most obvious differences are in the levels of sophistication and liquidity in national financial markets, but differences in financial practices can be much more profound. For example, banking practices in many Islamic countries are conducted according to the teachings of the prophet Mohammed as found in the Koran and other Islamic holy scriptures. According to these **Islamic banking** customs, bank depositors do not receive a set rate of interest but instead share in the profits and losses of the bank. Western banks attempting to open branch banks or offshore banking facilities in Islamic nations must adapt their operations to these cultural and religious norms.

Geographical Distance from the Parent

As if it were not enough that foreign operations must be conducted in a foreign business environment and between peoples with distinct cultures, foreign operations usually are conducted at a great distance from corporate headquarters. This means that some autonomy for local operating decisions must be taken away from managers at corporate headquarters and given to local managers.

During the 1970s and 1980s it became standard practice to organize operations around geographic rather than functional lines. Multinationals employed French to run their French operations, Japanese to run their Japanese operations, and Venezuelans to run their Venezuelan operations. The popular business press in Europe bemoaned the lack of "Euro-managers" able to shed the trappings of their native culture and manage effectively in new cultural settings. In recent years, multinationals have begun to return to organizing operations around product lines and to recentralize control at corporate headquarters. Although this trend owes much to advances in telecommunications and information technology, it also suggests that the search for the Euro-manager has been

---

Body Language

As if verbal language weren't enough of a barrier to communication, body language differs across cultures as well. In many settings, what we do with our bodies is even more important than what we say. (Voltaire wrote that "words were given to man to enable him to conceal his true feelings.") Some body language is universal, but a great deal of it is an accoutrement of our culture.

Eye contact is a good example. In the Western world, direct eye contact conveys confidence. Avoiding eye contact is taken as a sign of weakness and may even convey untrustworthiness. For this reason, in Western countries it is necessary for subordinates to show respect and meet the eyes of their superiors. In many Asian countries, however, subordinates show their respect by avoiding eye contact. In some Arab countries, excessive eye contact between a man and woman is thought to be disrespectful to the woman. The eyes may be the "windows to the soul," but be careful which window you look through.

at least partially successful. Job opportunities in cross-border business operations will continue to grow as barriers to cross-border trade progressively fall. The search for the Euro-manager is now an ongoing necessity rather than a luxury for the multinational corporation.

Cultural Distance from the Parent

Even more important than geographic distances are differences in culture. People and their cultural norms vary widely around the world. Being able to understand, manage, and adapt to cultural differences can make the difference between a successful and an unsuccessful international venture. For example, educational differences are especially important in global site selection because they are highly correlated with the skills, costs, and availability of various forms of labor. Unskilled labor tends to be both absolutely and relatively less expensive in countries with lower levels of education. Consequently, industries that employ large amounts of unskilled labor, such as clothing manufacturers, tend to source this input from countries with low labor costs. These are often, but not always, countries with relatively poorly developed education programs.

Skilled labor is most readily found in countries with advanced education programs. Research and development in technology-intensive industries such as electronics and biotechnology is almost invariably conducted in these countries. Companies with highly capable labor forces need not reside in developed countries, however. Because of high quality and low labor costs, computer programmers are increasingly being recruited by U.S. software houses from the East European states of the former Soviet Union. Cultural differences can have a material impact on the multinational's personnel practices, organizational form, distribution and marketing systems, and production technologies.

14.4 SUMMARY

The competitive advantages of multinational firms over local firms arise from differentiated products, proprietary technologies or technological processes, or other forms of barriers to entry. These goods market imperfections are preconditions for foreign direct investment.

The eclectic paradigm identifies three types of market imperfections benefiting the multinational corporation:

- Ownership-specific (O) advantages (from owning proprietary assets)
- Location-specific (L) advantages (from natural or human resource endowments)
- Internalization (I) advantages (from circumventing or exploiting market failures)

The corporation's internal market confers a competitive advantage on the multinational corporation if it allows the corporation to retain and extend its competitive advantages in one or more of the following ways:

- Maintain its oligopolistic position relative to local firms
- Capture and retain scale economies

- Control supplies and suppliers and protect the quality of its products
- Diversify into markets that are closed to portfolio investment
- Reduce the costs of information, negotiation, and dispute settlement
- Reduce conflicts of interest
- Take advantage of cross-border differences in tax systems

The most successful multinational firms will be those that

- Have the most pronounced ownership-specific (O) advantages
- Have access to location-specific (L) advantages, such as abundant natural or manufactured resources, low wage costs, and high labor productivity
- Can most successfully exploit their O-advantages and L-advantages through market internalization (I) advantages

To exploit these competitive advantages, the multinational corporation must overcome three additional sources of risk.

- Currency risk: the risk that currency values will change unexpectedly
- Political risk: the risk of an unexpected change in the political or regulatory environment
- Cultural risk: risk arising from dealing with an unfamiliar culture

Awareness of political and cultural risks is the first step in learning to deal with them and to internalize this knowledge to the competitive advantage of the multinational corporation.

KEY TERMS

Country risk	Location-specific advantages
Cultural risks	Market failure
Eclectic paradigm	Market internalization advantages
Expropriation	Ownership-specific advantages
Intellectual property rights	Political risks (macro and micro)
Islamic banking	Protectionism

CONCEPTUAL QUESTIONS

14.1 Why are product or factor market imperfections preconditions for foreign direct investment?

14.2 Describe the elements of the eclectic paradigm. What does the eclectic paradigm attempt to do?

14.3 What are ownership-specific advantages?

14.4 What are location-specific advantages?

14.5 What are market internalization advantages?

14.6 What are political risks?

14.7 What are cultural risks? Describe several types of cultural risk one might face when conducting business in a foreign culture.

The theory of the multinational enterprise is developed in the following (arranged in chronological order).

Richard H. Coase, "The Nature of the Firm," *Economica* 4, November, 1937, pages 386–405.

Richard E. Caves, "International Corporations: The Industrial Economics of Foreign Investment," *Economica,* February 1971, pages 1–27.

Peter J. Buckley and Mark Casson, *The Future of the Multinational Enterprise,* Macmillan, London, 1976.

Stephen Hymer, *The International Operations of National Firms: A Study of Direct Foreign Investment,* MIT Press, Cambridge, Mass., 1976.

Alan M. Rugman and Alain Verbeke, "Strategic Capital Budgeting Decisions and the Theory of Internalisation," *Managerial Finance* 16, No. 2, 1990, pages 17–24.

John H. Dunning, "Reappraising the Eclectic Paradigm in an Age of Alliances," *Journal of International Business Studies* 26, No. 3, 1995, pages 461–491.

Political risks are reviewed in

Stephen J. Kobrin, "Political Risks: A Review and Reconsideration," *Journal of International Business Studies,* Spring–Summer 1979, pages 67–80.

Cultural risk is reviewed in

Vern Terpstra and Kenneth David, *The Culture Environment of International Business,* 1991, South-Western College Publishing Co., Cincinnati, Ohio.

David Ricks, *Big Business Blunders: Mistakes in Multinational Marketing,* 1983, Irwin Publishing, Homewood, Illinois.

The timing of foreign direct investment is related to the eclectic paradigm in

Pietra Rivoli and Eugene Solario, "Foreign Direct Investment and Investment under Uncertainty," *Journal of International Business Studies* 27, No. 2, 1996, pages 335–357.

Strategy in the Multinational Corporation

Business is war.
Japanese folk wisdom

Overview

In the majority of multinational corporations, the finance team is responsible for the formulation and execution of global strategy.[1] Financial managers are in charge of allocating capital within the corporation. They are armed with an array of valuation concepts and tools that can assist management in protecting existing markets and expanding into new markets. The finance team is charged with executing financial strategies in both the goods markets (through their investment decisions) and the capital markets (through their financing decisions). In this position, the finance team is instrumental in determining how the multinational corporation sustains and extends its competitive advantages in existing products and markets and leverages its core competencies into new products and markets.

> *The finance team is charged with executing the firm's global strategies in both the goods and capital markets.*

Section 15.1 begins with a survey of entry modes into international markets. Entry modes include exporting, contract-based entry (such as licensing), and investment-based market entry. The form of entry into new markets is one of the most important decisions facing the multinational corporation. The market entry mode largely determines the opportunities, costs, and risks faced by the multinational corporation as it extends its product lines into new markets.

The multinational corporation must do everything that it can to protect its competitive advantages from foreign incursion and to leverage its core competencies into new products and markets. Section 15.2 describes the evolution of a typical multinational

---

1 A recent survey found that global strategy was being led by the finance team in more than half of corporate respondents. See "What's New in Financial Strategy" by J. Thackray, *Planning Review* 23, May/June 1995, pages 14–18.

corporation as it progresses through the various stages of its life cycle. Section 15.3 discusses how the multinational corporation can protect its existing and future products from competition. Appendix 15-A chronicles the growth of Merck & Co., a U.S. pharmaceutical company that achieved a series of remarkable international successes during the 1980s.

15.1 ENTRY INTO INTERNATIONAL MARKETS

As a general rule, new products are first introduced in the home market and only later are sold to foreign markets. This evolution proceeds at a different pace in different countries. New products tend to be distributed first in the most advanced countries and only later in less developed countries. Product evolution also proceeds at a different pace in different product markets. For example, the product life cycle of the pop culture shown on MTV is much shorter than the product life cycle in the aerospace industry. Product life cycles can often be extended by offering the product to international markets. Products that have reached maturity in their home markets may be ripe for sale elsewhere. But what is the best way to enter a foreign market? The choice of entry mode is the most important strategic decision made by the firm expanding into new markets. Once made, the choice of entry mode cannot be easily reversed.

The form of entry into new markets largely determines the opportunities, costs, and risks faced by the MNC.

Figure 15.1 displays the risks of foreign operations as a decreasing function of the multinational's knowledge of foreign markets. The foreign market is usually geographically and culturally distant. Unfamiliarity with the market is the biggest obstacle in the way of entry into a new and foreign market. As the producer's knowledge of the foreign market grows, the real and perceived risks of dealing with the foreign market decrease. Knowledge of foreign markets naturally increases with experience over time. With this increasing familiarity comes an increasing ability and willingness to take a more direct role in cross-border operations.

This section describes the advantages and disadvantages of several modes of foreign market entry. These foreign market entry modes are

- Export
- Contract-based (licensing)
- Investment

One important difference among these entry modes is whether the parent firm maintains control of the production process. In exporting, the parent transfers only the final good or service from the home to the foreign market; production is maintained in the home country. In foreign market entry through licensing, the rights to the production technology and other intangible assets are transferred from the domestic owner to a licensee in the foreign market for an agreed-on length of time. In investment entry, the parent preserves an ownership stake in the foreign assets, but it transfers production to the foreign market. In a joint venture, two or more partners share an investment by pooling their assets, including capital, human resources, and intellectual property rights. Another important difference among these foreign market entry modes is the resource commitment of the parent firm. In exporting and licensing, production remains in the

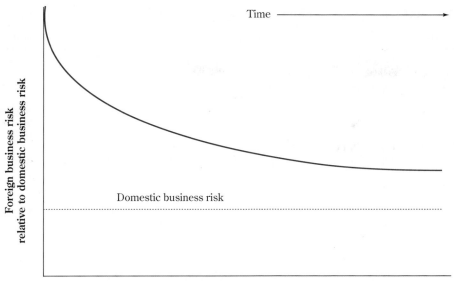

FIGURE 15.1
The Risks of Foreign
Operations as a
Learning Curve

home country and few resources need be committed to the promotion of international sales. In investment-based entry, production is transferred to the host country and controlled by the parent company. This requires a substantially larger commitment in capital, management time and effort, and other corporate resources. Required investment and ownership in a joint venture is negotiated between the partners.

Table 15.1 provides a summary of the key factors in the entry mode decision. Figure 15.2 presents a schematic view of this decision. Keep in mind that Table 15.1 and Figure 15.2 are only a general guide to market entry modes. Entry mode decisions must be made on a case-by-case basis.

Export-Based Foreign Market Entry

Firms that are just beginning to **export** their goods or services to foreign markets often make their initial sales through serendipity. Perhaps a foreign resident stumbled on their product or service while on vacation and, upon returning home, decided that it was just the thing she needed. Or perhaps a tourist visiting another country introduced the product to local residents. These initial foreign sales are usually more by chance than by design.

Initial cross-border sales usually come from direct contact between the manufacturer and final buyers in the foreign market. These sales are typically made over the phone or through the mail and products are shipped directly to the foreign resident without a formal marketing strategy. The growth of worldwide package delivery services has made this form of export activity easier today than it was years ago. Some small companies never evolve beyond this passive approach to international sales. For other companies, the decision not to actively pursue a foreign market is made consciously after weighing the opportunities, costs, and risks of international sales.

Initial cross-border sales usually come from direct contact between the manufacturer and final buyers in the foreign market.

TABLE 15.1 FACTORS INFLUENCING THE CHOICE OF ENTRY MODE INTO FOREIGN MARKETS

	Export-based		Contract-based		Investment-based	
	Foreign agents and distributors	Foreign sales branches or subsidiaries	Licensing and franchising	Foreign direct investment	Foreign acquisition or merger	Foreign joint venture
Resource commitment	Low	Moderate	Low	High	High	Moderate
Speed of market entry	Fast	Moderate	Fast	Slow	Fast	Moderate
Sales potential	Low	High	Moderate	High	High	High
Importance of import barriers	High	High	Low	Low	Low	Low
Importance of investment restrictions	Low	Low	Low	High	High	Moderate
Control of marketing and distribution channels	Low	High	Moderate	High	High	Moderate
Control over production	High	High	Low	High	High	Moderate
Potential loss of production technology	Low	Low	High	Moderate	Moderate	High
Problems in overcoming cultural distance	Low	Variable	Low	High	High	Variable
Political risk	High	High	Moderate	Moderate	High	Moderate
Political risk exposure	Low	Moderate	Moderate	High	High	Low

FIGURE 15.2
The Choice of Foreign Market Entry

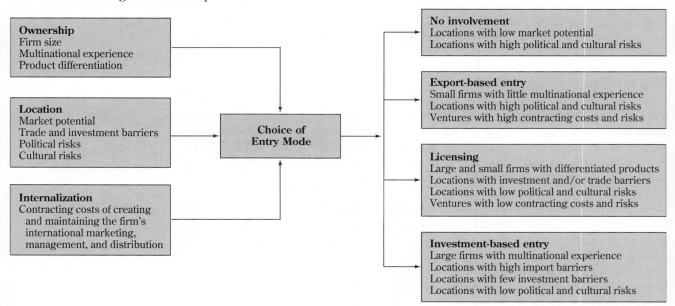

As the potential of the foreign market becomes apparent, the producer should begin to put a little more thought into the best way to gain entry into the foreign market. The producer can continue to be reactive and hope for the best, or the producer can take a pro-active stance and establish a more formal entry into foreign markets. Two effective proactive approaches to foreign market entry are the use of agents/distributors (based either in the domestic or in the foreign market) and the establishment of a foreign sales branch or subsidiary. These entry modes differ from contract-based and ownership-based entry modes in that the exported goods continue to be manufactured outside the target country.

Exporters cannot count on the sympathy of the host government, so foreign political risk and the cost of import barriers can be high. On the other side of the coin, barriers to investment in the foreign market are not an issue and the production technology is kept safely at home.

Agents and Distributors. A relatively low-risk mode of entry for a domestic manufacturer is to use a sales agent or distributor to handle promotion and distribution in the foreign market. The use of sales agents or distributors is an extremely easy entry into the export business for small domestic manufacturers without experience in export sales or knowledge of foreign markets. For the exporter, the key to success is in picking the right partner, one that shares the exporter's goals and is committed to the sales relationship.

A variety of foreign and domestic companies act as agents and distributors for domestic exporters in international markets. These agents, often called **export management companies,** can have from one to several hundred employees. Export merchants assume responsibility for marketing and distribution in the foreign markets. Hiring a sales agent requires little commitment in time and capital on the part of the producer relative to other forms of foreign market entry. With little investment at risk, the exporter is relatively insulated from the costs and risks of foreign sales. An additional advantage relative to producing the product in the foreign market is that the producer retains control of production. This ensures that the producer's quality standards are maintained and that its production technology stays at home.

A disadvantage of this entry mode is that the exporter's participation in its own export business is limited to manufacture of the exported goods. The manufacturer using a sales agent typically cannot control the marketing and distribution channels in the foreign market. This prevents the manufacturer from gaining value by internalizing the marketing and distribution functions of its export sales. Export sales into foreign countries also must overcome any import quotas and tariffs designed to protect local producers. If there is a chance that the government will manipulate its import quotas and tariffs in response to an increase in competition from abroad, the exporter is also exposed to political risk.

For a successful partnership with the manufacturer, export agents should be equipped in the following ways:[2]

Exporting through a foreign sales agent requires little resource commitment and insulates the exporter from the costs and risks of foreign sales.

_____

2 Robert W. Haigh reviews the performance of export management companies and the characteristics that make for success in "Export Management Strategies," *Columbia Journal of World Business* 29, No. 4, Winter 1994, pages 66–81.

- Technical knowledge of the product
- Country-specific experience and expertise, as well as marketing contacts in the foreign country
- Expertise in shipping, documentation, and trade credit
- Reliability and financial stability (avoid the fly-by-night start-up companies)

These are, of course, the same qualities that make for an effective in-house export department.

Domestic manufacturers without foreign export experience often find domestic export agents to be easier and more comfortable to deal with than foreign export agents. However, one risk of using a sales agent based in the domestic country is that the domestic agent may not be as familiar with the foreign market as a sales agent based in the foreign country. Agents already resident in the foreign market are familiar with the preferences of the market as well as with the peculiarities of the cultural and business environment.

A central point of contention in the relationship between the manufacturer and the sales agent is the termination or cancellation clause in the sales contract. The termination clause is a double-edged sword for both the manufacturer and the sales agent. With a strong termination clause, the producer can exercise more control over the agent, terminate the contract if the contractual performance criteria are not met, or even exit the market. Yet the sales agent must have some assurance of a continuing relation with the producer to fully commit to the sales arrangement. To avoid cross-border legal disputes, the contract must be legally binding in both countries and should identify the jurisdiction in which disputes are to be settled. The producer must consult with legal counsel in both countries to be sure that the contract meets the laws of each country and can be enforced in each country.

The termination clause creates a risk that the sales agent will not be fully committed to the relationship or may look only to short-term rather than long-term sales performance. This is a consequence of the manufacturer's desire to minimize its risk exposure in the foreign market. A further disadvantage of using an agent or distributor is that the local government is more likely to impose import controls and tariffs on a nonresident manufacturer. Offsetting this high political risk is the exporter's low exposure to political risk; the manufacturer has little resource commitment and can exit the market at low cost.

Operating a foreign sales branch allows the exporter to tap the full potential of the foreign market, but it requires experience and a larger resource commitment.

Foreign Sales Branches and Foreign Subsidiaries. As they become more familiar with foreign markets, exporters often decide to take a more active role in the marketing and distribution of their products. This can be accomplished by establishing a foreign sales branch or a foreign subsidiary. Foreign subsidiaries are incorporated in the host country, whereas foreign branches are treated as a part of the parent rather than as a separate legal entity. Because of this difference in legal and tax status, the choice between a foreign sales branch and a foreign sales subsidiary is often driven by tax considerations.[3] Foreign branches are the preferred mode of entry for firms in ser-

---

3 Foreign branches are also less than desirable when the parent firm is exposed to legal liability for the actions of its foreign affiliates. This consideration is especially important in industries that are prone to catastrophic accidents, such as petroleum, chemicals, and nuclear power.

vice industries, such as accounting, financial services, and legal services, as these firms follow their customers into foreign markets. Manufacturing firms, on the other hand, typically incorporate their foreign subsidiaries in the host country.

This mode of entry can offer greater sales potential in the foreign market than the use of a sales agent or distributor. Establishing a sales branch or subsidiary in the foreign market allows exporters to manage the marketing and distribution channels themselves. This can reduce the agency costs involved in hiring a sales agent to represent the manufacturer's interests in the foreign market. Having a branch office in the foreign country allows the manufacturer to be more aware of, and responsive to, changing conditions in the foreign market.

On the other hand, establishing a foreign sales branch/subsidiary comes with bigger risks because of the greater resource commitment on the part of the manufacturer. With an increased commitment to the foreign market, the manufacturer can find itself facing more business and political risk on its export operations. Moreover, if the manufacturer is unfamiliar with the culture of the foreign country or market, establishing a foreign branch can lead to unexpected delays, headaches, and, ultimately, losses. These costs and risks must be weighed against the higher sales potential when considering this mode of foreign market entry.

Contract-Based Market Entry

International Licensing. In an international **license agreement,** a domestic company (the licensor) with intangible assets (patents, trademarks, intellectual property, or technological expertise) allows a foreign company (the licensee) to market the licensor's products in a foreign country in return for royalties, fees, or other forms of compensation. The foreign licensee assumes the responsibility to produce, market, and distribute the good or service in the host country. To protect its reputation in both the domestic and foreign markets, the domestic owner of the trade or brand name uses the licensing agreement to ensure that a standardized product or service is delivered to the foreign market.

Licensing has several advantages for the multinational corporation. International licensing provides rapid and relatively painless entry into foreign markets. The resource commitment of the licensor is small, and typically no direct investment is made. Licensed products and services are produced in the host country, so import quotas or tariffs are not a hindrance. Along with international joint ventures, licensing is used when host governments require that some or all of the product be manufactured in the host country by local firms.

Although host governments often place limitations on the royalties that can be returned to the licensor, cultural and political risk exposures are low in a license agreement. Note that a limitation on royalty payments is not necessarily a political risk. Risk only exists when actual outcomes can deviate from expectations. Consequently, political risk over the royalty stream only exists if there is a chance that the host government will change the rules under which fees and royalties can be repatriated to the licensor.

Other Forms of International Licensing. International licensing agreements come in many varieties. For example, an international **franchise agreement** is a licensing agreement in which a domestic company (the franchisor) licenses its trade name and business system to an independent company (the franchisee) in a foreign market.

Licensing provides quick and relatively low-risk entry into foreign markets so long as the parent can protect its intellectual property rights.

Franchising is found most often in consumer service industries, such as fast foods (McDonald's), hotels (Holiday Inn and Hilton), and car rentals (Avis).

Yet another variation on the licensing theme is a **reciprocal marketing agreement**, in which two companies form a strategic alliance to comarket each other's products in their home markets. Production rights may or may not be transferred, depending on the participants. The reciprocal marketing agreement, like an international license agreement, is a written contract that specifies the rights and obligations of the partners.

Management contracts are a form of licensing agreement in which a company licenses its organizational and management expertise. In a management contract, experienced employees of the parent firm are sent in to organize operations and manage the marketing, production, or distribution processes. From the parent's perspective, management contracts are a way for the parent to maintain some control in situations in which the host government does not allow direct ownership of the foreign venture. From the client's perspective, management contracts are a way for developing countries and companies to acquire organizational and managerial skills that are not available locally.

Market Entry through Investment

Manufacturing firms typically use exports as their initial entry into international markets. Exporting is a low-risk way to acquire additional information about a foreign market. Unless the corporation already has experience exporting to a particular market, investment-based entry should come later in the product life cycle, usually when the product is in the mature stage in the domestic market. That is when the manufacturer begins to look for ways to extend the product life by penetrating new markets, by reducing operating costs, or both.

Entry into foreign markets can be accomplished through three types of foreign investment:

- Foreign direct investment
- Mergers and acquisitions
- Joint ventures

The relative popularity of each entry mode is displayed in Figure 15.3, based on a sample of 438 U.S. firms entering Europe during 1993.

Investment-based foreign market entry modes differ from exporting in that production is shifted to the foreign country, but ownership and control are retained by the parent corporation. Because a large resource commitment must be made in investment-based foreign market entry, great care must be taken before using one of these entry modes. The manufacturer must be far enough down the learning curve (Figure 15.1) to ensure that it can avoid the more obvious international marketing, production, and distribution blunders.

The potential for higher sales and lower costs are the main reasons for investment-based entry into foreign markets.

Producing a manufactured product in a foreign country has several potential advantages. The primary advantage is that foreign production can lead to higher sales in the foreign country and the neighboring region. People are more receptive to goods produced locally than to imported goods. Because local workers are employed in production, the multinational is less of an outsider than pure importers are. Another advantage is that, as a resident of the host country, the manufacturer can respond more quickly and more appropriately to changing market conditions in the host country.

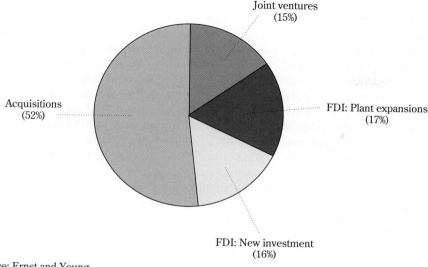

Joint ventures
(15%)

Acquisitions
(52%)

FDI: Plant expansions
(17%)

FDI: New investment
(16%)

Source: Ernst and Young

FIGURE 15.3
Market Entry Methods
Chosen by U.S. Companies
in Europe in 1993

Another motivation for investing in a foreign market can be lower labor or raw materials costs. Developing and newly industrializing countries (NICs) tend to specialize in labor-intensive industries because of their comparative advantage in labor costs. Shifting production to countries with low labor costs can greatly reduce the multinational corporation's operating costs. For example, worldwide production in the textile industry has largely shifted to China, India, Pakistan, and other countries with low labor costs. In the auto industry, as much as 75 percent of the cost of a new auto is in labor expense. A corridor of *maquiladoras* investment along the U.S.-Mexican border would not be there if it weren't for the lower labor costs of Mexican workers.[4]

Local production also avoids quotas and tariffs on imported goods and can reduce the risk of protectionism. Because of pressure from U.S. automakers and the U.S. Congress, Japanese automakers for many years adopted a "voluntary" quota on imported automobiles. This quota was intended to reduce the likelihood of protectionist measures being imposed by Congress. Japanese automakers invested heavily in North American plants, beginning with Honda's Marysville, Ohio, auto assembly plant in 1982. With production capacity in the United States, they were able to circumvent the self-imposed import quota without upsetting local politicians and the general public. By 1997, Japanese automakers are projected to have the capacity to produce 2.5 million autos annually in Kentucky and Tennessee alone. This foreign direct investment has created more than fifty thousand jobs in the region.[5]

4 The maquiladora program allows U.S. businesses to operate manufacturing facilities in northern Mexico on a duty-free basis so long as most of the output is exported to the United States. The program was established in 1966 and officially authorized by the Mexican government in 1983.
5 "The Automobile Industry and the Economic Development of Tennessee and the Southeast: New Investment Has Increased Production Capacity" by D. Mayes and M. Murray, *Survey of Business* 30, No. 1, Winter 1995, pages 41–52.

Although the potentials for higher sales and lower costs are the most compelling reasons for investment-based entry into foreign markets, there are other advantages as well. By having a diversified manufacturing base, the multinational corporation can more easily shift sales to where potential revenues are the highest and shift production to the lowest-cost plants. This may be in response to exchange rate movements, but it may also be in response to other factors. With an industrial base diversified across countries, multinational corporations are able to respond to changes in supply and demand as well as to other events in their product markets. For example, labor unions are seldom organized across borders. If a manufacturing plant in Ireland is threatening to go on strike, a multinational corporation with plants in other parts of the world is in a better position to weather the storm in Ireland than a company with only Irish manufacturing facilities.

A final potential advantage lies not in diversification but in vertical integration. Vertical integration can add value to the company to the extent that operating costs can be saved or revenues enhanced. The multinational corporation gaining market entry through a foreign manufacturing plant is vertically integrating its supply chain from production of the product through the final sale to foreign customers. The multinational corporation using a foreign manufacturing plant because of its cost advantages is integrating its supply chain backward to the source of its raw materials and labor inputs. The multinational corporation seeking the low labor and raw materials costs in the foreign market is integrating the supply chain backward into the factor inputs. Mature multinational corporations have often integrated their supply chains from the factor inputs (labor and raw materials) right through to the final marketing and distribution of their products.

Foreign Direct Investment. Building productive capacity directly in a foreign country is called **foreign direct investment (FDI)**. An advantage of foreign market entry through FDI is that it provides the multinational corporation with a permanent foothold into the foreign market. Export-based and contract-based entry modes are less able to provide this advantage.

Foreign direct investment is evaluated in much the same way as domestic investment. It differs from domestic investment in that it has an additional overlay of exchange rate risk, political risk, and cultural risk. These additional risks may or may not be offset by higher expected revenues or lower operating costs.

Foreign direct investment proposals should be analyzed with great care. Resource commitments on the part of the parent and the consequences of failure for the stakeholders (including managers) are high. FDI entails a substantial investment in capital, management time, and other corporate resources. Because of its importance in the success of the multinational enterprise, the next chapter is devoted to a review of cross-border capital budgeting analysis.

Foreign direct investment requires a large resource commitment on the part of the parent firm.

Cross-Border Mergers and Acquisitions. In foreign direct investment, the parent company *builds* productive capacity in a foreign country. In a **cross-border acquisition**, a domestic parent *acquires* the use of an asset in a foreign country. A company can acquire productive capacity in a foreign country in one of two ways:

- Cross-border acquisition of assets
- Cross-border acquisition of stock

A cross-border **acquisition of assets** is the most straightforward way to acquire productive capacity, because only the asset is acquired. None of the liabilities supporting that asset are transferred to the purchaser. A major consideration in an asset acquisition is the purchase price of the asset being acquired. Buying a manufacturing plant that has already been constructed in a foreign country is often less expensive than building the same plant through foreign direct investment.

In a cross-border **acquisition of stock**, a multinational corporation buys an equity interest in a foreign company. This is easiest to accomplish for publicly traded companies in countries with active equity markets. In these markets the purchaser can either make a friendly offer to management or make a (possibly hostile) offer directly to stockholders through the financial markets. In developing countries without active equity markets, a proposal to purchase stock must often be made to owners through the target firm's managers.

In a **cross-border merger**, two firms pool their assets and liabilities to form a new company. Stockholders trade their shares in the original companies for shares in the new company according to a negotiated exchange ratio. One of the firms is usually the aggressor in merger negotiations. Usually the shareholders of the more reluctant target company gain the most when old shares are exchanged for new shares.

Cross-border mergers are exceedingly difficult to consummate. Not only must a large proportion of stockholders in each company approve the merger (the proportion varies by company and by country), but the merger must also be approved by government agencies with jurisdiction over merger activity in each country. Mergers often have antitrust implications, and government agencies in different countries can have widely divergent views on what is in the public interest. Because of these cultural, legal, and financial impediments, cross-border mergers are less common than other forms of investment-based entry into foreign markets.

Chapter 19 compares the corporate governance systems of Germany, Japan, and the United States and addresses the topic of cross-border stock transactions in more detail.

Cross-Border Joint Ventures. In a **joint venture**, two or more companies pool their resources to execute a well-defined mission. Resource commitments, responsibilities, and earnings are shared according to a predetermined contractual formula. Joint ventures are useful when companies in a single industry or in complementary industries want to share the risk of a large venture, such as the development of a new product or market. A new, jointly owned company is usually created to accomplish the mission.

When embarking on a joint venture, companies in industries such as pharmaceuticals, electronics, and biotechnology must maintain control of their patents, trademarks, and production processes. Along with international licensing, a joint venture with a foreign partner is a relatively unattractive alternative when there is a risk that the foreign partner will behave opportunistically once the deal is struck. When the risk of losing control of the product is high, exporting and foreign direct investment are the preferred forms of market entry, because they maintain ownership and control of the firm's ownership-based advantages.[6]

---

6 John H. Dunning applies the eclectic paradigm to joint ventures and other forms of strategic alliances in "Reappraising the Eclectic Paradigm in an Age of Alliances," *Journal of International Business Studies* 26, No. 3, 1995, pages 461–491.

Section 15.4 discusses ways that the multinational corporation can maintain control of its ownership-based advantages when engaged in joint ventures.

Putting It All Together (Eclectically)

The eclectic paradigm (Chapter 14) states that the optimal mode of entry into a foreign market depends on the particular ownership-specific, location-specific, and internalization advantages available to the multinational corporation. Figure 15.2 maps these characteristics into the foreign market entry modes.

No foreign involvement is preferred when a market has low potential or when investment risks (including political and cultural risks) are high. When market potential is high but investment risks are significant, export entry is often preferred. This is especially true for small firms without international experience. Licensing is useful when a country has investment barriers or when political and cultural risks are high. Licensing may not be appropriate when the financial market (in particular, a licensee in the host country) is not able to properly price the assets of the multinational corporation. In licensing, care must be taken to ensure that a future competitor is not created once the technology or the technological process is transferred to the licensee.

Investment-based entry is most attractive when the firm has experience investing in this or another foreign market. This experience serves to reduce the cultural risk faced by the company. Investment-based entry is especially vulnerable to high political risks, because a substantial resource commitment must be made by the parent corporation. When it costs less to acquire companies in the foreign market than to build the assets, then a foreign acquisition is the preferred route. When the multinational corporation owns production technologies that do not exist in the foreign market, then foreign direct investment may be preferred. A joint venture can prove mutually beneficial when the multinational company believes that it can gain by sharing its competitive advantages with those of a company in the foreign market. As with licensing, care must be taken to ensure that the company's competitive advantages are not inadvertently transferred to the joint venture partner.

Although these general rules hold, the optimal mode of entry depends on the particular ownership and internalization advantages of the multinational corporation and on the advantages residing in the particular location.[7]

15.2 THE EVOLUTION OF THE MULTINATIONAL CORPORATION

A useful perspective on the behaviors and strategies of multinational corporations is provided by the **product cycle theory** of Raymond Vernon.[8] Product cycle theory views the products of the successful firm as evolving through four stages: (1) infancy, (2) growth, (3) maturity, and (4) decline (see Figure 15.4). Vernon observed that new

---

7 See Woodcock, Beamish, and Makino's "Ownership-based Entry Mode Strategies and International Performance," *Journal of International Business Studies* 25, No. 2, 1994, pages 253–273.

8 Raymond Vernon, "International Investment and International Trade in the Product Cycle," *Quarterly Journal of Economics,* May 1966, pages 190–207.

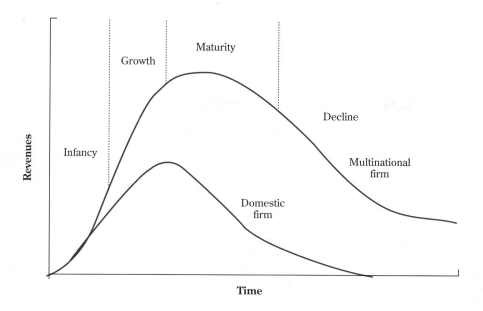

FIGURE 15.4
The Product Life Cycle and
the Multinational Firm

products are generally introduced and seasoned in the domestic market. Cross-border operations arise naturally in the evolution of these products as firms seek new markets or lower-cost factor inputs.

The remainder of this section lists strategies available to the multinational enterprise for exploiting product and factor market imperfections. Although these strategies are categorized according to the life cycle framework, the ways in which ownership-specific advantages are exploited depends on the multinational's advantages in internalizing the product and factor markets as well as the advantages offered by particular locations. Be forewarned that this list is neither exhaustive nor mutually exclusive. It merely illustrates some forms of positive-NPV activities designed to exploit the multinational's competitive advantages.

Infancy and Growth: Discovering Competitive Advantages

Infancy begins with the original conception of the product and extends through the research and development stage and the initial product launch. The corporation's mission in the infancy stage is to create ownership-specific advantages that can be exploited in the domestic and foreign product markets. This is an extremely critical stage in the product's life cycle, because many important marketing and production decisions are made.

The growth stage begins with a successful product launch and extends through market acceptance of the product. As the corporation seeks new markets for its products, it naturally turns to foreign markets in order to tap new sources of demand. To execute this strategy successfully, the multinational needs to provide something that is not being provided by local firms. Sometimes the multinational's advantage springs from a patent, a brand name, a perception of quality, or marketing expertise that is not available locally. In many cases, multinational corporations introduce new products that are costly to produce in the local market. Oligopolistic multinational corporations create competitive advantages for themselves by differentiating their products from their competitors' products in both domestic and foreign markets.

The Mature Stage: Milking the Cash Cow

The mature stage is generally the most profitable, so the corporation attempts to prolong this stage as long as possible. During this stage, the multinational fine-tunes its production and marketing policies in an effort to create value through revenue enhancement, cost minimization, and operating and financial risk reduction.

One of Vernon's most important observations was that multinationals move from domestic to international input and output markets primarily for *defensive* reasons as they seek to preserve their profit margins and extend their product life cycles in both home and export markets. Fear of losing an existing market is a great motivator and can drive a corporation to seek additional revenues through foreign operations. As an example, the late 1980s and early 1990s saw many cross-border partnerships in Europe as firms tried to position themselves for European economic and monetary union. Defensive strategies can be roughly categorized as revenue enhancing, cost minimizing, and financial in nature.

Defensive Strategies to Preserve and Enhance Revenues. Revenue-enhancing strategies can take many forms and can come about for a variety of reasons.

- **Preservation of market share.** When their foreign markets are threatened by local content requirements or import quotas, multinational corporations often respond by building manufacturing capacity directly in the foreign markets.

- **Follow the leader.** When competitors actively acquire foreign assets, a common competitive response is to acquire foreign assets as a hedge against the threat of falling behind in market share or production costs. This bandwagon phenomenon has been observed in many industries, especially those with free cash flow in excess of what is necessary to reinvest in all positive-NPV projects.

- **Follow the customer.** As domestic customers move overseas, service firms, such as banks and accounting firms, often follow their customers. Once the nuances of operating in a foreign location have been mastered, the firm can begin to serve the needs of local clients as well.

- **Lead the customer.** A foreign company attempting to gain access to a local market often seeks the service of a local firm to assist them in their market entry. This lead-the-customer practice occurs frequently in the banking and accounting sectors.

Defensive Strategies to Reduce Operating Costs. Opportunities to reduce operating expenses arise from a variety of sources and include potential savings in both variable and fixed expenses.

- **Low-cost raw materials.** Multinationals seek to gain access to low-cost raw materials, including both natural resources and manufactured factor inputs, to reduce costs and ensure enough supply to meet demand. For example, steel production flourished in Ohio and Pennsylvania in the United States because coal and iron ore occur naturally in this region.

- **Low-cost labor.** Many developing economies can thank low labor costs for their growth. For example, Asia's Little Dragons (including Malaysia, Singapore, Thailand, Laos, and Vietnam) have realized double-digit growth in GNP because of their comparatively low-cost but educated workforces. The threat of low-cost foreign labor is one of the major fears of labor in industrialized countries. For this reason, labor unions are among the most vocal opponents of trade agreements such as NAFTA and the European Union.

- **Economies of scale.** Manufacture of integrated circuits is an excellent example of a product for which there are large **economies of scale**. Manufacture of integrated circuits requires high development costs and large fixed costs of investment. Once a manufacturing plant is set up, variable production costs can be quite low. High start-up costs serve to insulate the corporation from competition.

- **Economies of vertical integration. Economies of vertical integration** utilize the firm's advantages in internalizing a market. Firms integrate vertically when it is costly to arrange the steps of a value-added production process through the external financial markets. Economies of scale also can be achieved by internalizing a stage of the production process that is used in several different products. For example, plastic is an input to a wide variety of consumer goods. A diversified firm with a product line dominated by plastics can internalize this stage of the value-added chain by manufacturing plastics in-house rather than buying this input from external sources.

- **Reduction of operating inefficiencies.** Once a multinational corporation develops a successful product, a great deal of effort is put into minimizing operating expenses. This is especially important when it is difficult for the multinational corporation to protect its ownership-specific advantage through patent protection, technological barriers, or other artificial or natural barriers to entry. The corporation must seek continuous improvement in its production processes in order to extract the maximum value possible out of a particular product.[9]

- **Knowledge seekers.** If knowledge can be acquired at less cost in foreign markets than it can be generated domestically, then firms will attempt to acquire knowledge from the less expensive source. For this reason, U.S. software firms in the biotechnology and computer industries are popular targets of acquirers from other developed countries.

- **Political safety seekers.** If conditions in a corporation's domestic country are highly uncertain, then foreign investment can be a better investment than domestic investment. This is especially prevalent in politically unstable countries and in countries in which currency convertibility is low. As an example, Russian banks often

---

9 A mathematician might observe that *continuous* improvement is unattainable in the real world. Let us say that improvements must be made discretely but very often.

place their dollar-denominated earnings in investments outside of Russia because Russia lacks bankruptcy and commerce laws.

Governments also create positive-NPV opportunities through tariff and nontariff trade barriers, preferential purchasing policies, tax incentives, and capital market controls.

Financial Considerations. Financial markets are not perfect, and a number of financial market imperfections can benefit the multinational firm at each stage of the product life cycle.

- **Financial economies of scale.** Decreased financing costs can arise from the large economies of scale in issuing debt and equity securities.

- **Access to new capital markets.** Decreased financial costs can arise in segmented capital markets if investors in one country are willing to pay a premium for the financial obligations of a foreign firm. Large multinationals may have greater access to international capital markets, resulting in lower costs of capital.

- **New sources of low-cost financing.** Multinationals with internationally diversified financing sources can more easily respond to changes in interest rates, tax rates, and capital controls. In this way, the multinational can gain access to funds at lower rates than local firms.

- **Indirect diversification benefits.** To the extent that international capital markets are segmented, multinational corporations can help their domestic investors diversify into foreign markets by providing indirect diversification benefits through their foreign operations.

- **Lower risk through international asset diversification.** Domestic exporters suffer when their domestic currency appreciates in real terms relative to other currencies. To reduce its exposure to currency risk, many multinationals seek to diversify their manufacturing facilities internationally. Large multinational corporations with geographically diversified product lines can reduce their bankruptcy risk relative to purely domestic firms.

- **Reduced taxes through multinational operations.** Multinational corporations can reduce their tax bill in many ways, including (1) transfer of net operating losses to profitable divisions, (2) utilization of unused debt capacity, (3) reinvestment of surplus funds (free cash flow) in nontaxable acquisitions as an alternative to paying dividends or repurchasing stock, (4) shifting production toward countries with low tax rates, and (5) shifting ownership toward countries with high tax rates and accelerated depreciation.

Decline—or Renewal?

The decline stage of existing products can be extended by selling into new foreign markets, sourcing from lower-cost foreign markets, and refining production processes. However, this is at best a rearguard strategy.

At the root of the multinational corporation's value as a going concern are its core competencies. Core competencies are the things that the corporation does well. To sustain the growth and value of the company, the multinational corporation must be able to leverage its core competencies into new products and technologies. Core competencies derive not from individual products or technologies but from the people and processes that manage them.

The multinational corporation must ensure that it does not engage only in defensive maneuvers. Cost cutting is important, but cost cutting can be copied and creates nothing new of value. Rather, the multinational corporation must plan for the future and renew itself with new products and services in order to achieve its full potential.

15.3 THE MULTINATIONAL CORPORATION'S COMPETITIVE ADVANTAGES

Intellectual Property Rights

At the root of the multinational corporation's competitive advantage over domestic firms are its intellectual property rights. **Intellectual property rights** include

- Patents
- Copyrights
- Trademarks
- Trade secrets

Intellectual property rights include patents, copyrights, trademarks, and trade secrets.

Most governments allow protection of specific intellectual property rights for a fixed length of time to encourage innovation. These protections provide a temporary monopoly to the inventor or creator.

Patents. In the United States, *patents* can be obtained on processes, products, machines, new chemical compounds, improvements on the processes, machines, or compounds, ornamental designs for products, and plants produced by asexual reproduction. In the United States, most patent protection lasts seventeen years; design patents last fourteen years. Patent protection lasts for shorter periods in most other countries. The United States follows a first-to-invent doctrine, whereas many other countries follow a first-to-file doctrine in which patent privileges go to the first individual or corporation to file a patent application. In Japan, patents can be filed on the idea of patentable creation; that is, before a process, machine, or compound is invented and refined. This makes patent law an important competitive weapon in Japan. Most countries grant patent protection to pharmaceuticals used in the treatment of disease, but many countries also regulate this industry and set prices on prescription drugs.

Copyrights. A *copyright* prohibits the unauthorized reproduction of creative works, including books, magazines, drawings, paintings, musical compositions, and sound and video recordings. Copyright protection in the United States lasts for the life of the creator plus an additional fifty years. Computer software is a good example of a creative work for which copyright laws vary greatly from country to country (see box). Although the United States and most other developed countries extend copyright protection to computer software, many developing countries do not.

Trademarks. A *trademark* is a distinctive name, word, symbol, or device used to distinguish a company's goods or services from those of its competitors. Trademark protection varies from country to country. Trademark protection in the United States is for ten-year terms. As it does with patents, the United States follows a first-to-invent policy by granting trademark protection to the first enterprise to commercially establish a trademark in the marketplace. Most other countries follow a first-to-file policy whether or not that individual or corporation has established the trademark in the marketplace. For this reason, multinational corporations can find their trademarks legally copied and used by competitors in foreign markets. If a local company already has trademark protection, the multinational can find itself competing against its own trademark. Registering a trademark in *all* possible future markets is a good idea for the multinational corporation with a distinctive trademark or trade name.

Trade Secrets. *Trade secrets* are ideas, processes, formulas, techniques, devices, or information that a company uses to its competitive advantage. In the United States, protection of trade secrets is extended so long as the owner takes reasonable steps to main-

---

The Modern Pirates of the High Seas

Developed countries, such as the United States, are fighting a fierce cross-border battle with developing countries over intellectual property right protection. The conflict basically comes down to the haves against the have-nots. To a company in the United States, the unauthorized use of another's intellectual property rights is called piracy. In China, pirated versions of software programs, such as Microsoft's Windows 95, are called "patriotic software" because of their ability to speed the country's modernization efforts at low cost. Despite promises by the Chinese government to crack down on copyright infringement, pirated Microsoft software is commonly found on the personal computers of government officials. The U.S. industry group Business Software Alliance estimated that 98 percent of the software sold in China during 1994 was sold illegally, with estimated losses to U.S. software firms of more than $350 million.

Microsoft and other software companies face rampant copyright infringement even in those countries that do extend copyright protection to computer software. Prior to the August 24, 1995, launch date of Windows 95, as many as fifty thousand CD-ROM discs with pirated versions of the software were estimated to be circulating in the Netherlands and Belgium. Industry antipiracy groups estimate that lost revenues in the software industry were more than $15 billion worldwide in 1994. This situation is only expected to get worse as advances in telecommunications and worldwide access to the Internet further expand the opportunities of software pirates.

Compiled from "U.S. Firms: Piracy Thrives in China" by James Cox, *USA Today,* August 23, 1995, page 2; "Microsoft Steps Up War on Pirates" by Louise Kehoe and Ronald van de Krol, *London Financial Times,* August 18, 1995, page 14; and "Software Groups Hail Piracy Win in China" by Louise Kehoe, *London Financial Times,* October 31, 1995, page 1.

tain secrecy. This category includes a wide range of ideas and processes that may or may not be patentable. The decision of whether or not to patent a trade secret is an important decision. Had Coca-Cola patented its formula for Coke, it would have lost its patent protection just prior to World War I. By keeping it a trade secret, Coca-Cola has squeezed an extra seventy years of life out of the formula.

Protecting the Multinational Corporation's Competitive Advantages

The multinational's competitive advantages can be lost in one or more of three ways. First, competitive advantages naturally dissipate as new products and technologies erode the value of old innovations. Managers must continually strive to leverage their core competencies into new products and new markets. Second, intellectual property rights can be stolen by competitors against the will of the multinational corporation. Third, the company's competitive advantages can be transferred, either intentionally or unintentionally, to licensees and joint venture partners. This transfer can come either with or without the knowledge and acquiescence of the multinational corporation. The rest of this section discusses each of these threats to the multinational corporation.

The Secret of Corporate Strategy: Maintaining and Extending Competitive Advantages. Management gurus Gary Hamel and C.K. Prahalad identify two different approaches that people take to corporate strategy.[10] The first approach follows conventional wisdom: "The secret of life is to be happy with what you have." This approach focuses on the problem of maintaining strategic fit. It emphasizes trimming ambitions to match available resources, identifying unsatisfied market niches, allocating resources to profitable products, and ensuring conformity with standard industry practices.

The second approach extends this wisdom: "The secret of life is to be happy with what you have, so get enough!" The emphasis here is in investing in core competencies, not just profitable product lines, to ensure the continued growth and success of the corporation. Rather than just squeezing the most out of current products, cross-functional organizational learning is used to create new core competencies, new competitive advantages, and, eventually, new products. By going outside the lines of the current blueprint for success, the multinational corporation can fully leverage its human and capital resources to create and achieve new goals.

Theft of Intellectual Property Rights. Theft of intellectual property rights is a growing international problem, especially for the multinational corporations of developed countries, such as the United States, Japan, and most of Western Europe. Developing countries are desperate for technologies that will improve their standards of living, and they often pay less attention to intellectual property rights than more developed countries do. The governments of less-developed countries often allow their local companies to acquire "by hook or by crook" any technology they can in fields such as

---

10 Gary Hamel and C. K. Prahalad. "Strategic Intent," *Harvard Business Review* 67, No. 3, 1989, pages 63–76. The "secret of life…" quotes used here are my own and not Hamel and Prahalad's.

pharmaceuticals, electronics, computer software, and publishing. Mechanisms for the protection of intellectual property rights are lax or nonexistent in many of these countries. Licensees sometimes steal technology with the implicit or even explicit cooperation of the host government. Intellectual property rights are vulnerable even in some developed and developing countries, such as Hong Kong, Italy, South Korea, and Taiwan. To make matters worse, patent and trademark rights are conferred by individual nations, so contractual restrictions on where and when the licensee can sell a product may not have force in other countries. When patent protection is suspect, the risk of losing production technology makes cross-border collaboration less attractive.

Sleeping with the Enemy. One way that the multinational corporation can extend the expertise of its people into new areas, new markets, and new technologies is by participating in strategic alliances such as joint ventures and reciprocal marketing agreements. As Prahalad and Hamel observed, "Unlike physical assets, [core] competencies do not deteriorate as they are applied and shared. They grow."[11] However, in the dynamic give-and-take of a strategic alliance lies the multinational corporation's biggest threat—the threat of an ally's looting the company of its competitive advantages and then competing head-to-head with its former partner. How does the multinational corporation allow its core competencies to grow through a strategic alliance without losing its competitive edge? This is the topic of the following section.

15.4 STRATEGIC ALLIANCES

The term **strategic alliance** is used to refer to any collaborative agreement between two companies that is designed to achieve some strategic goal. International licensing agreements, management contracts, and joint ventures are examples of strategic alliances. In industries with heavy research and development requirements, strategic alliances can reduce the cost and risk of product development. Strategic alliances are also used to penetrate foreign markets in which the domestic company has little expertise or experience.

In an international strategic alliance, multinational corporations frequently have love-hate relationships with their foreign partners. The partners offer strategic benefits, but these invariably come with strategic risks. Multinational corporations are most exposed to the potential loss of their competitive advantages in licensing agreements and international joint ventures.[12] In a joint venture, the incentive to act opportunistically and violate the terms of the agreement is great once the foreign partner has acquired the production technology. Armed with the ability to produce the goods itself, the partner can become a competitor in other international markets and even in the parent's domestic market. The multinational corporation using licensing or joint ventures must learn to find the right partner and then structure the deal to their (mutual) advantage.

As mentioned earlier, strategic alliances have been elevated to perhaps their highest form by the Japanese keiretsu system. Non-Japanese firms trying to enter the Japanese

---

11 C. K. Prahalad and Gary Hamel, "The Core Competence of the Corporation," *Harvard Business Review* 68, May–June 1990, pages 79–91.

12 As Shakespeare observed in *Henry IV,* "They sell the pasture now to buy the horse."

market have discovered that keiretsus are awfully hard to penetrate. For example, by 1990 more than one thousand Japanese parts suppliers were operating in the United States, but only one U.S. parts supplier was operating in Japan.[13] These Japanese business practices are coming under increased foreign criticism for their tendency to exclude foreign companies from Japanese markets and to create barriers to foreign investment in Japan.

Finding the Right Partner

The first and most important element in a successful partnership is in choosing the right partner.[14] In a successful partnership, neither party gains at the other party's expense. The partners must share a common goal. This seems like an obvious point, but it is truly the single most important element of any partnership. Once a partnership is formed, it is important for key executives in both companies to participate in the development and management of the partnership. Opportunism on the part of one or both partners is most likely to raise its ugly head when the partners lose the need or the will to work together. The final element is patience in structuring the deal so that the goals of the partnership and the means of obtaining them are clearly spelled out. The more complicated the deal, the more patience is required. Companies that can master these steps can gain access to new products and technologies, extend the life of their existing products, and reap the benefits of an increasingly integrated global village.

The Art of the Deal

In addition to finding the right partner, the multinational corporation can take several actions to limit its exposure to technology loss through international licenses and joint ventures.[15] These include

- Limiting the scope of the technology transfer to include only nonessential parts of the production process
- Limiting the transferability of the technology by contract
- Limiting dependence on any single partner
- Using only assets near the end of their product life cycle
- Using only assets with limited growth options
- Trading one technology for another
- Removing the threat by acquiring the stock or assets of the foreign partner

These remedies limit the ability and/or the willingness of the foreign partner to behave opportunistically and to become a competitor rather than a partner.

---

13 Tim Wise, "Mad as Hell," *World Trade,* June/July 1991, pages 28–32.

14 American author Jean Kerr observed: "Marrying a man is like buying something you've been admiring for a long time in a shop window. You may love it when you get it home, but it doesn't always go with everything else."

15 See "Collaborate with Your Competitors—and Win" by Gary Hamel, Yves L. Doz, and C. K. Prahalad, *Harvard Business Review* 67, January–February 1989, pages 133–139.

15.5 Summary

This chapter describes the advantages and disadvantages of several modes of entry into international markets. Entry modes can be categorized as follows:

- Export-based market entry
  - Agents and distributors
  - Foreign sales branches and foreign subsidiaries
- Contract-based market entry
  - Licensing
  - Franchising
  - Reciprocal marketing agreements
  - Management contracts
- Investment-based market entry
  - Foreign direct investment
  - Mergers and acquisitions (of assets or of stock)
  - Joint ventures

Two important dimensions along which these entry modes differ are in the resource commitment of the parent firm and in the degree of control that the parent firm maintains over its production processes and technologies.

The entry mode with the lowest immediate risk is exporting. This entry mode also requires the smallest resource commitment on the part of the parent firm. Although the resource commitment of contract-based entry is also relatively low, contract-based modes may come with higher risks, if the foreign partner can gain access to the parent firm's intellectual property rights, including its production processes and technologies. As the multinational corporation evolves away from exporting and contract-based entry toward investment-based entry, the firm must make a greater resource commitment and take greater risks in its pursuit of higher expected returns.

One of the most important objectives of the multinational is to renew its product lines and generate new advantages over its local and international competitors. There are four stages in the evolution of the multinational corporation's products: infancy, growth, maturity, and decline. Cross-border operations arise naturally in the evolution of the multinational corporation as the firm attempts to extend the half-life of its products by selling into and sourcing from new markets.

The multinational corporation's competitive advantages are based on its intellectual property rights, which include patents, copyrights, trademarks, and trade secrets. The multinational protects and renews its intellectual property rights through investment in its existing core competencies and development of new core competencies. Strategic alliances are one way to obtain access to new core competencies, but they come with the risk of losing control of existing assets.

Acquisition of assets

Acquisition of stock

Economies of scale

Economies of vertical integration

Export

Export management company

Foreign direct investment (FDI)

Franchise agreement

Intellectual property rights

Joint venture

License agreement

Management contract

Merger

Product cycle theory

Reciprocal marketing agreement

Strategic alliance

CONCEPTUAL QUESTIONS

15.1 Describe three broad modes of entry into international markets. Which of these modes requires the most resource commitment on the part of the MNC? Which has the greatest risks? Which offers the greatest growth potential?

15.2 What are the relative advantages and disadvantages of foreign direct investment, acquisitions/mergers, and joint ventures?

15.3 Describe the evolution of the MNC using product cycle theory.

15.4 Describe several defensive strategies that MNCs use during the mature stage of their products' life cycles.

15.5 How can the MNC protect its competitive advantages in the international marketplace?.

PROBLEMS

15.1 You work in the Corporate Strategy Division of Motorola Corporation. Motorola manufactures mobile communications devices (cellular telephones, pagers, and support equipment) and semiconductors. Your division is considering entry modes into the fast-growing markets of Southeast Asia. Design an entry strategy into Southeast Asia that will eventually lead to direct investment in the region. (One way of answering this question is to examine what Motorola has actually done in the past.)

SUGGESTED READINGS

A seminal work on global corporate strategy is

Gary Hamel and C. K. Prahalad. "Do You Really Have A Global Strategy?" *Harvard Business Review* 63, No. 4, 1985, pages 139–148.

Hamel and Prahalad's articles on corporate strategy are famous for going "outside the lines" and finding creative and insightful ways to add value to the corporation. Other articles of theirs include

Prahalad, C. K. "Strategic Choices in Diversified MNCs," *Harvard Business Review* 54, No. 4, 1976, pages 67–78.

Gary Hamel, Yves L. Doz, and C.K. Prahalad, "Collaborate with Your Competitors—and Win," *Harvard Business Review* 67, No. 1, January–February 1989, pages 133–139.

Gary Hamel and C. K. Prahalad, "Strategic Intent," *Harvard Business Review* 67, No. 3, 1989, pages 63–76.

C. K. Prahalad and Gary Hamel, "The Core Competence of the Corporation," *Harvard Business Review* 68, May–June 1990, pages 79–91.

Gary Hamel and C. K. Prahalad, "Strategy as Stretch and Leverage," *Harvard Business Review* 71, No. 2, 1993, pages 75–84.

Gary Hamel and C. K. Prahalad, "Competing for the Future," *Harvard Business Review* 72, No. 4, 1994, pages 122–128.

C. K. Prahalad, "Corporate Governance or Corporate Value Added? Rethinking the Primacy of Shareholder Value," *Journal of Applied Corporate Finance* 6, No. 4, 1994, pages 40–50.

Articles on entry modes into foreign markets include

Raymond Vernon, "International Investment and International Trade in the Product Cycle," *Quarterly Journal of Economics,* May 1966, pages 190–207.

Robert W. Haigh, "Export Management Strategies," *Columbia Journal of World Business* 29, No. 4, Winter 1994, pages 66–81.

A study of the performance of various investment-based entry modes appears in

C. Patrick Woodcock, Paul W. Beamish, and Shige Makino, "Ownership-Based Entry Mode Strategies and International Performance," *Journal of International Business Studies* 25, No. 2, 1994, pages 253–273.

An Example of Success: Merck & Co., Inc.

Merck, & Co., Inc. is one of the world's largest producers and distributors of prescription pharmaceuticals, with annual sales of more than $10 billion. Sales in this highly competitive industry come from two sources: patented drugs and generic drugs. New drugs require heavy investment in research and development (R&D), but successful products can yield enormous returns on investment. (Imagine the windfall to a pharmaceutical company able to create a cure for HIV.) Patent protection is seventeen years in the United States, but about one-third of this window of opportunity is needed to get Food and Drug Administration (FDA) approval of new products. After a patent expires, other companies can market generic versions of the same drug. Profit margins on generic drugs are much lower, but R&D investment is also much less than on new drugs.

The alternatives for building a portfolio of prescription drugs are the same as the four investment-based foreign market entry modes. In the last two decades, Merck & Co. has used all four entry modes as well as a variety of creative strategic alliances. Here is a chronology of Merck's most important strategic actions.

1970s   Merck *invests* heavily in R&D, spending about 50 percent more on every dollar of sales than its competitors in the prescription pharmaceutical industry. By the 1990s, this investment had produced nearly twenty products with annual sales exceeding $100 million.

1983   Merck *acquires* the rights to market Pepcid in the United States and Europe from Yamanouchi Pharmaceuticals of Japan.

1984   In the first acquisition of a controlling interest in a large Japanese company by a U.S. company, Merck *acquires* a majority stake in Banyu Pharmaceuticals Ltd.

1986   Merck forms a *strategic alliance* with ICI Americas, a U.S. subsidiary of U.K.-based Imperial Chemicals Industries PLC, to comarket drugs for hypertension and diabetes.

1989   Merck establishes a 50-50 *joint venture* with Johnson & Johnson to market Mylanta Natural Fiber Supplement through Johnson & Johnson–Merck Consumer Pharmaceuticals Co.

1989   Merck forms a *strategic alliance* with DuPont in which Merck trades marketing rights on some of its products for the right to develop DuPont's heart medicines.

1989   Merck forms a *strategic alliance* with ICI Americas to comarket Mylanta in exchange for comarketing rights to ICI's antidepressant drug Elavil.

1993   Merck *acquires* Medco Containment Services in a $6.6 billion cash-for-stock offer. Medco is a distributor of prescription drugs with more than $2 billion in 1992 sales. This vertical integration of Merck's R&D and production expertise with Medco's distribution capabilities initiated a wave of similar mergers in the health care field.

1994   Merck enters a 50-50 *joint venture* with the Swedish pharmaceutical firm Astra AB, called Astra Merck Inc., to develop and market prescription medicines that arise from Astra AB's research.

1995   Merck *divests* its Kelco specialty chemicals division to Monsanto for $1.08 billion as it refocuses on its core competencies in the prescription pharmaceuticals businesses.

Through this network of strategic alliances and the fruits of its R&D efforts, Merck enjoyed annual earnings growth higher than 25 percent and profit on sales of more than 20 percent during the 1980s. This string of successes earned Merck the highest score in Fortune magazine's Corporate Reputations Survey for four consecutive years, from 1986 through 1989.[16] Companies that are able to master the intricacies of partnering can reap the benefits of access to new products and technologies without having to develop their entire product line from scratch.

---

16 "America's Most Admired Corporations" by S. Smith and C. Davenport, *Fortune,* January 29, 1990, pages 58–92.

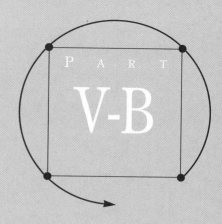

Multinational Corporate Finance

Cross-Border Investment Decisions

There is nothing more difficult to take in hand, more perilous to conduct, or more uncertain in its success, than to take the lead in the introduction of a new order of things.

Niccolò Machiavelli, *The Prince*

The chapters in Part 5B examine the multinational corporation's investment decisions. These investment decisions are the most important decisions made by any corporation, and they determine the firm's growth, prosperity, and longevity.

Chapter 16 presents the classic discounted cash flow framework for evaluating investment projects. Chapter 17 approaches the investment decision as a form of real option and points out some deficiencies in a naive application of the discounted cash flow framework. Chapter 18 discusses taxation of the multinational corporation's foreign-source income. Chapter 19 concludes this section with a discussion of mergers and acquisitions and the international market for corporate control.

16

Cross-Border Capital Budgeting

*Listen up, my Cossack brethren. We'll ride into the valley like the wind,
the thunder of our horses and the lightning of our steel striking fear in the hearts
of our enemies! …And remember—stay out of Mrs. Caldwell's garden.*

Gary Larsen, *The Far Side*

Overview

In principle, capital budgeting for cross-border investments is no different from capital budgeting for domestic investments. From the viewpoint of the parent firm, project value is still equal to the value of expected future cash flows from the investment discounted at an appropriate risk-adjusted discount rate. Projects should be undertaken by the parent firm if and only if the present value of the project cash flows exceeds the value of the initial investment.

Although the fundamental investment principle is the same, in practice many differences make cross-border investment decisions more interesting than their domestic counterparts.[1] Cross-border investment projects usually involve one or more foreign currencies, multiple tax rates and tax systems, and foreign political risk. Cross-border investment projects frequently involve special circumstances, such as capital flow restrictions that block funds in the host country, project-specific subsidies provided by the host government, or project-specific penalties imposed by the host government. To make matters even more complicated, valuing an investment project in the local currency of the host country often provides different values from valuation in the parent's domestic currency because the international parity conditions do not always hold. This chapter shows how to apply the discounted cash flow framework to each of these cross-border investment problems.

---

1 As in the Chinese curse "May your life be interesting," the word "interesting" is used here as a euphemism for "difficult."

To simplify the analysis, the discussions in this chapter assume that the foreign project is financed with 100 percent equity. This avoids the difficult issue of how the financing of a foreign project affects its value. We'll also assume that tax treatments in the foreign and domestic countries are the same. In practice, cross-border differences in taxes can have a huge influence on project valuation. These difficult topics are left to later chapters in order to focus on the fundamentals of cross-border capital budgeting for now.

16.1 THE ALGEBRA OF CROSS-BORDER INVESTMENT ANALYSIS

Discounted Cash Flows

In your first course in finance, you learned to value assets using the **discounted cash flow** (DCF) method. Consider a domestic company evaluating a domestic investment proposal. Project value according to the discounted cash flow method is calculated as follows:

1. Identify the expected future cash flows generated by the investment.
2. Identify the discount rate appropriate for the risk of the cash flows.
3. Discount the expected future cash flows at the risk-adjusted discount rate.

Algebraically, this can be written:

$$\text{NPV}_0^d = \sum_{t=0}^{T} [E[CF_t^d]/(1+i^d)^t] \tag{16.1}$$

where $CF_0^d = E[CF_0^d]/(1+i^d)^0$ is the initial (time t=0) investment. According to the discounted cash flow approach to project valuation, projects should be undertaken if and only if the net present value of the project is greater than zero.

In this approach, expected future cash flows are estimated according to two rules:

• Include only incremental cash flows.

• Include all opportunity costs.

The first rule says to include only incremental cash flows that are associated with the project in the capital budgeting analysis. Sunk costs that have already been spent, for instance, should not be included in the analysis. The second rule says to include all opportunity costs in the capital budgeting analysis. If building a manufacturing plant in Malaysia reduces sales from your Indonesian plant, then the reduction in sales from the Indonesian plant should be incorporated into the decision to invest in Malaysia. Lost sales from the Indonesian plant are an opportunity cost of opening the Malaysian plant.

Note that the discount rate depends on the risk of the cash flows. This is a more general and pervasive rule than you might think. In particular, you should

• Discount cash flows *in a particular currency* at a discount rate *in that currency*.

• Discount *nominal* cash flows at a *nominal* discount rate.

- Discount *real* cash flows at a *real* discount rate.
- Discount *before-tax* cash flows at a *before-tax* discount rate.
- Discount *after-tax* cash flows at an *after-tax* discount rate.
- Discount cash flows to *equity* at an *equity* discount rate.
- Discount cash flows to *debt* at the cost of *debt*.
- Discount cash flows to *both debt and equity* at a discount rate appropriate for *both debt and equity*.

For example, discounting dollar cash flows at a Japanese yen discount rate is inappropriate. Similarly, discounting nominal cash flows at a real discount rate makes no sense. Follow these rules and your valuations will be, if not accurate, at least internally consistent. Violate any one of these rules, and your valuations are guaranteed to miss the mark.

The Domestic Capital Budgeting Recipe

Implicit in the domestic capital budgeting recipe is an assumption that the cash flows and the discount rate are in the investor's functional currency. This is not generally the case for a cross-border investment project. Fortunately, if the international parity conditions hold, discounting foreign currency cash flows at the foreign discount rate is equivalent to discounting domestic currency cash flows at the domestic discount rate.

If the international parity conditions do not hold, all bets are off. For example, if forward exchange rates are biased estimates of future spot rates, so that forward parity does not hold, then the value of a foreign project depends on which currency is used to discount the expected future cash flows. The case in which the international parity conditions hold is much easier to handle, so we'll use this equilibrium condition as a starting point in this chapter. We'll return to deviations from the international parity conditions in a later section of the chapter.

The International Parity Conditions and Cross-Border Capital Budgeting

Suppose capital markets are (1) perfect, so there are no barriers to capital flows between the foreign subsidiary and the parent, and (2) symmetric, so taxes and investor preferences are identical in each country. Suppose further that the international parity conditions hold. In this (admittedly unlikely) setting, the value of a foreign investment is the same whether discounting is done in the foreign or in the domestic currency.

If markets are perfect and purchasing power parity holds, then value in the foreign currency is the same as value in the domestic currency.

This is easy to demonstrate with a little algebra. First, note that expected future cash flows in the domestic currency can be rewritten in terms of the foreign currency by translating at expected future spot exchange rates or, if they are available, at current forward exchange rates:

$$E[CF_t^d] = (E[CF_t^f]) \, E[S_t^{d/f}]$$
$$= E[CF_t^f]F_t^{d/f} \quad\quad (16.2)$$

Similarly, interest rate parity allows to restate nominal interest rates in the domestic currency in terms of nominal interest rates in the foreign currency, the forward exchange rate, and the spot rate.

$$\frac{(1+i^d)^t}{(1+i^f)^t} = \frac{F_t^{d/f}}{S_0^{d/f}} \quad \Leftrightarrow \quad (1+i^d)^t = (1+i^f)^t(F_t^{d/f}/S_0^{d/f}) \tag{16.3}$$

Substituting equations (16.2) and (16.3) into the numerator and denominator of (16.1), the domestic currency value of a foreign project can be restated as:

$$NPV_0^d = \sum_{t=0}^{T}[E[CF_t^d]/(1+i^d)^t] = \sum_{t=0}^{T}[E[CF_t^f]F_t^{d/f}/(1+i^f)^t(F_t^{d/f}/S_0^{d/f})]$$

After moving the spot exchange rate outside the summation and canceling the forward exchange rates in the numerator and denominator, net present value in the domestic currency can be rewritten:

$$NPV_0^d = (S_0^{d/f})\sum_{t=0}^{T}[E[CF_t^f]/(1+i^f)^t] = (S_0^{d/f})[NPV_0^f] \tag{16.4}$$

Both equations (16.1) and (16.4) are valid in that they value the cash flows of the project at an appropriate risk-adjusted discount rate. This suggests two alternative cross-border valuation recipes.

Recipe #1

Discount foreign currency cash flows at the foreign currency discount rate.

Recipe #2

Discount domestic currency cash flows at the domestic currency discount rate.

The details of these two equivalent approaches to project valuation are shown in Figure 16.1.

The good news is that these two methods give identical results when goods markets and financial markets are perfect and symmetric and the international parity conditions hold. The bad news, of course, is that international financial and (especially) goods markets are far from perfect, and, with the exception of interest rate parity, the international parity conditions are relatively poor predictors of financial prices. Before we move on to these more difficult issues, let's set the stage by illustrating these two capital budgeting recipes in a world in which there are no market imperfections and the international parity conditions hold.

16.2 AN EXAMPLE: WENDY'S RESTAURANT IN NEVERLAND

Peter Pan and Wendy are considering opening a restaurant in Neverland ("Turn right at the first star and then straight on 'til morning"). The land is governed by the dreaded

Recipe #1	Recipe #2
$NPV_0^d = S_0^{d/f} \left[\sum_{t=0}^{T} E[CF_t^f]/(1+i^f)^t \right]$	$NPV_0^d = \sum_{t=0}^{T} [E[CF_t^d]/(1+i^d)^t]$
	where $E[CF_t^d] = E[CF_t^f]E[S_t^{d/f}]$
Discounting in the Foreign Currency	*Discounting in the Domestic Currency*

1. Estimate expected future cash flows in the foreign currency.
2. Identify the foreign discount rate.
3. Find NPV in the domestic currency.
  a. Discount the foreign currency cash flows at the foreign currency discount rate.
  b. Convert foreign currency NPV to domestic currency at the spot exchange rate.
	1. Convert expected future foreign currency cash flows to the domestic currency.
	  a. Estimate cash flows in the foreign currency.
	  b. Estimate expected future spot rates of exchange.
	  c. Convert foreign currency cash flows to the domestic currency at predicted exchange rates.
	2. Identify the domestic discount rate.
	3. Find NPV in the domestic currency.
	  a. Discount domestic currency cash flows at the domestic discount rate.

If the international parity conditions hold, then these two NPVs are the same.	

FIGURE 16.1

Cross-Border Capital Budgeting Recipes

pirate Captain Hook—a vindictive tyrant with a consuming jealousy of Peter and Wendy (we'll deal with Hook in the section on "special circumstances").

Wendy's investment proposal is as follows. Wendy will purchase Captain Hook's ship and convert it into a fast-food restaurant with the appetites of the many pirates on the island as the target market. The ship is shipshape and Wendy (with a little help from Peter) can have the galley ready for business on January 1, 1999. Wendy will invest the necessary equity capital. Peter will invest his own human capital and serve as local manager. The workforce will consist of local Lost Boys.

The international parity conditions are known to hold (after all, this is an imaginary land), so equivalent assets have the same real required returns wherever they are traded. The real required return (r_F) on risk-free government bills is 1 percent per year in both U.S. dollars (Wendy's home currency) and Neverland crocs (the local currency). Interest and inflation rates as of December 31, 1998 (time $t = 0$) are as follows:

	U.S.		Neverland	
Nominal risk-free government T-bill rate	$i_F^\$ =$	10%	$i_F^{Cr} =$	37.5%
Real required return on T-bills	$r_F^\$ =$	1%	$r_F^{Cr} =$	1%
Expected inflation over each of the next four years	$p^\$ \approx$	8.91%	$p^{Cr} \approx$	36.14%
Nominal required return on restaurant projects	$i^\$ =$	20%	$i^{Cr} =$	50%
Real required return on restaurant projects	$r^\$ \approx$	10.18%	$r^{Cr} \approx$	10.18%

The 20 percent nominal required return on comparable U.S. investments is composed of expected inflation and a real required return on restaurant projects according to the Fisher equation $i^\$ = (1+p^\$)(1+r^\$) - 1 \Rightarrow (1.0891)(1.1018) - 1 = 0.2000$, or 20 percent. Because the parity conditions hold, the real required return of $r^\$ = 10.18$ percent on restaurant projects in the United States equals the real required return on restaurant projects in Neverland: $r^{Cr} = (1+i^{Cr})/(1+p^{Cr}) - 1 = 1.50/1.3614 - 1 = 0.1018$, or 10.18 percent.

The international Fisher relation ensures that the difference in nominal returns between Neverland and the United States is driven entirely by the difference in inflation between the two countries. Placing the dollar in the denominator of the international Fisher relation, both nominal interest rates and inflation are 25 percent per year higher in Neverland crocs than in U.S. dollars:

$$(1+i^{Cr})/(1+i^\$) \quad = (1+i_F^{Cr})/(1+i_F^\$) = (1+p^{Cr})/(1+p^\$)$$
$$= 1.5000/1.2000 = 1.3750/1.1000 \quad = 1.3614/1.0891$$
$$= 1.25$$

This implies that the forward premium on the dollar and the expected change in the spot exchange rate are also 25 percent per year, so the dollar (in the denominator of the foreign exchange rate) is expected to appreciate by 25 percent per year.

$$E[S_t^{Cr/\$}]/S_0^{Cr/\$} = F_t^{Cr/\$}/S_0^{Cr/\$} = (1.25)^t$$

The current spot rate of exchange between the U.S. dollar and the croc is Cr4.00/\$, so forward prices at the 25 percent annual forward premium are

Time	Date	Forward rate
t=0	12/31/98	Cr4.0000/\$
t=1	12/31/99	Cr5.0000/\$
t=2	12/31/00	Cr6.2500/\$
t=3	12/31/01	Cr7.8125/\$
t=4	12/31/02	Cr9.7656/\$

As a starting point, let's value the Neverland project assuming it is financed with 100 percent equity. This allows us to value the project as a pure investment, without any of the financing side effects caused by debt financing.

The following project-specific information is known about the Neverland proposal:

- The project will last four years, at which time Wendy grows up (only Peter stays young forever).
- An investment of \$10,000 (Cr40,000) on December 31, 1998, will purchase Captain Hook's ship.
- An additional \$6,000 (Cr24,000) will be needed to purchase inventory at that time. Increases in other current asset accounts are offset by increases in current liabilities, so the increase in net working capital (current assets minus current liabilities) is also \$6,000.

- Annual sales are expected to be Cr30,000, Cr60,000, Cr90,000, and Cr60,000 in nominal terms over the next four years.

- Variable operating costs (wages to Lost Boys) are 20 percent of sales.

- Fixed maintenance costs on the ship are Cr2,000 at the end of the first year, and they are expected to increase at the croc rate of inflation thereafter.

- The ship will be owned by the foreign subsidiary and depreciated on a straight-line basis over four years to a zero salvage value.

- The inventory balance will be sold at the end of the project and is expected to be worth Cr24,000 in real terms.

- The ship is expected to retain its Cr40,000 real value.

- Income taxes are 50 percent in both the U.S. and Neverland. Capital gains on the sale of the ship and inventory at the end of the project are also taxed at 50 percent.

- Assume all cash flows occur at the end of the year.

The cash flows of this cross-border business opportunity turn out to be quite simple, yet a multitude of real-world complications lurk within the framework of this simple, imaginary world. In the rest of this section we'll value Wendy's Neverland project in the absence of any real-world complications using equations (16.1) and (16.4) in turn. Section 16.3 analyzes violations in the international parity conditions and discusses the implications for financial management of the multinational firm. In Section 16.4, the dread pirate Captain Hook causes a number of investment and financing nightmares for Wendy and Peter as well as some additional business opportunities. These special circumstances frequently are a part of cross-border investments.

Recipe #1: Discounting in the Foreign Currency

Table 16.1 presents an overview of the Neverland project's cash flows. As in a domestic capital budgeting problem, the task is made simpler if we view the cash flow stream as being composed of three parts: (1) initial investment cash flows, (2) operating cash flows during the life of the project, and (3) terminal or end-of-project cash flows. The investment cash flows include the Cr40,000 cost of the ship and the Cr24,000 investment in net working capital. Cash flows from operations in this example are straightforward and can be computed from either of the equivalent equations:

$$CF = \text{Net income} + \text{Depreciation}$$
$$= [(\text{Revenues} - \text{Expenses} - \text{Depreciation})(1 - T)] + \text{Depreciation}$$

or

$$CF = \text{After-tax operating income} + \text{Depreciation tax shield}$$
$$= [(\text{Revenues} - \text{Expenses})(1 - T)] + [(\text{Depreciation})(T)]$$

Croc operating cash flows from these equations are shown in Table 16.1.

At the end of the project there are two extraordinary items—sale of the ship and sale of inventory. The value of the ship is expected to grow at the croc inflation rate to $(\text{Cr40,000})(1.3614)^4 = \text{Cr137,400}$ in year four. Because the ship is being depreciated to

TABLE 16.1 THE NEVERLAND PROJECT

Discounting in the Foreign Currency (Neverland Crocs)

	Time t=0 12/31/98	Time t=1 12/31/99	Time t=2 12/31/00	Time t=3 12/31/01	Time t=4 12/31/02
Purchase ship	(Cr40,000)				
Purchase inventory (Net working capital)	(24,000)				
Revenues		Cr30,000	Cr60,000	Cr90,000	Cr60,000
−Variable operating costs		(6,000)	(12,000)	(18,000)	(12,000)
−Fixed maintenance cost		(2,000)	(2,723)	(3,707)	(5,046)
−Depreciation		(10,000)	(10,000)	(10,000)	(10,000)
Taxable income		12,000	35,277	58,293	32,954
−Taxes		(6,000)	(17,639)	(29,147)	(16,477)
Net income		6,000	17,639	29,147	16,477
+Depreciation		10,000	10,000	10,000	10,000
Net cash flow from operations		16,000	27,639	39,147	26,477
Sale of ship					137,400 [a]
−Tax on sale of ship					(68,700) [b]
Sale of inventory					82,440 [c]
−Tax on sale of inventory					(29,220) [d]
$E[CF^{Cr}]$	(Cr64,000)	Cr16,000	Cr27,639	Cr39,147	Cr148,397
NPV^{Cr} (at i^{Cr}=50%)	(Cr137)				

Discounting in the Domestic Currency (U.S. Dollars)

Expected spot rates	Cr4.0000/$	Cr5.0000/$	Cr6.2500/$	Cr7.8125/$	Cr9.7656/$
$E[CF^\$]$	($16,000)	$3,200	$4,422	$5,011	$15,196
$NPV^\$$ (at $i^\$$=20%)	($34)				

Numbers are rounded to the nearest croc or dollar depending on the currency of denomination.

[a] $(Cr40,000)(1.3614)^4 = Cr137,400$
[b] $(Cr137,400)(0.5) = Cr68,700$
[c] $(Cr24,000)(1.3614)^4 = Cr82,440$
[d] $(Cr82,440 - Cr24,000)(0.5) = Cr29,220$

zero over the life of the project, the entire Cr137,400 amount is a capital gain. Capital gains taxes are 50 percent in Neverland, so a tax payment of Cr68,700 must be made to Hook's treasury at the end of year four. Inventory is also expected to grow in value at the croc inflation rate, so recovery of net working capital yields $(Cr24,000)(1.3614)^4 = Cr82,440$ after four years. If inventory is still carried at its historical cost of Cr24,000, there will be a taxable gain of $(Cr82,440-Cr24,000) = Cr58,440$ and a capital gains tax of Cr29,220. The resulting stream of nominal cash flows from the Neverland project is

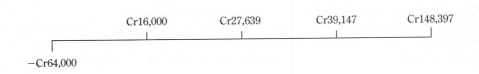

At the croc discount rate of 50 percent on comparable projects, Wendy's investment is worth less than zero; $NPV_0^{Cr} = -Cr137$. This is worth $NPV_0^{\$} = -\$34$ to Wendy at the Cr4/$ spot exchange rate.

Recipe #2: Discounting in the Domestic Currency

To discount domestic currency cash flows at the domestic discount rate, foreign currency cash flows should be converted into the domestic currency at forward exchange rates, if forward rates are available. Expected future croc cash flows after converting at the forward rates are shown at the bottom of Table 16.1. The net present value of the Neverland Project is $-\$34$ whether the cash flows are discounted in the foreign or in the domestic currency.

The NPV from the project perspective and from the parent perspective are equal in this example because the international parity conditions are assumed to hold. Compare this situation to one in which the required croc return on comparable projects in Neverland is 60 percent rather than 50 percent. In that case, NPV depends on whether discounting is done in crocs or in dollars. Tax differences and the size, timing, and form (dividend, interest, management fee) of cash flows back to the parent corporation further distort the picture.

If purchasing power parity holds, then valuation from the project and from the parent perspective are equivalent.

The Neverland example sets the stage, but cross-border business opportunities are never this easy to analyze in practice. Cross-border investment opportunities typically arrive amidst a bewildering array of financial market disequilibriums and imperfections—in addition to the goods market imperfections that form the core of the investment opportunity. The next several sections present a litany of disequilibriums and imperfections that confront cross-border projects. We'll first look at financial market disequilibriums that cause the international parity conditions to be violated. We'll then consider several project-specific circumstances commonly associated with cross-border business opportunities.

16.3 PARENT PERSPECTIVE VERSUS LOCAL PERSPECTIVE ON PROJECT VALUATION

The capital budgeting recipes in equations (16.1) and (16.4) yield consistent values when the international parity conditions hold. They can give conflicting results when the international parity conditions do not hold. Disequilibriums are most evident when there are not active forward exchange markets and Eurocurrency markets for one or both currencies, but persistent deviations from purchasing power parity occur even when interest rate parity is enforced through covered interest arbitrage in the foreign exchange and Eurocurrency markets.

Financial market imperfections affect the analysis as well. For example, if cash flows from the foreign project cannot be freely returned to the parent firm, then either or both of the above recipes may not be obtainable in the real world. The act of remitting cash flows to the parent firm is called **repatriation**, and repatriation restrictions can alter the value of foreign projects from the parent's perspective. If cash flows cannot be freely repatriated, then the equivalence of discounting in either the foreign or the domestic currency may not hold. These special circumstances are covered in section 16.4.

The act of remitting cash flows to the parent is called repatriation.

This section interprets the two cross-border capital budgeting recipes from the parent's perspective (as in equation (16.1)) and from the project's local perspective (as in equation (16.4)). It concludes with some recommendations for the financial manager when disequilibriums in the international parity conditions give different values depending on the perspective taken.

Project Valuation from the Parent's Perspective

The parent's perspective on project valuation is represented in Figure 16.2. The only relevant cash flows from the parent corporation's point of view are those that are to be remitted to the parent in its functional currency. After all, the parent's stakeholders care only about the size, timing, and riskiness of the expected future cash flows that it receives in its functional currency. For this reason, it is important to value foreign investment proposals in the functional currency of the parent and from the perspective of the parent. As a practical matter, this means discounting cash flows at the domestic required return only as they are remitted to the parent in the parent's functional currency. If cash flows from a foreign project can never be remitted to the parent and the parent's claim on these cash flows cannot be sold, then the project has no value to the parent's stakeholders, and there is no incentive to undertake the foreign investment project. From the perspective of the parent, the only relevant cash flows are those that are actually received in its functional currency.

Truly multinational corporations often issue debt and equity claims in several countries, so they have multiple functional currencies. In that case, foreign investments must return cash flows that can be converted into at least one of these functional currencies. As an example, British Petroleum has issued debt and equity securities in the United Kingdom, the United States, and continental Europe. Stakeholders in each of these countries demand a return on investment in their functional currency. If cash flows from foreign investment cannot ultimately be converted into something of value to these stakeholders, then foreign investment has no value.

FIGURE 16.2
The Parent's Perspective
on Project Valuation

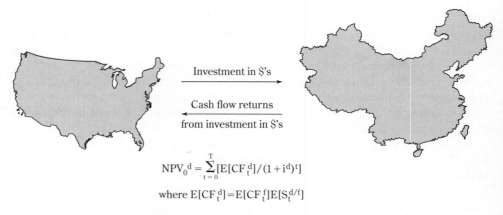

$$NPV_0^d = \sum_{t=0}^{T} [E[CF_t^d]/(1+i^d)^t]$$

where $E[CF_t^d] = E[CF_t^f]E[S_t^{d/f}]$

The parent ultimately requires that cash flows be remitted in its functional currency
(for example, dollars for a U.S. parent corporation).

Project Valuation from the Local Perspective

Initial returns on investment do not necessarily have to be repatriated to the parent in the parent's functional currency. For example, 3M Corporation had a small (several million dollar) investment in Beijing in the People's Republic of China during the early 1990s. 3M Corporation began as a sandpaper company, and its core competency remains applying coverings to backing materials. Its product line includes a wide assortment of products, ranging from photographic film to their ubiquitous Post-it notes. The company does not expect to recover dollar cash flows from its Beijing investment for some time. Rather, by gaining a foothold in this potentially huge market of more than 1 billion people, 3M hopes to earn a rate of return on funds invested in China that is above what can be earned elsewhere on projects of similar risk. If funds earned in China can be reinvested profitably in other Chinese investments, then eventually as repatriation restrictions are eased and the convertibility of the Chinese renminbi improves, these assets will have a large value in dollars. This local perspective on project valuation is shown in Figure 16.3.

Relevant cash flows from the project's local perspective are those that are earned by the project in the functional currency of the host country.

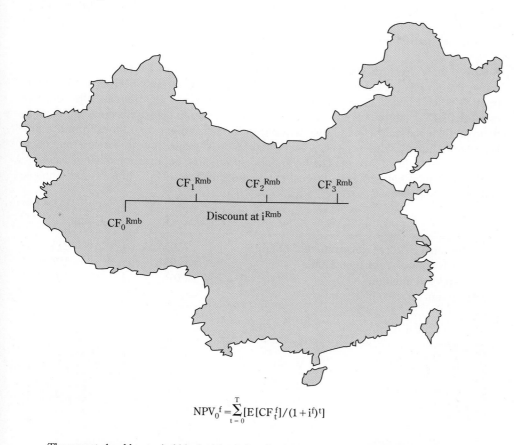

FIGURE 16.3
The Local Perspective on Project Valuation

$$NPV_0^f = \sum_{t=0}^{T} [E[CF_t^f]/(1+i^f)^t]$$

The parent should not mind blocked funds in a foreign country as long as (1) funds can earn their risk-adjusted rate of return in the local currency (for example, Chinese renminbi), and (2) funds can be repatriated to the parent sometime in the future.

How to Handle Valuation Differences

Covered interest arbitrage ensures that interest rate parity holds in the highly liquid interbank markets for foreign exchange and Eurocurrency transactions. Cash flows in these markets are contractual, so any disequilibriums result in an arbitrage opportunity. In contrast to the contractual cash flows of the foreign exchange and Eurocurrency markets, the operating cash flows of the multinational corporation's cross-border investments are both contractual and noncontractual in nature. Because the parity conditions do not in general hold for noncontractual cash flows, in practice there can be a substantial difference between project values calculated with the two cross-border capital budgeting recipes.

Consider the classification scheme in Figure 16.4. If both NPV^d and NPV^f are less than zero, then the project clearly should be rejected. Conversely, if both NPV^d and NPV^f are greater than zero, then the project should be accepted. The more ambiguous situations occur in the off-diagonal cells $NPV^d > 0 > NPV^f$ and $NPV^f > 0 > NPV^d$. The sections that follow provide some guidance on what to do in the "ambiguous" and "accept" situations.

To focus exclusively on disequilibriums in the international parity conditions, these examples assume there are no repatriation restrictions. Special circumstances such as repatriation restrictions are covered in Section 16.4.

Accepting a project for which $NPV^d>0$ and $NPV^f<0$ is tantamount to currency speculation.

Positive NPV for the Parent but Negative NPV for the Project. If $NPV^d > 0 > NPV^f$, the project looks attractive when viewed from the parent's perspective but unattractive when viewed from the project's local perspective. In this case, the positive expected NPV from the parent's perspective may be due to disequilibriums in the international financial markets and owe nothing to the investment cash flows from the project itself. Indeed, the project is expected to lose value in the foreign currency. Accepting this type of project is tantamount to speculating on foreign exchange rates.

Suppose nominal and real interest rates and inflation in U.S. dollars and Chinese renminbi are as follows.

	U.S.	China
Nominal risk-free government T-bill rate	$i_F^{\$} = 10\%$	$i_F^{Rmb} = 21\%$
Real required return on T-bills	$r_F^{\$} = 0\%$	$r_F^{Rmb} = 10\%$
Expected inflation	$E[p^{\$}] = 10\%$	$E[p^{Rmb}] = 10\%$
Current spot exchange rate	$S_0^{\$/Rmb} = \$0.20/Rmb$	

FIGURE 16.4
Valuation Differences
from the Parent and Local
Perspectives

		Parent's perspective in domestic currency d	
		$NPV_0^d < 0$	**$NPV_0^d > 0$**
Project's perspective in the foreign currency	**$NPV_0^f < 0$**	**Reject**	Look for better projects in the foreign currency
	$NPV_0^f > 0$	Lock in the local value in the foreign currency	**Accept**

If there are no barriers to cross-border capital flows, investors will prefer to borrow at the low U.S. real interest rates and lend at the high real renminbi rates. This will eventually force real interest rates back toward equilibrium and is likely to lead to a depreciation of the renminbi and an appreciation of the dollar.

In the short term, this adjustment in real interest rates and exchange rates may or may not occur. Suppose that the spot exchange rate is expected to hold its nominal value; that is, $E[S_1^{\$/Rmb}] = S_0^{\$/Rmb} = \$0.20/Rmb$. According to interest rate parity, renminbi should be selling at a 9.091 percent forward discount to the current spot rate.

$$(F_t^{\$/Rmb}/S_0^{\$/Rmb}) - 1 = [(1+i_F^{\$})/(1+i_F^{Rmb})] - 1 = (1.10/1.21) - 1 = -0.09091$$

Thus, the international parity conditions do not hold. If there is no forward exchange market for renminbi, then arbitrage activity will be unable to enforce interest rate parity. The fact that expected future spot exchange rates are not in equilibrium with the interest rate differential provides a financial opportunity (along with some risk) to multinational corporations active in the Chinese market.

Suppose 3M Corporation has identified a riskless investment in China with the following contractual cash flows:

At the 21 percent Chinese rate of interest, this investment is worth $NPV_0^{Rmb} = (+Rmb605/1.21) - Rmb525 = -Rmb25$. This is less than zero, which means that the investment has a negative value in the local currency. Translating the renminbi cash flows into dollars at the expected future exchange rate of $E[S_1^{\$/Rmb}] = \$.20/Rmb$, the project cash flows from the U.S. parent's perspective are as follows:

Net present value from the U.S. parent's perspective is $NPV_0^{\$} = \$121/1.10 - \$105 = +\$5$. This looks like a positive-NPV project from the U.S. parent's perspective.

Should 3M accept this project? The answer is "No" as long as there are better investment opportunities in the local Chinese market. As an alternative to this investment, consider an investment in a Chinese government bond at the 21 percent riskless renminbi interest rate. This generates the following renminbi cash flows:

This is a zero-NPV investment from the local Chinese perspective. At the expected end-of-period exchange rate of \$.20/Rmb, this riskless investment provides an expected end-of-period cash flow of $(\text{Rmb635.25})(\$.20/\text{Rmb}) = \$127.05$. Expected cash flows to the U.S. parent are then

$$
\begin{array}{l}
\qquad\qquad\qquad \$127.05 \\
\hline
-\$105 \qquad\qquad i_F^\$ = 10\% \qquad\qquad NPV_0^\$ = +\$10.9 \Rightarrow \text{Accept!}
\end{array}
$$

From the perspective of the U.S. parent, this is a 21 percent expected rate of return on the \$105 investment.

Investing in a zero-NPV government bond rather than a negative-NPV investment project avoids the negative NPV of the project and allows 3M to capture the full benefit of the expected real depreciation of the renminbi. If 3M decides to speculate on this capital market disequilibrium, it should speculate directly in the financial markets rather than through its negative-NPV investment project. By borrowing at $i_F^\$ = 10\%$ in the United States and investing an equivalent amount at $i_F^{Rmb} = 21\%$ in China, 3M can place a bet that the dollar will not appreciate by more than 10 percent in the coming year.

If the net present value of a proposed investment is negative when valued in the foreign currency and positive when valued in the domestic currency, the difference in value arises from a disequilibrium in the international parity conditions or from a repatriation restriction and not from the project itself. Under these conditions the parent corporation should continue to look for positive-NPV projects in the foreign currency. If the parent decides to speculate on future exchange rates, there is no reason to use the negative-NPV foreign project as the speculative instrument. A zero-NPV financial transaction allows the corporation to speculate directly and avoid the negative-NPV foreign project.

If $NPV^d < 0$ and $NPV^f > 0$, then the parent firm should try to capture the value of the project in the foreign currency.

Positive NPV for the Project but Negative NPV for the Parent. If $NPV^f > 0 > NPV^d$, the project looks attractive from the local perspective but not from the parent's perspective. In this case, the foreign investment project is worth more in the local economy than it is worth in the parent's domestic currency. The parent firm should try to realize the value of the project in the foreign currency and capture its positive NPV today. This value can then be transferred to the parent at today's exchange rates.

Suppose the following rates hold for U.S. dollars and Chinese renminbi:

	U.S.	China
Nominal risk-free government T-bill rate	$i_F^\$ = 21\%$	$i_F^{Rmb} = 10\%$
Real required return on T-bills	$r_F^\$ = 10\%$	$r_F^{Rmb} = 0\%$
Expected inflation	$E[p^\$] = 10\%$	$E[p^{Rmb}] = 10\%$
Current spot exchange rate	$S_0^{\$/Rmb} = \$0.20/\text{Rmb}$	

As before, suppose the current and expected future spot exchange rate is $E[S_t^{\$/Rmb}] = S_0^{\$/Rmb} = \$.20/\text{Rmb}$. Renminbi should be selling at a 10 percent forward premium to the current spot rate based on interest rate parity.

$$(F_t^{\$/Rmb}/S_0^{\$/Rmb}) - 1 = [(1+i_F^\$)/(1+i_F^{Rmb})] - 1 = (1.21/1.10) - 1 = +0.1000$$

Again, the international markets are not in equilibrium. Note, however, that this disequilibrium is in the opposite direction from the previous example.

3M's expected cash flows are the same as in the previous example.

$$\begin{array}{c} \text{Rmb605} \\ \llcorner\!\!\!\text{———————}\!\!\!\lrcorner \\ -\text{Rmb525} \qquad i_F{}^{Rmb} = 10\% \end{array} \qquad NPV_0{}^{Rmb} = +\text{Rmb } 25 \Rightarrow \text{Accept! (?)}$$

At the 10 percent Chinese interest rate, this investment is worth $NPV_0{}^{Rmb}$ = (+ Rmb605/1.10) − Rmb525 = + Rmb25. From the U.S. parent's perspective, the project cash flows and net present value are

$$\begin{array}{c} \$121 \\ \llcorner\!\!\!\text{———————}\!\!\!\lrcorner \\ -\$105 \qquad i_F{}^{\$} = 21\% \end{array} \qquad NPV_0{}^{\$} = -\$5 \Rightarrow \text{Reject! (?)}$$

This project looks like a winner from the foreign perspective but a loser from the parent's perspective. Should 3M reject this project? Not if it can somehow lock in the value of the project in the foreign currency and then capture this value in its own domestic currency.

Suppose 3M is able to borrow the initial investment from local investors at the relatively low 10 percent renminbi interest rate. Payoff on this loan will be (Rmb525)(1.10) = Rmb577.5. Project cash flows including the local financing are as follows.

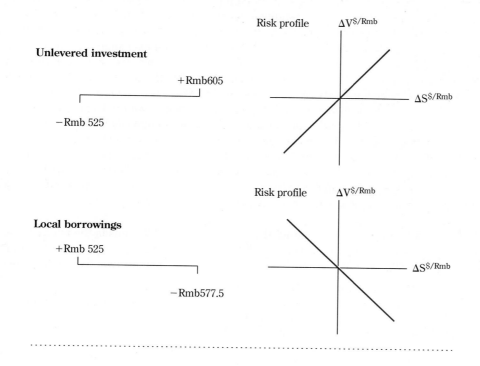

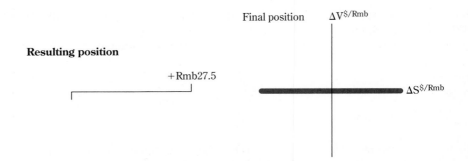

The resulting position has a value of Rmb25 when discounted at the 10 percent renminbi interest rate. This yields a positive net present value in dollars of (Rmb25) ($.20/Rmb) = $5.

If there are no active forward exchange or credit markets in Chinese renminbi, then 3M should try to lock in the positive foreign currency value in some other way. Perhaps the project could be sold to a local investor for whom the project has a positive net present value. By selling the project at its value in the foreign currency (NPV^f > 0), the parent firm could capture this value in its functional currency today. Alternatively, 3M could form a joint venture partnership with a local investor. If the project is attractive in the local currency, a local partner may be willing to form a joint venture partnership on terms that are advantageous to 3M. Each of these alternatives is a way of locking in the positive-NPV value in the local currency while reducing the parent firm's exposure to changes in the spot exchange rate during the life of the project.

In the real world, buying and selling foreign projects to take advantage of disequilibriums in the international parity conditions entails substantial sunk costs that may be difficult to recover.[2] Actively managing the firm's real assets (for example, by selling 3M's Chinese operations and then repurchasing them when exchange rates turn in the other direction) is much more costly than managing currency risk exposure through the financial markets. Active real asset management can also put the multinational corporation's intellectual property rights at risk. For example, if 3M sells its Chinese manufacturing plant to a local investor or shares its knowledge with a local joint venture partner, the local investor may soon become a competitor in other Asian markets.

This section focuses only on the sources and implications of valuation differences between the parent and project perspectives. Keep in mind that financial market disequilibriums are but one of a much broader set of strategic considerations. The benefits of trying to lock in a disequilibrium in the currency markets must be weighed against the costs of forgone real investment opportunities in the foreign markets.

Positive NPV for the Project and the Parent. Disequilibriums in the international parity conditions can result in valuation differences between the project's foreign currency perspective and the parent's domestic currency perspective. When both net

---

2 These strategic considerations are addressed in Chapter 17.

present values are positive, a comparison of the two tells us what to do. When $NPV^d > NPV^f > 0$, the corporation should invest in the foreign project. Depending on the corporate tolerance for currency risk, the corporation may consider leaving its foreign investment unhedged to take advantage of the expected real appreciation of the foreign currency. This is a risky strategy, however, and the corporation and its financial officer must be prepared to accept the consequences of their foreign exchange market speculation.

When $NPV^f > NPV^d > 0$, the corporation should invest in the project. It should then hedge its exposure to currency risk or otherwise try to capture the additional value of the project in the foreign currency. The value of the project in the foreign currency can then be realized today and passed back to the parent in its domestic (functional) currency.

When $NPV^f > NPV^d > 0$, the corporation should hedge its exposure to currency risk.

16.4 SPECIAL CIRCUMSTANCES IN CROSS-BORDER INVESTMENTS

Even if the international parity conditions hold, many country-specific and project-specific peculiarities that are encountered in practice make application of the two recipes difficult. Examples of such peculiarities are blocked funds, the availability of subsidized financing provided by the host government or by an international agency, negative-NPV tie-in projects, and the risk of expropriation.

Special circumstances in project valuation can often be valued separately as financial side effects.

Each of these special circumstances will be treated as a **side effect** of the project and will be valued separately from the project.

$$V_{\text{PROJECT WITH SIDE EFFECT}} = V_{\text{PROJECT WITHOUT SIDE EFFECT}} + V_{\text{SIDE EFFECT}}$$

Identifying a separate value for the project can help decompose the value of a project into its component parts and, hence, identify key value drivers. This in turn can help in negotiating the environment with the host government prior to investment. For example, knowing that a tax holiday is the major source of value in a foreign venture, a multinational corporation can structure the investment so that the parent's exposure to the risk of a change in the tax rules is minimized. This may mean taking profits in the early years of the project before the tax privilege can be revoked. Local debt and equity partners might also be employed, because they are likely to be more effective in lobbying the host government to keep the tax holiday in place. This section uses the Neverland example as a starting point and examines the effect of several special circumstances encountered in cross-border investment.

Blocked Funds

Blocked funds is one example of a repatriation restriction that can cause a discrepancy between the project value from the parent's perspective and from the local perspective. **Blocked funds** are cash flows generated by a foreign project that cannot be

Blocked funds cannot be immediately repatriated to the parent firm.

TABLE 16.2 AN EXAMPLE OF BLOCKED FUNDS IN HOOK'S TREASURE CHEST

	Time t=0 12/31/98	Time t=1 12/31/99	Time t=2 12/31/00	Time t=3 12/31/01	Time t=4 12/31/02
Project cash flows[a] without blocked funds					
Sale of ship					137,400.0
Tax on sale of ship					(68,700.0)
Sale of inventory					82,440.0
Tax on sale of inventory					(29,220.0)
CF from operations	(64,000.0)	16,000.0	27,639.0	39,147.0	26,477.0
CF without blocked funds	(64,000.0)	16,000.0	27,639.0	39,147.0	148,397.0
Incremental cash flows from blocked funds					
Blocked by Captain Hook		(8,000.0)	(13,819.5)	(19,573.5)	0.0
Release of blocked funds					41,393.0
Project cash flows with blocked funds					
	(64,000.0)	8,000.0	13,819.5	19,573.5	189,790.0

[a] All cash flows in Neverland crocs

immediately repatriated to the parent firm because of capital flow restrictions imposed by the host government. The corporation should compare an investment's returns to alternatives available in the local economy. If expected returns on investment are below comparable alternatives in the local economy, then the investment cannot compete with local alternatives. In this case, perhaps a foreign company should be hired to manage the investment locally. If returns are greater than local alternatives, then the multinational may have a reason for investing funds even if they cannot be easily remitted to the parent. Of course, the parent firm ultimately wants to move the funds out of the country and into its functional currency. Parent and project valuations may differ whenever funds cannot be freely converted into the functional currency of the parent.

Blocked funds are a classic form of financial side effect.

Blocked funds are a classic form of financial side effect. The loss in value from this side effect can be calculated in a fairly straightforward manner. Suppose that under current Neverland law 50 percent of foreign investor cash flow must be retained within Neverland until the investment is four years old. Blocked funds must be placed in Captain Hook's treasure chest and do not earn interest. Captain Hook has promised to return any blocked funds on December 31, 2002. Funds not blocked by the good captain can be remitted in the year they are earned. The cash flows of the project are then composed of blocked funds that must be invested in Hook's treasure chest and cash flow that can be repatriated to Wendy and reinvested in an asset of Wendy's choosing. The cash flows from this situation are shown in Table 16.2.

Suppose you are certain of retrieving funds from Hook's treasure chest. In that case, the appropriate discount rate on an "investment" in Hook's treasure chest is the $i_F^{Cr} = 37.5$ percent riskless rate of interest in crocs.

A Three-Step Procedure for Valuing Blocked Funds. Calculating the value of blocked funds requires a three-step procedure.

Step 1: Calculate the value of blocked funds assuming they are not blocked.

Funds are blocked in Neverland in the first three years of the project (1999 through 2001). Funds may be freely remitted to Wendy at the end of the project in year 2002. If blocked funds had been invested at the riskless croc discount rate of 37.5 percent per year, they would have grown in value to $(Cr8,000)(1.375)^3 + (Cr13,819.5)(1.375)^2 + (Cr19,573.5)(1.375)^1 = Cr73,838$. Discounted back to time zero (December 31, 1998) at the 37.5 percent riskless croc discount rate, this would have been worth Cr20,657 in present value.

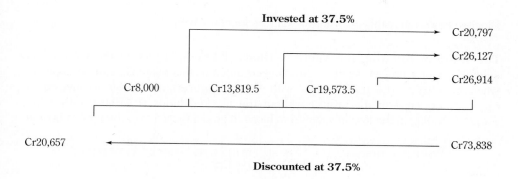

Step 2: Calculate the opportunity cost of blocked funds.

An investment in Hook's treasure chest is assumed to be riskless, so the required return on blocked funds is the riskless croc interest rate. However, the actual return is 0 percent, because payments into Hook's treasure chest earn no interest. With blocked funds, the accumulated balance as of time 4 is only $(Cr8,000 + Cr13,819.5 + Cr19,573.5) = +Cr41,393$. This has a present value of Cr11,580 at the riskless croc interest rate of 37.5 percent.

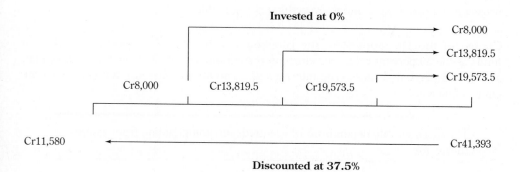

This is a negative-NPV investment. The opportunity cost of earning zero interest on the blocked funds is $Cr20,657 - Cr11,580 = Cr9,077$ at the 37.5 percent croc discount rate.

Step 3: Calculate the value of the project including the opportunity cost of blocked funds.

As calculated in the original Neverland example, the Neverland project is worth −Cr137 in the absence of blocked funds. The value (in this case, an opportunity cost) of the blocked funds is −Cr9,077. The value of the project with the blocked funds is then

$$V_{\text{PROJECT WITH SIDE EFFECT}} = V_{\text{PROJECT WITHOUT SIDE EFFECT}} + V_{\text{SIDE EFFECT}}$$
$$= -\text{Cr}137 - \text{Cr}9{,}077$$
$$= -\text{Cr}9{,}214$$

Blocked funds make this an even worse investment for Wendy.

Project side effects are often nego-tiated with the host government.

The Value of Knowing the Value of Blocked Funds. Knowing the value of any side effects of a project, such as the blocked funds in this example, can be important when negotiating the environment with the host government prior to investment. Suppose the value of the project without the blocked funds is Cr6,000 rather than −Cr137. Adding in the loss in value from blocked funds, the value of the project is then

$$V_{\text{PROJECT WITH SIDE EFFECT}} = V_{\text{PROJECT WITHOUT SIDE EFFECT}} + V_{\text{SIDE EFFECT}}$$
$$= +\text{Cr}6{,}000 - \text{Cr}9{,}077$$
$$= -\text{Cr}3{,}077$$

Rather than giving up on this negative-NPV project, Wendy should continue to negotiate with Captain Hook and try to structure the deal with the host government so that both parties can benefit. This is still a positive-NPV project for Wendy so long as the loss in value from blocked funds is less than Cr6,000. Knowing the value of the project without the blocked funds establishes Wendy's **reservation price**—the price below which she is unwilling to go. Separating the value of the project without the side effect from the value of the side effect will prove useful to Wendy in her negotiations with Captain Hook. In this example, Wendy may be able to exert some local political pressure on Captain Hook, because employment among Neverland's Lost Boys will increase if this project is approved. Remember, everything is negotiable.

Choice of the Discount Rate for Blocked Funds. Why not discount the blocked funds at the 50 percent required return on restaurant projects in Neverland rather than at the 37.5 percent riskless croc interest rate? The answer lies in a fundamental principle of finance:

The discount rate depends on where funds are going, not on from where they came.

The value of the project without the blocked funds reflects the 50 percent required return on restaurant projects in Neverland. Once cash flows from the restaurant project are earned, however, the appropriate discount rate on the next use of the funds depends on where they are invested. Cash flows generated by the Neverland project are **free**

cash flows in the sense that, in the absence of capital flow restrictions, these cash flows could be invested anywhere and not necessarily in the Neverland project. Because investments in Captain Hook's treasure chest are assumed to be riskless, the 37.5 percent riskless croc rate should be used to value the blocked funds. If blocked funds had been invested in another restaurant project in Neverland, then the appropriate discount rate would be the 50 percent required return on risky Neverland restaurant projects.

Subsidized Financing

The governments of emerging economies are sometimes willing to provide loans at below-market or subsidized rates in order to stimulate foreign direct investment in key strategic industries within the country. International agencies charged with promoting cross-border trade also occasionally offer financing at below-market rates. As a domestic U.S. parallel, the municipal bond (or "muni") market was born in the United States when the U.S. government allowed tax-free status for municipal debt in order to stimulate investment at the local level.

Subsidized financing is the mirror image of blocked funds that earn below-market rates of return. In the case of subsidized financing, the multinational pays rather than receives the below-market rate. As an example, suppose that as an investment incentive Captain Hook will provide Wendy with a Cr40,000 nonamortizing loan at a rate of 37.5 percent in Neverland crocs, even though corporate debt yields 40 percent in crocs. Interest payments on Cr40,000 at the 40 percent market rate would have been (Cr40,000)(0.40) = Cr16,000 per year. Hook only requires interest payments of (Cr40,000)(0.375) = Cr15,000 on the subsidized debt. This is a savings of Cr1,000 per year, or (Cr1,000)(1−0.5) = Cr500 in after-tax annual interest savings. Discounted at the 40% (1−T_C) = 20% *after-tax market cost of debt,* this interest subsidy has a value of Cr1,294. This value is a net gain to Wendy and a net loss to Hook and the taxpayers of Neverland.

An important question for Wendy to ask is whether this interest subsidy is separable from the Neverland project. In this example, Hook is likely to require that Wendy invest in the project in order to obtain the subsidized loan. When the subsidized financing is inseparable from the project, the value of the subsidized loan can be added to that of the project in making the investment decision. When subsidized financing is separable from the project, the additional value from the subsidized financing should not be allocated to the project. In this case, the manager's decision rule is simple: Take the subsidized loan (so long as there are no other strings attached, such as repatriation restrictions) and allow the subsidized debt to displace debt elsewhere in the firm. If the firm is optimally financed with 100 percent equity, so there is no other debt to displace, then the cost of the subsidized financing should be compared to the expected return on an investment of comparable risk. If the firm can invest the funds from the subsidized loan at a higher rate in a comparable-risk investment, then borrowing at the subsidized rate and investing at a higher market rate is a positive-NPV strategy.

Negative-NPV Tie-in Projects

Developing countries often require that foreign companies take on additional negative-NPV development or infrastructure projects in order to gain access to positive-NPV investments elsewhere in the economy. By tying approval of a project with a large positive NPV to an otherwise unattractive investment in the local economy, these governments hope to capture at least some of the gain on the attractive project for their residents. In this case, the value of the **negative-NPV tie-in project** should be subtracted from project value when making the investment decision.

Expropriation Risk

A multinational faces **expropriation risk** if there is a chance that the host government will seize the local assets of the firm. Expropriation risk is a country-specific political risk that, at least in theory, can be diversified away in a large portfolio. For this reason, finance theory suggests that the appropriate procedure in a discounted cash flow analysis is to adjust the cash flows rather than the discount rate.

Suppose Wendy estimates that there is a 50 percent chance that Captain Hook will seize all assets at the end of the fourth year. If this should happen, Wendy will have received repatriated dividends and interest through year three and will receive nothing thereafter. What is Wendy's expected net present value? The expected loss from the time $t = 4$ cash flow is

$$E[\text{loss from expropriation}] = (\text{Probability of loss})(\text{value of loss incurred})$$

The present value of this expected loss from expropriation can be calculated by discounting either in crocs or in dollars.

Alternative #1: Discounting in crocs

$$PV(E[\text{loss from expropriation}])$$
$$= (\text{probability of loss}) \ [E[CF_4^{Cr}]/(1+i^{Cr})^4]/(S_0^{Cr/\$})$$
$$= (\tfrac{1}{2}) \ [Cr148,397/(1.50)^4]/(Cr4.00/\$)$$
$$= \$3,664 \text{ at the } Cr4.00/\$ \text{ spot exchange rate}$$

Alternative #2: Discounting in dollars

$$PV(E[\text{loss from expropriation}])$$
$$= [(\text{probability of loss}) \ [E[CF_4^{Cr}]/E[S_4^{\$/Cr}]]/(1+i^{\$})^4$$
$$= (\tfrac{1}{2}) \ [Cr148,397/(Cr9.7656/\$)]/(1.20)^4$$
$$= \$3,664 \text{ at the } 10\% \text{ U.S. discount rate}$$

This financial side effect reduces the value of the Neverland project by $3,664.

The risk of expropriation is just one of many political risks. **Political risk** is the possibility that political events in a host country or political relationships between a host country and a parent country will adversely affect the value of assets in the host country. The risk of expropriation is an extreme case.

Does political risk affect the discount rate? It depends on your point of view. From the stakeholders' point of view, the answer depends on whether the political risk is diversifiable. In asset pricing theory, nondiversifiable risks are priced in the market and diversifiable risks are not priced. Thus, only nondiversifiable risks appear in the discount rate. Diversifiable risks should be included only in expected future cash flows and not in required returns. Because this expropriation risk is diversifiable in a large portfolio, it should affect only the expected cash flows from the Neverland project and not the required return.

From another point of view—the undiversified perspective of the project manager—political risk is certainly *not* diversifiable. Because of this agency conflict between shareholders and their managerial representatives, managers make decisions that may not be in the best interests of shareholders. The costs of getting managers to act in the best interests of shareholders are called *agency costs*.

Tax Holidays

Developing countries are often willing to offer tax holidays to promote foreign direct investment in their economies. A **tax holiday** usually comes in the form of a reduced tax rate for a period of time on corporate income from a project. As with other forms of subsidy, the project should be valued both with and without the reduced tax rate.

Host countries sometimes provide tax holidays as an inducement to investment.

$$V_{\text{PROJECT WITH TAX HOLIDAY}} = V_{\text{PROJECT WITHOUT TAX HOLIDAY}} + V_{\text{TAX HOLIDAY}}$$

Tax holidays are negotiable, and knowing how much the tax holiday is worth is valuable when the corporation negotiates the environment of the project with the host government.

For long-term projects that take a while before they begin to return positive cash flow, a tax holiday in the project's early years is not worth much. Indeed, if taxable income is expected to be negative for several years and losses can be carried forward, a tax holiday actually robs the firm of a valuable tax-loss carryforward. The firm would prefer to be subjected to a high tax rate during the early loss-making (and tax-credit-creating) years of a project. Calculating project value both with and without the tax holiday will help you to uncover situations such as this.

16.5 TAXES AND REMITTANCE OF CASH FLOWS TO THE PARENT FIRM

The U.S. government allows a foreign tax credit up to the amount of the taxes paid to a foreign government. Most other governments follow this convention as well. Suppose that two U.S. firms own foreign subsidiaries in Switzerland (corporate income tax rate 10 percent) and in Germany (56 percent), respectively. If each foreign subsidiary pays a dividend of $100 to its U.S. parents, the parents' U.S. income tax liabilities are as follows.

	Swiss Subsidiary	German Subsidiary
Remitted dividends ($U.S.)	$100	$100
Foreign income tax withheld	10	56
Net amount received	90	44
Included in U.S. income	100	100
U.S. income tax	35	35
Less foreign tax credit	10	35
Net U.S. tax payable	25	0
Total taxes paid	35	56

The net effect is that the total tax bill is based on the higher of the foreign and the domestic tax rates. Identifying the best way to remit capital back to the parent firm is an important decision in cross-border investment decisions. This decision is often determined by tax considerations.

The above example is intended only as a primer on international taxation. The example ignores a number of important tax considerations, including the effects of dividend withholding taxes, tax-loss carryforwards and carrybacks, income consolidation, and foreign tax credit limitations. An in-depth discussion of multinational taxation and tax strategy appears in Chapter 18.

16.6 SUMMARY

The presentation in this chapter simplified several aspects of cross-border investment and financial analysis. In particular, the chapter developed a discounted cash flow approach to cross-border capital budgeting. In this framework, we know that

- If the international parity conditions hold, discounting foreign currency cash flows at the foreign discount rate is equivalent to discounting domestic currency cash flows at the domestic discount rate.

- If the international parity conditions do not hold, then value depends on your perspective. The multinational firm can sometimes take advantage of market disequilibriums to enhance the value of its foreign investments.

- The discounted cash flow framework can handle many special circumstances commonly found in cross-border investment analysis. These include blocked funds, subsidized financing, negative-NPV tie-in projects, expropriation risk, and tax holidays.

The presentation in this chapter has neglected several important aspects of cross-border investment and financial management. In particular,

- The discounted cash flow framework developed in this chapter does not deal well with dynamic issues such as managerial flexibility in expanding or contracting a project.

- The impact of taxes on cross-border capital budgeting was only superficially covered.

- This chapter did not discuss the international market for corporate control. This market can be used (with varying difficulty, depending on the country) to acquire the stock or assets of companies in other countries and provides an alternative to foreign direct investment.

- This chapter did not deal with the impact of capital structure on the cost of capital and project value.

Each of these issues is addressed in the chapters that follow.

Blocked funds

Discounted cash flow

Expropriation risk

Free cash flow

Negative-NPV tie-in projects

Political risk

Repatriation

Reservation price

Side effect

Subsidized financing

Tax holiday

CONCEPTUAL QUESTIONS

16.1 Describe the two recipes for discounting foreign currency cash flows. Under what conditions are these recipes equivalent?

16.2 Discuss each cell in Figure 16.4. What should (or shouldn't) a firm do when faced with a foreign project that fits the description in each cell?

16.3 Why is it important to separately identify the value of any side effects that accompany foreign investment projects?

PROBLEMS

16.1 The following project-specific information is known about investment in a beer brewery in the small Central European country of Euro.

- The project will last two years. Operating cash flows are received at year-end.
- The inflation rate in Euro is 10 percent per year.
- All cash flows share the same nominal discount rate of 20% per year.
- An investment of Euro100,000 will purchase the land for the brewery. The land is to be sold after two years. The real value of the land is expected to remain constant at Euro100,000.
- Constructing the brewery will cost Euro50,000, payable at the start of the project. The brewery will be owned by the foreign subsidiary and depreciated on a straight-line basis over two years to a zero salvage value. The brewery is expected to be sold for its market value of Euro25,000 after two years.
- An investment in working capital of Euro50,000 is necessary. No additional investment in working capital is necessary, but the value of this investment is expected to grow at the rate of inflation.
- Annual sales are expected to be 5,000 barrels/year.
- Beer currently sells for Euro100 per barrel. The price of beer is expected to rise at the Euro rate of inflation.
- Variable operating costs are 20 percent of sales.
- Fixed operating costs are currently Euro20,000 per year and are expected to rise at the rate of inflation.
- Income and capital gain taxes are 40 percent in Euro.

a. Identify the expected future Euro cash flows of this project and value them at the appropriate Euro discount rate.

b. Suppose the current spot exchange rate is $S_0^{\$/Euro} = \$10/Euro$. The nominal discount rate on brewery projects in the United States is also 20 percent. Assuming the international parity conditions hold, calculate the dollar value of the brewery project using the capital budgeting recipe in equation (16.1). Value the project again using equation (16.4). Are these values the same?

16.2 You currently live in The-Land-of-Leisure (currency is the leisure-unit L), and you are considering investment in a diploma-printing shop in a foreign country called The-Land-of-Work (currency is the work-unit W). Financial markets are perfect and the international parity conditions hold in these two countries. The printshop investment will be financed with 100 percent equity. Interest and inflation rates are as follows.

	Leisure	Work
Nominal risk-free government T-bill rate	$i_F^L = 0\%$	$i_F^W = 50\%$
Real required return on T-bills	$r_F^L = 0\%$	$r_F^W = 0\%$
Expected future inflation	$p^L = 0\%$	$p^W = 50\%$
Real required return on printshop projects	$r^L = 10\%$	$r^W = 10\%$

The current spot exchange rate is W100/L and the following information is known.

- The project will last two years.
- An investment of W200,000 will purchase the land for the printshop. The real value of the land will remain constant throughout the life of the project. The land will be sold at the end of the project.
- Constructing the shop and purchasing the printing press will cost W200,000, payable at the start of the project. The shop and printing press will be owned by the foreign subsidiary and depreciated on a straight-line basis over two years to a zero salvage value. The shop and printing press are expected to have zero market value at the end of two years.
- Just-in-time inventory control will be used. No investment in working capital is necessary.
- Diplomas sell for W200 each in The-Land-of-Work. The price of a diploma is expected to remain constant in real terms. Annual sales are expected to be 2,000 diplomas per year in each of the next two years.
- Variable operating costs are 20 percent of sales.
- Fixed operating costs will be W45,000 in the first year, and they are expected to grow at the rate of inflation thereafter.
- Income and capital gain taxes are 50 percent in each country.
- Assume all operating cash flows occur at the end of the year.

a. What is the nominal required return on printshop projects in L? in W?
b. Identify expected future exchange rates $E[S_t^{W/L}]$ for each of the next two years.
c. Identify expected future cash flows CF_t^W on this foreign investment project. Discount these cash flows at the work-unit discount rate from part a to find NPV^W.
d. Translate the work-unit cash flows to leisure-units at the expected future spot rates from part b. Discount these cash flows at the leisure-unit discount rate from part a to find NPV^L. Is the answer the same as in part c? Why?

16.3 Consider the following investment:

$$+\text{DM200} \qquad +\text{DM500} \qquad +\text{DM300}$$

|_____|_____|_____|

$$\text{1 yr} \qquad\qquad \text{2 yrs} \qquad\qquad \text{3 yrs}$$

$-\text{DM600}$

The required rate of return on projects of similar risk in the U.S. is $i^{\$}$ = 15% and in Germany is i^{DM} = 11.75%. Inflation in the U.S. is expected to be $p^{\$}$ = 6% for the next several years. German inflation is expected to be p^{DM} = 3%. The current spot exchange rate between dollars and deutsche marks is $S_0^{\$/\text{DM}}$ = $0.5526/DM.

a. Assume the international parity conditions hold. Calculate $\text{NPV}^{\$}$ by converting deutsche marks to dollars at expected future spot rates and discounting in dollars. Then calculate $\text{NPV}^{\$}$ by discounting in marks and then converting into dollars at the current spot rate.

b. Suppose there is a 10 percent chance in each year that the government will seize your assets in Germany and that you will lose your investment. You expect your assets to return the original cash flows if your assets are not seized. What is the NPV of the project in dollars, assuming the international parity conditions hold?

c. Suppose the international parity conditions do not hold. Assume a DM discount rate of 11.75 percent. Expected future spot rates are as follows.

Time	0	1	2	3
$E[S_t^{\$/\text{DM}}]$	\$.5526/DM	\$.5801/DM	\$.6089/DM	\$.6392/DM

Using a DM discount rate of 11.75 percent and a dollar discount rate of 15 percent, calculate NPV using Recipes #1 and #2 from the chapter. Should you invest in the project? How do you respond to this market disequilibrium?

d. Repeat part c using the following expected future spot rates:

Time	0	1	2	3
$E[S_t^{\$/\text{DM}}]$	\$.5526/DM	\$.5575/DM	\$.5625/DM	\$.5676/DM

Should you invest in the project? How do you respond to this market disequilibrium?

16.4 Consider the example of blocked funds from the Neverland example in the chapter. As in the example, blocked funds (50 percent of operating cash flow) earn zero interest in Hook's treasure chest. Suppose an investment in Hook's treasure chest is not riskless and that the required return on Neverland bonds issued from the treasury is 40 percent. What is the opportunity cost of the blocked funds? What is the value of the project with the blocked funds?

Country-Specific Political Risk and the Cost of Capital (Advanced)[3]

Political risk affects the value of a foreign project through changes in expected future cash flows from the project. The treatment of expropriation risk in Chapter 16 explicitly recognizes this consequence of political risk. In many situations political risks are country-specific and, hence, diversifiable in a large portfolio. In these circumstances, the required return charged by investors remains unaffected by political risk despite higher total variability of return on foreign investment projects.

The idea that country-specific political risk is diversifiable, and thus should not increase the required return on investment, is difficult for many students and business practitioners to accept. This appendix uses the capital asset pricing model to demonstrate the diversifiability of country-specific political risk.

Country-Specific Political Risk in a One-Period CAPM World

Assume the perfect market conditions hold in a one-period world. Let $R_M \sim N(\mu_M, \sigma_M^2)$ represent the return on the world market portfolio and $R_A \sim N(\mu_A, \sigma_A^2)$ the return on investment in asset A in the absence of political risk. The covariance between R_A and R_M is denoted σ_{AM}. The systematic risk of asset A is measured by $\beta_A = \sigma_{AM}/\sigma_M^2$.

Suppose returns to asset A are subject to country-specific political risk of the following form:

$$R_B = R_A + I\,R_P \tag{16A.1}$$

where R_B includes returns to asset A and the influence of country-specific political risk R_P. The indicator variable $I = (0,1)$ takes a value of $I=0$ if political risk does not influence return and $I=1$ if political risk does influence return. The probability of political risk influencing return during the period is $E[I] = p$. If political risk affects returns ($I=1$),

---

3 Domingo Joaquin of Michigan State University contributed to this appendix.

then there is a return consequence $R_P \sim N(\mu_P, \sigma_P^2)$. The probability and the consequences of country-specific political risk are assumed to be jointly independent as well as independent of other elements of return, so that $\sigma_{AP} = \sigma_{PM} = \sigma_{IA} = \sigma_{IP} = \sigma_{IM} = 0$. Several properties of this structure are useful in the proofs that follow. First, note that $I^2 = I$, because I is either zero or one during the period. Also note that $E[R_A^2] = (\sigma_A^2 + \sigma_A^2)$ and $E[R_A R_P] = (\sigma_{AP} + \mu_A \mu_P)$.

In the general case, the expected impact of political risk $E[R_P] = \mu_P$ can be either positive, negative, or zero. Political risk is often presumed to detract from asset returns, that is $\mu_P < 0$. This is a realistic setting for the multinational corporation exposed to foreign political risk because the multinational is less likely to be helped by political events in foreign countries. To the extent that domestic firms are protected from foreign competition by their own governments, the impact of domestic political risk on domestic companies may be positive, such that $\mu_P > 0$. The general formulation in equation (16A.1) does not constrain the mean impact of political risk to be negative.

The expected return and variance of return in the presence of political risk are given by

$$E[R_B] = \mu_B = \mu_A + p\mu_P \tag{16A.2}$$

and

$$
\begin{aligned}
\text{Var}(R_B) = \sigma_B^2 &= E[R_B^2] - E[R_B]^2 \\
&= E[(R_A + I\,R_P)^2] - E[(R_A + IR_P)]^2 \\
&= E[R_A^2] + E[2\,I\,R_A R_P] + E[I^2\,R_P^2] - (E[R_A] + E[I\,R_P])^2 \\
&= (\sigma_A^2 + \mu_A^2) + 2p(\sigma_{AP} + \mu_A \mu_P) + p(\sigma_P^2 + \mu_P^2) - \mu_A^2 - 2p\mu_A\mu_P - p^2\mu_P^2 \\
&= \sigma_A^2 + p\sigma_P^2 + p(1-p)\mu_P^2 > \sigma_A^2 \tag{16A.3}
\end{aligned}
$$

for $\sigma_{AP} = 0$. Project-specific return variance with political risk is at least as great as project-specific variance without political risk, $\sigma_B^2 > \sigma_A^2$, because each of the terms $p\sigma_P^2$ and $p(1-p)\mu_P^2$ is nonnegative.

The covariance of return with the market portfolio when country-specific political risk is included is given by:

$$
\begin{aligned}
\sigma_{BM} &= E[(R_B - \mu_B)(R_M - \mu_M)] \\
&= E[R_B R_M] - 2\mu_B \mu_M + \mu_B \mu_M \\
&= E[(R_A + I\,R_P)R_M] - \mu_B \mu_M \\
&= E[R_A R_M] + E[I\,R_P R_M] - (\mu_A + p\mu_P)\mu_M \\
&= (\sigma_{AM} + \mu_A \mu_M) + p(\sigma_{PM} + \mu_P \mu_M) - \mu_A \mu_M - p\mu_P \mu_M \\
&= \sigma_{AM} \tag{16A.4}
\end{aligned}
$$

for $\sigma_{PM} = 0$. Systematic risk is measured by beta

$$
\begin{aligned}
\beta_B &= \sigma_{BM}/\sigma_M^2 \\
&= \sigma_{AM}/\sigma_M^2 = \beta_A \tag{16A.5}
\end{aligned}
$$

Consequently, the systematic risk of a project is unaffected by diversifiable, country-specific political risk. This is the conventional view of political risk. Country-specific political risks that are unrelated to returns on the world market portfolio affect project value through their impact on future cash flows, but they are not otherwise priced in the marketplace and do not require a higher return.

Political Risk in the Real World

Be aware that there are situations in which political and/or currency risk can result in higher required returns on foreign projects despite the diversifiability of these risks. First, managers are not as diversified as shareholders, so they may want to hedge total risk rather than just systematic risk. Similarly, bondholders are concerned with receiving their promised payment and may be more concerned with total risk. The analysis in this appendix also assumes that political risk is country-specific. If political risk on a project is related to changes in the market portfolio, then the systematic risk of the project will differ from the systematic risk of the project without political risk.

Finally, discounted cash flow methods do not work well when the business environment is uncertain. The next chapter examines how the presence of real options in investment projects can result in higher hurdle rates being charged on projects in uncertain environments even though the country-specific risks of cross-border investment are diversifiable.

Real Options and Cross-Border Investment

Keynes, in his most famous observation, noted that we are ruled by ideas and by very little else...and he was right in attributing importance to ideas as opposed to the simple influence of pecuniary vested interest. But the rule of ideas is only powerful in a world that does not change. Ideas are inherently conservative. They yield not to the attack of other ideas but to the massive onslaught of circumstance with which they cannot contend.

John Kenneth Galbraith, *The Affluent Society*

OVERVIEW

Chapter 16 introduced the NPV investment decision rule "Invest in all positive-NPV projects" and applied this rule to several situations encountered in cross-border capital budgeting. In market-based economies, this discounted cash flow approach to investment decisions is the overwhelming favorite among companies large and small. Yet companies employing discounted cash flow techniques occasionally make decisions that, at least on the surface, violate the NPV decision rule.

Exceptions to the NPV decision rule usually arise from one of two sources. A common source of conflict arises when management's incentives and objectives are inconsistent with those of other stakeholders, particularly those of equity holders. Managers are not as diversified as other stakeholders, so they tend to worry about the total risk rather than just the systematic risk of the firm. The objectives of managers can be partially aligned with those of stockholders through performance evaluation and the use of incentives in management employment contracts. However, some conflict between managers and stockholders will remain so long as these are not the same individuals. Debtholders are also concerned more with the total risk than with the systematic risk of the firm. The disparity between the objectives of debtholders and equityholders is lower when banks provide both debt and equity capital, as is common in Germany and Japan.

• •

*Options on real assets are
called real options.*

• •

The second source of conflict arises when the firm's investments involve one or more **real options**—options on real assets. This apparent conflict results from a failure to consider all of the opportunity costs of investment. The act of investing can be viewed as choosing to exercise an investment option on a real asset. Viewed in this way, an important opportunity cost of choosing to invest in a real asset is the forgone option of investing at a future date. Proper application of the NPV rule should consider *when* to exercise, and not just *whether* to exercise, an investment option. This timing option is difficult to value with the NPV rule and is often ignored.

Optionlike characteristics are present in decisions to expand, contract, suspend, and/or abandon an investment. Another set of real options involves management's flexibility in adapting the firm's production, marketing, and distribution systems to evolving circumstances and new information. Because these real options are difficult to value with NPV, managerial actions can sometimes appear to be inconsistent with the NPV rule.

An option pricing framework is a particularly useful valuation tool in the presence of uncertainty.[1] The environment of cross-border investment is even more uncertain than that of domestic investment because of the risks and uncertainties of dealing with foreign cultures. This chapter shows how the firm's cross-border investment opportunities are influenced by the presence of real options. These real options gain much of their value from managerial flexibility in moving both proactively and reactively in an uncertain world.

———————————————●———————————————

17.1 THE THEORY AND PRACTICE OF INVESTMENT

The Conventional Theory of Investment

According to the conventional theory of investment, presented in Chapter 16, the value of an investment is determined by discounting expected future cash flows at a risk-adjusted discount rate. According to this approach, the net present value of an investment that lasts T periods and has an initial cost of CF_0 can be written as

$$NPV = \sum_{t=0}^{T} [E[CF_t]/(1+i_t)^t] \tag{17.1}$$

According to this approach, projects should be undertaken if and only if the net present value of the project is greater than zero.

———————————————

1 Although this chapter illustrates the value of real investment options, it does so without the use of a formal option pricing theory. Appendix 8-A develops a binomial option pricing model for valuing situations like those found in this chapter. Interested readers should refer to the suggested readings at the end of this chapter.

Three Puzzles

Financial managers do not always follow the NPV rule, at least not in an obvious way. There are at least three situations in which violations of the NPV rule are likely to occur.

Puzzle #1: The Multinational's Use of Inflated Hurdle Rates. Multinational firms often impose higher hurdle rates on investments in countries with uncertain political, legal, and business environments despite the fact that country-specific political risk is diversifiable and, hence, should not command a higher required return.

Here is an example of this seemingly irrational managerial behavior. CMS Energy, a globally diversified multinational corporation listed on the New York Stock Exchange, has power-generation capacity in the United States, Canada, Columbia, Peru, Argentina, India, Pakistan, and the Philippines. Many of these markets are expected to experience higher than average growth in energy consumption. India, Pakistan, and the Philippines also offer dollar-denominated contracts and British-based legal systems, allowing CMS Energy to operate in those environments with a minimum of political risk. Despite the diversifiable nature of country-specific investment risks, CMS Energy requires a higher rate of return on investments in some countries, such as the Philippines, than on investments in other countries. CMS Energy refuses to invest in countries with high operating and political risks, such as the People's Republic of China.[2]

Is the use of inflated hurdle rates for investment in some countries and an outright refusal to invest in other countries a violation of the NPV decision rule? Not necessarily. Business practitioners usually have very good reasons for the actions they take. Energy production requires large, up-front development costs that cannot be recouped easily should the political situation in a foreign country deteriorate. Many times, investment is not made in positive-NPV projects because those projects are expected to have even higher NPVs in the future. For example, the Chinese government is still developing its rules for dealing with foreign investors, and there is a great deal of uncertainty about how the investment climate in China will evolve. Even if investing in China today would yield more than the opportunity cost of capital and a positive NPV, investment at some future date might yield even more value to a company like CMS Energy. This will give the Chinese government more time to become accustomed to dealing with foreign investors and to develop laws and customs regarding private ownership, bankruptcy, and commerce.

Puzzle #2: The Multinational's Failure to Abandon Unprofitable Investments. Firms often remain in markets even though they are losing money. This frequently happens when real exchange rates move against an exporting firm. For example, U.S. automakers suffered huge losses on both domestic and foreign sales in the mid-1980s as the dollar rose to unprecedented highs against most foreign currencies. The future looked bleak for U.S. automakers in the face of global overcapacity, stagnant markets at home, fierce competition from abroad, and an overvalued dollar. Why did U.S.

---

2 From a conversation with Victor J. Fryling, president of CMS Energy (April, 1994). See "CMS Energy's Adventures in Diversification" by Kelly M. Farr (*Public Utilities Fortnightly,* September 1994) for information on CMS Energy's worldwide investments.

automakers persist under these perilous circumstances? Clearly, the hope was that the dollar would fall back to normal levels and the automakers would return to profitability. The automakers had an option to abandon automobile production, but once abandoned it would be very difficult for them to reenter the global market for automobiles.

Puzzle #3: The Multinational's Entry into New and Emerging Markets. Firms often make incremental investments into new (especially emerging) markets even though at any given point in time further investment does not seem warranted according to the "Accept all positive-NPV projects" rule.

When a firm enters a foreign market for the first time, the only certainty is that management's initial cash flow forecasts will be wrong. Management often limits the size of initial forays into foreign markets so that it can assess the viability of the market and determine how to best structure the firm's entry. In these circumstances, management often states that the investment is being undertaken for "strategic" reasons. Are managers acting irrationally? Are strategic initiatives in violation of the NPV rule? Or, is the conventional application of the NPV rule incomplete?

The conventional discounted cash flow approach to valuation does not deal well with managerial flexibility in responding to uncertainty.

Are Financial Managers Irrational? Managers behaving in these ways are not acting irrationally. These three puzzles arise because of a failure of conventional discounted cash flow methods to properly incorporate the values of real options. Real options are options or optionlike features embedded in real investment opportunities. Like financial options, real investment options give the firm the option but not the obligation to pursue an investment opportunity. Whereas a financial option is based on an underlying financial asset, such as a share of stock or currency, the value of a real option depends on the *noncontractual* cash flows of a real investment opportunity.

Real options capture their value through resolution of uncertainty. With the arrival of new information about future investment outcomes, management can modify investment plans to fit the circumstance and make more informed investment choices. This provides **managerial flexibility** in the timing and scale of investment. Managerial flexibility is difficult to value with traditional discounted cash flow methods. Treating managerial flexibility as a form of real option allows us to bring to bear the full power of option pricing methods.

Timing and the Option to Invest

The NPV rule states that the firm should undertake all positive-NPV projects. Calculation of NPV is least complicated when an investment must be made immediately or lost forever. For such *now-or-never* projects there is no chance to wait for additional information, and the value of a project is simply the discounted value of the expected future cash flows net of the initial investment.

Timing is an important part of the option to invest.

If a project is not a now-or-never proposition, the firm has the option to delay the investment decision so it can obtain more information about future prices, costs and volume. Because of the option to delay investment, projects must compete not only with other projects but also with variations of themselves initiated at each future date. That is, the decision to invest in a project today must be compared with the alternative of investing in the same or similar projects at some future date. Hence, investment in a

Option Value = Intrinsic Value + Time Value

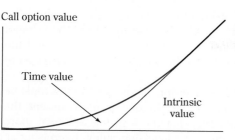

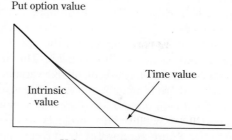

Option value determinants[a]	Call	Put
1. Underlying asset value	+	−
2. Exercise price	−	+
3. Riskless rate of interest	+	−
4. Time to expiration[b]	+	+
5. Volatility in the underlying asset	+	+

FIGURE 17.1
The Components of
Option Value

[a] A plus (+) indicates that an option increases in value with an increase in the given determinant while holding the other determinants constant. A minus (−) indicates a decrease in value, all else constant.
[b] American put options increase in value with an increase in the time to expiration. The positive relation between put option value and time to expiration need not hold for European put options. For typical values of the other parameters, European put options increase and then decrease in value as time to expiration is increased.

real asset is equivalent to exercising an investment call option. By exercising its option to invest, the firm is forgoing the opportunity to invest in the future. Consequently, a part of the exercise price is the opportunity cost of investing today rather than at some future date. The optimal time to invest is when the value of the forgone future investment is less than the value of investing immediately.

Because options are such an important part of the firm's investment decisions, it is useful to discuss the elements that make up an option's value. The value of a real or financial option can be divided into two distinct parts:

- The **intrinsic value** of the option if exercised immediately
- The **time value** of the option arising from the fact that the option need not be exercised today[3]

These two components of an option value are depicted graphically in Figure 17.1. Chapter 8 presents a similar discussion of the intrinsic value and the time value of an option.

---

3 The distinction between the intrinsic and the time value of an option is also discussed in the chapter on currency options.

The intrinsic and time values of an option are determined by the five variables listed at the bottom of Figure 17.1. The effect of an increase in each determinant on the value of a call or put option (holding the other determinants constant) is as shown in the figure. The intrinsic value of a call option is the value of the underlying asset minus the exercise price. The exercise price is simply the cost of the investment. As the value of the underlying asset increases, the option to invest falls further in-the-money and the investment becomes more valuable. The time value of the option to invest is a bit more complicated and depends on all five variables.

When there is an option to delay the investment decision, net present values must be calculated with great care. If applied without considering the timing of investment, the "invest in all positive-NPV projects" rule may mean that the firm forgoes even more attractive future versions of its current opportunities by investing today. Exercising an option today means accepting the intrinsic value and forgoing the time value of the option. The next section illustrates the way in which uncertainty over future prices affects the timing of the firm's investment decision.

17.2 MARKET ENTRY AND THE OPTION TO INVEST

The form and pace of market entry are the biggest concerns of the multinational firm facing uncertain conditions in foreign markets. Market entry is but one of a broader class of investment decisions that can fruitfully be viewed as real investment options. This section presents the decision to invest in a real investment opportunity as an option to invest and discusses the sources of value in this option.

An Option to Invest in a Natural Resource Project

In the presence of uncertainty, care must be taken in applying the NPV decision rule.

Crude oil is increasingly being produced from offshore oil wells. Such wells already exist in the North Sea and the Gulf of Mexico, and advances in seismic exploration techniques and in drilling and extraction technologies have opened up development of previously inaccessible regions of the ocean floor. The most promising deep-water prospects are located off the coasts of Angola, Brazil, Malaysia, Mexico, Namibia, the Philippines, the United Kingdom, and the United States. Oil has a very long shelf life so long as it is stored in the oil field itself. If not for a limited supply of oil reserves and competition for productive capacity in the oil industry, investments in oil wells could be delayed indefinitely.

Deep-sea oil exploration and extraction is an industry with large sunk costs.[4] For this reason, investment decisions in the crude oil industry critically depend on the expected future level of oil prices relative to the required investment costs. The value of any given development project ultimately depends on oil prices in the years following development. Because uncertainty in this setting is in the future level of prices, this uncertainty is called **price uncertainty**. Even though growth in oil supply and demand is relatively predictable, short- and long-term oil prices are difficult to predict. Oil prices are subject to unexpected

---

4 Deep sea oil rigs and sunk costs? Sorry about that. Hanging is too good for a man who makes puns; he should be drawn and quoted.

demand shocks, such as when winter temperatures in the northern hemisphere are unusually severe. Oil prices also are subject to unexpected supply shocks as a result of political upheaval. Political events affecting oil prices in the last several decades include the revolution in Iran, the Iran-Iraq War, the Persian Gulf War, and the (usually unsuccessful) oligopolistic actions of the Organization of Petroleum Exporting Countries (OPEC).

Because of such uncertainties, investments in the oil exploration industry are undertaken only when expected returns are substantially higher than required returns. Investments must have large positive NPVs before they attract capital. Projects with small positive NPVs relative to the initial sunk costs typically are not undertaken. This is an apparent violation of the conventional "invest in all positive-NPV projects" rule. In fact, the NPV rule still works if (and only if) we include the opportunity cost of investing today and forgoing the option to invest in the future. The following example illustrates the pitfall in applying the "invest in all positive-NPV projects" rule in a naive fashion. The basic insights of this example are extended to the general case in a later section.

An Example of the Option to Invest

Oil has been found in the deep waters of the Foinaven region west of the Shetland Islands. Suppose British Petroleum (BP) owns a lease to extract crude oil from the region and is considering the construction of a deep-sea oil rig. Construction costs on a deep-sea oil well are $I_0 = \$20$ million, and these costs are assumed to grow at a constant rate of $g = 10\%$ per year. The risk-free rate of interest is also $i = 10\%$, so the cost of the well is a constant $20 million in present value terms regardless of when construction begins. Crude oil is priced in dollars throughout the world, and the current price of oil is $P = \$20$ per barrel. Once a well is set up, BP's variable production costs to extract and refine the crude oil are $V = \$8$ per barrel. For simplicity, assume that there are no maintenance or other fixed production costs. The Foinaven well is expected to produce $Q = 200{,}000$ barrels per year in perpetuity. All cash flows are assumed to occur at the end of the year. Production can start immediately in which case the first cash flow will occur at the end of the first year.[5]

OPEC members are currently involved in a heated internal debate that will determine oil output and prices into the foreseeable future. If the OPEC members hold ranks, oil production will be limited and oil prices will rise to $30/bbl in perpetuity. If the oil cartel breaks up, production will rise and prices will fall to $10/bbl in perpetuity. This negotiation will be settled within one year. Once the new price is established, it is expected to remain at that level (either $10/bbl or $30/bbl) in perpetuity. BP estimates that an oil price rise and an oil price fall are equally probable.

Suppose there are two investment alternatives in this example: (1) BP can invest today or (2) BP can wait one year and reconsider the investment at that time. If BP invests today, it exercises its option to invest and incurs the sunk costs of investment.

---

5 Governments lease offshore sites for a finite number of years. The assumption of perpetual cash flows is for expositional convenience; the value of a perpetuity that begins today and continues forever is equal to the annual cash flow divided by the discount rate (CF/i). The assumption of a constant construction cost in today's dollars is also for expositional convenience.

The algebra of this alternative is simple. If BP invests today, perpetual cash flows begin in one year and the valuation equation is

$$\text{Invest today: } NPV_0 = \frac{(P - V)Q}{i} - I_0 \tag{17.2}$$

BP's option to invest expires in one year, and by delaying investment it can reduce uncertainty over future oil prices and make a more informed decision. If BP waits one year before making an investment, the valuation equation at time t=0 is:

$$\text{Wait one year: } NPV_0 = \left[\frac{(P - V)Q}{i} / (1+i) \right] - I_0 \tag{17.3}$$

where the present value of the initial investment is $I_0 = \$20,000,000$ regardless of when investment is made.

To keep matters simple, suppose that changes in oil price and in operating costs are unrelated to changes in the value of the market portfolio. Assuming that oil prices and market index levels are unrelated may or may not be a good assumption for an event as monumental as an agreement among OPEC members to curtail worldwide oil production. A credible agreement among OPEC members could precipitate a drop in debt and equity values around the world (along with a corresponding rise in the wealth of the OPEC nations). OPEC has found it increasingly difficult to act as an oligopolist because of increasing competition from non-OPEC oil-producing countries.[6]

To keep this example simple, assume that crude oil prices and production costs are unrelated to changes in the world market portfolio. Hence, the beta of this project is zero, and there is no systematic oil price risk. Future cash flows are then discounted at the risk-free rate of interest.[7]

Although the risk of oil price changes is assumed to be unsystematic, future oil prices are uncertain. As we shall see, uncertainty over future oil prices means that BP needs to be careful in its capital budgeting analysis. Failure to consider the opportunity cost of investing today rather than at some future date will misrepresent the value of the investment to BP.

The Intrinsic Value of the Option to Invest

The intrinsic value of an option is the value if exercised today.

The option to invest is displayed graphically in Figure 17.2. BP's option to invest is an **American call option**—an option to buy the investment project that is exercisable at any time.[8] The exercise price of BP's investment option is the $20 million initial cost of

---

6 The *London Financial Times* reports that non-OPEC capacity additions from already-discovered oil fields are likely to be 10 million barrels per day greater than present capacity by the year 2000 ("New Frontiers Open Up in the Deep Blue Sea" by Robert Corzine, November 11, 1994).

7 Systematic risk has no place in most option pricing models. Instead, a riskless arbitrage position is established with a replicating portfolio. The option position is then valued at the riskless rate of interest.

8 Recall that (1) a call option is an option to buy the underlying asset and (2) an American option is exercisable at any time until expiration of the option.

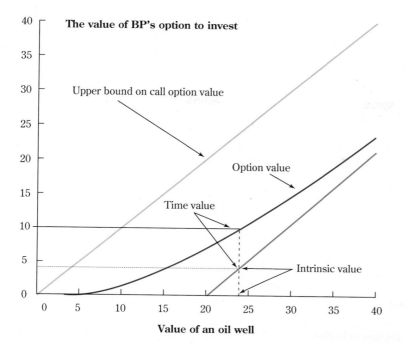

The value of BP's option to invest

Upper bound on call option value

Option value

Time value

Intrinsic value

Value of an oil well

FIGURE 17.2
The Investment Call Option

the project. The expected price level is $20/bbl and the variable costs are $8/bbl, so the expected contribution margin is $12/bbl in perpetuity. Expected production is 200,000 barrels per year, so expected cash flows are $2.4 million per year in perpetuity. With an initial investment of $20 million and a 10 percent cost of capital, the value of the oil well if investment is made today is

$$\text{NPV(investment today)} = \left[\frac{(\$20/\text{bbl} - \$8/\text{bbl})\,(200,000\text{bbl})}{0.10} \right] - \$20,000,000$$
$$= +\$24,000,000 - \$20,000,000$$
$$= +\$4,000,000 > \$0$$
$$\Rightarrow \text{Invest today (?)}$$

The value of the oil well is $24 million. With a $20 million exercise price, the net present value of the "invest today" alternative is $4 million. Following the conventional "Invest in all positive-NPV projects" decision rule, BP should apparently proceed with this investment immediately. But what about the time value of the option to invest?

The Time Value of the Option to Invest

Although tempting, the conclusion of the previous section is incomplete. The "invest today" alternative ignores the firm's **timing option**—the ability of the firm to postpone investment and to reconsider investment at a future date. In the BP example, the value of the well depends on the future price of oil. By delaying the investment decision while OPEC decides on its production quotas, BP can reduce its uncertainty over future oil prices. BP can then

The timing option reflects the firm's ability to postpone investment.

make a more informed investment decision based on new information. In particular, BP has an opportunity to avoid the negative outcomes of investment should oil prices fall.

Figure 17.3 shows a decision tree that can help formulate responses to uncertain future events. Our objective is to maximize the value of the oil well by following the optimal decision path. Just as in solving a maze, it is convenient to start at the end and work backward toward the beginning. The critical uncertainty facing BP is the future price of oil. Let the net present value of investment given an oil price of P_{oil} be written as $NPV | P_{oil}$. If OPEC can keep production down and prices up, then the price will be $30. If BP postpones the investment decision for one year and oil prices rise to $30/bbl, then the expected net present value of investment is

$$NPV \mid (P_{oil} = \$30) = \left[\frac{(\$30/bbl - \$8/bbl)\,(200,000bbl)}{0.10} / 1.10 \right] - \$20,000,000$$

$$= \left[\frac{\$4,400,000}{0.10} / (1.10) \right] - \$20,000,000$$

$$= \$20,000,000 > \$0$$

$$\Rightarrow \text{Invest in one period if } P_{oil} = \$30$$

FIGURE 17.3 Uncertainty and the Option to Invest

Initial investment	I_0	= $20,000,000
Price of oil	P_0	= $20/bbl
	P_1	= $30 or $10 with equal probability
Variable production cost	$8/bbl	
Expected production	200,000 bbl/year	
Discount rate	i	= 10%

Invest today

$$NPV_0 = \left[\frac{(\$20/bbl - \$8/bbl)\,(200,000\ bbls)}{0.10} \right] - 20,000,000 \quad \Rightarrow NPV(\text{invest today}) = +\$4,000,000$$

Invest in one year

Invest at $P_{oil} = \$30$

$$NPV_0 = \left[\frac{(\$30/bbl - \$8/bbl)\,(200,000\ bbls)}{0.10} / 1.10 \right] - 20,000,000 \Rightarrow NPV \mid (P_{oil} = \$30) = +\$20,000,000$$

Invest at $P_{oil} = \$10$

$$NPV_0 = \left[\frac{(\$10/bbl - \$8/bbl)\,(200,000\ bbls)}{0.10} / 1.10 \right] - 20,000,000 \Rightarrow NPV \mid (P_{oil} = \$10) = -\$16,363,636 \quad \overset{\$0}{\nearrow}$$

$$\Rightarrow NPV(\text{wait one year}) = [\text{Prob}(P_{oil} = \$10)]\,(NPV \mid P_{oil} = \$10) + [\text{Prob}(P_{oil} = \$30)]\,(NPV \mid P_{oil} = \$30)$$

$$= (\tfrac{1}{2})\,(\$0) + (\tfrac{1}{2})\,(\$20,000,000) = +\$10,000,000$$

Option value	=	Intrinsic value	+	Time value
NPV (wait one year)	=	NPV (invest today)	+	Additional value from waiting one year
$10,000,000	=	$4,000,000	+	$6,000,000

If BP postpones the decision for one year and oil prices fall to $10/bbl, then the expected net present value of investment at $10/bbl is

$$\text{NPV} \mid (P_{\text{oil}} = \$10) = \left[\frac{(\$10/\text{bbl} - \$8/\text{bbl})(200,000\text{bbl})}{0.10} / 1.10 \right] - \$20,000,000$$

$$= \left[\frac{\$4,400,000}{0.10} / 1.10 \right] - \$20,000,000$$

$$= -\$16,363,636 > \$0$$

$$\Rightarrow \text{Do not invest in one period if } P_{\text{oil}} = \$10$$

By postponing the investment for one year, BP can choose to not invest if oil prices fall to $10/bbl. If BP does not invest, then the net present value of this path of the decision tree is $0.

To determine whether it is worthwhile to wait one year before making its investment decision, BP must consider the probabilities of $P_{\text{oil}} = \$30$ and $P_{\text{oil}} = \$10$. Prices may rise or fall with equal probability, so $\text{Prob}(P_{\text{oil}}=\$10) = \text{Prob}(P_{\text{oil}}=\$30) = \frac{1}{2}$. The expected net present value of delaying the investment decision for one period is an equally weighted average of the NPVs from the "invest in one period given $P_{\text{oil}} = \$30$" and the "do not invest in one period given $P_{\text{oil}} = \$10$" outcomes.

$$\text{NPV(wait one year)} = [\text{Prob}(P_{\text{oil}}=\$10)]\,(\text{NPV} \mid P_{\text{oil}}=\$10) + [\text{Prob}(P_{\text{oil}}=\$30)]\,(\text{NPV} \mid P_{\text{oil}}=\$30)$$

$$= (\tfrac{1}{2})\,(\$0) + (\tfrac{1}{2})\,(\$20,000,000)$$

$$= +\$10,000,000 > \text{NPV(invest today)} > \$0$$

$$\Rightarrow \text{Wait one period before deciding to invest}$$

This is $6 million greater than the value of the option to invest today, so BP should wait until OPEC announces its production quotas before making its investment decision. The decision to wait is summarized at the bottom of Figure 17.3.

Consider the components of the value of the option to invest.

Option Value	=	Intrinsic Value	+	Time Value	(17.4)
NPV(wait one year)	=	NPV(invest today)	+	Opportunity cost of investing today	
$10,000,000	=	$4,000,000	+	$6,000,000	

By investing today, BP forgoes an investment alternative with an expected value of $10,000,000. Thus the intrinsic value, the "invest today" NPV, does not include the $6 million value of the timing option. The value of this timing option is the opportunity cost of investing today.

The time value of the option to invest reflects the opportunity cost of investing today.

Failure to recognize this timing option can result in a firm's investing prematurely and failing to capture the maximum potential value of its real assets. This opportunity cost can be avoided by investing at the most opportune time.

A Resolution of Puzzle #1: Use of Inflated Hurdle Rates

The NPV rule says to accept all positive-NPV projects, which is the same thing as saying "Accept all projects with expected returns that exceed their required returns." Yet firms in many industries require hurdle rates that are well above their cost of capital before they invest in a new project. At first glance this seems to be at odds with the NPV rule. It is not. The oil well example illustrates why firms require above-market hurdle rates in uncertain environments.

> Firms demand higher hurdle rates in uncertain environments because of the option value of waiting for additional information.

If the uncertainty over future oil prices increases, management will demand even higher hurdle rates before investing. This is true even if the additional risk is entirely diversifiable and the required return of investors does not change. Exercising the investment option means giving up the option of investing at some future date when more information will be known about the likely payoffs on the investment. Once exercised, the option to invest cannot be costlessly reversed. This lost option is the opportunity cost of investing today.

17.3 Uncertainty and the Value of the Option to Invest

The Determinants of Option Value

Reductions in uncertainty allow the firm to avoid making investment decisions that turn out to be wrong. In the BP example, the fall in oil prices is behind the incentive to delay investment in the oil well. British Petroleum can avoid the 50 percent probability of a loss by delaying the investment decision one period. Consider the change in price from $20/bbl to either $10/bbl or $30/bbl. For the "invest now or never" alternative, an increase in oil price from $20/bbl to $30/bbl results in an increase in value relative to the expectation. Similarly, a $10/bbl decrease in price to $10/bbl results in an offsetting loss in value. Each of these is equally likely to occur, so BP is equally exposed to an increase and to a decrease in oil price if it invests today. If the option to invest is exercised early, BP cannot benefit from new information. The "wait one year" strategy allows BP to forgo investment when oil prices fall. For this reason, the incentive to delay investment is driven entirely by bad news—the size and probability of unprofitable outcomes.

Time value also reflects managerial flexibility.

The value of the option to delay investment can also be viewed as the value of managerial flexibility. By delaying the investment decision, the firm gains flexibility. In the BP example, if oil prices turn out to be lower than expected, the firm can refuse to invest and avoid the loss in value associated with low oil prices. In option terminology, the investment option is out-of-the-money, and the firm should leave its option to invest unexercised. If oil prices rise, however, the firm can exercise its investment option and capture the higher NPV arising from the higher oil prices. In addition to depending on the underlying asset value and the exercise price, the value of the timing option depends on the discount rate (risk-free rate of interest), the option's time to expiration, and the volatility of the underlying asset, as shown in Table 17.1.[9]

---

9 Depletion of the oil reserve has been omitted from the analysis. Depletion of a natural resource can be treated in much the same way that dividends on a dividend-paying stock are treated in the valuation of a stock option. See the technical references at the end of this chapter.

TABLE 17.1 OPTION VALUE DETERMINANTS

Option value determinant	BP example	Increasing this determinant changes option value in the indicated direction
Price of the underlying asset	P_{oil}	+
Exercise price of the option	$20 million	−
Risk-free rate of interest	10%	+
Time to expiration of the option	one year	+
Volatility of the underlying asset	σ_{Poil}	+

Increases in the discount rate generally make the future less important than the present. Thus, the $20 million exercise price of BP's option to invest becomes less of an impediment in present value terms, which causes the oil investment to look more attractive today. The value of the option to invest thus increases with an increase in the discount rate through an increase in the time value of the option to invest.[10]

Time to expiration is a key determinant of the value of the timing option. In general terms, the time to expiration of the option to invest in a natural resource, such as an oil well, should correspond to the period of the lease on the natural resource. If the option to invest can be extended indefinitely into the future, then the firm has even more flexibility and the investment has additional time value. Conversely, if the time to expiration is reduced to zero, this is a now-or-never project and there is no timing option. Increases in the ability to delay an investment decision thus increase time value as well as the value of the option to invest, although at a diminishing marginal rate. Changes in option value from changes in time to expiration diminish as the time to expiration is lengthened, so the biggest gains from increases in time to expiration occur in the earliest periods of the investment horizon.

The most important determinant of the value of the timing option on real assets is uncertainty in the future value of the real asset itself. Uncertainty is the major reason why firms are reluctant to jump wholeheartedly into economies undergoing rapid change, such as the People's Republic of China and the states of the former Soviet Union. The value of the option to invest increases with an increase in the volatility of the underlying asset or, equivalently, with an increase in price or input cost uncertainty.

Exogenous versus Endogenous Uncertainty

There are really two types of managerial flexibility. When price or input cost uncertainty is outside the firm's control, it is called **exogenous uncertainty**. Here, information is revealed about price or cost as time unfolds, but the firm cannot uncover new information through its investment activities. In the example of BP's option to invest, oil prices

Uncertainty is endogenous when the act of investing reveals information about price or cost.

---

10 Jonathan E. Ingersoll, Jr., and Stephen A. Ross developed the impact of changes in interest rates on the value of the timing option in "Waiting to Invest: Investment and Uncertainty," *Journal of Business* 65, Vol. 1, pages 1–30.

were assumed to be outside BP's control. In contrast, uncertainty is called **endogenous uncertainty** when the act of investing reveals information about price or cost. Endogenous uncertainty can create an incentive to speed up investment in order to gain more information about likely future prices and costs. Endogenous uncertainty can also create an incentive to invest in projects that appear to be losers. The examples in the remainder of this section deal with exogenous price and input cost uncertainty.

Exogenous Price Uncertainty

Option values increase with an increase in the volatility of the underlying asset. Greater uncertainty over future oil prices results in a higher value for the option to wait and a greater incentive for BP to postpone investment. In the BP example, if oil price volatility increases, then BP can gain even more value from rises in price and can still avoid investing if prices fall. Suppose the current price is $20/bbl and that oil prices will either rise to $35/bbl or fall to $5/bbl with equal probability.[11] Based on information available at time t=0, the net present value of the "invest today" alternative is as in the original example:

$$\text{NPV(invest today)} = \left[\frac{(\$20/bbl - \$8/bbl)\,(200,000bbl)}{0.10} \right] - \$20,000,000$$

$$= +\$4,000,000$$

$$\Rightarrow \text{Invest today}\,(?)$$

If BP waits one year before making its investment decision, NPV depends on the path of oil prices as follows:

$$\text{NPV} \mid \left(P_{oil} = \$35\right) = \left[\frac{(\$35/bbl - \$8/bbl)\,(200,000bbl)}{0.10} /1.10 \right] - \$20,000,000$$

$$= +\$29,090,909$$

$$\Rightarrow \text{Invest in one period if } P_{oil} = \$35$$

$$\text{NPV} \mid \left(P_{oil} = \$5\right) = \left[\frac{(\$5/bbl - \$8/bbl)\,(200,000bbl)}{0.10} /1.10 \right] - \$20,000,000$$

$$= -\$25,454,545$$

$$\Rightarrow \text{Do not invest in one period if } P_{oil} = \$5$$

This NPV is less than zero, so BP will not invest if price falls to $5 per barrel. In other words, NPV|P_{oil} = $5 is $0. The NPV of the "wait one year" strategy is then

---

11 In this example we'll assume that BP must continue to produce oil even though the $5/bbl price of oil is below the $8/bbl cost of producing and refining the oil. The option to abandon losing projects will be discussed shortly.

$$\text{NPV(wait one year)} = [\text{Prob}(P_{oil}=\$5)](\text{NPV}|P_{oil}=\$5) + [\text{Prob}(P_{oil}=\$35)](\text{NPV}|P_{oil}=\$35)$$
$$= (\tfrac{1}{2})(\$0) + (\tfrac{1}{2})(\$29,090,909)$$
$$= +\$14,545,455 > \text{NPV(invest today)} > \$0$$
$$\Rightarrow \text{Wait one period}$$

Just as in the original example, the option value is the sum of the intrinsic value and the time value.

Option Value	=	Intrinsic Value	+	Time Value
NPV(wait one year)	=	NPV(invest today)	+	Opportunity cost of investing today
$14,545,455	=	$4,000,000	+	$10,545,455

An increase in the uncertainty over future oil prices makes the timing option to delay the investment decision even more valuable and the opportunity cost of premature investment even more deleterious than in the original example.

Exogenous Input Cost Uncertainty

Suppose there is exogenous input cost uncertainty in the preceding example. To focus on one variable at a time, suppose oil prices will remain constant. Do more volatile production costs increase or decrease the time value of the option to invest?

As with uncertainty over output prices, the value of the option to wait increases with increases in exogenous uncertainty over future operating costs. Suppose oil sells for $20/bbl and that oil processing costs will either rise to $V_{oil} = \$12$/bbl or fall to $V_{oil} = \$4$/bbl with equal probability in one year. The net present value of the "invest today" alternative is still

$$\text{NPV(invest today)} = \left[\frac{(\$20/\text{bbl} - \$8/\text{bbl})(200,000\text{bbl})}{0.10} \right] - \$20,000,000$$
$$= +\$4,000,000$$
$$\Rightarrow \text{Invest today (?)}$$

If BP waits one year, it can resolve its uncertainty over future operating costs:

$$\text{NPV}|(V_{oil} = \$12) = \left[\frac{(\$20/\text{bbl} - \$12/\text{bbl})(200,000\text{bbl})}{0.10} / 1.10 \right] - \$20,000,000$$
$$= -\$5,454,545$$
$$\Rightarrow \text{Do not invest in one period if } V_{oil} = \$12$$

BP will not invest if variable processing costs rise to $12 per barrel. If processing costs fall to $4 per barrel, on the other hand, the investment looks attractive:

$$\text{NPV}|(V_{oil} = \$4) = \left[\frac{(\$20/\text{bbl} - \$4/\text{bbl})(200,000\text{bbl})}{0.10} / 1.10 \right] - \$20,000,000$$
$$= -\$9,090,909$$
$$\Rightarrow \text{Invest in one period if } V_{oil} = \$4$$

The NPV of the 'wait one year' strategy is then

$$\text{NPV(wait one year)} = [\text{Prob}(V_{oil}=\$12)](\text{NPV}|V_{oil}=\$12) + [\text{Prob}(V_{oil}=\$4)](\text{NPV}|V_{oil}=\$4)$$
$$= (\tfrac{1}{2})(\$0) + (\tfrac{1}{2})(\$9{,}090{,}909)$$
$$= +\$4{,}545{,}455 > \$0$$
$$\Rightarrow \text{Wait one period}$$

Option value is decomposed as follows.

Option Value	=	Intrinsic Value	+	Time Value
NPV(wait one year)	=	NPV(invest today)	+	Opportunity cost of investing today
$4,545,455	=	$4,000,000	+	$545,455

Exogeneous uncertainty creates an incentive to postpone investment.

This form of exogenous input cost uncertainty has the same effect as exogenous output price uncertainty. Exogenous uncertainty in either input costs or output prices creates uncertainty in operating cash flows and an incentive to postpone investment. By waiting for additional information regarding the level of expected future operating cash flows, the firm can choose to invest or not to invest at a later date, depending on the arrival of new information.

17.4 MARKET EXIT AND THE ABANDONMENT OPTION

An Example of the Abandonment Option

Abandoning a losing venture is always an option when events do not work out as planned. But abandonment usually entails some up-front costs. As an example, suppose British Petroleum invested in an offshore oil well in the Foinaven field and that oil prices have subsequently fallen to $10/bbl. The well is producing 200,000 barrels per year as expected. Unfortunately, the oil is of lower quality than expected, so extraction and refinement costs have risen to $12/bbl. This means that BP is losing $2/bbl on every barrel it pumps. Her Majesty's government wants to prevent abandoned oil wells from developing into ecological disasters and requires that any well that is not producing at capacity be capped and the platform dismantled and removed. BP estimates this abandonment cost at $2 million. For simplicity, let's assume that BP must make the abandonment decision either immediately or in one period and that the risk-free interest rate is 10 percent. The situation is summarized in Figure 17.4.

If oil prices ($10) and extraction and refinement costs ($12) are certain to remain at these levels into the indefinite future or if BP must make its abandonment decision either now or never, then BP will want to shut down operations as soon as possible. By abandoning the project now, BP can avoid the $2/bbl loss. This is equivalent to a net cash inflow of $2/bbl on every barrel produced. The expected net present value of abandoning the well immediately is

$$\text{NPV(abandon today)} = -\left[\frac{(\$10/\text{bbl} - \$12/\text{bbl})\,(200{,}000\text{bbl})}{0.10}\right] - \$20{,}000{,}000$$

$$= +\$4{,}000{,}000 - \$2{,}000{,}000$$

$$= +\$2{,}000{,}000 > \$0$$

$$\Rightarrow \text{Abandon immediately (?)}$$

If oil prices and refinement costs are certain to remain at these levels, then the timing option has no value and BP should pay the $2 million abandonment cost to avoid the $4 million loss from operating the well. This is the intrinsic value of the abandonment option.

If there is uncertainty over future prices and costs, then abandoning the project has an opportunity cost—loss of the option to continue to operate the oil well if circumstances change for the better. For instance, if there is an equal probability that oil prices will rise to $15/bbl or fall to $5/bbl and stay at that level in perpetuity, BP may want to continue production for another period and observe the new oil price level before

FIGURE 17.4 Uncertainty and the Option to Abandon

Initial investment	$I_0 = \$2{,}000{,}000$
Price of oil	$P_0 = \$10/\text{bbl}$
	$P_1 = \$5$ or $\$15$ with equal probability
Variable production cost	$\$12/\text{bbl}$
Expected production	200,000 bbl/year
Discount rate	$i = 10\%$

Abandon today

$$\text{NPV}_0 = \left[\frac{(\$10/\text{bbl} - \$12/\text{bbl})\,(200{,}000\text{ bbls})}{0.10}\right] - 2{,}000{,}000 \quad \Rightarrow \text{NPV(abandon today)} = +\$2{,}000{,}000$$

Abandon in one year

Abandon at $P_{\text{oil}} = \$15$

$$\text{NPV}_0 = \left[\frac{(\$15/\text{bbl} - \$12/\text{bbl})\,(200{,}000\text{ bbls})}{0.10}/1.10\right] - 2{,}000{,}000 \quad \Rightarrow \text{NPV}\,|\,(P_{\text{oil}} = \$15) = -\$7{,}454{,}545 \quad \$0$$

Abandon at $P_{\text{oil}} = \$5$

$$\text{NPV}_0 = \left[\frac{(\$5/\text{bbl} - \$12/\text{bbl})\,(200{,}000\text{ bbls})}{0.10}/1.10\right] - 2{,}000{,}000 \quad \Rightarrow \text{NPV}\,|\,(P_{\text{oil}} = \$5) = +\$10{,}727{,}273$$

$$\Rightarrow \text{NPV(wait one year)} = [\text{Prob}(P_{\text{oil}} = \$15)]\,(\text{NPV}\,|\,P_{\text{oil}} = \$15) + [\text{Prob}(P_{\text{oil}} = \$5)]\,(\text{NPV}\,|\,P_{\text{oil}} = \$5)$$

$$= (\tfrac{1}{2})\,(\$0) + (\tfrac{1}{2})\,(\$10{,}727{,}273) = +\$5{,}363{,}636$$

Option value	=	Intrinsic value	+	Time value
NPV (wait one year)	=	NPV (abandon today)	+	Additional value from waiting one year
$5,363,636	=	$2,000,000	+	$3,363,636

making its abandonment decision. If prices rise to $15 per barrel, the expected net present value of this wait-and-see strategy is

$$\text{NPV} \mid (P_{\text{oil}} = \$15) = -\left[\frac{(\$15/\text{bbl} - \$12/\text{bbl})(200{,}000\text{bbl})}{0.10} / 1.10\right] - \$20{,}000{,}000$$

$$= -\$7{,}454{,}545 < \$0$$

$$\Rightarrow \text{Do not abandon in one year given } P_{\text{oil}} = \$15$$

In this case, BP will continue operating the well, and the NPV of this alternative will effectively be zero. If prices fall to $5/bbl, however, then BP will want to abandon the well rather than lose $7 on every barrel.

$$\text{NPV} \mid (P_{\text{oil}} = \$5) = -\left[\frac{(\$5/\text{bbl} - \$12/\text{bbl})(200{,}000\text{bbl})}{0.10} / 1.10\right] - \$20{,}000{,}000$$

$$= +\$10{,}727{,}273 > \$0$$

$$\Rightarrow \text{Abandon in one year given } P_{\text{oil}} = \$5$$

With an equal probability of prices rising to $15/bbl or falling to $5/bbl, the expected net present value of delaying the abandonment decision for one year is

$$\text{NPV(wait one year)} = [\text{Prob}(P_{\text{oil}} = \$5)](\text{NPV} \mid P_{\text{oil}} = \$5) + [\text{Prob}(P_{\text{oil}} = \$15)](\text{NPV} \mid P_{\text{oil}} = \$15)$$

$$= (\tfrac{1}{2})(\$10{,}727{,}273) + (\tfrac{1}{2})(\$0)$$

$$= +\$5{,}363{,}636 > \$0$$

$$\Rightarrow \text{Wait one period before deciding whether to abandon}$$

This is greater than the "abandon today" alternative by $3,363,636.

The values of options on real assets are driven by the same parameters that determine the values of options on financial assets. The value of the abandonment option depends on the value of the underlying asset, the volatility of the underlying asset, the exercise price, the level of interest rates, and the time to expiration of the option.

A Resolution of Puzzle #2: Failure to Abandon Unprofitable Investments

Market exit and abandonment decisions are another form of **American option.** For British Petroleum, the abandonment decision can be thought of as an American call option in which BP can opt to buy out or dispose of the project's negative cash flows. The exercise price of the option is the $2 million sunk cost of abandonment. If exercised today, the abandonment option has an intrinsic value of $2 million. Of course, if BP chooses to abandon the well, it forgoes the positive operating cash flows should oil prices rise. The time value of the option—the value of leaving the abandonment option unexercised and postponing the abandonment decision—is $3,363,636. The total value of the abandonment option is the sum of these two parts.

Option Value	=	Intrinsic Value	+	Time Value
NPV (wait one year)	=	NPV (invest today)	+	Opportunity cost of abandoning today
$5,363,636	=	$2,000,000	+	$3,363,636

Failure to consider the time value of the abandonment option will lead BP to abandon the oil well prematurely.

Other market exit and abandonment decisions come in the form of American put options. For example, if the oil well can be sold to a competitor for $1 million, then BP holds an American put option to sell the underlying asset (the oil well) at an exercise price of $1 million. As with American call options, the values of American put options depend on the value of the underlying asset and it's volatility, the exercise price, the time to expiration of the option, and the time value of money.

The time value of the option to abandon is the flip side of the option to invest. In an uncertain environment, a firm that has some control over the timing of its investments will wait until expected returns are well above required returns before it invests. This results in hurdle rates that are well above investors' required returns. Similarly, firms will delay their abandonment decisions in the presence of uncertainty until the expected savings from abandonment are well above the up-front costs of abandoning a project. This provides us with the reason why firms continue to operate under adverse conditions.

The option to abandon is the flip side of the option to invest.

Firms continue to operate in unfavorable environments when there is a chance that prospects will improve and the sunk costs of abandonment can be avoided.

The time value of the option to invest arises from the ability to avoid negative outcomes should oil prices fall. Conversely, the time value of the abandonment option arises from the firm's ability to participate in positive outcomes should oil prices rise. That is, investment options gain value from bad news whereas abandonment options gain value from good news. Because of the value of the timing option, firms adopt a wait-and-see attitude before incurring sunk investment or abandonment costs.

Multinational firms often see the value of their investments rise and fall with changing real exchange rates. An increase in a country's real exchange rate makes goods manufactured in that country relatively more expensive on world markets. A fall in the real value of a currency makes that country's output relatively inexpensive on world markets. When the real value of the dollar was at its peak in the mid-1980s, U.S. manufacturers complained that their products were too expensive relative to foreign competitors' products. Similarly, as the yen appreciated in real terms against other currencies during the mid 1990s, Japanese manufacturers complained that they were losing sales to foreign competitors. Real changes in currency values inevitably provoke a call for government intervention to reverse the misfortunes of domestic businesses. The time value of the abandonment option is the reason multinational firms choose to weather the storm and persist in foreign markets despite adverse exchange rate conditions.

*Endogeneous uncertainty
creates an incentive to speed
up investment.*

Real options can create incentives for firms to invest in projects that, at least on the surface, look like negative-NPV projects. This is particularly true when there are endogeneous price or cost uncertainties tied to the project. When uncertainty is endogenous, the act of investing reveals information about the value of the investment option. In this case, firms have an incentive to speed up investment in order to gain additional information and resolve the uncertainty.

Endogeneous Price Uncertainty and the Value of Follow-up Projects

Suppose that the quality of oil produced by the Foinaven oil field cannot be determined until oil production begins. If the oil is high quality it will sell for \$30/bbl in perpetuity, and if it is low quality it will sell for \$10/bbl in perpetuity. Again, these two outcomes are equally likely. Variable production costs are \$12 per barrel and the initial investment is \$20,000,000. The intrinsic value of an oil well is less than zero.

$$\text{NPV(invest today)} = \left[\frac{(\$20/\text{bbl} - \$12/\text{bbl})\,(200,000\text{bbl})}{0.10} \right] - \$20,000,000$$

$$= -\$4,000,000 < \$0$$

$$\Rightarrow \text{Do not invest today (?)}$$

If the investment option is viewed as a now-or-never proposition, BP should not invest.

But suppose that this oil well is only the first of ten wells that BP might drill. If constructed, each well will be identical to the others and produce 200,000 barrels of oil per year in perpetuity. If BP were to invest in all ten oil wells today, the expected net present value of all ten wells would be −\$40,000,000. Viewed as a now-or-never decision, this is clearly not a good investment.

In this example, the act of investing reveals information about the price of oil and the value of the option to invest. BP can gain information about the potential of additional wells by investing in a single exploratory well. For simplicity, assume the quality of the oil and, hence, its market price are known in one year after the first well is drilled. (As in the original example, we'll ignore abandonment costs.)

If the oil is low quality and sells for \$10/bbl, BP should not produce oil at a \$12 cost that is above the \$10 oil price. The initial investment will be lost:

$$\text{NPV} | (P_{\text{oil}} = \$10) = -\$20,000,000$$

$$\Rightarrow \text{Do not invest further given } P_{\text{oil}} = \$10$$

On the other hand, if the oil is high quality, each well will have a net present value of

$$\text{NPV} | (P_{\text{oil}} = \$30) = \left[\frac{(\$30/\text{bbl} - \$12/\text{bbl})\,(200,000\text{bbl})}{0.10} / 1.10 \right] - \$20,000,000$$

$$= +\$16,000,000$$

$$\Rightarrow \text{Invest in additional wells given } P_{\text{oil}} = \$30$$

Additional investment can occur at time t=1. Given an oil price of $30/bbl, each of the nine additional wells will be worth $16,000,000/(1.10) = $15,545,454.50 > $0 as of time zero. The expected value of the decision to drill an exploratory well is then

NPV (invest in exploratory well)
$$= \text{Prob}(P_{oil}=\$10)] \, (NPV|P_{oil}=\$10) + [\text{Prob}(P_{oil}=\$30)] \, (NPV|P_{oil}=\$30)$$
$$= (\tfrac{1}{2})[-\$20,000,000] + (\tfrac{1}{2})[(1)(\$16,000,000) + (9)(\$15,545,454.50)]$$
$$= +\$63,454,545 > \$0$$
$$\Rightarrow \text{Invest in exploratory well}$$

Investing in the exploratory well reveals additional information about the potential of the Foinaven oil field and allows BP to make a more informed decision about its future investments.

In the original example of the option to invest, uncertainty was exogeneous and there was always value in waiting. In this example, there is an incentive to invest early because BP cannot determine the quality of the oil until after investment is made in the exploratory well. Including the value of follow-up projects can be important when uncertainty is endogeneous and the act of investing reveals information that otherwise would remain undiscovered.

A Resolution of Puzzle #3: The Multinational's Entry into New Markets

Multinational corporations often make small investments into emerging markets and new technologies even though the expected return on investment appears to be less than the cost of capital. In option pricing terms, the firm is purchasing an out-of-the-money call option that entitles it to make further investments if conditions improve.

Firms investing in new markets and technologies are purchasing a call option that entitles them to purchase additional call options if conditions warrant further investment.

By acquiring information that helps it make a better assessment of future opportunities, a firm can withdraw when its experience in a new market or technology suggests a negative outcome, and it can continue to invest when the outlook is positive.

17.6 OPTIONS WITHIN OPTIONS

Hysteresis: Entry and Exit Strategies in Combination

In the presence of uncertainty, firms impose hurdle rates that are higher than investors' required returns because of the investment timing option. Similarly, once a firm is invested, it will not abandon the investment until the gain from disinvestment is large enough to overcome the alternative of waiting for the situation to improve and thereby avoiding the sunk costs associated with abandonment. When the investment and abandonment options are considered in combination, the firm faces two thresholds. A suffi-

Hysteresis occurs when both entry and exit costs are high.

ciently high level of expected return over the return required by investors is necessary to induce the firm to invest. Similarly, a sufficiently high level of expected loss is necessary to induce the firm to pay the sunk costs of abandonment and disinvest. Because of these twin thresholds, firms' investment behaviors can appear "sticky"—firms sometimes fail to enter markets that appear attractive and, once invested, persist in operating at a loss. This behavior is called **hysteresis**. It is characteristic of multinational firms because of the high entry and exit costs and high uncertainty associated with foreign activities. In many cases, unanticipated changes in real exchange rates drive foreign investments into and then out of profitability, and then back again.

Because the option to invest and the option to abandon are two sides of the same coin, they are called switching options.[12] A **switching option** is a sequence of options in which one option is exchanged for another upon exercise. Many other investment decisions facing the firm can be characterized as switching options, including the suspension/reactivation and expansion/contraction decisions.

Suspension and Reactivation of Foreign Projects

Another switching option occurs when a firm considers the joint problem of suspension and/or reactivation of an existing project. Suspension of a project is often less costly than outright abandonment and retains the option to reactivate the project if and when conditions improve.

Suppose an energy company has invested considerable sunk costs in a coal-powered electricity generating plant for an energy-poor southern province in the People's Republic of China. Shortly after the plant begins operations, a competitor constructs a nuclear power plant in a nearby location. Once the nuclear-powered plant is in operation, the managers of the coal-fired plant find that they cannot compete on price with the nuclear-powered plant. The managers of the coal-powered plant have four options:

1. Downsize the scale of the plant and operate at a smaller capacity
2. Operate at a loss in the hopes that energy prices will rebound
3. Exercise their option to abandon the plant
4. Suspend operations or "mothball" the plant until energy prices rebound

Alternative 1 may not be viable. There are large economies of scale in energy production, and downsizing operations would result in higher costs per kilowatt produced. Alternatives 2 and 3 are the classic "to abandon or not to abandon" decision. If management decides to abandon the project, there is a good probability that its relationship with the Chinese government will be spoiled, thus forcing the firm to forgo positive-NPV projects elsewhere in China. Alternative 4 is a less costly alternative to abandonment and retains the option to reactivate the plant at a later date should coal prices fall or nuclear power fall into disfavor.

Once a foreign operation has been mothballed, the firm has purchased an American call option to reactivate the plant. Conversely, when the firm exercises the option to reactivate a foreign operation, it is simultaneously purchasing an American option to suspend operations. This is an example of a switching option.

---

12 See Peter Carr, "The Valuation of Sequential Exchange Opportunities," *Journal of Finance* 43, Vol. 5, 1988, pages 1235–1256.

Expansion and Contraction of Foreign Projects

Yet another example of a switching option comes in the form of managerial flexibility to expand or contract investments as new information arrives. As in the case of the multinational's entry into new and emerging markets, managers gain experience as they operate in new markets, and this experience helps them to "rightsize" their investments. If conditions look better than anticipated, the firm can exercise its option to increase its investment. If conditions look worse than anticipated, the firm can exercise its option to reduce its investment. Of course, exercise of each of these options brings with it additional expansion/contraction options.

The *scale* of investment has a great influence on the firm's operating flexibility. The term **operating leverage** is used to refer to the trade-off between fixed and variable costs in the operation of the firm. In this context, fixed costs reflect a cost accountant's attempt to allocate the initial sunk cost across production volume. Given an initial sunk cost, higher output allows the sunk cost to be allocated across more output and results in lower total costs per unit. Larger investments often result in lower variable costs per unit as well. Per-unit cost savings arising from a larger investment in plant and equipment are called **economies of scale**. In general, the smaller a firm's financial commitment to a project, the greater its operating flexibility.

As an example, suppose Ford Motor Company is building an automobile assembly plant in Brazil and is trying to decide whether to fully or only partially automate the plant. Fully automating the plant involves high fixed (sunk) costs and low variable costs per unit. Partial automation involves lower fixed costs and higher variable costs. The parameters of Ford's operating decision are shown in Figure 17.5. At the expected level of sales indicated in Figure 17.5, full automation is expected to minimize total costs and maximize profitability. Should sales not reach expectations, the low fixed costs and high

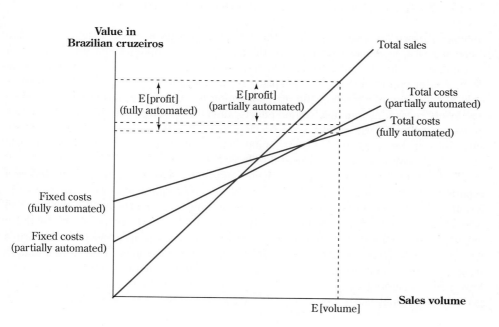

FIGURE 17.5
Ford's Operating
Leverage Decisions

variable costs of a partially automated plant can still result in a profitable investment. This is the classic version of the firm's operating leverage decision.

Viewed as a real option, the operating leverage decision is not a now-or-never choice. Full automation provides higher expected profits at the expected sales level in Figure 17.5, but full automation is less flexible than partial automation because of the high required sunk investment cost. Profitability can be maintained over a broader range of output with a partially automated plant. Perhaps more important, the scale of investment in a partially automated plant can be increased more easily if sales turn out to be higher than expected. The option to expand a partially automated plant is often omitted in traditional analyses of operating leverage. The partially automated plant comes with an American call option to increase the scale of investment should circumstances turn out favorably. The exercise price of the option is the incremental cost of upgrading the plant to a fully automated plant. As with the option to invest, the intrinsic value of the option is the value if exercised today, and the time value is the additional value of the option if the decision is postponed pending the arrival of additional information.

Conversely, the fully automated plant comes with an option to downsize the investment in plant and equipment to a less automated plant. The downsized plant would rely more on variable costs such as labor and less on capital investment in plant and equipment. Ford may be able to ship some of the machinery back to the United States for use on more lucrative projects there. The option to decrease the scale of investment is also an American option. With a smaller investment in plant and equipment, Ford may be able to make the Brazilian operation successful at a lower sales volume. Ford's decision on the optimal operating leverage of its Brazilian subsidiary must reflect this trade-off between the scale of investment and operating flexibility.

17.7 ASSETS-IN-PLACE VERSUS GROWTH OPTIONS

Assets-in-place are assets in which the firm has already invested. Suppose we value these assets in isolation from the growth (and flexibility) options that the firm has in expanding its current operations or in moving into new or related operations. If no expansion or contraction of assets-in-place is allowed, then the value of assets-in-place reflects the value of operating the firm according to the existing product mix, production levels, marketing and distribution efforts, and cost structures. In this case, valuation of assets-in-place is straightforward following the NPV rule—discount expected future cash flows at the opportunity cost of capital. The value of assets-in-place is the intrinsic value of the firm's current investment in real assets.

Growth options capture management's flexibility in responding to an uncertain world.

Flexibility in the management of existing and future assets can then be viewed as a separate source of value. Valuing managerial flexibility requires that we value many different kinds of options, including the options to enter new markets, exit existing and possible future markets, expand or contract the product line, suspend or reactivate existing and possible future investments, and develop follow-up projects to the firm's existing assets. These potential future investments arise because of the firm's unique position in the real goods markets and its brand names, patents, technological know-how, and managerial culture and expertise. These intangible assets are referred to as **growth options** because they capture the value of management's flexibility in responding to an uncertain world. Growth options reflect the positive-NPV decisions that the firm is likely to make in the future. In an option pricing framework, the value of growth options reflects the time value of the firm's current investment in real assets as well as the option value (including both intrinsic and time value) of the firm's potential future investments.

Firm value is the sum of the value of assets-in-place and the value of growth options:

$$V_{FIRM} = V_{ASSETS-IN-PLACE} + V_{GROWTH\ OPTIONS} \qquad (17.5)$$

Financial statements do not accurately capture the value of assets-in-place, and they typically ignore growth options entirely. The firm's financial statements reflect the sunk costs of investment and the accumulated returns to investment in the form of retained earnings. Although growth and abandonment options typically do not show up on the firm's financial statements, the market value of the firm's debt and equity reflects the market's assessment of the value of these hidden assets.[13] The market can assess the value of the firm's assets-in-place as well as its growth options and, hence, can assign a value to managerial flexibility in the firm's investment decisions.

17.8 WHEN THEORY FAILS

Why NPV Has Difficulty Valuing Managerial Flexibility

The net present value rule says to accept all positive-NPV projects. It requires that *only incremental cash flows* be included in the analysis and that *all opportunity costs* be included in the analysis. Although the NPV rule can faithfully value assets-in-place, it has difficulty with the many real options that accompany the firm's real assets.

The problem lies in the opportunity cost of capital.[14] In the Capital Asset Pricing Model (CAPM), identification of the opportunity cost of capital is handled by assuming normally distributed returns and a single market factor so that the discount rate is determined by a project's beta—its covariance with the market portfolio. The Arbitrage Pricing Theory (APT) also assumes normally distributed returns but allows the possibility of factors other than the market index. The contribution of factor F to the opportunity cost of capital for an asset is then determined by the asset's sensitivity to the factor according to $\beta_{j,F} = \rho_{j,F}\ (\sigma_j/\sigma_F)$. Normal distributions are completely described by their means, standard deviations, and correlations with other assets, and both the CAPM and the APT take advantage of this fact.

---

13 There are instances in which the value of growth options appears on the balance sheet. For example, under the purchase method of merger accounting in the United States, intangible assets are capitalized on the balance sheet and the value of growth options appears as *goodwill*.

14 An excellent discussion appears in "Project Valuation and Uncertainty: When Does DCF Fail?" by Nalin Kulatilaka and Alan J. Marcus, *Journal of Applied Corporate Finance* 5, No. 3, 1992, pages 92–100.

The discounted cash flow approach to project valuation is unable to adequately capture the opportunity cost of capital for an option. Even if the distribution of future cash flows can be estimated, the appropriate discount rate is ambiguous for three reasons:

- Options are always more volatile than the assets on which they are based.
- The volatility of an option changes with changes in the value of the underlying asset.
- Returns on options are inherently nonnormal.

Degree of Option Volatility. Options are always more volatile than the assets on which they are based. Options are levered investments, and small changes in the value of the underlying real or financial asset result in larger changes in option values. Consequently, options are always more volatile than the underlying assets on which they are based. Higher volatility on the option than on the underlying asset means that the systematic risk of the option is also greater than that of the underlying asset, assuming the beta of the underlying asset is positive.

Consider BP's investment option. In the original example, the value of the cash inflows from the oil well was

$$\text{Value} = \frac{(P - V)Q}{i} - I_0 = \frac{(\$20 - \$8)(200{,}000)}{0.10} = \$24{,}000{,}000$$

The intrinsic value of the option to invest at an exercise price of $20 million was $4 million. Suppose the value of the oil well increases by 50 percent, to $36 million. The intrinsic value of the option on this asset increases by 300 percent, from $4 million to $16 million.[15] This illustrates the general rule that the option is more volatile than the underlying asset.

Changing Degree of Option Volatility. The volatility of an option changes with changes in the value of the underlying asset. Suppose the value of the oil well rises another 50 percent, from $36 million to $54 million. The intrinsic value of the investment call option rises from $16 million to $34 million. This is an increase of 112.5 percent. Although the option is still more volatile than the underlying asset, the percentage increase in option volatility at this higher oil price level is less than the percentage increase at the lower oil price level. This illustrates a general rule: The volatility of a call option falls as the value of the underlying asset rises, although call option volatility never falls to the level of volatility in the underlying asset. Conversely, the volatility of a put option rises as the underlying asset value rises and the put option goes further out-of-the-money. This varying volatility has a devastating consequence for the discounted cash flow valuation method. The risk of a call or put option depends on the value of the underlying asset, so no single discount rate reflects the opportunity cost of capital as the value of the underlying asset evolves throughout the life of the option.

---

15 It is simplest to focus on the intrinsic value of the option and treat the option as if it expires immediately. The general result prevails when the time value is included; the volatility of an option is always greater than the volatility of the underlying asset so long as the volatility of the underlying asset is greater than zero.

Distribution of Option Returns. Returns on options are inherently nonnormal. Even if underlying asset returns are normally distributed, returns on options are not normally distributed. An easy way to see this is to observe that the distribution of call option values is truncated, or cut off, at the exercise price. Only that portion of a call option to the right of the exercise price is of value to the option holder. This means that conventional risk measures are not sufficient to fully describe the risk of an option. Neither standard deviation of return nor beta captures the asymmetric nature of option risk.

In combination, these three characteristics make determining the opportunity cost of capital on an option a messy and unrewarding affair. Option pricing models handle this problem by constructing a *replicating portfolio* that mimics the payoffs on the option.[16] Arbitrage arguments are then used to determine option values against the offsetting replicating portfolio. This eliminates the need to determine the opportunity cost of capital. For this reason, the only discounting conducted in an option valuation exercise is done at the risk-free rate of interest. This works especially well for options that are contractually written against an underlying asset whose value is observable, such as oil, interest rates, or currency values. For the noncontractual cash flows associated with real assets, underlying asset values are often unobservable and determination of the distributional characteristics of the underlying asset is even more difficult to assess.

Limitations of the Option Pricing Approach to Project Valuation

Because financial options are traded in a competitive financial market with few trading frictions, financial options are usually zero-NPV investments. Valuation of financial options, such as currency options, is relatively straightforward. Real options are another matter entirely. Financial options are easier to value than real options for the following reasons:

- Financial markets have few market imperfections that impede the law of one price from ensuring that identical assets sell for the same price.

- Exercise prices on financial options are contractually written on a single financial asset whose price is readily observable in the financial market.

- The process generating returns is relatively stable over the short (typically nine-month) maturities of most financial options.

Three characteristics of real options make them difficult to value with option pricing methods.

Relation of the Underlying Asset to Option Value. Option pricing methods are simplest to apply when option value depends on a single financial price. The oil price examples of this chapter were intentionally chosen to reduce this dimension of the option valuation problem. Yet the value of a real option usually depends on a myriad of factors that can be difficult to identify and can interact in complex ways. The value of a manufacturing plant, for example, depends on a variety of cost and revenue streams that

---

16 Appendix 8-A demonstrates the construction and use of a replicating portfolio.

interact through price and volume. Discounted cash flow methods are also subject to this criticism, but option valuation methods are particularly sensitive to the assumptions underlying the analysis. This is especially true of the assumptions regarding the process (or processes) governing returns to the underlying asset.

The Underlying Asset's Return-Generating Process. Once the asset (or assets) underlying the option are identified, option pricing methods require an assumption about the process governing returns to the underlying asset. Identifying this process is difficult, and it is a critical step in solving for option value. Once the return-generating process is identified, option values can be found either analytically (such as in the binomial and Black-Scholes models) or by numerical methods. Most financial options are of relatively short maturity, and the assumption of a stationary, instantaneous normal distribution is reasonable. Most real options are long-lived and the processes that generate returns are seldom stationary (or even normal) over the life of the option.

Unobservable Prices, Market Frictions, and Option Values. Option pricing models rely on a replicating portfolio (composed of the underlying asset and riskless borrowing or lending) with the same payoffs as the option. An assumption of costless arbitrage then ensures that the value of the option is equal to the value of the replicating portfolio.

There are two obstacles to costless arbitrage between a real option and its replicating portfolio. First, most real options have values that are unobservable. This means that arbitrage cannot use market prices to ensure comparability between the option and its replicating portfolio. Second, imperfections in the markets for real assets are much more prominent than in the financial markets. As a consequence of these two differences between real and financial assets, real option values can diverge from their theoretical values; costless arbitrage cannot ensure that the value of the option is equal to that of the replicating portfolio.

Discounted Cash Flow and Option Pricing as Complements

The discounted cash flow and option pricing approaches to project valuation should be viewed as complements. Each approach has advantages and disadvantages. For example, constructing a decision tree of possible future scenarios can assist the financial manager in formulating competitive responses to various situations. Yet a decision tree can only capture a few of the future possibilities. Option pricing methods start with an assumption about the distribution of project values and determine the value of the option to invest from this distribution. If both valuation methods are applied to a real investment opportunity, they reinforce each other and provide a second opinion regarding the value of the investment. Managers will have more confidence in their valuation if the NPV and option value estimates are close than if they are far apart.

17.9 SUMMARY

A key variable faced by every cross-border investment is uncertainty. Currency, political, and cultural risks are the most prominent additional risks in cross-border investment, but business risk on foreign projects can also be higher than that of domestic projects.

When uncertainty is high, the multinational corporation's real investment opportunities often possess optionlike characteristics. Real options found in cross-border investment opportunities include

- The option to invest
- The option to abandon
- Options to expand or contract
- Options to suspend or reactivate
- Growth options and follow-up projects

Option values can be decomposed into the value of the option if exercised today and the value of waiting.

$$
\begin{array}{llll}
\text{Option Value} & = & \text{Intrinsic Value} & + & \text{Time Value} & \quad (17.4) \\
\text{NPV(wait)} & = & \text{NPV(invest today)} & + & \text{Opportunity cost} \\
& & & & \text{of investing today}
\end{array}
$$

Option pricing methods are particularly useful for identifying the time value of a real option.

Conventional discounted cash flow valuation techniques run into trouble when the firm's investments include real options. Discounted cash flow and net present value are difficult to apply to real options for the following reasons.

1. Options are inherently riskier than the underlying asset on which they are based.
2. The risk of an option changes with changes in the value of the underlying asset.
3. Returns to options are not normally distributed.

Despite the difficulties in applying discounted cash flow techniques to cross-border valuation, we should not let what we do not know about valuation get in the way of what we do know. Discounted cash flow techniques are useful in many circumstances, particularly when an investment decision must be made immediately or forgone entirely.

Option valuation is simplest to implement when option values are contingent on a single financial price variable. Even when project value depends on many factors and encompasses many interacting variables, viewing the project as a package of options can help place a cross-border project into the proper perspective. In particular, firm value can be decomposed into the value of assets-in-place and the value of growth options.

$$
V_{\text{FIRM}} = V_{\text{ASSETS-IN-PLACE}} + V_{\text{GROWTH OPTIONS}} \qquad (17.5)
$$

Option valuation can be used to complement a conventional discounted cash flow analysis when valuing an investment that includes real options.

KEY TERMS

American call option
American put option
Assets-in-place
Economies of scale
Endogenous uncertainty
Exogenous uncertainty
Growth options
Hysteresis

Intrinsic value
Managerial flexibility
Operating leverage
Price uncertainty
Real options
Switching options
Time value
Timing option

CONCEPTUAL QUESTIONS

17.1 What is a real option?

17.2 In what ways can managers' actions seem inconsistent with the "accept all positive-NPV projects" rule? Are these actions truly inconsistent with the NPV decision rule?

17.3 Are managers who do not appear to follow the NPV decision rule irrational?

17.4 Why is the timing option important in investment decisions?

17.5 What is exogeneous uncertainty? What is endogeneous uncertainty? What difference does the form of uncertainty make to the timing of investment?

17.6 In what ways are the investment and abandonment options similar?

17.7 What is a switching option? What is hysteresis? In what way is hysteresis a form of switching option?

17.8 What are assets-in-place? What are growth options?

17.9 Why does the NPV decision rule have difficulty in valuing managerial flexibility?

17.10 What are the shortcomings of option pricing methods for valuing real assets?

PROBLEMS

17.1 (Exogenous price uncertainty and the option to invest)

A proposed brewery in the East European country of Dubiety will produce a beer—dubbed the "Dubi Dubbel"—for Grolsch N.V. of the Netherlands. In response to the thrust to integrate East European markets, a number of other West European brewers have announced plans to produce and sell beer in the Dubi market. If too many breweries open, beer prices will fall. If some of these investment plans do not materialize, prices are likely to rise. The price of beer is determined exogeneously and will be known with certainty in one year. Grolsch management must decide whether to begin production today or in one year. The following facts apply to the investment decision.

Initial investment	I_0 = D200,000,000; rises by 10% each year
Expected price of beer	P_0 = D50 per bottle in perpetuity
Actual price of beer in a year	P_1 = either D25 or D75 with equal probability
Fixed production cost	D10,000,000 per year
Variable production cost	D10 per bottle
Expected production	1,000,000 bottles per year forever
Tax rate	0%
Discount rate	i = 10%

a. Draw a decision tree that depicts Grolsch's investment decision.
b. Calculate the NPV of investing today as if it were a now-or-never alternative.
c. Calculate the NPV (at t=0) of waiting one year before making a decision.
d. Calculate the NPV of investing today, including all opportunity costs.
e. Should Grolsch invest today or wait one year before making a decision?

17.2 (Exogeneous price uncertainty and the option to abandon)

Grolsch management has gone ahead with the brewery investment in Problem 17.1. The market has grown increasingly competitive, and nearly all of the brewery investments in Eastern Europe are losing money. To make matters worse, variable production costs are higher than expected (D20/bottle). Grolsch has also discovered (much to its dismay) that employment laws in Dubiety specify that employees cannot be laid off so long as the brewery is open; Grolsch must either produce at capacity or close the brewery. Several competitors are considering abandoning the market. If they do not abandon, the price will remain constant at D15/bottle in perpetuity. If they do abandon, the price will rise to D35/bottle. Assume Grolsch's abandonment decision does not influence competitors' abandonment decisions, so price uncertainty is exogenous. The following facts apply to the abandonment decision.

Cost of abandoning brewery	I_0 = D10,000,000; rises by 10% each year
Current price of beer	P_0 = D15 per bottle in perpetuity
Price of beer in a year	P_1 = either D15 or D35 with equal probability
Fixed production costs	D10,000,000 per year
Variable production cost	D20 per bottle
Expected production	1,000,000 bottles per year forever
Tax rate	0%
Discount rate	i = 10%

a. Draw a decision tree that depicts Grolsch's investment decision.
b. Calculate the NPV of abandoning today as if it were a now-or-never alternative.
c. Calculate the NPV (as of t=0) of waiting one year before making a decision.
d. Calculate the NPV of abandoning today, including all opportunity costs.
e. Should Grolsch abandon this losing venture today?

17.3 (Endogeneous price uncertainty and growth options)

The "Dubi Dubbel" investment of Problem 17.1 is one of five brewery investments that Grolsch is considering in Eastern Europe. The quality of the beer produced by the Dubi brewery will provide Grolsch with information on the quality of beer that it can expect from the other five investments. Grolsch will not know the quality of beer, and, hence, the price at which the beer will sell, until production begins. The situation is similar to Problem 17.1.

Initial investment	I_0 = D200,000,000; rises by 10% each year
Expected price of beer	P_0 = D50 per bottle in perpetuity
Actual price of beer in a year	P_1 = either D25 or D75 with equal probability
Fixed production cost	D10,000,000 per year
Variable production cost	D10 per bottle
Expected production	1,000,000 bottles per year forever
Tax rate	0%
Discount rate	i = 10%

a. Draw a decision tree that depicts Grolsch's investment decision.
b. Calculate the NPV of investing today as if it were a now-or-never alternative.
c. Calculate the NPV (as of t=0) of waiting one year before making a decision.

d. Calculate the NPV of investing today, including all opportunity costs.

e. Should Grolsch invest today? What is different in this problem from the setting in Problem 17.1, and how does it affect Grolsch's investment decision?

17.4 (Advanced problem on competitive strategy)

In Problems 17.1 and 17.2, how might Grolsch's investment/abandonment decisions be different if its decisions influence competitors' decisions and vice versa?

SUGGESTED READINGS

A unified treatment of many of the topics in this chapter appears in
Avinash K. Dixit and Robert S. Pindyck, *Investment under Uncertainty,* Princeton University Press, Princeton, N.J., 1994.

A review of this pathbreaking text appears in
Eduardo S. Schwartz, *Journal of Finance* 49, No. 5, 1994, pages 1924–1928.

Financial Management devoted an entire special issue (Vol. 22, No. 3, 1993) to real options. The following articles in this issue are particularly illustrative.
"Real Options and Interactions with Financial Flexibility" by Lenos Trigeorgis

"Reversion, Timing Options, and Long-Term Decision Making" by David G. Laughton and Henry D. Jacoby

"Creating Value by Spawning Investment Opportunities" by Eero Kasanen

"Case Studies in Real Options" by Angelien G.Z. Kemna

When and why discounted cash flow methods prove insufficient to value real options is discussed in
Nalin Kulatilaka and Alan J. Marcus, "Project Valuation and Uncertainty: When Does DCF Fail?" *Journal of Applied Corporate Finance* 5, No. 3, 1992, pages 92–100.

Valuation of offshore oil leases is developed in
James L. Paddock, Daniel R. Siegel, and James L. Smith, "Option Valuation of Claims on Real Assets: The Case of Offshore Petroleum Leases," *Quarterly Journal of Economics* 103, August 1988, pages 479–508.

Daniel R. Siegel, James L. Smith, and James L. Paddock, "Valuing Offshore Oil Properties with Option Pricing Models," *Midland Corporate Finance Journal* 5, Spring 1987, pages 22–30.

Managerial flexibility is valued as an option in
Alexander J. Triantis and James E. Hodder, "Valuing Flexibility as a Complex Option," *Journal of Finance* 45, June 1990, pages 549–565.

Lenos Trigeorgis and Scott P. Mason, "Valuing Managerial Flexibility," *Midland Corporate Finance Journal* 5, Spring 1987, pages 14–21.

The nature of endogeneous uncertainty, sequential options, and the learning curve are discussed in
Carl W. Kester, "Today's Options for Tomorrow's Growth," *Harvard Business Review,* March/April 1984, pages 153–160.

Taxes and Multinational Business Strategy

The only thing that hurts more than paying an income tax
is not having to pay an income tax.

Lord Thomas R. Duwar

OVERVIEW

The perfect market assumption that there are no taxes or, more generally, that there is no difference in tax rates across business activities, is obviously simplistic. The many differences in national tax rates and tax systems can make tax planning a major source of value for the multinational corporation. This chapter shows how a multinational's income from foreign operations is taxed and how tax planning can lessen the multinational's tax liability, maximize after-tax return on investment, and maximize corporate value.

A word of caution before we begin this journey into national tax codes and international tax planning: International taxation is an exceedingly technical area that requires a detailed knowledge of two or more (often incompatible) tax systems. If the advice "Consult with your tax accountant" applies to domestic business, it applies tenfold to international business. This chapter is intended as an introduction to international taxation and is not meant to be your sole reference on international taxation and tax planning. You should consult with your tax accountant before proceeding with a new international venture.

18.1 NATIONAL TAX SYSTEMS AND INTERNATIONAL TAX TREATIES

The Objectives of National Tax Policy

We often hear that the only sure things in life are death and taxes. Taxes are collected to pay for public services, including police and fire protection; roads and other infrastructure projects; social programs, including welfare; and national defense. A **national tax policy** refers to the way in which a nation chooses to allocate the burdens of tax collections across its residents.

Tax Teutrality: A Level Playing Field. A starting point in our discussion of national tax policy is the concept of **tax neutrality**. A neutral tax is one that does not interfere with the natural flow of capital toward its most productive use. Tax neutrality was implicit in our perfect market assumption of frictionless markets. Taxes are a form of market friction, but so long as they fall equally on all business activities, they are a neutral friction and do not reallocate capital away from its natural destinations.

There are two (often competing) forms of tax neutrality.

- *Domestic tax neutrality* ensures that incomes arising from foreign and from domestic operations are taxed similarly by the domestic government.
- *Foreign tax neutrality* ensures that taxes imposed on the foreign operations of domestic companies are similar to those facing local competitors in the host countries.

Domestic tax neutrality attempts to put the foreign and domestic operations of domestic multinationals on an even footing so that export activity and international trade are not disadvantaged. Foreign tax neutrality attempts to preserve the viability of domestic multinationals relative to their foreign competitors by ensuring that an undue tax burden is not imposed on domestic companies doing business in foreign lands.

Violations of Tax Neutrality. In practice, national governments have quite different social, political, and economic agendas, and they are only too willing to use taxation to implement these policy objectives. Consequently, the ideal of tax neutrality is almost impossible to achieve. For example, with a corporate income tax rate of 42 percent in Germany and 20 percent in Liechtenstein, it is impossible for U.S. tax authorities to ensure that taxes imposed on the foreign operations of U.S. multinationals are similar to those of local competitors in Germany and Liechtenstein and still maintain domestic neutrality. Because national governments use tax policy to promote the welfare of their own domestic businesses, they cannot attain the twin objectives of domestic and foreign tax neutrality.

Because taxes are never truly neutral, businesses need tax planning. Multinational corporations are especially well positioned to take advantage of cross-border differences in tax rates and tax systems. The remainder of this section describes four deviations from tax neutrality that are important determinants of multinational tax planning and business strategy. These deviations are

- Different tax rates on income from different tax jurisdictions
- Different tax rates on income from different organizational forms
- Different tax rates on income from different asset classes
- Different tax rates on income from different financing instruments

Income received from different tax jurisdictions is often taxed at different rates. Some countries, such as Sweden, choose to impose relatively high taxes to finance ambitious social welfare programs. Other countries, such as Luxembourg, choose relatively low tax rates to attract foreign capital. Still other countries, including Canada, France, and the Netherlands, fully exempt the earnings of foreign operations from domestic taxation. Differences in tax codes can be important considerations in market entry and exit decisions, in intrafirm transfer pricing decisions, and in how the multinational corporation repatriates income from its foreign operations.

Income received from different legal organizational forms in the same tax jurisdiction may be taxed at different rates. Many countries tax the foreign branch income of domestic firms as it is received but delay taxes on subsidiaries of domestic firms incorporated in a foreign country until income is repatriated to the parent. This is the general rule in the United States, although there are limitations on the type of foreign income that qualifies under this rule (this is covered in a later section on Subpart F income). Other countries tax different legal forms at different rates. Withholding taxes on dividend, interest, and royalty distributions also influence the choice of organizational form. For these reasons, a multinational must consider the tax consequences of its choice of organizational form when operating in foreign countries and entering new markets. Multinational corporations based in the United States usually choose to incorporate their foreign operations in the host country. Operating as a foreign branch is a less popular organizational form for U.S. corporations. On the other hand, financial institutions incorporated in the United States commonly choose to organize their foreign operations as foreign branches.

Income received from different types of assets in the same tax jurisdiction, such as active business income versus passive investment income, is often taxed at different rates. In the United States, losses on one type of income cannot be used to offset gains on another type of income. Many other countries make some distinction for tax purposes between different forms of income.

Returns on financial securities are taxed differently depending on whether the financing instrument is debt, equity, a debt-equity hybrid (such as preferred stock), or an equity-linked security (such as a stock option or warrant). On the other side of the contract, the tax treatment of financial expenses is different for payments to different classes of creditors, such as employees (wages payable), customers (trade credit), banks (interest), and shareholders (dividends). For example, interest expense is tax deductible in most countries, whereas dividend payments usually are not. Different corporate and personal tax treatments on interest and dividend payments mean that different capital structures are preferred in different tax jurisdictions.

National tax policies thus help determine the types and locations of assets held by the multinational corporation, the organizational forms in which it chooses to operate, and the way in which the multinational corporation finances its domestic and foreign operations.

National Taxes on Foreign-Source Income

The major issues in international taxation revolve around the fact that income earned from foreign operations—**foreign-source income**—generally falls under two or more tax jurisdictions. Countries around the world generally apply one of two different tax regimes to income earned by multinational corporations incorporated within their borders:

- A worldwide tax system
- A territorial tax system

In a **worldwide tax system**, the multinational's worldwide income is taxed by the home country as this income is repatriated to the parent company. Income from foreign corporations usually is not taxed until it is repatriated to the parent, as long as it is reinvested in an active business outside of the home country. A foreign tax credit for income taxes paid to a foreign government prevents double taxation of foreign earned income. This tax regime is used in the United States, the United Kingdom, and Japan.

In a **territorial tax system** only domestic income is taxed. Income from outside the home country is not taxed as long as it is earned in an active business. This tax regime is used in Hong Kong, France, Belgium, and the Netherlands, among others. Still other countries, such as Canada and Germany, use a territorial system for income earned in countries with which they have a tax treaty and a worldwide system for income earned in nontreaty countries. The intent of both the worldwide and the territorial tax systems is to avoid double taxation of foreign-source income.

Bilateral tax treaties ensure some consistency in the treatment of foreign-source income.

Although the details of national income tax systems vary, bilateral tax treaties ensure some consistency in the tax treatment of foreign-source income. Many of these tax treaties follow the *Model Treaty of the Organization for Economic Cooperation and Development* (OECD). Tax treaties are intended to ensure that the foreign operations of each nation's multinational corporations are not tax-disadvantaged relative to local competitors in the foreign country. Bilateral tax treaties also largely remove the threat of double taxation of foreign-source income.

Explicit versus Implicit Taxes

Explicit Taxes. National governments impose many different kinds of **explicit taxes**, including

- Corporate and personal income taxes
- Withholding taxes on dividends, interest, and royalties
- Sales and value-added taxes
- Property and asset taxes
- Tariffs on cross-border trade

The costs of doing business in a foreign country depend in large part on the types and levels of explicit taxes imposed by the host government. Table 18.1 lists tax rates on corporate income, personal income, and capital gains, and withholding tax rates on dividend and interest income for forty-three countries.

Country	Top corporate income tax rate	Dividend withholding tax rate	Interest withholding tax rate	Top personal income tax rate	Capital gains tax rate
Argentina	30	0	12	30	0
Australia	33	15	10	47	regular rates
Austria	34	5/12.5	0	50	0
Bahamas	0	0	0	0	0
Belgium	41	5/15	0/10	46	0
Bermuda	0	0	0	0	0
Brazil	25	15	25	25	regular rates
Canada	38	10/15	15	29	regular rates
China	30	20	20	20	0
Denmark	34	5/15	0	66	regular rates
Egypt	42	n/s[b]	n/s	20	2
Finland	25	5/15	0	35	25
France	33	5/15	0	25	19
Germany	42	5/15	0	52	0
Greece	35	n/s	n/s	40	0
Hong Kong	18	0	regular rates	25	0
Hungary	40	10/20	0	44	regular rates
India	65	20	20	40	20
Indonesia	15	15	0/15	20	regular rates
Ireland	40	0	0/27	n/s	40
Israel	37	13/15/25	10/18	48	0
Italy	36	5/10/15	15	51	15/25
Japan	38	10/15	10	20	20
Korea	34	10/15	12	20	10/20
Liechtenstein	20	4	4	*[c]	regular rates
Luxembourg	33	5/7.5	0	33	26
Malaysia	34	0	0/20	34	0
Mexico	34	0	5/10	30	0
Netherlands	35/40	5/15	0	35	20/38
New Zealand	38	30	15	33	0
Norway	0	15	0	28	regular rates
Russia	32	n/s	0	30	regular rates
Saudi Arabia	45	n/s	n/s	0	regular rates
Singapore	27	27	27	27	0
South Africa	40	15	0	43	0
Spain	35	10/15	10	25	regular rates
Sweden	30	5/15	0	25	25
Switzerland	10	5/15	5	12	0
Taiwan	20/25/35	20/35	20	20	0
Thailand	30	10	15	37	0
Turkey	46	0/10/15	10	50	0
United Kingdom	33	0	0	40	regular rates
United States	35	—	—	28	28

[a] Local taxes not included

[b] n/s = not specified

[c] Taxed as an addition to personal income at those tax rates.

Source: Compiled from *1994 International Tax Summaries,* Coopers & Lybrand International Tax Network, Editor: George J. Yost, III, John Wiley & Sons, Inc.

Corporate income taxes are charged on the corporation's taxable income. As might be expected, there is little consistency in how sovereign nations define taxable income. Countries following a territorial tax system typically do not tax foreign-source income, but countries following a worldwide tax system usually tax foreign-source income as it is repatriated to the parent company.[1] Whether countries follow worldwide or territorial tax systems, the net effect of most bilateral tax treaties is to make foreign-source income taxable at the higher of the two national corporate income tax rates.

Withholding taxes on dividend distributions are the norm, especially for dividend payments to nonresidents. Withholding taxes on dividend distributions are intended to ensure that the taxable dividend income of residents is reported to the tax authorities in the host country. For dividend distributions to nonresidents, such as a multinational parent firm in another country, withholding taxes also compensate the host government for lost tax revenues from forgone personal income taxes in the host country. The dividend withholding tax rate is most frequently 5 percent between countries with bilateral tax treaties, but it varies from 0 percent on cross-border dividend distributions from Hong Kong and the United Kingdom to more than 25 percent on some dividend distributions from Austria and Germany.

Withholding taxes on interest and royalty payments are imposed less frequently. Governments that withhold taxes on interest payments are also likely to withhold taxes on royalty payments. As an example of why governments impose interest withholding taxes, the German Bundesrechnungshof (or taxing authority) estimated in the late 1980s that 65 percent to 70 percent of all interest income received by individuals in West Germany went unreported.[2] Germany instituted several tax law changes in the early 1990s in an effort to increase reporting compliance. First, the level at which interest income becomes taxable was raised to several thousand marks in order to help break the tradition of noncompliance. Second, a withholding tax on interest payments by corporations and banks was instituted and administered through the banking system. This withholding tax can be partially recovered by those declaring their interest income to the government. Finally, penalties for noncompliance were increased. Prior to these tax law changes, most nonreporters were not discovered until death or divorce brought them before the taxing authority. German taxpayers now have greater incentives to report their interest income.

In lieu of the state sales taxes popular in the United States, many countries around the world use **value-added taxes** (also called *ad valorem taxes* or *VATs*). A value-added tax is a sales tax collected at each stage of production in proportion to the value added during that stage. Each of the countries in the European Union uses a value-added tax. Although the merits of value-added taxes are periodically debated in the United States, proposals to institute a value-added tax have met strong resistance in the U.S. Congress.

---

1 As mentioned in Chapter 14, in the 1980s the State of California attempted to tax the worldwide income of all foreign companies doing business in California. After much political brouhaha and numerous lawsuits brought by both foreign and domestic businesses, California formally dropped this taxation system in 1994.

2 Wolf Bay and Richard Stehle, "Elimination of the Double Taxation of Dividends: Is the German Experience Relevant for the USA?," Augsburg University (Germany), working paper, 1992.

Tax policy is a competitive tool that local and national governments can use to attract businesses that might not otherwise locate in a particular tax jurisdiction. Developing economies can use tax holidays to attract foreign investment and promote development in key regions and industries. Countries that actively employ tax policy to attract investment include China, Hungary, Ireland, Malaysia, and the United States (see box on Puerto Rico). Low taxes or tax subsidies in the form of tax relief or tax holidays allow locations to overcome some of the handicaps that make a particular location less desirable than competing locations.

Implicit Taxes. The law of one price requires that equivalent assets sell for the same price. Because investors care about after-tax returns (as opposed to before-tax returns), the law of one price can be restated as: *Equivalent assets sell to yield the same after-tax real rate of return.* Not all taxes are neutral, and higher before-tax required returns are demanded on highly taxed assets and organizational forms and in high-tax jurisdictions. Lower expected returns on assets subject to lower tax rates are a form of **implicit tax.**

The law of one price imposes an implicit tax on assets in low-tax jurisdictions.

Here is an example of an implicit tax. Suppose a multinational corporation can invest $100,000 in Country H to yield $112,500 for a pretax return of $i_H = 12.5\%$. Corporate income in Country H is taxed at a relatively high rate of $t_H = 60\%$. After-tax return in Country H is then $i_H(1-t_H) = (0.125)(1-0.60) = 0.50$, or 5 percent. Alternatively, the corporation can invest $100,000 in Country L and endure a lower corporate tax rate of $t_L = 40\%$. If a pretax return of $i_L = 12.5\%$ can also be earned in this country, then $100,000 can be turned into $107,500 after taxes for an after-tax return of $i_L(1-t_L) = (0.125)(1-0.40) = 0.075$, or 7.5 percent.

This situation cannot persist. Investors will eventually begin to move their investments toward the low-tax country and away from the high-tax country. This activity will continue until, in equilibrium, expected after-tax rates of return are equal across all countries.

The law of one price requires that expected after-tax real rates of return on comparable-risk assets are equal across all countries.

In this example, this means that

$$1+ i_H(1-t_H) = 1+i_L(1-t_L)$$
$$i_H/i_L = (1-t_L)/(1-t_H)$$
$$= (1-0.40)/(1-0.60)$$
$$= 1.5 \tag{18.1}$$

In equilibrium, pretax returns in Country H will be 50 percent higher than pretax returns in Country L to compensate for the higher income tax in Country H. For example, if prices are bid up in the low-tax country until before-tax returns fall to $i_L = 10\%$, then prices in Country H will fall and before-tax expected rates of return will rise until $i_H = 15\%$ in equilibrium. The higher prices and lower expected returns in country L are a form of implicit tax on earnings in that country.

Explicit and Implicit Taxes in Puerto Rico

The Commonwealth of Puerto Rico is an example of a location where low taxes have been used successfully as a competitive tool for attracting new businesses. Under the "possessions corporation" provisions of Section 936 of the U.S. Internal Revenue Code, 90 percent of qualified manufacturing income earned in Puerto Rico is exempt from U.S. taxation for the first five years of operations, and 75 percent is exempt for the next five years. Additional tax relief is available for up to thirty-five years if operations are located in remote regions away from the capital of San Juan. To qualify for exemption from U.S. income taxes, 80 percent of the employees must come from Puerto Rico and be employed at least twenty hours per week. A withholding tax of 10 percent discourages U.S. companies from immediately repatriating earnings from Puerto Rico. The withholding tax falls 1 percent per year to zero after ten years if earnings are reinvested in Puerto Rico.

These subsidies are an attempt by the U.S. Congress to make investment in U.S. possessions more attractive to U.S.

businesses. Tax subsidies were deemed necessary to overcome a history of poor development and a shortage of skilled workers in Puerto Rico and other U.S. possessions. Poor infrastructure (especially transportation and telecommunications), relatively undeveloped banking facilities, and language differences (Spanish rather than English) also contribute to making Puerto Rico a less-than-desirable site for manufacturing operations. Tax subsidies have made an important contribution to the Puerto Rican economy, which is blessed with some of the best ports in the Caribbean. Puerto Rico is home to many high-margin manufacturing industries, including pharmaceuticals, electronics, and petrochemicals.

Tax subsidies have also spawned a variety of implicit taxes. Demand for local labor has resulted in high minimum wages. The resulting high operating costs are a form of implicit tax on operations in Puerto Rico. The withholding tax on earnings in Puerto Rico has also contributed to relatively low before-tax returns on Puerto Rican assets.

18.2 TAXATION OF FOREIGN-SOURCE INCOME IN THE UNITED STATES

Foreign-source income from a foreign branch is taxed as it is earned.

In the United States, the Internal Revenue Service (IRS) is responsible for collecting taxes and ensuring that individuals and corporations follow the U.S. tax guidelines. The treatment of foreign-source income depends on how foreign operations are organized. **Foreign branches** of a U.S. corporation are treated as a part of the parent rather than as a separate legal entity. Income earned from a foreign branch is taxed in the U.S. as it is earned in the foreign country.

On foreign-source income from an affiliate that is incorporated in a foreign country, the United States allows a **foreign tax credit (FTC)** against domestic U.S. income taxes up to the amount of foreign taxes paid on foreign-source income. If a U.S. parent company owns more than 50 percent of a foreign corporation either in terms of market value or voting power, the foreign subsidiary is called a **controlled foreign corporation (CFC)**. Income from a CFC is taxed only when funds are repatriated to the parent company in the United States in the form of dividends, interest, royalties, or management fees. Earnings from foreign corporations that are between 10 percent and 50 percent owned by a U.S. parent are called Subpart F income, which is taxed on a pro rata basis according to sales or gross profit. The rest of this section describes U.S. taxation of foreign-source income from foreign corporations.

Foreign Tax Credits and FTC Limitations

Foreign Tax Credits for a Single Foreign Subsidiary. The amount of the foreign tax credit applied to the U.S. parent's taxable income depends on both the amount and the form of taxes paid to the foreign government. Foreign taxes used in the computation of the foreign tax credit include foreign income taxes as well as foreign withholding taxes on dividend distributions to the parent.

Consider the foreign subsidiaries of three different U.S.-based multinational corporations as shown in Table 18.2. The foreign subsidiaries are located in Switzerland, Italy, and Germany. Let's first suppose that these are the only foreign businesses of each parent firm so that we do not have to bother with limitations on foreign-source income pooled across several foreign subsidiaries. (The overall limitation on foreign tax credits is the topic of the next section.) After translating foreign-source incomes into dollars, each subsidiary has $1,000 of taxable income. Corporate income tax rates are 28 percent in Switzerland, 36 percent in Italy, and 50 percent in Germany.[3] The highest corporate income tax rate in the United States is 35 percent. Withholding taxes on dividend distributions to the U.S. parent of each foreign subsidiary are 5 percent in each foreign country.[4]

The parents' foreign and domestic income tax liabilities shown in the top portion of Table 18.2 assume that the full $1,000 is repatriated from each subsidiary. The foreign-source income of each controlled foreign corporation is taxed as it is earned in the foreign country (line e). An additional tax on the dividend distribution to the U.S. parent is withheld by each foreign country (line h). The declared dividend net of the dividend withholding tax is available to the U.S. parent (line j). Total foreign tax (line i) is the sum of the foreign income tax (line e) and the foreign dividend withholding tax (line h).

With a 100 percent dividend distribution, 100 percent of foreign-source income is taxed as it is received in the United States (line k). The tentative U.S. income tax on each subsidiary is then $350 (35 percent of $1,000 on line l). This is the amount of tax that would have been due had the income been earned in the United States. With a 100 percent dividend distribution, each subsidiary provides a tax credit equal to total foreign taxes paid (line m). If the tentative U.S. tax is larger than the foreign tax credit, as is the case for the subsidiary in Switzerland, then the U.S. parent must pay the difference between the tentative U.S. tax and the foreign tax credit (line n). If the foreign tax credit is larger than the tentative U.S. tax, as is the case for the subsidiaries in Italy and Germany, then no additional taxes are due. If these subsidiaries are the sole foreign operations of their respective parents, then the total foreign and domestic taxes of these three foreign subsidiaries is $1,267.

Multiple Foreign Subsidiaries and the Overall FTC Limitation. The previous example assumed that the three foreign subsidiaries were owned by three different U.S. parent firms and that these were the sole foreign operations of the respective U.S.

*The intent of the foreign tax credit
is to avoid double taxation of
foreign-source income.*

---

3 Much of the political and taxing power in Switzerland resides in twenty-five cantons (provinces). The maximum national corporate income tax rate is 9.8 percent. Each canton adds its own income tax, so that combined national and cantonal tax rates range from 22 percent to 35 percent.
4 Withholding taxes for countries with U.S. tax treaties range from 5 percent to 15 percent. See Table 18.1.

TABLE 18.2 REPATRIATION OF ACTIVE FOREIGN-SOURCE INCOME

Tax Statements as Single Subsidiaries of Three U.S. Parents

			Switzerland	Italy	Germany
a		Dividend payout ratio	100%	100%	100%
b		Foreign dividend withholding tax rate	5%	5%	5%
c		Foreign tax rate	28%	36%	50%
d		Foreign income before tax[a]	1000	1000	1000
e	Less	Foreign income tax (d*c)	280	360	500
f		After-tax foreign earnings (d.−e)	720	640	500
g		Declared as dividends (f*a)	720	640	500
h		Foreign dividend withholding tax (g*b)	36	32	25
i		Total foreign tax (e+h)	316	392	525
j		Dividend to U.S. parent (d−i)	684	608	475
k		Gross foreign income before tax (d)	1000	1000	1000
l		Tentative U.S. income tax (k*35%)	350	350	350
m	Less	Foreign tax credit (i)	316	392	525
n		Net U.S. taxes payable [max(l−m, 0)]	34	0	0
o		Total taxes paid (i+n)	350	392	525
p		Net amount to U.S. parent (k−o)	650	608	475
q		Total taxes as separate subsidiaries (Σo)		1,267	

Consolidated Tax Statement as Subsidiaries of One U.S. Parent

r	Overall FTC limitation (Σk*35%)	1,050
s	Total FTCs on a consolidated basis (Σi)	1,233
t	Additional U.S. taxes due [max(0, r−s)]	0
u	Excess tax credits [max(0, s−r)]	183
	(carried back 2 years or forward 5 years)	

[a] All income and tax amounts are in U.S. dollar equivalents.

parents. In this setting, the FTC limitation is simple to apply. The foreign tax credit in any year is the minimum of foreign taxes paid and the U.S. tax that would have been paid if the income was earned in the United States. The net effect is that the U.S. parent pays current-year taxes at the higher of the two rates.

Multinational corporations based in the U.S. and owning more than one foreign subsidiary face an overall limitation on foreign tax credits. The total FTC on earnings from active foreign businesses is limited to the amount of U.S. tax attributable to foreign-source income. Total foreign income is pooled or consolidated across all foreign subsidiaries, so that losses in some countries are offset by gains in other countries. When the U.S. tax rate is a constant fraction of a multinational's worldwide income, such as 35 percent, the **overall FTC limitation** is calculated as:

The overall FTC limitation applies to consolidated income.

$$\text{Overall FTC limitation} = (\text{Total foreign-source income})(\text{U.S. tax rate}) \qquad (18.2)$$

Now assume the three foreign subsidiaries in Table 18.2 are all owned by the same U.S. parent. Total foreign-source income across the three foreign subsidiaries is $3,000. At the 35 percent U.S. tax rate, the overall FTC limitation is ($3,000) (0.35) = $1,050 (line r). The $1,233 sum of the foreign tax credits is greater than the tentative U.S. tax of $1,050, so the U.S. multinational owning these three foreign subsidiaries has excess foreign tax credits of $1,233 − $1,050 = $183 (line u). Excess foreign tax credits can be carried back two years or forward five years in the United States.

Other Limitations on Foreign Tax Credits

The Tax Reform Act of 1986 and Income Baskets. The **Tax Reform Act (TRA) of 1986** instituted changes to the U.S. tax code that affect the way multinational corporations are taxed on their foreign operations. The 1986 TRA categorized taxable income into a variety of income baskets:

Income baskets limit the value of foreign tax credits to U.S. multinationals.

- Active income
- Passive income
- High-withholding-tax interest income
- Export financing interest
- Financial service income
- Foreign sales corporation (RSCs) and domestic international sales corporations (DISCs)
- Other income

Active income is income earned from participation in an active business. This category includes

- Dividends received from active subsidiaries
- Management fees received from active subsidiaries
- Interest received from more-than-50-percent-owned subsidiaries
- Income from active foreign branches

Passive income is income, such as investment income, that does not come from an active business. This category includes

- Dividends received from less-than-10-percent-owned owned companies
- Interest from less-than-50-percent-owned subsidiaries or unrelated parties
- Rents and royalties not derived from an active business
- Income from commodities and currency transactions
- Dividends, interest, rents, royalties, and Subpart F income (see below) to the extent attributable to the passive income of controlled foreign corporations
- Passive income from the sale of property
- Foreign personal holding company income

High-withholding-tax interest income is interest income (with the exception of export financing interest) that has been subject to a foreign gross withholding tax of 5 percent or more. (Although many countries impose a withholding tax on dividend distributions, only a few withhold taxes on interest payments.)

Export financing interest is interest income derived from goods manufactured in the United States and sold outside the United States as long as not more than 50 percent of the market value of the goods is imported into the United States.

Financial service income is derived from financial services, such as banking, insurance, leasing, and financial service management fees. Interest rate, currency, and commodity swap income is also allocated to this basket.

Foreign sales corporations (FSCs) and *domestic international sales corporations (DISCs)* are specialized sales corporations that are classified into a separate income basket. Tax losses from this income basket cannot be used to offset active income.

Additional classifications apply to a variety of other forms of income. Losses in one category of income can only be used to offset gains in that same income category. For example, passive gains on currency transactions cannot be used to offset losses from an active foreign investment, such as a foreign branch. Because tax losses in one category cannot be pooled with gains from another category, the value of foreign tax credits to U.S. multinationals is greatly reduced. This also means that the tax consequences of various forms of income distribution must be explicitly considered as U.S. multinationals organize their foreign operations.

Subpart F Income. Taxing foreign-source income only when it is repatriated to the parent corporation allows multinational corporations to shift sales to foreign subsidiaries and avoid current taxation. To reduce tax-avoidance abuses, **Subpart F** of the 1962 Revenue Act modified the rule that foreign-source income is taxed only as it is repatriated to the parent. According to Subpart F, shareholders owning 10 percent or more of a foreign corporation must include a pro rata share of the Subpart F income of the foreign corporation in their own gross income. This makes Subpart F income taxable when it is earned, whether or not it is remitted to the parent. The most important category of Subpart F income is **foreign base company income**. Foreign base company income includes the following.

The Subpart F income of a foreign subsidiary is taxed as it is earned on a pro rata basis.

- *Foreign holding company income.* Passive income from dividends, interest, management fees, royalties, rents, net foreign currency and commodity gains, and income from the sale of non-income-producing property. These sources of income do not arise from an active business.

- *Foreign base company sales income.* Active income derived from transactions between related parties when the goods are both produced and sold outside the United States. An example is sales of auto parts from a Mexican subsidiary of General Motors to an assembly plant owned by a Canadian subsidiary of GM.

- *Foreign base company service income.* Active service income derived from transactions between related parties when the services are both produced and sold outside the United States. An example is information services sold from a Canadian subsidiary to a Mexican subsidiary of General Motors.

Subpart F also includes a number of less common sources of income: (1) income from the insurance of U.S. risks, such as premiums from health, life, and property insurance; (2) any increase in earnings invested in U.S. property; (3) income that is related to international boycotts; and (4) income from illegal foreign bribes (see box *La Mordida*).

Once income is identified as belonging to the Subpart F categories, the gross income net of expenses is *deemed paid* to the parent firm and must be included in the parent's taxable income whether or not it is actually repatriated to the parent. Because of the Subpart F rules, active income from related-party transactions that take place outside the United States and all passive foreign-source income is taxed in the United States as it is earned.

The Subpart F rules contain several additional provisions. The most important of these is the so-called "5-70 rule," which states that

- If Subpart F income is less than the minimum of $1 million or 5 percent of the gross income of the parent firm, then foreign base company income is set to zero.

- If Subpart F income is more than 70 percent of the parent firm's total gross income, the entire gross income of the foreign subsidiary is treated as foreign base company income. This income is then subject to several additional limitations.

Subpart F makes it much more difficult for multinational corporations to avoid taxes by using tax havens and the transfer pricing schemes discussed in Section 18.3. Along with the separate income baskets created by the 1986 Tax Reform Act, these changes caused foreign tax credit limitations to be binding for many more U.S. businesses.

Allocation of Income and Expenses. Another limitation on the usefulness of foreign tax credits comes in the form of **allocation-of-income rules**. When not all profits are repatriated to the parent, the U.S. tax code applies the allocation-of-income rules to determine what portion of earnings are taxable and how interest, R&D, and other expenses are to be allocated between domestic-source and foreign-source income. The general rule is that income and expenses should be allocated to the tax jurisdiction in which they are earned. These rules are important because of the different tax rates that can apply to foreign-source and domestic-source income.

The Tax Reform Act of 1986 allocates interest expense according to the proportion of foreign and domestic assets on the MNC's consolidated financial statements. Thus, regardless of whether the parent or a foreign subsidiary issues debt, the proportion of interest that is allocated to foreign- and domestic-source income depends on the firm's proportion of foreign and domestic assets and not on which entity actually issued the debt.

According to current tax law, 50 percent of the research and development expenses of U.S. MNCs are allocated to domestic-source income, with the remainder allocated to foreign- and domestic-source income according to the proportion of either sales or gross income from foreign and domestic sources. Expenses that do not directly arise from an income-related activity (such as the general and administrative expenses of operating the home office) are allocated to foreign- and domestic-source income according to the proportion of either sales or gross income from foreign and domestic sources.

These allocation-of-income rules also are important because the size of the MNC's FTC limitation depends on how income and expenses are allocated. Tax shields can be lost altogether if foreign taxing authorities do not follow the IRS's guidelines. For

La Mordida—*"The Little Bite"*

One of the income baskets created under Subpart F of the 1962 Revenue Act is a basket for illegal foreign bribes. Bribery is not commonly practiced in the United States, so this income basket seems strange from a U.S. perspective. In other countries it is quite common for government bureaucrats and the managers of private businesses to use bribes as they conduct their daily business.

Suppose that you are the sales representative of International Business Machines (IBM) for all of South America. You are in the process of negotiating a large contract to supply personal computers to the Venezuelan government. Your competitors from Hong Kong are offering to pay the local official in charge of computer acquisitions a modest sum in an effort to secure the contract. If you stick to your (American) principles and refuse to pay *la mordida* (the little bite), there is a good chance that you will lose the contract. On the other hand, you are fairly sure that you can secure the contract if you offer a bribe. What should you do?

In the United States, the 1977 Foreign Corrupt Practices Act specifically outlawed the use of bribery as a way to promote the business interests of U.S. corporations and their foreign affiliates. This act requires that U.S. multinationals compete with local firms in foreign markets according to U.S. rules—rules that are sometimes in conflict with local convention. Because bribes are commonplace in many countries and the competitors of U.S. firms do not have to follow the U.S. rules, this act puts U.S. firms at a competitive disadvantage in securing sales contracts and in transporting goods in countries where bribery is commonplace.

Lockheed Corporation holds the dubious distinction of having paid the largest fine in U.S. history for violating the Foreign Corrupt Practices Act. In February 1995 Lockheed admitted in a U.S. court that it bribed an Egyptian official to arrange the sale of three transport aircraft in 1988. The fine for this act was $24.8 million.

---

example, allocating home office expenses to a foreign subsidiary reduces the FTC limitation and increases the U.S. tax liability. If the foreign taxing authority does not recognize these as tax-deductible expenses, the FTC limitation is reduced even though taxes in the foreign country are not reduced. The portion of home office expense that is allocated to the foreign country is simply lost. Along with income baskets and the Subpart F rules, the allocation-of-income rules further limit the usefulness of foreign tax credits.

18.3 TAXES AND THE LOCATION OF FOREIGN OPERATIONS

Global Site Selection: In Pursuit of After-Tax Returns

MNCs have a tax incentive to shift operations toward low-tax countries when the overall FTC limitation is binding.

U.S.-based multinationals have a tax incentive to shift operations toward countries with low income tax rates, particularly when the overall FTC limitation is binding. If the overall FTC limitation is binding, unused foreign tax credits from high-tax countries absorb the additional U.S. taxes due on foreign-source income from countries with low tax rates. To illustrate the effect of shifting operations toward low-tax foreign jurisdictions, suppose sales are shifted from the German to the Swiss subsidiary in the example of Table 18.2. Then the German taxable income falls to $0 while Swiss taxable income rises to $2,000. This situation is shown on the right-hand side of Table 18.3.

TABLE 18.3 EFFECT OF SHIFTING SALES TOWARD LOW-TAX COUNTRIES

Tax Statements as Single Subsidiaries of Three U.S. Parents

			Tax statements without shifting			Shift sales to Switzerland and away from Germany		
			Switzerland	Italy	Germany	Switzerland	Italy	Germany
a		Dividend payout ratio	100%	100%	100%	100%	100%	100%
b		Foreign dividend withholding tax rate	5%	5%	5%	5%	5%	5%
c		Foreign tax rate	28%	36%	50%	28%	36%	50%
d		Foreign income before tax[a]	1000	1000	1000	2000	1000	0
e	Less	Foreign income tax (d*c)	280	360	500	560	360	0
f		After-tax foreign earnings (d−e)	720	640	500	1440	640	0
g		Declared as dividends (f*a)	720	640	500	1440	640	0
h		Foreign dividend withholding tax (g*b)	36	32	25	72	32	0
i		Total foreign tax (e+h)	316	392	525	632	392	0
j		Dividend to U.S. parent (d−i)	684	608	475	1368	608	0
k		Gross foreign income before tax (d)	1000	1000	1000	2000	1000	0
l		Tentative U.S. income tax (k*35%)	350	350	350	700	350	0
m	Less	Foreign tax credit (i)	316	392	525	632	392	0
n		Net U.S. taxes payable [max(l−m, 0)]	34	0	0	68	0	0
o		Total taxes paid (i+n)	350	392	525	700	392	0
p		Net amount to U.S. parent (k−o)	650	608	475	1300	608	0
q		Total taxes as separate subsidiaries (Σo)		1,267			1,092	

Consolidated Tax Statement as Subsidiaries of One U.S. Parent

r	Overall FTC limitation (Σk*35%)			1,050			1,050	
s	Total FTCs on a consolidated basis (Σi)			1,233			1,024	
t	Additional U.S. taxes due [max(0, r−s)]			0			26	
u	Excess tax credits [max(0, s−r)]			183			0	
	(carried back 2 years or forward 5 years)							

a All income and tax amounts are in U.S. dollar equivalents.

The overall FTC limitation is still 35 percent of $3,000, or $1,050. Once German sales are shifted to Switzerland, total foreign taxes paid on the two remaining foreign subsidiaries ($1,024) is $26 less than the FTC limitation of $1,050. This means that $26 in additional taxes are due the U.S. tax authorities. Shifting sales from Germany to Switzerland in this example reduces the U.S. parent's total tax bill in the current fiscal year by $1,233 − $1,050 = $183. Excess tax credits in the U.S. are correspondingly reduced by $183.

In the base case without shifting sales, total taxes depend on whether the $183 excess tax credit can be applied against foreign taxes paid in other years. If the overall FTC limitation is binding in other years, then the $183 excess tax credit cannot be carried backward or forward and would simply be lost to the corporation. Shifting sales to Switzerland will then capture a $183 reduction in current year taxes.

In this example, Switzerland is the tax-preferred location because of its low tax rates. However, this is not the whole story. Operations in Switzerland are likely to face an implicit tax as multinationals from around the world shift their operations toward Switzerland in pursuit of Switzerland's tax advantages. In the absence of capital flow restrictions, this flow of foreign capital will squeeze profit margins in Switzerland, and before-tax expected returns will fall. For example, winegrowers flooding the Swiss market in an attempt to reap profits in this low-tax country will drive wine prices down, and profit margins will deteriorate. Falling profit margins mean lower before-tax expected returns on investment in Switzerland. Conversely, before-tax profit margins in Germany will rise to compensate for the relatively high German tax rates. This process will continue until, in equilibrium, after-tax expected returns are equal across all countries.

Implicit taxes also must be considered as the MNC makes its global location decisions.

Explicit taxes are just one of many factors to be considered in decisions about global locations of operating and financing affiliates. Implicit taxes also must be taken into account as the multinational corporation makes its global location decisions. Minimizing explicit taxes cannot be the overriding criterion in multinational site selection because of the many and subtle forms of implicit taxes faced by the multinational corporation. For example, when governments offer tax incentives to attract foreign investment it is usually because they cannot compete for capital without these incentives. These countries are likely to have a poorly educated workforce, inadequate physical or legal infrastructures, poor communications systems, or other handicaps that lead either to higher operating costs or to lower final goods prices. Multinational corporations must assess the after-tax, rather than before-tax, expected returns on investment. To the extent that before-tax expected returns are driven down by low explicit tax rates, multinationals may choose to locate elsewhere. The criteria determining site selection for a foreign operation should thus include, but not be dominated by, tax considerations.

Tax-Haven Affiliates

Because of the costs of moving capital to and from the parent firm, some multinationals have set up wholly owned **tax-haven affiliates** in countries with low tax rates. Bermuda and the Bahamas, for instance, have no income taxes. Offshore affiliates in countries such as these typically own stock in the overseas subsidiaries of the parent company and are used to direct the multinational's capital to where it is needed.

Several location-specific factors determine site selection for tax-haven affiliates. The country should have low taxes on foreign-source income and low withholding tax rates on dividends repatriated to the parent firm. The country's currency should not be too volatile. Allowing local firms to freely conduct trade in the Eurocurrency markets is an easy way for countries to allow tax-haven affiliates to reduce their exposure to local currency risk. The country should have low political risk so that the tax-haven affiliate and its parent need not be overly concerned about changing local laws and regulations. The location should have sound physical, legal, and communication infrastructures to support the financial services activities conducted by the tax-haven affiliates located within its borders. A local population that is sophisticated in the uses of financial products is a plus.

The TRA of 1986 largely eliminated the tax benefits of tax-haven affiliates.

The Tax Reform Act of 1986 requires that income taxes be paid on offshore banking, shipping, and airline income. Previously, taxes did not have to be paid until dividends were remitted to the parent firm. Tax-haven affiliates are often financial in nature, and these captives are categorized as banks by the U.S. tax code. This has greatly reduced and in many cases eliminated the tax benefits of tax-haven affiliates for U.S.-based multinational corporations. Tax-haven affiliates are still popular for multinational corporations based in countries with territorial tax systems and in some other countries with worldwide tax systems.

Re-invoicing Centers

Even though many of the tax benefits of tax-haven affiliates to U.S. multinational corporations have been eliminated by the Tax Reform Act of 1986, many multinationals still find it convenient to maintain offshore financial affiliates. In many cases, these take the form of **re-invoicing centers** that are used to channel funds to and from the multinational's far-flung operations. These re-invoicing centers also often manage the MNC's currency risk exposures. The U.S. tax system is a large part of the reason that U.S. MNCs tend to conduct their currency risk management off-shore.[5] The factors that go into site selection for re-invoicing centers are the same as those for tax-haven affiliates.

Re-invoicing centers are used to channel funds between the MNC's overseas operations.

Transfer Pricing and Tax Planning

Transfer prices must be set on intracompany sales from one unit of the firm to another. Section 486 of the Internal Revenue Code requires that transfer prices be set as if the transaction were an *arm's-length transaction* between unrelated parties. Most countries have transfer pricing guidelines similar to those in the United States. Management of transfer prices is most advantageous in the following situations:

- For businesses with operations in more than one tax jurisdiction
- For businesses with high gross operating margins
- For businesses with intermediate or final products for which there is no market price

Firms whose ownership-advantages come in the form of patents or other intangible assets are prime candidates for aggressive tax management, because these assets often have high margins and no market prices with which to identify arm's-length pricing. Companies that market high-technology products, such as semiconductors and prescription drugs, fit this category.

Firms with intangible assets, such as patents, are more aggressive in their transfer pricing policies.

The potential for transfer price abuses is particularly high when the firm is exposed to different tax rates on different sources of income, such as through operations in different countries. Transfer pricing is a particularly powerful tax-management tool when intracompany transfers involve intangible assets, such as royalties, services, and high-margin goods, for which there is no market price. In these cases, the MNC can use transfer prices to shift expenses toward countries with high tax rates. This can minimize total taxes and maximize the value of foreign investment.

---

5 See Andrea S. Kramer and J. Clark Heston, "An Overview of Current Tax Impediments to Risk Management," *Journal of Applied Corporate Finance* 6, No. 3, 1993, pages 73–81.

Because of the potential for abuse, the IRS closely monitors the transfer pricing policies of multinational corporations. If the IRS disagrees with a taxpayer's transfer prices, it can unilaterally make an adjustment to the tax returns. Appeals of the IRS's transfer pricing decisions can take years to resolve, and more than one company has gone through Chapter 11 reorganization to avoid the extra tax bite. For example, Storage Technology produced disk storage devices in Puerto Rico during the late 1970s to take advantage of Puerto Rico's "possessions corporation" tax status. Most of the company's revenues but none of the R&D expenses were allocated to the Puerto Rican subsidiary. The resulting earnings were exempt from U.S. income tax. The IRS challenged Storage Technology's transfer prices and allocation of R&D expense. Storage Technology declared bankruptcy in 1983 largely to avoid the back taxes due on earnings from its Puerto Rican manufacturing facilities.

Consider the example in Table 18.4. FoodCorp, Inc. is a diversified, U.S.-based MNC with operations in Argentina and Hungary. The Argentinean subsidiary of FoodCorp exports beef to the FoodCorp subsidiary in Hungary. The 40 percent corporate income tax rate in Hungary is greater than the 30 percent rate in Argentina. How should these subsidiaries of FoodCorp price their goods to reduce their worldwide taxes?

Under an arm's-length transfer pricing policy, FoodCorp sets the price equal to the market price, which results in $5,000 in revenues for its Argentinean subsidiary. Revenues to this subsidiary are costs of goods sold to the Hungarian subsidiary. The good news is that the Hungarian subsidiary enjoys a 50 percent markup over its cost and nets $5,000 in taxable income. The bad news is that income in Hungary is taxed at a relatively high 40 percent rate. Income from the combined Argentinean-Hungarian operation is effectively taxed at 38 percent under the low markup policy.

Suppose FoodCorp increases the transfer price by 60 percent, resulting in revenues of $8,000 to its Argentinean subsidiary and cost of goods sold to its Hungarian subsidiary. FoodCorp could justify this inflated price by claiming that only top-quality beef is being exported to Hungary. This contention is difficult for the tax authorities to challenge without monitoring both the quality of the beef being shipped and the market prices for medium-grade and top-grade beef. The issue will be further complicated from

TABLE 18.4 TRANSFER PRICING AND TAX PLANNING FOR FOODCORP, INC.

	Low transfer price			High transfer price		
	Argentinean subsidiary	Hungarian subsidiary	Consolidated	Argentinean subsidiary	Hungarian subsidiary	Consolidated
Revenue	$5,000 ⌐	$10,000	$10,000	$8,000 ⌐	$10,000	$10,000
Cost of goods sold	3,000 └→	5,000	3,000	3,000 └→	8,000	3,000
Other expenses	1,000	1,000	2,000	1,000	1,000	2,000
Taxable income	1,000	4,000	5,000	4,000	1,000	5,000
Taxes	300	1,600	1,900	1,200	400	1,600
Net income	700	2,400	3,100	2,800	600	3,400
Effective tax rate on foreign operations		38%			32%	

the government's perspective if comparable beef sells for the equivalent of $5,000 in Argentina and $8,000 in Hungary. In any case, FoodCorp's effective tax rate falls from 38 percent to 32 percent with the higher transfer price.

The key to understanding the impact of transfer pricing on the worldwide tax liability is to recognize that taxes can be reduced by shifting taxable income toward low-tax jurisdictions (Argentina) and away from high-tax jurisdictions (Hungary).

18.4 TAXES AND ORGANIZATIONAL FORM: FOREIGN BRANCH OR FOREIGN SUBSIDIARY?

Most MNCs incorporated in the United States conduct their foreign operations through controlled foreign corporations (CFCs). Controlled foreign corporations are foreign corporations owned more than 50 percent either in terms of market value or voting power. CFCs are incorporated in the host country and are governed by the laws and tax rules of the host country. Income from CFCs is not taxed by the U.S. government until it is repatriated to the U.S. parent company in the form of dividends, interest, royalties, or management fees. Foreign governments usually impose a withholding tax on dividend distributions to the parent as compensation for lost tax revenues from forgone personal income taxes in the host country.

MNCs often use controlled foreign corporations to conduct their foreign operations.

A smaller amount of foreign business is conducted by U.S. MNCs through foreign branches. Foreign branch income is fully taxable by the parent's home country as it is earned. The immediate taxability of foreign branch income is often the overriding tax consideration that leads U.S. MNCs to organize foreign operations as subsidiaries rather than as branches. This is especially true for foreign operations located in countries with low tax rates. Operating as a foreign branch subjects foreign-source income to the higher domestic tax rates immediately. In contrast, foreign subsidiaries can reinvest abroad without having to pay the higher domestic tax rates until funds are repatriated back to the parent.

Foreign branches do have some tax advantages over foreign subsidiaries. Income earned through a foreign branch is taxed as it is earned by the government of the country in which the parent company is incorporated. This creates a tax advantage for the foreign branch organizational form for start-up operations that are expected to lose money for a number of years. Losses from foreign branch operations are immediately deductible against domestic income, so there is a tax incentive to establish start-up operations that are expected to lose money for a number of years as foreign branches. The foreign branch can be incorporated in the host country once foreign operations become profitable, although previously deducted losses must be recaptured as income. Withholding taxes also do not need to be paid on foreign branch income as it is repatriated to the parent, because it is not a dividend distribution. Finally, transfers of property to foreign branches are not a sale to a separate legal entity and, hence, are not taxable.

Despite these tax advantages of foreign branches, foreign subsidiaries are the preferred mode of foreign operation for most U.S. MNCs. There are several other reasons for incorporating in the host country. First, incorporation in the host country helps limit the liability of the parent company on its foreign operations. The MNC's exposure to the activities of each foreign subsidiary is limited to the assets of that subsidiary. This limit on liability is not absolute, as Union Carbide discovered when its subsidiary in India suffered a major ecological and human disaster at a chemical plant in Bhopal, India. If it can be shown that the parent company had effective control of the subsidiary despite the legal separation of the two, then attorneys can "pierce the corporate veil" and claim that the parent is culpable for the activities of the foreign subsidiary. There is still the difficult issue of which country has jurisdiction over disputes.

Disclosure requirements imposed by a host country also can favor incorporating in the host country over operating as a foreign branch. Some countries require that firms operating within their borders disclose information on their worldwide operations. The worldwide operations of a foreign subsidiary are limited to those of the subsidiary, but the worldwide operations of a foreign branch include those of the parent. MNCs use foreign subsidiaries when they would be hurt by publicly disclosing sensitive information on their worldwide operations.

Foreign branches are most frequently found in the banking and insurance industries because the 1986 Tax Reform Act does not allow them to use all of their foreign tax credits when they operate with foreign subsidiaries.[6] National tax policies also influence the choice of organizational form for foreign affiliates, because most nations tax branches and subsidiaries differently. Finally, the treatment of royalties, management fees, and expenses paid to the home office varies across countries.

18.5 TAXES AND CROSS-BORDER INVESTMENT ACTIVITY

In equilibrium, after-tax returns should equalize across countries as corporations adapt their investment and financing strategies to take advantage of cross-border tax differentials. Because of higher taxes, equilibrium before-tax returns in high-tax countries should be higher than before-tax returns on similar investments in low-tax countries to compensate for higher taxes. Lower expected and required returns in low-tax countries are a form of implicit tax that cannot be credited against the parent corporation's tax liabilities. The law of one price equalizes after-tax returns so that countries with high (low) explicit taxes have low (high) implicit taxes. In equilibrium, there should be a single worldwide required return on after-tax income of a particular risk.

The existence of implicit taxes has an interesting effect on the MNC's incentives to acquire or invest in foreign assets. The effect of implicit and explicit taxes is country-specific in that it depends on how foreign-source income is treated by the MNC's home country. For U.S.-based MNCs, the most important tax variable affecting foreign investment is whether the firm has excess foreign tax credits (FTCs). The interaction of the FTC limitation on foreign source income with the tax rate of the host country is summarized in Figure 18.1.

---

6 See Scholes and Wolfson, *Taxes and Business Strategy: A Planning Approach,* 1992, page 298.

Tax Status of U.S. Buyer	Host Country Tax Rate	
	Low	High
Excess FTCs	neutral	neutral
No excess FTCs	unattractive	attractive

FIGURE 18.1
Foreign Tax Credits and the Attractiveness of Foreign Investment

Overall FTC Limitation Reached—Excess FTCs

When a U.S. MNC has reached its overall FTC limitation and has excess foreign tax credits, foreign-source income earns the equilibrium after-tax market rate of return, and there is no tax incentive to invest or disinvest internationally. In this case, investments in low-tax countries consume some of the MNC's excess FTCs, so the effective tax rate on income from low-tax countries is equal to the low foreign tax rate. This means that the after-tax rate of return on investments in low-tax countries equals the worldwide equilibrium after-tax return. On the other hand, excess FTCs generated on income from high-tax countries generally goes unused, so the effective tax rate on income from high-tax countries is equal to the high foreign tax rate. As with investment in low-tax countries, the effective after-tax rate of return is equal to the worldwide equilibrium rate. Consequently, when a U.S.-based MNC has excess FTCs, the tax status of the host country is not a factor in the MNC's investment decisions.

Overall FTC Limitation Not Reached—No Excess FTCs

An interesting result arises when the MNC has not yet reached its FTC limitation and there are no excess foreign tax credits. When there are no excess FTCs, foreign source income from low-tax countries is taxed at the higher U.S. rate. This provides a disincentive toward investing in low-tax countries. Conversely, foreign source income from high-tax countries generates excess FTCs that can be used to offset the U.S. tax liability on the MNC's existing operations in low-tax countries. This creates an incentive to invest in high-tax countries. The net result is an incentive to invest in high-tax countries and avoid low-tax countries when the MNC has not yet reached its overall FTC limitation.[7]

---

7 For a discussion of the effect of explicit and implicit taxes on foreign investment and some empirical evidence consistent with the tax effect described here, see Gil Manzon, David Sharp, and Nickolaos Travlos, "An Empirical Study of the Tax Consequences of U.S. Tax Rules for International Acquisitions by U.S. Firms," *Journal of Finance* 49, No. 5, 1994, pages 1893–1904.

18.6 SUMMARY

National tax policies play an important role in the business strategies of the multinational corporation. In the absence of other factors, the objective of multinational tax management is to minimize taxes and maximize after-tax earnings. But the multinational corporation does not operate in a vacuum. Although the attractiveness of cross-border investment and financing opportunities depends on national tax policies, it also depends on a host of nontax factors that relegate tax management to an important but ultimately supportive role in the strategies and operations of the multinational corporation. One of these factors is the existence of implicit taxes in the form of lower rates of return in low-tax countries.

The United States follows a worldwide tax system in which foreign-source income is taxed by the U.S. as it is repatriated to the parent company. Foreign branches are legally a part of the parent company, so income is taxed as it is earned in the foreign country. Income from affiliates that are incorporated in a host country is taxed as it is repatriated to the parent in the form of dividends, interest, management fees, transfer prices, or royalties. The U.S. tax code allows a foreign tax credit (FTC) against domestic U.S. income taxes up to the amount of foreign taxes paid on foreign-source income.

For a large multinational corporation paying U.S. income taxes at the maximum rate, the overall FTC limitation on earnings from active foreign businesses is

$$\text{Overall FTC limitation} = (\text{Total foreign-source income})(\text{U.S. tax rate}) \qquad (8.2)$$

Excess FTCs can be carried back two years or forward five years. Other portions of the U.S. tax code further limit the tax deductibility of business expenses. These limitations include

- Separate income baskets for income from different sources, such as for active versus passive income
- Subpart F rules that specify pro rata taxation (based on sales or gross profit) for income from foreign corporations that are between 10 percent and 50 percent owned by a U.S. parent
- Allocation-of-income rules that determine how income and expenses are allocated between foreign and domestic U.S. operations

These limitations influence how the overall FTC limitation is applied to different tax jurisdictions, organizational forms, asset classes, and financing instruments.

International tax planning is more complicated than domestic tax planning, but the opportunities for increasing the value of the firm through tax planning are correspondingly greater. The international business environment provides the multinational corporation with a number of opportunities that are either not available to the domestic firm or are available in a greatly diminished form. These include

- A variety of tax rates and tax systems
- Transfer prices between affiliates in different tax jurisdictions
- The ability to shift both production and sales across national borders
- Tax-haven affiliates and re-invoicing centers for channeling offshore funds to where they are most needed

- Tax treatments for asset classes, financing instruments, and organizational forms (foreign branch versus subsidiary) that can differ across countries

Because of these opportunities, tax planning is even more important for the multinational corporation than for its domestic counterpart.

KEY TERMS

Allocation-of-income rules
Controlled foreign corporation (CFC)
Explicit taxes
Foreign base company income
Foreign branch
Foreign-source income
Foreign tax credit (FTC)
Implicit tax
National tax policy

Overall FTC limitation
Re-invoicing centers
Subpart F income
Tax-haven affiliate
Tax neutrality
Territorial tax system
Transfer prices
Value-added taxes
Worldwide tax system

CONCEPTUAL QUESTIONS

18.1 What is tax neutrality? Why is it important to the multinational corporation? Is tax neutrality an achievable objective?

18.2 What is the difference between an implicit and an explicit tax? In what way do before-tax required returns react to changes in explicit taxes?

18.3 How are foreign branches and foreign subsidiaries taxed in the United States?

18.4 How has the U.S. Internal Revenue Code limited the ability of the multinational corporation to reduce taxes through multinational tax planning and management?

18.5 Are taxes the most important consideration in global location decisions? If not, how should these decisions be made?

PROBLEMS

18.1 India imposes a 65 percent tax on corporate income. Thailand's maximum corporate income tax rate is 30 percent. If pretax returns in Thailand are 10 percent, how much must pretax returns be in India for the law of one price to hold?

18.2 Salty Solutions, Inc., has manufacturing facilities in Hong Kong and India. Each facility earns the equivalent of $10 million in foreign-source income before tax.

a. Use Table 18.2 and the tax rates from Table 18.1 to calculate the overall U.S. tax liability (or excess FTC) of Salty Solutions.

b. Suppose Salty Solutions is able to shift operations so that pretax income is $20 million in Hong Kong and zero in India. What is the U.S. tax liability (or excess FTC) under this scenario?

c. Suppose Salty Solutions is able to shift operations so that pretax income is $20 million in India and zero in Hong Kong. What is the U.S. tax liability (or excess FTC) under this scenario?

18.3 Quack Concepts, Inc., produces its patented drug Metafour (a duck extract used as an antioxidant) in both Puerto Rico and the United States. The effective marginal tax rate is 35 percent in the United States and 5 percent in Puerto Rico. No additional taxes are due in the United States from Puerto Rican sales. Quack sells Metafour to U.S. consumers for $10 per bottle and has annual sales of 100,000 bottles.

a. Because the patent is an intangible asset, Quack has wide latitude in the transfer price that it sets on sales from its Puerto Rican manufacturing subsidiary back to the U.S. parent company. Quack's cost of goods sold is $1/btl in Puerto Rico. Fill in the following table and calculate the effective tax rate on Metafour sales for a low transfer price of $1/btl and for a high transfer price of $10/btl.

	Low transfer price ($1/btl)			High transfer price ($10/btl)		
	P.R.	U.S.	Consolidated	P.R.	U.S.	Consolidated
Revenue						
Cost of goods sold						
Taxable income						
Taxes						
Net income						
Effective tax rate						

b. Suppose the cost of goods sold is $0.50/btl if Metafour is manufactured at Quack's U.S. plant. Where should Quack produce Metafour, based on tax considerations alone? Conduct your analysis using a transfer price of $1/btl on internal sales from the Puerto Rican plant to the U.S. parent corporation.

SUGGESTED READINGS

A comprehensive treatment of the issues in this chapter appears in
    Myron S. Scholes and Mark A. Wolfson, *Taxes and Business Strategy: A Planning Approach,* 1992, Prentice Hall, Englewood Cliffs, New Jersey.

For a discussion of the role of taxes on foreign investment activity see
    Gil B. Manzon, Jr., David J. Sharp, and Nickolaos G. Travlos, "An Empirical Study of the Consequences of U.S. Tax Rules for International Acquisitions by U.S. Firms," *Journal of Finance* 49, No. 5, 1994, pages 1893–1904.

    Myron S. Scholes and Mark A. Wolfson, "The Effects of Changes in Tax Laws on Corporate Reorganization Activity," *Journal of Business* 63, No. 1, Part 2, 1990, pages S141–S164.

    Henri Servaes and Marc Zenner, "Taxes and the Returns to Foreign Acquisitions in the United States," *Financial Management* 23, No. 4, 1994, pages 42–56.

Additional articles on taxes and tax planning include
    Andrea S. Kramer and J. Clark Heston, "An Overview of Current Tax Impediments to Risk Management," *Journal of Applied Corporate Finance* 6, No. 3, 1993, pages 73–81.

    James Brickley, Clifford Smith, and Jerold Zimmerman, "Transfer Pricing and the Control of Internal Corporate Transactions," *Journal of Applied Corporate Finance* 8, No. 2, 1995, pages 60–67.

Corporate Governance and the International Market for Corporate Control

Make no little plans; they have no magic to stir men's blood.
Daniel Hudson Burnham

OVERVIEW

Corporate governance refers to the way in which major stakeholders exert control over the modern corporation. The rights of the firm's stakeholders in corporate governance are determined by each nation's laws, legal institutions and conventions, and regulatory framework. These national systems influence many aspects of economic life, including

- The way in which capital is allocated within and between national economies
- The opportunities available to individual and institutional investors and to individual, corporate, and governmental borrowers
- Ownership and control of the corporation

Although national legal systems share many common elements, they are also shaped by many unique political, social, and economic forces. These unique forces manifest themselves in country-specific differences in corporate governance systems. In turn, national corporate governance systems have a great influence on the ways in which corporations are governed and perform, including the frequency and form of cross-border mergers, acquisitions, and divestitures.

The Anglo-American model of corporate governance of the United Kingdom and the United States is characterized by dispersed equity ownership, a large proportion of public debt and equity issues, and a relatively independent management team. The bank-based systems used in continental Europe and Japan rely on concentrated owner-ship (in the hands of a lead bank or the firm's business partners or both) of both debt and equity capital and a management team that is closely monitored by the principal owners.

These disparate systems of corporate governance result in dissimilar markets for corporate control. Corporate control contests in the United States and the United Kingdom tend to be large-scale, aggressive, financially motivated, arm's-length deals that often involve private investors and other corporations. Hostile acquisitions in these markets often prompt equally forceful defensive maneuvers by the management of tar-get firms. In Japan, corporate takeovers are typically managed from inside (rather than in the public markets) by the corporation's main bank or by its business partners or by both. The market for corporate control in Germany is intermediate between the Anglo-American and Japanese systems.

After briefly presenting some merger and acquisition (M&A) terminology and a description of the major corporate stakeholders, this chapter examines national differ-ences in corporate ownership and control, using Germany, Japan, and the United States for illustration. The pace and form of cross-border merger and acquisition activity are then examined, along with a discussion of the elements that make for multinationality in the modern corporation.

19.1 THE TERMINOLOGY OF MERGERS AND ACQUISITIONS

A firm can obtain control over the assets of another firm in three direct ways:[1]

- Through acquisition of another firm's assets
- Through merger or consolidation
- Through acquisition of another firm's stock

Chapter 16 covers acquisition of another firm's assets. Mergers and acquisitions (M&A) of stock involve corporate control issues and are covered in the remainder of this chapter.

In a **merger**, one firm absorbs another. The acquiring firm usually retains its name and legal status. All assets and liabilities of the target firm are merged into the acquiring firm. A **consolidation** is like a merger except that an entirely new firm is created. Whenever firms merge or consolidate, one firm usually serves as the acquiring firm with the other firm as a target firm. The acquiring firm's management usually retains its management role in the merged firm. The target firm's management may or may not be retained. In an **acquisition** of stock, the acquiring firm purchases some or all of the equity of another firm. Acquisitions are sometimes followed by a merger after the acquiring firm obtains a controlling interest in the target firm. An acquisition of stock can be in any amount up to 100 percent of the acquired firm's stock. Acquisitions of stock of 50 percent or less are referred to as *partial acquisitions*.

---

1 There are a number of indirect ways of obtaining control over the assets of another firm, including joint ventures and collaborative alliances.

Whenever one firm is acquired by or merged with another, the hope of the participants is that the combined entity will have more value than the sum of the parts (as in 2+2=5). Cross-border mergers and acquisitions derive their value from more efficient utilization of the competitive advantages of the acquiring or acquired firm or of both. This additional value is called **synergy** and is measured as

$$\text{Synergy} = V_{AT} - (V_A + V_T) \qquad (19.1)$$

where V_A and V_T are the values of the acquiring firm A and the target firm T prior to the announcement of the merger or acquisition, and V_{AT} is the post-acquisition value of the combined firm.

The purchase price paid to the shareholders of the target firm includes the preacquisition value of the target and an **acquisition premium** paid to target shareholders.

$$\text{Acquisition premium} = \text{Purchase price} - V_T \qquad (19.2)$$

If the target is publicly traded, the convention is to assume informationally efficient markets and to define the acquisition premium as the difference between the purchase price and the preacquisition market value. In this case, target shareholders will never sell for less than their preacquisition market value, so the acquisition premium to preacquisition price is always positive. (Empirical results for publicly traded firms are presented in a later section.) If the target firm is not publicly traded, the preacquisition value V_T is not easily identified, and target firm shareholders may end up selling for more or less than the fair market price.[2]

Whether the *acquiring* firm wins or loses depends on whether the synergies created by the merger or acquisition outweigh the acquisition premium paid to the target firm. The gain to the acquiring firm can be stated as

$$
\begin{aligned}
\text{Gain to acquiring firm} &= \text{Synergy} - \text{Acquisition premium} \\
&= [V_{AT} - (V_A + V_T)] - [\text{Purchase price} - V_T] \\
&= V_{AT} - (\text{Purchase price} + V_A) \qquad (19.3)
\end{aligned}
$$

Acquiring shareholders win if the synergy created through the acquisition is greater than the acquisition premium paid to target shareholders. If only one or a few target firms offer the competitive advantages that acquiring firms desire, then the target firm's position will be enhanced as it negotiates with its suitors. The bargaining position of an acquiring firm is greatest when there are many potential targets but only a few acquiring firms in a position to make an offer.

Cross-border mergers and acquisitions are conducted within the rules and conventions established by national governments and their regulatory bodies. Consequently, it is useful to describe how national financial regulations affect the patterns of corporate ownership and the structures of corporate governance in different countries. This is the topic of the rest of this chapter.

---

2 As they say, "If you can't spot the sucker at the table, you're probably it."

19.2 CROSS-BORDER DIFFERENCES IN CORPORATE GOVERNANCE

This section describes how the regulation of financial institutions and the structure of national capital markets affect ownership and control of the modern corporation. Differences in national legal and financial systems largely determine how firms raise capital and how stakeholders exercise control over corporate decisions.

The Supervisory Board: An Agent of the Principal Stakeholders

Corporations in most industrialized economies have a **supervisory board** charged with monitoring and supervising the management team on behalf of the stakeholders. The composition of the supervisory board and its powers and responsibilities vary widely across countries. In the United States this supervisory board is called the board of directors and is usually controlled by management. The typical NYSE/AMEX firm in the

---

The Creation of Akzo Nobel

The pharmaceuticals and chemicals industries saw a wave of mergers and acquisitions during the late 1980s and the 1990s as companies in these industries sought synergies through complementary product lines, expansion into new markets, and economies of scale.

On November 6, 1993 (a Saturday), Netherlands-based Akzo Chemicals announced a takeover of Sweden's Nobel Industries for SK16 billion (more than $2 billion). The European Commission approved consolidation of the two companies into Akzo Nobel in February 1994. Many industry analysts hailed the consolidation as a dream fit of these two companies. Akzo Nobel predicted pretax savings of $100 million over three years as a result of the consolidation. Based on more than $11 billion in annual sales, Akzo Nobel is the world's seventh largest chemicals producer and the world's largest paint producer.

Nobel's and Akzo's share price performances (after subtracting changes in their respective national stock market indices) over the months surrounding the consolidation are shown at right. Nobel shareholders were the clear winners in this takeover. Nobel's A shares rose 25 percent over the weekend of the announcement. The gain or loss to Akzo's shareholders is more difficult to determine. The blip in Akzo's share price just prior to the announcement

was the result of Akzo's higher-than-expected earnings for the third quarter of 1993 after a turnaround in the European chemicals industry. Akzo's share price fell by 6 percent over the weekend of the announcement. As usual in a corporate takeover, the target firm shareholders were the clear winners.

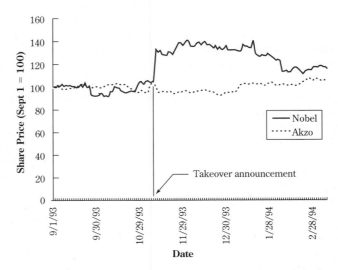

United States has about twelve board members, more than half of whom are outsiders who have no other direct affiliation with the corporation.

In Continental Europe the supervisory board commonly includes outside directors who have no other business links with the corporation as well as representatives of banks and of labor. For example, German boards have a two-tier structure, with a management board consisting solely of inside managers and a supervisory board consisting solely of outside directors representing shareholders, the lead bank or banks, and employees.

In Japan it is rare for a board member to come from a group other than the corporation's management or from a close affiliate of the corporation, such as another member of the firm's keiretsu or the firm's main bank. The board of a typical Japanese corporation from the first section of the Tokyo Stock Exchange has twenty-three board members but only one outsider.[3] Governance of most large Japanese corporations is thus dominated by an inner circle of inside managers, their bankers, and their major business partners.

Private versus Public Capital Markets: The Importance of Commercial Banks

Table 19.1 summarizes the role of banks in the two predominant systems of corporate governance in operation today:

TABLE 19.1 CROSS-BORDER DIFFERENCES IN CORPORATE GOVERNANCE SYSTEMS

System of corporate governance	Examples	Composition of supervisory board	Bank participation in equity market	Role of banks in corporate governance	Hostile acquisitions
Bank-based	Germany	Outside directors, bankers, labor representatives	Limited equity ownership Underwriting	Shared control between the lead bank and the corporation	Rare; possible with the support of lead bank and 75% of shareholders
	Japan	Inside managers, bankers, keiretsu members, business partners	Limited equity ownership No underwriting	Cooperative with bank and other keiretsu members Bank intervenes only in financial distress	Rare; blocked by equity share cross-holdings within keiretsu or with business partners
Market-based	United States	Inside managers, outside directors	Banks prohibited from owning equity except in trust Trusts limited to passive 5% ownership of any firm	By law, banks are not allowed an active voice in corporate governance	Possible through proxy contests and tender offers

---

3 The composition of Japanese boards is described in two articles by Jun-Koo Kang and Anil Shivdasani: "Firm Performance, Corporate Governance, and Top Executive Turnover in Japan," *Journal of Financial Economics* 38, May 1995, pages 29–58, and "Does the Japanese Governance System Enhance Shareholder Wealth? Evidence from the Stock-Price Effects of Top Management Turnover," *Review of Financial Studies* 9, Winter 1996, pages 1061–1095.

- The market-based system used in the United States and the United Kingdom.
- The bank-based systems used in continental Europe and Japan

The United States and the United Kingdom use a **market-based system** of corporate governance in which the supervisory board (the board of directors in the United States) represents a dispersed set of shareholders and often includes outside directors that have little contact with the corporation except through their role on the supervisory board. Continental Europe and Japan use a **bank-based system** of corporate governance in which the supervisory board is dominated by bankers and other corporate insiders.

Commercial banks are much more important to the domestic economy in a bank-based system than in a market-based system. Table 19.2 compares the size of U.S. banks within the U.S. economy to the sizes of banks in Germany and in Japan relative to the sizes of their respective economies. In 1994, the five largest U.S. banks controlled assets worth $962 billion. Gross National Product (GNP) in the United States during 1994 was $6,727 billion. The five largest U.S. banks thus held a stake in assets equal to 14.3 percent of U.S. GNP.

The ratio of assets controlled by the five largest German banks ($1,258 billion) to German GNP ($1,829 billion) was 68.8 percent — more than four and a half times the comparable U.S. figure. The ratio of the assets of the five largest Japanese banks ($2,860 billion) to Japanese GNP ($4,634 billion)was about the same, at 61.7 percent. Clearly, the largest U.S. banks have lagged behind large German and Japanese banks in terms of their relative importance to the domestic economy.

The Role of Commercial Banks in Corporate Governance

Bank-based and market-based systems of corporate governance reflect the relative importance of private and public capital markets to a nation's economy. Historically, banks have been the primary source of capital in nearly every nation. The evolution of each nation's financial system is thus inextricably linked to the growth and development of commercial banks and the laws governing commercial banking. In the United States and the United Kingdom, increasing restrictions on commercial banking have coincided with the growth of public capital markets.

TABLE 19.2 ASSETS CONTROLLED BY COMMERCIAL BANKS[a]

	United States	Japan	Germany
Assets of five largest banks	$962 billion	$2,860 billion	$1,258 billion
GNP	$6,727 billion	$4,634 billion	$1,829 billion
Ratio of assets/GNP	14.3%	61.7%	68.8%
Assets/GNP relative to the U.S.	—	4.32	4.81

[a] Bank assets and GNP figures are for 1994. GNP data is from *International Financial Statistics* (a publication of the International Monetary Fund).

This section tours the corporate governance systems of the United States, Germany, and Japan to illustrate the way in which each nation's unique history, culture, and legal and regulatory institutions influence that nation's financial and banking markets and the national and international markets for corporate control. The corporate governance systems described here are not exhaustive of all the possible systems. Rather, they are illustrative of the variety of corporate governance systems around the world.

The United States: A Market-Based System of Corporate Governance. Relative to banks in many other countries (including Japan and Germany), commercial banks in the United States are constrained in *where* and in *how* they conduct their business. As to the *where*, the National Banking Act of 1863 confined national commercial banks to a single location. The McFadden Act of 1927 later allowed bank branches only to the extent permitted by state law. Only within the last thirty years have state laws allowed entry to out-of-state banks. Branches of foreign banks are an even more recent innovation in the United States.

Banks have also been prohibited in *how* they conduct their business. In particular, they face the following prohibitions on equity-related activities:

- Banks cannot own stock for their own account
- Banks cannot actively vote shares held in trust for their banking clients
- Banks cannot make a market in equity securities
- Banks cannot engage in investment banking activities

U.S. banks have been limited in the types of financial securities activities that they can pursue. The most important of these limitations on banking operations was imposed by the Glass-Steagall Banking Act of 1933. This act had two important consequences for the U.S. financial system. First, Glass-Steagall barred commercial banks from operating as investment bankers, brokers, or equity market makers. Second, Glass-Steagall barred commercial banks from owning stock except in trust for their banking clients. The Bank Holding Company Act of 1956 later limited banks' trust activities to *passive* ownership in no more than 5 percent of a corporation's stock. These geographic and product market restrictions permitted the growth of only relatively small, regional banks with limited product lines. These limitations largely removed banks from corporate boardrooms and prohibited banks from taking an active role in corporate governance except during bankruptcy.

> *In the U.S., banks have not been permitted to take an active role in corporate governance.*

Germany: A Bank-Based System of Corporate Governance. Commercial banking in Germany has evolved along quite different lines from banking in the United States. In addition to being the primary suppliers of debt capital to German corporations, German banks control equity capital in three ways that are not available to U.S. banks:

> *German banks are the most important voice in the boardrooms of large German corporations.*

- Through ownership of stock for their own account and through bank-controlled mutual funds and investment companies

- By serving the German corporation as investment bankers
- By actively voting the shares of their banking clients, including both trust and brokerage customers

German law allows commercial banks to own stock for their own account and to engage in investment banking and brokerage activities. Commercial banks in Germany also own and control a variety of mutual funds and investment companies. In the U.S., these equity investments and investment banking and brokerage activities would violate the Glass-Steagall Banking Act and the Bank Holding Company Act. Along with control over equity and the equity voting mechanism, the investment banking and brokerage activities of German banks have allowed them to largely capture the market for new issues of both debt and equity in Germany.

In contrast to U.S. law, German law gives banks *Vollmachtstimmrecht*—the authority to vote on behalf of their banking clients. German banks obtain revocable proxies from their brokerage customers that allow the bank to vote their shares. Banks advise the shareholders of their intentions prior to voting and, unless instructed otherwise, vote the shares on behalf of their brokerage customers.[4] German banks have a near monopoly on brokerage activities in Germany, so this allows German banks to control a large percentage of shares in German corporations.

Large publicly traded corporations in Germany are called *Aktiengesellschaft* (AG).[5] The German equivalent of the U.S. board of directors is the *Aufsichtsrat*, which literally translated means "supervisory board". The management (or *Vorstand*) reports to the supervisory board. German law stipulates the representation of various stakeholders on the supervisory board. There are twenty-one seats on the supervisory board for most corporations over DM20 million in equity capitalization. If there are at least two thousand employees in the company, then ten of these seats are elected by employees and eleven are filled by shareholders. The chairman of the supervisory board represents shareholders and has the twenty-first vote. The number of seats and the proportion held by equity and by employees varies for smaller companies and for companies in different industries. German banks control the Aufsichtsrat in large part through their dominance of the equity seats on the board.

German banks' control over the equity portion of the Aufsichtsrat also allows them to control the proxy mechanism by which shares are voted. In the United States the Chief Executive Officer (CEO) controls the proxy mechanism, especially if he or she also chairs the board of directors. In Germany the CEO is prohibited from serving on the supervisory board. Without a corporate insider at the head of the supervisory board, German managers must filter their proxy solicitations through a supervisory board that is controlled by the company's bankers. This allows commercial banks to control both

---

4 German Corporations Code (*Aktiengesetz*) Section 135(1)–(2) of 1992 requires that commercial banks obtain revocable proxies from their brokerage clients and that these proxies be renewed every fifteen months.

5 Small corporations in Germany are called *Gesellschaft mit beschränkter Haftung* (GmbH) or "corporation with limited liability." AG are allowed to issue securities to the public, whereas GmbH are not. The GmbH form is far less popular in Switzerland where the acronym GmbH is jokingly referred to as *Gesellschaft mit beschränkter Hoffnung* or "corporation with limited hope."

the equity portion of the Aufsichtsrat as well as the proxy mechanism by which equity shares are voted. Through their large debt and equity stakes and their dominance of the supervisory board, German banks exert a great deal of influence in corporate boardrooms.

One last characteristic of the German system of corporate governance should be noted. Publicly held companies account for only about 20 percent of sales by German companies, and only about one-fifth of these are exchange-listed.[6] The vast majority of German businesses are unincorporated small- to medium-sized businesses called *Mittlestand* companies. These are often owned and controlled by a single family. Conflicts of interest between owners and managers are reduced or eliminated in these businesses because owners and managers are one and the same. These family-owned businesses usually maintain a close relationship with a single bank.

Japan: A Bank-Based System of Corporate Governance. As in Germany, corporate governance in Japan is an example of a bank-based system. However, the role of commercial banks in Japan is actually somewhere between the U.S. and German systems. Banks have far less formal influence in Japan than in Germany but a far greater role than in the United States. Their role is more that of partner than banker, at least from a Western perspective.

Prior to World War II, the largest firms in Japan were family-owned conglomerates called **zaibatsu**. These family-owned firms typically used a single main bank that was controlled by the family. The main bank, in turn, provided both debt and equity capital to the zaibatsu. After World War II, the postwar office of the Supreme Commander of Allied Powers (SCAP) tried to break up the zaibatsu and impose American-style Glass-Steagall limitations on Japan's financial system. SCAP prohibited Japanese banks from owning more than 5 percent of any nonbank company and separated investment from commercial banking activities.

Despite this constraint on equity participation, Japanese banking evolved along different lines from banking in the United States. Whereas banks in the United States were limited to a single geographic region and could not actively exercise the votes of their shares held in trust, Japanese banks were nurtured by the Japanese government and became truly national in scope. They also became actively involved in corporate governance.

The traditional zaibatsu have reemerged in modern form in a Japanese institution called the **keiretsu**. Keiretsu are collaborative groups of vertically and horizontally integrated companies with extensive cross-holdings of each others' shares and with a major Japanese bank or corporation at the center. Many of the firms in these keiretsu are also linked through their customer/supplier relations. In many ways, the Japanese system of competition is *cooperative within* each keiretsu and aggressively *competitive between* keiretsu. The six major keiretsu in Japan today are named after the main bank or major corporation. The number of core companies and the most recognizable members of each group are[7]

Keiretsu play a key role in Japanese corporate governance

---

6 Figures from "Silly Slogans of Stakeholders," *London Financial Times*, September 11, 1995, page 10.
7 From "Mighty Mitsubishi Is on the Move," *Business Week*, September 24, 1990, pages 98–107.

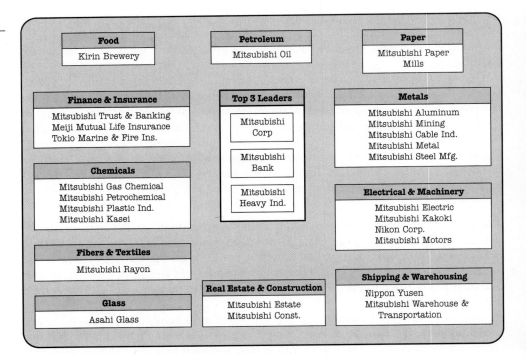

FIGURE 19.1
The Mitsubishi Keiretsu

- Mitsubishi   28 core companies (Mitsubishi Bank, Kirin Beer)
- Mitsui   24 core companies (Toyota, Toshiba)
- Sumitomo   20 core companies (NEC, Sumitomo Heavy Industries)
- Dai-Ichi   47 core companies (Seibu Department Stores, Yokohama Rubber)
- Fuyo   29 core companies (Nissan, Canon)
- Sanwa   44 core companies (Teijin, Kobe Steel)

The first three of these are actually prewar zaibatsu that reemerged after the Allied occupation. The last three are new collaborations that have emerged since the war. The members of the Mitsubishi keiretsu are shown in Figure 19.1. The keiretsu system commands a prominent role in Japanese business life.

This collaborative form of governance results in some interesting characteristics. Although stock ownership is restricted to no more than 5 percent of the outstanding stock of any corporation, the accumulation of cross-holdings by other keiretsu members means that keiretsu members often collectively control a majority of the stock of other keiretsu members. The corporation and its top management team are closely monitored (both formally and informally) by their keiretsu partners. The Japanese convention is for the senior officers of the companies in each keiretsu to meet in a monthly "president's council." At these meetings, top managers discuss topics of mutual interest to the members of the keiretsu and formulate business strategy. Keiretsu members also frequently exchange employees on temporary assignments to learn the other's business and to promote interaction among the partners.

TABLE 19.3 INSTITUTIONAL OWNERSHIP OF DOMESTIC AUTOMAKERS[a]

	United States	Japan	Germany
Largest domestic automaker	General Motors	Toyota	Daimler-Benz
Largest institutional owner	Michigan State Treasury	Sakura Bank	Deutsche Bank
Percent owned by largest institutional owner	1.4%	4.9%	41.8%
Percent owned by five largest institutional owners	5.7%	21.6%	78.4%

[a] From Mark J. Roe, "Some Differences in Corporate Structure in Germany, Japan, and the United States," *The Yale Law Journal* 102, 1993, pages 1927–2003. Reprinted by permission of The Yale Law Journal Company and Fred B. Rothman & Company.

Concentration of Equity Ownership

An important consequence of a nation's relative emphasis on a market-based or a bank-based system is in the concentration of ownership in the firm. In a market-based system, such as in the United Kingdom and the United States, ownership is diffusely held across a large number of outside investors. In Germany's bank-based system, ownership and control are concentrated in the hands of a single institution. In Japan's bank-based system, ownership and control rest with a small group of business partners through reciprocal relationships and shared cross-holdings within the keiretsu.

One difference between bank- and market-based systems is in the concentration of equity ownership.

The automobile industry is at the heart of the national economies of Germany, Japan, and the United States, so it is interesting to compare the ownership structure in this industry across these three countries. Table 19.3 lists the largest automaker in each country along with the percentage of shares controlled by the largest institutional shareholders. These ownership distributions are typical of large firms in Germany, Japan, and the United States and they illustrate the relative power of commercial banks in these economies.

In the United States banks cannot own stock directly and cannot actively vote the shares of stock owned through their trust accounts. The largest institutional owner of General Motors is the Michigan State Treasury, which owns only 1.4 percent of GM's outstanding shares. Without banks to supply equity capital, U.S. corporations rely heavily on public issues of stock. This has fragmented the ownership of large corporations among many institutional and individual investors.

Consider the institutional ownership of Daimler-Benz in Germany. Deutsche Bank directly or indirectly controls more than 40 percent of Daimler-Benz's outstanding shares of stock. Direct control arises through ownership of Daimler-Benz stock and through bank-controlled mutual funds and investment companies. Indirect control springs from the bank's power to vote the shares owned by its brokerage customers. Along with its services as lender and investment banker, this concentration of equity ownership provides Deutsche Bank with a singularly powerful voice in company affairs. In recognition of this position, Deutsche Bank is considered Daimler-Benz's *Hausbank* (house bank) and the chair of the supervisory board is customarily a Deutsche Bank executive. The next two largest investors in Daimler-Benz (Dresdner Bank and Commerzbank) control an additional 30 percent of outstanding shares.

Although no single shareholder owns more than 5 percent of Toyota, collectively the five largest shareholders own more than 20 percent of Toyota's outstanding shares. This is typical of the ownership structure of large Japanese corporations. Japanese banks are prohibited from owning more than 5 percent of the equity of any single company, but in combination with other keiretsu members they typically control up to one-third of the equity of each keiretsu member. Because of reciprocal trade and reciprocal equity ownership, Japanese managers seek the blessings of the other members of their keiretsu before undertaking major new projects. The primary role served by banks in the Japanese keiretsu and in Japanese corporate governance places their corporate governance system closer to that of Germany than of the United States, although Japanese banks by themselves are not necessarily the dominant keiretsu member as the Hausbank is in Germany.

Shareholder Activism

In recent years, shareholders have become increasingly vocal in the United States as well as in other parts of the world, and their influence in corporate boardrooms is growing. Individual shareholders, working through shareholder rights groups and groups promoting or lobbying against particular special interests, exert their voting power more and more on environmental issues and on the ethics of investment. Environmental groups such as Greenpeace lobby in the popular press—often successfully.

Barriers to shareholder activism in the United States relative to other countries include the lack of concentrated ownership and corporate managerment control of the proxy mechanism. Thus, shareholder activism is most effective in the United States when it is led by one or more large institutional investors. Despite increasing levels of shareholder activism both by large institutional shareholders and by special interest groups, managers of U.S. firms enjoy relative independence from their major stakeholders.[8]

19.3 THE INTERNATIONAL MARKET FOR CORPORATE CONTROL

Regulation of Mergers and Acquisitions

In many countries, regulation of the *conduct* of takeovers is separated from competitive issues, such as antitrust considerations. Many countries also have a separate agency to regulate foreign acquisitions. Foreign ownership of key industries, such as defense and communications, is commonly either barred outright or subjected to closer scrutiny than domestic acquisitions.

In the United States, the Securities and Exchange Commission regulates the conduct of takeovers. The Justice Department and the Federal Trade Commission regulate

---

8 See Bernard S. Black, "Institutional Investors and Corporate Governance: The Case for Institutional Voice," *Journal of Applied Corporate Finance* 5, No. 3, 1992, pages 19–32; Marc J. Epstein, "Corporate Governance and the Shareholders' Revolt," *Management Accounting* 74, No. 2, 1992, pages 32–35.

economic and antitrust issues. Many industries also have their own regulatory bodies, such as the Federal Reserve Board (banking), the Federal Communications Commission (broadcasting), the Interstate Commerce Commission (railroads and trucking), and the Transportation Department (airlines).

In Germany takeover conduct is governed by the Stock Exchange Commission. Competitive issues fall under the jurisdiction of the German Antitrust Authority. In Japan the Fair Trade Commission has jurisdiction whenever 10 percent or more of a company changes hands. In France the Treasury is responsible for regulating the conduct of an acquisition, and the Monopolies Commission reviews antitrust considerations.

In the United Kingdom takeover rules are determined by the City Panel on Takeovers, a self-regulatory agency of the London Stock Exchange. The Monopolies and Mergers Commission handles antitrust issues and has the power to stop mergers and acquisitions that it considers anticompetitive. Rather than having a separate regulatory body for each industry, the Secretary of State for Trade and Industry regulates all U.K. industries. Governmental policies are more likely to be consistent across industries with a single regulatory body, but the cost of this regulatory consistency in the United Kingdom is the lower level of regulatory expertise in any single industry.

Hostile Acquisitions

With dispersed equity ownership in the United States, acquiring or merging with another firm is relatively easy. Mergers and acquisitions are much more difficult in Germany and Japan because of the concentration of equity ownership. Obtaining control of an uncooperative corporation in these countries is difficult without the support of the lead bank or banks and other prominent stakeholders.

The Anglo-American tradition of the United States and the United Kingdom (as well as Australia and Canada) is to trust the "invisible hand" of the marketplace in corporate governance issues. In these market-based economies, dispersed equity ownership has led to price-oriented, arm's-length transactions that take place in a relatively competitive marketplace. The actions of the various stakeholders are separated by contract in many ways and by legal force, such as through Glass-Steagall's prohibition on banks' activities in the equity markets. Public proxy contests are much more common in the U.S. and U.K. equity markets than in countries with bank-based governance systems. Control contests are also much more likely to be hostile in countries with market-based governance systems.

Although there are several thousand takeovers in Japan yearly, most of these are friendly acquisitions between related companies and the sums involved are usually small relative to the size of the Japanese stock market.[9] A small number of private investors in Japan engage in **greenmail**—buying shares on the open market in the hope that the corporation's business partners will buy back the shares at inflated

Hostile acquisitions are more common in the United States and the United Kingdom than in Germany and Japan.

9 W. Carl Kester, *Japanese Takeovers: The Global Contest for Corporate Control*, Harvard Business School Press, 1991.

prices.[10] Aside from the occasional greenmail, most acquisitions in Japan tend to be between related companies.

Foreign acquisitions of Japanese firms are extremely rare given the size of the Japanese economy and the number of Japanese acquisitions of non-Japanese companies. *Euromoney* magazine reports that foreign acquisitions of Japanese companies fell from just forty-three in 1992 to thirty-five in 1993.[11] This was only a small fraction of the level of acquisition activity elsewhere in Southeast Asia, Europe, and the United States. About one-half of these foreign acquisitions were friendly takeovers of Japanese joint venture partners or transfers of control from one non-Japanese company to another.

Three impediments make a hostile foreign acquisition of a Japanese company difficult. The first and weakest barrier is a requirement that foreign bidders notify the Japanese Ministry of Finance of their intention to acquire a Japanese company. The Ministry of Finance and the Japanese Fair Trade Commission can delay acquisitions (especially foreign acquisitions) for a "suspense period" that can last for several months. This allows target management time to erect takeover defenses.

A second and more important barrier to hostile foreign acquisitions is a cultural aversion to hostile and aggressive social behavior. Japanese business practices place a heavy emphasis on reciprocity and cooperation. Keiretsu members strive for harmony within the keiretsu group, and they prize trust, loyalty, and friendship in their business dealings. It is not surprising that most Japanese find American-style takeovers to be repugnant. Institutional owners and other keiretsu members strongly resist foreign intrusion into their keiretsu relationships.

In Japan, the keiretsu structure makes hostile acquisitions difficult.

The third and most powerful barrier to a hostile foreign acquisition of a Japanese firm is the convention of reciprocal share cross-holdings among the members of each keiretsu. These cross-holdings ensure that a large fraction of outstanding shares are in the hands of friendly business partners, including the keiretsu's main bank. When faced with a hostile acquisition, Japanese managers rely on the shares held by their business partners as a source of stability during turbulent times.

These barriers to foreign control in Japan are gradually weakening in the face of falling regulatory barriers to foreign acquisitions and the financial crisis brought on by the fall in Japanese equity share values during 1990 and 1991. The fall in share values caused a massive retrenchment in Japanese industry and jeopardized the Japanese tradition of lifetime employment. Although the opportunities for non-Japanese companies to acquire Japanese firms may be growing, mergers and acquisitions of Japanese companies with non-Japanese companies are still the exception rather than the rule.

In Germany, the structure of the supervisory board makes hostile acquisition difficult.

Hostile takeovers in Germany are also rare, but for different reasons than in Japan. The largest impediment to a hostile acquisition in Germany is the structure of the German supervisory board. A majority of the stock in large public corporations is controlled by the corporation's Hausbank, so the cooperation of this bank is essential. Support of the labor force is also necessary, because employees control one-half of the seats on the supervisory boards of public corporations with more than two thousand employees. This effectively eliminates the practice (more commonly seen in the United

---

10 Japanese corporations are prohibited from repurchasing their own shares.
11 Geoff Dyer, "Hopes Unrealistic," *Euromoney*, February 1994, pages 10, 12.

States) whereby a hostile buyer moves production of a major product to a foreign site to reduce costs.

Several other impediments help to block hostile acquisitions in Germany. Takeover guidelines are enforced by commercial banks, which also control the corporation through their extensive stock holdings and through the supervisory board. Takeover guidelines require that all shareholders must be paid the same price even if they have previously accepted a lower bid for their shares. German corporation law also requires that a supermajority of 75 percent of shareholders approve a takeover and prohibits golden parachutes to management. For all of these reasons, hostile takeovers in Germany are rare. Friendly takeovers are much more common and account for nearly all of corporate merger and acquisition activity.

Top Executive Turnover and Firm Performance

The Agency Costs of Corporate Governance. There is a built-in tension between the various stakeholders in the corporation. Each stakeholder has an incentive to pursue his or her own selfish interest. These interests are often in conflict with those of other stakeholders, especially during times of financial distress. Different corporate governance systems manage these tensions between the stakeholders and their attendant costs differently.

Debt and equity shareholders hire the management team to run the corporation through the mechanism of the supervisory board. In this principal-agent relationship, management serves as an **agent** of other stakeholders. This requires that the activities and performance of management be monitored by other stakeholders. The costs of monitoring management and ensuring that it acts in the best interest of other stakeholders are called **agency costs**.

Large institutional owners can monitor management more easily than small investors.

When East Meets West

In April 1989, U.S. investor and legendary "greenmailer" T. Boone Pickens of Mesa Petroleum launched the first hostile takeover attempt of a Japanese company by a foreign investor. Pickens paid more than $800 million for a 26.4 percent stake in Koito Manufacturing Co., an auto parts supplier (mostly to Toyota) that is listed on the first section of the Tokyo Stock Exchange. As Koito's largest shareholder, Pickens demanded disclosure of financial data and a seat on Koito's board.

Koito's management went into action, lining up their Japanese investors and business partners. Full-page ads were placed in the American press decrying Pickens's "blatant attempt at greenmail." With the bulk of Koito's shares in friendly Japanese hands (Toyota held 19 percent of the equity) and with the backing of the Japanese Ministry of Finance (which found infringements of Japanese law in Pickens's share-transfer documents), Koito successfully denied Pickens a seat on the board. Pickens eventually sold his interest in Koito to a Japanese investor.

Concentrated ownership of public corporations in Germany and Japan provides a strong incentive for financial institutions in those countries to monitor management performance. Corporate management also is more easily monitored by the lead bank in Germany or by closely affiliated members of the keiretsu in Japan than by a dispersed set of equity owners as in the United States. Control of the supervisory board provides institutional owners in Germany and Japan with the means by which to monitor management. Consequently, bank-based systems can greatly reduce the agency costs that arise between managers and other stakeholders.

Without a single source of capital such as in Germany and Japan, corporations in the United States and the United Kingdom rely much more extensively on public capital markets. Without equity capital from commercial banks and with dispersed institutional ownership, U.S. managers have not often had to face a dominant stakeholder or stakeholders, so they operate more or less unfettered by outside concerns, at least in comparison to managers in Germany and Japan.

Corporate Governance and Top Executive Turnover: Why, When, and How. One test of a corporate governance system is in how it deals with poorly performing managers. Replacement of inefficient managers should result in an increase in the value of poorly performing companies. In the market-based governance systems of the United States and the United Kingdom, control contests over the supervisory board are often held as proxy contests over seats on the board. The public takeover market is a vehicle of last resort for disgruntled shareholders. In a bank-based governance system, top executive turnover is much more likely to be initiated by the lead bank (as in Germany) or by the principal shareholders (as in Japan).

There are cross-border similarities in why *and* when *top executives are replaced.*

The empirical evidence suggests that there are similarities in *why* and *when* top management is replaced in the United States, Germany, and Japan.[12] In each country, the likelihood that top management will be replaced is greater for firms reporting poor earnings performance or a sharp decline in share price. Further, empirical evidence in each country indicates that firm performance tends to improve after turnover in the top management of poorly performing companies.

The major difference among these three countries is in the mechanism by which top management is replaced—the *how* of top executive turnover. Turnover in the ranks of top executives is usually initiated by the supervisory board. In all three countries the likelihood of top executive turnover in poorly performing firms is positively related to the concentration of equity ownership and to the proportion of outsiders on the board.

In the United States, any attempt to replace top management must be channeled through the board of directors. The board of directors represents shareholders and is responsible for initiating any change in top management. Corporate control contests occur either as proxy contests for seats on the board or as hostile takeover contests to

---

12 See Steven N. Kaplan, "Top Executives Rewards and Firm Performance: A Comparison of Japan and the United States," *Journal of Political Economy* 102, 1994, pages 510–546; Steven N. Kaplan, "Top Executives, Turnover, and Firm Performance in Germany," *Journal of Law, Economics, and Organization* 10, 1994, pages 142–159; Steven N. Kaplan and Bernadette A. Minton, "Appointments of Outsiders to Japanese Boards: Determinants and Implications for Managers," *Journal of Financial Economics* 36, 1994, pages 225–258; and Jun-Koo Kang and Anil Shivdasani, "Firm Performance, Corporate Governance, and Top Executive Turnover in Japan," *Journal of Financial Economics* 38, May 1995, pages 29–58.

replace the board. These contests are conducted in the financial marketplace between largely unrelated investors. These corporate control contests are highly public and they often receive a great deal of coverage in the financial press.

If there is a main bank in the Japanese keiretsu, it usually takes the initiative in replacing the management of poorly performing keiretsu members. Turnover in the ranks of the firm's top executives is greater in bank-dominated keiretsu than in keiretsu that do not include a main bank. In Germany the lead bank usually takes the initiative in replacing top executives. In each country, poor earnings or stock price performance is likely to lead to the appointment of outside directors—from the lead bank in Germany and from other keiretsu members in Japan. Outside appointments to the board are often followed by a turnover in top management and are more than likely followed by an improvement in firm peformance.

These empirical findings suggest that there is more than one way for a corporate governance system to successfully deal with nonperforming managers and to resolve the agency problems that inevitably exist between managers and other stakeholders in the firm.

19.4 A RECENT HISTORY OF CROSS-BORDER MERGERS AND ACQUISITIONS ACTIVITY

Cross-border mergers and acquisitions were a rarity as recently as 1970. For example, during 1968 there were only sixteen cross-border deals out of more than four thousand mergers and acquisitions involving U.S. firms.[13] Figures 19.2 and 19.3 chronicle the explosive growth in the number and value of the merger and acquisition activities of U.S. firms, especially cross-border deals. Figure 19.3 is in constant 1990 U.S. dollars, so the increase in the value of cross-border acquisitions is not due to inflation.

During the late 1970s and the 1980s cross-border deals became commonplace and the values involved skyrocketed. In 1982 there were 264 cross-border mergers and acquisitions involving U.S. firms.[14] This accounted for 10.9 percent of all mergers and acquisitions involving U.S. firms. The value involved was $6.3 billion. In 1995 there were 1,422 cross-border deals involving U.S. firms. This was 24.1 percent of all M&A activity involving U.S. firms. The total market value involved was $103.2 billion. Table 19.4 lists the largest cross-border merger or acquisition involving a U.S. firm from 1983 to 1995.

Japanese companies went on a buying spree in the late 1980s, gobbling up U.S. companies at an unprecedented rate. At least part of the reason for this acquisition binge was the run-up in Japanese share prices during the 1980s. The rise in the value of the yen during the late 1980s also helped to make foreign assets look cheap relative to Japanese assets. Because Japanese banks can and do own substantial equity interests in their keiretsu members, the rise in Japanese share prices in the late 1980s benefited both the large corporations and their main banks and left them with a great deal of buying power on international markets. The fall in Japanese share prices in the early 1990s resulted in a fall in value and a cash flow crisis for the entire Japanese financial

13 Sarkis Khoury, *Transnational Mergers and Acquisitions in the United States*, Lexington Books, Lexington, Mass., 1980, page 22.

14 The figures in this paragraph are from the May/June 1990 and March/April 1996 issues of *Mergers and Acquisitions*.

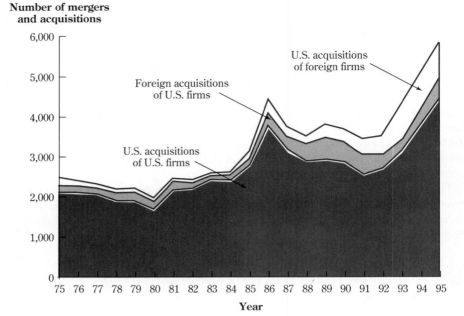

FIGURE 19.2
Number of Mergers and
Acquisitions Involving
U.S. Firms

Compiled from *Mergerstat* and *Mergers and Acquisitions*, various issues.

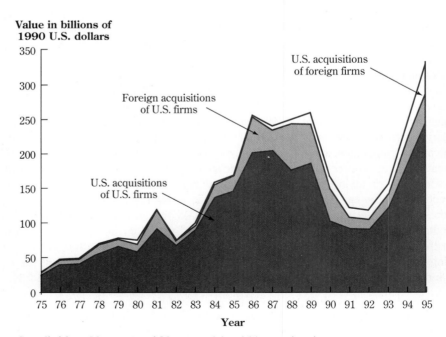

FIGURE 19.3
Value of Mergers and
Acquisitions Involving
U.S. Firms

Compiled from *Mergerstat* and *Mergers and Acquisitions*, various issues.

TABLE 19.4 LARGEST MERGERS INVOLVING A U.S. FIRM

Year	Buyer (Country)	Seller (Country)	$ Billions
1983	Broken Pop Properties (Australia)	General Electric (U.S.)	
1984	Broken Hill Proprietary Co. (Australia)	Utah International Co. (U.S.)	2.4
1985	Royal Dutch/Shell Group (Netherlands)	Shell Oil (U.S.)	5.6
1986	Unilever (Netherlands)	Cheesebrough-Pond's (U.S.)	3.1
1987	British Petroleum (U.K.)	Standard Oil, Ohio (U.S.)	7.8
1988	Campeau (Canada)	Federated Department Stores (U.S.)	6.5
1989	Beecham Group PLC (U.K.)	SmithKline Beecham Corp. (U.S.)	8.3
1990	Philip Morris (U.S.)	Jacobs Suchard AG (Switzerland)	3.8
1991	Matsushita Elec. Indus. (Japan)	MCA (U.S.)	6.9
1992	Philip Morris (U.S.)	Freia Marabou (Norway)	1.6
1993	Hanson PLC (U.K.)	Quantum Chemical Corp. (U.S.)	3.2
1994	Roche Holding AG (Switzerland)	Syntex Corp. (U.S.)	5.3
1995	Hoechst AG (Germany)	Marion Merrell Dow (U.S.)	7.1

Source: *Mergers and Acquisitions*, various issues.

system. This drastically reduced the rate of Japanese acquisitions of non-Japanese assets and at least partially opened the door to foreign acquisitions within Japan.[15]

In Europe the pace of mergers and acquisitions increased in the 1980s as businesses responded to political efforts to increase European integration and harmonization. Survival strategies in a unified Europe are focused on cross-national alliances to take advantage of price and cost differences, to diversify operations and reduce operating risk, and to gain footholds and growth options into new markets. Buying an existing business in another location is often easier than establishing a new investment from scratch. The signing of the Maastricht Treaty in December 1991 provided fresh impetus to activity in the European market for corporate control. The number and value of cross-border deals involving European companies is now only slightly less than those of intra-national deals in Europe.

Table 19.5 displays the involvement of West European countries in cross-border reorganization activity. The biggest buyers of European companies were the United States and the United Kingdom. The major targets within Western Europe were in the United Kingdom and Germany during 1995. The largest cross-border deal within Europe in 1995 was Swiss Bank Corporation's $3.16 billion acquisition of the investment banking division of the United Kingdom's S. G. Warburg Group PLC. Another deal of interest was the Internationale Nederlanden Groupe (ING) acquisition of Barings PLC for $1.07 billion. Barings Bank had collapsed after unauthorized trading by a single employee in its Singapore office lost $1.4 billion on futures and options speculation.

---

15 Practical advice for investing in Japan is provided by Nicholas E. Benes in "Glimmers of Hope for the Inbound Acquisition in Japan," *Mergers and Acquisitions*, July/August 1995, pages 25–30.

TABLE 19.5 VALUES OF CROSS-BORDER M&A DEALS INVOLVING WEST EUROPEAN COUNTRIES[a]

	Acquiring countries								Target countries						
	1995	1994	1993	1992	1991	1990	1989		1995	1994	1993	1992	1991	1990	1989
Belgium	3.9	1.7	–	–	–	–	–		0.8	1.4	1.7	0.7	–	–	–
Denmark	0.2	–	0.2	1.0	–	–	–		0.5	–	–	–	–	–	–
France	6.5	4.6	2.1	7.3	10.8	13.3	9.1		3.4	15.6	8.4	9.5	6.0	7.9	4.7
Germany	14.8	5.0	4.4	1.6	7.4	2.1	4.5		6.8	4.5	2.7	6.0	6.3	5.9	3.3
Hungary	–	–	–	–	–	–	–		1.9	–	1.3	–	–	–	–
Italy	1.7	–	0.2	5.6	3.4	1.4	1.9		3.1	10.0	3.6	1.8	–	–	–
Netherlands	5.8	11.2	1.8	–	–	–	–		2.7	1.9	1.7	5.1	2.3	1.2	2.1
Norway	–	–	–	–	–	–	–		–	–	1.8	–	–	–	–
Spain	–	–	1.0	–	–	–	–		1.1	3.6	1.8	4.6	4.8	4.8	3.0
Sweden	4.3	0.5	1.7	1.1	–	–	–		2.3	5.6	1.4	1.5	–	–	–
Switzerland	4.8	1.3	–	4.3	–	–	–		3.9	1.2	–	1.9	–	–	–
United Kingdom	20.2	8.3	8.0	3.8	6.1	8.3	3.2		17.5	14.5	7.8	8.6	23.1	21.5	13.3
U.S. & Canada	–	22.6	12.6	7.8	15.3	10.0	5.1								
Number of cross-border deals in Western Europe	1548	1512	1,193	1,269	1,377	1,067	898								
Value of cross-border deals in Western Europe	86.9	61.3	37.2	58.0	37.3	73.0	48.9								

[a] Values in billions of U.S. dollars. The missing value indicator "–" indicates no information rather than a value of zero.
Source: *Mergers and Acquisitions*, various issues.

19.5 THE EVIDENCE ON DOMESTIC MERGERS AND ACQUISITIONS

The U.S. market for corporate control has received more attention than other markets because of its international prominence and the fact that information on mergers and acquisitions in the U.S. is more readily available than in other countries. Although other national markets have been studied less extensively, some common themes have emerged in studies of domestic mergers and acquisitions:

- Who wins
- The influence of "free cash flow"
- The importance of the tax environment

The discussion in the rest of this section is not intended as an exhaustive review of the evidence on domestic mergers and acquisitions. Rather, the focus is on those characteristics of the domestic market that remain important in cross-border merger and acquisition activity.

Studies of mergers and acquisitions in domestic markets find that it is a sellers' market. The shareholders of target firms capture large positive gains, whereas shareholders of buying firms may or may not gain depending on the circumstances.

Acquisition premiums in the United States have averaged from 35 to 55 percent when measured from share price one month prior to the acquisition announcement. Returns to target firms tend to be larger in acquisitions than in mergers.[16] Returns to target firms are also larger when there are multiple bidders, which suggests that an increase in competition for target firms drives up premiums.

Although the shares of target firms go up in price at the time of an acquisition or merger announcement within the United States, returns to the shareholders of acquiring firms are mixed. On average, acquiring firms either receive no net gain or slightly overpay for target firms. This is consistent with a competitive domestic market for corporate control, because acquiring firms are forced to pay nearly full value for the target firm.[17]

In the U.S. equity markets, the return to the acquiring firm when an acquisition is announced is related to the **method of payment** used to finance the acquisition. Offers of stock are associated with large negative returns to acquiring firms, but cash offers generate little share price movement on average for domestic U.S. acquisitions.[18] The commonly accepted explanation for this is that offers of stock (rather than cash) are taken by the market as a *signal* that management believes the stock is overvalued.

Julian Franks and Robert Harris found similar results for acquisitions within the United Kingdom.[19] On average, target firms receive large positive premiums, but the share prices of acquiring firms either do not change or rise only slightly. Franks and Harris found returns to both acquiring and target firms within the United Kingdom were comparable in size to those in the United States after controlling for the method of payment. As in the United States, returns to target firms were higher when there were multiple bidders for the target firm.

Free Cash Flow and Gains to the Acquiring Firm

Managers with a substantial ownership stake in the firm are much more likely to use cash or debt to finance an acquisition than stock. Owner-managers have two reasons for avoiding new stock offers to finance acquisitions. First, their large equity shareholdings are prima facie evidence that they believe their shares to be undervalued by the market.

---

16 Jensen and Ruback reported gains to target firms of 29 percent for acquisitions versus 16 percent for mergers.

17 See, for example, Michael Bradley, Anand Desai, and E. Han Kim, "Synergistic Gains from Corporate Acquisitions and Their Division Between the Stockholders of Target and Acquiring Firms," *Journal of Financial Economics* 21, No. 1, 1988, pages 3–40.

18 Nickolaos G. Travlos, "Corporate Takeover Bids, Methods of Payment, and Bidding Firms' Stock Return," *Journal of Finance* 62, No. 4, 1987, pages 943–963.

19 Julian R. Franks and Robert S. Harris, "Shareholder Wealth Effects of Corporate Takeovers: The U.K. Experience 1955–1985," *Journal of Financial Economics* 23, No. 2, 1989, pages 225–250.

If they believe that their shares are undervalued, then a stock offer would dilute their ownership stake and rob them of some of this latent value. Second, financing acquisitions with stock dilutes their ownership position in the firm. With a smaller vote in company affairs, managers risk loss of control.

Michael Jensen suggested that losses to acquiring firm shareholders are related to **free cash flow**.[20] Free cash flow is defined as cash flow that is available to the firm after all positive-NPV investments have been exhausted in the firm's main line of business. According to Jensen's hypothesis, managers with control over large amounts of free cash flow are more likely to spend it on wasteful investments, such as overpriced acquisitions, rather than paying these sur-plus funds as a dividend or repurchasing the firm's debt or equity securities. The U.S. evidence is consistent with Jensen's hypothesis. Firms with higher free cash flow are more likely to engage in acquisitions that destroy rather than create value for their shareholders.

Tax Reasons for Domestic Mergers and Acquisitions

Finally, tax laws can influence domestic merger and acquisition activity. Tax laws influence the treatment of tax-attribute carryforwards and carrybacks, such as operating losses, capital losses, investment tax credits, and foreign tax credits. The value of unused carryforwards can be realized more quickly and more fully through merger with a profitable firm than if the firm with unused carryforwards is left to generate taxable income on its own. Mergers and acquisitions also can facilitate asset sales to change to a more accelerated depreciation schedule, to step up the book value of an asset to its fair market value and thus increase the depreciation deduction, and to realize taxable losses in order to generate an immediate tax deduction.

In the United States, the Economic Recovery Tax Act (ERTA) of 1981 encouraged asset sales by allowing acquiring firms to step up the depreciable basis and to change the depreciation schedule to an accelerated cost recovery system (ACRS). The Tax Reform Act (TRA) of 1986 later removed these tax incentives for mergers and acquisitions. Provisions of the 1986 TRA on asset purchases went into effect on January 1, 1987. Empirical evidence shows that changes in U.S. tax laws influenced domestic acquisitions of U.S. companies during the 1980s.[21] Indeed, the last quarter of 1986 saw a surge in merger and acquisition activity as corporations scrambled to consummate their acquisitions under the old, more favorable tax rules.

It is important not to overemphasize the importance of tax considerations to the pace of merger and acquisition activity and the returns to buyers and sellers.[22] Taxes are but one of many factors that influence reorganization activity. Nevertheless, mergers and acquisitions can facilitate the transfer and realization of these tax benefits.

---

20 Michael C. Jensen, "Agency Costs of Free Cash Flow," *American Economic Review* 72, No. 2, 1986, pages 323–329.

21 Myron S. Scholes and Mark A. Wolfson, "The Effects of Changes in Tax Laws on Corporate Reorganization Activity," *Journal of Busin*ess 63, No. 1, Part 2, 1990, pages S141–S164.

22 For example, Alan Auerbach and David Reishus found that tax considerations are a relatively unimportant source of takeover gain in "The Effects of Taxation in the Merger Decision," in A. Auerbach, ed., *Corporate Takeovers: Causes and Consequences*, University of Chicage Press for NBER, Chicago, Illinois, 1988, pages 157–190.

19.6 THE INTERNATIONAL EVIDENCE ON MERGERS AND ACQUISITIONS

539

Chapter 19 Corporate
Governance and the
International Market for
Corporate Control

The value created in cross-border mergers and acquisitions should bear some resemblance to that of domestic deals, so it is useful to begin a discussion of cross-border M&A activity with an extension of the domestic evidence to cross-border acquisitions. Most of this evidence involves the cross-border activities of U.S. firms, although an increasing number of studies are examining M&A activity in non-U.S. markets. Some of the lessons from domestic markets extend to cross-border mergers and acquisitions. However, there are also some differences in the factors that influence cross-border reorganization activity.

A Reinterpretation of the Domestic Variables

The Winners and the Losers in Cross-Border Mergers and Acquisitions. In sharp contrast to the literature on domestic acquisitions, several recent studies have found that gains to both acquiring firms and target firms in cross-border mergers and acquisitions are on average positive. For example, Constantinos Markides and Christopher Ittner examined the acquisitions by U.S. corporations of 276 foreign firms in sixteen countries over the period 1975 to 1988 and found that wealth gains to U.S. acquirers were on average positive (about 0.5 percent in the days surrounding the announcement).[23] This result is opposite that of domestic mergers and acquisitions, in which acquiring firms tend either to lose or to gain only slightly depending on the method of payment. Jun-Koo Kang found similar wealth gains for Japanese firms acquiring U.S. firms (again of about 0.5 percent in the days surrounding the announcement).[24] These findings suggest that cross-border mergers and acquisitions create value for shareholders of *both* acquiring and target firms.

Cross-border acquisitions tend to result in gains for both buyers and sellers.

Free Cash Flow and Profitability. Several authors have found that returns to acquiring firms are negatively correlated with the profitability of the acquiring firm in mergers and acquisitions that cross the U.S. border.[25] That is, the higher the acquiring firm's profitability (net income divided by sales), the lower the return to the shareholders of the bidding firm. This is consistent with Jensen's free cash flow hypothesis and the domestic evidence. The cross-border evidence substitutes "profitability" for "free cash flow" because of the difficulty in identifying the free cash flow of firms with accounting practices and disclosures that differ from U.S. accounting principles.

23 Constantinos C. Markides and Christopher D. Ittner, "Shareholder Benefits from Corporate International Diversification: Evidence from U.S. International Acquisitions," *Journal of International Business Studies* 25, No. 2, 1994, pages 343–366.

24 Jun-Koo Kang, "The International Market for Corporate Control," *Journal of Financial Economics* 34, 1993, pages 345–371.

25 See, for example, Markides and Ittner, "Shareholder Benefits." John Doukas found that the negative correlation between free cash flow and bidder returns is greatest for firms with low Tobin's q (the ratio of market value to replacement cost of assets). See Doukas, "Overinvestment, Tobin's q, and Gains from Foreign Acquisitions," *Journal of Banking and Finance* 19, October 1995, pages 1285–1303.

Tax Reasons for Cross-Border Mergers and Acquisitions. If taxes play a role in domestic mergers and acquisitions, then they should play an even greater role in cross-border mergers and acquisitions. National taxes on foreign source income are complex and vary by country. Cross-border differences in tax rates and tax regimes should allow the multinational corporation with geographically diversified operations to arbitrage across tax jurisdictions. In turn, the ability of the MNC to arbitrage tax asymmetries depends on the way in which foreign source income is taxed in the parent's home country.

The empirical evidence suggests that markets do react to firm-specific tax-related advantages around the time of cross-border acquisition announcements. For example, Manzon, Sharp, and Travlos found that returns to the foreign targets of U.S. firms are sensitive to changes in U.S. tax laws.[26] Firms with no excess FTCs that invest in high-tax countries earn positive abnormal returns in excess of similar firms that invest in low-tax countries.[27] This evidence suggests that the market responds favorably to a foreign acquisition that enhances the MNC's ability to repatriate after-tax funds and unfavorably to an acquisition that is likely to trigger additional taxes.

The Advantages of Multinationality

A growing body of literature examines factors related to the success of the multinational corporation on its forays into cross-border mergers and acquisitions. In general, the empirical findings are consistent with the eclectic paradigm introduced in Chapter 14. The eclectic paradigm categorizes the MNC's competitive advantages into ownership-specific, location-specific, and market internalization advantages. According to this theory of the firm, multinational corporations are successful when they can

- Create and maintain intangible *ownership-specific advantages*, such as brand names, patents, copyrights, proprietary technology or technological processes, or marketing or management expertise
- Obtain privileged access to *location-specific advantages*, such as natural or manufactured resources, low taxes or wage costs, markets for the firm's products, or high labor productivity
- Successfully exploit their ownership-specific and location-specific advantages through *market internalization advantages*

For cross-border mergers and acquisitions to make sense, the MNC must enjoy advantages over local firms in internalizing the markets for its intangible assets and in capitalizing on the firm-specific and location-specific advantages of its foreign acquisitions. Of course, even if an MNC can identify a foreign acquisition possessing firm-specific or

---

26 Gil B. Manzon, Jr., David J. Sharp, and Nickolaos G. Travlos, "An Empirical Study of the Consequences of U.S. Tax Rules for International Acquisitions by U.S. Firms" *Journal of Finance* 49, No. 5, 1994, pages 1893–1904.

27 Similarly, Henri Servaes and Marc Zenner found that returns to the U.S. targets of foreign acquirers responded to changes in U.S. tax laws in "Taxes and the Returns to Foreign Acquisitions in the United States," *Financial Management* 23, No. 4, 1994, pages 42–56.

location-specific advantages that the MNC can turn to its advantage, these advantages are of no use if the purchase price is too high.

Multinationality and Intangible Firm-Specific Assets. Markides and Ittner, among others, found that multinational corporations tend to spend more heavily than domestic firms on research and development (R&D) and on advertising to create and promote intangible firm-specific advantages.[28] International expansion benefits the MNC by allowing it to exploit these intangible assets on a larger scale and across a greater range of markets than its domestic competitors. Not only do MNCs tend to have higher R&D and advertising expenses than domestic firms, but the returns to acquiring firms are also related to their level of investment in intangible assets. Several authors found higher gains to acquiring firms with intangible assets such as brand names and in industries that were technologically intensive or had high advertising expenditures.[29]

Using Tobin's q as a measure of firm value, Morck and Yeung found that the positive impact of spending to create and promote the firm's intangible assets increases with a firm's multinationality.[30] Tobin's q is equal to the market value of firm assets divided by the replacement cost of firm assets. Morck and Yeung found that multinationality itself has little relationship to the returns of acquiring firms after controlling for R&D and advertising expense. Morck and Yeung concluded from this that multinationality has little value in and of itself. Multinationality must be accompanied by intangible firm-specific assets to be of value to the corporation.

Multinationality and the Relatedness of the Target Firm. Multinationality also benefits the MNC by providing access to a more diverse stock of assets and, therefore, better prepares the MNC to seize opportunities as they arise. For example, Markides and Ittner found that acquisitions of companies in related businesses result in strong positive gains to acquiring firms, whereas acquisitions of unrelated businesses result in shareholder losses, on average.[31] This is consistent with companies possessing firm-specific advantages successfully expanding their enterprise into other markets through acquisition. As in the domestic capital market, Markides and Ittner found that horizontal acquisitions into unrelated businesses in other countries result in losses for the shareholders of acquiring firms. This result is consistent with Morck and Yeung in that international diversification per se does not appear to be of value.[32] MNCs need intangible advantages to be able to increase their market values through international acquisition.

Prior International Experience. The experience gained through multinational operations can itself be of value if it reduces the costs and increases the efficiency with which

MNCs spend more heavily on R&D and advertising to create and promote their products.

Acquisitions in related businesses lead to bigger gains than in unrelated businesses.

28 Markides and Ittner, "Shareholder Benefits."
29 For example, Thomas Horst, "Firm and Industry Determinants of the Decision to Invest Abroad," *Review of Economics and Statistics* 54, August 1972, pages 258–266; and Stephen G. Grubaugh, "Determinants of Direct Foreign Investment," *Review of Economics and Statistics* 69, February 1987, pages 149–151.
30 Randall Morck and Bernard Yeung, "Why Investors Value Multinationality," *Journal of Business* 64, No. 2, 1991, pages 165–187.
31 Markides and Ittner, "Shareholder Benefits."
32 Morck and Yeung, "Why Investors Value Multinationality."

• •

*Prior international experience is
a valuable asset in expanding
internationally.*

• •

the MNC internalizes product and factor markets for its intangible assets and exploits its ownership and locational advantages. As an example, the international scope of the multinational corporation can confer advantages in manufacturing industries such as electronics and semiconductors as the MNC shifts production to those plants that have the lowest production cost. The international scope of the MNC can also confer market power if it preempts competitors from gaining sufficient scale to compete on an international level or from exploiting their own intangible assets in new locations. Consequently, firms that expand their multinational network through mergers and acquisitions should see their share prices rise when these deals are announced.

In fact, several authors have found positive abnormal returns to the shareholders of MNCs announcing cross-border acquisitions. This is presumably because MNCs are better able to translate their international experience into more effective use of their firm-specific and location-specific advantages. Doukas and Travlos examined the gains to U.S.-based MNCs acquiring foreign assets through international acquisition.[33] They found that shareholder returns are largest for MNCs entering foreign markets in which they are not already operating. Returns are especially large for MNCs entering emerging markets through acquisition. Returns are not significantly different from zero for firms entering markets in which they are already operating and for firms entering the international arena through a foreign acquisition for the first time.

In a similar vein, Harris and Ravenscraft found that the premiums paid to the U.S. targets of foreign acquirers (40 percent) are almost double those paid to the U.S. targets of U.S. acquirers (26 percent).[34] This is presumably because the U.K. acquirers can exploit the intangible assets of the U.S. targets better than the U.S. acquirers can exploit these same assets. This additional value is then reflected in the higher price that the U.K. acquirers are willing to pay for the U.S. targets.

19.7 EXCHANGE RATES AND CROSS-BORDER ACQUISITIONS

One additional macroeconomic factor may affect the pace of cross-border M&A activity—change in the relative purchasing power of two currencies as reflected in the real exchange rate.

Casual observation suggests that foreign acquisitions of domestic assets increase when the real value of the foreign currency is high relative to the domestic currency. The conventional wisdom is that a depreciation of the domestic currency increases the purchasing power of foreign residents relative to domestic residents, which results in a

---

33 John Doukas and Nickolaos G. Travlos, "The Effect of Corporate Multinationalism on Shareholders' Wealth: Evidence from International Acquisitions," *Journal of Finance* 63, No. 5, December 1988, pages 1161–1175.

34 Robert S. Harris and David Ravenscraft, "The Role of Acquisitions in Foreign Direct Investment: Evidence from the U.S. Stock Market," *Journal of Finance* 66, No. 3, July 1991, page 836.

competitive advantage in corporate control contests. This popular conception of the impact of purchasing power is intuitively appealing. Anyone who has traveled to a foreign country has felt the impact of exchange rates on the purchasing power of their domestic currency.

Yet this text has stressed at several points that corporate financial policy is irrelevant in a perfect capital market.[35] This irrelevance proposition has an interesting consequence for the relation between exchange rates and the pace of cross-border mergers and acquisitions. In a perfect capital market, all corporations have equal access to frictionless capital markets and costless information. This means that there is no advantage to a foreign (or domestic) bidder in corporate control contests. For example, changes in the real exchange rate may mean that foreign bidders are wealthier than domestic bidders. But the fact that either firm can gain access to additional capital at prevailing market prices means that it is no easier for one firm than another to raise funds in order to bid on another firm. Consequently, neither foreign nor domestic bidders have an advantage in takeover contests in a perfect capital market.

For there to be an advantage to a foreign or domestic firm in raising capital, one or more market imperfections must preferentially benefit one bidder over another. Several capital market imperfections can potentially lead to a bidding advantage, depending on the MNC's country of residence. Froot and Stein have suggested that such an advantage can arise when there is an informational asymmetry between corporate insiders and outside investors that makes new outside capital more expensive than internally generated funds.[36] According to their theory, a fall in the value of the domestic currency results in an increase in the cash position of foreign corporations relative to domestic corporations. Foreign firms have additional cash on hand, so they need not raise additional capital through the external markets to mount a bidding campaign. Domestic firms, on the other hand, suffer a decrease in their relative wealth and must tap the external markets if they want to initiate or join a bidding contest. The lower cost of internal funds confers an advantage on foreign firms over domestic firms in bidding contests for both foreign and domestic target corporations when the domestic currency falls in value.

The converse occurs when a foreign currency falls against the domestic currency. To the extent that domestic firms enjoy an increase in wealth relative to foreign firms, they will have more cash on hand and will not have to tap the external capital markets to mount an acquisition bid. Foreign firms are relatively cash constrained and will be more likely to need to access external capital before they can mount a bidding contest. A fall in the foreign currency thus benefits the domestic acquirer relative to its potential foreign competitors.

An informational asymmetry between inside and outside stakeholders is not the only capital market imperfection that results in an advantage to the foreign firm when the domestic currency falls in value. Any capital market imperfection that results in higher costs on external capital will result in a competitive advantage for the firm that has

---

35 The perfect capital market assumptions include rational investors, frictionless capital markets, and equal access to costless information and to market prices.

36 Kenneth A. Froot and Jeremy C. Stein, "Exchange Rates and Foreign Direct Investment: An Imperfect Capital Markets Approach," *Quarterly Journal of Economics* 106, 1991, pages 1191–1217.

access to internally generated funds. Underwriting fees and transactions costs on new debt and equity issues are examples of other imperfections that raise the cost of external capital.

Consistent with the implications of these theories, empirical studies generally confirm that the level of foreign acquisitions is positively related to the value of the domestic currency.[37] Moreover, gains to bidding firms are found to be positively related to the strength of the domestic currency. For example, acquiring firms based in the U.S. gain from an appreciation of the dollar.[38] Similarly, gains to Japanese bidders rise with an appreciation of the yen.[39] Domestic firms are both (1) more likely to acquire foreign companies and (2) more likely to benefit from the foreign acquisition when the domestic currency is strong.

A relative corporate wealth effect similar to that proposed by Froot and Stein may be the dominant effect. Kathryn Dewenter examined the relation of exchange rate changes to foreign direct investment (FDI) and found that the exchange rate has no power to explain FDI beyond that explained by change in the relative corporate wealth of foreign and domestic firms and the overall level of investment.[40] Dewenter measured relative corporate wealth as the dollar value of a foreign stock market divided by the dollar value of the U.S. market. The relative corporate wealth variable dominated the exchange rate variable in her sample of foreign acquisitions of U.S. target firms. A firm with high relative corporate wealth was both more likely to acquire a foreign firm and more likely to see a share price appreciation upon announcing the foreign acquisition.

A strong domestic currency leads to both more foreign acquisitions and to higher bidder returns.

19.8 A CAVEAT

It should be pointed out that theoretical and empirical research into cross-border mergers and acquisitions is still in its infancy. Further empirical work will surely modify and extend the conclusions reported here. Moreover, as markets are increasingly integrated across national borders the gains that we have seen in the past may be harder to achieve in the future. Finally, the factors that influence the winners and the losers in cross-border acquisitions are likely to change. The growing international market for corporate control provides the multinational financial manager with an exciting and challenging opportunity to consolidate existing operations, to preempt potential competitors from entry into existing and future markets, and to protect and expand the value of future operations.

---

37 See, for example, Markides and Ittner, "Shareholder Benefits."

38 See Markides and Ittner, "Shareholder Benefits," and Harris and Ravenscraft, "Role of Acquisitions."

39 Jun-Koo Kang, "International Market for Corporate Control."

40 Kathryn L. Dewenter, "Do Exchange Rate Changes Drive Foreign Direct Investment?" *Journal of Business* 68, No. 3, 1995, pages 405–433.

19.9 SUMMARY

545

Chapter 19 Corporate
Governance and the
International Market for
Corporate Control

This chapter described corporate governance and the markets for corporate control with an emphasis on Germany, Japan, and the United States. Corporate governance systems have many common elements, but they have unique features as well. The systems in these three countries are merely three examples of an infinite number of possible national systems.

Although a supervisory board represents the major stakeholders in each country, the composition, powers, and responsibilities of the supervisory board vary across countries. In the market-based system of corporate governance used in the United States, the board is elected by a diverse set of shareholders. In the United States, commercial banks are prohibited from taking an active role in corporate governance by the Glass-Steagall Act. In the bank-based systems of Germany and Japan, banks supply equity as well as debt capital and play a much more prominent role on the supervisory board and in monitoring and supervising the management team.

There are important differences even within the bank-based corporate governance systems of Germany and Japan. In Germany the lead bank supplies both debt and equity capital and serves as investment banker and market maker for public equity offerings. Because the lead bank controls the mechanisms by which the corporation raises capital, the lead bank plays a very powerful role in corporate affairs. The role of commercial banks in Japan is intermediate between that in Germany and the United States. In Japan, power is shared within the keiretsu, a network of companies linked through share cross-holdings and business partnerships. Keiretsu are centered around a major industrial corporation or a large commercial bank. Influence in a keiretsu depends on the prominence of the corporation within the keiretsu.

The structure of these corporate governance systems influences top executive turnover and the market for corporate control. In the United States, management is much more likely to be disciplined through the public equity markets through (possibly hostile) corporate takeovers. Hostile acquisitions are much less common in Germany and almost nonexistent in Japan because of the concentration of equity ownership in the hands of the lead bank in Germany and in other keiretsu members in Japan. A hostile acquisition is simply not possible in Germany or Japan without the cooperation of the major stakeholder or stakeholders.

Acquisition premiums paid to target firm shareholders are roughly comparable in domestic and in cross-border acquisitions. However, the shareholders of acquiring firms are much more likely to gain in a cross-border acquisition than in a domestic acquisition. The shareholders of acquiring firms tend to gain in cross-border acquisitions when the firm

- Has intangible assets such as patents or trademarks
- Has prior international experience
- Is entering a market for the first time
- Is acquiring a firm in a related line of business
- Does not have excess profitability that is being wasted on unnecessary investments

Finally, a firm is much more likely to acquire foreign assets when there has been a recent appreciation of its domestic currency.

KEY TERMS

Acquisition	Greenmail
Acquisition premium	Keiretsu
Agency costs	Market-based system
Agent	Merger
Bank-based system	Method of payment
Consolidation	Supervisory board
Corporate governance	Synergy
Free cash flow	Zaibatsu

CONCEPTUAL QUESTIONS

19.1 What does the term "corporate governance" mean? Why is it important in international finance?

19.2 In what ways can one firm gain control over the assets of another firm?

19.3 What is synergy?

19.4 What is the difference between a private and a public capital market? Why is this difference important in corporate governance?

19.5 Describe several differences in the role of commercial banks in corporate governance in Germany, Japan, and the United States.

19.6 Why are hostile acquisitions less common in Germany and Japan than in the United Kingdom and the United States?

19.7 How is turnover in the ranks of top executives similar in Germany, Japan, and the United States? How is it different?

19.8 Who are the likely winners and losers in domestic mergers and acquisitions that involve two firms incorporated in the United States?

19.9 In what ways are the winners and losers in cross-border mergers and acquitions the same as in domestic mergers and acquisitions? In what ways do they differ?

19.10 Why might the shareholders of bidding firms lose when the bidding firm has excess free cash flow or profitability?

19.11 How are gains to bidding firms related to exchange rates?

PROBLEMS

19.1 Suppose Axle Company of the United States acquires Mobile Company of the United Kingdom. The value of Axle stock on the NASDAQ in the United States is $3 billion. Mobile sells on the London Stock Exchange for the pound sterling equivalent of $1 billion. Axle pays a 20 percent acquisition premium to acquire Mobile. The synergy created through the merger of Axle's wheel products with Mobile's transmission products adds 10 percent to the value of the combined firm. How much should Axle's shareholders gain or lose through this acquisition?

SUGGESTED READINGS

547

Chapter 19 Corporate
Governance and the
International Market for
Corporate Control

Corporate governance systems in various countries are discussed in the following.

W. Carl Kester, *Japanese Takeovers: The Global Contest for Corporate Control*, Harvard Business School Press, 1991.

W. Carl Kester, "Japanese Corporate Governance and the Conservation of Value in Financial Distress," *Journal of Applied Corporate Finance* 4, No. 2, 1991, pages 98–104.

W. Carl Kester, "Governance, Contracting, and Investment Time Horizons: A Look at Japan and Germany," *Journal of Applied Corporate Finance* 5, No. 2, 1992, pages 83–98.

Merton Miller, "Is American Corporate Governance Fatally Flawed," *Journal of Applied Corporate Finance* 6, No. 4, 1994, pages 32–39.

Hesna Genay, "Japan's Corporate Groups," *Economic Perspectives*, January/February 1991, pages 20–30.

Erik Berglof and Enrico Perotti, "The Governance Structure of the Japanese Financial Keiretsu," *Journal of Financial Economics* 36, No. 2, 1994, pages 259–284.

Stephen Prowse, "Corporate Governance in an International Perspective," *Bank for International Settlements, BIS Economic Papers* 41, 1994.

Mark J. Roe, "Some Differences in Corporate Structure in Germany, Japan, and the United States," *Yale Law Journal* 102, 1993, pages 1927–2003.

Domestic mergers and acquisitions have been studied in

Michael Bradley, Anand Desai, and E. Han Kim, "Synergistic Gains from Corporate Acquisitions and Their Division between the Stockholders of Target and Acquiring Firms," *Journal of Financial Economics* 21, No. 1, 1988, pages 3–40.

Julian R. Franks and Robert S. Harris, "Shareholder Wealth Effects of Corporate Takeovers: The U.K. Experience 1955–1985," *Journal of Financial Economics* 23, No. 2, 1989, pages 225–250.

Michael C. Jensen, "Agency Costs of Free Cash Flow, Corporate Financing, and Takeovers," *American Economic Review* 76, No. 2, 1986, pages 323–339.

Michael C. Jensen and Richard S. Ruback, "The Market for Corporate Control," *Journal of Financial Economics* 11, No. 1, 1983, pages 5–50.

Nickolaos G. Travlos, "Corporate Takeover Bids, Methods of Payment, and Bidding Firms' Stock Return," *Journal of Finance* 62, No. 4, 1987, pages 943–963.

The gains to shareholders in cross-border mergers and acquisitions are discussed in

John Doukas, "Overinvestment, Tobin's q, and Gains from Foreign Acquisitions," *Journal of Banking and Finance* 19, October 1995, pages 1285–1303.

John Doukas and Nickolaos G. Travlos, "The Effect of Corporate Multinationalism on Shareholders' Wealth: Evidence from International Acquisitions," *Journal of Finance* 63, No. 5, 1988, pages 1161–1175.

Robert S. Harris and David Ravenscraft, "The Role of Acquisitions in Foreign Direct Investment: Evidence from the U.S. Stock Market," *Journal of Finance* 66, No. 3, 1991, pages 825–845.

Jun-Koo Kang, "The International Market for Corporate Control," *Journal of Financial Economics* 34, 1993, pages 345–371.

Gil B. Manzon, Jr., David J. Sharp, and Nickolaos G. Travlos, "An Empirical Study of the Consequences of U.S. Tax Rules for International Acquisitions by U.S. Firms" *Journal of Finance* 49, No. 5, 1994, pages 1893–1904.

Constantinos C. Markides and Christopher D. Ittner, "Shareholder Benefits from Corporate International Diversification: Evidence from U.S. International Acquisitions," *Journal of International Business Studies* 25, No. 2, 1994, pages 343–366.

Randall Morck and Bernard Yeung, "Why Investors Value Multinationality," *Journal of Business* 64, No. 2, 1991, pages 165–187.

The impact of the macroeconomic environment on cross-border acquisitions and foreign direct investment is discussed in

Kathryn L. Dewenter, "Do Exchange Rate Changes Drive Foreign Direct Investment?" *Journal of Business* 68, No. 3, 1995, pages 405–433.

Kenneth A. Froot and Jeremy C. Stein, "Exchange Rates and Foreign Direct Investment: An Imperfect Capital Markets Approach," *Quarterly Journal of Economics* 106, 1991, pages 1191–1217.

Myron S. Scholes and Mark A. Wolfson, "The Effects of Changes in Tax Laws on Corporate Reorganization Activity," *Journal of Business* 63, No. 1, Part 2, 1990, pages S141–S164.

Myron S. Scholes and Mark A. Wolfson, *Taxes and Business Strategy: A Planning Approach*, 1992, Prentice-Hall, New Jersey.

Top executive turnover as a means of restructuring poorly performing companies is discussed in

Jun-Koo Kang and Anil Shivdasani, "Firm Performance, Corporate Governance, and Top Executive Turnover in Japan," *Journal of Financial Economics* 38, May 1995, pages 29–58.

Jun-Koo Kang and Anil Shivdasani, "Does the Japanese Governance System Enhance Shareholder Wealth? Evidence from the Stock-Price Effects of Top Management Turnover," *Review of Financial Studies* 9, Winter 1996, pages 1061–1095.

Steven N. Kaplan and Bernadette A. Minton, "Appointments of Outsiders to Japanese Boards: Determinants and Implications for Managers," *Journal of Financial Economics* 36, 1994, pages 225–258.

Steven N. Kaplan, "Top Executives, Turnover, and Firm Performance in Germany," *Journal of Law, Economics, and Organization* 10, 1994, pages 142–159.

Steven N. Kaplan, "Top Executives Rewards and Firm Performance: A Comparison of Japan and the United States," *Journal of Political Economy* 102, 1994, pages 510–546.

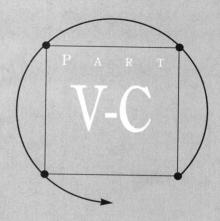

Multinational Corporate Finance

Financial Management of the Multinational Corporation

When I look back on all these worries I remember the story of the old man who said on his deathbed that he had had a lot of trouble in his life, most of which never happened.

Winston Churchill

The firm's operating and investment decisions determine the maximum potential worth of the corporation. Given the firm's asset mix, the financial manager must attempt to establish financial policies that capture this maximum potential value. These financial policies include the firm's choice of financial leverage, management of working capital, and risk management policies.

Chapter 20 discusses the elements of multinational capital structure and how capital structure relates to the firm's capital costs. Chapter 21 discusses financial management of the flow of value within the multinational corporation, particularly the short-term cash flows that facilitate efficient operation of the firm's assets. Chapter 22 concludes the book with a discussion of currency risk management, including both financial market hedges and operating hedges using the firm's real assets.

Multinational Financial Structure and Cost of Capital

A banker is someone who will give you a loan if you can provide sufficient evidence that you don't need one.

Anonymous

OVERVIEW

Financial (or capital) structure refers to the proportion of debt and equity capital and to the particular forms of debt and equity chosen to finance the assets of the firm. Management must choose the amount of debt as well as its maturity, seniority, indenture provisions, conversion features, callability, and whether it should be fixed or floating rate. Financial structure is an important determinant of the firm's overall cost of capital. The financial manager maximizes the value of the corporation's investment cash flows by minimizing the firm's after-tax cost of capital. This "optimal" financial structure also maximizes the value of shareholder's equity.

The opportunities as well as the complexities of financial strategy for the multinational corporation are many times greater than for the firm confining itself to the domestic goods and financial markets. Unless it is large and well known internationally, the domestic firm usually issues its debt and equity securities in its own domestic market. In contrast, the multinational corporation has flexibility in choosing the markets and currencies in which it issues its debt and equity securities. By accessing unsatisfied demand for its financial securities in international markets, the MNC can increase its value by lowering its costs of debt and equity capital. This chapter describes financial strategies that multinational corporations follow in pursuit of these objectives.

20.1 THE MULTINATIONAL CORPORATION'S COST OF CAPITAL

An important issue in multinational capital budgeting is whether the risks of cross-border operations result in higher or lower required returns on the part of investors and, hence, a higher or lower cost of capital for the MNC. The answer in any particular circumstance is "It depends." This section introduces several factors that influence the cost of capital on foreign projects relative to comparable domestic projects. The influence of these factors on the cost of capital is summarized in the rest of this section and in Table 20.1.

Financial Market Integration/Segmentation and the Cost of Capital

Financial Market Integration. International financial markets are **integrated** if real after-tax required returns on assets of identical risk are the same in every country. This is a consequence of the law of one price, which states that identical assets sell for the same price. The perfect market assumptions are sufficient to ensure that financial markets are both informationally efficient and integrated across national borders. In a perfect financial market, asset prices take into account national differences in tax rates, inflation rates, and foreign exchange rates. Financial market arbitrage drives real after-tax rates of return to equality across national markets. Because real after-tax required returns on assets of identical risk are the same in every country, the MNC cannot raise funds more cheaply in one location or currency than in another.

The International Asset Pricing Model (IAPM) provides a way to estimate the required return and cost of capital on a project in an integrated capital market. According to this model, the discount rate on a foreign or domestic project is determined by the security market line:

$$R_j = R_F + \beta_j (E[R_W] - R_F) \tag{20.1}$$

where R_j is the required return on asset j, R_F is the riskless rate of interest, $E[R_W]$ is the expected or required return on a diversified market portfolio, and β_j is a measure of the systematic risk of R_j relative to the market portfolio. In an integrated financial market, the appropriate market portfolio (R_W) is a globally diversified portfolio of securities weighted according to their market values. The relevant risk in determining the appropriate discount rate on a foreign or domestic project is the beta of the project relative to the world market portfolio. National market indices have no role in the pricing of systematic risk in an integrated financial market.

Financial Market Segmentation and Cross-Border Financial Opportunities. At the other end of the continuum from integrated financial markets is complete financial market segmentation. A national financial market is **segmented** from other markets if the required rate of return in that market is independent of the required rate of return on assets of comparable risk in other national markets. Like complete integration, this extreme is found in theory but not in practice. Regardless of the ruthlessness with which political authorities attempt to segment a national market, there are invariably some cross-border price leakages. The law of one price is a powerful force, and people will find a way to profit from price disparities. Market segmentation, like market integration, is never complete.

TABLE 20.1 THE COST OF CAPITAL ON FOREIGN INVESTMENT: IS IT HIGHER OR LOWER THAN ON DOMESTIC INVESTMENT?

	Higher	Same	Lower
Financial market integration versus segmentation	If foreign investment must be (at least partially) financed locally, the MNC may face a higher cost of capital on its foreign investment.	In an integrated financial market, the MNC's cost of capital does not depend on where it raises funds.	MNCs with access to foreign capital markets may gain access to investors with lower real after-tax required returns.
Operating risks	Operating risks may be positively related to events elsewhere in the world.	Country-specific operating risks are unrelated to events elsewhere in the world, so they are diversifiable.	Operating risks may be negatively related to events elsewhere in the world.
Political risks	Political risks may be positively related to events elsewhere in the world.	Country-specific political risks are unrelated to events elsewhere in the world, so they are diversifiable.	Political risks may be negatively related to events elsewhere in the world.
Currency risk	Foreign currency values may be positively related to the relevant market portfolio.	Diversifiable risks should not be priced in the marketplace and should not be reflected in the cost of capital.	Foreign currency values may be negatively related to the relevant market portfolio.

Factors contributing to financial market segmentation arise from a violation of any of the perfect market assumptions, including prohibitive transactions costs, different legal and political systems, regulatory interference (such as barriers to financial flows or to financial innovation), differential taxes or tax regimes, informational barriers (such as disclosure requirements), home asset bias (investors' tendency to buy financial assets in their own country), and differential investor expectations.

The extent of national market segmentation depends on the importance of each of these capital market imperfections to cross-border capital flows. Although fewer barriers occur in the financial markets than in the real goods markets, they can nevertheless affect the MNC's financing decisions.

For a completely segmented market, a local rather than a global security market line is appropriate in the context of the Capital Asset Pricing Model. In a completely segmented financial market, the discount rate on a project is determined according to

$$R_j = R_F + \beta_j \left(E[R_M] - R_F \right) \qquad (20.2)$$

where R_M is the local or domestic market portfolio. The relevant risk in determining the appropriate discount rate is the beta of the asset relative to the domestic market portfolio.

Financial market segmentation can lead to financial opportunities for the multinational corporation. Investors in foreign countries are sometimes willing to pay a higher price than domestic investors for debt or equity securities that provide them with additional investment opportunities or diversification benefits. In these circumstances, MNCs with established reputations in foreign markets can gain access to debt and equity financing at real rates of return that are below those available in the MNC's home country. If other domestic companies cannot gain access to the higher prices paid by foreign investors, then the MNC with access to international financial markets will enjoy a cost of capital advantage in obtaining funds. Figure 20.1 depicts the situation in which the MNC's cost of capital is below that available domestically.

The presence of different national tax rates and national tax systems also creates investment and financing opportunities for the MNC that are not available to the domestic firm. For example, earnings retained in most foreign subsidiaries are not subject to U.S. taxes until they are repatriated to the U.S. parent. If corporate income tax rates in a foreign country are below those in the United States, then the United States is in essence making a tax-deferred loan to the U.S. parent until the funds are repatriated and taxes must be paid. Similarly, tax rates on interest expense differ greatly across countries. By borrowing through foreign affiliates exposed to high tax rates, multinationals may be able to increase the value of their interest tax shields, reduce taxes paid, and maximize overall firm value. This is similar to using transfer prices to shift operating expenses toward countries with high tax rates.

Financial market segmentation less frequently results in a higher cost of capital on foreign investment. A higher cost of capital could arise if a foreign government requires that at least a part of the MNC's foreign investment be financed locally. Governments in developing countries sometimes require that foreign investments be shared with local investors or with the government itself. For example, prior to 1992, investments in India were required by the national government in Delhi to be at least 50 percent owned by

FIGURE 20.1
The Multinational
Corporation's Cost of
Capital under Segmented
Financial Markets

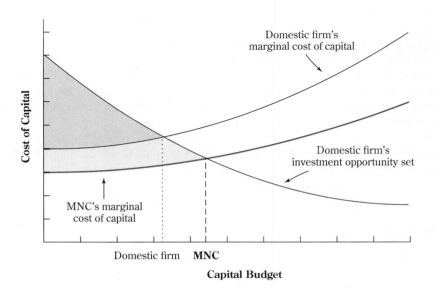

local investors. Many countries have imposed similar local-ownership requirements at some point in their history.

Although local-ownership requirements affect expected returns on foreign investments, these requirements do not necessarily affect required returns on foreign investment or the MNC's cost of capital. Because the MNC invests the capital and requires a return, investors in the MNC should determine required returns on the MNC's foreign investments. This is why the cash flows of such financial side effects as subsidized financing and blocked funds (see Chapter 16) are discounted at the market rate of interest from the perspective of investors in the MNC and not at local rates of interest in the foreign markets.

The Indirect Diversification Benefits of Cross-Border Investments

An objective of multinational financial strategy is to minimize the firm's cost of capital given its investment policy. If investors already have access to international markets through portfolio investment, then the MNC cannot provide anything to investors that investors cannot already capture for themselves through international portfolio diversification. In this case, diversification into international markets will not add value to the firm in and of itself. The MNC may be able to better employ its intangible assets in international markets than in domestic markets, but the added value arises from the investment itself and not from international diversification per se.

MNCs provide indirect diversification benefits into markets that do not allow portfolio investment.

However, if investors are restricted from some national markets by capital flow barriers, then the MNC may be able to provide **indirect diversification benefits** through corporate investment into these restricted markets. Cross-border portfolio investment is restricted by local governments in many emerging markets and even in some developed economies. Multinational corporations often can invest in these countries through joint ventures with local partners or directly through foreign subsidiaries or branch offices.

For example, foreign portfolio investment into India was prohibited until 1992. Foreign companies desiring access to the Indian market prior to 1992 were required to enlist a local joint venture partner. Although the barriers to portfolio diversification into the Indian securities market have been reduced (see box), MNCs that have established operations in the Indian market may still provide some indirect diversification benefits to non-Indian investors.

In these circumstances, MNCs may be able to achieve investment opportunities and diversification benefits that individual investors and portfolio managers cannot replicate through the financial markets. These indirect diversification benefits can lead to lower required returns on investments in foreign countries and a correspondingly lower cost of capital to the parent firm in its own national market.[1]

---

1 For conflicting views on the indirect diversification benefits of MNCs, compare Bertrand Jacquillat's and Bruno Solnik's "Multinationals Are Poor Tools for International Diversification" (*Journal of Portfolio Management,* Winter 1978, pages 8–12) with Ali M. Fatemi's "Shareholder Benefits from Corporate International Diversification" (*Journal of Finance* 39, December 1984, pages 1325–1344).

The Operating Risks of Cross-Border Investments

Investments in emerging markets can offer higher expected returns than investments in developed markets, but they come with higher operating risks. Supplier relations, employee relations, and distribution channels are more standardized in developed markets than in emerging markets. This ensures some predictability in the conduct of business. High political uncertainty and the lack of business and legal conventions in emerging economies can lead to some unpredictable returns on investment. For these reasons, the total operating risks of foreign investment are greater than on similar domestic investment.

Whether higher total risk translates into higher systematic risk on foreign investment depends on the correlation of returns with the relevant market portfolio. The systematic risk or beta of an asset is equal to

$$\beta_j = \rho_{j,M} \, (\sigma_j / \sigma_M) \tag{20.3}$$

The economies of emerging countries seldom move in step with those of developed countries. Total risk (σ_j) on a foreign investment may be higher than on a comparable domestic investment, but this increase can be more than offset by a decrease in the investment's correlation ($\rho_{j,M}$) with the relevant (domestic or global) market index. This means that systematic, nondiversifiable operating risks may actually be less on investments in emerging markets than on investments in developed markets, despite the higher total risk of foreign projects. Whether the systematic operating risk of a foreign project is higher or lower than a comparable domestic project depends on the particular project and on whether the domestic or the global market model is used to estimate the required return.

The Political Risks of Cross-Border Investments

Foreign political risk is the risk that the foreign business environment will change unexpectedly. Foreign political risks arise either because of unexpected changes in the business environment within a host country or because of unexpected changes in the relationship of the domestic government to the government of the host country. Foreign political risk comes in many forms including unexpected changes in the foreign operating environment arising from repatriation restrictions, taxes, local content regulations, local ownership limitations, business and bankruptcy laws, foreign exchange controls, and expropriation.

Foreign political risks increase the variability of outcomes on foreign investment projects, often to the detriment of the multinational corporation. Whether these higher total operating risks on foreign investment also lead to higher required returns for the MNC's investors depends on whether the events leading to these risks are related to the relevant market portfolio of the MNC's investors. If the additional layer of risk is positively related to the market portfolio, these risks will increase investors' required returns and the MNC's cost of capital. If they are negatively related to the market, these risks will decrease investors' required returns and the MNC's cost of capital.

If foreign political risks are unrelated to the market portfolio of the MNC's investors, the MNC's cost of capital will remain unaffected by foreign political risks. Most political risk is of this type. Political events are usually country-specific and only rarely are related to events outside a particular country. So, although political risk usually increases the total variability of returns, in most cases political risks are diversifiable and do not impact the MNC's cost of capital.

Currency Risk and the Cost of Capital

If financial markets are perfectly integrated across national borders, investors can insulate themselves against currency risk by holding internationally diversified portfolios of assets. If financial markets are segmented, however, domestic investors may not be able to diversify currency risk through international portfolio diversification. Consequently, whether currency risk exposure is a systematic risk that matters to investors depends on whether investors have access to a sufficient number and variety of financial market alternatives for them to hedge themselves against currency risk.

In a perfect financial market, currency risk is a diversifiable risk, so it does not affect the required returns of diversified investors. In such a market, investors can reduce or even eliminate the currency risk exposures of their investment portfolios through their own portfolio hedging and diversification strategies. In the International Asset Pricing Model (IAPM) of Chapter 12, for example, currency risk was hedged by holding the world stock market portfolio and a country-specific hedge portfolio to eliminate any remaining exposure to currency risk.

This is not to say that the MNC should not hedge its exposure to currency risk. In the real world of imperfect financial markets, hedging can increase the firm's expected

Currency risk is diversifiable and does not affect the cost of capital.

The Required Return on Investments in India

For many years, foreign direct investment in India has been prohibited by the Indian government, except for joint ventures with a local partner. Foreign portfolio investment was prohibited until 1992, when up to 24 percent of the stock in individual Indian companies was opened to registered foreign institutional investors. These restrictions on goods and capital market investments have segmented the stock market of India from other national and world markets.

Union Carbide India Limited (UCIL) is a joint venture between the government of India and the U.S.-based multinational Union Carbide. From the perspective of UCIL, project risk on investments in India should be measured against the Indian stock market. The returns on UCIL's investments are highly correlated with business activity in India, so the covariance of returns and, hence, the systematic risk (or beta) of UCIL's investments are about the same as the risk of the Indian market as a whole.

In contrast, the relevant risk of Union Carbide's equity investors depends on the covariance of investments in India with alternatives in the equity markets outside India. Because business activity in India is only loosely related to business activity elsewhere in the world, the covariance of return between investments in India and other national markets or the world market is less than the correlation between investments in India and the stock market in India. This means that the cost of capital of an MNC investing in India is less than that of the Indian subsidiary. In this case, the MNC is providing indirect diversification benefits to its investors that are not available elsewhere in the capital markets.

cash flows by reducing expected taxes, bankruptcy costs, and agency costs.[2] Outside investors cannot hedge against these drains on individual firms. Management also has an incentive to hedge currency risk because managers are relatively undiversified and receive a disproportionate amount of their current and future wealth from their employment with the firm. Although hedging currency risk can increase the MNC's expected future cash flows, it is unlikely to reduce the MNC's cost of capital unless the MNC's investors are unable to diversify against currency risk through the financial markets. Evidence presented in Chapters 11 and 12 suggests that indeed this is the case. For companies operating in freely floating currencies and in markets without governmental restrictions on capital flows, currency risk is largely diversifiable and does not affect the cost of capital.

20.2 MULTINATIONAL COST OF CAPITAL AND PROJECT VALUATION

Whether you are valuing a project, a firm, or any other real or financial asset, you should follow one basic valuation rule:

Use an *asset-specific* discount rate that reflects the opportunity cost of capital.

An investment must stand or fall on its own merits. For a proposed capital budgeting project, this requires a *project-specific* discount rate. A corollary of this rule is that you should estimate expected cash flows and required returns based on what the asset will look like in the future and not based on what the asset looks like today or has looked like in the past. This point is particularly important for cross-border project valuation, because the performance of a foreign project may be very different from that of similar domestic projects. Of course, experience on similar domestic projects and on other foreign projects is useful in helping to form expectations of future performance on a new investment in a foreign land.

There are two discounted cash flow approaches to valuing a foreign or domestic investment project: (1) weighted average cost of capital (WACC) and (2) adjusted present value (APV). These two valuation approaches deal with the debt capacity of a foreign project in different but complementary ways. The WACC approach discounts after-tax cash flows to debt and equity at a weighted average of the after-tax required returns on debt and equity. The APV approach attempts to separate the all-equity value of an asset from the value of any financing side effects. In each method, the discount rate should reflect the systematic risk of the cash flows that are being discounted.

Each valuation method brings a unique perspective to the cross-border investment decision, so it is worth evaluating international investment proposals under both methods. This allows you to form a second opinion on the value of a foreign project. If the two methods give similar values, you will probably have confidence that your estimates are

---

2 See Chapter 6 on the rationale for hedging currency risk.

in the right ballpark. If the two valuation methods yield vastly different values, you will have less confidence in your valuation estimates.

The WACC Approach to Project Valuation

According to the **weighted average cost of capital (WACC)** approach to project valuation, after-tax cash flows to debt and equity are discounted at a rate that reflects the after-tax required returns on debt and equity capital.

$$NPV = \sum_{t=0}^{T} \frac{E[CF_t]}{(1+i_{WACC})^t} \qquad (20.4)$$

where $E[CF_t]$ is the expected cash flow at time t and i_{WACC} is the weighted average cost of capital. The WACC is calculated according to

$$i_{WACC} = [(B/V_L)\, i_B\, (1-T_C)] + [(S/V_L)i_S] \qquad (20.5)$$

where

B = the market value of corporate bonds
S = the market value of corporate stock
$V_L = B + S$ = the market value of the firm
i_B = the required return on corporate bonds B
i_S = the required return on corporate stock S
T_C = the marginal corporate tax rate

Discounting after-tax cash flows to debt and equity at the weighted average cost of capital is the most commonly used method for project valuation in multinational corporations.

The discount rate i_{WACC} should reflect the target or optimal mix of debt and equity and not the mix that is actually raised to finance a particular project. The target debt capacity of a foreign project is the amount of debt that the firm would choose to borrow if the project were financed as a stand-alone entity. In Figure 20.2, the target debt capacity of the firm is the point at which the weighted average cost of capital is minimized.

The firm's existing WACC is only appropriate as a discount rate on a proposed new investment under the following conditions:

- The project has the same systematic business risk as the rest of the firm.
- The optimal financial structure of the project is identical to that of the firm.

If a project has the same risk and debt capacity as the existing assets of the firm, then the firm's WACC can be used to discount cash flows from the project. If the project has different systematic business risk or can support a different level of debt, then the corporatewide capital costs and debt capacity should not be used to value the project. In this case, you must estimate a project-specific cost of capital that depends on the systematic risk and target debt capacity of the project.

Only in rare circumstances is the debt capacity of a foreign project identical to the proportion of debt that is actually used to finance the project. For example, if an MNC borrows £50 million to finance a project in the United Kingdom, the debt capacity of this

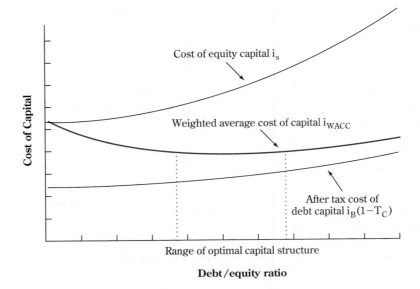

Figure 20.2

The Multinational
Corporation's Cost of Capital
Using the WACC Approach

project is not necessarily £50 million. Some of this debt may be used to support other assets of the firm. The corporate treasurer simply may have seized this opportunity to tap the pound sterling debt market for additional capital. Firms often accumulate several projects under one or more large securities issues to take advantage of the substantial economies of scale in the transactions costs that accompany debt and equity flotations.

The Cost of Debt. The **yield to maturity** (YTM) on debt is the discount rate that equates the present value of promised future interest payments to the current market value of the debt B. For a bond issue with maturity T and promised cash flows CF_t, yield to maturity is the rate i_B that satisfies the equality

$$B = \sum_{t=1}^{T} \frac{CF_t}{(1+i_B)^t} \tag{20.6}$$

This is just the internal rate of return on the bond issue. If the risk and debt capacity of foreign assets are similar to those of other firm assets, the yield to maturity on existing debt in a particular currency can be used as the cost of capital on foreign projects. If the corporation's debt is not publicly traded, the yield to maturity can be estimated from the yield on publicly traded debt with similar characteristics (debt rating, maturity, currency of denomination, seniority, callability, and convertibility).

There is one hazard in using yield to maturity as the required return on low quality debt issues. The yield to maturity calculation is based on promised cash flows, not on expected cash flows. If there is default risk, then expected cash flows are less than promised cash flows, and yield to maturity overstates investors' true required return. This in turn overstates the firm's true cost of debt capital. This is less of a problem on high-quality debt than on low-quality debt, because the difference between promised and expected cash flows on high-quality debt is small. The yield to maturity on low-quality debt can significantly overstate bondholders' true required return and the firm's cost of capital.

International bond issuers sometimes pay Standard & Poor's or Moody's a fee for rating their bonds. These issuers have the option of not publishing their bond rating. Low quality issuers usually choose either to not have their bonds rated or to not publish their ratings if they feel a rating is lower than they deserve. For these lower quality issues, investors must estimate the creditworthiness of the bond issue themselves. MNCs that do publish their bond ratings tend to have high quality debt.

The Cost of Equity. The most common way to estimate the required return on the equity of a publicly traded corporation is to regress the company's equity returns on a stock market index according to the **market model** regression:

$$R_i = \alpha_i + \beta_i R_M + e_i \qquad (20.7)$$

The regression estimate of the equity beta β_i is then plugged into the security market line in equation (20.1) or (20.2) (depending on the extent of market segmentation) to arrive at an estimate of the required return on equity. If the company is not publicly traded or if a project-specific equity beta is needed for valuation of a proposed investment, an estimate of beta, and, hence, required return, can be obtained from the beta of a publicly traded *pure-play* firm that is concentrated in the same industry as the project. An ideal pure play will have the same systematic business risk and debt capacity as the project.

The world's capital markets are not yet fully integrated, with investors in many countries exhibiting strong home equity biases. For this reason, a national market index is usually chosen as the market return R_M for use in the security market line. In the

Weighted Average Cost of Capital: An Example

Suppose the market value of debt is $100 million, the market value of equity is $200 million, the before-tax cost of debt is 10 percent, the before-tax cost of equity is 20 percent, and the corporate tax rate is 40 percent. What is the weighted average cost of capital?

From equation (20.5), the WACC is

$$\begin{aligned}
i_{WACC} &= (B/V_L)\, i_B\, (1-T_C) + (S/V_L)\, i_S \\
&= (\$100M/\$300M)\,(0.10)\,(1-0.40) \\
&\quad + (\$200M/\$300M)\,(0.20) \\
&= 0.153, \text{ or } 15.3\%
\end{aligned}$$

The before-tax cost of debt is 10 percent. The after-tax cost of debt is only 6 percent because every dollar of interest expense reduces corporate taxes by 40 cents. The after-tax cost of equity is the same as the before-tax cost because capital gains and dividend payments on equity are not a tax-deductible expense for the corporation.

United States an equity market index, such as the S&P 500 or the NYSE Composite, is conventionally chosen for the market return by U.S. companies and equity investors. Similarly, Japanese residents prefer to use a Japanese market index, such as the Nikkei 225. For economic, cultural, and geographic reasons, investors in Europe have less home equity bias than investors in the United States and Japan. Nevertheless, European investors tend to use their own national market index as the market portfolio, although some European institutional investors are beginning to use an all-European index instead.

For investments in developed economies, the security market line is still the most popular method for identifying equity required returns. Arbitrage Pricing Theory (APT) is less frequently used to estimate the required return on equity. However, the use of APT in portfolio investment and cost of capital decisions is on the rise. Moreover, some evidence indicates that the factors that determine risk premiums in emerging capital markets are different from those in developed markets.[3]

The Adjusted Present Value Approach to Project Valuation

Investment-Financing Interactions on Foreign Projects. The traditional weighted average cost of capital approach to valuation assumes that the firm's investment and financing decisions are determined independently. If only life were so simple. The MNC with access to international financial markets faces financing decisions that affect both the cost of capital and expected future returns on investment. This is particularly true when there are government incentives attached to the foreign project or there are tax differences between the home and foreign countries. Consequently, the value of an international investment project almost always depends on the way it is financed.

For example, governments are sometimes willing to provide debt financing for selected projects at below-market interest rates in order to promote foreign investment and achieve their policy objectives. International agencies, such as the financing branch of the World Bank, also occasionally facilitate foreign investment through below-market loans. Because subsidized financing is tied to a particular investment project, a decision to accept subsidized financing is both an investment and a financing decision.

A large part of the value of an investment derives from the way the investment is financed. Cross-border differences in tax rates result in different interest tax shields, depending on whether the parent or a foreign subsidiary issues the debt. Cross-border differences in real interest rates and in real exchange rates result in different costs of capital, depending on the currency in which debt or equity securities are issued. Interactions between the investment and financing decisions mean that the debt capacity of a foreign project varies, depending on the level and riskiness of cash flows from the project, the country in which the project is located, and other project-specific factors. Because of these interactions, investment and financing decisions on cross-border projects cannot be made in isolation. The dependency between the investment and financing decisions should always be kept in mind when evaluating foreign projects.

---

3 See Claude B. Erb, Campbell R. Harvey, and Tadas E. Viskanta, "Country Risk and Global Equity Selection," *Journal of Portfolio Management* 21, Winter 1995, pages 74–83.

The Adjusted Present Value Equation. It is useful to have an idea of how much of the value of a foreign project is from the investment itself and how much of the value is from the way in which it is financed. The **adjusted present value (APV)** approach to project valuation attempts to separate these two sources of value.

$$V_L = V_U + PV(\text{financing side effects}) \qquad (20.8)$$

V_L is the value of a levered project. V_U represents the market value of a project in the absence of financial leverage. This value is simply the present value of cash flows from an unlevered project discounted at an unlevered cost of equity. The last term, PV(financing side effects), represents the present value of any financing side effects that arise as the project's debt capacity is employed. This approach can be used either for project valuation or for valuation of the firm itself.

Adjusted present value is the present value of the project, assuming all-equity financing, plus the present value of any financing side effects minus the initial investment:

$$
\begin{aligned}
APV &= V_L - \text{Initial investment} \\
&= V_U + PV(\text{financing side effects}) - \text{Initial investment} \qquad (20.9)
\end{aligned}
$$

In a perfect capital market *without corporate taxes,* the present value of financing side effects is zero. This is a consequence of the irrelevance proposition presented in Chapter 6: "If financial markets are perfect, then corporate financial policy is irrelevant." In the real world, with interest tax shields adding to value and costs of financial distress subtracting from value at higher levels of debt, the value of financing side effects can be important.

The Unlevered Cost of Equity. Calculating an APV begins with an estimate of the value of a project as an all-equity investment. This in turn requires an estimate of the unlevered cost of equity.

The **systematic business risk** or **unlevered beta** of a project, β_U, is the beta of the project as if it were financed with 100 percent equity. Business risk is the risk of operating cash flows. It is often measured as the standard deviation of Earnings Before Interest and Taxes, or σ_{EBIT}. Systematic business risk is the systematic or nondiversifiable portion of total business risk; that is, the portion of σ_{EBIT} that is related to movements in the market portfolio. Systematic business risk is also referred to as the firm's unlevered beta, β_U, or the beta of the EBIT stream such that $\beta_U = \beta_{EBIT}$.

If a publicly traded pure play (that is, a firm concentrated in the same industry as the project) can be found with similar systematic business risk and no debt in its capital structure, then the beta of this pure play can be used as a proxy for the unlevered beta of the project. Using this unlevered pure-play beta in the security market line of equation (20.1) or (20.2) yields an estimate of the unlevered cost of equity.

The Value of Financing Side Effects. If financial markets are perfect, there are no financing side effects and the value of the levered firm is equal to the value of the unlevered firm. If markets are not perfect, financial market imperfections can introduce a number of **financing side effects**. One important financing side effect is the tax deductibility of interest payments. This tax deduction results in interest tax shields to the firm using debt to finance its investments. Other financing side effects are deadweight costs that detract from the value of a project. The most important deadweight costs are costs of financial distress, including the agency costs that arise between managers and shareholders. These costs become more prominent at higher levels of debt. The financial manager's objective is to determine at what debt level the decrease in value from costs of financial distress begins to overtake the increase in value from interest tax shields. This optimal capital structure can be very difficult to determine because expected future costs of financial distress are not directly observable.[4]

APV and Project Valuation When Special Circumstances Exist. Chapter 16 identified several special circumstances commonly attached to foreign investment projects. These special circumstances include blocked funds, subsidized financing, negative-NPV tie-in projects, expropriation risk, and tax holidays. Chapter 16 treated each of these special circumstances as a separate side effect of the foreign investment project. Although not all of these side effects are financial in nature, the approach to project valuation in Chapter 16 separated the value of the side effect from the value of the project without the side effect.

$$V_{\text{PROJECT WITH SIDE EFFECT}} = V_{\text{PROJECT WITHOUT SIDE EFFECT}} + V_{\text{SIDE EFFECT}} \qquad (20.10)$$

The spirit of equation (20.10) is the same as that of adjusted present value in equation (20.8).

Knowing the components of the value of a foreign project can prove beneficial when negotiating the environment of a foreign project with a host government. For example, if project value springs entirely from a tax holiday that could be taken away at the whim of a new political regime, then the project is highly exposed to political risk. And unlike such political risks as expropriation, it is difficult to ensure against loss of a tax holiday through agencies such as the U.S. government's Overseas Private Investment Corporation (OPIC) or the World Bank's Multilateral Investment Guarantee Agency (MIGA). If the project has a negative NPV when the tax subsidy is removed, then the MNC may choose to forgo the foreign project entirely rather than be at the mercy of the foreign government. Alternatively, the MNC can continue to search for positive-NPV projects on which the government will still confer the tax holiday.

20.3 CAPITAL STRUCTURE THEORY AND PRACTICE

Capital Structure in a Perfect World

The Modigliani-Miller Model: Capital Structure in a No-Tax World. Chapter 6 introduced the perfect market assumptions of Franco Modigliani and Merton Miller

---

4 Isik Inselbag and Howard Kaufold apply the APV approach to the present value of interest tax shields in "How to Value Recapitalizations and Leveraged Buyouts," *Journal of Applied Corporate Finance* 2, No. 2, 1989, pages 87–96.

(hereafter MM).[5] MM's contribution to finance was in identifying the conditions under which financial policy does not matter. MM began with the perfect market assumptions:

- Frictionless markets (including no corporate or personal taxes)
- Equal access to market prices
- Rational investors
- Equal access to costless information

To these perfect market assumptions, MM added three other assumptions:

- The existence of homogeneous business risk classes, so there are perfect substitutes or pure plays for every asset
- Homogeneous investor expectations
- Perpetual cash flows[6]

Rational investors operating in a perfect financial market will not allow different prices for identical assets to exist simultaneously. This means that in MM's stylized world the law of one price holds in all places and at all times. Financial markets in an MM world are perfectly integrated.

Equal access to perfect financial markets has an important consequence—individual investors can replicate any financial action that the firm can take. Because of equal access to perfect financial markets, the firm's financial policies and strategies become irrelevant. Investors can create "homemade" financial transactions that are equivalent to anything the firm can create. This is Miller's and Modigliani's famous **irrelevance proposition**:

If financial markets are perfect, then corporate financial policy is irrelevant.

The value of an asset is then solely determined by the value of expected future *investment* cash flows and not by the way in which it is financed.

The assumption of perfect financial markets is a far cry from the real world. Yet the perfect market assumptions provide us with a first step in understanding the workings of the imperfect and vastly more complex real world. In a perfect financial market, financial policy is irrelevant. The converse is that one or more of the perfect market assumptions must be important if financial policy is to matter.

If financial policy is to increase firm value, then it must either increase the firm's expected future cash flows or decrease the discount rate in a way that cannot be replicated by individual investors.

---

5 Franco Modigliani and Merton Miller, "The Cost of Capital, Corporation Finance and the Theory of Investment," *American Economic Review* 48, June 1958, pages 261–297.

6 The assumption of perpetual cash flows yields a simple algebraic solution to the capital structure problem, because the value of a perpetuity is the annual cash flow divided by the discount rate: $V = CF/i$.

The Modigliani-Miller Model: Capital Structure with Corporate Taxes. Modigliani and Miller later added corporate taxes to their basic model.[7] The tax deductibility of interest payments on corporate debt yields the following.

MM PROPOSITION I WITH CORPORATE TAXES:

$$V_L = V_U + T_C B \qquad (20.11)$$

where V_L = market value of the levered firm
V_U = market value of the unlevered firm (that is, financed with 100% equity),
B = market value of the firm's bonds
T_C = firm's marginal tax rate

According to this proposition, the value of the levered firm is equal to the value of the unlevered firm plus the present value of the tax shield from the use of debt.[8] An interest rate i_B is paid on debt. Because this debt is a perpetuity, the size of the periodic interest payment is $i_B B$ in perpetuity. The tax shield is T_C percent of the interest payment in each period, or $T_C(i_B B)$. Discounting this interest tax shield at the cost of debt yields the present value of the future tax shields, $T_C(i_B B)/i_B = T_C B$. The cost of debt is the appropriate discount rate because the tax shields are dependent on making the interest payments.

The particular algebraic form of MM Proposition I is driven by MM's assumption of perpetual cash flows. The intuition, however, is quite general. Interest payments on debt are tax deductible at the corporate level, whereas dividend and capital gain payments to equity are not. Financial leverage can add to the value of the firm by providing the corporation with a reduction in taxes through the interest tax shield. Because taxes are assessed at the corporate level, this reduction in corporate taxes cannot be replicated by individual investors. In the absence of costs of financial distress or other market imperfections, the corporation unambiguously gains as it adds more debt to its capital structure and the firm should use as much debt as possible in an MM world.

According to MM Proposition II, the required return on levered equity is equal to the required return on unlevered equity i_U plus a premium for financial leverage.

MM PROPOSITION II WITH CORPORATE TAXES:

$$i_S = i_U + \left(\frac{B}{S}\right)(i_U - i_B)(1 - T_C) \qquad (20.12)$$

7 Franco Modigliani and Merton Miller added corporate taxes in "Corporate Income Taxes and the Cost of Capital: A Correction," *American Economic Review* 53, June 1963, pages 433–442.
8 Miller later extended the MM model to personal taxes on stocks and bonds as well as corporate taxes in "Debt and Taxes," *Journal of Finance* 32, June 1977, pages 261–275. See Problem 20.4 at the end of this chapter.

Warning: Use of the MM Model Can Be Hazardous to Your Health

Be careful that you do not try to apply equations (20.11) through (20.14) to a real-world cost of capital or capital structure problem. The MM model is set up in the absence of any real-world complications (except corporate taxes), so these equations are of little use in real valuation situations. In the MM world, the size of the tax shield is directly proportional to the amount of debt issued by the company. No matter how much debt is issued, there are no other drains on the system, such as costs of financial distress or agency conflicts between the various stakeholders in the firm. The implication is that the firm should issue as much debt as possible—up to 100 percent of the value of the firm. This is a nonsensical result. In the real world, the only companies that are financed with 100 percent debt are those that are in financial distress.

Equation (20.13) is particularly seductive in that it appears to provide an adjustment to beta for differences in financial leverage. Keep in mind that the assumptions that

underlie equation (20.13) are the same ones that suggest the firm issue 100 percent debt in equation (20.12). Although equation (20.13) might be useful for making adjustments for small differences in leverage, attempting to adjust beta with equation (20.13) can actually lead to worse beta estimates than simply ignoring differences in financial leverage.* A more reliable strategy for estimating a firm's cost of capital is to begin with the beta of a publicly traded pure play company in the same industry and country and with similar financial leverage. Using the beta of a publicly traded pure play will ensure that your beta estimate is at least in the right ballpark.

---

* See Kirt C. Butler, Rosanne M. Mohr, and Richard R. Simonds, "The Hamada and Conine Leverage Adjustments and the Estimation of Systematic Risk for Multisegment Firms," *Journal of Business Finance and Accounting* 18, November 1991, pages 885–901.

---

where   S = market value of the firm's stock
           B = market value of the firm's bonds
           i_S = required return on the stock of the levered firm
                 (the cost of levered equity)
           i_U = required return on the unlevered firm (the cost of unlevered equity)
           i_B = required return on the firm's bonds (the cost of debt)
           T_C = firm's marginal tax rate

Robert Hamada combined the MM and CAPM assumptions and derived the following relation between the systematic risk or beta of equity (β_S) and financial leverage:[9]

LEVERED BETA:

$$\beta_S = \beta_U + \beta_U \left(\frac{B}{S} \right)(1 - T_C) \tag{20.13}$$

---

9 Robert Hamada, "The Effects of Capital Structure on the Systematic Risk of Common Stock," *Journal of Finance* 27, May 1972, pages 435–452.

Equations (20.12) and (20.13) state that the systematic risk (and hence required return) of levered equity is equal to the systematic risk (and hence required return) of unlevered equity plus a premium for financial leverage. As with MM Proposition I, the particular algebraic forms of equations (20.12) and (20.13) are determined by MM's assumption of perpetual cash flows.

Optimal Capital Structure: The Rest of the Story

An important omission in the Modigliani-Miller model is the assumption that there are no costs of financial distress. Financial distress costs include

- **Direct costs**—directly incurred during bankruptcy or liquidation proceedings
- **Indirect costs**—indirectly incurred prior to formal bankruptcy or liquidation

Direct costs of financial distress include court costs and attorney fees. Indirect costs include lower sales and higher operating and financial expenses as managers tend to the causes and side effects of financial distress rather than running the business. Indirect costs also include the **agency costs** that arise from conflicts of interest between managers and other stakeholders during financial distress.

Costs of financial distress rise at higher levels of debt as stakeholders contend for the firm's remaining resources. These costs affect expected future cash flows to debt and equity investors as well as the required returns of these investors. As capital costs begin to rise at higher levels of debt, the costs of financial distress eventually begin to dominate the interest tax shields from additional debt. The optimal capital structure includes an amount of debt that minimizes the cost of capital and maximizes the value of the firm, given the nature and scale of the firm's investments.

20.4 FINANCING FOREIGN OPERATIONS

Balancing the Needs of the Parent with the Needs of the Project

From the parent corporation's perspective, the financial structure of foreign affiliates should be driven by the objectives of the parent corporation. Corporate financing of both domestic and foreign projects should be done at the corporate level with the goal of minimizing the overall cost of capital of the multinational corporation, given the risk and expected returns of the corporation's assets. Financing sources should be shifted toward those subsidiaries and currencies with relatively low real after-tax borrowing costs and away from subsidiaries and currencies with relatively high borrowing costs. In this setting, the capital structure of each individual project is subordinate to the corporation's overall capital structure.

Financial managers also must pay attention to how they finance each individual project. Foreign investments are made in economic, political, and cultural environments that can have an important influence on the activities of the multinational corporation. The foreign environment brings many nonfinancial factors into the multinational corporation's financing decisions. To reduce the costs and risks of foreign operations, financing choices often must be tied to local norms.

	Internal sources	External sources
Multinational corporation's home country	Cash flow from the parent and from affiliates in the parent's home country	New debt or equity financing (usually issued or guaranteed by the parent corporation)
Foreign project's host country	Cash flow from existing operations in the host country	Local debt or equity from institutions or markets in the host country
International financing sources	Cash flow redistributed from other foreign affiliates	Eurobonds Euroequity Swaps Project finance

The risk of expropriation is one of these real-world factors. A multinational corporation's exposure to expropriation risk is greatest when the MNC fails to tie its foreign projects into local communities.[10] One response is to finance foreign projects with as much local debt and equity as possible. This reduces the consequences of expropriation because less of the corporation's own money is at risk. Local financing also reduces the probability of expropriation because locally financed projects belong not just to the foreign MNC but to local investors as well.

Although reducing the cost of capital is a primary objective of the financial manager, the weight given to location-specific factors is much greater on foreign projects than on domestic projects.

Sources of Funds for Foreign Projects

Table 20.2 categorizes the financing sources available to the multinational corporation along two dimensions: (1) whether funds are raised from internal or from external sources and (2) the location of the market in which funds are raised.

Internal versus External Sources of Funds. The preferred source of financing for both domestic and foreign investment is internally generated cash flow from operations.[11] Cash flow comes from earnings from operations and from noncash charges, such as depreciation. Internally generated funds can come from existing operations in the host country or in the parent's home country. Internal funds can also be redistributed from other foreign affiliates.

Internally generated funds are preferred because they indicate that the corporation has **free cash flow**—cash flow available beyond that needed to finance the firm's other positive-NPV activities. Financing foreign projects with internally generated funds avoids the transactions costs associated with new securities issues. Financing investments with

---

10 See David Bradley's "Managing Against Expropriation," *Harvard Business Review,* July–August 1977, pages 75–83.

11 A review of capital structure theory and practice and a discussion of the pecking order of financial sources appears in Stewart C. Myers, "The Capital Structure Puzzle," *Journal of Finance* 39, July 1984, pages 575–592.

internally generated cash also allows managers to avoid the discipline of the financial markets.

The form of the financing becomes important when funds are to be repatriated to the parent corporation or redistributed to other foreign affiliates. Vehicles for repatriating funds to the parent include

- Interest payments on debt
- Lease payments on operating and financial lease agreements
- Royalties
- Management fees
- Dividend payments on equity

With the exception of dividend payments on equity, each of these repatriation vehicles promises a stream of contractual cash flows to the supplier of capital.

The multinational corporation faces a transfer pricing problem in setting rates of return on these internal financial transactions. In external financial markets, purchasing power parity ensures that real after-tax rates of return tend toward equilibrium. The multinational corporation is not similarly constrained in setting rates of return on its own internal transactions.

Tax planning plays an important role in how the multinational corporation structures its internal financial transactions. Taxes depend on the form of income in any single tax jurisdiction as well as on bilateral tax treaties between different tax jurisdictions. The multinational corporation can reduce its tax liability by shifting internal sales toward low-tax countries and internal expenses (including interest payments) toward high-tax countries.

To avoid abuses of the tax code, most countries specify that transfer prices must be set at arm's-length or market prices. In the United States, this is required by Section 486 of the Internal Revenue Code. It is difficult to defend aggressive pricing on debt and lease contracts because market prices are readily observable. The multinational corporation has slightly more discretion in the rates that it sets on royalties and management fees because no market prices are available. For this reason, many countries place a limit on the royalties that can be repatriated to the parent. A limit of 5 percent of sales is common on royalty payments to foreign owners.

Firms without pools of internally generated funds must tap external sources for additional capital to fund their foreign operations. In addition to domestic sources of debt and equity capital, the multinational corporation has access to a variety of international sources of capital. These include[12]

- International equity
- International bonds
- Project finance
- Swaps

---

12 A comprehensive summary of overseas financing appears in the Winter 1992 special issue of *Financial Management*. See also Marr, Trimble, and Varma, "Innovation in Global Financing: The Case of Euroequity Offerings," *Journal of Applied Corporate Finance* 5, Spring 1992, pages 50–54.

International Equity Markets. Securities trade tends to gravitate toward the most liquid market, and this is usually a company's local stock market. For this reason, national stock markets are predominantly local markets. A non-U.S. investor wishing to buy or sell IBM often chooses the New York Stock Exchange despite the fact that IBM has multiple listings in London, Tokyo, Paris, and several other national exchanges. Nevertheless, corporations have begun appealing to investors in other countries by offering equity securities directly in foreign markets. Equity issues that are offered directly to investors in international markets are called *Euroequity* or *global equity* issues.

Most securities in the United States are issued in registered form. The convention in most West European securities markets is to issue securities in bearer form. Investors in these markets prefer bearer securities to retain their anonymity—sometimes in order to avoid taxation. To allow U.S. corporations to compete for capital in international securities markets, the 1986 Tax Reform Act allowed U.S. corporations to issue securities in bearer form directly to foreign investors.[13] To further reduce the costs of overseas financing, the U.S. Treasury Department defined **targeted registered offerings** to foreign financial institutions and exempted such securities issues from the information-reporting and tax-withholding requirements of the 1986 act. To qualify as a targeted registered offering, four requirements must be satisfied.

- The registered owner must be a financial institution in another country.
- Interest coupons or dividends must be paid to this registered financial institution.
- The issuer must certify that it has no knowledge that a U.S. taxpayer is the owner of the security.
- The issuer and any registered financial institutions must follow SEC certification procedures.

The foreign financial institution then maintains an over-the-counter secondary market in the securities. Targeted registered offerings allow U.S. corporations access to overseas sources of equity financing that they otherwise might not be able to access.

Foreign corporations seeking access to U.S. investors typically use either American shares or American depository receipts. **American shares** are issued directly to U.S. investors through a transfer agent in accordance with SEC regulations. American shares pay dividends in the currency of the multinational corporation's home country. **American depository receipts (ADRs)** are derivative securities that are backed by a pool of foreign shares held in trust by a U.S. investment banker or broker. ADRs pay dividends in dollars and trade on U.S. exchanges just as other U.S. equities do. Multinational corporations based in the United States also can use depository receipts to appeal to investors in foreign markets.

International Bond Markets. An **international bond** is a bond that is traded outside the country of the issuer. International bonds can be categorized into two types. A **foreign bond** is a bond issued by a domestic borrower in the internal market of a

---

13 Prior to the 1986 Tax Reform Act, U.S. corporations could issue bearer securities to foreign investors only through an offshore finance subsidiary.

foreign country and denominated in the currency of that country. A **Eurobond** is traded in a market outside the borders of the country in which the Eurobond is denominated. A Eurobond is called a **global bond** when it trades in one or more internal (foreign or domestic) bond markets as well as in the external Eurobond market. Only a few global bonds have been issued, and these have been issued by large AAA-rated borrowers, such as the World Bank.

An advantage of a foreign bond is that it helps tie the foreign subsidiary of a multinational corporation into the local community. Raising funds in the bond market of a host country is one way to ensure that the multinational corporation is viewed as a good corporate citizen by local residents. It also partially insulates the foreign subsidiary against foreign political risk. A disadvantage of a foreign bond is that it is regulated and taxed by authorities in the foreign market. In contrast, Eurobonds are exempt from such regulation and taxation because they trade outside the jurisdiction of any single nation.

Nearly the full panoply of bond types is available in the Eurobond market. Eurobonds have been issued in each of the following forms:

- Fixed-rate Eurobonds
- Floating-rate Eurobonds (typically at a spread over LIBOR)
- Zero-coupon Eurobonds
- Equity-linked Eurobonds (convertible Eurobonds or Eurobonds with warrants)
- Eurobonds with detachable warrants that allow purchase of additional bonds, currency, or a commodity (typically gold or oil) at a fixed price for a set period of time
- Eurobonds with call or put options, granted to the issuer or the bondholder or both to buy or sell the bonds to the other party at a fixed exercise price
- Dual currency Eurobonds that pay interest in one currency and principal in another
- Currency option Eurobonds (a form of dual currency bond) that give either the bondholder or the issuer the option to select the currency denomination at each coupon date

Many of these bond features involve a call or put option, so option pricing models are especially useful for valuing both domestic and international bonds.

Project Financing. **Project financing** is a way for a project sponsor to raise nonrecourse financing for a specific project. Three characteristics distinguish project financing from other forms of financing.

- The project is a separate legal entity and relies heavily on debt financing.
- The debt is contractually linked to the cash flow generated by the project.
- Government participation comes in the form of infrastructure support, operating or financial guarantees, rights-of-way, or assurances against political risk.

The hallmark of project financing is that claims on the project are contractually tied to the cash flows generated by a single asset. When a corporation finances an investment project from internally generated funds, cash flows from the project are commingled with cash flows from other projects. Contractually tying cash flows to the asset being financed effectively unbundles the project from other assets of the firm and allows the market to value the project as a stand-alone entity. Debt and equity have a claim on project cash flows, but not on the assets or cash flows of the corporation sponsoring the project.

Project financing works best for finite-lived, tangible assets that offer reliable cash flow streams capable of supporting high debt levels. Ownership of the project is transferred at the end of the project either to the project sponsor or to the host government. In a build-operate-own (BOO) contract, the project sponsor assumes ownership of the project at the end of the contract life. On a build-operate-transfer (BOT) project, ownership is transferred to the host government.

Candidates for project financing include natural resource developments, toll roads and bridges, and power generation projects, because such projects usually possess advantages that are tied to a particular location. Reliable cash flows permit the project to borrow against future revenues, which are sometimes guaranteed by selling the output in advance of construction. This allows cash flows to be contractually allocated to those most willing and able to bear the risks (and reap the rewards) of the project.

Examples of projects that were funded by project financings include the Channel Tunnel between England and France, the EuroDisney theme park outside Paris, the Orange County (California) and Cuernavaca-Acapulco (Mexico) toll roads, and oil exploration and development in the Forties Field in the North Sea off the coast of England. Project financing has become a popular way to fund infrastructure development projects, such as roads and power generation, in countries with emerging capital markets and a shortage of capital.

Quite often, commitments are made by the project sponsor or by supporting governments, suppliers, or customers to ensure that cash flow projections and debt payments will be met. Infrastructure projects, natural resource development projects, and power

---

Project Finance through the Ages

Suppose you live in Devon, England, and have discovered a rich vein of silver on your property. England is in a recession, and lenders in "the City" (London) are unwilling to lend you money to construct a silver mine. Desperate for funds to invest in your future, you arrange for an Italian bank to finance construction of the silver mine in return for the entire revenue stream from the mine for a period of one year. Both parties can benefit from this arrangement. The bank is assured of a good return on its investment through its contractual claim on project cash flows. You get your silver mine after one year and minus a few tons of ore. This example of project finance actually took place—in the year 1299.

Project financing was a popular way to fund international ventures throughout the Middle Ages and the Renaissance. Oceanic voyages to America and the Far East were financed by governments and merchant banks, with the proceeds distributed to the project sponsor at journey's end. Christopher Columbus's voyage to the New World was financed in this way by the Queen of Spain. As international trade flourished, fleets of ships were eventually brought under one corporate banner and the need to fund journeys on a trip-by-trip basis declined.

This example is retold in John W. Kensinger's and John D. Martin's "Project Finance: Raising Money the Old-Fashioned Way," *Journal of Applied Corporate Finance* 1, No. 3, 1988, pages 69–81.

generation are high priorities for the governments of developing countries. Government contributions increase the expected return and reduce the risk to other project participants. Although governments may make assurances to reduce the political risk of the project, these assurances are not always honored. Just weeks before the planned opening of a project-financed toll road in Thailand, the Thai government reduced the toll by a third and unilaterally seized operational control of the highway in violation of the project's thirty-year build-operate-transfer agreement.

Swaps. Swaps provide the financial manager with a useful way to transform the corporation's existing liabilities into new forms. In a swap contract, one asset or liability is exchanged for another and then reexchanged at a later date. The most popular swap contracts are:

- Currency swaps
- Interest rate swaps
- Commodity swaps
- Debt-for-equity swaps

A **currency swap** allows the corporation to exchange an obligation in one currency for an obligation in another. Currency swaps are used to hedge against foreign exchange risk. An **interest rate swap** trades fixed- and floating-rate interest payments in a single currency. Interest rate swaps are used to hedge against interest rate risk. A **commodity swap** trades fixed and floating commodity prices either on a single commodity or between two different commodities. Commodity swaps are used to hedge against commodity price risk. A **debt-for-equity swap** trades debt for equity. An example is a swap of ten-year Treasury bonds for an equivalent notional amount of the NYSE Composite index. Swap contracts often include one or more options that cap prices in one direction or another.

20.5 THE INTERNATIONAL EVIDENCE ON CAPITAL STRUCTURE

Identifying the determinants of capital structure in an international setting is somewhat more difficult than in a domestic setting—yet potentially more rewarding. Financial and accounting data are difficult to obtain in many countries and, when available, are subject to widely divergent accounting conventions. There is also a great deal of heterogeneity among national tax and bankruptcy codes, legal and financial institutions, and markets for corporate control.

This variability in national systems is both a blessing and a curse for cross-border studies of capital structure. Although variability in business environments limits the inferences that may be drawn from studies of capital structure in different national markets, cross-border studies are also potentially more revealing of the underlying determinants of capital structure. This section examines the empirical evidence on the determinants of capital structure choice by domestic and multinational corporations.

Evidence from the U.S. Capital Markets

Many factors influence the firm's capital structure decision. Empirical studies of the capital structure of corporations in the United States have generally agreed on the following:[14]

- Leverage increases with
  - Fixed assets
  - Nondebt tax shields
  - Growth opportunities
  - Firm size

- Leverage decreases with
  - Earnings volatility
  - Advertising and research/development expenditures
  - The probability of bankruptcy or default
  - Profitability
  - The uniqueness of the product

Evidence from International Capital Markets

Raghuram Rajan and Luigi Zingales conducted an interesting cross-border study of the international determinants of capital structure.[15] Rajan and Zingales presented balance sheets representing typical nonfinancial companies from each of the G-7 countries (Canada, France, Germany, Italy, Japan, the United States, and the United Kingdom) based on Standard & Poor's Global Vantage international financial database. These balance sheets appear in Table 20.3.

At first glance, companies in the United Kingdom and Canada appear to have the lowest debt, with debt ratios (defined as total debt to book value of assets) of 57.8 percent and 60.3 percent, respectively. However, these balance sheets are distorted by cross-border differences in accounting practices. Rajan and Zingales reported leverage ratios after making some adjustments for these accounting differences. Adjusted debt-to-capital ratios are reported at the bottom of Table 20.3. Rajan and Zingales concluded that, with the exception of the United Kingdom and Germany, adjusted debt ratios were from 33 to 39 percent in each of the G-7 countries. Leverage in Germany and the United Kingdom was somewhat lower than in the other five countries, with debt-to-capital ratios of 18 percent and 16 percent, respectively.

---

14 See the summary in "The Theory of Capital Structure" by Milton Harris and Artur Raviv, *Journal of Finance* 46, March 1991, pages 297–355, especially the table on page 334.

15 From Raghuram G. Rajan and Luigi Zingales, "What Do We Know about Capital Structure? Some Evidence from International Data," *Journal of Finance* 50, Vol. 1, December 1995, pages 1421–1460.

TABLE 20.3 BALANCE SHEETS FOR NONFINANCIAL FIRMS IN G-7 COUNTRIES, 1991

	United States	Japan	Germany	France	Italy	United Kingdom	Canada
Assets							
Cash and short-term investments	11.2%	18.4%	8.8%	10.3%	10.5%	11.4%	8.2%
Accounts receivable/debtors	17.8	22.5	26.9	28.9	29.0	22.1	13.0
Inventories	16.1	13.9	23.6	17.4	15.6	17.7	11.0
Current assets—other	2.9	3.0	0.1	1.7	1.6	3.7	1.9
Current assets—total	48.0	57.7	59.4	58.3	56.5	54.7	33.2
Fixed assets (tangible)	36.3	28.7	32.7	24.4	32.4	41.3	51.6
Investment and advances—equity	1.4	1.4	1.4	3.4	1.9	1.5	4.8
Investment and advances—other	3.1	9.4	3.4	4.9	4.1	1.2	2.9
Intangible assets	7.6	0.8	2.4	8.5	2.6	0.9	4.7
Assets—other	5.8	2.9	0.7	0.7	3.3	0.5	3.7
Assets—total	100.0%	100.0%	100.0%	100.0%	100.0%	100.0%	100.0%
Liabilities							
Debt in current liabilities	7.4%	16.4%	9.9%	11.6%	16.2%	9.6%	7.3%
Accounts payable/creditors	15.0	15.4	11.5	17.0	14.7	13.7	13.3
Current liabilities—other	11.0	10.4	8.7	17.0	12.2	16.7	2.8
Current liabilities—total	33.4	42.2	30.0	43.4	43.2	40.0	23.1
Deferred taxes	3.2	0.1	0.8	1.3	1.5	0.9	4.4
Long-term debt	23.3	18.9	9.8	15.7	12.1	12.4	28.1
Minority interest	0.6	0.9	1.6	3.9	3.4	1.1	2.0
Reserves—untaxed	0.0	0.0	1.7	0.0	0.0	0.0	0.0
Liabilities—other	5.8	4.8	28.7	6.3	7.8	3.4	2.6
Liabilities — total	66.1	66.8	72.0	68.8	67.4	57.8	60.3
Shareholders' equity	34.1	33.2	28.0	31.2	32.6	42.2	39.7
Total liabilities and shareholders' equity	100.0%	100.0%	100.0%	100.0%	100.0%	100.0%	100.0%
Debt-to-capital ratios adjusted for accounting differences	33%	37%	18%	34%	39%	16%	37%

Source: Standard & Poor's Global Vantage database as reported by Raghuram G. Rajan and Luigi Zingales, "What Do We Know about Capital Structure? Some Evidence from International Data," *Journal of Finance* 50, Vol. 1, December 1995, pages 1421–1460.

Rajan and Zingales then examined the relation of firm characteristics to financial leverage. The results of their analysis are presented in Table 20.4 and summarized below.[16] Rajan and Zingales found that in the international capital markets

- Leverage increases with
  - Asset market-to-book ratios
  - The proportion of fixed to total assets
  - Firm size

---

16 Rajan and Zingales, "What Do We Know about Capital Structure." Earlier attempts to document the international determinants of capital structure include Lee Remmers, Arthur Stonehill, Richard Wright, and Theo Beekhuisen, "Industry and Size as Debt Ratio Determinants in Manufacturing Internationally," *Financial Management* 3, No. 2, 1974, pages 24–32, and Arthur Stonehill, Theo, Beekhuisen, Richard Wright, Lee Remmers, Norman Toy, Antonio Pares, Alan Shapiro, Douglas Egan, and Thomas Bates, "Financial Goals and Debt Ratio Determinants: A Survey of Practice in Five Countries," Financial Management 4, No. 3, 1975, pages 27-41.

- Leverage decreases with
  - profitability

The most striking result in Table 20.4 is the consistency across countries for all variables except firm size. Each of these relations is found in the domestic U.S. market. Whether the other relations found in the U.S. are also found in international markets

TABLE 20.4 FACTORS CORRELATED WITH DEBT TO BOOK AND MARKET CAPITAL

The estimated model is: $\text{Leverage}_{[\text{Firm } i]} = \alpha + \beta_1 \text{Tangibility}_i + \beta_2 \text{Market-to-book Ratio}_i + \beta_3 \text{Log Sales}_i + \beta_4 \text{Profitability}_i + \varepsilon_i$. The intercept coefficient is not reported. Variable definitions are as follows. *Leverage* is adjusted debt to adjusted debt plus book value of adjusted equity in 1991. *Tangibility* is the ratio of fixed assets to the book value of total assets. *Market-to-book* is the ratio of the book value of assets less the book value of equity plus the market value of equity all divided by the book value of assets. *Logsale* is the logarithm of net sales. *Profitability* is earnings before interest, taxes, and depreciation divided by book value of assets. All explanatory variables are four-year averages (1987–90). Standard errors are in parentheses. See the original article for additional details.

Variable	United States	Japan	Germany	France	Italy	United Kingdom	Canada
Book Capital							
Tangibility	0.50[c]	1.41[c]	0.42[b]	0.53[b]	0.36	0.41[c]	0.26[c]
	(0.04)	(0.18)	(0.19)	(0.26)	(0.23)	(0.07)	(0.10)
Market-to-book	−0.17[c]	−0.04	−0.20[c]	−0.17[b]	−0.19	−0.13[c]	−0.11[c]
	(0.01)	(0.04)	(0.07)	(0.08)	(0.14)	(0.03)	(0.04)
Logsale	0.06[c]	0.11[c]	−0.07[c]	0.02	0.02	0.026[c]	0.08[c]
	(0.01)	(0.02)	(0.02)	(0.02)	(0.03)	(0.01)	(0.01)
Profitability	−0.41[c]	−4.26[c]	0.15	−0.02	−0.16	−0.34	−0.46[b]
	(0.1)	(0.60)	(0.52)	(0.72)	(0.85)	(0.30)	(0.22)
Number of observations	2079	316	175	117	96	522	264
Pseudo R^2	0.21	0.29	0.12	0.12	0.05	0.18	0.19
Market Capital							
Tangibility	0.33[c]	0.58[c]	0.28[a]	0.18	0.48[b]	0.27[c]	0.11
	(0.03)	(0.09)	(0.17)	(0.19)	(0.22)	(0.06)	(0.07)
Market-to-book	−0.08[c]	−0.07[c]	−0.21[c]	−0.15[b]	−0.18[a]	−0.06[b]	−0.13[c]
	(0.01)	(0.02)	(.06)	(0.06)	(0.11)	(0.03)	(0.03)
Logsale	0.03[c]	0.07[c]	−0.06[c]	−0.00	0.04	0.01	0.05[c]
	(0.00)	(0.01)	(0.02)	(0.02)	(0.03)	(0.01)	(0.01)
Profitability	−0.6[c]	−2.25[c]	0.17	−0.22	−0.95	−0.47[b]	−0.48[c]
	(0.07)	(0.32)	(0.47)	(0.53)	(0.77)	(0.24)	(0.17)
Number of observations	2207	313	176	126	98	544	275
Pseudo R^2	0.19		0.14	0.28	0.12	0.19	0.30

[a] Significant at the 10 percent level.
[b] Significant at the 5 percent level.
[c] Significant at the 1 percent level.
Source: Raghuram G. Rajan and Luigi Zingales, "What Do We Know about Capital Structure? Some Evidence from International Data," *Journal of Finance* 50, Vol. 1, December 1995, pages 1421–1460.

will have to await future research. The rest of this section discusses Rajan's and Zingales's findings in more detail.

The Fixed-to-Total Asset Ratio and Asset Tangibility. The ratio of fixed assets to total assets is a measure of the **tangibility** of the firm's assets. Tangible assets can be used as collateral to secure debt. Because it is backed by a tangible asset, secured debt is less susceptible to the agency problems that plague unsecured debt issues. For example, one of the risks with unsecured debt is that the firm will shift into riskier assets once the debt is sold. This shifts risk from equity to debt and, hence, shifts value from debt to equity. The corporation can partially insure debt holders against opportunistic, risk-shifting behavior on the part of management or equity or both by securing debt with a tangible asset. All else equal, this reduction in agency costs results in an increase in equity value. This suggests that firms with a high proportion of tangible assets are more likely to use debt.

Indeed, higher leverage is positively associated with the tangibility of assets (measured by the ratio of fixed to total assets) in each of the G-7 countries, and it is statistically significant at a 5 percent level in every country except Italy. The conclusion that firms use more debt when their assets are tangible is consistent across all of the G-7 countries, despite the wide variation in the role of banks and in the market for corporate control in these countries.

The Asset Market-to-Book Ratio and the Firm's Investment Opportunities. Rajan and Zingales use the market-to-book ratio of a firm's assets as a measure of **growth options** or real investment opportunities.[17] Capital structure theory suggests that the market-to-book ratio should be negatively related to leverage for two reasons. First, if firms issue stock when their stock price is high relative to earnings or book value, then leverage should be negatively related to the market-to-book ratio. Second, because highly levered companies that are in financial distress are more likely to pass up profitable investment opportunities, firms with high growth opportunities should tend to use less debt in their capital structure in order to avoid financial distress.[18]

Market-to-book ratios in Table 20.4 are negatively correlated with leverage in each of the countries. The correlation coefficient is statistically significant at 5 percent in five of the seven countries. Rajan and Zingales found that this negative relation was driven by firms with high market-to-book ratios within each country. The relation is weaker or is absent in firms with low market-to-book ratios. This suggests that the negative relation between leverage and market-to-book ratios may be driven by the tendency of firms to issue equity when stock price is high.

Firm Size and Leverage. Large firms are more likely to be diversified than small firms. In the presence of bankruptcy costs, the diversification of large firms allows the cash flows generated by some of the firm's assets to *coinsure* cash flows of other corpo-

---

17 The market-to-replacement cost ratio (Tobin's q) would have been preferable as a measure of growth opportunities, but replacement cost data were unavailable for firms in most of the G-7 countries.

18 Michael C. Jensen and William Meckling refer to this as the *underinvestment incentive* in "Theory of the Firm: Managerial Behavior, Agency Costs, and Capital Structure," *Journal of Financial Economics* 3, No. 4, 1976, pages 305–360.

rate assets. This **coinsurance effect** can add value to the firm by reducing the expected costs of financial distress. Consequently, large diversified firms should be able to support higher levels of debt, other things held constant.

In Table 20.4, the relation between firm size (logsale) and leverage is generally positive and frequently statistically significant. The exception is Germany, where larger firms tend to be less levered.

Profitability and Leverage. The effect of profitability on leverage is ambiguous. Profitable firms can finance expansion internally and thereby avoid external capital markets. This suggests that profitable firms should have less leverage than unprofitable firms.[19] On the other hand, the larger cash flow of the profitable firm can support more debt and can thereby generate higher tax shields. Thus, higher debt levels should be forced on managers in countries with efficient markets for corporate control.[20] Managers may prefer to avoid the discipline imposed by higher debt levels in countries with less efficient markets for corporate control.

The evidence in Table 20.4 indicates that profitability and leverage are negatively related in the majority of the G-7 countries. Again, the exception is Germany, although the coefficient for Germany is not statistically significant.

20.6 SUMMARY

In an integrated financial market, real after-tax rates of return are equal on equivalent assets. In such a world, multinational corporations do not enjoy financing advantages over local firms. In the real world of segmented financial markets, the multinational corporation with access to alternative sources of capital is often able to lower the cost of debt and equity capital through its financing decisions. This chapter describes some of the considerations that must be in the mind of the financial manager as he or she implements the corporation's financial policy.

19 See Stewart C. Myers and Nicholas S. Majluf, "Corporate Financing and Investment Decisions When Firms Have Information that Investors Do Not Have" *Journal of Financial Economics* 13, No. 2, 1984, pages 127–221.
20 Michael C. Jensen, "Agency Costs of Free Cash Flow, Corporate Financing, and Takeovers," American Economic Review 76, No. 2, 1986, pages 323–339.

KEY TERMS

Adjusted present value (APV)

Agency costs

American depository receipts (ADRs)

American shares

Coinsurance effect

Direct versus indirect costs of financial distress

Financial (capital) structure

Financing side effects

Free cash flow

Growth options

Indirect diversification benefits

Integrated versus segmented financial markets

Interest rate, currency, commodity, and debt-for-equity swaps

International (foreign, Euro-, and global) bonds

Market model

Miller and Modigliani's irrelevance proposition

Project financing

Systematic business risk (unlevered beta)

Tangibility

Targeted registered offerings

Tax clienteles

Weighted average cost of capital (WACC)

Yield to maturity

CONCEPTUAL QUESTIONS

20.1 What distinguishes an integrated from a segmented capital market?

20.2 What factors could lead to capital market segmentation?

20.3 Are risks higher or lower on cross-border investment?

20.4 Does the required return on a project depend on who is investing the money or on where the money is being invested?

20.5 When can the firm's weighted average cost of capital be used as a discount rate on a foreign project?

20.6 Does the value of a foreign project depend on the way it is financed?

20.7 When is the adjusted present value approach to project valuation most useful?

20.8 Does corporate financial policy matter in a perfect financial market?

20.9 What does the Modigliani-Miller (MM) capital structure model tell us about capital structure in the real world?

20.10 What is a targeted registered offering and why is it useful to the corporation?

20.11 What is project financing and when is it most appropriate?

20.12 How can a swap allow the multinational corporation to tap new sources of capital?

20.13 What evidence is there on the international determinants of corporate capital structure? How is the international evidence similar to the domestic U.S. evidence?

PROBLEMS

20.1 The systematic risk (beta) of Grand Pet is 0.8 when measured against the Morgan Stanley Capital International (MSCI) world market index and 1.2 against the London Financial Times 100 (or FTSE 100) stock index. The annual risk-free rate in the United Kingdom is 5 percent.

a. If the required return on the MSCI world market index is 10 percent, what is the required return on Grand Pet stock in an integrated financial market?

b. Suppose the U.K. financial markets are segmented from the rest of the world. If the required return on the FTSE 100 is 10 percent, what is the required return on Grand Pet stock?

20.2 Find Grand Pet's weighted average cost of capital under each of the following scenarios.

a. Grand Pet has a market value debt-to-equity ratio of 33 percent. Grand Pet's pretax borrowing cost on new long-term debt in the United Kingdom is 6 percent. Grand Pet's beta relative to the Footsie 100 is 1.2. The risk-free rate in the United Kingdom is 5 percent, and the market risk premium over the risk-free rate is 10 percent. Interest is deductible in the United Kingdom at the marginal corporate income tax rate of 33 percent. What is Grand Pet's weighted average cost of capital in the U.K. market?

b. Grand Pet can borrow in the Europound market at a pretax cost of 5 percent. International investors are willing to tolerate a 50 percent debt-to-equity mix at this cost of debt. With a 50 percent debt-to-equity ratio, the beta of Grand Pet is 0.8 against the MSCI world index. The required return on the world market portfolio is 10 percent. What is Grand Pet's weighted average cost of capital under these circumstances?

c. Suppose Grand Pet is expected to generate after-tax operating cash flow of £1 billion in the coming year and that this is expected to grow at a g=3% rate in perpetuity. The valuation equation $V_0 = CF_1/(i-g)$ can value Grand Pet's cash flow stream, given CF_1 is the coming year's cash flow, i is the weighted average cost of capital, and g is the growth rate of annual cash flow. Find the value of Grand Pet using the weighted average costs of capital from the scenarios in parts a and b.

20.3 Suppose Grand Pet uses an APV approach to project valuation.

a. Grand Pet's latest investment proposal is to produce nonalcoholic beer for dogs in the United States. Initial investment will be £100 million and will produce a single after-tax cash flow of £8 million after one year. The brewery will be sold for £100 million at the end of the year. Assume there are no tax effects on sale of the brewery. An all-equity company that produces a similar brand of doggy beer trades on the London Stock Exchange and has an all-equity discount rate of 8 percent. What is the value of Grand Pet's project as an all-equity investment?

b. Suppose the project can support up to £25 million in debt at a pretax cost of debt of 6 percent. Principal and interest on the debt (as well as the interest tax shield) are due in one year. Grand Pet's corporate tax rate is 33 percent. What is the value of Grand Pet's project as a levered investment?

c. Suppose Grand Pet's project produces after-tax cash flow of £8 million per year in perpetuity. What are the unlevered and levered APVs from parts a and b? Assume perpetual debt at an interest rate of 6 percent.

20.4 Merton Miller extended the MM capital structure model to include personal as well as corporate taxes.[21] The value of the levered firm in Miller's world with personal taxes on dividend and capital gain income at an average rate T_S and interest income on bonds at a rate T_B is

$$V_L = V_U + (1 - [(1-T_C)(1-T_S)/(1-T_B)]) B$$

where the remaining terms are the same as in MM's proposition in equation (20.11). Corporate income tax rates are 0 percent, 18 percent, and 33 percent in Bermuda, Hong Kong, and the United Kingdom, respectively. Personal tax rates on interest income are 0 percent, 25 percent, and 40 percent, respectively. Individuals from each of these countries face effective tax rates on equity incomes of 0 percent, 0 percent, and 40 percent, respectively.

a. Use Miller's equation to find how much value the tax shield on a $100 million bond would add to the individuals in each of these three countries. Assume perpetual bonds and ignore costs of financial distress.

b. If these tax rates are faced by a majority of the residents in each country, in which country would you expect to find the most debt financing? In which country would you expect to find the most equity financing?

c. Suppose these markets are integrated, so after-tax rates of return on equivalent assets are equal in each of these countries. In which country would you expect to find the highest real pretax cost of debt? Where would real pretax required returns on equity be the highest?

21 Merton Miller, "Debt and Taxes," *Journal of Finance* 32, June 1977, pages 261–275.

Part 5C Multinational Corporate Finance

Capital structure and cost of capital in a Modigliani-Miller world are developed in the following articles:

Franco Modigliani and Merton Miller, "The Cost of Capital, Corporation Finance, and the Theory of Investment," *American Economic Review* 48, June 1958, pages 261–297.

Franco Modigliani and Merton Miller, "Corporate Income Taxes and the Cost of Capital: A Correction," *American Economic Review* 53, June 1963, pages 433–442.

Robert Hamada, "The Effects of Capital Structure on the Systematic Risk of Common Stock," *Journal of Finance* 27, May 1972, p. 435–452.

Milton Harris and Artur Raviv, "The Theory of Capital Structure," *Journal of Finance* 46, March 1991, pages 297–355.

Isik Inselbag and Howard Kaufold, "How to Value Recapitalizations and Leveraged Buyouts," *Journal of Applied Corporate Finance* 2, Summer 1989, pages 87–96.

Merton Miller, "Debt and Taxes," *Journal of Finance* 32, June 1977, pages 261–275.

Articles on the cost of capital to the multinational corporation include

Ian Cooper and Evi Kaplanis, "Home Bias in Equity Portfolios and the Cost of Capital for Multinational Firms," *Journal of Applied Corporate Finance* 8, Fall 1995, pages 95–102.

Claude B. Erb, Campbell R. Harvey, and Tadas E. Viskanta, "Country Risk and Global Equity Selection," *Journal of Portfolio Management* 21, Winter 1995, pages 74–83.

Dennis E. Logue, "When Theory Fails: Globalization as a Response to the (Hostile) Market for Foreign Exchange," *Journal of Applied Corporate Finance* 8, Fall 1995, pages 39–48.

René M. Stulz, "Globalization of Capital Markets and the Cost of Capital: The Case of Nestlé," *Journal of Applied Corporate Finance* 8, Fall 1995, pages 30–38.

For divergent views on the indirect diversification benefits of MNCs, compare the following articles.

Ali M. Fatemi, "Shareholder Benefits from Corporate International Diversification," *Journal of Finance* 39, December 1984, pages 1325–1344.

Bertrand Jacquillat and Bruno Solnik, "Multinationals are Poor Tools for International Diversification," *Journal of Portfolio Management* 4, Winter 1978, pages 8–12.

A comprehensive summary of overseas financing appears in the Winter 1992 special issue of *Financial Management.* Related sources include

M. Wayne Marr, John L. Trimble, and Raj Varma, "On the Integration of International Capital Markets: Evidence from Euroequity Offerings," *Financial Management* 20, Winter 1991, pages 11–21.

M. Wayne Marr, John L. Trimble, and Raj Varma, "Innovation in Global Financing: The Case of Euroequity Offerings," *Journal of Applied Corporate Finance* 5, Spring 1992, pages 50–54.

John W. Kensinger and John D. Martin, "Project Finance: Raising Money the Old-Fashioned Way," *Journal of Applied Corporate Finance* 1, Fall 1988, pages 69–81.

Here is another source of information on project finance: The *Journal of Project Finance* published by Institutional Investor, Inc., 488 Madison Avenue, New York, NY 10022.

Attempts to document the international determinants of capital structure include

J. McDonald, "The Mochiai Effect: Japanese Corporate Cross-Holdings," *Journal of Portfolio Management* 16, Fall 1989, pages 90–95.

Raghuram G. Rajan and Luigi Zingales, "What Do We Know about Capital Structure? Some Evidence from International Data," *Journal of Finance* 50, December 1995, pages 1421–1460.

Lee Remmers, Arthur Stonehill, Richard Wright, and Theo Beekhuisen, "Industry and Size as Debt Ratio Determinants in Manufacturing Internationally," *Financial Management* 3, No. 2, 1974, pages 24–32.

Stephen E. Skomp and C.W.R. Ward, "The Capital Structure Policies Of U.K. Companies: A Comparative Study," *International Journal of Accounting* 19, No. 1, 1983, pages 55–64.

Arthur Stonehill, Theo Beekhuisen, Richard Wright, Lee Remmers, Norman Toy, Antonio Pares, Alan Shapiro, Douglas Egan, and Thomas Bates, "Financial Goals and Debt Ratio Determinants: A Survey of Practice in Five Countries," *Financial Management* 4, No. 3, 1975, pages 27–41.

Richard H. Pettway, Takashi Kaneko, and Michael T. Young, "Further Evidence of Unsatisfied Clienteles in International Capital Financing," *Financial Review* 30, November 1995, pages 857–874.

Agency costs are discussed in

Michael C. Jensen, "Agency Costs of Free Cash Flow, Corporate Financing, and Takeovers," *American Economic Review* 76, No. 2, 1986, pages 323–339.

Michael C. Jensen and William Meckling, "Theory of the Firm: Managerial Behavior, Agency Costs, and Capital Structure," *Journal of Financial Economics* 3, No. 4, 1976, pages 305–360.

Stewart C. Myers, "The Capital Structure Puzzle," *Journal of Finance* 39, July 1984, pages 575–592.

Stewart C. Myers and Nicholas S. Majluf, "Corporate Financing and Investment Decisions When Firms Have Information that Investors Do Not Have" *Journal of Financial Economics* 13, No. 2, 1984, pages 127–221.

Multinational Treasury Management

If something can go wrong, it will
Murphy's Law

OVERVIEW

As corporations grow beyond their traditional domestic markets and become multinational in scope, they must develop a financial system capable of managing the transactions and the risks of the individual operating divisions and of the corporation as a whole. The treasury division of the multinational corporation fulfills this role. The multinational corporation's treasury has evolved into a form of corporate bank that manages cash flows within the corporation and between the corporation and its external partners. The modern corporate treasury performs the following functions:

- Determining the firm's overall financial goals
- Managing the risks of domestic and international transactions
- Arranging financing for domestic and international trade
- Consolidating and managing the financial flows of the firm
- Identifying, measuring, and managing the firm's risk exposures

Treasury must set policies and establish guidelines for how the operating divisions of the firm are to interact with each other. Treasury also must coordinate the interaction of the firm with its various external constituents, including suppliers, customers, banks, creditors, equity investors, and governments. Consequently, treasury management has both an internal and an external dimension.

This chapter covers the first four functions. The fifth function—risk management—is covered in Chapter 22.

21.1 Setting the Firm's Financial Goals and Strategies

The highly competitive and fast-changing global marketplace demands that corporations continuously reassess their business and financial strategies. The process of creating a strategic business plan includes the following steps:

- Identifying the firm's core competencies and potential growth opportunities
- Evaluating the business environment within which the firm operates
- Formulating a comprehensive strategic plan for turning the firm's core competencies into sustainable competitive advantages
- Developing robust processes for implementing the strategic business plan

The strategic plan should incorporate all of the corporation's existing businesses. The plan should promote the refinement of existing core competencies and the development of new ones. The plan should be flexible to adapt to the exigencies of the global marketplace. Finally, the plan should be continually updated and revised so that it is a dynamic, living guide rather than a static anchor for the firm.

Financial strategy should complement the overall business plan.

Financial strategy should complement the overall strategic business plan. Financial strategy should not stand as an island apart from other operations. A properly conceived strategic financial plan integrates and promotes the core operations of the corporation and furthers the goals and objectives of the corporation's overall business strategies.

21.2 Managing the Costs and Risks of International Trade

International trade is hazardous because you often do not know with whom you are dealing. Exporters must take extra precautions to ensure payment from faraway foreign customers. Importers must protect themselves against late shipments and goods or services of inferior quality. When disputes arise, claimants often must pursue their grievances through foreign legal systems and on the home turf of their trading partners.

No single doctrine defines international commercial law. Each nation recognizes a slightly different set of legal principles within its domestic borders. It is not surprising that international shipments are more difficult than domestic shipments. This section describes how the multinational corporation can manage the costs and risks of cross-border trade and protect itself against trade and legal disputes.

Managing the Costs and Risks of International Shipping

Cross-border trade can be cumbersome and time-consuming due to the logistics involved in shipping goods from one country to another. In addition to geographic distance, there is often a wide cultural distance between buyer and seller. These difficulties can be overcome through the use of specialists to coordinate the carriage of goods. In many cases, a **freight shipper** (or **freight forwarder**) is used to coordinate the logistics of transportation. These agents select the best mode of transportation and arrange for a particular carrier to handle the physical shipment of goods.

International sales conform to Murphy's Law: "If something can go wrong, it will." For this reason, it is advisable to clearly specify the terms of trade *in writing,* including who is responsible for insurance coverage, who bears the risk of loss during shipping, who pays for transportation and loading/unloading of the goods, and who is responsible for export/import clearance. Because each of these is customarily specified in writing, cross-border shipments are accompanied by a bewildering array of documentation. Documentation includes

- *Commercial invoice*—a document that describes the merchandise, identifies the buyer and the seller, and specifies delivery and payment terms
- *Packing list*—an itemization of the number of packages and contents of a shipment
- *Certificate of origin*—a document certifying the country of origin of the goods, required by some nations
- *Shipper's export declaration (SED)*—a document required by the U.S. Department of Commerce on export shipments valued over $500
- *Export license*—permission required before some governmentally regulated goods can be exported
- *Bill of lading*—a contract between the owner of goods (usually an exporter) and a commercial carrier, issued by the carrier when it receives goods for shipment
- *Dock receipt*—a document indicating that the goods have been delivered to a dock for transportation by a carrier
- *Warehouse receipt*—a document indicating that the goods have been delivered from a carrier to a warehouse
- *Inspection certificate*—third-party certification that goods meet certain specifications, sometimes required by the buyer, a bank financing the transaction, or a governmental agency
- *Insurance certificate*—proof of insurance for goods in transit, often required by sales contracts

Arranging transport can be quite time-consuming. Many commercial banks have a shipping subsidiary or affiliate that arranges the carriage of goods for their banking clients. This arrangement facilitates communication between the exporter, its bank, and the carrier and, thus, reduces shipping costs.

Managing the Costs and Risks of International Payments

A major barrier to international trade is that each nation has jurisdiction over business transactions within its national borders and imposes its own unique legal system on these transactions. Cross-border trade is forced to contend with two or more legal systems.

Most of the nations in Western Europe and Latin America use a *civil law* system in which laws are codified as a set of rules. The United Kingdom and many of its former colonies (including the United States) use a *common law* system that relies heavily on the decisions of judges in previous court cases. Both civil and common law systems are offshoots of ancient Roman law. They differ in their emphasis on legal rules and on specific case examples.

TABLE 21.1   METHODS OF PAYMENT ON INTERNATIONAL TRADE

	Time of payment	Goods available to buyer	Risk to seller	Risk to buyer
Cash in advance	Before shipment	After payment	None (unless legal action is taken by buyer)	Relies on seller to to ship goods as agreed
Open account	After buyer receives shipment as agreed	Before payment	Relies on buyer to pay account as agreed	None (unless legal action is taken by seller)
Documentary collection				
Sight draft	Payable on presentation of draft to buyer	After payment	Buyer may refuse pay when documents are presented—goods must be shipped home or sold under duress in the foreign country	Same as L/C
Time draft	On maturity of draft	Before payment	Relies on buyer to pay draft; otherwise same as sight draft	Legal consequences if an accepted draft is not honored by buyer
Documentary credits				
Letter of credit (L/C)	Payable when shipment is made	After payment	Low risk if seller meets terms of L/C that has been issued or confirmed by a creditworthy bank; risk of nonpayment due to currency unavailability	Relies on seller to ship goods described in trade documents; L/Cs are more time-consuming to arrange than other payment methods

Other legal systems in frequent use around the world include Islamic, communist, and socialist systems. *Islamic law* is based on the teachings of the prophet Mohammed in the Koran and other holy scriptures. In practice, Islamic law combines elements of civil law and common law. Communist and socialist countries, such as China, Russia, Cuba, and Vietnam, have historically used centrally planned economies and seldom recognize private property rights. In recent years, laws in communist and socialist nations have changed radically as these nations have adapted their legal systems to support market-based rather than state-based economies.

International trade is handicapped by this wide divergence in national legal systems. Disagreements between parties are frequent and are difficult to settle because the legal issues span two or more legal jurisdictions. The United Nations *Convention on Contracts for the International Sale of Goods* (CISG) was created to standardize and codify the legal rules under which international sales are made. Many countries have ratified the CISG, including the United States, Canada, Mexico, Russia, France, and Germany. The United Kingdom and Japan are among the nations that have not ratified the CISG.

Exporters need to assure payment and importers need to assure delivery of quality goods.

In this uncertain trade environment, exporters must have assurance that they will receive payment on the goods that they ship, and importers must have assurance that they will receive the goods that they expect. There are four ways that exporters can arrange for payment:

- Open account
- Cash in advance
- Documentary collections
- Documentary credits

The characteristics of these payment methods are summarized in Table 21.1. These international payment mechanisms differ in the protection provided the buyer and seller, as shown in Figure 21.1. Which payment terms are adopted in any particular sale depends on the bargaining positions of the buyer and the seller, on industry conventions, and on the probability and the consequences of default.

Open Account. Most domestic sales are made on **open account**. Under an open account arrangement, the seller delivers the goods directly to the buyer. The seller then bills the buyer for the goods under agreed-upon payment terms such as "net 30" (payment is due in 30 days) or "1/10, net 60" (1 percent discount if paid in 10 days, otherwise the net amount is due in 60 days). This arrangement is most convenient for the buyer.

Sales on open account are an unattractive payment mechanism for most exporters. First, the exporter must pay for the inputs to produce its goods well before it ships the goods and receives final payment. Second, the exporter is exposed to credit risk because the buyer may default on payment. An open account is appropriate only when the buyer and seller have established a long-term relationship and the credit record of the buyer is good.

Cash in Advance. **Cash in advance** requires the buyer to pay for the goods prior to shipment. This affords the greatest protection to the seller of goods. The cost of this protection to the seller may be a reduced sales price. Cash in advance is least convenient for the buyer since the buyer must trust the seller to make delivery in a timely manner and in good condition. Cash in advance is used when the buyer has a poor credit history or where demand far outstrips supply. It is seldom used when the buyer and seller have a long and satisfactory (that is, dispute-free) relationship.

Seller's Perspective	Payment Mechanism	Buyer's Perspective
Highest risk trade terms		Most advantageous trade terms
	Open account Draft Letter of credit Cash in advance	
Lowest risk trade terms		Least advantageous trade terms

FIGURE 21.1

The Methods of
International Payment

Documentary Collections. Commercial banks are in the business of assuming credit and collection risks. Commercial banks are also in the business of facilitating trade, even if buyers and sellers are in different countries. By bringing one or more commercial banks into the transaction to assist in shipment and collections, the total costs of international transactions can be reduced.

The documentary collection is the instrument most frequently used as an international payment mechanism. In a documentary collection, the seller draws a **draft** (also called a **trade bill** or **bill of exchange**) payable to itself on the buyer. With a draft, the buyer (the drawer) instructs another party (the drawee—either the buyer or its bank) to pay the seller (the payee) according to the terms of the draft. A **sight draft** is payable on demand, whereas a **time draft** is payable at a specified future time. The drawee (either the buyer or its bank) is liable to the seller if it accepts the draft by signing it. A time draft that is drawn on and accepted by the buyer is called a **trade acceptance**. A time draft that is drawn on and accepted by a commercial bank is called a **banker's acceptance**. The shipping documents giving control over the goods are released to the buyer only when the buyer or its commercial bank pays the draft or accepts the draft for payment.

The draft and the trade documents are then presented to a commercial bank. If the buyer and seller cannot agree on a single bank to serve as go-between, they can each retain a bank to represent their own individual interests. The trade documents giving control over the goods are released to the buyer only when the buyer or its commercial bank pays the draft or accepts the draft for payment.

Banker's acceptances are especially useful in international trade. An exporter holding a banker's acceptance can sell it at a discount to reduce accounts receivable and speed payment on the sale. The discount from the face value of the acceptance depends on the time value of money and on the reputation of the accepting bank. Selling a banker's acceptance is only possible if the banker's acceptance is *negotiable*. To be negotiable, a banker's acceptance must meet five requirements. It must

- Be in writing
- Be signed by the bank
- Contain an unconditional payment guarantee upon receipt of the trade documents
- Be payable on demand (a sight draft) or at a specified time (a time draft)
- Be payable *to order* or *to bearer*.

The holder of such a banker's acceptance is said to be a *holder in due course* and is legally protected against disputes that may arise relating to the transfer of goods from seller to buyer.

Figure 21.2 illustrates how trade can be accomplished through a banker's acceptance. After negotiating the terms of trade (A), the exporter sends an invoice to the importer (B). The importer writes a time draft drawn on its bank (C). The bank accepts the draft by signing it and forwards it to the exporter (D). The exporter then initiates shipment of the goods (E). Upon receipt of the goods, the warehouse signs the trade documents indicating that the shipment meets the specified terms of trade and is in good condition (F). The trade documents are then sent to the importer's bank by the exporter (G). Upon receipt of the trade documents, the bank either sends payment to

FIGURE 21.2
Payment through a Banker's Acceptance

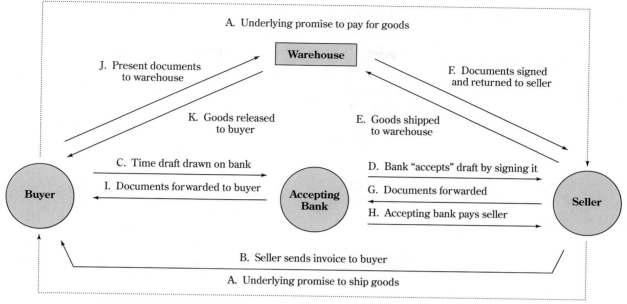

A. Buyer and seller negotiate trade terms.
B. Seller sends an invoice to the buyer with the agreed-upon trade terms.
C. Buyer writes a time draft written on a creditworthy bank agreeable to both parties.
D. Bank "accepts" the draft by signing it and thereby guarantees payment upon receipt of the trade documents.
E. Goods are shipped to a warehouse in the buyer's country.
F. Shipping documents are signed by the warehouse and returned to the seller.
G. Completed trade documents are sent to the accepting bank.
H. Bank honors its acceptance and pays seller.
I. Issuing bank forwards trade documents to the buyer.
J. Buyer presents documents to the warehouse.
K. Buyer collects goods from warehouse.

the exporter or stands by its promise to pay at the specified future date (H). The trade documents are forwarded to the importer (I). Finally, the importer presents the trade documents to the warehouse (J) and collects the goods (K). The timing of the payment from the importer to the bank depends on the importer's cash flow needs, its credit standing, and its relationship with the bank.

Documentary Credits.

The biggest risk faced by an exporter is that the buyer will default on payment, pay too little in an attempt to renegotiate the terms of trade, or pay too late. This risk can be greatly reduced by having the importer's bank issue a **letter of credit (L/C)** that guarantees payment upon presentation of the trade documents specified in the letter of credit. Like a banker's acceptance, the letter of credit protects the exporter because payment is guaranteed by a commercial bank rather than the importer.

A letter of credit guarantees payment upon presentation of the trade documents.

The *Uniform Rules and Usances of the International Chamber of Commerce* describes two legal principles surrounding the international letter of credit.

Letters of credit have facilitated cross-border trade for many centuries. Yet they are not infallible. Since 1995 many Chinese importers have postponed payments on letters of credit or insisted on renegotiating contracts over such apparently innocuous problems as misspellings, imprecise wordings, and even the color of the official stamps.*

Failure to honor letters of credit will ultimately raise the costs of doing business in China both for Chinese companies and for their non-Chinese business partners.

* See "Exporters Angry as Chinese Postpone Payments," *London Financial Times,* Sept. 1, 1995, page 10.

- Independence principle—the letter of credit is independent of the sales transaction
- Strict compliance principle—the issuing bank must honor the letter of credit upon receipt of the documents specified in the letter of credit

The independence and strict compliance principles protect the right of the exporter to payment under the terms of the letter of credit. This substitutes the credit standing of the issuing bank for that of the buyer.[1]

A letter of credit is termed *irrevocable* if payment is conditional upon receipt of the trade documents identified in the letter of credit. If the letter of credit stipulates additional conditions under which the buyer or the issuing bank can declare the letter of credit invalid, the letter of credit is called a *revocable* letter of credit. Nearly all letters of credit are irrevocable. In fact, if the letter of credit says nothing about revocability, it is assumed to be irrevocable under international law. With the exception of cash in advance, the irrevocable letter of credit provides exporters with the highest level of assurance that payment will be made.

Under an *unconfirmed letter of credit,* the buyer instructs its bank to issue a letter of credit. This promises the exporter that payment will be made by the issuing bank upon receipt of the documents specified in the letter of credit. Whether the issuing bank requires the buyer to pay for the letter of credit in advance or at some later date depends on the creditworthiness of the buyer and on its banking relationships. In an unconfirmed letter of credit, the exporter is still exposed to the risk that the issuing bank will default or delay payment. This risk can be substantial in some developing countries (see box).

One way to mitigate the default risk of the issuing bank is for the letter of credit to be *confirmed* by a bank selected by the exporter (called the *advisory* bank). The advisory bank confirms that the terms of trade, required documents, and letter of credit are in good order and that the issuing bank is in good financial health. Upon confirming that

---

1 Under U.S. law, the buyer can prevent the issuing bank from honoring the letter of credit if the buyer can demonstrate fraud in the transaction (for example, shipment of substitute or inferior goods). This is the only exception to the independence and strict compliance principles. Consequently, commercial banks have a stake in ensuring that the terms of trade are met by both parties.

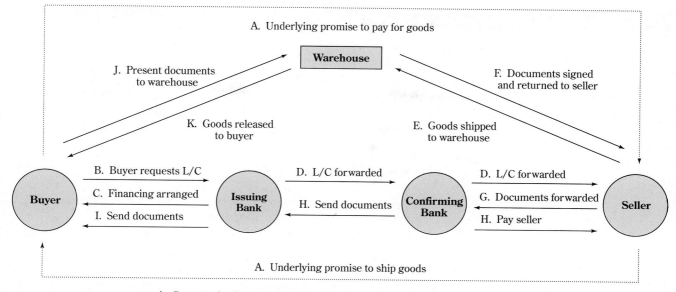

A. Underlying promise to pay for goods

J. Present documents to warehouse

Warehouse

F. Documents signed and returned to seller

K. Goods released to buyer

E. Goods shipped to warehouse

Buyer

B. Buyer requests L/C
C. Financing arranged
I. Send documents

Issuing Bank

D. L/C forwarded
H. Send documents

Confirming Bank

D. L/C forwarded
G. Documents forwarded
H. Pay seller

Seller

A. Underlying promise to ship goods

A. Buyer and seller negotiate trade terms.
B. Importer applies for a *letter of credit* (L/C) from an *issuing bank*.
C. Issuing bank arranges payment with buyer, usually through a line of credit.
D. Letter of credit is sent to *confirming bank* in the seller's country and then to seller.
E. Goods are shipped to a warehouse in the buyer's country.
F. Shipping documents are signed by the warehouse and returned to the seller.
G. Completed documents are sent to the confirming bank.
H. Confirming bank pays seller and sends documents to issuing bank.
I. Issuing bank forwards documents to the buyer.
J. Buyer presents documents to the warehouse.
K. Buyer collects goods from warehouse.

FIGURE 21.3
Payment through a Confirmed Letter of Credit (L/C)

this is indeed the case, the advisory bank promises payment to the exporter regardless of whether the issuing bank honors its obligation. The letter of credit is then called a *confirmed letter of credit*. Payment terms on a confirmed letter of credit primarily depend on the default risk of the bank originally issuing the letter of credit. The sequence of events in international trade under a confirmed letter of credit is similar to the sequence of events under a banker's acceptance. An illustration appears in Figure 21.3.

Countertrade

Countertrade refers to a variety of barterlike techniques used to exchange goods or services without exchanging money. Countries with inconvertible currencies or limited reserves of hard currency often use countertrade to preserve hard currency, promote foreign trade, and attract key industries. Companies from industrialized countries participate in countertrade to gain a foothold in developing markets and to diversify operations. Countertrade is difficult to negotiate and execute, but it is often the only way for countries without hard currency to pay for manufactured goods or for multinational

Countertrade involves an exchange of goods or services without the use of cash.

corporations to gain access to developing markets. Estimates of the importance of countertrade to international commerce vary widely, typically falling in a range from 10 to 40 percent of international trade.[2]

Countertrade can take many forms:

- *Barter*—an exchange of goods without the use of money. Barter is easiest to arrange when the values of the goods being exchanged are the same and the shipments take place at the same time.
- *Compensation trade*—a form of barter in which one of the flows is partly in goods and partly in hard currency.
- *Counterpurchase*—a barter arrangement in which one contract is conditional upon fulfillment of another.
- *Switch trade*—a counterpurchase agreement in which the owner of the conditional contract has the right to sell its claim to another party.
- *Offsets*—countertrade that is required as a condition of trade; common for defense-related exports, such as jet fighters (especially in the Persian Gulf).
- *Buy-back*—an agreement to build a turnkey plant in exchange for specific amounts of the plant's output, usually over a period of years. For example, Chrysler may build an automobile manufacturing plant in China and provide training to local employees in exchange for a certain number of vehicles over several years.

Some multinational corporations with a high proportion of their business in developing countries rely heavily on countertrade. For example, Coca-Cola has traded syrup for Lada automobiles to extract value from its Russian joint venture. In a similar deal, PepsiCo traded soft drinks for Russian vodka. Countertrade is most suited to large firms with diversified markets and products and experience in international markets. These companies are better able to assume and manage the costs and risks of countertrade.

Barter exchange companies help to complete the market in cross-border countertrade. These companies trade bartered goods and services among their members. The International Reciprocal Trade Association estimates that the value of countertrade transactions through barter exchange companies in the United States and Canada was $2.6 billion in 1982. By 1992, countertrade through these intermediaries had grown to $6.5 billion. Countertrade is likely to continue to be useful to companies and countries operating in markets that lack hard currencies.

21.3 FINANCING INTERNATIONAL TRADE

Money does not grow on trees, so someone must finance a sale of goods between the time an order is made and the time the goods are received by the buyer. When a sale is paid for in advance, the buyer is providing financing for the seller. When a sale is made on open account, the seller is providing the financing to the buyer. The international

---

2 An estimate of 10 to 15 percent appears in "The Case for Countertrade," N. Gilbert, *Across the Board,* May 1992, pages 43–45. An estimate of 40 percent appears in "Worldwide Money Crunch Fuels More International Barter," C. Miller, *Marketing News,* March 2, 1992, page 5. Other estimates are usually between these two.

TABLE 21.2 METHODS OF PAYMENT AND THE FINANCING OF INTERNATIONAL TRADE

	Financing for seller	Financing for buyer
Cash in advance	Financing provided by buyer	Because the transaction is not secured, financing usually must come from some other source
Open account	Accounts receivable can be discounted to the bank or sold to a factor; long-term receivables can be sold to a forfaiter	Financing provided by seller
Documentary collection		
Trade acceptance	Trade acceptances can be discounted, or sold to a bank at a discount to face value, either with or without recourse	In an accepted time draft, the seller extends credit to the buyer
Banker's acceptance	Banker's acceptances are negotiable and can be sold at a discount to face value	The buyer's bank charges a fee in the form of a compensating balance, a required line of credit, or an outright transaction fee
Documentary credits		
Letter of credit (L/C)	In the United States, exporters do not borrow against or discount L/Cs; in some other countries, L/Cs can be discounted or used as collateral	L/Cs tie up buyer's borrowing capacity; bank fees for unconfirmed L/Cs range from 0.125% to 0.5% of the face amount; confirmed L/Cs add another 0.05% to 0.5%

payment methods in Section 21.2 allow someone other than the buyer or seller, such as a commercial bank, to provide financing for international trade. These financing alternatives are described below and summarized in Table 21.2.

The Exporter's Perspective

The corporation's sources and uses of cash can be categorized as follows.

- Sources of cash
  - A decrease in an asset account
  - An increase in a liability account
- Uses of cash
  - An increase in an asset account
  - A decrease in a liability account

As an exporter manufacturers goods, work-in-process inventory is increased. An increase in inventory is an increase in an asset account and, therefore, is a use of cash. When a sale is booked on open account, the asset is transferred out of inventory and into accounts receivable. If the sale is made through a trade acceptance or a banker's acceptance, the acceptance is a negotiable instrument and may be considered a marketable security. Whether the sale resides in accounts receivable or in marketable securities, the exporter is now in a position to recoup its investment in working capital and to capture a gain on the sale.

International payment methods create financing sources in one of the following ways.

- A decrease in a current asset account
  - Sell short-term accounts receivable to a *factor,* such as a commercial bank
  - Sell medium-term or long-term accounts receivable to a *forfaiter,* such as a commercial bank
  - Sell a marketable security, such as a trade or banker's acceptance, at a *discount* to face value
- An increase in a current liability account
  - Borrow against an asset, such as accounts receivable or inventory

Each of these sources of financing has an opportunity cost. As with every other financial transaction, the exporter must shop around for the best value. The least cost financing method in any particular circumstance depends on competitive conditions in the exporter's goods and financial markets, on the exporter's borrowing capacity, and on the exporter's relationship with its bank.

Sell a Current Asset. Credit risks are high on export sales and collections are likely to be costly. For this reason, many small exporters are unwilling or unable to support an in-house credit and collections department. One alternative is for the exporter to **factor** or sell accounts receivable at a discount to face value to a third party, such as a commercial bank, that is better able to bear the costs and risks of credit assessments and collections. Most factoring is done on a nonrecourse basis, although when credit risks are high the factor may insist on recourse financing.

Factors have a comparative advantage over in-house credit departments in bearing international credit and collection risks. Because of the volume of trade that they service, factors can

- Maintain greater access to credit information on foreign customers
- Diversify credit and collection risks over a broader customer base

Factors' comparative advantage in credit and collections is greatest over small firms with a high proportion of export sales and geographically dispersed customers.

Forfaiting resembles factoring but involves medium- to long-term receivables (with maturities of one year or longer) and larger transactions (for example, more than $100,000). Forfaiting is commonly used by West European banks to finance export sales to Eastern Europe. Financial markets in Eastern Europe are poorly developed, and East European importers find it difficult to obtain capital locally. West European manufacturers find that they can increase sales by arranging financing for their East European customers. Unfortunately, political risk is high in many of these countries and the importers tend to be poor commercial risks as well. In these circumstances, neither importers nor exporters are well positioned to assume the risks of international trade.

Through long years of exposure to the East European markets, West European banks have developed expertise in estimating and managing commercial and political risks in Eastern Europe. In a typical forfaiting arrangement, a commercial bank purchases a medium-term receivable with a one- to five-year maturity from an exporter at a discount and without recourse to the exporter. The bank provides the financing and assumes the credit and collection risks for the exporter. The receivable is typically denominated in an actively traded, convertible currency, such as the U.S. dollar, German mark, or Swiss franc.

A trade acceptance is a time draft that a buyer draws on itself. Commercial banks are willing to accept trade acceptances at a discount to face value. This process, known as **discounting**, allows exporters to receive the face value of their trade acceptances less interest and commissions. Discounting may be done with or without recourse. Trade acceptances discounted with recourse require the seller to pay the bank the face value of the draft should the buyer fail to pay the bill when due. Trade acceptances discounted without recourse release the seller from this responsibility. The bank assumes the credit risk on trade acceptances discounted without recourse, so bank fees and interest rates on discounts without recourse are higher than on acceptances discounted with recourse.

> *Discounting is the purchase of a promised payment at a discount from face value.*

A banker's acceptance is a time draft drawn on a commercial bank. When the bank accepts the time draft, it promises to pay the holder of the draft a stated amount on a specified future date. For this service, banks charge a fee that is taken out of the face value of the acceptance at maturity. Maturities range up to 180 days on banker's acceptances. In recent years, the outstanding balance of banker's acceptances has remained over $100 billion and has financed around one quarter of U.S. international trade.[3]

Like trade acceptances, banker's acceptances are negotiable instruments that can be sold at a discount to face value. The size of the discount reflects the time value of money. Discount rates on prime banker's acceptances are near the discount rates on prime commercial paper. For large firms with access to the commercial paper market, the cost of commercial paper (including placement fees and back-up lines of credit) is frequently lower than the cost of banker's acceptances. Small and medium-sized firms without access to the commercial paper market are more likely to use banker's acceptances to finance their international trade.

The costs and risks of documentary collections (including both trade acceptances and banker's acceptances) can be reduced by insuring them against commercial and political risks through national or international trade insurance agencies, such as the U.S. government's *Export-Import Bank (Eximbank)*. Eximbank provides guarantees and insurance against credit and political risks for U.S. companies engaged in international trade. The all-in cost of these discounted drafts includes the discount rate on the draft along with any bank fees and insurance premiums.

Borrow against a Current Asset. An exporter can lower its financing costs by using current assets as collateral. Accounts receivable and inventory balances are often used as collateral to reduce the interest cost on bank lines of credit and short-term loans.

---

3 Robert K. La Roche, "Bankers Acceptances," Federal Reserve Bank of Richmond *Quarterly Review,* Winter 1993, page 77.

Marketable securities and bank demand deposits can be used as compensating balances to reduce the risk of nonpayment to the bank on short-term borrowings. The use of collateral provides insurance to the bank and thereby reduces the costs charged by the bank.

In some countries, such as Hong Kong, letters of credit also can be discounted or used as collateral for bank borrowings. In the United States, letters of credit are not typically discounted or used as collateral on bank loans.

The Importer's Perspective

The most convenient method of payment for the importer is to purchase on open account. In this case, the exporter extends credit to the importer. The least convenient method of payment for the importer is cash in advance. This requires that the buyer obtain a source of cash prior to purchase, either by reducing an asset account or increasing a liability account. Payment of cash in advance may be undesirable or even impossible for some importers, in which case other sources of financing are needed.

The All-in Cost of Export Financing

Suppose a bank charges an acceptance fee of 2 percent per year compounded semiannually (or 1 percent per six months) on a six-month banker's acceptance with a face value of $1 million. The fee, equal to $(0.01)(\$1,000,000) = \$10,000$, is taken out of the face value at maturity. If an exporter chooses to hold the acceptance until maturity rather than sell it to the market, the exporter will receive $990,000 at maturity. This acceptance fee may be well worth paying, because it greatly reduces the credit risk of the receivable to the exporter.

An exporter can convert the banker's acceptance into cash by selling it to the market on a discount basis (much like a Treasury bill). There is a fairly active secondary market in banker's acceptances. Suppose the current discount rate on prime banker's acceptances is 8 percent compounded semiannually. An exporter selling this acceptance to the market will receive $(\$990,000)/(1.04) = \$951,923$.

If the exporter's opportunity cost of capital on accounts receivable financing is 10 percent compounded semiannally, then the exporter will benefit by selling the acceptance at the lower 8 percent rate. At the 10 percent discount rate, the receivable is only worth $(\$990,000)/(1.05) = \$942,857$. Selling the acceptance for

$951,923 results in a gain of $9,066 in net present value to the exporter.

It is sometimes useful to look at the total or **all-in cost** of trade financing, including the bank's acceptance fee. If this exporter sells the acceptance for $951,923, it forgoes the $1 million face value of the receivable. The resulting cash flows look like this:

The all-in cost of this acceptance to the exporter is

$$(\$1,000,000/\$951,923) - 1 = 0.0505, \text{ or } 5.05 \text{ percent per six months}$$

The effective annual cost is $(1.0505)^2 - 1 = 0.1036$, or 10.36 percent. This cost includes the 1 percent semiannual cost of obtaining the acceptance from the bank as well as the 4 percent semiannual cost of discounting the acceptance with the bank. The all-in cost of other export financing methods can be found in a similar manner.

In an accepted trade draft, the seller extends credit to the buyer. This credit does not come free of charge—the seller will try to cover its shipping, credit, and collection costs in the payment terms offered to the buyer. The terms agreed to in a banker's acceptance include these costs, as well as any bank fees, required lines of credit, and compensating balance requirements that the bank demands for accepting the draft.

Letters of credit also tie up the importer's borrowing capacity. Bank fees on unconfirmed letters of credit range from one-eighth to one-half percent of the face amount of the letter of credit. Another one-twentieth to one-half percent is charged if the letter of credit is confirmed by a bank in the seller's country. Whether the buyer or the seller ultimately bears the shipping and financing costs is determined by their respective bargaining positions and abilities.

21.4 MANAGING THE MULTINATIONAL CORPORATION'S CASH FLOWS

Treasury's management of financial cash flows has both an internal and an external dimension. Activities in this area include

- Cash management
  - Managing the general ledger
  - Multinational netting
  - Forecasting funds needs

- Managing relations between the operating divisions of the firm as well as with the firm's external partners, suppliers, and customers
  - Credit assessment, credit approval, and credit limit monitoring
  - Setting or negotiating transfer prices between the firm's operating divisions
  - Determining the required return (or hurdle rate) on new investments

Individual business units within the corporation transact with other business units within the corporation as products are moved through the corporate value chain. Treasury serves as a central clearinghouse for the cash flows associated with the interactions of these business units. Treasury is also involved in either setting or negotiating internal transfer prices on intracompany transactions. Consolidating all of these operations in the treasury division allows the treasury to monitor and forecast the company's funds needs, minimize its transactions costs, manage the firm's exposure to operating and financial risks, and take advantage of market opportunities as they arise.

Cash Management

To effectively manage the corporation's financial resources, the multinational treasury must implement a cash management system that tracks cash receipts and disbursements. The multinational treasury has several cash management tools at its disposal. Chief among these cash management tools is a process called **multinational netting** in

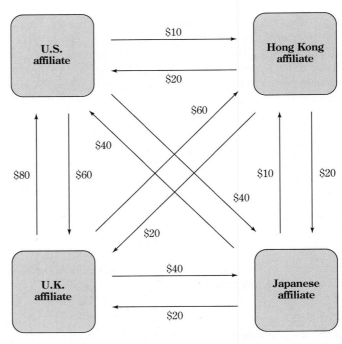

FIGURE 21.4
The Internal Cash Flows of
a Multinational Corporation

Receiving affiliate	Paying affiliate				Total receipts
	U.S.	U.K.	Hong Kong	Japan	
United States	0	80	20	40	140
United Kingdom	60	0	20	20	100
Hong Kong	10	60	0	10	80
Japan	40	40	20	0	100
Total payments	110	180	60	70	420

which intrafirm fund transfers are minimized by "netting" offsetting cash flows in various currencies. By monitoring and maintaining control over cash receipts and disbursements, the multinational treasury is also in an excellent position to forecast the cash needs of the corporation. This section discusses the netting and forecasting processes.

Multinational Netting. Centralizing control over cash receipts and disbursements in the treasury allows the modern corporation to minimize the number of transactions that take place both within the corporation and between the corporation and the external markets. For the multinational corporation, this begins with a process of multinational netting of transactions in each currency. Consider the intrafirm transactions of the U.S.-based multinational corporation depicted in Figure 21.4. Intrafirm transactions for this company include

- A total of $140 paid to the U.S. parent
- A total of $100 paid to the U.K. affiliate

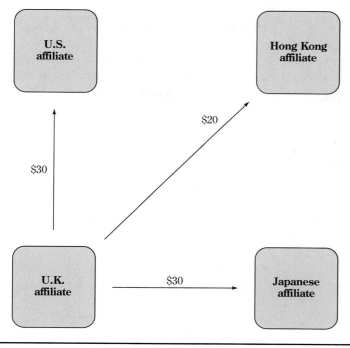

	Gross		Net	
	Receipts	Payments	Receipts	Payments
United States	140	110	30	0
United Kingdom	100	180	0	80
Hong Kong	80	60	20	0
Japan	100	70	30	0
Total payments	420	420	80	80

FIGURE 21.5
Cash Flows after
Multinational Netting

- A total of $80 paid to the Hong Kong affiliate
- A total of $100 paid to the Japanese affiliate

Total payments among the operating units of this firm are $420 without any netting of cash flows. Figure 21.5 shows how funds transfers can be reduced to $160 by eliminating redundant cash flows. In most multinational corporations, intrafirm transactions are reconciled at the end of each month, and internal debits and credits are allocated across the operating divisions according to the net amount due each division. By coordinating the cash flows of its operating divisions, the treasury can minimize the transactions costs involved in running its operations.

Multinational netting of transactions eliminates offsetting cash flows.

Forecasting Funds Needs. By tracking cash flows to and from the firm's external suppliers and customers and serving as a central clearinghouse for intrafirm transactions, the treasury can ensure that each operating division has sufficient funds to run its operations. When cash is in short supply, the treasury can use its banking relations to draw upon its established lines of credit. When there is temporarily excess cash in the system, the treasury can pay down obligations or invest in money market instruments in the currencies of its choice. By forecasting funds needs, the treasury can use multinational netting both across operating divisions and over time to minimize the number and size of transactions in the external financial markets. By consolidating intrafirm transactions and serving as a single source of funds, the treasury can obtain funds from the source that minimizes the firm's cost of capital.

Managing Internal and External Relations

Credit Management. Managing international credit relations is a good deal harder than managing domestic relations because of cross-border differences in laws, business conventions, information availability, banking relations, and political systems. The risks of multinational credit can be managed through the payment mechanisms and trade finance vehicles described earlier in this chapter.

Transfer Pricing. When market prices are not available, the corporate treasury has a great deal of latitude in setting transfer prices on intracompany transfers of intermediate goods. All else constant, the multinational corporation has a tax incentive to

- Shift revenues toward low-tax jurisdictions
- Shift expenses toward high-tax jurisdictions

Transfer pricing decisions should be made to benefit the corporation as a whole. Nevertheless, individual units are subject to performance standards and have incentives to maximize sales prices and minimize costs on each transfer of goods and services. This can create disputes within the multinational corporation because headquarters determines transfer prices for tax reasons and not according to the value added at each stage of the production process.

If transfer prices differ from market values or from the individual units' next best alternatives, then separate sets of books can be kept for tax and for internal management accounting purposes. Tax records reflect the transfer price reported to the tax authorities, but management accounting records reflect the transfer price used internally. In this way, individual units are not rewarded or penalized for artificial transfer prices that are set for reasons that are out of divisional managers' control.

Identifying Divisional Costs of Capital. Disputes also arise among operating divisions over hurdle rates on new investment. Theory states that managers should use a discount rate that reflects the opportunity cost of capital on a project in order to maximize shareholder wealth. However, managers are often more interested in maximizing the corporate resources over which they have control. This can result in artificially low hurdle rates as managers try to justify new investments. The chief financial officer must insist that market-based hurdle rates are used within the company in the evaluation of new investment proposals. Treasury is often in a good position to identify required returns on new investments, because it is relatively detached from the managerial fiefdoms of the operating divisions.

The goal of treasury management is to allow the core business activities of the corporation to attain their potentials. To add to corporate value, the officers of the treasury must

- Determine the firm's overall financial goals
- Manage the risks of international transactions
- Arrange financing for international trade
- Consolidate and manage the financial flows of the firm
- Identify, measure, and manage the firm's risk exposures

The first four of these functions were discussed in this chapter. The last function—risk management—is important enough to warrant separate treatment and is covered in the next chapter.

KEY TERMS

All-in cost	Freight shippers (freight forwarder)
Banker's acceptance	Letter of credit (L/C)
Cash in advance	Multinational netting
Countertrade	Open account
Discounting	Sight draft
Draft (trade bill, bill of exchange)	Time draft
Factoring	Trade acceptance
Forfaiting	

CONCEPTUAL QUESTIONS

21.1 What is multinational treasury management?

21.2 What function does a firm's strategic business plan perform?

21.3 Why is international trade more difficult than domestic trade?

21.4 Why use a freight forwarder?

21.5 Describe four methods of payment on international sales.

21.6 What is a banker's acceptance, and how is it used in international trade?

21.7 What is discounting, and how is it used in international trade?

21.8 How is factoring different from forfaiting?

21.9 What is countertrade? When is it most likely to be used?

21.10 What is multinational netting?

21.11 How can the treasury division assist in managing relations among the operating units of the multinational corporation?

PROBLEMS

21.1 Fruit of the Loom, Inc., has a banker's acceptance drawn on Banque Paribas with a face value of $10 million due in ninety days. Paribas will take out an acceptance fee of $10,000 at maturity. Fruit of the Loom's U.S. bank is willing to buy the acceptance at a discount rate of 6 percent compounded quarterly.
   a. How much will Fruit of the Loom receive if it sells the banker's acceptance?
   b. What is the all-in cost of the acceptance, including Paribas's acceptance fee?

21.2 Suppose Fruit of the Loom, Inc., sells $10 million in accounts receivables to a factor. The receivables are due in ninety days. The factor charges a 2 percent per month factoring fee as well as the face amount for purchasing the accounts receivable from Fruit of the Loom on a nonrecourse basis.
   a. How much will Fruit of the Loom receive for its receivables?
   b. What is the all-in cost of the acceptance, including Paribas's acceptance fee?

21.3 Refer to the following set of transactions. Identify the net transactions within this system by filling in the table below the figure. Draw a new set of transactions like those below to identify which division pays funds and which division receives funds after multinational netting of transactions.

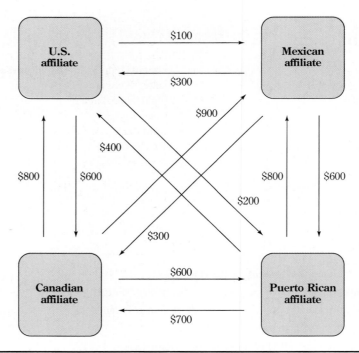

	Paying affiliate					Net	
Receiving affiliate	U.S.	Can.	Mex.	P.R.	Total receipts	Receipts	Payments
United States							
Canadian							
Mexican							
Puerto Rican							
Total payments							

Multinational treasury management is discussed in the following articles:

Robert K. Ankrom, "The Corporate Bank," *Sloan Management Review* 35, Winter 1994, pages 63–72.

James Brickley, Clifford Smith, and Jerold Zimmerman, "Transfer Pricing and the Control of Internal Corporate Transactions," *Journal of Applied Corporate Finance* 8, No. 2, Summer 1995, pages 60–67.

Venkat Srinivasan and Yong H. Kim, "Payments Netting in International Cash Management: A Network Optimization Approach," *Journal of International Business Studies* 17, Summer 1986, pages 1–20.

Useful references on countertrade include

Erwin Amann and Dalia Marin, "Risk-Sharing in International Trade: An Analysis of Countertrade," *Journal of Industrial Economics* 42, No. 1, March 1994, pages 63–77.

R. Mirus and B. Yeung, "Economic Incentives for Countertrade," *Journal of International Business Studies* 27, No. 3, Fall 1992, pages 27–39.

Cynthia C. Ryans, "Resources," *Journal of Small Business Management* 32, No. 4, October 1994, pages 73–77.

Piet Sercu and Raman Uppal, *International Financial Markets and the Firm,* 1995, South-Western Publishing Co., Cincinnati, Ohio, pages 542–546.

Measuring and Managing Exposure to Currency Risk

Far better an approximate answer to the right question, which is often vague, than an exact answer to a wrong question, which can always be made precise.

John W. Tukey

OVERVIEW

Along with new opportunities, the multinational corporation is exposed to a variety of new business risks on its foreign operations. Chapter 14 classified these risks as

- Currency risk—the risk that currency values will change unexpectedly
- Political risk—the risk of an unexpected change in the political or regulatory environment
- Cultural risk—risk arising from dealing with an unfamiliar culture

Management of these risks is a critical objective of the multinational corporation. Cultural risks primarily affect the marketing and human resource management functions of the corporation, but they also surface in purchasing, materials and logistics management, accounting, and finance. Political risks are present in all ventures, but they are particularly prominent in foreign operations.

In Chapter 21 we saw how the corporate treasury can manage the costs and risks of international trade, arrange financing, and manage the cash flows and the funds needs of the corporation. This chapter discusses measurement and management of exposure to currency risk in the multinational corporation.

Financial Goals and Strategies as Complements to the Overall Business Plan

The corporation's financial policies must be formulated at the highest levels of management and faithfully implemented on an ongoing basis to meet the changing needs of the corporation. Failure to set risk management guidelines and then monitor the corporation's risk management activities can expose the firm to financial loss or even ruin.

The way that the firm deals with currency risk is a key element of financial policy. Management must decide whether currency risk exposure will be managed, how actively these risk exposures will be managed, and whether the firm is willing to take speculative positions in the pursuit of its business and financial objectives. Failure to take action in hedging currency risk is a de facto decision to take a speculative position in foreign exchange. Yet the firm can go well beyond a passive posture toward currency risk as it attempts to squeeze as much value as possible from the firm's operating cash flows.

Many commercial and investment banks include speculation among their core competencies. For manufacturing and service firms, a better use of the corporate treasury is as a complement to the other business activities. Short-term speculative profits from the treasury's financial market operations are usually due to chance and not to any enduring expertise in anticipating market movements. Even more important, other business units are unlikely to operate at peak effectiveness if speculative activity in the treasury is distracting top management from running the company's core businesses. A financial strategy of taking speculative positions that are independent of the firm's operating cash flows is, in the long run, likely to destroy shareholder wealth.

This is not to say that the treasury should avoid speculative positions. Treasury may choose to leave a forward exposure unhedged when it believes that forward prices will not yield as much value as future spot prices. But choosing to leave an existing operating cash flow unhedged is vastly different from taking outright speculative positions in the financial markets for speculation's sake. Taking informed but unhedged positions on forward transactions is also a far cry from ignoring currency risk entirely. Treasury adds the most value to the multinational corporation when the treasury functions are designed to complement rather than compete with the other business operations of the enterprise.

The Five Steps of a Currency Risk Management Program

There are five steps that the corporate treasury must take in evaluating and managing the firm's exposure to currency risk.

1. Identify those currencies to which the firm is exposed.
2. Estimate the firm's sensitivity to changes in these currency values.
3. Decide whether to hedge currency exposures in accordance with the firm's overall risk management policy.
4. Select an appropriate hedging instrument or hedging strategy.
5. Monitor the firm's evolving exposures and revisit the above steps as necessary.

Management of currency risk should not be a one-time affair. Exposures to currency risk change over time with changes in exchange rates and in the geographic and product mix of the firm. Management should monitor and periodically reassess its risk management strategies in light of changing market conditions and the evolving state of the company.

22.2 IDENTIFYING EXPOSURES TO CURRENCY RISK

Economic exposure to currency risk is defined as change in the value of future cash flows due to unexpected changes in currency values. **Translation (accounting) exposure** to currency risk is defined as change in financial accounting statements arising from unexpected changes in currency values.[1] Economic exposure is far more important than translation exposure to the value of the multinational corporation because it involves actual cash flows. Translation exposure involves accounting income and not cash flows, so it affects firm value only if managerial behavior or the firm's tax liability is influenced by translation exposure. The body of this chapter deals with economic exposure to currency risk. Translation exposure is a lesser concern and is covered in Appendix 22-A.

Economic exposure is important because it involves cash flows.

Economic Exposure to Currency Risk

Economic exposure to currency risk can be further decomposed into transaction exposure and operating exposure.

- **Transaction exposure** is defined as change in the value of *contractual* cash flows (that is, cash flows to *monetary* assets and liabilities) due to unexpected changes in currency values.

- **Operating exposure** is defined as change in the value of *noncontractual* cash flows (that is, cash flows to *nonmonetary* or *real* assets) due to unexpected changes in currency values.

Transaction exposure is easier to measure and manage than operating exposure and is therefore given the most attention by financial managers. Although measurement and management of operating exposure are more difficult, operating exposure is usually the more important long-term exposure because it involves the firm's core businesses.

Transaction Exposure to Currency Risk. Transaction exposure is the exposure of monetary (contractual) assets and liabilities to currency risk. The size, timing, and currency of denomination of the cash flows associated with monetary assets and liabilities are contractually determined. This makes measuring the exposure of monetary contracts to currency risk relatively straightforward. Parts 2 and 3 of this text present a detailed treatment of currency risk hedging with derivative securities.

---

1 The distinction between economic and accounting exposure to currency risk was first introduced in Chapter 5.

Contracts with fixed, nominal foreign currency cash flows are exposed to two sources of risk: foreign currency risk and domestic inflation risk. Consider the currency exposure of a U.S.-based corporation with a contractual cash inflow of DM1 million due in six months. This is a contractual cash flow denominated in marks, so a 25 percent nominal depreciation of the mark results in a 25 percent nominal drop in the dollar value of this asset. As a secondary effect, the dollar value of the expected future cash inflow may change in value unexpectedly if U.S. inflation is other than expected over the six months. Exchange rates are more volatile than inflation in most countries, so currency risk is the dominant effect. Countries with high inflation develop specialized methods for dealing with purchasing power risk, such as pegging all financial contracts to an inflation index. When this is done, inflation is passed through to prices, and currency risk remains the dominant effect.

Operating Exposure to Currency Risk. Define the value of real assets in the domestic currency V^d as the present value of expected future after-tax operating cash flows in the domestic currency $E[CF_t^d]$ discounted at an appropriate risk-adjusted discount rate i^d in the domestic currency.

$$V^d = \Sigma_t \, E[CF_t^d]/(1+i^d)^t \tag{22.1}$$

Evidence presented elsewhere in this text suggests that foreign exchange risk is largely diversifiable, so it should not affect the discount rate in equation (22.1).[2] Hence, the firm's competitive position is altered by currency risk only to the extent that unexpected changes in currency values affect future operating cash flows.

Operating exposure to a foreign currency can be defined as the percentage change in the domestic currency value of real assets $v^d = \%\Delta V^d$ resulting from a percentage change in the spot rate of exchange $s^{d/f} = \%\Delta S^{d/f}$.

Change in the value of operating cash flows is called operating exposure.

$$\text{Operating exposure}^f = (\%\Delta V^d/\%\Delta S^{d/f}) = v^d/s^{d/f} \tag{22.2}$$

This measure of operating exposure is displayed graphically in Figure 22.1. The value of monetary (contractual) cash flows denominated in a foreign currency changes one-for-one with changes in foreign currency values. This is reflected in the lines of slope +1 (for assets denominated in a foreign currency) and −1 (for liabilities denominated in a foreign currency). The value of real assets can change more or less than one-for-one. Lines are drawn in Figure 22.1 for real assets with a two-for-one ($\beta=2$) and one-for-two ($\beta=+\frac{1}{2}$) sensitivity to the exchange rate.

The noncontractual operating cash flows of the firm's real assets are affected primarily by changes in *real* exchange rates and not just by changes in nominal exchange rates. Relative purchasing power parity predicts that nominal exchange rates will change with differential inflation. Hence, unexpected change in the nominal exchange rate is synonymous with change in the real exchange rate according to relative purchasing power parity. In contrast to nominal exchange rate changes that merely reflect

---

2 Chapter 11 discusses empirical evidence regarding the diversifiability of currency risk. Appendix 16-A demonstrates the diversifiability of country-specific political risk.

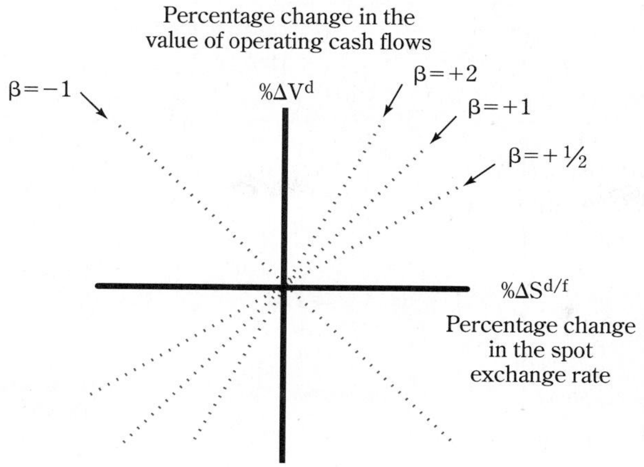

FIGURE 22.1
Operating Exposure
to Currency Risk

inflation differentials, change in the real exchange rate impacts the competitive position of the multinational corporation.

Operating cash flows may be earned in more than one currency. Using the forward rate for currency c as a predictor of future spot exchange rates $F_t^{d/c} = E[S_t^{d/c}]$, equation (22.1) can be restated as

$$V^d = \Sigma_t \, \Sigma_c \, F_t^{d/c} \, E[CF_t^c] / (1+i^d)^t \qquad (22.3)$$

where the summation over c refers to the currencies in which the company receives its operating cash flows. (For the domestic currency, the forward rate is simply $F_t^{d/d} = 1$.)

To focus on revenues and costs, suppose that the foreign and domestic tax environments are identical and that there are no noncash charges, such as depreciation. Operating cash flows can then be decomposed into revenues less operating expenses and taxes:

$$
\begin{aligned}
CF_t^d &= (\text{Revenues}_t^d - \text{Expenses}_t^d)(1-T_C) \\
&= (S_t^{d/c})[(\text{Revenues}_t^c - \text{Expenses}_t^c)(1-T_C)] \qquad (22.4)
\end{aligned}
$$

Again, the underlying cash flows could be denominated in the domestic or in the foreign currency. Operating exposure to currency risk depends on the operating exposure of both revenues and expenses. These separate effects are developed in the next section.

Operating Exposure and the Competitive Environment of the Firm

Operating exposure to currency risk depends on the degree of market segmentation or integration for the firm's inputs and outputs. Figure 22.2 classifies firms according to whether input costs and output prices are determined locally or in a competitive global marketplace. The degree of market integration or segmentation determines the extent to which local prices are correlated with foreign exchange rates. The sign of the exposure to foreign currency values appears in parentheses in each cell of the matrix.

		Revenues	
		Local	Global
Operating expenses	Local	**Domestic firms** (0)	**Exporters** (+)
	Global	**Importers** (−)	**Global MNCs and importers/exporters of globally competitive goods** (+, −, or 0)

FIGURE 22.2
A Taxonomy of Exposures
to Foreign Currency Risk

....

*Segmented markets are insulated
from currency risk exposure.*

....

When markets for goods or factors of production (labor and materials) are completely segmented from other markets, prices are determined entirely in the local market. In contrast, prices in globally integrated markets are determined by worldwide supply and demand, and they fluctuate one-for-one with exchange rates. Real-world prices typically fall somewhere between these two extremes. Labor costs are usually determined by supply and demand in the local market. Commodity prices (oil, metals) are more likely to be set in global commodity markets.

Domestic firms with revenues and expenses that are locally determined are the least sensitive to currency movements. This is the case when local markets are segmented from foreign markets. For example, service industries that rely heavily on local labor are relatively insensitive to currency fluctuations. Labor is not very mobile, and wages paid for labor typically move with domestic inflation rather than with foreign currency values. Consequently, local labor costs tend to be less dependent on foreign exchange rates than most other factor inputs are. Local service companies also tend to compete with other local companies and not with global companies, so both revenues and operating expenses depend more on the local economy than on foreign exchange rates.

Importers buy their goods in competitive world markets and sell them in local markets. If the local market is segmented from other markets (shown in the lower-left block of Figure 22.2), the importer has a negative exposure to foreign currency values. If the importer competes in goods such as oil or electronics for which there is a competitive global market (lower-right block), then local prices move with foreign exchange rates. In this case, both revenues and costs are exposed to currency risk. The direction of the exposure depends on which effect (revenues or costs) dominates.

Exporters face the opposite problem. The classic exporter manufactures goods in the local economy and sells the output in competitive global markets. If the local market is segmented from other markets (upper-right block), the exporter is positively exposed to foreign currency values. If the exporter competes in goods both manufactured and sold in competitive global markets (lower-right block), then both costs and revenues move with foreign currency values.

For the multinational corporation, both revenues and operating expenses are likely to be sensitive to foreign currency values. The nature of the multinational corporation's exposure to currency risk depends on the particular products and markets in which it competes. Seldom are revenues matched one-for-one with operating expenses, so measuring and managing currency risk becomes an everyday activity of the multinational corporation.

An Example of Operating Exposure to Currency Risk

The Operating Exposures of U.S. Firms. To illustrate the effects of the competitive environment on operating exposure, consider the situation of the four U.S.-based companies (local, importer, exporter, and global) shown in Table 22.1. In the base case that runs down the left-hand column, each firm faces per-unit prices and costs of $1,000 and $800, respectively. These prices and costs will continue to hold for firms operating in local markets. Suppose that firms operating in integrated global markets compete with Japanese companies, and must take the yen price for their goods. At the current spot exchange rate of $.0100/¥, yen prices and costs are ¥100,000 and ¥80,000, respectively.

The right-hand columns of Table 22.1 show the impact of a 25 percent appreciation of the yen (or, equivalently, a 20 percent depreciation of the dollar) on each U.S. firm. Prices and costs of firms operating in locally segmented markets are unaffected by exchange rate changes, so locally determined dollar prices and costs remain $1,000 and $800, respectively. In contrast, the prices and costs of firms competing in global markets move with the yen. A 25 percent appreciation of the yen raises the dollar prices of yen-based goods to (¥100,000)($.0125/¥) = $1,250 and the dollar costs of yen-based goods to (¥80,000)($.0125/¥) = $1,000.

An appreciation of the yen has the following effects on the contribution margins of these U.S. firms. The local firm operating in segmented U.S. markets faces constant dollar prices and costs and sees no change in contribution margin. The importer faces constant yen costs, and so it suffers from a depreciation of the dollar. The exporter is able to sell its output at constant yen prices, so it gains from an appreciation of the yen. The U.S. firm operating in globally competitive markets sees no change in its yen prices and costs. The 25 percent appreciation of the yen is passed through both prices and costs, so its contribution margin in dollars also increases by 25 percent.

TABLE 22.1 THE OPERATING EXPOSURES OF U.S. COMPANIES

	Base case		Per unit price or cost in dollars at $.0125/¥			
	In dollars	at $.01/¥	Local	Importer	Exporter	Global
Price	$1,000	¥100,000	$1,000	$1,000	$1,250	$1,250
Cost	$800	¥80,000	$800	$1,000	$800	$1,000
Contribution margin	$200	¥20,000	$200	$0	$450	$250
Percentage change			0%	−100%	125%	25%

TABLE 22.2 THE OPERATING EXPOSURES OF JAPANESE COMPANIES

	Base case		Per unit price or cost in dollars at $.0125/¥			
	In yen	at $.01/¥	Local	Importer	Exporter	Global
Price	¥100,000	$1,000	¥100,000	¥100,000	¥80,000	¥80,000
Cost	¥80,000	$800	¥80,000	¥64,000	¥80,000	¥64,000
Contribution margin	¥20,000	$200	¥20,000	¥36,000	¥0	¥16,000
Percentage change			0%	80%	−100%	−20%

The Operating Exposures of Japanese Firms. Now consider the same four types of firms operating in Japan, as shown in Table 22.2. In the base case, dollar prices and costs are $1,000 and $800, or ¥100,000 and ¥80,000 at the $.0100/¥ exchange rate. The effect of a 25 percent appreciation of the yen (and a corresponding 20 percent depreciation of the dollar) on these Japanese firms appears in the right-hand columns of Table 22.2. Local prices and costs are again determined in the local currency, which in this case is the Japanese yen. The prices and costs of globally competitive goods are determined in the foreign currency, which in this case is the U.S. dollar.

As for the U.S. firms, the competitive positions of these companies depend on whether prices and costs move with the local currency or with global price levels. For the firm operating in a segmented Japanese market, local prices and costs remain ¥100,000 and ¥80,000, respectively, and the contribution margin remains ¥20,000 per unit. Japanese importers are helped by the rise in the yen as they buy goods at reduced yen prices in globally competitive markets. Japanese exporters are hurt by the increase in the yen, because they must compete against relatively inexpensive dollar-priced goods. The Japanese firm competing for inputs and outputs in global markets sees no change in its dollar prices and costs. This global competitor sees a 20 percent decrease in its contribution margin in yen because of the 20 percent depreciation of the dollar against the yen.

The Operating Exposures of Importers and Exporters. In Tables 22.1 and 22.2, the exposure of each U.S. firm was opposite that of its Japanese counterpart. For example, a U.S. and a Japanese exporter face opposite exposures to the value of the yen (or to the dollar). The operating exposures in Tables 22.1 and 22.2 are examples of a general rule. Regardless of where they reside:

A real appreciation of the domestic currency helps importers and hurts exporters.

- A real appreciation of the foreign currency helps exporters and hurts importers.
- A real depreciation of the foreign currency helps importers and hurts exporters.

Or, equivalently,

- A real appreciation of the domestic currency helps importers and hurts exporters.
- A real depreciation of the domestic currency helps exporters and hurts importers.

Companies competing in markets that are either entirely local or entirely global are exposed to a lesser degree of currency risk.

The Exposure of Shareholders' Equity

Shareholders' equity has a residual claim on the assets of the firm after all the financial obligations of the firm have been satisfied. As such, equity absorbs the transaction exposure of **net monetary assets** (monetary assets less monetary liabilities) as well as the operating exposure of real assets.

Consider the common size balance sheet of a domestic exporter shown in Figure 22.3. For simplicity, this exporter's balance sheet is set up in cents (rather than percents) based on a one-dollar unit of the firm. Forty cents of every dollar in this firm is invested in monetary assets denominated in a foreign currency. Only twenty cents of every dollar is in monetary liabilities denominated in the foreign currency. This leaves net monetary assets of 20 cents exposed to transaction risk. If the foreign currency appreciates by 10 percent, firm value in the domestic currency will appreciate by $(20¢)(0.10) = 2¢$ as foreign monetary assets rise by 4 cents and foreign monetary liabilities rise by 2 cents in value. As the residual owner of the firm, equity gains the net 2 cents in value when the foreign currency appreciates by 10 percent.

This exporter has invested 35 cents of every dollar in real assets. The real assets of an exporter are positively exposed to foreign currency values, the magnitude of this operating exposure may be more or less than one-for-one. As the foreign currency appreciates, the purchasing power of foreign customers increases. If the exporter retains the foreign currency price, then its contribution margin increases on the same sales volume (assuming other exporters do not change their price). If the exporter retains the existing contribution margin in its local currency, then exports increase as the foreign currency appreciates.

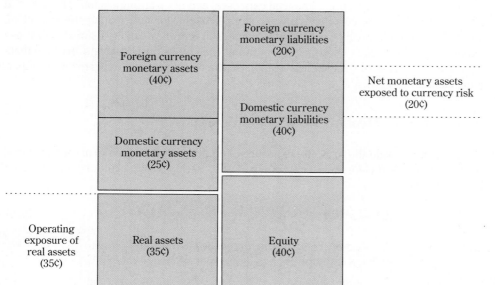

Figure 22.3
The Exposure of
Shareholders' Equity

The exporter's optimal pricing strategy depends on the price elasticity of demand that it faces on global markets.[3] **Price elasticity of demand** is defined as minus the percentage change in quantity demanded for a given percentage change in price.

$$\text{Price elasticity of demand} = -(\%\Delta Q)/(\%\Delta P) \qquad (22.5)$$

For a price elasticity of one, a 1 percent increase in price results in a 1 percent decrease in quantity sold. This leaves sales revenue unchanged. Elasticities greater than one result in a decrease in revenue with an increase in price. Elasticities less than one (inelastic demand) result in an increase in revenue with an increase in price. The firm's price elasticity of demand is an important component of the firm's operating exposure to currency risk.

The exposure of shareholders' equity to currency risk is thus the sum of the transaction exposure of net monetary assets and the operating exposure of the firm's real assets.

22.3 ESTIMATING EXPOSURES TO CURRENCY RISK

There are two perspectives that you can take toward the measurement of economic exposure. The first approach views the firm from outside and measures the impact of exchange rate changes on the market value of the firm's equity or net worth. The market value of equity is equal to the value of total (monetary and real) assets less monetary liabilities, so it reflects the net economic exposure of the corporation to currency risk. Net economic exposure is equal to the operating exposure of the firm's real assets net of any transaction exposure from the firm's monetary assets and liabilities.

The second approach attempts to separately identify the currency risk exposure of revenues, operating expenses, financial expenses, and net working capital. This internal or managerial view of currency risk exposure is useful for anticipating the impact of, and formulating competitive reaction to, changes in currency values. Estimates of these exposures are best done by management rather than by external analysts, because management has access to detailed information on the firm's past and expected future operating cash flows.

Market-Based Measures of Economic Exposure

Viewed from outside the firm, the exposure of equity to currency risk can be measured by the slope coefficient in a regression of the market value of equity on the spot exchange rate.

$$R_t^d = \alpha^d + \beta^f s_t^{d/f} + e_t^d \qquad (22.6)$$

where
$$R_t^d = \text{equity return in the domestic currency d}$$
$$s_t^{d/f} = \text{percentage change in the spot exchange rate } S^{d/f}$$

---

3 Price elasticity of demand was first introduced in Chapter 5.

Equation (22.6) decomposes the change in firm value into two parts: a part that is exposed to currency risk ($\beta^f s_t^{d/f}$) and a part that is independent of currency risk ($\alpha^d + e_t^d$). The regression coefficient β^f captures the sensitivity of equity to changes in the spot exchange rate.

Exposure to currency risk can be thought of as a regression coefficient.

If a particular firm is not exposed to changes in the value of a foreign currency, the regression in equation (22.6) yields a slope coefficient of $\beta^f = 0$. Changes in the spot exchange rate then have no power to explain changes in equity value. The *coefficient of determination* (or r^2) of this regression is zero. If there is a relation between currency values and equity values, then the slope coefficient in equation (22.6) is nonzero. The greater the equity exposure, the greater the magnitude of β^f. This conceptualization of currency risk exposure as a regression coefficient is illustrated in Figure 22.1.

Consider an exporter that is positively exposed to foreign currency values. Daimler-Benz (see box) is a German exporter with a significant exposure to the dollar. Suppose a slope coefficient of $\beta^\$ = +0.1$ is estimated using past D-B stock returns and exchange rate changes in the following regression.

$$R_t^{DM} = \alpha^{DM} + \beta^\$ s_t^{DM/\$} + e_t^{DM} \tag{22.7}$$

According to this estimate of economic exposure, a 10 percent increase in the value of the dollar is associated with a 1 percent increase in the value of Daimler-Benz equity.

Exchange Rate Exposure at Daimler-Benz

Many individual investors and professional fund managers classify Daimler-Benz (D-B) as a German company in their portfolio allocation decisions. D-B is legally incorporated in Germany and has its principal listing on the Frankfurt Stock Exchange. Yet more than 20 percent of D-B sales are in North America. D-B shares trade in dollars on the New York Stock Exchange in the form of American depository receipts (ADRs). Should these dollar-denominated ADRs be treated as mark-denominated or as dollar-denominated investments in portfolio allocation decisions?

D-B's shares are actively traded on both the Frankfurt and New York stock exchanges, so the law of one price should hold. Indeed, financial arbitrage ensures that the value of D-B's ADRs on the NYSE are equal (within the bounds of transactions costs) to the value of D-B shares trading on the Frankfurt exchange. Because these prices move together, the currency exposure of dollar-denominated ADRs in New York is identical to that of D-B shares trading in Frankfurt.

D-B exports its automobiles all around the world, but its manufacturing facilities are located in Stuttgart, Germany. This means that most of D-B's operating expenses are in marks. For a German exporter such as D-B, a real appreciation of the mark raises D-B's costs relative to its competitors in other countries. Conversely, a real depreciation of the mark lowers D-B's costs relative to its foreign competitors.

The currency mismatch between its inflows and outflows exposes D-B's operating cash flows to significant currency risk. D-B's principal currency exposures are to the dollar and the pound, because most of its foreign sales are to the United States and Great Britain. Yet D-B is also indirectly exposed to the yen because several of its major competitors are Japanese. D-B's currency exposure is thus a mixture of exposures to the dollar, pound, and yen and to a variety of other currencies.

In fact, a firm such as Daimler-Benz has revenues and expenses in a number of currencies, so it is exposed to a number of currency risks. A more inclusive measure of D-B's currency exposure can be estimated with the following multiple regression:

$$R_t^{DM} = \alpha^{DM} + \beta^{\pounds} s_t^{DM/\pounds} + \beta^{\$} s_t^{DM/\$} + \beta^{\yen} s_t^{DM/\yen} + \ldots + e_t^{DM} \tag{22.8}$$

where the coefficients $\beta^{DM/\pounds}$, $\beta^{DM/\$}$, and $\beta^{DM/\yen}$ represent exposures to the pound, dollar, and yen. This multiple regression approach reminds us that a firm such as Daimler-Benz has exposure not just to a single currency but to a number of currencies, depending on the nature and geographic scope of its operations and on those of its competitors.[4]

Regressions based on historical relationships can be unsatisfactory as indicators of current and expected future economic exposure. Regressions are necessarily backward looking. As the mix of international sales and costs changes over time, regressions based on historical data provide biased measures of foreign exchange exposure. Regression coefficients based on historical performance also do not allow the financial manager to perform what-if analyses on the impact of various financial market or real asset hedges. This creates a need for a forward-looking measure of economic exposure. It is to this topic that we turn to next.

An Insider's View of Currency Risk Exposure

Unbundling revenues and costs can help in understanding currency risk exposure.

We can develop a better sense of the sensitivity of the firm's operating cash flows to currency risk by unbundling the revenues and costs of the firm and examining the sensitivity of each to changes in foreign exchange rates. Using historical accounting data from internal operations, managers can estimate the following regressions for each major business unit.

$$\%\Delta Revenue_t^d = \alpha_{Rev}^d + \beta_{Rev}^f s_t^{d/f} + e_t^d \tag{22.9}$$

$$\%\Delta Expenses_t^d = \alpha_{Exp}^d + \beta_{Exp}^f s_t^{d/f} + e_t^d \tag{22.10}$$

Separating these two components of cash flow allows the manager to determine to what extent revenues and costs are exposed in different business units. Armed with estimates of the past sensitivity of revenues and expenses to currency risk, managers are in a better position to assess the exposure of the company's future operating cash flows.

Several decision support tools have proved useful in making the step from a descriptive estimate of currency risk exposure to a prescriptive risk management system. These tools include scenario analysis, decision trees, and Monte Carlo simulation. **Scenario analysis** is a process of asking "What if?" In assessing currency risk exposure, scenario analysis consists of asking

"What if real exchange rates change?"

---

4 When the independent variables in a multiple regression are correlated, the standard errors around the slope coefficients are large and the slope coefficients become imprecise. Spot rates in equation (22.8) are related through their common dependence on the mark, so multicollinearity is always a concern in equation (22.8). The firm is considered to be exposed to a particular currency only if the slope coefficient is statistically significant (for example, at a 5 percent significance level).

Scenario analysis evaluates the impact on the firm of a few representative exchange rate scenarios. **Decision trees** can be used in conjunction with scenario analysis to assess the possible responses of the firm to currency fluctuations. Decision trees are graphical representations of sequential decisions and allow managers to ask such questions as

"What if real exchange rates appreciate and we follow this course of action?

or

"What if real exchange rates appreciate and our competitors respond in this way?"

The principal benefit of this approach is in forcing the manager to try to anticipate future events and to establish proactive strategies for dealing with these events. Monte Carlo simulation is similar to scenario analysis, but it uses the entire distribution of exchange rates rather than just a few representative scenarios.[5]

Each of these modeling techniques begins with a forecast of future exchange rates and exchange rate volatilities. Given these forecasts, the impact of variations in the exchange rates on revenues and operating expenses is estimated from past and expected future exchange rate sensitivities. The procedure is as follows.[6]

1. Identify the distribution of future exchange rates.
2. Estimate the sensitivity of revenues and operating expenses to changes in exchange rates.
3. Determine the desirability of hedging, given the firm's risk management policy.
4. Identify the hedging alternatives and evaluate the cost/benefit performance of each alternative, given the forecasted exchange rate distributions.
5. Monitor the position and revisit steps 1 through 4 as necessary.

Estimates of the operating exposure of revenues and operating expenses can help the financial manager understand the components of the firm's exposure to currency risk. In combination with the net exposure of monetary assets and liabilities, this can assist the financial manager or treasurer in formulating a plan for managing exposures to currency risks.

A Caveat on Exposure Measurement

Measurements of currency risk exposure that are based on the past relationship between operating cash flows and exchange rates are appropriate only if the historical relationship is expected to persist into the future. Measures built on past results will not work for evolving businesses and for newly acquired business units. These situations

Scenario analysis helps the manager to be proactive rather than just reactive in an uncertain environment.

---

5 The use of simulation in currency risk management is described in "Identifying, Measuring, and Hedging Currency Risk at Merck" by Judy Lewent and John Kearney, *Journal of Applied Corporate Finance* 2, No. 4, 1990, pages 19–28.

6 This is essentially the same list as the one given in Section 22.1 at the beginning of this chapter (see "The Five Steps of a Currency Risk Management Program"). The difference is in the level of detail allowed by the decision support tools.

call for a heavier-than-usual dose of managerial judgement. Questions that management should ask include

- What is likely to happen to exchange rates and to our business in the future?
- How has the relationship between exchange rates and operating cash flows changed?
- How might our competitors respond to a change in exchange rates?

Although answers to these questions are difficult to find, it is essential that managers ask these questions so they are proactive rather than merely reactive to changes in foreign exchange rates.

22.4 To Hedge or Not to Hedge: Formulating a Risk Management Policy

To ensure that the corporate treasury's hedging and risk management strategies are consistent with the overall goals of the corporation, top management must be actively involved in formulating the corporation's risk management policy and monitoring its implementation. This sounds obvious, but most derivative-related losses that hit the newspaper headlines result from a failure to follow this simple rule. A framework for setting the corporation's risk management policy appears in Figure 22.4.

The first decision that management must make is whether it is willing to take speculative positions in foreign exchange. Two forecasting approaches—technical analysis and fundamental analysis—are available to the firm that feels it possesses the expertise and the risk tolerance to take speculative positions in foreign currencies. **Technical analysis** uses recent exchange rate movements to predict the direction of future exchange rate movements. Technical models have achieved some success in forecasting near-term exchange rates. **Fundamental analysis** uses macroeconomic data (such as forecasts of inflation, GNP growth, and the money supply) to forecast long-term exchange rates.

Some (In)famous Derivatives-Related Losses

Derivatives-related losses have appeared in the financial and popular press with increasing frequency in recent years. This is not a coincidence. With the increasing use of derivative instruments for corporate risk-hedging purposes, more mistakes are bound to occur. Here are three of history's biggest derivative-related losses.

Loss ($ billions)	Firm	Derivative product
1.58	Showa Shell Sekiyu	Currency forwards
1.45	Kashima Oil	Currency derivatives
1.34	MG Corp (Metallgesellschaft)	Crude oil futures

Of course, for every loser there is a winner on the other side of the contract. But the winners seldom make the headlines.

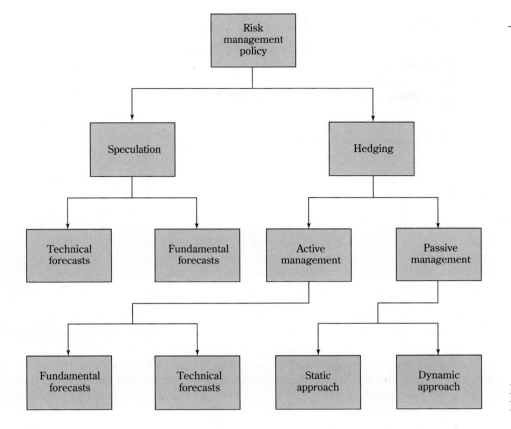

FIGURE 22.4
Risk Management Policy

Although fundamental forecasting models have difficulty beating forward exchange rates as predictors of future spot rates, they are nevertheless popular with practitioners.

The firm that is unwilling to take outright speculative positions must still decide whether it will take a passive or an active approach to hedging its exposures to currency risk. A passive approach does not try to anticipate currency movements. Instead, a passive approach assumes that financial markets are informationally efficient. Passive hedging strategies can be applied in a static or in a dynamic manner. A static approach hedges exposures as they are incurred and then leaves these hedges in place until maturity. A dynamic approach continually reviews the corporation's underlying exposures and its currency risk hedges and revises these positions as necessary.

Active management also hedges currency risk exposures, but it does so selectively. As with speculation, forecasts are made of future currency movements. If exchange rates are predicted to move in a favorable direction for the corporation, then management may decide to leave the position exposed to currency risk. Currency hedging is undertaken if exchange rates are predicted to move in an unfavorable direction. The hedging decision then depends on the volatility of currency values, the size of the exposure, the exchange rate forecasts, and the corporation's (that is, managers') tolerance for risk.

22.5 CURRENCY RISK MANAGEMENT

*Currency risk exposures within
the corporation often cancel
each other out.*

In a multinational corporation, one business unit's exposure to currency risk is often offset by the exposure of another business unit within the corporation. Currency risk management begins with the process of **multinational netting**, which identifies these offsetting currency exposures.[7] The treasury of the multinational corporation is well positioned to identify and manage offsetting foreign currency positions and risk exposures. The exposure of the corporation as a whole is found by consolidating and then netting the exposures of the individual assets and liabilities.

Hedging the Currency Risk Exposures of Individual Operating Units

The managers of individual business units often wish to hedge their units' exposures, so they can stabilize the accounting income or cash flow of their individual units. In these cases, treasury can write *internal* hedging contracts (such as currency forwards or options) for the business units. By writing contracts internally and netting exposures whenever possible, the number and value of external financial market transactions can be minimized. Consolidating and netting exposures rather than hedging each individual exposure allows managers of individual units to hedge as needed while avoiding the costs (commissions and bid-ask spreads) of hedging in external financial markets.

*Operating divisions should
be charged market prices for
internal currency hedges.*

What price should the treasury charge for this service? In transfer pricing decisions on intermediate goods in manufacturing industries, there are often no market prices available. In contrast, the treasury has access to market prices on financial hedges through its financing activities and commercial and investment banking relations. The treasury should charge financial market prices for hedging the currency risk exposure of individual business units within the firm. Market prices allow the treasury to benchmark the costs of hedging and to determine the savings from hedging internally rather than going to the market for each individual transaction.

Managing Transaction Exposure to Currency Risk

Managing Transaction Exposure in the Financial Markets. Table 22.3 reviews the characteristics of financial market hedges of transaction exposure to currency risk. Financial market hedging instruments include[8]

- Currency forwards
- Currency futures
- Money market hedges[9]
- Currency options
- Currency swaps

---

7 A related discussion appears in the cash management section of Chapter 21.

8 Parts 2 and 3 treat each of these contracts in detail.

9 A money market hedge replicates a forward contract by borrowing in one currency, lending in another, and covering the transaction in the spot market.

Vehicles	Advantages	Disadvantages
Currency forwards	Provides an exact hedge of transactions of known date and amount (near-term or long-term)	Bid-ask spreads can be large, especially on long-dated forwards and forwards in infrequently traded currencies
Currency futures	Low-cost hedge if the amount and maturity match the underlying exposure; low-risk hedge because of daily marking-to-market	Exchange-traded futures come in only a limited number of currencies and maturities; daily marking-to-market can cause a cash flow mismatch
Money market hedge	Forward positions can be built in currencies for which there are no forward markets	Relatively expensive hedge; may not be feasible if there are constraints on borrowing or lending in the foreign currency
Currency options	"Disaster hedge" insures against unfavorable currency movements	Option premiums reflect the value of the option, so these can be expensive
Currency swaps	Low-cost switch into other currencies or payout structures (e.g., fixed versus floating)	Not the best choice for near-term exposures; better for long-term exposures

Financial market hedges are most appropriate for hedging transaction exposures because their contractual payoffs can be matched to the underlying foreign currency transaction exposures. Payoffs on currency forwards, futures, and swaps are symmetric, so these financial market hedges can be used to minimize the variability of hedged positions. Currency options have a somewhat different role to play. Because of their asymmetric payoffs, currency options are typically used as an insurance policy against an appreciation or depreciation of the foreign currency. An option to buy one currency (a currency call option) is simultaneously an option to sell another currency (a put option), so currency options can protect against a currency appreciation or depreciation. (If you fear an appreciation of a currency, buy a call option on that currency. If you fear a depreciation, buy a put option on that currency.) Currency options are less frequently used for speculation by multinational corporations.

Financial market hedges are well suited for transaction exposures.

Hedges of long-term transaction exposures are best done with long-dated currency forward contracts or currency swaps. A one-time cash flow with a distant transaction date is best hedged with a long-dated forward contract or, when forward markets are illiquid, with a money market hedge. Long-term contracts with periodic cash flows are best hedged with a currency swap. Exchange-traded currency futures and options are near-term contracts and are unable to effectively hedge distant cash flows against currency risk. Investment banks are willing to create customized contracts (including currency futures and options) to hedge long-term contractual exposures, but these hedges come at a high price.

If a financial market hedge is expensive or simply unavailable in a particular currency, a **currency cross-hedge** can be formed using a related currency. For example, bid-ask spreads on Belgian franc forward contracts are large for maturities longer than

TABLE 22.4 CORPORATE USE OF CURRENCY RISK MANAGEMENT PRODUCTS

Type of product	Used often (A)	Used occasionally (B)	Used once or twice (C)	Never heard of –	Percentage of adoption (A+B+C)
Forward contracts	72.3%	17.9%	2.9%	0.0%	93.1%
Foreign currency swaps	16.4	17.0	19.3	1.2	52.7
Over-the-counter currency options	18.8	19.4	10.6	6.5	48.8
Foreign currency futures contracts	4.1	10.7	5.3	1.2	20.1
Exchange-traded currency options	3.6	6.5	7.1	3.6	17.2
Exchange-traded futures options	1.8	3.0	4.2	4.2	9.0
Foreign currency warrants	1.8	1.2	1.2	22.3	4.2
Cylinder options	7.0	9.9	11.7	8.8	28.6
Synthetic "homemade" forwards	3.0	8.9	10.1	12.5	22.0
Synthetic "homemade" options	3.0	7.8	7.8	12.0	18.6
Participating forwards , etc.	4.1	7.0	4.7	16.4	15.8
Forward exchange agreements, etc.	3.6	3.0	8.3	18.3	14.9
Compound options	0.0	2.4	1.2	44.2	3.6
Break forwards, etc.	0.6	1.2	1.2	34.7	3.0
Hindsight/lookback options, etc.	0.0	0.6	1.2	47.9	1.8

Source: Kurt Jesswein, Chuck C.Y. Kwok, and William R. Folks, Jr., "What New Currency Risk Products
Are Companies Using and Why?" *Journal of Applied Corporate Finance* 8, Fall 1995, pages 115–
124.

two years. Because the value of the Belgian franc is highly correlated with the German
mark, a cross-hedge using the actively traded mark can eliminate a good portion of the
currency risk of the Belgian franc. The effectiveness of this currency cross-hedge
depends on the correlation between the German mark and the Belgian franc. Cross-
hedges using a related currency can cost less than a hedge in thinly traded currencies and
can be nearly as effective. Management may decide to accept a bit of risk on a DM cross-
hedge to avoid the large bid-ask spreads on long-dated Belgian franc forward contracts.

*Forwards are the most popular
currency hedge.*

Table 22.4 presents the results of a survey of the financial officers of 173 large U.S.
corporations regarding their use of financial derivatives in currency risk hedging.[10] The
currency forward contract is the instrument of choice for these firms when the size and
timing of a contractual cash flow is known in advance. Approximately 50 percent of
these financial managers have also used currency options and currency swaps.

Managing Transaction Exposure through Operations. Transaction exposure can
be reduced by timing cash flows within the corporation to offset the corporation's
underlying currency exposures. This process is known as **leading and lagging**. For
example, if a U.S. parent firm is short French francs, the parent can accelerate franc
repatriations from its foreign affiliates. This is known as *leading*. Similarly, the U.S.
parent can delay or *lag* franc payments to its foreign affiliates. Of course, the French franc
balance of the foreign affiliates will change correspondingly. Leading and lagging works
best when the currency needs of the individual units within the corporation are opposite.

10 See also the "Wharton Survey of Derivatives Usage by U.S. Non-Financial Firms," by Bodnar, Hayt,
Marston, and Smithson, *Financial Management* 24, Summer 1995, pages 104-114.

Although leading and lagging can be beneficial to the corporation as a whole, it also tends to distort the rates of return earned by the various affiliates. This calls for some sort of internal recognition of the sacrifice made by the affiliates that pay the leading or receive the lagging cash flows. In essence, leading and lagging is a form of loan from one unit of the firm to another. One alternative for solving the incentive problems created by leading and lagging is to charge market interest rates on these intracompany loans.

Many national governments place limits on corporate leading and lagging.[11] For example, Japan places a 360-day limit on leading and lagging payments on both import and export activities. Most Latin American countries and many Asian countries place even more restrictive limits on leading and lagging and, in some cases, on multinational netting as well. There are no limits on leading and lagging activities in the United States, the United Kingdom, Canada, and Mexico. Managers should check the local regulations concerning leading and lagging before getting too aggressive in applying this cash management tool.

A benefit of corporate international diversification is that cash inflows and outflows occur in many currencies and not in just one or a few currencies. Diversified multinational operations provide a *natural hedge* of transaction exposure—when one currency is depreciating, another currency must be appreciating. Geographically diversified multinational corporations, such as Coca-Cola and PepsiCo, have relatively low transaction exposure to currency risk because they have cash inflows and outflows in a wide variety of currencies.

Managing Operating Exposure to Currency Risk

Managing Operating Exposure in the Financial Markets. Financial market hedges that can be used to hedge operating exposures to currency risk include

- Financing a project with local debt capital
- Selling the local currency with long-dated forward contracts
- Using currency swaps to acquire financial liabilities in the local currency
- Using roll-over hedges to repeatedly sell the local currency using short-term forward contracts

Borrowing in the local currency creates financial cash outflows that are in the same currency as the operating cash inflows. This is a natural way to reduce the exposure of both the parent and the subsidiary to foreign currency fluctuations. Selling short-term or long-dated forward contracts and swapping into the local currency are other ways to achieve the same objective.

The main advantage of a financial market hedge is that the sunk costs of investing and disinvesting in financial instruments are low compared to the sunk costs of investing/disinvesting in real assets. The main disadvantage is that contractually based

Financial market hedges cannot completely hedge operating exposures.

---

11 Business International Corporation publishes an annual survey of national limits on leading and lagging in its *Business International Money Report.*

financial market hedges cannot fully hedge against the uncertain operating cash flows of the firm's real assets.

Hedging operating exposure with a financial market hedge does not reduce the operating exposure itself. Rather, it offsets this operating exposure with a financial hedge that (hopefully) has an opposite exposure to currency risk. Thus, it changes the transaction exposure of the firm in a way that offsets the operating exposure of the firm. Financial market hedges are contractual, whereas operating cash flows are not. Thus, a financial market hedge is almost certain to over- or underhedge an operating exposure.

Suppose Duracell International, Inc., expects operating cash flow of ¥100 billion next year from battery sales to Japan. At a forward rate of $.0100/¥, the resulting expected cash flow is worth $1 billion. Duracell can hedge the expected operating cash flow of ¥100 billion by selling ¥100 billion forward.

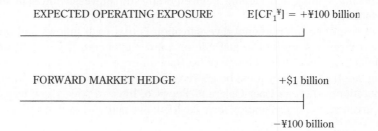

The expected value of this hedged position is $1 billion.

Suppose operating cash flow could be as little as ¥50 billion or as much as ¥150 billion. When combined with a forward sale of ¥100 billion, the resulting yen payoffs are

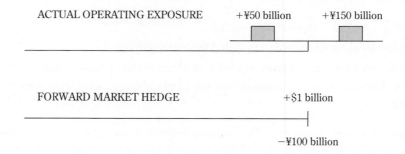

The expected payoff of the yen side of this hedged position is still zero, but the actual payoff will be +¥50 billion or −¥50 billion depending on operating cash flow. The net exposure then depends on operating performance.

Because of this mismatch between the certain cash flows of the contractual hedge and the uncertain cash flows of the underlying operating exposure, it is important for managers to undertake an analysis of the likely performance of financial market hedges. Managers should assess the performance of financial market hedges in the following ways.

- Vary pro forma operating performance within reasonable limits.
- Vary the exchange rate and assess the resulting competitive position of the firm.
- Assess the interaction of operating performance to exchange rate changes.

The effectiveness of various financial market hedges can then be investigated:[12]

- Vary the amount of the hedge.
- Vary the term or maturity of financial market hedges.
- Vary the striking price of currency options.

In many cases, management will choose to hedge less than the expected cash flow. For example, Duracell may choose to sell only ¥50 billion forward rather than the full ¥100 billion expected operating cash flow. This reduces the sensitivity of operating performance to the exchange rate while avoiding overhedging.

Managing Operating Exposure with the Firm's Real Assets. Multinational corporations often manage their transaction exposure through the financial markets and manage their operating exposure by diversifying their operations across a number of currencies and geographic regions. Financial market hedges can be easily reversed should conditions warrant, but hedges achieved through management of the firm's real assets can involve substantial sunk costs and are not freely reversible. The costs of hedging through operations are less onerous for a large multinational corporation with diversified operations than for a smaller firm that is less diversified geographically. Large diversified firms face lower sunk costs when shifting production or sales between countries because they are more likely to have established operations in these countries. The diversified multinational corporation has a natural advantage in responding to real changes in currency values because of the diversity of its international operations.

Real asset hedges are more difficult to construct than financial hedges but also longer lasting.

Two dimensions to diversification can benefit the multinational corporation. First, multinational corporations have varying degrees of international diversification across countries and geographic regions. International diversification can add to corporate value by insulating the diversified multinational from the vagaries of currency risk. Second, firms engaged in international operations often have diversified product lines.

At least one author has found an interaction between product and geographic diversification. Rakesh Sambharya found that single-product multinational corporations tended to diversify geographically, and multinational corporations that have many unrelated businesses tended to concentrate their international efforts in a small number of countries or regions.[13] Sambharya interpreted this as evidence that managers have difficulty managing both product market and geographic diversity.

Operating strategies for reducing the firm's sensitivity to changes in real exchange rates are listed in Table 22.5 for each component of operating cash flow. When local markets are segmented from global competition, local prices are "sticky" and real changes in foreign exchange rates cause changes in real asset values. For example, a real appreciation of the domestic currency typically helps importers and hurts exporters. In the presence of real foreign exchange rate changes, the multinational corporation operating

The MNC can shift sales and production to take advantage of changes in real exchange rates.

12 These variations are described in "Identifying, Measuring, and Hedging Currency Risk at Merck" by Judy Lewent and John Kearney, *Journal of Applied Corporate Finance* 2, No. 4, 1990, pages 19–28.
13 Rakesh B. Sambharya, "The Combined Effect of International Diversification and Product Diversification Strategies on the Performance of U.S.–Based Multinational Corporations," *Management International Review* 35, No. 3, 1995, pages 197–218.

TABLE 22.5 OPERATING HEDGES WITH THE FIRM'S REAL ASSETS

Cash flow component	Hedging strategy
Revenue	Shift marketing efforts to countries with overvalued currencies
Variable cost	Source inputs from countries with undervalued currencies
	Shift production to countries with undervalued currencies
Fixed costs	Build production facilities in countries with undervalued currencies
	Acquire productive capacity from countries with undervalued currencies

in geographically diversified markets can shift its marketing efforts toward countries with overvalued currencies and away from countries with undervalued currencies.[14]

By shifting the firm's marketing efforts toward countries with overvalued currencies, the multinational corporation creates a spectrum of favorable pricing alternatives. Suppose local production costs are at least partially segmented from global competition. If the local currency price is retained, prices in the overvalued foreign currency fall and sales should increase. If the foreign currency price is retained, the contribution margin in the local currency can be increased with no fall-off in sales. Of course, each of these marketing strategies presumes that local costs do not increase with the rise in foreign currency values. If input costs are integrated with other global markets, then any change in currency values is reflected in both prices and costs.

By maintaining geographic diversity, the multinational corporation is in a better position than the domestic firm to recognize and respond to cross-border differences in factors of production, including materials, labor, and capital. Multinational corporations can take advantage of cross-border differences in labor and materials costs by shifting production toward countries with undervalued currencies. Diversifying production and sales across countries also partially hedges the multinational corporation against country-specific political risks. In combination, these strategies for dealing with real foreign exchange changes allow the multinational corporation to enhance revenues and reduce costs while taking advantage of the benefits of international portfolio diversification to keep the total risk of the firm at a minimum.

22.6 SUMMARY

The body of this chapter deals with economic exposure to currency risk. Economic exposure has two components:

- Transaction exposure is change in the value of contractual cash flows due to unexpected changes in currency values.

- Operating exposure is change in the value of noncontractual cash flows due to unexpected changes in currency values.

---

14 The terms "overvalued" and "undervalued" refer to relative changes in real foreign exchange rates and not to overvaluation or undervaluation in any absolute sense.

The contractual cash flows of transaction exposure are relatively easy to manage with financial market hedges. Operating exposure is more difficult to measure and manage because it involves uncertain future cash flows. Operating exposure is often the more important exposure because it involves the corporation's core businesses and not just current (monetary) assets and liabilities.

KEY TERMS

Currency cross-hedge	Operating exposure
Decision trees	Price elasticity of demand
Economic exposure	Scenario analysis
Fundamental analysis	Technical analysis
Leading and lagging	Transaction exposure
Multinational netting	Translation (accounting) exposure
Net monetary assets	

CONCEPTUAL QUESTIONS

22.1 What is the relationship between the risk management directives in the financial plan and the overall business plan of the corporation?

22.2 What is economic exposure to currency risk and why is it important?

22.3 Identify the five steps that the corporate treasury must take to evaluate and manage its economic exposure to currency risk.

22.4 How is an importer affected by a real depreciation of the domestic currency? An exporter? A diversified multinational corporation competing in globally competitive goods and financial markets?

22.5 What is meant by the statement "Exposure is a regression coefficient"?

22.6 How can management improve upon market-based measures of the firm's economic exposure to currency risk?

22.7 What is the difference between technical and fundamental forecasts of exchange rates?

22.8 What is multinational netting, and how can it assist the multinational corporation?

22.9 What alternatives are there for hedging transaction exposure to currency risk through the financial markets?

22.10 What alternatives are there for hedging operating exposure to currency risk through the financial markets? Can these provide perfect hedges against operating exposure?

22.11 What alternatives are there for hedging operating exposure to currency risk through management of the firm's real assets? Do diversified multinational corporations have an advantage over local firms in hedging operating exposure with their real assets?

SUGGESTED READINGS

Operating exposure to currency risk is discussed in

Eugene Flood, Jr., and Donald R. Lessard, "On the Measurement of Operating Exposure to Exchange Rates: A Conceptual Approach," *Financial Management* 15, No. 1, 1986, pages 25–36.

Philippe Jorion, "The Exchange-Rate Exposure of U.S. Multinationals," *Journal of Business* 63, No. 3, 1990, pages 331–346.

Operating exposure to political risk is discussed in

David Bradley, "Managing Against Expropriation," *Harvard Business Review,* July–August 1977, pages 75–83.

Diversification in the multinational corporation is discussed in

Rakesh B. Sambharya, "The Combined Effect of International Diversification and Product Diversification Strategies on the Performance of U.S.-Based Multinational Corporations," *Management International Review* 35, No. 3, 1995, pages 197–218.

Studies of firms' hedging policies and practices appear in

Gordon M. Bodnar, Gregory S. Hayt, Richard C. Marston, and Charles W. Smithson "Wharton Survey of Derivatives Usage by U.S. Non-Financial Firms," *Financial Management* 24, Summer 1995, pages 104-114.

Kurt Jesswein, Chuck C. Y. Kwok, and William R. Folks, Jr., "What New Currency Risk Products Are Companies Using and Why?" *Journal of Applied Corporate Finance* 8, Fall 1995, pages 115–124.

Judy C. Lewent and A. John Kearney, "Identifying, Measuring, and Hedging Currency Risk at Merck," *Journal of Applied Corporate Finance* 2, No. 4, 1990, pages 19–28.

Peter J. Maloney, "Managing Currency Exposure: The Case of Western Mining," *Journal of Applied Corporate Finance* 2, No. 4, 1990, pages 29–34.

Measuring and Managing Accounting Exposure

Accounting exposure (also called **translation exposure**) refers to the impact of exchange rate changes on the parent firm's financial statements. Accounting exposure exists when the *functional currency* of a foreign affiliate is different from the *reporting currency* in which the parent firm prepares its own financial statements (normally the currency of the parent's home country). A key measure of accounting exposure under any translation method is **net exposed assets**, which refers to the book value of assets that are exposed to currency risk less the book value of liabilities that are exposed to currency risk. Accounting measures of net exposed assets depend on which assets and liabilities are considered to be exposed to foreign currency risk by a particular accounting method.

Measuring Accounting Exposure

In the United States, the Generally Accepted Accounting Principles (GAAP) contained in the *Financial Accounting Statements* (FAS) of the Financial Accounting Standards Board specified two methods for translating the financial statements of foreign affiliates:

- The temporal (or monetary/nonmonetary) method of FAS #8
- The current rate method of FAS #52

Each of these will be discussed in detail, because these methods are representative of the translation methods used in other countries.

The Temporal or Monetary/Nonmonetary Method of FAS #8 (1975). The **temporal (monetary/nonmonetary) method** of foreign currency translation was introduced by FAS #8 in the United States and was used from 1976 through 1981. FAS #8 applied the following rules:[15]

---

15 FAS #8 was a temporal method that allowed inventory to be translated at the current exchange rate if domestic inventories were shown at market value on the balance sheet. The monetary/nonmonetary method is similar except that inventory is treated as a nonmonetary asset that is recorded at historical cost.

TABLE 22A.1 AN EXAMPLE OF THE TEMPORAL METHOD OF FAS #8

	Value in FF	Dec '96 value at $.25/FF	Dec '97 value at $.20/FF		Translation gains or losses	
Assets						
Cash and marketable securities	FF10,000	$2,500	$2,000	Exposed assets	−$500	
Accounts receivable	FF10,000	$2,500	$2,000		−$500	
Inventory	FF10,000	$2,500	$2,000		−$500	
Plant and equipment	FF30,000	$7,500	$7,500		$0	
Total assets	FF60,000	$15,000	$13,500		−$1,500	
Liabilities						
Accounts payable	FF10,000	$2,500	$2,000	Exposed liabilities	−$500	
Short-term debt	FF10,000	$2,500	$2,000		−$500	
Long-term debt	FF20,000	$5,000	$4,000		−$1,000	
Net worth	FF20,000	$5,000	$5,500		+$500	Net exposure
Total liabilities and net worth	FF60,000	$15,000	$13,500		−$1,500	

- Monetary (contractual) assets and liabilities are translated at the current exchange rate (that is, at the exchange rate prevailing on the date of the financial statement).
- All other assets and liabilities are translated at historical exchange rates (that is, the rates that prevailed on the date the items were entered on the balance sheet).
- With the exception of depreciation and cost of goods sold (COGS), income statement items are translated at the average exchange rate over the reporting period.
- Depreciation and COGS are directly related to real (nonmonetary) assets and are translated at the historical rate.

The temporal method correctly values monetary assets and liabilities at the current exchange rate according to $P^d = P^f S^{d/f}$. However, by leaving nonmonetary assets and liabilities at their historical cost in the domestic currency, the temporal method implicitly assumes that the domestic currency values of real assets are unaffected by changes in nominal exchange rates. This would be the case if relative purchasing power parity holds in both goods and financial markets, so that nominal exchange rate changes reflect inflation differentials alone. It is unlikely to hold when there are changes in real exchange rates.

Suppose a U.S. parent using the temporal method establishes a French manufacturing affiliate during 1996. The end-of-year balance sheet translated at the then-prevailing rate of $.25/FF is shown in Table 22A.1. Table 22A.1 also shows the balance sheet effect of a change in the nominal exchange rate from $.25/FF to $.20/FF during 1997. If inflation is equal in France and the United States, then this also reflects a 20 percent real depreciation of the franc.

For the temporal method, net exposed assets are equal to monetary assets less monetary liabilities. Net exposed assets in Table 22A.1 are (FF30,000 − FF40,000) = −FF10,000. As the franc falls from $.25/FF to $.20/FF, the dollar value of exposed assets falls by $1,500 (from $7,500 to $6,000). The dollar value of exposed liabilities falls by $2,000 (from $10,000 to $8,000). Exposed liabilities fall by more than exposed assets, so the net effect is a translation gain of $500 that flows through net income into retained earnings. For most firms, the value of monetary assets is less than that of monetary liabilities, so a depreciation (appreciation) of a foreign currency results in a translation gain (loss).

Accounting exposure to currency risk under FAS #8 caused more than a few sleepless nights for the managers of publicly traded firms. Managers like to have control over the factors that influence reported income. Under FAS #8, translation gains or losses were reflected in reported earnings and, hence, in the retained earnings account on the balance sheet. Restatements of balance sheet accounts sometimes overwhelmed operating performance in the income statement and negatively affected reported earnings. This made the temporal method unpopular with corporate managers. Under FAS #8, they might have had a profitable year but still reported negative earnings because of currency translation adjustments.

The Current Rate Method of FAS #52 (1981). FAS #52 introduced the **current rate method** in the United States in 1981 to isolate the effect of translation changes from net income. The current rate method applies the following rules:

- With the exception of common equity, all assets and liabilities are translated at the current rate (the rate of exchange in effect on the date of the balance sheet).
- Common equity is translated at historical exchange rates (the rates prevailing on the date that items were entered on the balance sheet).
- The firm has a choice of translating income statement items at
  - The average exchange rate for the reporting period
  - The exchange rates prevailing on the dates that the various income statement items were entered on the company's books
  - A weighted average exchange rate for the period
- Dividends paid are translated at the current exchange rate.
- Any imbalance between the book value of assets and liabilities is recorded as a separate equity account called the **cumulative translation adjustment** (CTA).

Table 22A.2 presents an example of translation exposure under the current rate method. Under this method, net exposed assets equal the net worth of the firm (total assets minus monetary liabilities). In the example of Table 22A.2, net exposed assets are equal to the entire net worth of the foreign affiliate: (FF60,000 − FF40,000) = +FF20,000. A fall in the value of the franc from $.25/FF to $.20/FF produces a change of -$1,000 in the book value of the foreign affiliate.

Gains or losses caused by translation adjustments are not included in the calculation of net income. Rather, they are placed into the cumulative translation adjustment account in the equity section of the balance sheet. Even though this change is only cosmetic, in that it affects only accounting performance and not the cash flows of the firm, it does relieve managers of the burden of explaining poor earnings outcomes due solely to balance sheet translation effects.

TABLE 22A.2 AN EXAMPLE OF THE CURRENT RATE METHOD OF FAS #52

	Value in FF	Dec '96 value at $.25/FF	Dec '97 value at $.20/FF		Translation gains or losses
Assets					
Cash and marketable securities	FF10,000	$2,500	$2,000	Exposed assets	−$500
Accounts receivable	FF10,000	$2,500	$2,000		−$500
Inventory	FF10,000	$2,500	$2,000		−$500
Plant and equipment	FF30,000	$7,500	$6,000		$1,500
Total assets	FF60,000	$15,000	$13,500		−$3,000
Liabilities					
Accounts payable	FF10,000	$2,000	$2,500	Exposed liabilities	−$500
Short-term debt	FF10,000	$2,000	$2,500		−$500
Long-term debt	FF20,000	$4,000	$45,000		−$1,000
Net worth	FF20,000	$4,000	$5,500		−$1,000] Net exposure
Total liabilities and net worth	FF60,000	$15,000	$10,000		−$3,000

Which Translation Method Is Most Realistic? The temporal and current rate methods treat the real assets of the firm differently. The temporal method retains real assets at historical cost and passes any change in net translation exposure through the income statement. The current rate method adjusts the book value of real assets for exchange rate changes and then treats any change in net translation exposure as a cumulative translation adjustment to owners' equity. Which method more accurately reflects changes in the market values of assets, liabilities, and cash flow? This depends on the nature of the firm and its functional currency, operating environment, and economic exposure to currency risk.

Both the temporal and the current rate methods correctly value monetary assets and liabilities. The difference lies in their treatment of the firm's real assets and operating exposure. The monetary/nonmonetary method assumes that the value of the firm's real assets are unaffected by changes in currency values. The current rate method assumes that real assets are fully exposed to exchange rate changes. For most firms, the truth is somewhere between these two positions.

The most obvious effect of a fall in a foreign currency value is to decrease the value of foreign assets according to $P^d = P^f S^{d/f}$. However, a fall in the local currency also tends to increase the competitiveness of local industries and to increase their value in the local currency (that is, increase firm value P^f in the foreign currency). This increase in local currency value may or may not offset the immediate decrease from the currency depreciation. Consequently, these two accounting methods are simplifications of the true operating exposure of real assets.

Corporate Hedging of Translation Exposure

Translation exposure involves reported income statement and balance sheet accounts and may or may not involve cash flows. To the extent that it does not involve cash flows, management of translation exposure is unlikely to add to shareholder value. In this respect, measurement and management of exposures that are related to cash flows (that is, the firm's economic exposure) are much more important objectives of the firm.

One aspect of translation exposure management can influence firm value even if it is not directly related to the operating cash flows of foreign affiliates. Managerial performance evaluations should ideally be tied to economic performance—to underlying cash flows and values—and not merely to accounting profits. Nevertheless, many managers are evaluated based on accounting performance simply because it is easier to measure accounting flow than economic performance. If they are not allowed to hedge, risk-averse managers may forgo value-creating investments that would expose them to too much currency risk. Allowing managers to hedge against accounting exposure may reduce the agency costs of managers.[16] If this is so, hedging translation exposure can increase shareholder wealth.

To Hedge or Not to Hedge: Recommendations for Translation Exposure

The decision of whether to hedge translation exposure to currency risk must be made on a case-by-case basis. Nevertheless, here are some general recommendations:

- Do not hedge translation exposure in the capital markets except as a by-product of hedging an economic exposure.

- If hedging of translation exposure is deemed necessary to align managerial incentives with shareholder desires, the corporate treasury should use market prices for quoting the hedging costs to the individual units. These exposures should only be hedged internally, not in the external financial markets.

- Structure managerial performance evaluation and compensation in a way that does not reward or penalize managers for unexpected changes in currency values. This can be done by benchmarking divisional performance to other firms or divisions with similar exposures to currency risk.

- The capital structure of foreign affiliates should use local sources of debt and equity capital to the extent permitted by the corporation's overall financial goals. This will minimize both the translation and (more important) the economic exposure of the foreign affiliate.

With nonzero agency costs, accounting income performance can impact real costs. Providing a way for managers to reduce this source of uncertainty will ultimately benefit shareholders and other corporate stakeholders.

---

16 This is discussed by Raj Aggarwal in "Management of Accounting Exposure to Currency Changes: Role and Evidence of Agency Costs," *Managerial Finance* 17, No. 4, 1991, pages 10–22.

KEY TERMS

Accounting (translation) exposure
Cumulative translation adjustment (CTA)
Current rate method
Net exposed assets
Temporal (monetary/nonmonetary) method

SUGGESTED READINGS

Accounting exposure to currency risk is discussed in

Raj Aggarwal, "Management of Accounting Exposure to Currency Changes: Role and Evidence of Agency Costs," *Managerial Finance* 17, No. 4, 1991, pages 10–22.

Ray Ball, "Making Accounting International: Why, How, and How Far Will It Go?" *Journal of Applied Corporate Finance* 8, No. 3, Fall 1995, pages 19–29.

Kathleen M. Dunne and Theresa P. Rollins, "Accounting for Goodwill: A Case Analysis of the U.S., U.K., and Japan," *Journal of International Accounting, Auditing and Taxation* 1, No. 2, 1992, pages 191–207.

Charles H. Gibson and Nicholas Schroeder, "U.K. Firms on the NYSE: An Analysis of Readability Traits," *Journal of International Accounting, Auditing and Taxation* 3, No. 1, 1994, pages 27–40.

Michael H. Moffett and Douglas J. Skinner, "Issues in Foreign Exchange Hedge Accounting," *Journal of Applied Corporate Finance* 8, No. 3, 1995, pages 83–94.

Clyde P. Stickney, Roman L. Weil, and Sidney Davidson, *Financial Accounting: An Introduction to Concepts, Methods, and Uses,* 6th ed., Exhibit 14.4, "Summary of Generally Accepted Accounting Principles for Major Industrialized Countries," copyright 1991 by Harcourt Brace Jovanovich, Inc.

Glossary

Accounting (translation) exposure: Changes in a corporation's financial statements as a result of changes in currency values. (Contrast with *economic exposure*.)

Acquisition of assets: In an acquisition of assets, one firm acquires the assets of another company. None of the liabilities supporting that asset are transferred to the purchaser.

Acquisition of stock: In an acquisition of stock, a multinational corporation buys an equity interest in another company.

Acquisition premium: In a merger or acquisition, the difference between the purchase price and the preacquisition value of the target firm.

Active fund management: An investment approach that actively shifts funds either between asset classes (*asset allocation*) or between individual securities (*security selection*).

Active income: In the U.S. tax code, income from an active business as opposed to passive investment income.

Adjusted present value: A valuation method that separately identifies the value of an unlevered project from the value of financing side effects.

Agent: Someone who represents another. In corporate governance terminology, management is the agent of the principal stakeholders in a principal-agent relationship.

Agency costs: The costs of monitoring management and ensuring that it acts in the best interest of other stakeholders.

All-in cost: The percentage cost of a financing alternative, including any bank fees or placement fees.

Allocation-of-income rules: In the U.S. tax code, these rules define how income and deductions are to be allocated between domestic-source and foreign-source income.

Allocational efficiency: The efficiency with which a market channels capital toward its most productive uses.

American option: An option that can be exercised anytime until expiration. (Contrast with *European option*.)

American shares: Shares of a foreign corporation issued directly to U.S. investors through a transfer agent in accordance with SEC regulations.

American terms: A foreign exchange quotation that states the U.S. dollar price per foreign currency unit. (Contrast with *European terms*.)

Andean Pact: A regional trade pact that includes Venezuela, Colombia, Ecuador, Peru, and Bolivia.

Appreciation: An increase in a currency value relative to another currency in a floating exchange rate system.

Arbitrage Pricing Theory (APT): A asset pricing model that assumes a linear relation between required return and systematic risk as measured by one or more factors according to $R_j = \mu_j + \beta_{1j}F_1 + \ldots + \beta_{Kj}F_K + e_j$.

Asia-Pacific Economic Cooperation Pact (APEC): A loose economic affiliation of Southeast Asian and Far Eastern nations. The most prominent members are China, Japan, and Korea.

Ask (offer) rates: The rate at which a market maker is willing to sell the quoted asset.

Asset allocation policy: The target weights given to various asset classes in an investment portfolio.

Assets-in-place: Those assets in which the firm has already invested. (Compare to *growth options*.)

Association of Southeast Asian Nations (ASEAN): A loose economic and geopolitical affiliation that includes Singapore, Brunei, Malaysia, Thailand, the Philippines, Indonesia, and Vietnam. Future members are likely to include Burma, Laos, and Cambodia.

At-the-money option: An option with an exercise price that is equal to the current value of the underlying asset.

Autarky: In models of international trade, a situation in which there is no cross-border trade.

Balance of payments: The International Money Fund's accounting system that tracks the flow of goods, services, and capital in and out of each country.

Bank-based corporate governance system: A system of corporate governance in which the supervisory board is dominated by bankers and other corporate insiders.

Banker's acceptance: A time draft drawn on and accepted by a commercial bank.

Basis: The simple difference between two nominal interest rates.

Basis point: Equal to 1/100 of one percent.

Basis risk: The risk of unexpected change in the relationship between futures and spot prices.

Basis swap: A floating-for-floating interest rate swap that pairs two floating rate instruments at different maturities (such as six-month LIBOR versus thirty-day U.S. T-bills).

Bearer bonds: Bonds that can be redeemed by the holder. The convention in most West European countries is to issue bonds in registered form. (Contrast with *registered bonds*.)

Beta (β): A measure of an asset's sensitivity to changes in the market portfolio (in the CAPM) or to a factor (in the APT). The beta of an asset j is computed as $\beta_j = \rho_{j,k} (\sigma_j/\sigma_k)$, where k represents a market factor (such as returns to the market portfolio in the Capital Asset Pricing Model).

Bid rate: The rate at which a market maker is willing to buy the quoted asset.

Blocked funds: Cash flows generated by a foreign project that cannot be immediately repatriated to the parent firm because of capital flow restrictions imposed by the host government.

Bond equivalent yield: A bond quotation convention based on a 365-day year and semiannual coupons. (Contrast with *effective annual yield*.)

Call option: The right to buy the underlying currency at a specified price and on a specified date.

Capital account: A measure of change in cross-border ownership of long-term financial assets, including financial securities and real estate.

Capital asset pricing model (CAPM): A theoretical asset pricing model that relates the required return on an asset to its systematic risk.

Capital market line: The line between the risk-free asset and the market portfolio that represents the mean-variance efficient set of investment opportunities in the CAPM.

Capital markets: Markets for financial assets and liabilities with maturity greater than one year, including long-term government and corporate bonds, preferred stock, and common stock.

Capital (financial) structure: The proportion of debt and equity and the particular forms of debt and equity chosen to finance the assets of the firm.

Cash in advance: Payment for goods prior to shipment.

CHIPS (Clearing House Interbank Payments System): Financial network through which banks in the United States conduct their financial transactions.

Closed-end fund: A mutual fund in which the amount of funds under management is fixed and ownership in the funds is bought and sold in the market like a depository receipt.

Coinsurance effect: An effect whereby the diversification of a large firm allows the cash flows generated by some of the firm's assets to "coinsure" cash flows of other corporate assets.

Commodity price risk: The risk of unexpected changes in a commodity price, such as the price of oil.

Commodity swap: A swap in which the (often notional) principal amount on at least one side of the swap is a commodity such as oil or gold.

Comparative advantage: The rule of economics that states that each country should specialize in producing those goods that it is able to produce relatively most efficiently.

Consolidated income: The sum of income across all of the multinational corporation's domestic and foreign subsidiaries.

Consolidation: A form of corporate reorganization in which two firms pool their assets and liabilities to form a new company.

Continuous quotation system: A trading system in which buy and sell orders are matched with market makers as the orders arrive, ensuring liquidity in individual shares.

Controlled foreign corporation (CFC): In the U.S. tax code, a foreign corporation owned more than 50 percent either in terms of market value or voting power.

Convertible bonds: Bonds sold with a conversion feature that allows the holder to convert the bond into common stock on or prior to a conversion date and at a prespecified conversion price.

Convex tax schedule: A tax schedule in which the effective tax rate is greater at high levels of taxable income than at low levels of taxable income. Such a schedule results in *progressive taxation.*

Corporate governance: The way in which major stakeholders exert control over the modern corporation.

Correlation: A measure of the covariability of two assets that is scaled for the standard deviations of the assets ($\rho_{AB} = \sigma_{AB}/\sigma_A\sigma_B$ such that $-1 \leq \rho_{AB} \leq +1$).

Countertrade: Exchange of goods or services without the use of cash.

Country risk: The additional risk brought on by conducting business in a particular foreign country.

Coupon swap: A fixed-for-floating interest rate swap.

Covariance: A measure of the covariability of two assets ($\sigma_{AB} = \sigma_A\sigma_B\,\rho_{AB}$).

Cross-hedge: A cross-rate futures hedge that does not involve the domestic currency.

Cultural risks: The risks of dealing with unfamiliar business and popular cultures.

Cumulative translation adjustment (CTA) : An equity account under FAS #52 that accumulates gains or losses caused by translation accounting adjustments.

Currency coupon swap: A fixed-for-floating rate non-amortizing currency swap traded primarily through international commercial banks.

Currency cross-hedge: A hedge of currency risk using a currency that is correlated with the currency in which the underlying exposure is donominated.

Currency of reference: The currency that is being bought or sold. It is most convenient to place the currency of reference in the denominator of a foreign exchange quote (see *Rule #2* in Chapter 3).

Currency (foreign exchange) risk: The risk of unexpected changes in foreign currency exchange rates.

Currency swap: A contractual agreement to exchange a principal amount of two different currencies and, after a prearranged length of time, to give back the original principal. Interest payments in each currency are also typically swapped during the life of the agreement.

Current account: A measure of a country's international trade in goods and services.

Current account balance: A broad measure of import-export activity that includes services, travel and tourism, transportation, investment income and interest, gifts, and grants along with the trade balance on goods.

Current rate method: A translation accounting method (e.g., FAS #52 in the United States) that translates monetary and real assets and monetary liabilities at current exchange rates. FSA #52 places any imbalance into an equity account called the "cumulative translation adjustment".

Dealing desk (trading desk): The desk at an international bank that trades spot and forward foreign exchange.

Decision trees: A graphical analysis of sequential decisions and the likely outcomes of those decisions.

Debt capacity: The amount of debt that a firm chooses to borrow to support a project.

Debt-for-equity swap: A swap agreement to exchange equity (debt) returns for debt (equity) returns over a prearranged length of time.

Deliverable instrument: The asset underlying a derivative security. For a currency option, the deliverable instrument is determined by the options exchange and is either spot currency or an equivalent value in futures contracts.

Delta-cross-hedge: A futures hedge against both a maturity and a currency mismatch.

Delta-hedge: A futures hedge against a maturity mismatch.

Depository receipt: A derivative security issued by a foreign borrower through a domestic trustee representing ownership in the deposit of foreign shares held by the trustee.

Depreciation: A decrease in a currency value relative to another currency in a floating exchange rate system.

Derivative security: A financial security whose price is derived from the price of another asset.

Devaluation: A decrease in a currency value relative to another currency in a fixed exhange rate system.

Difference check: The difference in interest payments that is exchanged between two swap counterparties.

Direct costs of financial distress: Costs of financial distress that are directly incurred during bankruptcy or liquidation proceedings.

Direct terms: The price of a unit of foreign currency in domestic currency terms, such as $.6548/DM for a U.S. resident. (Contrast with *indirect quote*.)

Discounted cash flow: A valuation methodology that discounts expected future cash flows at a discount rate appropriate for the risk, currency, and maturity of the cash flows.

Discounting: Purchase of a promised payment at a discount from face value.

Discretionary reserves: Balance sheet accounts that are used in some countries to temporarily store earnings from the current year or the recent past.

Domestic bonds: Bonds issued and traded within the internal market of a single country and denominated in the currency of that country.

Domestic International Sales Corporation (DISC): In the U.S. tax code, a specialized sales corporation whose income is lumped into the same income basket as a foreign sales corporation.

Draft (trade bill, bill of exchange): A means of payment whereby a drawer (the importer) instructs a drawee (either the importer or its commercial bank) to pay the payee (the exporter).

Eclectic paradigm: A theory of the multinational firm that posits three types of advantage benefiting the multinational corporation: ownership-specific, location-specific, and market internalization advantages.

Economic exposure: Change in the value of a corporation's assets or liabilities as a result of changes in currency values.

Economies of scale: Achieving lower average cost per unit through a larger scale of production.

Economies of vertical integration: Achieving lower operating costs by bringing the entire production chain within the firm rather than contracting through the marketplace.

Effective annual yield: Calculated as $(1+i/n)^n$, where i is the stated annual interest rate and n is the number of compounding periods per year. (Contrast with *bond equivalent yield*.)

Efficient frontier: The mean-variance efficient portion of the investment opportunity set.

Efficient market: A market in which prices reflect all relevant information.

Emerging stock markets: The stock markets of emerging economies. These markets typically have higher expected returns than established markets but also higher risk.

Endogenous uncertainty: Price or input cost uncertainty that is within the control of the firm, such as when the act of investing reveals information about price or input cost.

Equity-linked Eurobonds: A Eurobond with a convertibility option or warrant attached.

Eurobonds: Fixed rate Eurocurrency deposits and loans and Eurocurrencies with longer maturities than five years.

Eurocurrencies: Deposits and loans denominated in one currency and traded in a market outside the borders of the country issuing that currency (e.g., *Eurodollars*).

Eurodollars: Dollar-denominated deposits held in a country other than the United States.

European currency unit (ECU): A trade-weighted basket of currencies in the European Exchange Rate Mechanism (ERM) of the European Union.

European exchange rate mechanism (ERM): The exchange rate system used by countries in the European Union in which exchange rates are pegged within bands around an ERM central value.

European Monetary System (EMS): An exchange rate system based on cooperation between European Union central banks.

European option: An option that can be exercised only at expiration. (Contrast with *American option*.)

European terms: A foreign exchange quotation that states the foreign currency price of one U.S. dollar. (Contrast with *American terms*.)

European Union (EU): Formerly the European Economic Community, a regional trade pact that includes Belgium, France, Germany, Italy, the Netherlands, Portugal, Spain, and the United Kingdom (England, Wales, Northern Ireland, and Scotland).

Exercise price: The price at which an option can be exercised (also called *the striking price*).

Exogenous uncertainty: Price or input cost uncertainty that is outside the control of the firm.

Explicit tax: A tax that is explicitly collected by a government; includes income, withholding, property, sales, and value-added taxes and tariffs.

Export: An entry mode into international markets that relies on domestic production and shipments to foreign markets through sales agents or distributors, foreign sales branches, or foreign sales subsidiaries.

Export financing interest: In the U.S. tax code, interest income derived from goods manufactured in the United States and sold outside the United States as long as not more than 50 percent of the value is imported into the United States.

Export management company: A foreign or domestic company that acts as a sales agent and distributor for domestic exporters in international markets.

Expropriation: A specific type of political risk in which a government seizes foreign assets.

External market: A market for financial securities that are placed outside the borders of the country issuing that currency.

Factoring: The sale of accounts receivable at a discount to face value to factors that are willing and able to bear the costs and risks of credit and collections.

Financial engineering: The process of innovation by which new financial products are created.

Financial innovation: The process of designing new financial products, such as exotic currency options and swaps.

Financial markets: Markets for financial assets and liabilities.

Financial policy: The corporation's choices regarding the debt-equity mix, currencies of denomination, maturity structure, method of financing investment projects, and hedging decisions with a goal of maximizing the value of the firm to some set of stakeholders.

Financial price risk: The risk of unexpected changes in a financial price, including currency (foreign exchange) risk, interest rate risk, and commodity price risk.

Financial service income: In the U.S. tax code, income derived from financial services such as banking, insurance, leasing, financial service management fees, and swap income.

Financial (capital) structure: The proportion of debt and equity and the particular forms of debt and equity chosen to finance the assets of the firm.

Financial strategy: The way in which the firm pursues its financial objectives.

Fixed exchange rate system: An exchange rate system in which governments stand ready to buy and sell currency at official exchange rates.

Foreign base company income: In the U.S. tax code, a category of Subpart F income that includes foreign holding company income and foreign base company sales and service income.

Foreign bonds: Bonds that are issued in a domestic market by a foreign borrower, denominated in domestic currency, marketed to domestic residents, and regulated by the domestic authorities.

Foreign branch: A foreign affiliate that is legally a part of the parent firm. In the U.S. tax code, foreign branch income is taxed as it is earned in the foreign country.

Foreign direct investment (FDI): The act of building productive capacity directly in a foreign country.

Foreign exchange broker: Brokers serving as matchmakers in the foreign exchange market that do not put their own money at risk.

Foreign exchange dealer: A financial institution making a market in foreign exchange.

Foreign exchange (currency) risk: The risk of unexpected changes in foreign currency exchange rates.

Foreign sales corporation (FSC): In the U.S. tax code, a specialized sales corporation whose income is lumped into the same income basket as that of a domestic international sales corporation.

Foreign-source income: Income earned from foreign operations.

Foreign tax credit (FTC): In the U.S. tax code, a credit against domestic U.S. income taxes up to the amount of foreign taxes paid on foreign-source income.

Forfaiting: Factoring that involves medium- to long-term receivables (six months or longer) and large transactions (i.e., more than $100,000).

Forward discount: A currency whose nominal value in the forward market is lower than in the spot market. (Contrast with *forward premium*.)

Forward market: A market in which trades are made for future delivery according to an agreed-upon delivery date, exchange rate, and amount.

Forward parity: When the forward rate is an unbiased predictor of future spot exchange rates.

Forward premium: A currency whose nominal value in the forward market is higher than in the spot market. (Contrast with *forward discount*.)

Franchise agreement: An agreement in which a domestic company (the franchisor) licenses its trade name and/or business system to an independent company (the franchisee) in a foreign market.

Free cash flow: Cash flow after all positive-NPV projects have been exhausted in the firm's main line of business.

Freely floating exchange rate system: An exchange rate system in which currency values are allowed to fluctuate according to supply and demand forces in the market without direct interference by government authorities.

Freight shippers (freight forwarders): Agents used to coordinate the logistics of transportation.

Fundamental analysis: A method of predicting exchange rates using the relationships of exchange rates to fundamental economic variables such as GNP growth, money supply, and trade balances.

Futures commission merchant: A brokerage house that is authorized by a futures exchange to trade with retail clients.

Futures contract: A commitment to exchange a specified amount of one currency for a specified amount of another currency at a specified time in the future.

General Agreement on Tariffs and Trade (GATT): A worldwide trade agreement designed to reduce tariffs, protect intellectual property, and set up a dispute resolution system. The agreement is overseen by the *World Trade Organization (WTO)*.

Generalized autoregressive conditional heteroskedasticity: A time series model in which returns at each instant of time are normally distributed but volatility is a function of recent history of the series.

Global bond: A bond that trades in the Eurobond market as well as in one or more national bond markets.

Gold exchange standard: An exchange rate system used from 1925 to 1931 in which the United States and England were allowed to hold only gold reserves while other nations could hold gold, U.S. dollars, or pounds sterling as reserves.

Gold standard: An exchange rate system used prior to 1914 in which gold was used to settle national trade balances. Also called the "classical gold standard."

Goodwill: The accounting treatment of an intangible asset such as the takeover premium in a merger or acquisition.

Greenmail: Buying shares on the open market in the hope that the target's business partners will buy back the shares at inflated prices.

Growth options: The positive-NPV opportunities in which the firm has not yet invested. The value of growth options reflects the time value of the firm's current investment in real assets as well as the option value of the firm's potential future investments.

Hedge funds: Private investment partnerships with a general manager and a small number of limited partners.

Hedge portfolio: The country-specific hedge portfolio in the *International Asset Pricing Model* serves as a store of value (like the risk-free asset in the *CAPM*) as well as a hedge against the currency risk of the market portfolio.

Hedge quality: Measured by the r-square in a regression of spot rate changes on futures price changes.

Hedge ratio: The ratio of derivatives contracts to the underlying risk exposure.

Home asset bias: The tendency of investors to overinvest in assets based in their own country.

High-withholding-tax interest income: In the U.S. tax code, interest income that has been subject to a foreign gross withholding tax of 5 percent or more.

Historical volatility: Volatility estimated from a historical time series.

Hysteresis: The behavior of firms that fail to enter markets that appear attractive and, once invested, persist in operating at a loss. This behavior is characteristic of situations with high entry and exit costs along with high uncertainty.

Implicit tax: Lower (higher) before-tax required returns on assets that are subject to lower (higher) tax rates.

Implied volatility: The volatility that is implied by an option value given the other determinants of option value.

Income baskets: In the U.S. tax code, income is allocated to one of a number of separate income categories. Losses in one basket may not be used to offset gains in another basket.

Index futures: A futures contract that allows investors to buy or sell an index (such as a foreign stock index) in the futures market.

Index options: A *call* or *put option* contract on an index (such as a foreign stock market index).

Index swap: A swap of a market index for some other asset (such as a stock-for-stock or debt-for-stock swap).

Indication pricing schedule: A schedule of rates for an *interest rate* or *currency swap*.

Indirect costs of financial distress: Costs of financial distress that are indirectly incurred prior to formal bankruptcy or liquidation.

Indirect diversification benefits: Diversification benefits provided by the multinational corporation that are not available to investors through their portfolio investment.

Indirect terms: The price of a unit of domestic currency in foreign currency terms such as DM1.5272/$ for a U.S. resident. (Contrast with *direct terms*.)

Informational efficiency: Whether or not market prices reflect information and thus the true (or intrinsic) value of the underlying asset.

Integrated financial market: A market in which there are no barriers to financial flows and purchasing power parity holds across equivalent assets.

Intellectual property rights: Patents, copyrights, and proprietary technologies and processes that are the basis of the multinational corporation's competitive advantage over local firms.

Interbank spread: The difference between a bank's offer and bid rates for deposits in the Eurocurrency market.

Interest rate risk: The risk of unexpected changes in an interest rate.

Interest rate swap: An agreement to exchange interest payments for a specific period of time on a given principal amount. The most common interest rate swap is a fixed-for-floating coupon swap. The notional principal is typically not exchanged.

Intermediated market: A financial market in which a financial institution (usually a commercial bank) stands between borrowers and savers.

Internal market: A market for financial securities that are denominated in the currency of a host country and placed within that country.

International Asset Pricing Model (IAPM): The international version of the CAPM in which investors in each country share the same consumption basket and purchasing power parity holds.

International Bank for Reconstruction and Development: Also called the *World Bank*, an international organization created at Breton Woods in 1944 to help in the reconstruction and development of its member nations.

International bonds: Bonds that are traded outside the country of the issuer. International bonds are either *foreign bonds* trading in a foreign national market or *Eurobonds* trading in the international market.

International Monetary Fund (IMF): An international organization that compiles statistics on cross-border transactions and publishes a monthly summary of each country's balance of payments.

International monetary system: The global network of governmental and commercial institutions within which currency exchange rates are determined.

In-the-money option: An option that has value if exercised immediately.

Intrinsic value of an option: The value of an option if exercised immediately.

Investment opportunity set: The set of possible investments available to an individual or corporation.

Investment philosophy: The investment approach—active or passive—pursued by an investment fund and its managers.

Islamic banking: A form of banking popular in some Islamic countries in which bank depositors do not receive a set rate of interest but instead share in the profits and losses of the bank.

Joint venture: An agreement of two or more companies to pool their resources to execute a well-defined mission. Resource commitments, responsibilities, and earnings are shared according to a predetermined contractual formula.

Keiretsu: Collaborative groups of vertically and horizontally integrated firms with extensive share cross-holdings and with a major Japanese bank or corporation at the center.

Law of one price: The principle that equivalent assets sell for the same price. The law of one price is enforced in the currency markets by financial market arbitrage.

Lead manager: The lead investment bank in a syndicate selling a public securities offering.

Leading and lagging: Reduction of transaction exposure through timing of cash flows within the corporation.

Less developed country (LDC): A country that has not yet reached the level of industrial organization attained by developed countries.

Letter of credit (L/C): A letter issued by an importer's bank guaranteeing payment upon presentation of specified trade documents (invoice, bill of lading, inspection and insurance certificates, etc.).

License agreement: A sales agreement in which a domestic company (the licensor) allows a foreign company (the licensee) to market its products in a foreign country in return for royalties, fees, or other forms of compensation.

Limited flexibility exchange rate system: The International Monetary Fund's name for an exchange rate system with a managed float.

Liquid market: A market in which traders can buy or sell large quantities of an asset when they want and with low transactions costs.

Liquidity: The ease with which an asset can be exchanged for another asset of equal value.

Location-specific advantages: Advantages (natural and created) that are available only or primarily in a single location.

Loanable funds: The pool of funds from which borrowers can attract capital; typically categorized by currency and maturity.

London Interbank Bid Rate (LIBID): The bid rate that a Euromarket bank is willing to pay to attract a deposit from another Euromarket bank.

London Interbank Offer Rate (LIBOR): The offer rate that a Euromarket bank demands in order to place a deposit at (or, equivalently, make a loan to) another Euromarket bank.

Long position: A position in which a particular asset (such as a spot or forward currency) has been purchased.

Macro risks: Political risks that affect all foreign firms in a host country.

Management contract: An agreement in which a company licenses its organizational and management expertise.

Managerial flexibility: Flexibility in the timing and scale of investment provided by a real investment option.

Margin requirement: A performance bond paid upon purchase of a futures contract that ensures the exchange clearinghouse against loss.

Market-based corporate governance system: A system of corporate governance in which the supervisory board represents a dispersed set of largely equity shareholders.

Market failure: A failure of arms-length markets to efficiently complete the production of a good or service. In the *eclectic paradigm*, the multinational corporation's *market internalization advantages* take advantage of market failure.

Market internalization advantages: Advantages that allow the multinational corporation to internalize or exploit the failure of an arms-length market to efficiently accomplish a task.

Market maker: A financial institution that quotes *bid* (buy) and *offer* (sell) prices.

Market model (one-factor market model): The empirical version of the *security market line*: $R_j = \alpha_j + \beta_j R_M + e_j$.

Market portfolio: A portfolio of all assets weighted according to their market values.

Market risk premium: The risk premium on an average stock; $(E[R_M] - R_F)$.

Market timing: An investment strategy of shifting among asset classes in an attempt to anticipate which asset class(es) will appreciate or depreciate during the coming period.

Marking to market: The process by which changes in the value of futures contracts are settled daily.

Mean-variance efficient: An asset that has higher mean return at a given level of risk (or lower risk at a given level of return) than other assets.

Mercosur: The "common market of the South," which includes Argentina, Brazil, Paraguay, and Uruguay in a regional trade pact that reduces tariffs on intrapact trade by up to 90 percent.

Merger: A form of corporate acquisition in which one firm absorbs another and the assets and liabilities of the two firms are combined.

Method of payment: The way in which a merger or acquisition is financed.

Micro risks: Political risks that are specific to an industry, company, or project within the host country.

Miller and Modigliani's irrelevance proposition: If financial markets are perfect, then corporate financial policy (including hedging policy) is irrelevant.

Monetary assets and liabilities: Assets and liabilities with contractual payoffs.

Money markets: Markets for financial assets and liabilities of short maturity, usually less than one year.

Money market yield: A bond quotation convention based on a 360-day year and semiannual coupons.

More flexible exchange rate system: The International Monetary Fund's name for a floating exchange rate system.

Multinational corporation: A corporation with operations in more than one country.

Multinational netting: Elimination of offsetting cash flows within the multinational corporation.

National tax policy: The way in which a nation chooses to allocate the burdens of tax collections across its residents.

Nationalization: A process whereby privately owned companies are brought under state ownership and control. (Contrast with *privatization*.)

Negative-NPV tie-in project: A negative-NPV infrastructure development project that a local government requires of a company pursuing a positive-NPV investment project elsewhere in the economy.

Net asset value: The sum of the individual asset values in a closed-end mutual fund. *Closed-end funds* can sell at substantial premiums or discounts to their net asset values.

Net currency exposure: Exposure to foreign exchange risk after netting all intracompany cash flows.

Net exposed assets: Exposed assets less exposed liabilities. The term is used with market values or, in translation accounting, with book values.

Net monetary assets: Monetary assets less monetary liabilities.

Net position: A currency position after aggregating and canceling all offsetting transactions in each currency, maturity, and security.

Nonintermediated debt market: A financial market in which borrowers (governments and large corporations) appeal directly to savers for debt capital through the securities markets without using a financial institution as intermediary.

Nonmonetary assets and liabilities: Assets and liabilities with noncontractual payoffs.

North American Free Trade Agreement (NAFTA): A regional trade pact among the United States, Canada, and Mexico.

Notional principal: In a swap agreement, a principal amount that is only "notional" and is not exchanged.

Offer (ask) rates: The rate at which a market maker is willing to sell the quoted asset.

Offering statement: In the United States, a shortened registration statement required by the Securities and Exchange Commission on debt issues with less than a nine-month maturity.

Official settlements balance (overall balance): An overall measure of a country's private financial and economic transactions with the rest of the world.

Open account: The seller delivers the goods to the buyer and then bills the buyer according to the terms of trade.

Open-end fund: A mutual fund in which the amount of money under management grows/shrinks as investors buy/sell the fund.

Operating exposure: Changes in the value of a corporation's real (nonmonetary) assets as a result of changes in currency values.

Operating leverage: The trade-off between fixed and variable costs in the operation of the firm.

Opportunity set: The set of all possible investments.

Operational efficiency: Market efficiency with respect to how large an influence transactions costs and other market frictions have on the operation of a market.

Out-of-the-money option: An option that has no value if exercised immediately.

Outright quote: A quote in which all of the digits of the bid and offer prices are quoted. (Contrast with *points quote*.)

Overall balance: (*See official settlements balance.*)

Overall FTC limitation: In the U.S. tax code, a limitation on the FTC equal to foreign-source income times U.S. tax on worldwide income divided by worldwide income.

Ownership-specific advantages: Property rights or intangible assets, including patents, trademarks, organizational and marketing expertise, production technology and management, and general organizational abilities, that form the basis for the multinational's advantage over local firms.

Parallel loan: A loan arrangement in which a company borrows in its home currency and then trades this debt for the foreign currency debt of a foreign counterparty.

Passive income: In the U.S. tax code, income (such as investment income) that does not come from active participation in a business.

Payoff profile: A graph with the value of an underlying asset on the x-axis and the value of a position taken to hedge against risk exposure on the y-axis. Also used with changes in value. (Contrast with *risk profile*.)

Pegged exchange rate system: The International Monetary Fund's name for a fixed exchange rate system.

Pension liabilities: A recognition of future liabilities resulting from pension commitments made by the corporation. Accounting for pension liabilities varies widely by country.

Perfect market assumptions: A set of assumptions under which the law of one price holds. These assumptions include frictionless markets, rational investors, and equal access to market prices and information.

Periodic call auction: A trading system in which stocks are auctioned at intervals throughout the day.

Points quote: An abbreviated form of the *outright quote* used by traders in the interbank market.

Political risk: The risk that a sovereign host government will unexpectedly change the rules of the game under which businesses operate. Political risk includes both *macro* and *micro risks*.

Price elasticity of demand: The sensitivity of quantity sold to a change in price ($-\%\Delta Q/\%\Delta P$).

Price uncertainty: Uncertainty regarding the future price of an asset.

Private placement: A securities issue privately placed with a small group of investors rather than through a public offering.

Privatization: A process whereby publicly owned enterprises are sold to private investors. (Contrast with *nationalization*.)

Product cycle theory: Product cycle theory views the products of the successful firm as evolving through four stages: (1) infancy, (2) growth, (3) maturity, and (4) decline.

Production possibilities schedule: The maximum amount of goods (for example, food and clothing) that a country is able to produce given its labor supply.

Progressive taxation: A convex tax schedule that results in a higher effective tax rate on high income levels than on low income levels.

Project financing: A way to raise nonrecourse financing for a specific project characterized by the following: (1) the project is a separate legal entity and relies heavily on debt financing and (2) the debt is contractually linked to the cash flow generated by the project.

Prospectus: A brochure that describes a mutual fund's investment objectives, strategies, and position limits.

Protectionism: Protection of local industries through tariffs, quotas, and regulations that discriminate against foreign businesses.

Public securities offering: A securities issue placed with the public through an investment or commercial bank.

Put option: The right to sell the underlying currency at a specified price and on a specified date.

Random walk: A process in which instantaneous changes in exchange rates are normally distributed with a zero mean and constant variance.

Real appreciation/depreciation: A change in the purchasing power of a currency.

Real exchange rate: A measure of the nominal exchange rate that has been adjusted for inflation differentials since an arbitrarily defined base period.

Real options: An option or optionlike feature embedded in a real investment opportunity.

Reciprocal marketing agreement: A strategic alliance in which two companies agree to comarket each other's products in their home market. Production rights may or may not be transferred.

Registered bonds: Bonds for which each issuer maintains a record of the owners of its bonds. Countries requiring that bonds be issued in registered form include the United States and Japan. (Contrast with *bearer bonds*.)

Registration statement: In the United States, a statement filed with the Securities and Exchange Commission on securities issues that discloses relevant information to the public.

Re-invoicing centers: An offshore financial affiliate that is used to channel funds to and from the multinational's foreign operations.

Repatriation: The act of remitting cash flows from a foreign affiliate to the parent firm.

Reservation price: The price below (above) which a seller (purchaser) is unwilling to go.

Revaluation: An increase in a currency value relative to other currencies in a fixed exchange rate system.

Rights of set-off: An agreement defining each party's rights should one party default on its obligation. Rights of set-off were common in *parallel loan* arrangements.

Risk profile: A graph with the value of an underlying asset on the x-axis and the value of a position exposed to risk in the underlying asset on the y-axis. Also used with changes in value. (Contrast with *payoff profile*.)

R-square (the coefficient of determination): The percent of the variation in a dependent variable (a y-variable) that is "explained by" variation in an independent variable (an x-variable).

Rule #1: Always keep track of your currency units.

Rule #2: Always think of buying and selling the currency in the denominator of a foreign exchange quote.

Scenario analysis: A process of asking "What if?" using scenarios that capture key elements of possible future realities.

Security market line (SML): In the CAPM, the relation between required return and *systematic risk* (or *beta*): $R_j = R_F + \beta_j (E[R_M] - R_F)$.

Security selection: An investment strategy that attempts to identify individual securities that are underpriced relative to other securities in a particular market or industry.

Segmented market: A market that is partially or wholly isolated from other markets by one or more market imperfections.

Set-of-contracts perspective: A view of the corporation as the nexus of a set of legal contracts linking the various stakeholders. Important contracts include those with customers, suppliers, labor, management, debt, and equity.

Sharpe index: A measure of risk-adjusted investment performance in excess return per unit of total risk: $SI = (R_P - R_F)/(\sigma_P)$.

Short position: A position in which a particular asset (such as a spot or forward currency) has been sold.

Short selling: Selling an asset that you do not own, or taking a short position.

Side effect: Any aspect of an investment project that can be valued separately from the project itself.

Sight draft: A draft that is payable on demand.

Signaling: The use of observable managerial actions in the marketplace as an indication of management's beliefs concerning the prospects of the company.

Special drawing right (SDR): An international reserve created by the International Monetary Fund and allocated to member countries to supplement foreign exchange reserves.

Spot market: A market in which trades are made for immediate delivery (within two business days for most spot currencies).

Stakeholders: Those with an interest in the firm. A narrow definition includes the corporation's debt and equity holders. A broader definition includes labor, management, and perhaps other interested parties, such as customers, suppliers, and society at large.

Stamp tax: A tax on a financial transaction.

Stationary time series: A time series in which the process generating returns is identical at every instant of time.

Stock index futures: A futures contract on a stock index.

Stock index swap: A swap involving a stock index. The other asset involved in a stock index swap can be another stock index (a stock-for-stock swap), a debt index (a debt-for-stock swap), or any other financial asset or financial price index.

Strategic alliance: A collaborative agreement between two companies designed to achieve some strategic goal. Strategic alliances include international licensing agreements, management contracts, and joint ventures as special cases.

Striking price: The price at which an option can be exercised (also called the *exercise price*).

Subpart F income: In the U.S. tax code, income from foreign subsidiaries owned more than 10 percent and *controlled foreign corporations* that is taxed on a pro rata basis as it is earned.

Subsidized financing: Financing that is provided by a host government and that is issued at a below-market interest rate.

Sunk costs: Expenditures that are at least partially lost once an investment is made.

Supervisory board: The board of directors that represents stakeholders in the governance of the corporation.

Swap: An agreement to exchange two liabilities (or assets) and, after a prearranged length of time, to reexchange the liabilities (or assets).

Swaption: A swap with one or more options attached.

Swap book: A swap bank's portfolio of swaps, usually arranged by currency and by maturity.

SWIFT (Society for Worldwide Interbank Financial Transactions): Network through which international banks conduct their financial transactions.

Switching options: A sequence of options in which exercise of one option creates one or more additional options. Investment-disinvestment, entry-exit, expansion-contraction, and suspension-reactivation decisions are examples of switching options.

Syndicate: The selling group of investment banks in a public securities offering.

Synergy: In an acquisition or merger, when the value of the combination is greater than the sum of the individual parts: $Synergy = V_{AT} - (V_A + V_T)$.

Synthetic forward position: A forward position constructed through borrowing in one currency, lending in another currency, and offsetting these transactions in the spot exchange market.

Systematic business risk (unlevered beta): The systematic risk (or beta) of a project as if it were financed with 100 percent equity.

Systematic risk: Risk that is common to all assets and cannot be diversified away (measured by *beta*).

Tangibility: Tangible assets are real assets that can be used as collateral to secure debt.

Targeted registered offerings: Securities issues sold to "targeted" foreign financial institutions according to U.S. SEC guidelines. These foreign institutions then maintain a secondary market in the foreign market.

Tax arbitrage: Arbitrage using a difference in tax rates or tax systems as the basis for profit.

Tax clienteles: Clienteles of investors with specific preferences for debt or equity that are driven by differences in investors' personal tax rates.

Tax-haven affiliate: A wholly owned affiliate that is in a low-tax jurisdiction and that is used to channel funds to and from the multinational's foreign operations. (The tax benefits of tax-haven affiliates were largely removed in the United States by the Tax Reform Act of 1986.)

Tax holiday: A reduced tax rate provided by a government as an inducement to foreign direct investment.

Tax neutrality: Taxes that do not interfere with the natural flow of capital toward its most productive use.

Tax preference items: Items such as tax-loss carryforwards and carrybacks and investment tax credits that shield corporate taxable income from taxes.

Technical analysis: A method of forecasting future exchange rates based on the history of exchange rates.

Temporal (monetary/nonmonetary) method: A translation accounting method (such as FAS #8 in the United States) that translates monetary assets and liabilities at current exchange rates and all other balance sheet accounts at historical exchange rates.

Territorial tax system: A tax system that taxes domestic income but not foreign income. This tax regime is found in Hong Kong, France, Belgium, and the Netherlands.

Time draft: A draft that is payable on a specified future dare.

Time value of an option: The difference between the value of an option and the option's *intrinsic value*.

Timing option: The ability of the firm to postpone investment (or disinventment) and to reconsider the decision at a future date.

Total risk: The sum of *systematic* and *unsystematic risk* (measured by the standard deviation or variance of return).

Trade acceptance: A *time draft* that is drawn on and accepted by an importer.

Trade balance: A country's net balance (exports minus imports) on merchandise trade.

Trading desk (dealing desk): The desk at an international bank that trades spot and forward foreign exchange.

Transaction exposure: Changes in the value of future cash flows as a result of changes in currency values.

Transfer prices: Prices on intracompany sales.

Translation (accounting) exposure: Changes in a corporation's financial statements as a result of changes in currency values.

Unbiased expectations hypothesis: The hypothesis that forward exchange rates are unbiased predictors of future spot rates. (See *forward parity*.)

Unlevered beta (systematic business risk): The *beta* (or *systematic risk*) of a project as if it were financed with 100 percent equity.

Unlevered cost of equity: The discount rate appropriate for an investment assuming it is financed with 100 percent equity.

Unsystematic risk: Risk that is specific to a particular security or country and that can be eliminated through diversification.

Value-added tax: A sales tax collected at each stage of production in proportion to the value added during that stage.

Warrant: An option issued by a company that allows the holder to purchase equity at a predetermined price prior to an expiration date. Warrants are frequently attached to *Eurobonds*.

Weighted average cost of capital: A discount rate that reflects the after-tax required returns on debt and equity capital.

Withholding tax: A tax on dividend or interest income that is withheld for payment of taxes in a host country. Payment is typically withheld by the financial institution distributing the payment.

World Bank: See *International Bank for Reconstruction and Development*.

World Trade Organization (WTO): Created in 1994 by 121 nations at the Uruguay Round of the *General Agreement on Tariffs and Trade (GATT)*. The WTO is responsible for implementation and administration of the trade agreement.

Worldwide tax system: A tax system that taxes worldwide income as it is repatriated to the parent company. Used in Japan, the United Kingdom, and the United States.

Yield to maturity: The discount rate that equates the present value of promised future interest payments to the current market value of the debt.

Zaibatsu: Large family-owned conglomerates that controlled much of the economy of Japan prior to World War II.

Subject Index

Name Index

Federal Deposit Insurance
    Corporation (FDIC),
    61–62
Fiat, 21, 31, 43
Finnerty, Joseph, 339, 348
Flood, Eugene, Jr., 630
Folks, William R., Jr., 122, 171,
    624, 629–630
Ford Motor Corporation, 237
Franks, Julian, 537
French, Kenneth R., 180, 198,
    278, 290, 330, 348, 381
Frenkel, J.A., 145
Froot, Kenneth A., 138, 140,
    145, 543–544, 548
Fryling, Victor J., 463
Fuyo, 526

G

Garman, Mark, 225
Genay, Hesna, 547
General Motors Corporation,
    21, 64–65, 269, 283, 342,
    378–379, 397, 504, 527
Gernon, Helen, 363
Gibson, Charles H., 636
Giddy, Ian H., 225
Glen, Jack, 361
Goldberg, L.G., 266
Goldman Sachs & Co., 359
Goodman, Stephen H., 140, 145
Grauer, Frederick L., 347
Greyhound, 272
GTE, 121
Gupta, Manoj, 339, 348

H

Haigh, Robert W., 407, 426
Hamada, Robert, 567, 582
Hamel, Gary, 421–423, 425–426
Hansell, S., 258
Hanweck, G.A., 266
Harris, Milton, 575, 582
Harris, Robert S., 537
Harvey, Campbell R., 334, 347,
    381, 562, 582
Heisenberg, Werner, 117
Henriksson, Roy, 361
Heston, J. Clark, 509, 516
Hietala, Pekka T., 314, 323
Hill, Joanne H., 198
Hilliard, Jimmy E., 225
Hilton, 410
Hino, Hisaaki, 380
Hodder, James E., 492
Holiday Inn, 410

Honda, 21, 411
Horst, Thomas, 541
Hull, John, 225
Hussein, Saddam, 70
Hymer, Stephen, 387–388, 402

I

ICI Americas, 427–428
Ikeda, Shinsuki, 348
Imperial Chemicals Industries
    PLC, 427
Ingersoll, Jonathan E., Jr., 180,
    473
Inselbag, Isik, 564, 582
International Bank for
    Reconstruction and
    Development. *See* World
    Bank.
International Business
    Machines (IBM),
    237–238, 506, 571
Ito, Takatoshi, 370, 381
Ittner, Christopher D., 539, 548

J

Jacoby, Henry D., 492
Jacquillat, Bertrand, 323, 350,
    380, 555, 582
Janakiramanan, S., 323,
    354–355, 380
Japan Air Lines (JAL), 68
Jensen, Michael C., 538, 547,
    578–579, 583
Jesswein, Kurt, 122, 171, 624,
    629–630
Joaquin, Domingo, 458
Johnson & Johnson, 38, 427
Jones, Charles P., 381
Jorion, Philippe, 134, 144,
    312–313, 322, 341–342,
    348, 357, 375–376,
    380–381, 630

K

Kaneko, Takashi, 583
Kang, Jun-Koo, 521, 532, 539,
    544, 547–548
Kaplan, Steven N., 532, 548
Kaplanis, Evi, 319–320, 323, 582
Kapner, Kenneth R., 257
Kasanen, Eero, 492
Kaufold, Howard, 564, 582
Kearney, John, 619, 627, 630
Kehoe, Louise, 420
Keim, Donald B., 381
Kemna, Angelien G.Z., 492

Kensinger, John W., 573, 582
Kerr, Jean, 423
Kester, W. Carl, 492, 529, 547
Khomeini, Ayatollah, 329
Khoury, Sarkis, 533
Kim, Dong-Soon, 355, 380
Kim, E. Han, 537, 547
Klemkosky, Robert C., 369, 381
Kobrin, Stephen J., 392, 402
Kohlhagen, Steve W., 225
Koito Manufacturing Co., 531
Kolodny, Richard, 380
Kon, Stanley, 361
KPMG Peat Markick, 363
KPN, 283
Kramer, Andrea S., 509, 516
Krugman, Paul R., 44
Kulatilaka, Nalin, 485, 492
Kwan, Clarence C.Y., 347
Kwok, Chuck C.Y., 84, 122, 171,
    624, 629–630

L

La Roche, Robert K., 597
Laughton, David G., 492
Lee, Charles, 355, 380
Lee, Chen-Few, 361
Lee, Jason, 361
Leeson, Nick, 166, 210
Leontief, Wassily, 44
Lerman, Zvi, 312, 322
Lessard, Donald R., 630
Levich, Richard M., 145, 281
Levine, Ross, 111, 145
Levy, Haim, 312, 322
Lewent, Judy, 244–246, 619, 627
Lewis, J., 258
Lim, Joseph, 355, 379
Lin, Weng-Ling, 370, 381
Litzenberger, Robert, 247, 258
Lloyd's of London, 396
Lloyds Bank, 64
Lockheed Corporation, 506
Logue, Dennis E., 582
Lorinc, Marek, 382

M

Madura, Jeff, 225
Majluf, Nicholas S., 579, 583
Makino, Shige, 426
Malaikah, S.K., 317, 322
Maloney, Peter J., 630
Malthus, Thomas Robert, 45
Manzon, Gil, 513
Manzon, Gil B., Jr., 516, 540,
    547

Marber, Peter, 273, 382
Marché à Terme des
    Instruments Financiers
    (MATIF), 174–175
Marcus, Alan J., 485, 492
Marin, Dalia, 605
Mark, Nelson C., 111, 145
Markides, Constantinos C., 539,
    548
Markowitz, Harry, 293
Marr, M. Wayne, 582
Marshall, John F., 257–258
Martin, John D., 573, 582
Mason, Scott P., 492
Matsushita Electric Industrial
    Company, 275, 289
Mavrodi, Sergei, 271
Mayes, D., 411
McDonald, J., 171, 582
McDonald's Corporation, 71,
    92, 356, 410
Meckling, William, 578, 583
Medco Containment Services,
    428
Meek, Gary K., 363
Mello, Antonio S., 198
Merck & Co., Inc., 427
Mercosur, 1, 7, 19
Merrill Lynch, 268, 286, 346
Mesa Petroleum, 531
Metallgesellschaft A.G., 191
MG Refining and Marketing
    (MGRM), 191
Microsoft Corporation, 420
Midland Bank, 266
Miller, Merton and Franco
    Modigliani (MM), 150,
    152–154, 165, 335–336,
    341, 345, 458–459,
    565–568, 580–581
Min, Sang Kee, 380
Minton, Bernadette A., 532, 548
Mishkin, Frederic S., 111, 144
Mitsubishi, 21–24, 31, 286,
    525–526
Mitsui, 23, 526
Mitterrand, François, 282, 397
Modigliani, Franco and Merton
    Miller (MM), 150,
    152–154, 165, 335–336,
    341, 345, 458–459,
    565–568, 580–581
Moffett, Michael H., 636
Mohr, Rosanne M., 567
Monsanto, 428

Some Useful Rules and Formulas

Chapter 3 The Foreign Exchange and Eurocurrency Markets   Equation

Rule #1   Always keep track of your currency units.

Rule #2   Always think of buying or selling the currency in the denominator of a foreign exchange quote.

Foreign currency premium or discount (direct quotes) = $[(F_t^{d/f} - S_0^{d/t})/S_0^{d/t}](n)$ (3.1)

Foreign currency premium or discount (indirect quotes) = $[(S_0^{f/d} - F_t^{f/d})/F_t^{f/d}](n)$

     Where n = The number of compounding periods per year   (3.4)

Chapter 4 International Parity Conditions

nominal rate of interest

$$i = \left(1+p\right)\left(1+r\right) - 1$$

inflation   *real rate*

Exchange rate determination: $P_t^d/P_t^f = S_t^{d/f}$ (4.1)

Cross exchange rates: $S^{d/e}\, S^{e/f}\, S^{f/d} = 1$ (4.3)

Interest rate parity: $F_t^{d/f}/S_0^{d/t} = (1+i^d)^t/(1+i^f)^t$ (4.4)

International parity conditions:

$$F_t^{d/f}/S_0^{d/t} = E[S_t^{d/f}]/S_0^{d/t} = (1+i^d)^t/(1+i^f)^t = (1+E[p^d])^t/(1+E[p^f])^t$$

Chapter 5 The Nature of Foreign Exchange Risk

Percentage change in the real exchange rate: $x_t^{d/f} = S_t^{d/f}/S_0^{d/t}\,(1+p^f)^t/(1+p^d)^t - 1$ (5.2)

Chapter 7 Currency Futures and Futures Markets

A futures delta-cross-hedge: $s_t^{d/f_1} = \alpha + \beta\, fut_t^{d/f_2} + e_t$ where $\beta = \rho_{s,fut}(\sigma_s/\sigma_{fut})$ (7.11)

Chapter 8 Currency Options and Options Markets

Put-call parity: $Call_T^{d/f} - Put_T^{d/f} + K^{d/f} = F_T^{d/f}$ (8.1)

Black-Scholes option pricing model: $Call = P \cdot N(d_1) - e^{-iT} \cdot K \cdot N(d_2)$ (8A.2)

    where $d_1 = [\ln(P/K) + (i+(\sigma^2/2))T]/(\sigma\sqrt{T})$ and $d_2 = (d_1 - \sigma\sqrt{T})$

Currency option pricing model: $Call^{d/f} = e^{-i^fT} \cdot [S^{d/f} \cdot N(d_1)] - e^{-i^dT} \cdot K^{d/f} \cdot N(d_2)$ (8A.5)

    where $d_1 = [\ln(S^{d/f}/K^{d/f}) + (i^d - i^f + (\sigma^2/2))T]/(\sigma\sqrt{T})$ and $d_2 = (d_1 - \sigma\sqrt{T})$

Chapter 9 Currency Swaps and Swaps Markets

Bond equivalent yield = Money market yield * (365/360)

Chapter 11 International Portfolio Diversification

Return on foreign investment: $(1+R^d) = (1+R^f)(1+s^{d/f})$ (11.7)

Expected return on foreign investment: $E[R^d] = E[R^f] + E[s^{d/f}] + E[R^f\, s^{d/f}]$ (11.8)

Variance on foreign investment: $Var(R^d) = Var(R^f) + Var(s^{d/f}) + Var(R^f\, s^{d/f}) + 2Cov(R^f, s^{d/f})$ (11.9)